# Psalms
# in
# Ordinary
# Voices

# Psalms in Ordinary Voices

*A Reinterpretation of the 150 Psalms by Men, Women and Children*

*edited by*
Andrea Ayvazian

*photographs by*
Ellen Augarten

White River Press
Amherst, Massachusetts

White River Press edition published 2011

Privately published 2007

White River Press
PO Box 3561
Amherst, MA 01004

www.whiteriverpress.com

Cover design by Rebecca Neimark, Twenty-Six Letters, www.twentysixletters.com
Interior design by Ann Chiara
All photographs by Ellen Augarten, www.ellenaugartenphotography.com

Printed in the United States of America

ISBN: 978-1-935052-31-9


Library of Congress Cataloging-in-Publication Data

Psalms in ordinary voices : a reinterpretation of the 150 Psalms by men, women and children / [collected by] Andrea Ayvazian and [photography by] Ellen Augarten.
     p. cm.
ISBN 978-1-935052-31-9 (pbk. : alk. paper)
1.   Bible. O.T. Psalms--Paraphrases, English. I. Ayvazian, Andrea. II. Augarten, Ellen, 1950- III. Bible. O.T. Psalms. English.
BS1440.P825 2010
223'.205209--dc22
                            2010020372

*For Michael and Sasha*
*with unending love and enduring gratitude*
*A.A.*


*For Mark, Libby and Noah*
*with love*
*E.A.*

# *Preface*

## *by Bill McKibben*

A confession: I've always loved the Psalms, but mostly for their glorious
language. All those lyres sounding and leviathans spouting, all that oil
shining on brows, those glorious cedars of Lebanon, the roaring floods.
Despite that, though, the Psalms never meant as much to me as I thought
they should. Part of it, maybe, is that I haven't yet wandered into the
valley of the shadow; my life's been less traumatic than many, and perhaps
not as demanding of constant comfort. But more, I think, it's just that
so much of the writing is over the top. All the browbeating and breast
baring, the constant lamenting, the God-praising that sounds to a modern
ear like some kind of bizarre sucking-up. All those eager demands that
one's enemies die particularly nasty deaths. To my ear it often came out
sounding like opera.

Which is why the Psalms reconfigured in this new collection seem
to me so moving. For the most part they're quieter, written not so much
in the language of our time as in the volume of our time. The despair is
quieter, the exultation more personal. Less wailing, less trumpeting. But
no less pain, and no less hope, and no less feeling. And that in turn is why
the photographs are so crucial, with their reminder that this is us talking.
That these deep emotions come from ordinary people, just as they must
have done originally. And of course ordinariness is the most moving thing
of all—the recognition that roughly six billion of us are going through
these trials, dealing with these feelings, as we make our short journeys
through this life.

New translations from the Bible only occasionally clarify. Usually
they manage to strip away emotional power, and leave only simpleness
as recompense. But these Psalms are not translations—they're more like
improvisations, riffs on the images and the moods of the original. You
can recognize the theme in many cases, but that theme is refreshed.
The intonation of the pulpit reading drops away, the rhythm of the
conversation wells up. These writers have performed a great service, given
a great gift. To hear these phrases stripped down and then restored in a
tone we instantly recognize as real is, in a certain way, to hear them again
for the first time. Praise be!

# Table of Contents

# Introduction

## by The Rev. Dr. Andrea Ayvazian

The Holy Bible is a messy book—full of drama and intrigue, hope and despair, loyalty and betrayal, sin and righteousness, violence and compassion. Every human emotion is found in the Bible: love, hate, envy, anger, forgiveness, revenge, joy, grief, fear, gratitude, and so on. And nowhere are these feelings more abundantly expressed than in the 150 Psalms in the Hebrew Scriptures.

The Psalms are a diverse collection of devotional poetry, laments, hymns of praise, blessings and curses, songs of thanksgiving, and words of wisdom and instruction. John Calvin called the Psalms "the mirror of man" because the full range of feelings, hopes, imaginings, and experiences of the Israelite people is conveyed with raw honesty, vivid images, profound insights, and prophetic visions. Praised by Martin Luther as "a Bible in miniature," the Psalms lift up universal struggles with divine revelation, personal and collective identity, doubt and faithfulness. Most of all, the Psalms reflect human beings' deep longing for a sense of reverence for and closeness with God.

No one has been able to determine precisely when the Psalms were written. The range of dates found in the scholarly literature speculating about the origins of the Psalms spans 800 years—from the tenth to the second century B.C.E. Biblical historians believe that some of the Psalms were written by David in the tenth century B.C.E. Other Psalms may have been composed in the era when kings ruled Israel before the exile in 587–6 B.C.E. Still others make reference to the exile and may have been written in the centuries following it. Although commonly referred to as "The Psalms of David," scholars agree that while David may have written some of the Psalms, these hymns, laments, and words of wisdom and praise were composed by many different poets including Asaph, Ethan the Ezrahite, Heyman the Ezrahite, the Korahites and many others. What emerges when one studies this complex and multi-layered book is that writing the Psalms was an ongoing process that involved many authors and spanned centuries, possibly close to a millennium.

### Old Truths Reborn

The Book of Psalms is read more often than any other book of the Bible, possibly because the Psalms speak to us in deeply personal ways about religious faith and struggle. Because they are so often read and widely loved, they have been the subject of considerable attention by authors and poets. The Psalms have been rewritten using inclusive language, reinterpreted by theologians, translated anew by clergy and laypeople, recast in haiku, and refashioned in a distinctly female voice. The Psalms continue to have relevance and appeal in all these forms because each retelling of the beloved poems and songs speaks to our deep spiritual needs and aspirations.

*Psalms in Ordinary Voices* joins the proud tradition of revisiting the Psalms. This book is also born from a love of the 150 ancient hymns, poems, and prayers—a love reflected in my dog-eared Bible with its soiled pages and scribbling in the margins. Wrestling with the Bible, in particular with the Psalms, deepens one's spiritual journey by bringing the feelings, wisdom, and guidance of its ancient authors to bear on the trials and joys of contemporary life.

### This Book's Beginning

The genesis of *Psalms in Ordinary Voices* reaches back several years to my brief stint as a Sunday-school teacher when my son was in the seventh grade. Each week I tried to find a story, activity, art project, or field trip that would make the stories in the Bible—distant and strange to these twelve year olds—relevant in the minds of those MTV-watching, computer-savvy, thoroughly trendy young people.

After we read Psalms aloud one week and studied their origins the next, I asked these young people to tell me what they heard when I read some Psalms line by line. Taking this assignment surprisingly seriously, the boys and girls reworded the Psalms with a depth and simplicity that brought me to the edge of tears. Realizing this moment should not be lost, I distributed pencils and paper to everyone. They dutifully wrote their own interpretation of Psalm 23 as I read it slowly, stopping after every line.

Andrew Stone, a baseball player who sang in the children's choir, wrote:

> The Lord is my keeper.
> I will not want for He has provided.
> He makes me rest in beautiful places, with water to refresh my soul.
> He guides me to right decisions for He feels it is good.

Jonny Carbaugh, a quiet boy who liked to play soccer and poker, wrote:

> The Lord guides me, I will not want.
> I relax in His field.
> He guides me to blue water.
> He revives my spirit.
> He takes me the right way in His name.

Andy Carbaugh, Jonny's twin brother, also an athlete and a sweet child, wrote:

> The Lord is my leader
> So I do not want anything I don't need.
> He makes me rest peacefully in paradise.
> He leads me to the peacefulness of still waters.
> He restores my soul.
> He points me in the right direction
> For His sake and mine.

I shared the rewritten Psalms with the young people's parents and the church pastor. Quickly, copies circulated throughout the congregation and parishioners asked for more. The idea of creating a book of Psalms written by everyday people grew from that Sunday-school class, the congregation's response, and the initial offerings from family and friends who tried their hands at rewriting Psalms in contemporary language.

### "God is Still Speaking ..."

The theological underpinning of this book is the belief that God is still speaking to, in, and through us. I believe that, through our own words and actions, God's presence is felt in contemporary society. Years ago, I gave a sermon about how we are the continuing story of God moving in individual lives and through history. I held a Bible in one hand while I preached. At the close of the sermon, I ripped the back cover off the Bible to symbolize that the story is not finished; we are the current chapter, and there will be chapters that follow us.

I believe that we should wrestle with the Bible, to bring it into current time, to retell the stories, and to rewrite the songs. The more we find ways to bring the Bible's words and lessons into our daily lives, the more that ancient text becomes relevant and useful today.

To me, these 150 rewritten Psalms are individual gifts from each of the writers to each of you readers. The simplicity, honesty, yearning, and joy found in these contemporary Psalms draw the reader in close and beckon the divine. Whether standing in a forest or seated at an urban café, these writers have lived with the words of an ancient and beloved text, worked with its meaning and images, and made a few lines of a sacred book their very own. May you travel with them into new territory in a familiar landscape and find anew the presence of God.

### Its Own Little Miracle

The creation of this book has been nothing short of its own little miracle.

The project was inspired by adolescents who tackled the challenge with a matter-of-fact nonchalance—as if rewriting Psalms in their own voices was an everyday occurrence. I recognized that finding other contemporary Psalmists might be more of a challenge. In fact, I reached out to about 250 individuals before finding 150 willing to try their hand.

Early on, I realized that the book had to reflect the beauty and diversity of God's family. The "ordinary" people writing Psalms in their own voices had to be a cross-section of the human community. That wonderful challenge meant that I spent time in prisons and nursing homes, on the streets with homeless folks, and in garages with auto mechanics. I also talked to physicians and judges, sheriffs and lawyers, teenagers, teachers, hair stylists, and school-bus drivers. People were intrigued, intimidated, offended, honored, delighted, and baffled. Some said no, many said yes, and the work began.

Some folks studied their Psalm for weeks and then labored over every word. Others read their Psalm a few times, put it away, and wrote what emerged directly from their hearts. Some found they needed a partner to work with; most wanted to work alone. Every person turned in his or her Psalm with some trepidation, but all felt that the experience of bringing ancient feelings and experiences into this millennium had changed them in some way. I extend a deep and heartfelt thank you to each Psalm writer. You tackled something hard, wrote with grace and beauty, and together we created an unusual book of enduring value.

The idea of pairing a photograph of each Psalmist with the text developed organically, since only photographs could convey the precious diversity in age, ethnicity, sexual orientation, profession, social class, and physical ability. I knew that the book needed portraits taken by a professional who would photograph the writers where they lived, worked, studied, or played, to put the contemporary Psalmists in context.

Finding Ellen Augarten to collaborate with on this book was a great gift, and working with her has been a joy. Together we have spent many hours coaching and coaxing our Psalm writers to believe in their own words, laughing with them while they were photographed, and imagining with them the release of this book. Thank you, Ellen, for your professionalism, flexibility, patience, humor, and tremendous artistic skill. The portraits complete this book in a way that nothing else could.

When one college student turned in her finished Psalm, she spoke out loud what many others may have thought in silence. "Just think," she said in wistful tones, "someone might actually hold your book and pray using my Psalm. That is totally awesome." She is right.

# Psalms
in
Ordinary
Voices

# Psalm 1

*by Marcelle Walters*
FIRST GRADE TEACHER

The Lord lifts up the person who will not tolerate an unkind word.

The Lord rejoices in the one who refuses to allow sexist, racist,
and intolerant remarks.

Our God holds high those people who walk away from any gathering
that excludes the poor, the unfortunate, the unforgivable.

Each of us will be honored and judged equally if we practice and
believe in justice and fairness to all.

We must contemplate and move toward this end.

Our Savior will guide us, even nourish us throughout this struggle.

We will rise like the evergreen, planted by the water, no matter what
the season is, true to form.

When faced with racism, sexism, ageism, homophobia, God's path
will lead us to do what is just, what is right.

Our courage will allow others to follow suit, growing to become a
groundswell.

The unenlightened will linger, weak and eventually lost like the chaff
from the wheat.

Our Lord knows that this is a difficult task and will be our wellspring
along the way.

# Psalm 2

*by Jim Moynihan*
PLUMBER

Why do we act (argue and fight) against each other?

Who are these kings of the earth and rulers who think and act against others (the Lord and His people)?

All should be free from overbearers and tyrants. Our belief in the Lord will give us power to love and serve each other.

Those in Heaven laugh at our smallness and pettiness. In the Lord we are all one.

Why do I fear my God? Is it that I do not know, trust, love?

This place, this earth, is part of your eternal kingdom.

Do I recognize the Christ that is my brother/sister? Have I accepted you into my life, my heart?

We are Sons/Daughters—God's love is unconditional.

Ask, and we all share in His love. As we believe and accept Christ's love, our happiness will be beyond the measures of the earth.

God will lead us with strength and conviction even at our most fragile times. Can I let Him lead? Will I accept my role?

We all take the same message. Listen to the Lord (Christ) and each other. Do I take the time to hear?

Live at/in peace with each other (honor and love). You will have peace in the Lord.

Happy and blessed are those who believe and act with kindness; they believe and live in the Lord's peace.

# *Psalm 3*

## by Tricia Sohl and Mark Dickstein
CONSULTANTS

The Transformative All

So many viciously taunt me—
so many, so many.
They laugh and ridicule me.
They call my beliefs
The opiate crutch of wishful thinking.

But my life flows together in faith,
which shields and elevates me.
It subdues my doubts
and lets me hold my head up high.
I reach out and sense a larger presence.
I feel watched over and no longer alone.

When I go to sleep at night, I rest at ease
And feel safe again when I awake in the morning,
So that no amount of disdain can
Stir in me turmoil or despair.

Envelop me with your overriding presence,
that I may continue impervious
To those who, lacking in understanding, lash out,
For they also are in need of blessing.

The world seems against me
Because they don't understand.
They think it weak
To persist in such beliefs
… but it is my strength that I do.

# Psalm 4

## by Brenda E. Millette
### PROFESSOR EMERITUS OF NURSING

Joy and Peace in the Lord

A song to God on strings:

Please listen to me, God! You have helped me in the past. Once again, please hear me and attend to my needs.

Why are we, his people, apt to persist in listening to the cynics and prevaricators? Is it a way to strengthen our belief in our own power?

We should know by now that the Lord truly hears us and values our words. I know he will hear me when I speak to him.

We shouldn't be as fearful as we are, but should carefully and sincerely consider the Lord's teachings. Quietly and at rest, we need to reflect on His way.

All we need to do is to follow the directions He has given and continue to always hope and trust.

There are those who would always ask who will help us? Lord, shine your warmth and beauty on us all.

God, you have given me more joy than the richest person could ever obtain.

I sleep deeply, peacefully and securely, Lord, because I know you alone will always care for me.

# *Psalm 5*

### *by Kathryn D. Foran*
### PEACE AND SOCIAL JUSTICE WORKER

Morning clouds streak the sky
    in rows
That parallel the rows
    of roadside corn.
Beneath the pavement the roots of trees
    reflect their branches.
The shadows of birds swim
    in the river like the ghosts
    of fish.
Everywhere the earth's a metaphor
    for heaven.

And every dawn's a repetition
    of the ancient verses,
the pleas and sighs of sunrise—
as every morning I look
    for you here, O Lord,
wondering if all I have of you
    are echoes and psalms.

*Lord, in the morning you hear*
    *my voice;*
*in the morning I plead my case*
    *to you, and watch.*

I watch my path.
I watch, but cannot see beyond
    my step in salted sand;
I see only myself
    and the unlikely
crayfish suddenly before me,
    far from water.

*Lead me, O Lord, in your*
          *righteousness*
*because of my enemies;*
*make your way straight before me.*

And what if my only enemy
          is that small and lost
hard-shelled part of myself,
          the ego clawing the air?

The crawdad turns its accusing pincers to me.
Its mottled exoskeleton
is no shield against the grind of cars,
          against their loud and boastful motors.
The only way to save it
          is to cover it with my light jacket,
lift it up, deliver it to the river.

Beneath the bridge
          which is no temple
I turn the crayfish out of my coat—
a ritual without the flutes
          and words of David.
The water laps my footprints,
          absorbing them.
And I, who turn to metaphor, plead,
*Let it be so, O Lord—*
You the water's robe
          skimming the shore,
          swathing me,
You the hands delivering me,
You my only shield.

# Psalm 6

*by Philip Hall*
MINISTER, RETIRED


O Lord, please do not rage against our trashed times.
I am clinging to the edge
Of headlines that stick like Napalm—
Wars, cold hatreds, revenge, desperate isolation.
My bones ache with anguish. Go easy.
You could—with good cause—let your hammer fall.
But hear me. I am clinging to the edge
Of a world going out of control.
My tear-drenched eyes look to your mercy—how long?—
Your steadfast love is the only flicker of light.

O Lord, turn;
Deliver me;
Save me from Sheol.
Where praise withers and souls gasp,
And fade into screaming silence.

I am tired.
Nights of weeping bring no rest.
I am held only by my tear-drenched couch.

I am clinging to the edge
Of the city dump,
Where old consolations lie rusting at my feet.

The purveyors of hatred and revenge seem to be winning.
My grief-wrenched spirit longs for peace and justice.
But maybe the Lord's ears are attentive
To the sounds of my weeping?

The Lord does receive my stumbling prayers.
Blinding self-righteousness and endless violence cannot stand
Forever, you are our only hope.

# *Psalm 7*

*by Robert Garvey*
SHERIFF

O, Lord, I put my faith and trust in you. I ask you to save me and deliver me from all who persecute me. Deliver me before they tear me to pieces, leaving nothing to save.

But, dear God, if I am guilty of harming my enemies, if I am guilty of bringing ill to him who was at peace with me, then let him take my life and destroy my honor.

Rise in thy anger, Lord, lift thyself up in the face of my enemies' rage. Rise up to judge as you have commanded. Your people will gather about you, Lord, and for their sake you will return on high.

The Lord shall judge all people. Judge me, O Lord, according to goodness and integrity in me. O, Lord, let the evil of the wicked come to an end, but reward the just, for goodness should reign.

God judges the righteous and is angry at the wicked. His weapons are ready. He will search out and find those who do not repent. Sinners who continue to create mischief and falsehoods will fail. Their evil deeds come back on them and violence will descend on them.

I will praise the justice and goodness of the Lord and will sing praise to his name.

# Psalm 8

## By Anne Fitzgerald-Pittman
STUDENT

For the best musician to play on the guitar

O, the delight at the magnificence of the world and its creation!

From babes grow those who have the skills and strengths to overcome adversity, so that they can bring peace to the wrongdoer and the righter of wrongs alike.

When I ponder all that has been created, the accomplishments of humans, the sky above, all that is in the world, the question follows:

What are people? Why do we prevail?

We are honored with the faculty to do great things; with glory and tribute we have been blessed.

We are endowed with the responsibility for all deeds done and global welfare.

I am awed by the diversity of the world, the ant and the buffalo, all things.

Birds in the air, fish in the sea, every part of the whole is astounding.

O, the delight at the magnificence of the world and its creation!

# *Psalm 9*

*by Ivy Tillman*

INFORMATION TECHNOLOGY PROFESSIONAL

You amaze me!
Your many wonderful gifts fill me
Until I am so high
That my joy spills out in song,
And I overflow with thanks and praise!

You know my enemies inside and out:
Those who with or without intent come to harm me,
But also myself—my pride, my ego, my will.
When You turn aside,
Confused, we scatter.

I don't know why, but You love me.
You tell me the truth about me,
And speak to my heart of how things should be.
You draw me back from my confusion;
You help me and care for me.
You let us know the wrongs we've done,
Let us feel the pain;
Then You forgive us—
Soothe and heal us—
'Til I hardly remember who harmed who or why...

My enemies have yielded:
Past actions ground to dust;
Selfishness, conceit and vanity swept away.
Forgiven, only the memories—and repentance—
Remain.

But You hold us—my enemies and me—always,
Leading, teaching, correcting;
Representing all of us justly and fairly.
You hold us fiercely, sheltering us
When we are lost and shaken in mind or body.

And so we trust You,
Whose name we don't even know:
You never let go!

O my people,
Have you heard of this amazing God,
Who lives here and now
Hear how she shows her love!

She holds the victim and the oppressor.
He hears the screams and whispers—
God, help me!—from the pain to body and spirit.
God holds me, feels what I feel, cries in my despair,
And rescues me when I've nearly lost hope.

Hosanna!
Hallelujah!

Often I take a prideful fall;
I suffer in my selfishness.
Its value obscured by clouds of arrogance,
You give me another gift:
Choice, fair and free.

I walk the road I choose,
Damaging as it may be,
And You allow it.

If I choose to ignore the cries of the needy,
Someone else will do that job.
If I choose to turn my back to the condition of the poor,
You will find someone else who won't.
And if I am in need, You will help even me.

You AMAZE me, God!
How arrogant we must seem,
How small in defying You.
Bring us into your presence!
Show us who we are.

# Psalm 10

*by Michael Hurley*

JOURNEYMAN PAINTER,
MASTER SARGEANT IN THE AIR FORCE RESERVE

Whenever affliction arises we always think God should help us, but as we all know it may not be his due time.

We see the wicked man rejoice in his own lust—boasting and bragging about his wit and wealth. He blesses himself which blasphemes the Lord.

Shall God not break the arm of this wicked man? Why does he not destroy this man's power to harm others?

All man's evil is organic and any infraction of one commandment involves the breaking of all of them.

Should the Lord not open this man's eyes to behold the content of his evil? Though all evil is futile, maybe this man speaks thus because evil has not touched him in a lifetime?

The wicked man has many ways to hide his evil. Even if evil is futile this man should be feared because he does not possess the desires of the meek.

If he had this quality he might accept correction without resentment. But he continues in his evil ways hiding behind the hypocrisy of those many men who are in authoritative positions.

He needs to call God for help in repairing his wicked heart which has been overgrown to the point where right and wrong are blurred.

God helps when man's help ceases to exist. The man who is saved will be terrible no more!

# Psalm 11

*by Donna Russell*
ADMINISTRATIVE ASSISTANT

Help us in this self-centered world.
Many people today have turned
away from God.
Protect us from the people who lie
to make themselves look better.
People who are in control have taken the support
away from our poor and sick,
it makes the cycle more vicious for them.
We turn toward your promise of hope.
Keep all of us safe until the tide turns
away from selfishness
and toward your way of hope.

# Psalm 12

*by Paul Sorrentino*
CAMPUS MINISTER

Oh God, help.
  I am alone,
      I can trust no one.
No one cares about You.

Prodigal liars surround me.
      Plagiarism is rampant.
Words are used only to manipulate—
      to get one's way.

Everyone is two-faced,
  and they think they can get away with it,
      because You are not in their equation.

LORD, put a stop to their arrogance.

God says, "I see the pain of those mistreated,
  I hear their prayers 24/7
      I will come to their aid,
      I will rescue them from injustice."

We can always trust content from God.
  There are never viruses with God's attachments,
      His files are always uncorrupted.

Or, to change the image,
  the LORD's words are as perfect
      as twenty-four-carat gold.
We can depend on the LORD,
      God will protect us and keep us safe.

 It is an upside down world:
      what is wrong is valued,
      what is right is not.

# Psalm 13

*by Sharon Aminia*
CHEF

Lord, have you abandoned and forgotten me?
It has been so long since I felt your presence—
I pray constantly, I call out for you, and I yearn with all my being,
     and still I am unanswered.

O lonesome me!
Without you, my God, my life is miserable.
Each heartbreaking day turns to sleepless night
     as my soul yearns for you.
My troubled mind cries out for the happiness and joy
     that have gone out of my life.
Life is not important without you.
I feel my life ebbing away.

What has happened?
What have I done or not done?
Please answer me!

Non-believers cannot be right!
You have been there for me and will be again.
I must trust in you and your mercy, for your bounty sustains me.
I will praise you evermore.

# Psalm 14

## by Elizabeth Carr
### CHAPLAIN

"The soul's greatest malaise is laziness. I don't mean laziness of the hands,
but of the sleeping heart."

—Max Jacob


The fool says in his heart, "There is no God"
while endlessly busy, too busy to stop,
to breathe, to be silent, to savor the Good,
to keep a Sabbath.

And God says, "You are my Beloved"
while gifting us with skies, stars, giraffes,
cactus, lilies, bison, trout, bees and people—
each one precious in God's eyes.

God looks at us, seeks us,
wanting only our Love and Mercy shared.
We are so busy, busy with war, oil, bottom lines,
while Mt. Kilimanjaro's snow melts and the ozone withers.

You are devouring my people and for what?
for hearts of stone? for ulcers? for war?
for lonely comforts?
You live in fear and never call on me.

Come back to me. I who am your Mother,
Father, Sister, Brother, Lover, Companion, Friend;
the Peace you need, the Mystery that beckons,
I live in the hearts of the just and I shelter the poor.

I am your Living God and you my cherished ones.
My mercy is yours. Seek me and
Your heart bursts with New Life.
All together we dance.

# *Psalm 15*

*By Jennifer Ladd*
CLASSISM TRAINER

The Character of the Enspirited Human

Oh All That Is—who shall attain cosmic awareness and who shall become enlightened?

She who walks with integrity, works for justice, and speaks truthfully from her heart.

He that harms no one in speech, thought or deed.

She who can challenge wrong,

While holding the heart of the wrong-doer in the light.

He who uses money thoughtfully and

For the good of the whole (to which he belongs).

She and he who do these things shall be "like trees standing by the water: They shall not be moved."

# Psalm 16

*by Melissa B. Simon*
STUDENT

Do not abandon me, Adonai
      In you I find a constant companion
My salvation, You are my beloved
      My one and only
You are a true creator, with you
      I can do anything
Those who seek falsely
      Shall not benefit from your goodness
As for me, I swear devotion only to You
      Never will I stray to another
My G-D is all that I am
      And all I know
I am proud to be from a blessed people
      Chosen by You for a holy birthright
Never-ending prayers I utter to you
      My conscience and salvation
Showing me the way when I am blind
      Lending me Your ears so I can hear
I praise our G-D who guides me
      Because I know your ways
I am always aware of Your presence
      Never will I refrain from singing Your praises
Because of You, the sun shines and the wind blows
      My heart rejoices
My soul is lifted
      My body is full of life
You will not abandon me
      Nor will You stray from Your most high purpose
You show me the True path
      In The Eternal's presence
I am unafraid
      Arm in arm with Your goodness
Forever is endless.
      Amen.

# Psalm 17

*by Memory Bandera*
Student

David's prayer. Listen to my righteous cause, O Lord.

Attend to my sob, pay heed to my prayer, that it not go out of a deceitful mouth.

You know my heart and ways. Judge me as you shall find, and let me not fall under the judgment of man; do not be deceived, do justice between me and my enemies.

Even if you scrutinize my heart and inspect me in the hours of darkness,

Even if you put me on trial, you will uncover nothing.
I have refrained from words that might be considered inflammatory or seditious by my enemies; I have decided that my mouth will not fall into transgression.

Though the wicked provoked me to do evil for evil, your word kept me back from the actions of the aggressive.

My steps have held to your pathways; my feet have not slipped.

I call on you, because I know you will pay attention to my call;
listen to me and consider my plea.

Display the wonder of your loving kindness, you who save by your loyal hand those who seek protection in you from their rivals.

Take much care to preserve me; envelop me with your protection from my enemies for their cruelty cannot be satisfied.

They seal up their cold hearts, and they are puffed up with pride.

They have chased me down, they now enclose me with a vigilant gaze, to toss me to the ground.

They are akin to a lion ravenous for prey, and squatting in cover.

When they rise up against me, Arise Lord;
stop their rage, seize and cast them down.

Lord, save me by your heavenly power from such men, who have bartered heaven for earth, and have gotten the portion they desired; their sons have abundant wealth, and they stock up inheritable wealth for their children.

Through righteousness, my happiness will eventually be in seeing you.

I draw comfort against all assaults, knowing I will someday see the face of the Lord.

# Psalm 18

## by Sheila Peltz Weinberg
### Rabbi

How do we withstand the trials of being alive?
Where is the resting place amidst the constant change and confusion?

To seek to serve,
To try to love,
To hope to feel a greater Love—that is our home, our place of refuge,
our comfort and our strength.

We learn from David—king, warrior, lover, sinner, singer of songs—a
man who had plenty of trials and tribulations.

"God's love is my stronghold," says David.

Sometimes, God's love appears only when we are desperate and feel
encircled by the bonds of death itself.

And God appears like a blazing light—shaking the earth and rocking
our mountains.

A huge force, grasping thunderbolts, scattering arrows, and scooping
us out of the deepest waters...

Flying through our lives, mounted on a cherub (what a sight!),
swooping through our fears on the wings of wind...

Releasing us into a spacious consciousness, where we are safe and at
ease.

Sometimes I experience God's love when I understand things.
I understand the law of cause and effect.
I understand that we have choices that shape our future experience.
Things are not random.
My efforts toward goodness and devotion bear blessed fruit.
And the result of hatred and ill will is more of the same.

For You, my God.

# *Psalm 19*

*by Jeannie J. Cooper*
MOTHER AND HOUSEWIFE

How I love to study the skies!
There is so much there to read,
Such beauty, yet fury beyond
The power of man to create,
Only God Himself, a Being beyond description.

God speaks in so many ways,
If we but listen!
In growing things I see His work.
And hear His voice in the songs of birds.

My camera captures the heavenly scene
Of clouds piling upon each other
And changing shapes.
Daily I stand in awe
Watching trees respond to the wind
And plants come alive in the rain.
At night I gaze at the stars
And am thrilled to be able to see them!

God's laws must be obeyed, not questioned.
Though I do my best
There is sin within me.
And I pray for forgiveness
Help me, O God, to do only
What is right.

# *Psalm 20*

*by Gary Shaw*
CUSTODIAN

The Lord my God will help you when you are in need
and His name will protect you.
He will send you help from on High and remember
all the good that you have done.

God will give you the desire of your heart
and help all of your good plans succeed.

We will shout for joy and lift up
the name of the Lord when you are victorious.

We know that the Lord saves His people
with the power of His right hand.

Some people trust in material things
but we will trust in the Lord our God.
Those who trust in material things will fail and fall,
but those who trust in God will stand.

The Lord answers all our prayers.

# *Psalm 21*

## *by Kathryn S. White*
### PRIEST

I celebrate your strength, O God;
     I rejoice in the wonders of your creation.

You have filled my heart with blessings.
     You have answered my every prayer.

My life is a cherished life.
     I am adorned with rings on my fingers
     and jewels around my neck.

I prayed that I might live to see my children's children,
     and you have made it so.

Friends and strangers honor me;
        my efforts turn to gold because of You.

My joy will extend forever,
        my gladness in your presence, O God.

All my trust I offer to you, Holy One.
        Your love is the rock on which I rest.

You reach out and confront your challengers.
        You do not let go of the ones who attack you.

The sheer power of your presence
        sears them with white hot flames.

Your anger will overcome them,
        and they shall be overcome.

Their children will know your power;
        their descendants will not stand against you.

In spite of their hatred of you,
        their attempts to bring you down,
        they will not succeed against you.

For you, O God, will send them away.
        You, O God, will banish them forever.

Rise up, O Holy One, and show us the power of your presence,
        and make our voices sing with joy.

# Psalm 22

## by Marianne MacCullagh
### MOTHER AND MINISTER

Alone, and crying
      Seeking You, but not finding You
My cries echo silence in the morning and at night.

You
      You are
            You are the Holy One
                  Your ears have heard cries like these before.

Scorned and hated
      Mocked and despised
Abandoned by those who do not know You

But You know me
      You have known me.
All of my life is Yours.
      Let me hear You now

Surrounded by an evil that would devour me.
      The strength to escape, or fight, is gone.
Helpless, threatened, stripped of everything

Come close!
      Aid, deliver, save, rescue me from this evil.
My trust is in You alone.

Now will my mouth sing.
      My joy will not be stopped.
Know the Holy One! Sing and praise!
      The Holy One hears even the smallest cry and answers.

From person to person and land to land
      Far and wide and near, the songs will rise to heaven.

We will remember.
      We will remember and serve.
            We will remember always and serve only You.

# *Psalm 23*

*by Sasha Klare-Ayvazian*
STUDENT

The Lord is my guide, and the Lord is all I need
We sit together and watch the sky
We walk together and are grateful for the water
The earth is beautiful and my soul is pure
The earth is beautiful, but not perfect
Together, we must continue to do the good work that must be done

We must keep seeking justice
We must keep fighting inequality
We must cherish and protect the earth,
          at any cost.
And united we will do so much

The Lord will stay with me
And guide my path.
The Lord is with us all, guiding and supporting, and compelling
us on all of our paths

We must keep working for goodness and mercy
And then we can share the bounty of the earth together.

# *Psalm 24*

## *by Thelma Wong and Sarah Bellows Meister*
### STUDENTS

Of David

This gentle earth and all that it cradles,
     each life, each possibility for hope,
     was born of goodness and of grace,
     founded in love and cast in kindness.

Who shall reach the highest heights
     to stand in communion with the Good?
Those whose lives are marked by service,
     who mend what they find broken,
     be it places, lives, or hope.
They shall find themselves always blessed,
     as they have blessed the lives they touch.
For such is sacred community:
     a circle of souls in harmony, turning towards each other.
Selah.

O Sisters, open your hearts—
     that comfort and love may come in!
O Brothers, open your hearts—
     that comfort and love may come in!
Lift up your hearts in eternal compassion!
Lift up your hearts in perpetual peace!
What act is more sacred?
What prayer is more holy?
Open your hearts,
     and dwell humbly and gently in truth.
Selah.

# *Psalm 25*

## *by Crystal Hayes*
MOTHER, STUDENT, ACTIVIST

We must live through our souls so that we may live through God.

We live in our bodies, but we experience the world through our souls.

Our souls feel love, our bodies feel pleasure; our souls know sacred and spiritual beauty, our bodies only know illusions; our souls give lovingly, gently, and tenderly, our bodies kill, hate, and injure.

In the physical world our bodies are not our own. Our bodies continually commit sins, causing catastrophic harm to the planet whenever we spite, betray, hate, and lust.

When we live through our bodies, we subject ourselves to our most basic animal nature, living in wanton hyper-consumption of every aspect of life, indulging in the media, food, sex, greed, and violence—we are vulgar in our bodies.

God wants us to live through our sacred souls.

The holy truth of divine love, righteous kindness, honorable trust, and living as decent human beings who compassionately care for one another and ourselves.

Only through a relationship with God, who speaks to us through the soul, are we able to connect with our high nature of being on the planet. When we fail to do this, we surrender to the lowest nature of our being.

We are rendered helpless to survive the pain that those who live in their low nature inflict upon us.

We cannot survive the hate of our enemies, their cowardly acts, spoiled hearts, and cruel words, because we are not able to see those individuals as troubled spirits living through their disturbed bodies.

The only protection from such a fate is through seeking the covenant of God that requires that we live through our souls so God can work for us and through us. Amen.

# Psalm 26

*by Norma Akamatsu*
CLINICAL SOCIAL WORKER

To Ron

Uphold my conviction, O God,
to live with integrity
and trust in you absolutely.
Put me to the test,
my heart and my mind,
I remain focused on your love
and walk with resolute faith in you.

I avoid the dishonest and dissemblers.
I despise those who cause harm
and I will refuse the company of the malevolent.

I hold a *mala* of the purest wood
sitting in meditation, O God,
I whisper my thankfulness
and wonder at your creation.

O God, I cherish this earth
and celebrate nature's splendor.
Don't throw me in with the despicable,
Nor throw my life in with the violent
who hold weapons in one hand and
bribes in the other.

My path is to walk in my integrity,
Redeem me, and with kindness.
I stand in equanimity
and when we all gather together, I will
bless God.

# Psalm 27

*by John P. Webster*
MINISTER

The Lord is my light and my salvation
Without whom I stagger blind in the darkness.
With God I can face uncertainty with conviction—
The unknown with inner confidence.

The Lord is my light and my salvation,
With God my fulfillment and destiny abide.
His mercy and grace are the Source of life's blessings.
Without God life is empty and hollow
No Word feeds us with meaning,
Our souls hunger for something sensed but unknown.
In a world of junk food, we starve for the Bread of Life.

The Lord is my light and my salvation
No person or thing will I fear
The Lord is the strength of my life,
Of whom should I be afraid? I can't think of a soul.

Life has shown us hazards along the way.
Tragedy brings loss and bereavement when least expected.
Sacred bonds are broken, trust and loyalty prove more
Fragile than we thought. Our own faithlessness to God's Way
Is challenged in our souls, but through it all stands God
With Faithfulness and Grace, God stands secure.
I would have fainted, passed out, given up had I not seen
            and believed in the goodness of the Lord
            in the land of the living.

One thing only do I desire of the Lord.
That I may seek and live in God's Presence.
I have known His shelter from threatening storms,
A Father's love shining with grace and mercy
Welcoming the lost to the protection of His home.
To live with God is to live with love, blessed with Peace
            In the search for truth.
To live with God is to abide with beauty that nurtures the souls we are.
In God's presence the quest goes on for truth, and God responds with joy
To our questioning minds.
So one thing have I asked of the Lord,
That I will seek after:  That I may dwell in the house of the Lord
All the days of my life,
To behold the beauty of the Lord, and to worship in His temple
Praise God from whom all blessings flow.

# *Psalm 28*

*by Adin Thayer*
PEACE ACTIVIST

I call upon You, O Lord, my foundation, and pray that You respond.
If You are silent, I will fall like others who are without hope.

I call to You, I call upon You to hear my plea.

Do not leave me with those who do wrong, those who pretend peace but
have no peace in their hearts. To those who behave unjustly, give what
they deserve for their wrongdoing, and do not allow them to prosper.

Because they ignore Your works and Your teaching, You shall destroy
them, they shall not be allowed to live outside Your teaching.

I praise You for receiving my prayer. You are my strength, my protector,
and my spirit. My trust in You has answered my need. Therefore I rejoice
with my heart and praise You with my words.

You are the strength of all who truly seek You. May You care for us, Your
people, may You protect and provide for us forever.

# *Psalm 29*

## *by Bessie Nicodemus*

Give praise to God for all His glory and strength,
Praise the glory of God's name.
Give God your respect.

You can hear God's name on the sea,
You can hear God's name in the thunder,
You can hear God's name everywhere.
God's name is powerful and majestic.

God's voice breaks the Cedars—even the Cedars of Lebanon.
His voice makes Lebanon and Sirion shake like young calves.
God's voice can walk through fire,
God's voice shakes the desert of Kadesh,
God's voice gives life to the animals in the forest,
And in the temple everyone praises His glory.

God rules over all the seas, He rules forever.
God gives strength to His people, and blesses them with peace.

# *Psalm 30*

*by Gina M. Finocchiaro*
PASTOR

Dark nights welcome shadows of doubt
creeping into my mind and soul.
My body convulses with racks of pain,
with fever of illness, with sorrow of fear.
My clamor rising to the heavens
   "O God, my God, I want to be well.
   Please, O Gracious One, heal me."
I cry through fits of tears.

Alas, the sun crackling through to my eyes,
the shimmers of a new day beginning,
a new hope for renewal and strength.

Today, O God, I am here because you have seen me
through that night, my battles, wayside and fallen.
Forever and forever more, my God, I will praise you.
  Restoreth my health you have
  Restoreth my soul you have
  Restoreth my faith
Forever and always.

And to all now, I beckon:
  Come before God with your sack loaded of burdens
  Come before God with your cups overfilled of tears
  Come before God with your bundles tied of pains
  And cry out for God's help—always near.
  Exchange your sorrow for God's joy.

  Together then we thank our God
  We dance and do not mourn
  We sing and do not bellow
  We rest and do not fret.

  Sing praises unto God, O faithful friends
  Sing praises unto God, O joyous souls
  Sing praises unto God, O grateful ones

  All forgiving is our God
  All loving is our God
  Forever and always more.

# *Psalm 31*

*by Carol Dick*
TEACHER

I avoid those who cling to worthless idols,
        and put my trust in the eternal Lord.
You have not shackled me to temporal things,
You have set me free.
When my strength fails,
And when fear is all around,
I will trust in You.

Let lies be silent.
Let your Truth prevail.
How great is your goodness.
Love the Lord, who protects the faithful.
Take courage, all you who wait
        for the Lord.

# Psalm 32

*by Tanya Kopec*
FAMILY DAYCARE PROVIDER

Those who know their sins are forgiven can live in bliss.
We are freed from living in deceit.

When we do not confess our sins to the Lord,
we carry a burden and feel worn down.
When we completely confess our sins to the Lord
and know all are forgiven, the burden is lifted and we are released.

All faithful people shall pray to you, Lord, in times of need.
We can rest knowing that your deliverance protects us.

We will be instructed by you and you will guide us and watch over us.
We shall obey.

Those who are wicked will suffer,
but those who submit to the Lord's ways will be sheltered by His love.

All you righteous people, be glad and rejoice to the Lord
always with singing and praise.

# Psalm 33

*by Sarah Cutler*
YOGA TEACHER

Know that God is in everything.
Feel God's enormous presence.
Radiate joy, peace, and love.

In all you do, in all you are, Child of the Divine,
create and participate in Divine Beauty.
Praise God with the instrument of your life!
Make music to God with all that is around you.
Create anew the melodies of your life
in loud shouts and quiet whispers.

God is the creative Pattern,
that gives order and clarity to the Universe.
God's love fills the Universe and
informs every just and loving thing.
Divine word and intention made the Universe;
the Breath of God brought life to all Beings.

Form and formlessness, boundless yet binding.
God contains the ocean as in a bottle
and encompasses all the deep places of darkness or fear.
Do you not yet feel awe?

The pattern woven by Divine Intention
is greater than the council of any nation.
With God, all plans fall apart.
But to let go, to surrender to the weaving of God in the Universe,
to listen to the still small Presence inside,
is to let magic unfold.

This Knowledge of the Divine and
trust in Creation
will uphold the people of all ages.

Joy and contentment is to all
who realize the Sacred among them
Knowing and known by God, this Divine Family
is the heir to the Kingdom.

It is not in things, but in trust and openness
that you gain Power.
Neither a ruler's army
nor a militant's strength offers protection.
Tank or gun, education or cunning, all of these are vain hopes;
no tool and no object can provide what God will not,
for the successful have surrendered their attempt to control the outcome
of God's weaving in the Universe.

God is present to those who are awed by the Sacred
and to those who believe in and witness Divine Love.
This Love will carry your soul into Life
and will feed you in famine, inspire you in drought, and sustain you in
hardship.

Our souls crave to be touched and held by God,
who weaves us into the Universe and offers us sanctuary.
We rejoice because we Know Divine Love,
and we trust, surrendering into the Creative Pattern of the Universe.

O God, Holy One, Source of Creation,
let us know, live, and manifest Your Love.
We let go, and trust in You.

# *Psalm 34*

## *by The Davis Family*

In loving memory of Doris Eloise Allen Davis
Beloved mother and grandmother

We have ancestors who have passed through the journey of time
and have become angels who stand by our sides to guide and protect us.
As we find our way in our journey,
we feel their presence and listen to their warnings.

The message is clear and resonates within this Psalm. It is nothing new.
We have heard it before when we were once children ourselves.
Now we have the blessings of children to guide and to raise,
and the message is even more powerful.

Respect ... always with respect with words and action.
Truth ... always keep truth within our lips.
Humility ... growing up is a joyous journey
but we find ourselves in foolish confidence.
Deceit, greed, and jealousy have ways of self-consumption.

Recognize that we are not perfect and to know
perfection is to understand
and to acknowledge that there is Only One.

When fear confronts us and engulfs us with hopelessness and despair,
 stand tall and be humbled by the presence of the Spirit.

To know Him is to know that we are always protected,
that our prayers are heard
and that He stands by our sides in our journey.

"Glorify the Lord with us; let us exalt His name together."

# Psalm 35

### by Louis J. Mitchell and krysia lycette villón
SEMINARY STUDENT AND WRITER/POET

Lord, stand for me. Stand and defend me against my attackers. Block their way and shield me with your strength. Let me know that you are my protection. Confuse their thoughts and make them ashamed and guilty for wanting to hurt me. Haunt them with their malicious words, for without reason, they have planned to destroy me. Let them stumble into the trap they have laid for me.

I will shout with joy for my safety from their harm. I will shout and praise—"Lord, who is like you?"

My enemies lied and blamed me for things that I did not do or say. I was a Christian to them: showing empathy when they were sick, mourning with them in their losses. But they celebrated my hardships—individually and collectively. They laughed at me. They mocked me. They scorned me.

Lord, how long will you sit and witness their cruelty without saving me? I will praise you—alone and among my brothers and sisters. Please do not let my enemies gloat—they are liars and deceivers. They hate me for no reason.

Lord, please do not stay quiet. Come close to me. Be my shield and my sun. Judge me as you will and stand up for me against their gloating and lies. Let their shame, guilt and confusion be their undoing. Let them rejoice in your name for my salvation, knowing that it is you who saves and condemns.

And I will praise you. I will praise you out loud, every moment of every day.

# Psalm 36

*by Eliete Brasil*
RESIDENTIAL COUNSELOR

An oracle cannot see that he is wicked and a sinner.
He is not fearful of God.
His words are false.
He had to commit himself to evil and cannot see that he is wrong.
God, your mercy and fidelity reach the sky.
Your justice is like the highest mountain.
O Lord, you preserve animals and humans.
How precious is your kindness.
All men can find refuge in the shadow of your wings.
You give them drink from your river.
God, you are the fountain of life.
Still giving your love to the people who already know you.
Show your love to those who need to know you.
Do not let the wicked come to me.
The evildoers are down and will not rise up again.

# *Psalm 37*

*by Sujata Rege Konowitz*
EDUCATOR

All scripture comes to us for a reason.
This is my lesson today about envy, desire, and not losing faith.
I may notice prosperity in others and feel envy.
Why? Why is good coming to others and seemingly not to me?

As I question this I must look closer at myself and toward my God.

| Trust | —trust all is right in my world |
|-------|--------------------------------|
| Delight | —delight at where I am presently |
| Commit | —commit to remaining faithful and hopeful |
| Rest | —rest and find patience and joy in the wait |

There may be those who acquire prosperity through ill acts, but it will be short lived. Their ill ways may come full circle to hurt them. Trust that prosperity acquired in good ways will bring with it an abundance of peace and long lasting joy.
Find the goodness and the God in myself and live from that place.
Delight in even the little that comes to me in this way. It is far better than all the riches that may come from any wicked ways. Depart from evil and do good. For it is only goodness that continues on, can change the world and truly lives forever.
If I fall, I must hold onto my faith and remain hopeful remembering that God is still with me even when it is difficult to feel the presence within myself. I am blessed even in my most difficult hour.
When I can see my own prosperity, I won't feel envy. I will know what I have is perfect and find a place to rest in that knowing. There is joy to be had in my present and peace in my future.

# *Psalm 38*

### *by Lois K. Happe*
PASTOR

Please, please, God, don't punish me any more—
     I feel your rejection in every fiber of my being.
I am crushed by the weight of your displeasure;
     your wrath torments me without reprieve.

When I consider my wretchedness,
     I am overwhelmed with revulsion and disgust;
     my whole being gags on the sickness of my soul.
There is no cure for the pestilence that infects every cell of my body.
     There is no purge for the shame that racks me night and day.
I fast but there is no relief;
     I scour my insides, but there is no catharsis;
     I cannot retch enough to uproot my wickedness.

O God, you know what I yearn for;
        you hear my pleas far into the night.

My heart aches, and I am weary unto death.
My friends avoid me
        and my family is in despair.
Other women look upon me with scorn;
        they flaunt their slender bodies in my face,
        and taunt me with their gracefulness.
What can I do with this reproach?
        I sit silent in my condemnation.

So I wait for you, O God,
        wait for your word of forgiveness,
        wait for your word of absolution.

Don't let the eyes of my enemies see how ugly I am;
        don't let them gloat in their smug assurance.
I cannot go on much longer;
        my shame is relentless,
        my guilt is endless.
I confess my unworthiness;
        my imperfection is constantly before my eyes.

My enemies, however, are strong and confident;
        they hate me and accuse me.
No matter what I do,
        they condemn me in their hearts.

Do not abandon me, O God;
        Do not hide from me or leave me alone.
Hear my cry of desperation.
        Have mercy upon me, O God of hope and healing.

# Psalm 39

*by Renee Fall*
GRANT WRITER

Sometimes I keep my complaints to myself,
so others cannot relish my suffering
or say I told you so.

But my silence eats away at me.
I am angry and confused;
I need to question:

God, how long are my days?
Life seems short to me,
yet to you my life must be a split second in eternity.

We're all here such a brief time,
what difference do we really make?
Why do we work to better ourselves and the world,
when soon we're gone and we will never know the
results?

What is my purpose here,
and how long should I hope to live?
Can't you spare me the suffering?
Is this all a part of your plan?
It does me in.

God, please hear my need and respond.
I know, like all the rest I'm just passing through.
Please lighten my heart
before you end my days.

# Psalm 40

## by Tracey Sutphin and Kristie Miller
### OFFICE ADMINISTRATOR AND PHYSICIAN

Faith Persevering in Trial

There was a time in which I needed God desperately, so I prayed for Him patiently, and in time I could see that He heard my prayers.

My life had been overwhelming me, my troubles felt like quicksand trying to swallow me, and the Lord pulled me out of it so that I was steady on my own two feet.

I am now a different person, and I am sharing my story of how the Lord helped me, so that everyone will know of His power, and trust in His greatness.

Those who trust in the ways of God will be blessed. God teaches us not to succumb to pride, and to listen carefully for the truth.

Lord, you have been so generous in your acts of kindness, and you have shown us the path of goodness in so many ways that it is hard to recall them all.

You have shown me that you do not require us to sacrifice ourselves, but instead to follow your teachings.

I am delighted to follow your path, and your law of goodness is now in my heart, a part of me.

I have been sharing your goodness with everyone around me.

I tell everyone of how you were there for me when I needed you, and how you saved me with your love and kindness

Lord, I thank you for letting me feel your love and tenderness as much as possible, for this kindness keeps me going.

In my life I have felt surrounded by difficulties, challenges, and at times I feel that my sins are so numerous that I am ashamed.
O Lord, show me your way, help me

Let those who bring negativity and
destruction to my life think twice before they challenge me.

Let those who look towards you and bring you into their lives find happiness and love. Let them sing your praises.

Those of us that are poor and need direction will find the help we need in the Lord. Please hurry, my God.

# *Psalm 41*

*by Karen V. Hurd*
TEACHER

God is pleased with those who are kind to the poor.
He never forgets them when they are in need.
He is always protecting them, day and night. Even when their enemies
speak falsely of them, he will never leave their side.
He takes care of them when they are sick and when they cannot care for
themselves.

Oh, God, I beg of you to heal me and be kind to me because I have hurt
you and I am sorry.

My enemies sit around and whisper: When will he die? I thought that
they were my friends but that was not true. They care little about me. As
they leave, they laugh and make fun of me.

They gossip among themselves about what they will do when I am gone.

They say that it is just a matter of time and that I will never leave this bed.

Even the person I trusted the most, to whom I told my innermost
thoughts, has turned against me.

Oh, God, please do not leave me. Heal me, so I can pay them back.

I know that you will never leave me nor let my enemies get the best of me.

You have kept me because of my integrity, and have placed me in your
presence forever.

May God be praised!

# Psalm 42

## by Lauren E. Snead
### ARTIST AND MUSICIAN

My heart and soul are thirsty for Love
I feel a void, a hole longing to be filled
I recognize the emptiness and I turn to Love

Why is my soul so empty?
Why do I feel so alone?
I drink from the endless fountain of Love
I am nourished and fulfilled,
I remember and feel Love in my life

Love, I need you to reach
the depths of my emptiness
Love, Kindness and Peace,
be with me through each day

In the evening I am filled with song
I sing my joy,
and I pray through music

Yet Love, when you are so strong
Love, when you are so present
Love, when you are so sturdy
Why don't I feel you sometimes?
Where do you go?
Why must I mourn?

I turn to Love over and over again
To lift my spirits, to lift my soul
To fill my being, to fill my heart

I put my hope and trust in Love
Forever, for always
LoveGodLove

# *Psalm 43*

*by Susan Burggraf*
COLLEGE PROFESSOR

My Lord, in this moment it feels like you have abandoned me.
I feel like an outcast and scapegoat by others who obviously do not see
      your light in me.

Save me from this heaviness and oppression I am burdened by!
Please guide me home to you, to your sanctuary where I am held by your
      love.

I call to you, but my own anxiety is screaming too loud for me to hear you.
I am miserable and my vision is clouded by my loneliness.
Nevertheless, I pray and open my heart in yearning to once again feel
      your calm, your Presence in my heart.

Your Presence purifies my sight and restores me to feeling your love even
      by those who oppress me.

Oh, Precious Lord who brings only joy and delight, I take refuge in you,
      in the sanctuary my yearning has made for you in my open, grateful
      heart.

# Psalm 44

*by Peter Ives*
MINISTER

We have heard with our ears, O God
Our mothers and fathers have told us of Your deeds
In their days, in the days of old
Other nations faltered
But You helped them to grow
Others experienced affliction
But You set them free
Not by themselves did they become Your people
But by Your right hand
And by the light of Your countenance

You have been our Lord and our God
Through the power of Your love,
We have triumphed over adversities.
Through Your goodness,
We have overcome obstacles before us.
It wasn't by our own strength alone
But You who helped us find a way out of no way.

To You O Lord we give thanks and praise

But now, You have cast us off and forsaken us
We feel like sheep waiting to be slaughtered.
We feel weak and powerless
We feel You have sold us down the river
And we have no value in Your eyes
We feel persecuted and ridiculed
A laughingstock among peoples.
All this has happened to us
Even though we have not forgotten You
Or departed from Your ways.

So why have You left us broken in our broken places?
Why have You covered us in deep darkness?
If we had forgotten Your name or prayed to other gods,
You would have discovered it,
For You know the secrets of our hearts.
Instead, it feels that we are being led toward destruction,
Like we are sheep for the slaughter.

Why do You sleep, O Lord? Awake!
Don't abandon us forever.

# *Psalm 45*

*by Janet Aalfs*
POET, MARTIAL ARTIST, TEACHER

Wild Lilies: Shoshannim

*My tongue is the pen of a ready writer,*
my hands leaves of praise
wind carries, words etch. Sun

infusing shadows, I read
between the lines, mortal,
immortal, ancient voices rise.

I listen to the song
unfettered, smell the blossom
not bred, follow the woman who leads

and follows well
but is not led
into forgetting.

*Scepter of equity*, ready tongue,
pen dipped in *myrrh and aloe, cassia*
planted long before the word

of mystery was made
to shrink in the thrones of men.
Common heart of the law

ignited, *logos* wise within
and beyond, I sing
from roots older and deeper

than meet the eye. Fueled
by the frank-incense of truth
I breathe the infinite

winds of justice strong
and kind *to be remembered*
*in all generations.* Anointed

*in oils of gladness*, my pen
a grateful tongue set free.

# Psalm 46

*by Marion VanArsdell*
TEACHER

God is our comfort and our support, beside us
when we are most in need.

So we will not be afraid even when the world is
filled with change and insecurity.

Even though the very waters of the earth are
troubled and earthquakes shake the mountains.

There is a river steady and calm that carries the
promise of peace to God's city, a holy place.

God is there in the midst of the city and will
protect and sustain that place.

Though evil surrounds us and threatens our
security, God's voice can calm the world.

The Lord of all time is with us. The God of our
ancestors is our hiding place.

Look again at the works of the Lord, how he has
laid waste to evil.

God brings an end to wars, breaking the bow and
the spears, burning the chariots.

Listen then and know that I am God. I will
triumph over disbelief and be honored in all parts
of the world.

The Lord of all time is with us still. The God of
our ancestors is our comfort in all of our troubles.

# Psalm 47

*by Jennifer Leary*
TEACHER

People rally in large groups to make themselves heard.

Let's all come together!

Every man, woman and child.

People of every race, color, religious background and sexual preference.

Let's make ourselves heard as we celebrate our higher power!

Let's rejoice in the fact that we can worship "our God" in any way we choose and give thanks for all the good He or She brings to us.

# Psalm 48

*by Kathy Silva*
CORRECTIONAL OFFICER

God is great, and we should always praise him
       anywhere and everywhere we go.

Every city is his and he should be praised in them
       to the fullest.

People come together within his cities
       who don't love or praise God, and who suffer.

Some people think their suffering is because of God,
       which causes them to be afraid of him.

This fear causes them not to love him.

Love God, honor him, and walk with him in your life.

Teach your children of his goodness and his love
       so they too may walk with him forever.

For his cities are filled with happiness and contentment,
       only if you can see it.

# Psalm 49

*by Korri Piper*
ADMINISTRATIVE ASSISTANT

A Song for the People of Korah, by the Chief Musician

All God's creatures great and small, pay heed to what I say!
Prince, pauper, servant or Sheba, bend your ear I may.

For my notes compose a melody strong and sound,
As each pitch harmonizes the truth comes unbound.

If fear strikes my drum when enemies take hold
Shall my rhythm be drowned out by the clank of their gold?

Midas's fortune ten times over could not place you in God's favor.
Death: a blind escort to sultans and sitar players on the road to the
Creator.

The prophet shall pass and likewise the fool,
As their fortunes sink to the depths of a spiritless pool.

They will reach their graves with the earth as their beds.
Though in life pillows of satin cradled their heads.

To this denouement come the fool and his flock:
The lack of God's light at the end of the clock.

The Banshee's chariot leaves the dead behind devoid of all sorrow,
She knows God's children will dance in the sun on their graves tomorrow.

# Psalm 50

*by Don Carr*
TAX ACCOUNTANT

The Lord God has spoken, reaching the earth all day long.
God arrives out of the lovely spot Zion, and He shines brightly,
Coming in fire and storm and with plenty of noise.
In order to judge His people, He will call from on high to the
skies and the land.
He is the judge himself, obviously righteous,
And wants to reach the people who have made a contract
with Him by sacrificing.
God calls Israel, His chosen people, to listen
As He makes clear how He judges them.

He says that He does not condemn their continual burnt offerings
And the sacrifices they place before Him.
But He makes it clear that He will take neither
The bull from their home nor the goat from their herd.
After all, He needs nothing they could offer inasmuch as
He owns the whole of creation: all of the wild beasts
Of the fields and the woods and the domestic cattle too.
Were He hungry, He wouldn't ask them for anything
Since they can't really possess His property.
Even so, He encourages their vows and gratitude,
Saying that He will save His faithful when they encounter misfortune.

God also has words for the wicked people,
Asking how they even dare to speak those words
Of the covenant or that describe good behavior.
He says the wicked hate to learn the correct ways
And they turn away from His words.
These nasty persons conspire with thieves
And become involved with adulterers.
He speaks at length about their lies and slander,
Saying they will even speak ill of their own brothers.
He continues with a warning to those who have not yet been punished
For their vile ways and therefore assume that God is like them,
Willing to countenance evil behavior and do nothing.

God tells them to think it over, how they have ignored Him.
They could be in grave danger because He threatens
To tear them apart and they will have no chance of escape at all.
But He does say that He is pleased by the righteous who
glorify God with praise.
So they have that hope. In such a case (if they reform)
He will set them right,
And He will reform such people's ways so they cease speaking evil
And they shall find the salvation that God provides.

# *Psalm 51*

### *by Denise Karuth*
### ADVOCATE

Judge me kindly, O God, as you are always loving;
As you are always kind, blot out my wrongs.
Wash from me every trace of my unjust, unfair nature,
And cleanse me of my self-centeredness.

For I know my misdeeds,
And my actions lie heavy on my heart.
All my wrongs are, ultimately, against you,
I have failed in love as you watched,
So that you are right to sentence me and blameless for
holding me accountable.

Indeed, I was born straying, a wandering sheep when my mother conceived me.

You desire truth at the core of all beings;
Therefore teach me wisdom in my innermost heart.
Purify me with sacred herbs and I shall be clean,
Wash me, and I shall be whiter than snow.
Let me hear joy and gladness;
Let even my brokenness be joyful.

Look not on my wrongs, and blot out all my unjust, unfair ways.

Create in me a clean heart, O God, and uphold a willing spirit within me.

Do not banish me from your presence,
And do not take your holy spirit from me.
Renew in me the joy of your saving grace,
And uphold a willing spirit within me.
Then I will teach wrongdoers your ways,
And your lost sheep will return to you.
Deliver me from the violence I have done, O God, O God who redeems me, and I will sing aloud of your deliverance.
O God, restore my hope, and my words will be filled with your praise.
For you have no delight in grand gestures;
If I were to make a show of giving, you would not be pleased.

The gift acceptable to God is a willing spirit.
O God, you will embrace a willing and contrite heart.
Care for Creation in your joy, O God;
Establish peace and safety in the ruined city,
Then you will delight in true gifts;
In offerings that reflect and increase your love;
Then these things will be offered to you.

# *Psalm 52*

*by Nancy Pick*
SCIENCE WRITER


Traitor!
(Ahimelech was one
in the eyes of Saul,
for he helped the enemy David—
gave him bread
and sword.)
Saul says
Ahimelech has a tongue
like a razor.

Yet the story is not Saul's to tell.
For David wins, of course.
In the Psalms,
David gets to write whatever he wants,
His version
summons all Saul's righteous anger
toward Ahimelech,
the evil one,
the liar.

Saul put that traitor to death.

Traitor?
In the end, we must love Ahimelech
if we would love David
the writer,
the king.
It is all a matter of perspective.

I see both sides of everything.
Perhaps this is what comes of reading too many novels.

# Psalm 53

*by Hannah Todd*
STUDENT

I passed a man in the street
He cried of injustice.
I saw a poet on T.V.
She talked of the war.
I heard a newspaper reporter;
He said people were starving.
The magazines said the billionairess, well,
She bought a new car.

If I stood on Mount Everest,
Or floated through space,
All I would see are the corrupt and the foolish;
The few who do good are lost in the shade.
Those who are highest,
Who influence most,
Who run the great nations,
They've all become lost.
They all believe there is no one to watch them,
No one to catch them,
No one who cares.

Who are they that block the good from sight?
Who are they that they swallow upright
Like a terrible leviathan, leaving behind
Only charred excrement,
Absent of life?
They are those that preach G-d,
While G-d stands behind them,
Ignored, abused, and weeping with fright.

It's time to turn them to face what they're doing,
It's time to turn them to see what they've done,
Their bones will be scattered, their shame brought upon them,
And G-d will stand smiling when goodness has won.
Those with compassion, those with understanding,
Those who have strived to make everything fair,
They will revive and rejoice in the sun.

# Psalm 54

### by Steven Siclari and Edward Lockhart
#### SALON OWNERS

Hi, God.

Yeah, it's me again. I know it might seem like I only talk to you when I'm in trouble, but I do think about you a lot.

Well, you're right, I'm in trouble. My first thought was to promise you all kinds of new things. My second thought was maybe I should try to catch up on the stuff I already owe you.

So ... please, please, please, help me this one time and I'll do all those things I promised.

I REALLY do promise.

Thanks, God.

# *Psalm 55*

*by Tim Button*
STUDENT

If I could reach with my teeth I would have no need to pray for annexation.

I would gnaw through the rope woven from 10,000 umbilical cords tying me to this antediluvian appendage.

I would emancipate myself from my brothers, my sisters, the throng of conjoined humanity.

I would refuse to share their stagnant blood in which creeps a rot cascading from the root out.

I would clip their wagging tongues which drip cyclopean philosophy. I would pluck out my own heart before it ferments, but I cannot.

The fires of ancestral hubris have fused me to this malignant apostate stitched together from the heads of unbaptized babies.

A sea of countless orifices ejaculate unnecessary humors and pedestrian sounds down into my ears and mouth.

Under this cacophony I am drowning, my lungs filling with the lukewarm drool of the living dead; I am sinking into complacent flesh.

Before my eyes are flooded with reptilian milk I ask you to amputate my complaint and in the fraction of silence reach in and remove me.

Tear down the walls of this scale-model Pandemonium and cremate the blind maelstrom masturbating inside.

Ignore the jigsaw pleas for forgiveness for even the leanest of masks is marbled with fat.

Collect their ashes, feed them to me, and I will turn dense and opaque on nitrogen rich comeuppance.

Nurture me and I will grow to be an uncut monument to the Divinity of natural tools.

# Psalm 56

### by Lisa Freitag-Keshet and Meirav Kalfon Keshet
#### RABBI AND MARKETING MANAGER

In honor of Maor Kalfon, z'l
A defender of Israel,
and a man "who walked in the light that shines on the living."

For the leader concerning the community of Israel likened to a silent dove when they are far from their cities. A Psalm of David when the Philistines seized him at Gat.

God, be compassionate to me for I am tired of the hardships of war.

The armies of my enemies pursued me today, Boundless GOD.

In these times of fear, in you Adonai I will place my trust.

By GOD, I will rejoice.
By GOD, I will trust.
I shall not fear the doings of flesh and blood.

All through the day, I was pressed by the evil pursuits of my enemies.

They gathered and surrounded me; they stalked me,
waiting to take my soul.

For their evil, punish them with great might.
You will bring my enemies down, My GOD.

You are who determines my fate.
Keep my tears in your cup.
Those are the tears that you have written for me in your book.

Surely, my enemies will turn back on the day that I will call to you.
I believe, for GOD is with me.

By GOD, I will rejoice.
In Adonai, I will rejoice.
In GOD, I put my trust.
I shall not fear.
What can a human do to me?

Your blessings are upon me, Oh GOD.
Hence, I will offer thanks to you.

For you have rescued my soul from death,
and removed me from harm's way.
That I may walk with GOD in the light that shines on the living.

# *Psalm 57*

*by Laurie Walhovd*
ENTREPRENEUR

How fragile this earthly life,
How thin the line between joy and despair.
Let me rest where I can feel your glory,
alone at your feet, yet wrapped in love.

I look to what my eyes can see;
I look down, disgraced, discouraged, disheartened.
But when I raise my eyes, Oh Lord,
And look beyond what I understand,
A gentle stirring quickly leaps
To thunderous JOY
For I see your truth.

When I see clearly my joy
Streaming from the love in your eyes
My strength grows from under your shield
My protection, within your teaching.
I begin to understand...
That even what is painful,
is part of your great plan.

My courage rides on the direction of your
Merciful breath,
While my sorrow and fear
Fly through the heart of the gentle forest
Transformed in your light
As they soar high and far away.

I place my life in your hands, Father!
In you alone will I seek solace
For my weary spirit
My journey is safe and noble
My burden is light
If to you, I submit my will.

# Psalm 58

*by Françoise Harrison*
TEACHER AND WRITER

A Psalm for the Media

Do you print what's true?
Do you ignore all falsehoods?
Speak of justice?

Not at all. You slant the facts
And feature scandal, every issue.
Your writers, fed on lies
Before their birth,
Now feed their poisoned information
Into their computers,
Avoiding honest sources

Whose goal is to inform
Not sell unwanted goods
Or cause good folks to riot.

Break their contracts, O Lord!
Crash their computers!
Let them have no hard copy,
No backup floppy!

Just like Siegfried and like Roy,
Make tigers of the press
All disappear before our eyes.
Like yesterday's celebrities,
May they see their famous names
Removed from precious A-lists.

Honest folks will cheer
As you turn the pages of the 'zines
Into Pooper Scoopers.
Good folks will shout
While shredding the spreadsheets
Of the rumor mongers.
The couch potatoes will finally take notice,
Praise the God of decent TV programs,
And say, "There's justice, after all.
God's taken charge, at last!"

# Psalm 59

*by Cappie Glica*
GRANDMOTHER

We are faced with temptations and challenges every day.

They are difficult to escape and often are hidden or disguised in very subtle ways. Likewise, in today's world it can be difficult to distinguish those who may have ulterior motives as they approach us.

In our day-to-day interactions with others, can we always know who is our friend and who may wish to harm us in some fashion?

We need to be strong, rely on our beliefs and our faith in God.

Take strength from our faith and believe in ourselves.

Do not falter in our faith and in the knowledge that God is with us and watching over us.

# Psalm 60

## by Jenny Fleming
### WOMEN'S HEALTH NURSE PRACTIONER

O God, I despair that you are not with us as
     violence reigns once again, historic lands destroyed
     and precious lives wasted.

     I lament the suffering of men, women and children
     experiencing terror, hardship and death.

     I petition you to help us find a way forward to peace and justice
     and to reaffirm all that is lovely in life.

In stillness, I hear you, God.

I hear you speak words of reassurance, comfort and hope:

     "Always know that I am with the peacemaker,
     with those who work for justice and love,
     with those who defend the poor and support the weak."

O God, I hear your promise now,
     that armies, bombs and people bent on deceit and destruction
     will not be the final word,
     that despite setbacks, and even defeat,

Your love and your goodness will prevail.

# Psalm 61

*by Chris Perry*
HOMELESS BROTHER

Please God, hear my request for forgiveness.
I ask for your healing and power to make me well.

Lead me to a place that is closer to the heavens,
God, you are my fortress against my enemies.

Let me live by your truth and your will, forever.
Wherever you are is where I want to be, too.
O God, you have heard what I have promised,
You have given me hope in what I believe in.

Let me walk in the path of Jesus for all my life,
As he walks with me let him walk with my family
And the rest of the people who live on the earth
And all the planets everywhere!

Jesus will always be the King, forever.
His love will be with you forever,
For eternity!

God, I will always worship you and praise you.
I will sing your songs every day.
I will live my promises,
As you protect me and watch over my spirit.

# Psalm 62

*by Caryn Markson and Peggy Gillespie*
PSYCHOLOGIST AND JOURNALIST/WRITER

During this lifetime
we have witnessed people
commit acts of unspeakable cruelty
towards other people
and destroy the precious balance
of the natural world. Greed
turns rain forests into desolate landscapes
and contaminates sweet jasmine air. Greed
sends soldiers, soldiers, and more soldiers seeking
weapons of mass destruction
with weapons of mass destruction,
knocking villages down like they
were tumbling fences, killing families
as easily as pushing over
a tottering wall in their way.

Where is God, the salvation,
the rock, the refuge
for those wide-eyed children watching
in silence the slaughter of their parents?
We ask, dear heart,
who can we trust?
We wait for your answer in silence.

Not everyone recognizes that the arms
of God are holding them. Not everyone
remembers that their arms are the arms of God.
When falsehood and attack happen
from the outside, we must hold
fast in our hearts to the God that is our very heart.
When the world around us is ruled by
harshness and lies, our leaders betraying us,
pretending to love and care for us
with blessings, prayers, and promises
that camouflage acts of cruelty,
we can never be betrayed
by the true God within.

We must remember
that we are never lost
when we take refuge in God—our very heart.
If our soul is at rest in the God we hold
in our hearts, we stand firm.
The God in our hearts is our rock,
our salvation, our refuge.
If we trust in God, we will never be shaken.

# *Psalm 63*

### *by Kizzi Buchmelter*
MOTHER AND TEACHER

Ahh, Love. You are the true God I eagerly seek. Your powers can soothe a burning soul and mend a breaking heart. You are always there, yet not always seen.

I look for You, Love, in my family and in myself.

Your positive presence is far better than any of life's materialistic treasures. You are forever cherished by me.

I will honor You and protect Your name for as long as I am able.

I see You, Love, as I watch my beautiful children learn and grow, loving themselves and others. I can sense Your calming presence each time I smile at an angry, evil face.

You have lovingly embraced me when I was in doubt and faced with deceit. You gave me a caring hand to make sure I would not unconsciously slip between the cracks of Hate. You stand a great mirror in front of me whenever I am selfish, naive or pessimistic.

Love, You blessed me with my mothers, sisters, husband and children—all of whom helped shape the thoughtful, beautiful, loving person I am today.

Those who try to destroy my love will in turn destroy only themselves— leaving them alone and scared, vulnerable to Hate.

All should praise You, Love, like the true God You are, praise You with true sincerity in their actions, not just with preached words.

Accept Love into your life. You will then involuntarily learn to love yourself and others, helping to shape this world into a more trusting, secure, beautiful place for all.

# Psalm 64

*by Bill Zimmer*

ADMINSTRATOR, DEPARTMENT OF MENTAL RETARDATION

How can it be, Lord,
That your most precious
Gift to us—
The magic of words that makes us
But a little lower than the angels—
Can be twisted into weapons
More wounding than knives?

That which makes us
Most human—
The transformation, through
words, of the mundane into the
Holy—
Can, alternately,
Char the soul
in baseness and hatred.

We deceive ourselves, Lord,
As we deceive others,
Denying ill intent
while we ambush the innocent
and the inarticulate
with subtle, but piercing,
Invective.

Those who mesmerize with
words,
But whose haughtiness
masks malevolence,
Must be humbled by your
Magnificent poetry,
And shamed for their perversion
of your most sacred
Gift.

# Psalm 65

*By Laurie Priest and Annie Harrison*
TEACHERS

We sing praises to you, God, and ask that you hear our prayers.

We want to walk with you in faithfulness, but we are only human and ask that you forgive our shortcomings.

May we honor you with loving care of all living things, recognizing our interdependence and grateful for your many blessings. We know that to you all life must return.

You set glaciers in motion to carve our mountains, and your rain feeds the rivers that shape our fertile valleys. You provide us with more than we need and we thank you, God, for the elements of nature that sustain.

You are a just and merciful God, and we delight in the diversity of your creation. Forgive us, God, for the greed and gluttony that threaten our planet. We join our sisters and brothers around the world in prayers for peace.

We give thanks, gracious God, for a warm home in winter and an abundant harvest in fall. We thank you for the spring rains and the summer sun. We, your daughters, vow to live in harmony with the seasons, and we promise to honor you by our deeds.

Hear our song of praise and thanksgiving, God, and hear our prayer that all life may cheer and sing for joy.

# Psalm 66

*by Barry Werth*
WRITER

The Isley Brothers said it best, I think.

They said they want You to know,
They want You to know right now,
That You've been good to us,
Better than we've been to ourselves.

And that if You ever leave us
We don't want nobody else.

But then You go and test us,
And bring enslavement.
And holocausts.
Why?
If You're so great how can You be so terrible?

The answer is, But You don't turn us away, afterwards.
You hear our pleas
And listen to our praises,
And don't refuse us the kindness we seek.
You put fear in our enemies and
Deliver us from narrow places.

Weeeeelllll!

You know You make me want to shout
Kick my heels up and shout
Throw my hands up and shout
Throw my hands back and shout
Don't forget to say You will
Don't forget to say yeah yeah yeah yeah yeah
(Say You will)

# Psalm 67

### by Emily Dines, Mae V. Smith, Sally J. Lemaire, and Patricia LaFreniere

THE HAYDENVILLE CONGREGATIONAL CHURCH WRITERS' WORKSHOP

God, we reflect our inner light
like a prism—like a rainbow.
Open your heart to us, dear Lord,
and show us the way to peace.

RAIN YOUR BLESSINGS ON US!

Help us through our turmoil
to better understand each other.
Teach us Thy way—
the world awaits.
Come now or come later
but come as fast as you can.

LET THE PEOPLE SAY AMEN!

Direct our spirits to feed the hungry,
house the homeless,
heal the wounded,
and lift their sorrow.

LET JOY EMERGE!

Bring peace to our earth.
Judge us wisely,
for we are all created
uniquely in your image.

LET THE PEOPLE SAY AMEN!

Dear God, you have blessed us
in so many ways.
Help us to be humble caretakers
in this world full of need.
AMEN.

# *Psalm 68*

## *by Amy Rothenberg*
### NATUROPATHIC PHYSICIAN, MOTHER, ARTIST

Riding the ancient and modern skies
Through weather hard or soft
Our God of love and nature and time
Using every possible instrument
Playing the chords,
       measuring the breath,
       monitoring the evolution of days.

And we, below, riding too,
Ear to the drumbeat,
Keeping time, like it's ours to keep
Savoring berries and minutes and touches of love
Or wincing at dissonant rhythms, the chords awry
While regardless
The hard or soft breaths
We know as life
       inhaled, exhaled, the expanding lung
       full and open-mouth,
       singing your glory, selah.

# Psalm 69

### *by Lenore Reilly Carlisle*
### ASSISTANT PROFESSOR

God, save me, for I am drowning.
I find it happens often.
Drowning in paper.
Drowning in debt.
Drowning in sorrow.
Drowning in the deep despair that comes from watching a world
      gone wrong.

God knows I am not perfect, that I have made mistakes.
Thankfully, God forgives.
Sadly, the world often doesn't.
It seems the world defines faithfulness in tight terms,
        so little room for forgiveness:
Faith is a perfect circle. A loop of rope around your neck?
Stumble and you'll see how tightly bound you are by the circle of faith,
        how quick the Unforgiving Faithful are to set you free.

In the dark of night I call out,
Sometimes in a whisper,
Sometimes in a cry of anguish.
I'm crushed between my own cry for mercy
and my cry for God to punish those who are so punishing.
The very forgiveness I ask for myself
I would also ask God to deny those who try to hurt me.
How dare I pray such a prayer?

God hears me.
Somehow, even in the midst of the rage,
I trust that God will listen long enough to heed only my final prayer.
Like the waters that would drown me, the rage subsides.
At last, one pure prayer rises above the floods like a bird in flight,
A winged prayer of hope and forgiveness.
And I know these things to be true:
God hears the poor. He will not forsake those who are in pain
        or held captive.
God sees those who have been pushed to the margins of life.

They will somehow be embraced and returned
        to the heart of humankind.
God whispers to us all. A just and kind world is the rightful inheritance
        of all people who are truly faithful.

Perhaps I will not drown after all.

# Psalm 70

*by Justin David*
HUSBAND, FATHER, RABBI

For the leader, a Psalm of David, to shout out

Rescue me, Goddammit!
Come on,
Help me out,
Give me shelter!

They would love to destroy me,
But they'll wind up
Looking stupid,
Backing off,
Tails between their legs.
The whole time yelling,
"Get him!  Get him!"

Finding You is my only
Joy. In You I know love,
Compassion, constancy.

You never leave.
But I can't hold on.

So now,
Here I am,
Poor and
Pathetic.

Help me out,
Give me shelter,
You're all I've got ...

This is no time to wait!

# *Psalm 71*

*by Laura Reed*
PEACE ACTIVIST

Dear God, I look to you for refuge;
please keep me safe and secure.

You are such an inspiration to me.
I can always turn to you when I am in
trouble; you willingly lend your ear
and offer guidance.

Let me look to you as a rock of
refuge and as my home when I
need strength.

Please rescue me from the hands of
the selfish and greedy, from the grasp
of those who are unjust and cruel.

For you give me hope and I have
trusted in you since I was young,
despite my many doubts and
disappointments.

You have always been a force in my life, starting with the miracle of my
birth and my mother's love. Thank you for nurturing me and caring for
me.

Although I cherish many, you provide a special sense of love, hope, and
renewal.

Let my words convey the power of your love; let my spirit feel your
presence.

Please do not abandon me when I am old, or neglect me when I lose my
strength.

For those who wish to harm me are keeping watch for their chance to take
advantage of me when I am vulnerable.

Let not my enemies (both within and without) say, "God has forgotten her, pursue and seize her, for there is none to deliver her."

Please stay by my side; keep me from wanting to give up when others hurt me or I am in pain.

Let all those who are cruel to living creatures change their ways and feel compassion.

Never let me give up hope and help me to appreciate all that I am blessed with each day.

When I speak, fill my words with your message of peace and justice for all, for you make anything possible.

Help me to appreciate and build upon the extraordinary potential of all that is around us.

You have taught me from my childhood; I am still in awe of all I experience.

When I am old and gray, please give me special care so I may pass along your blessings to all the generations to come.

Your spirit is all encompassing. How can I comprehend it?

You have known my troubles and helped me to heal. From the depths of my sadness you have renewed me and helped me to find happiness again.

Comfort me and make me more compassionate and honorable.

You have been important in my life and your faithful presence makes me feel better. I will do my best to be true to all you represent.

In my thoughts, I give you thanks and praise. How can I convey all that you mean to me in words?

You will always be a part of me, as I am a part of you. Please forgive those who have hurt me, for they cannot touch the thrill of what I feel.

# Psalm 72

*by Misha Herscu*
STUDENT

When there is no one
To help, to keep you alive
Then God will come, then

God's enemies fall
God will help good in rising
Justice is God's rule

God ever governs
Creator of all that lives,
Ruling in splendor

Judgment to the King
Advice to the Emperor
Only purest truth

# Psalm 73

*By Deborah Heimel-Karpman and Hannah Heimel-Karpman*
DOMESTIC VIOLENCE AGENCY MANAGER AND PROGRAM DIRECTOR

Alarm clock
    Hot water
        Creased clothing
           Car
               Work
                  Car
                     Gym
                         Television
                            Down comforter
                               Sleep

All that we have
A warm home in winter
A cool home in summer
Two cars
Vacations
Full closets
And cupboards

Friends
Movies

Dinner
Parties
Family

Jobs
That turn the wheel
Of our lives

Yet inside ourselves
It is simplicity we crave

In the stillness of the synagogue
In the rhythm of the davening
In the ritual of the fast
The apples and the honey
The light filtered through
Blue stained glass

The time
To stand
On Shabbat
and remember
Who I am
And those who came before me.

In the stillness of the church
In the cadence of the Our Father
In the ritual of the rosary
The bread and the wine
The light filtered through
The multi-colored glass

The time
To kneel
On Sunday
And remember
Who I am
And He who came before me.

# Psalm 74

## by Leslie Fraser
### MULTIFAITH MINISTER

Why, God, does your sacred heart burn inside of us?

Why stoke this fire, this flame of hope, if not to consume every hindrance
we put in love's way?
> The fire each time, fueled by oxygen, the breath—
> This is what makes the divine heart breathe.
> The flaming heart, the heart on fire, expands and contracts,
> in and out, out and in.
> In this duality of love on fire lives the all-in-all.

We stand in the ruins of your temple, feeding burnt offerings to the
fire inside.

Oh Yahweh, free us from the enemies that separate us from our divinity.

Transform us into love, Kwan Yin. Liberate us from pain, Green Tara.

Comfort and console, sweet Jesus. Unite us, Allah, with the law of oneness.

Oh God, how do we live when miracles cease and your prophets leave us?
> Look to your own hearts, and let the pain you feel be transformed.
> Out of all the hurt you can imagine, when given to God, is born a
> new Jerusalem.
> It is not possible to fight the past, to win old wars.
> Turn your face towards the not-yet-known and feed your fears to
> the fire.
> Let them be consumed.

We know that you know—
> No beginning, no end; no birth, no death.
> Just change, ever change:  creator, creating, created.
> Love becoming more love
> And what is not love, released to be love.

We know that you know—
> There is nothing that is not love,
> Never was and never can be.
> There is only your own not knowing, your own terror terrorizing
> the planet.

Feed it to the burning heart. Fan the flames. See red.

# *Psalm 75*

## *by Ted Hamel*
### GROUNDSKEEPER

Thank you, God, for all you do and have done; you are indeed wonderful.

I decree that at a time that I appoint, a fair and impartial judgment for all mankind will transpire.

I will bring strength to all living creatures of the land.

So do not brag nor toot your horn. Be not boastful or full of yourself.

It does not come from the four corners of the earth, or from the wilds of the wilderness.

It is not for us to condemn nor to heap praise. That judgment comes from God.

The world's evil will try to drain and drag down all in its path.

But sing praise to God for he will condemn the wicked and the righteous shall find jubilation in his name.

# Psalm 76

*by Marisa Labozzetta*
WRITER

God is present everywhere on this earth,
     and desires that all live in freedom.
Therefore, with power greater than that of any army,
     he struck down invaders who brought the violence of war
     to the holy city of Jerusalem.

Applaud God's victories in the name of justice.
Those who seek to abuse others should fear God's anger,
     for God condemns all oppressors and their weapons of war
     and will stop perpetrators in their tracks.

But God can turn even the evil intentions of men and women
     into his own good purposes.
So ask God's help to exchange your negative energy for positive energy.
Vow to promote only good, peace, and social justice on this earth,
     and follow through with your promises,
     always remembering that God is more powerful
          than any human ruler.

# Psalm 77

*by Stevie Converse*
STUDENT

I feel utterly and completely alone.

I cry out.
I cry out a desperate plea for recognition.
My hands are outstretched, reaching, waiting.
My troubled heart keeps me from sleeping.
I stay up all night praying,
        hoping to hear an answer from You.
There are no words to describe my despair.
I realize the depth of my grief,
        and I know that You can help me move through it.

I recall
the young and carefree girl I used to be.
In the darkness I look deep into my heart,
in the stillness I search my spirit,
       hoping to find her.
Perhaps I can recover my vitality by remembering my past.
The change was gradual and I don't understand how it happened.
Have You changed too?
Is that why You have forgotten me?
Is that why You have stopped loving me?
Has Your own anger finally destroyed Your compassion?

I'll remember
Your past and all the amazing things You've done,
       and hope they will serve as a reminder of Your great strength and
       wholeness.
You are the one who truly works wonders.
You created order out of chaos,
       and separated the earth from the sky and parted the seas
       and there was much fear and trembling in the universe.
Now You are guiding all of us toward the evolving truth of our being,
       and this process is also terrifying and confusing.
New truths emerge from great upheavals.

Steadfast commitment and lifelong practice are required
to attain wisdom and enlightenment,
to find peace within my soul,
and my way back to You.

# Psalm 78
*in Haiku*

*by L. Fred Ayvazian*
PHYSICIAN

Hear the Lord teaching
God's wisdom, for then, for now,
For eternity

# Psalm 79

*by Chris Rohmann*
WRITER

Forgive us, oh God, for naming other humans heathens, fortifying our temple walls against them, bricked by arrogance and mortared with fear.

Their bodies lie in heaps, as iron birds scream overhead and steel behemoths crush them into dust.

Blood runs like water, the graveyards overflow.

Our friends are ashamed, our enemies scorn and mock us.

How can we pretend our hubris is God's anger, our violence his jealous rage?

We pour down wrath upon the infidels, lay waste to lands that call you by another name.

As if heaven had a single ladder's entrance, as if people everywhere see you with a single face.

Oh, forgive us for our past and present crimes; let your tender mercies heal our warring hearts. Our souls are thin and ragged, laid so low.

Help us find salvation from our mission of salvation, to see the sin in trading sin for sin; teach us to speak your name in countless tongues.

We know there are those who call us the heathens, and cry out to their god for blood revenge: servants executing their master's will.

But transform our lust for vengeance into a passion for justice, let the prison be a place of mercy, the torture cell become a sanctuary, the scaffold a new symbol of lives reprieved.

And make the world our neighborhood, where cruel reproachful thoughts redouble sevenfold in our consciences, till we reproach ourselves, and think again.

So we, the shepherds of your mercy, may pasture thankfully in peace, and live in grateful knowledge of forgiveness.

# Psalm 80

*by Richard A. Bondi*
Priest

Listen to us O Lord, our God.
You who guide us in all our journeys,
You who are over all nations and lands.
Show us your power and rescue us.

Heal us O God and have mercy that we may live!

How long will you, O Lord, refuse to listen to our supplications?
We are in dismay at the great suffering that is ours.
We are despised by all around us.
We have become a joke to those who hate us.

Heal us O God and have mercy that we may live!

You have called us and formed us into your people.
You have created a place for our community
        and given us space to worship you.
We have grown strong and powerful in your sight.
We have multiplied over the face of the earth.

But now we lie naked and exposed to all
We have no defense, we are consumed by all who desire us.

O Lord God, look at us now and recognize our suffering.
Remember your love for us of old.
Punish those who have tried to destroy us,
        let them experience your anger and fury against them.
Once again show your chosen ones your support.
We will never leave you again as we once did.
Restore us and let us sing your praise again.

Heal us O God and have mercy that we may live!

# Psalm 81

*by Jackilynn Wood*
TEACHER

Raise your voice and sing!
Sing with joy to the spirit of the
Earth and abundance.
Gather in community, and sing together.
Sing together under the blessed light
of the Full Moon Mother.

Sing in celebration and gratitude.
Sing in reverence.

And then, listen.
Find a quiet spot in your day
perhaps as you wash dishes,
make a cup of tea,
bathe your baby,
or pick flowers for the dinner table.

Listen to the voice of that which is greater than all of us.
Listen to the voice of that which is within all of us.
Listen for the steady beat of the songs we sing.

The voice will grow within you,
and when you are ready,
your truth will be revealed to you.

As you drive to work,
study in the library,
travel away from home,
you will come to understand
that the universe will provide.

The Creator, with infinite love,
has offered us all that we could need.
We are blessed and nourished.
We are comforted in our loneliness.
We are challenged to grow and learn
All we need to do is open our hearts to
what is true.
There is enough.
We are enough.
*Selah.*

# Psalm 82

*by Myaisha Hayes*
STUDENT

Stand with God in the powerful church and you will look upon the Gods

But how long will you look upon them and not to the evil?

Help the poor and helpless, watch over them because they

Are the ones who need your help. Give the poor a role in their own lives.

Turn them away from the hands of evil

They may be in the spirit of evil but they have a role in the universe

Let them die like every other. Let them make mistakes like every other

But make them special in their own way like the royal Might of God

Help us not to judge the whole earth.

# Psalm 83

*By Alexis Chapman*
STUDENT

O Goddess, do not keep silence; how do I hold thy peace or stillness?

For behold, my deepest shadows arise in a great commotion of noise and confusion; those that seek to sicken my soul speak in many tongues from many heads.

They lay crafty snares against my self-worth, they consult together and turn me from my hidden wisdom.

They say, "Come, let us desecrate her living body which is that of the Goddess; let her not remember her many names! Let her stumble and forget the sacred way!"

Yea, they conspire with one accord; against me they make a covenant—

The shadow of despair, and hopelessness, and bitter pity
Turn me against myself, against my lovers, against you.

For depression, guilt and self-hate have joined them; they are the strong arm of Distrust.

Remind me, Goddess, that I hold both crescent sword and full, round cauldron in my hands,

And may cut down my shadows to reveal seeds yearning for dark, fertile ground.

Make my movements noble and wise, my breath as royal lines of spider webs.

I say, "Let me claim my body as Her body, my mind as Her mind, and my spirit ever Her spirit."

O Goddess, make me like a sudden storm, like rain within the wind.

As fire consumes the shadows, my flame sets the mountains ablaze with northern lights;

So do I pursue them with Thy tempest and terrify them with Thy blizzard which is my own!

Fill the faces of my shadows with the reflection of myself and let them know my name forever, O Goddess.

Let them be turned to silver and shine forever; let them plant themselves in my darkest places, now brighter than they were before.

Let them know that I, with many, art a song of the Goddess, complete and whole within the Earth.

# Psalm 84

## by Bob Lamothe
LOCKSMITH

Your home is a beautiful place, O Creator of all
My soul longs to be at your home with you
My heart and my being sing with joy at your presence
Even the birds of the earth seek to live near you
The swallow builds her nest and has her young by your altar
O Great One, my God and Creator
Fortunate are those who live with you
And they are forever speaking of your Greatness
Fortunate is the person whose strength is in you, Lord
They will go to any length to reach you and your dwelling place
As they pass through the valley of sorrow it becomes a spring
        for the thirsty
And the early rains refill all of the pools
They are filled with your strength
Until they reach and appear before you, Lord
Please listen to my prayer my Great God
Behold that our shield is you, Lord
And cast your loving gaze upon our smiling faces
For a day with you, Lord
Is better than a thousand anywhere else
I would rather be a doorkeeper at your house
Than hang out with evil or wicked people
You, Lord, are the sunshine that warms the earth
And the shield that protects your people
For the Lord gives Love and Mercy
To all those who seek to live with Honor
Oh, My Dear God
How truly Blessed is the one
Who trusts in You!

# Psalm 85

## by Kevin Hurley
### INMATE

A sacred reading for Korah's people

Lord, you have given life to the world and all that inhabit it.

You forgave your loyal followers for the crimes that they have committed. You took into account all of their faults and you still forgave them.

You are not angry and bitter towards them any more because you realized that everyone makes mistakes.

We learn from these mistakes, no matter how severe they are, and are asking for a second chance.

Will we join you in heaven or will we have to spend eternity in hell? Will your anger stop with us or will we be plagued with it forever?

Wouldn't you like us to join you in heaven so we can be together?

Show us how much you love us and give us the one gift that we ask for, a second chance. Let us join you and the rest of the angels in heaven when we leave this realm.

I wait for God to grant me peace so that I can stop battling the demons inside. With this gift I will once again become whole and share all I have been through with others so that they will not make the same mistakes I did.

He will answer my prayers and we will meet in the afterlife.

God and the devil have battled over my soul and goodness has prevailed. I am to be spared from an eternity of damnation.

God has seen inside my soul and he grants me another chance at life because he feels that I am righteous.

This is truly a blessing from God and I will live a righteous and meaningful existence.

God has saved a seat for me next to him. When I die he will be awaiting me with open arms.

# Psalm 86

*by Vicha Hajdamowicz*
OFFICE MANAGER

Lord, hear my prayer
For I am oppressed and poor
And therefore weak to Satan's lure

Lord, give me strength
Mortal passions weaken my body to these deeds
Yet my soul is searching for peace, forgiveness; of heavenly needs

Lord, save my soul
I pray you hear me and lead me home
For Lord only you can save this wretched soul

Lord, teach me love
So I may be your servant and walk without blame
To be gentle and worthy to speak your name

Lord, you give me a sign
But I am blind and cannot see
That the sign you give
Breathes the love in me

Lord hear my prayer
Lord hear my plea
Lord save my soul and comfort me.

# Psalm 87

*by Gemma Rachel Laser*
STUDENT

From all corners of the earth they come,
The people who are blessed
To live in a holy land.
They speak of mountains, rivers, deserts, mesas.
They grow mangoes in the morning
And plant wheat fields late at night.

When people ask,
"Where does your family come from?"
They always smile when I answer.
"Ah," they say,
"It's good to come from sacred ground."

I bend down and touch the earth,
In my hands I find the answers I have been missing.
I kneel very close and whisper,
"Thank you for bringing me home."

In every land the earth will heal you,
The earth will fill you full of secret love and wisdom.
In every land you will see the mark of holy dreams and sacred stories,
For in every land you will find the footprints
Telling you that Divine Love has been walking there.

Lift up your voice to the wind!
shout out the name in your heart!
Raise up the name of your homeland in praise
And you will hear a thousand voices cry,
"Oh, yes!
We know this place.
We have seen it in our dreams and dreamed it in our hearts.
It is a holy land,
Touched by the Hand that guides us all!"

In the night, under a shining sky,
The poet and musician both remember
That their singing tongues
Forever flow from this precious source,

Like water from a crystal stream.

# Psalm 88

*by Allen M. Hart, with Mildred Hart*
ARTIST AND ART MANAGER

Like Job, I cry out in my alienation.
Art alone sustains me in my helplessness.
I cry out to you to be delivered from my agony.
My dear Mildred, along with my crimson red paint, comfort me when
      all seems lost.
We gain our strength from love,
and the beauty of nature, art and music that surrounds us.

# *Psalm 89*

## *by Rich Fournier*
### MINISTER

My dear God, the hills are alive with the sound of music
singing your praise. I too feel like singing my heart out,
telling everyone "how great thou art."
For You have promised to tenaciously love us forever.
Chapter and verse I could give
where You solemnly covenanted to uphold us,
despite our shortcomings, and to give us a guarantee
of a Davidic future and a victorious hope.

And there is none like unto You.
For heaven and earth, the sea and
all living things, live and move
and have their being in You.

Blessed are we upon whose souls
Your countenance has shined.
We, who take tentative steps

on the timid trails we call our lives,
are blessed indeed by a divine love
wilt not let us go.

But truth be told, dear God,
You confuse me.
I love to tell the story of
Your power and Your love,
and Your promises for our
sovereign kingdom and
our glorious future.
And yet...

Our present reality cannot be denied.
There's a quaking in my heart and
a shaking in my faith
for we are bereft of Your presence.
We have been deserted, abandoned, and
delivered to our enemies
to be mocked and killed.

My God, my God, why have You
forsaken us, forgotten us? Has
Alzheimer's set in?
Where is Your steadfast love of old?
My heart breaks, and the only
song I can muster is "O come...
and ransom captive Israel, that
mourns in lonely exile here."

How long must we wait
for You to remember us and
for You to be true to Your own promises?

For now we see in a glass darkly...
Maybe someday face to face.
But in the meantime,
night and fog.

# *Psalm 90*

*by Kathy Alexander and Denice Yanni*
LOVER OF LIFE AND TEACHER

I
The constancy of the Holy is our inheritance.
It is spoken on the lips
of our mothers and fathers;
It is embodied in our flesh—
breath carrying the whisper of
life's call in every cell;
It is present in the stars
that break open new worlds
of light.
Yes, the Holy holds all beings
with faithful expectation;
the call of the sacred in humans
is repeated.

II

How can we know this stretch of time
       Where a life is lived and lost?
       Where a sun sets and a new day begins?
       Where flowers blossom and then fade?
A universe of sights and sounds opens before us,
       yet it is but a moment.
We walk the earth from day to day;
       the Holy echoes from everlasting to everlasting
Still, we cannot escape our smallness;
       the anger that contorts our gentle hearts;
       the fatigue that slackens our intent;
       the self-centeredness that obstructs purposeful action.
We cause pain in each other's lives.
Seventy is the sum of our years
       or eighty, if we are strong;
Yet we drift ceaselessly,
       quiet defeats, diminishing our spirits
       over time.

III

Teach us to honor our days and nights!
To be vigilant, that we may cultivate
       wisdom of spirit.
Let the sacred open and uplift us
       that we may continue our journey
       with strong hearts and hands.
This, then, is how we will carve out a path
       creating a world of joy and compassion,
       of justice and peace.
And this is how we will be true
       to our ancestors,
       passing on an inheritance
       of Holiness amidst us.
May all prosper from this vow!
May all prosper!

# *Psalm 91*

## *by Michael Klein-Berndt*
### CUSTODIAN

Those that aspire for peace and serenity need but one thing...

Those that are from park ave or park bench need but one thing...

Faith ... reliance on something greater than ourselves.

Release self will, you will be granted trust.

Trust will gain serenity and walk you on the road towards grace...

All of this can be had ... with small children steps

practiced and built on daily ... faith can relieve fear

practiced and built on daily ... faith can soothe turmoil

Life will bring heartache or joy ... measures of each bring new understandings

It is a God of your understanding opening your heart

It is a God of your understanding moving through others to teach us new things

It is a God of your understanding...

# Psalm 92

*by David Aminia*
JEWISH CLERGY

A song for the Sabbath day

It is very good to sing praises to God
To declare every morning and every evening and talk about your glory and
our faith in you.

All things that you have created make me very happy,
therefore I sing with joy and happiness.

As we look around the universe we notice your designs and artistic works,
yet it is beyond our understanding. If one thinks more about it, one
cannot comprehend it any more.

Your enemies will be like fading grass, but you will deal with them because
you are the Supreme Being.

But you have made us aware of all your goodness and kindness, and
provided beauty and fragrant oil all around us.

I have seen the destruction and doom of my enemies. Those who do good
deeds will flourish like palm trees and thrive like cedar trees.

Those who plant goodness and kindness in their hearts and deeds will
flourish and enjoy happiness and joy all their lives, and proclaim God's
love and justice, and believe that God has no imperfections.

# Psalm 93

*By Budge Hyde*
PROFESSOR OF ART

The Sovereign is dressed as a royal personage; He exercises supreme authority, and dignity.

With firmness doth the Sovereign strengthen and encircle his world.

His chair is eternal: He persists indefinitely.

With Noah's waves ascending, Oh Sovereign, floods overflow, pitching with loud utterance; the waters repeatedly undulate, disturb, and continually surge.

The ranking Sovereign is mightier than the howling outcry,

Yeah, than the mighty disturbance of the sea.

Thy declarations are inevitable; sanctity is thy residence,

O Lord, indefinitely.

# Psalm 94

## by Darien McFadden
### PSYCHOLOGIST

God, you have the ability to retaliate. Do something.

Show yourself, God, and reward the kind-hearted.

God, how long shall cruel people be allowed to win?

How long are you going to allow them to say the nasty and cruel things they say?

They hurt the good people of the world. They berate the lonely, the isolated and those who are vulnerable.

Yet they say, "God is on our side, not yours."

Listen up, you religious bullies, you idiots. When will you learn?

Don't you realize the God who made us all is smart enough to get what you're doing?

God gets it. He knows you are being cruel.

God, take care of the kind-hearted, until the idiots of the world get what's coming to them.

Because, eventually, what goes around, comes around.

I've often asked myself, "How are these people able to get away with this cruelty?"

If it wasn't for you, God, maybe I would have given up hope for the world.

When I have felt like, "I can't take this any more," you have shown me that good still exists in the world.

Thoughts of you have the tendency to clear my head.

Will the cruel and cold-hearted of the world really have the right to condemn others?

They claim to speak "the word of God" and condemn others who just want to live a life being true to themselves.

But you'll take care of it, God. Eventually, they'll get what's coming to them.

# Psalm 95

*by Paul S. Kuzeja*
RESEARCH FIELD ASSISTANT

God is this glorious Creation.

God is the little rivulets from which we sip as we lay on our bellies while resting during a journey. These happy trickles join again and again until God tumbles and then roars out of the mountains in torrents.

When you remember to watch the sun sink to rest, remember also that God will be there in the sunrise tomorrow.

In a handful of soil taken from beneath your feet, every pebble and tiny creature in your palm proclaims itself God as loudly as the largest Oak tree, the dignified Rhinoceros, or the Tuna as it flashes above the sea. In the summer, when the Whippoorwill cries into the secret wee hours, or in the winter, when the Great Horned Owl claims the dusk, God is in every stirring.

God is everywhere you choose to look—among grains of soil, along a footpath, or in the clear night sky.

And yet God is so much greater than this beauty before you, and as much as you would love to behold it forever, you cannot, for time is very short.

This you must understand because you will not always be at peace, nor will you always behold God with a light and carefree heart. Your pain will always try to wrench you from God, from all that is. You will wonder how God could let you suffer so much when there is such beauty as proof of God's love for you. You are not the first or the last to ask this.

You cannot know God's ways and reasons, but you can know that life with God brings you into God's great house. There you will always be welcome, even though there are so many rooms that there will always be mystery.

# Psalm 96

*by Chris Brown*
GROUNDSKEEPER

Be thankful
Be thankful and in awe
Be aware of this great mystery.
        We are all a part of it.
Wondrous is the spirit of all living things,
        not always gentle nor merciful, but not to be feared.
Too easily do we lose sight of what really matters—
        the earth, the sky, the air we breathe.
Peace and tranquility are found here.
        Strength and meaning are found within.
This is not for us alone, but to be shared unconditionally.
Give the spirit a proper name, one that speaks of essence.
        Give in return for what has been received.
Be thankful and in awe of all you see.
This world will proceed as it will.
        We join in its shaping, for better or worse,
        and must accept our part in its outcome.

# Psalm 97

*by Li-Ling Waller*
WEIGHT WATCHERS LEADER

Omnipotent One!
The world rejoices in you!
Fairness and justice are your cornerstones.
We see your power in the lightning
        as it flashes across the world,
We feel your strength as the very earth
        trembles beneath us!
How mighty you truly are!

Heaven sings of your goodness and
Rays of sun that shine through the clouds
        allow us to see your glory!
False idols are put to shame in the glory of
        your magnificence!
You are most high!

You adore those who hate evil and
        protect those who are faithful.
You plant seeds of goodness and light within our souls
        so that we may shine with your heavenly light!
Celebrate and thank the Lord!

# Psalm 98

*by Chuck Hommes*
CABINET MAKER

A Psalm of great joy and love, to the creation of a world of beauty and life.

A world that protects and sustains us.

We should never take our lives for granted, but continue to embrace life and nature to make our voices heard through our music, our song, our deeds.

To protect the "sea and all that fills it, the world and all that live in it," by letting nature be who she is.

For in the end, it will be Humankind who will be judged for how we treat this world.

# *Psalm 99*

### *by Beverly Daniel Tatum*
#### COLLEGE PRESIDENT

God is in control, breathing Life into our very being;
Let our souls tingle with the knowledge of God's creative Power;
God's Love surrounds us and cradles those who will come and those who
      have gone;
All are in God's loving care; let our souls rejoice with gratitude.

Even the most powerful warring nation cannot claim God's Power,
For God is a God of Peace. God's Love transcends all and God's Peace
      surpasses all understanding.
Let our hearts be still in God's presence.

And what does God's Love require of us?
Throughout the ages it is the same: to act justly and to love mercy
      and to walk humbly with our God.
Let us listen and follow directions. Let our actions be our song of praise.

Harriet Tubman and Sojourner Truth are among God's praiseful servants,
      and Martin Luther King among many that called upon God
      for help.
They called and God answered.
They heard God's voice and followed God's instructions.

They called to God for guidance and God replied.
They were not perfect as we are not perfect.
God used them as they were and magnified their willingness to serve into
      mighty acts of transformation.
Give thanks to the God who can use us in our imperfection, and
offer yourself for God's service.
God's Love will surround you and guide you all your days.

# Psalm 100

*by Janet Grevstad*
BUSINESS MANAGER AND VOLUNTEER, RETIRED

Let everyone sing praise to the Lord!
Cheerfully do his will;
Seek him with a joyful heart!

Remember, the Lord is God!
Our lives are his gift; he needs our love.
We are his family; he watches over us.

Approach God with a song on your lips.
Let your soul fill with gladness.
Count your blessings, and be grateful for each of them.
Glorify his name.

For our God is good:
He is with us every step of the way; his grace enfolds us.
His boundless love will endure for all generations.
Hallelujah!

# Psalm 101

## by Beverly Sabourin
### WIFE, MOTHER, BUSINESS OWNER

In My Own Voice of Prayer to God

Father, the song of my life is how you entered my heart and made it new.

Just as King David committed to leading his people with good behavior and a perfect heart, I commit to being a godly example to all whose lives I touch.

Lord, I can be easily distracted by the world's enticements.

As David would not allow anyone to slander his or her neighbor, I will try to value my neighbors just as you do.

As David would not allow anyone to work under him who is of a proud spirit, help me to remember that you will exalt me when I humble myself.

As David selected only the faithful of the land to live in his house and serve him, may I remember that you take great delight in my faithful service to you.

I commit to being an honest woman and to being filled with integrity.

As King David spoke of destruction towards evildoers in his kingdom, there will be a time when destruction will come to all of those who have not trusted in Christ.

Please use me in pointing people to you.

For it is in Jesus's name, who is the way, the truth, and the life, that I pray.

Amen.

# Psalm 102

## by David Arfa
STORYTELLER AND ENVIRONMENTAL EDUCATOR

God help me, please help. Where are You?
I am lost and I have fallen into a pit. I have
no escape.
Cold, damp stones wall me in. Impenetrable
fog surrounds me.
Raging eyes meet mine. Arms with long
fingers and sharpened nails reach toward me.
One fist grabs my throat, the other pounds
my chest and knocks the breath out of me.
Bees sting my belly; rats climb my calves.
God help me!
I am close to death. Even my scream is
trapped.
Where are You?

Now I am caught high in this tree.
Murderers are down below laughing,
drinking wine, and building a fire. It is
only a matter of time until they see me.
Why have You turned Your Face?

My arms ache from holding tight to this branch. Bark is pressing into my
ribs, scraping my cheek. I dare not sleep and risk falling. I dare not breathe
and risk drawing their attention. Then I will surely die. I lie awake bathed
in fear. How long must I wait for You? God, why won't You help me?

Nearby, bats begin to fly from a hollowed tree. Some chase the night
moths rising from the embers below. An owl slowly announces itself,
and in the distance, a casual reply. The murderers settle under blankets. I
begin to notice the toads are calling, like every summer night, in the trees
around me. A gust shakes the top branches, I allow my eyes the freedom
to glance upwards and I am soothed by a glimpse of starlight flickering
through the canopy.

I smile as the wind rushes over me. I let the breeze cool my clammy hands
and sweaty forehead. I slowly lift my head away from the branch and
I catch a gust in the neck of my shirt. I gladly let it swirl where it may,

freely flowing between shirt and body, raising goose-bumps and erasing stickiness. I loosen my foot's grip from the branch and then free my entire leg, lifting it behind me. My cuff is open to the wind. Air rises within, curving around ankle and bare calf, surging past knees and thighs, circling my entire body. I close my eyes and let my nose drink in the fresh air.

I quietly push myself upright and let the tree support my back. Breathing fully, I feel Your Presence in the darkness. I am able to remember that You are always present. Even in that first fish who, long ago, risked life without water; and it was You who allowed that hearty egg, eons before chickens clucked, to withstand the dryness of land. And still earlier, You were present in the first cells of life, the first rains, and before Earth and Stars. And You are here tonight, inside these raucous tree toads, chilling winds, and me! Wonder of Wonders. How could I have forgotten?

Below, moving shadows catch my eye. I watch a snake slide between the sleeping murderers and slip into the wine flask, silently sipping until engorged. And then, in the darkness, wine-red venom is spewed back into that flask. The viper hides away as the morning birds begin to sing. With the first light of dawn, I see the murderers stir and reach to quench their thirst. I want to stop them, but I am afraid. One by one, they drink from their flask and fall over like snapped branches in a sudden gust.

The shock of survival makes me numb. I blink in disbelief. I wait in silence before I climb down. My arms bury the bodies, but my eyes do not see, my ears do not hear. I leave and wander down a trail by the stream, soothed by flowing water. Slowly, I begin again, searching for my home.

Resting by a patch of blackberries, my mind wanders back. If the snake did not appear? If the murderers were to see me and take their axes to the tree? What then? Could I truly believe that the whole earth is filled with Your Glory? That there is, was, and will be no place devoid of You? Present at the origins of life and in cold stones that trap? In the breathing forest and the heart of murderers?

I slowly breathe in the warm fragrance of fruit, green leaves, and soil. Surprisingly, I listen, as I whisper blessings for the berries in my hand and for coming to this place.

# Psalm 103

*by Liddy Gerchman Barlow*
PASTOR

Bless the Lord, my soul.

    You have been hurried; now slow down; be mindful. Turn all that you are to your work of blessing.

Bless the Lord, my soul.

    Give thanks: God has made you whole again, has filled your body with food, your enemies with mercy, and your friends with kindness. Because of God, your life overflows with goodness. You have everything you need.

Bless the Lord, my soul.

    God is by your side, for you no less than for Moses. God knows your failings, but sees past them to know you as you are. Your sins wither away in God's sight.

Bless the Lord, my soul

    for you will wither, too. Watch the grass and the flowers flourish for a season and die, and know the same will happen to you. You will not die to God, for God goes on and on. Souls to come, your grandchildren's grandchildren, will know abundance too.

Bless the Lord, my soul.

    Spread the blessing to everyone, everywhere. All people, bless the Lord! Angels and saints, bless the Lord! All creation in all corners of the universe, bless the Lord! But as all these blessings thunder, do not forget:

Bless the Lord, my soul.

# Psalm 104

## by Damiano Razzoli
JOURNALIST

All, improvviso la pioggia terge loro i volti,
Le lacrime scorrono via sciolte in acque celesti

L'oceano accarezza loro i piedi sul crocevia polveroso
del tempo, la canzone silenziosa è goccia dorata

Mi ascolti, lo dico ancora, mi ascolti?
L'amore venne creato nel vuoto
Mi ascolti, lo dico ancora, mi ascolti?

Zitto, è sempre luce una melodia

Prateria e respiro sono talmente vasti d'accogliere
il segreto in grazia d'ali e liturgia di fiori

And suddenly the rain is washing their faces,
The tears are flowing away, melted in celestial waters

The ocean caresses their feet at the dusty crossroads
Of time, the silent song is a drop of brilliance

Do you hear me, I say again, do you hear me?
The love was created in emptiness
Do you hear me, I say again, do you hear me?

Hush, the light remains a melody

Prairie and breath are wide enough
to welcome a secret with the grace
of wings and a hymn of flowers

# Psalm 105

*by Emikan Sudan*
COUNSELOR, PHOTOGRAPHER, ASTROLOGER

Just as God, The Great Spirit, helped Moses
many, many years ago
fulfilling the Covenant, the Compact, the Principles
that we live, breathe and practice today.
So too today shall we
one people under the sky, uphold our Pledge
to the New Covenant
presented by Jesus Christ, The Prophet
Messenger, the Revolutionary
A message so revered for its simplicity
"for us to love one another"
One People
One Love
One World
One Spirit/Above
Some may kill the Revolutionaries
but you cannot kill the Revolution
for God is Change
A metamorphosis that encompasses
not only the Soul, but Mind and Body
A transformation of the Diaspora
from the physical nation building struggles
to an acceptance of ALL IS ONE
MOTHER FATHER GOD
all working as One People, WOMAN/MAN
One being that unfolds
its petals Rose & Gold
Miracles happen ... don't lose Sight
Divine Spirit, Life and Light
then truly once again
can we sing praises up high
to the Lord who has shown us the Way!

# Psalm 106

*by George Singfield*
EDUCATOR – SPECIAL POPULATIONS

In obedience to the Great Commandments of long ago, we continue striving—today—recognizing and integrating those past covenants in our daily lives. Therefore:

Please hear us, O Great One, who has dominion over all and who steadily watched over us, who occupies this sphere of wonder-of-wonders.

We continually call upon you to lend your grace on our behalf, to live, love, succeed and multiply.

We have also committed to honor you and one another, in the service of perpetuating attitudes and behaviors of: respect, honesty, and fair treatment towards all.

Above all, we committed to those tenets you provided, to lead and guide us toward greater wisdom, gratitude and forthrightness of faith.

Although there are, and have been, times when we did not adhere to and follow the path of your shining light, upon recognition and realization, we do humble ourselves—sometimes, in guilt and shame—but never with a lack of respect for your continued love and tolerance for our shortcomings.

Oh, source and center of our inner peace and balance, we call upon all those inner resources you've imbued us with to sustain us in withstanding the sometimes-attractive as well as contorted temptations of life that we tend to let overwhelm us.

As we look upon the horizon of tomorrow, may we find increasing strength in the beauty and endless bounties that continually flow from our trough of sustainment.

By your Grace, may we be elevated in wisdom to a level that will continually mine the love, patience and spiritual energy you've provided; so our children will be able to inherit, enjoy and prudently perpetuate the riches and sustenance of our Mother Earth, from whence we arose (through you) and to which we are destined to return.

# Psalm 107

*by Phil and Josee Radzikowski*

Engineer Officer and Infantry Officer, United States Army

"Praise the L-rd, for he is good,
His steadfast love is eternal!"
Thus let the redeemed of the L-rd say,
Those He redeemed from adversity,
Whom He gathered in from the lands,
From east and west,
From the north and from the south.

Some left to find themselves in the big city,
Amongst the crowd,
And found no place to grow roots.
Weary and lonely,
Their spirits failed.
In their bitter isolation they cried out to the L-rd,
And the L-rd brought them companionship.
G-d showed them how to confide
To reach a settled state.

Let them praise the L-rd for his everlasting love,
        His patience with mankind;
For he has shown the lost their souls,
And grew roots for the lonely.

Some did things no human should ever know.
They perpetrated cruelty on mankind.
They were locked in a circle of violence,
Shutting everything good and heavenly out.
Because they turned away from the gift of life,
Thumbed their noses at the higher power,
G-d humbled their pride through suffering.
They had no one to help them.
In their pain they cried out to the L-rd,
And G-d's mercy rescued them from despair.
G-d brought them into the light,
And made them see the errors in their lives.
Let them praise the L-rd for his love,
For he shattered their lives of hopelessness and opened the doors of
        possibility.

Let them praise the L-rd for his benevolence,
Let them be thankful and spread his love with charitable deeds.

There are those who challenge G-d out of necessity.
They live off of G-d's good will,
They have seen the work of the L-rd
And the wonders he creates.
By his word he destroyed their livelihood
With hurricanes, tornadoes, floods and earthquakes,
Destruction spreading to all, leaving no one safe.
They staggered around, lost and hopeless.
In their adversity, they cried out to the L-rd,
And he rescued them from his creation.
He steadied the earth and the birds sang.
They rejoiced when all was quiet and began to rebuild all that was
            destroyed.
Let them praise the L-rd for his steadfast love,
His merciful attention to all mankind.
Let them spread the word of his mercy to all mankind, and celebrate with
the rulers of the land.

When civilization overcrowds land, wastes resources and destroys
            natural habitats,
He allows man to suffer from his own ambition and gluttony.
He fills the rivers with fish, fertilizes the land, and feeds the hungry.
He allows man to prosper and families to grow.
He blesses them and they thrive.
He will not let civilization fall,
Despite civilization's way of war and destruction,
He will create peace from destruction, misery and sorrow.
He pours contempt on heartless men
And thrusts them into the unknown.
Through his love and support,
He will pick up the humble and provide resources.
He provides greatness through inspiration and direction through insight.

The upright see it and rejoice,
The mouths of all wrongdoers are stopped.
The wise man will take note of these things,
He will consider the steadfast love of the L-rd.

# Psalm 108

*by Christine and Jim Foudy*
ADMINISTRATIVE ASSISTANT AND EDITOR

We sing the praises of a higher power.
We know this force by many names:
God, Yawheh, Mother Earth, Jehovah,
Great Spirit, Brahma, Almighty.
They are one, guiding the world and
dwelling as a spirit within each of us.

We lift our voices to share the belief
that day-to-day, hour-to-hour
connecting to our higher power
sustains the soul as food nourishes the body,
opens the mind to new ideas,
and prepares the heart for unseen possibilities.

When we are in touch with our higher power,
we are able to recognize the harmony in the world;
we have respect for all forms of life,
all cultures, creeds and points of view;
we accept the mysteries of the universe.
When we act from a spiritual place
we offer thanks to our higher power
and bless those with whom we interact.

Countering the false prophets of greed and gluttony,
the spirit offers peace of mind,
strength in the face of adversity,
an understanding and acceptance of our fears and vulnerabilities,
hope in days of darkness and self-doubt,
power to the weak and a check on the powerful.

Blessed be our spirits
that draw strength from a higher power
and, through conscious action,
sing its praises.

# Psalm 109

*by Gordon Pullan*
PASTOR

The silence of God is my death.

You see, in the absence of God speaking up for me—and I'm talking about speaking out loud and clear—there are people wagging their tongues at my backside as if they know, really know, who I am.

They spit their words of hate at me as if they can judge the intentions of my heart by their reactions to my actions.

But they don't know that my heart is full of love and that my actions come from love. They don't know that secretly I pray for them. "God give them understanding. God give them compassion." But the silence of my God is my death.

So, in the absence of a booming voice from a burning bush or even a murmur from a misty mountain, those who were once my friends now reward me evil for good and hatred for my love.

They say, "A good district attorney could find something to charge him with. His love is not natural. And then when he is found guilty, everyone will see that he had no right to pray for us. Let him die from his sin. Let someone more righteous have his position, his possessions, his posterity. Send the children-of-his-lie away—far away—so that they can never play with our children again. Send them away to live with the guilt of their father. Send them away to live with a name that is stained. Send them away without aid. Sell their house to someone more desirable. And give the proceeds to someone worthy of our charity. Why? Because his kindness was false. He pursued the poor and helpless even to their spiritual deaths.

Even as he swore his good desires, his desires swore his maliciousness. And he wrapped himself with that desire as if it were a coat to shield him. But the storm of sin is internal and the beautiful colors of the coat will bleed inward, soaking into his body like water and into his bones like oil. So that his coat will become a straitjacket, coloring and discoloring his whole life."

What do they know, I say. They wear their own straitjackets.

But you, my God, what is your excuse? What is restraining you from helping me? There are no supreme straitjackets.

Your chosen absence leaves me starved. So much so that I feel like a shadow lost in the night.

Being no more than a shadow of the man I once was.

And seeing how I have withered, people see me and shake their heads.

What is your excuse, God? Help me and save me, if you still will, through your love. Break your silence.

And through your love, let others know that it was your will and it was your voice.

I can take their curses, if the only blessing I receive is that of yours.

Give me a blessing. Let the ones who wag their fingers be constrained by those very straitjackets they wish to wrap me in.

The silence of my God would be my death. But my God speaks and I speak back with words of thanks and praise.

Because God is justice and justice cannot be silent.

# Psalm 110

## by Paki Wieland
### PEACE AND JUSTICE ACTIVIST

You are the promise of the divine.
You are chosen now as
You have been chosen and you
Will be chosen
Forever and for all time.

Awakening to the spirit within,
You recognize your enemies, the shortcomings:
the ego, the self-will.
These enemies,
As they entropy and decay, become
The rich soil through which
Your being is nourished.

The great spirit moves beside and within and through you.
In you, this spirit becomes
Humanity.

From the womb,
From the day you were born,
You are named
Gift of the cosmos.

Spirit flows through the waters
Spirit flows through your human life.
In communion,
We drink those flowing waters.

# Psalm 111

*by Jake Wartenberg*
STUDENT

Honor the Lord!
I will thank God with every part of me
Along with my friends
Wonderful is everything God has done
And everyone who enjoys them ponders his deeds.
His work is great and he acts justly all the time.
Everyone knows the great things he has done
And he is kind and full of mercy.
He gives those who fear him food;
And he keeps his promise forever.
He has shown those who follow him his power
By giving them land.
Everything he does is fair and even;
All of his rules can be trusted.
They will always be there and won't change,
And will be listened to well and fairly.
He saved the people who follow him
And he has made the agreement permanent.
Faultless and perfect is He.
Fear of God is the beginning of wisdom;
So it is smart to fear God.
People will honor him forever.

# Psalm 112

## by Mary Bowne Brandt
### COMMUNITY VOLUNTEER

Gentle spirit, constant companion
You are my river, filling me, your pond,
Flowing in from many sources
Raindrops from the sky, springs bubbling up from the mud,
Brooks streaming in and around from many directions
Water everywhere
Some evaporates, but will return
Most stays with me, in me,
At least for a while.
So much is alive,
Breathing, growing, dying,
Within and around me, one of your myriad pools.

Each season is its own
Some so active, with lots of wriggling, blooming, feeding, growing,
Other times seem calmer, frozen over for short or longer stretches

Dormant, gathering the energy for another season,
Dying back, decaying, to be reborn in another form or generation at just
the right time.
Through it all, I'm grateful for the present,
This time and these gifts, glorious all,
Knee-deep in all that has gone before, life-giving muck,
Holding the promise and the lessons of this season, and others past and
soon to be.

I take it all in,
The water and all it brings my way,
The water and all it gives to the world around me,
Aware and appreciative, sometimes oblivious or blind.
Mostly I simply be.
But I've witnessed the dry periods, and endured the unfulfilled promises
When your beauty is in short supply,
When I am depleted and haven't much to share in my world.
Other times I am fed by many, too many, sources.
I am filled too full
My banks overflow

But I trust in this season also, witnessing the fullness of all the
ways of being
Knowing from my depths that, sooner or later,
The waters will return to that level,
No drought, no flood.

Once again, I am able to see my world in a new light,
Blessing dragonflies, leaves, mud, and the breeze,
I see the beauty and promise of each breath and ripple and reflection.
Reaching from the depths to clouds high above,
I am filled with gratitude for sun and rain and life, at one with my home.
My source,
You are the giver,
The constant and renewable source of
Just what I need and no more.

# Psalm 113

### by Shamshad Sheikh
#### MUSLIM ADVISOR AND CHAPLAIN

Praise the Lord

What this message means to me is that
      God is worthily and deservedly praised.
God (Allah) is loving, the most Merciful and most Beneficent.
We worship God alone five times a day.
      The only authority deserving worship.
Praying five times a day and fasting in the month of Ramadan
      means remember God and thank God
      for all the gracious gifts we enjoy every moment of our lives.
Allah created man and woman and the entire universe.
He is the master of heaven and of Earth.
We begin our day with the name of God and end our day with his name.
God is loving and protecting
He takes care of us at every step of our lives.
God will never put us through something he knows we cannot handle.
God is the guardian and leads us from darkness to light.

We are all Allah's creation in this temporary world
      and shall be returning back to him.

# Psalm 114

*by Susan E. Pennison*

TECHNICAL SERGEANT, MASSACHUSETTS AIR NATIONAL GUARD

Israel was born from the slaves of Egypt,
and it became God's holy place, and they
became His people.

Nature took note of God's presence among
these people as they journeyed from Egypt to Israel.

The sea and the River Jordan receded, as though
kneeling with respect and humbleness.

The mountains and hills ran, for they
were ashamed of their sin.

The earth shook and danced at the awe-inspiring
power of God, as He turned rocks and stones to water,
to nourish it and the people.

# Psalm 115

### by Brianna Martineau and Holly Martineau
#### ARTIST, MOTHER AND FUNDRAISER

Where is God?
God is everywhere. In strength. In love. In faith.

Our Lord God is all around us, not of silver or gold.
Although God is not of our physical world,
we hear God's words, feel God's touch
and know God's love for us.

We have faith God is among us,
even though we do not see with our eyes, touch with our hands,
hear with our ears or smell with our noses.

Believe and trust in God.
Have faith God will protect you.
God is aware of and has faith in us; blessing our lives.
Our faith in God enriches us and our lives.

God watches over the heavens while we have responsibility for the earth.
We praise God by caring for what we have been given.
When we are no longer of the earth,
we pass its care to those we have nurtured.
Our passage to heaven is ours to make with our God together.

Have faith in God, forever.

# Psalm 116

*by Rosa Ibarra*
ARTIST/PAINTER

I love God with all of me because
He listens to my voice and to my prayers.
I know deeply inside my being that
God is the provider of all my needs.

I feel the strength of my steps
As I walk in the right path.
I have doubts along the way
Have wronged many and hurt others
But God has never left me.

All is Divine and has its Divine purpose.
God is Compassion for He is Eternal Love
I was hurting and I was comforted
I have stopped crying and my soul is calm.
I go on with life, blessing every moment.
I am here walking among the living
I thank God for everything, even the Opponent
Because I know deeply inside my being
That He is forever, the provider of all of my needs.

# Psalm 117

*by Anya Spector*
STUDENT

God is great.
God will not lie.
God will say the truth forever.
We are grateful to God
for our land and our country
and our city and our home.

# *Psalm 118*

### *by Patricia Romney*
#### PSYCHOLOGIST

Dear Heavenly Father, I thank you.

You who awaken the world each morning
You who bring us out of our nightmares and
our lonely nights.

All praise and thanksgiving.

I suffered and cried out to you, my God.
You answered me and widened my path.
You gave me courage, and opened my heart.

Look at me, my God
Once rejected and tossed aside
I, your servant,
am now made new in You.

You, my God, are always there
Ever-present for us to call on, depend on, and love.

Dear Heavenly Father
Mother of our Souls
I salute you. I praise you.
I glorify you. I thank you.

In the face of danger
You protect us all.
In a struggle with enemies
You secure us all.
In the presence of war
You call us to love.

We salute you. We praise you.
We glorify you. We thank you.

Dear Heavenly Father
Mother of my Soul.
Fill me with your light
Let me live in your fullness
Let me rest in your arms.

For You God are all good.
Father and mother to my soul.
My lover and my friend.

You God are all I hope for
Thank you, my God
You are all I need.

# Psalm 119

*by Penny Gill*
PROFESSOR

Oh, Great One,
I long to hear your voice.
In the darkest hours of the night,
I wonder, where is my path?
Who am I to be?
What am I to do?

You called Sarah and Abraham out of their homeland.
You sent Noah out on the flooded earth.
You led Miriam and Moses out of Egypt.
David you brought from his sheep.
When Jonah preferred death to Nineveh, you would not be thwarted.
So Jonah met the great fish.

Our times are different now, Oh Great One.
Even Jonah could hear your voice.
But we cannot. We no longer turn an ear to you.
We have forgotten you speak to us.
We do not know the way into deep silence.
We have ceased to wait upon your presence.

You created us from the stuff of stars
to be your home on earth.
You write your name in our hearts.
You inscribe "Beloved" on our foreheads.

The lineaments of my soul reveal your presence.
I feel your breath at my back.
You green me into new life.
You are the very marrow of my bones.
Gladness rises in me.
It is joy to follow your lead.
In your presence I am whole and well.
Fear melts like morning mist in the bright sun.
I dance with our friends who know You.

# Psalm 120

### by Eli Epstein-Deutsch
#### STUDENT

To God—
From everywhere, lies ring out from the lips of my countrymen
and reverberate in my ears and body. Harshly, like the sound
of artillery shells against buildings. Shaking the ground.
Treacherous untruths, stamped out by presses of the greedy and unjust
reach my eyes like a flash of blinding white light
shattering the comfort of darkness
And it stings.

Born into a land of ignorance and mistrust
my sole voice is drowned out before it reaches even my own ears.
Alone I work for peace, but
To no effect.
Still we are hurtling down the path to war.
Deliver us.

# Psalm 121

*by Pauline Bassett*
ATTORNEY

When I am troubled and feel lost and alone, I look to the sky, seeking help.

When I see the beauty of God's world around me, I am reminded of God's love and I feel comforted.

I know God will give me the strength to face all that troubles me.

God will protect me from all that I fear.

God is with me always, whether I am awake or asleep, whether I am at home or out in the world, whether I am filled with joy or with sadness.

God is with me always, from this time forth and for evermore.

# Psalm 122

*by Lan Katz*
EDUCATOR

A Song of Physical Ascent to Spiritual Heights.

We are all uplifted when we are close to God.

We yearn for a place where we can feel close to God.

We look for a spiritual place in our physical world, so that we may live contemplative and spiritual lives.

We pray for the peace of our land.

May our land be secure and peaceful, and the people prosper so that we may spend time in the house of the Lord.

May peace be with us all.

# Psalm 123

*by Andrew Stone*
STUDENT

To you, O God, I pay attention
because you are where I wish to be.
Watch as your people find the source
of their Master
like a young duckling
looks to its mother for warmth
till happiness comes upon us.

Comfort us O Lord.
Be near to us.
Be kind to us
because we have had too much pain.
For too long
evil has been upon us
from the lazy and the ungrateful.

# Psalm 124

### *by Gwen Agna*
#### ELEMENTARY SCHOOL PRINCIPAL

In my work, we must be on the same side;

In my work, children and parents, caregivers and teachers, community folks make up the team;

In my work, there is love and trust, tension and stress, but no "us" against "them";

In my work, our souls must come together and we find God within us;

In our work, we witness, miracles happen, joy abounds;

In our work, it is up to us

To learn from the pain, the sadness, the dark within and without us;

Our days together are heaven on earth.

Amen.

# Psalm 125

*by Barbara Harlow*

Divine love is available to us everywhere, all the time.
If our hearts are open, abiding Divine love sustains us and guides us.

Sometimes our hearts can close down a bit, or a lot, and we become
    susceptible to fear, or ignorance, or greed, or hatred.
We might turn to things like drugs and alcohol, sex, loud music,
    shopping, harsh judgment, mindless consumption, violence,
    or war.

Though it may take strength and courage and practice,
    it is in opening our hearts that we become restored
    to the Divine love of God
    and to forgiveness and compassionate right action
    toward ourselves and others.

Peace requires a steadfast practice of open-heartedness.

# Psalm 126

*by Ivan Anderson*
<small>STUDENT</small>

The only way to get something for nothing is to be lucky.
It's easy to be thankful when you're lucky.
Everyone wants to be lucky.

If I can't be lucky
       I'll just have to be ready.

# Psalm 127

## by Women Inmates

A home built without the Lord's presence
    is built in vain.
Without God by your side,
    your efforts go to waste.
You can work all day, all night
    and it will be for naught.

Daughters are made in the image of God;
    our children are our reward.
What arrows are to a warrior,
    a child is in a mother's arms.
Happy is a woman surrounded by family,
    just as a warrior is happy
    with a quiver full of arrows.
Proud is a woman who stands at the gate
    with God and her children by her side.

# Psalm 128

## by Annalise Hamel

Happiness is given to those who follow in the ways of our God.
You get what you earn, and earn what you get.
Those around you will be fruitful and bring you joy and good spirits.

Your children will follow what you teach them.
But your time with them goes fast, as they learn and grow.

You will be blessed by all of this if you follow our God.

May God bless you from Zion and may you see the good doings
of Jerusalem, and learn from and follow their ways.
And do good all the days of your life.

May you live long enough to see the future of our world,
your children's children,
and may they be taught the way you taught your children.

Peace be on Israel!

# Psalm 129

*by Sandra E. North*
OFFICE MANAGER

Each year, before the onions can be planted,
The harvest of rocks must first be extracted
From the earth.

"I don't know where they come from,"
The farmer says, shaking his head,
"But there are always
More of them."
The land does not care—
It grows both rocks and onions well.

The sun sits heavily,
Slung into a yoke on my back,
As I trace my way between the furrows
That the plow has already made.
Someone has to drag these
Shards of that fossilized field
Down into the brush.

By some strange act of geology,
Each is heavier than the last. I grow
Tired of having to make my way
Back and forth
Without disturbing the soil,
So I hurl one out to the sun
Like a gnarled discus.
It doesn't go far.

"I know it's hard
To carry the burden for so long,"
Says the farmer, "But I'd rather
Grow onions than rocks.
Be careful where you throw stones."

# Psalm 130

*by Ruth Cowan*
COLLEGE COUNSELOR, RETIRED


Waiting for God's Help
A Song of Growing

From the darkness of my secret shadow places I reach out to you,
    O Lord; I am so scared.
Listen to my crying! I know you are near.
    Please hear the desperation in my voice! I am hurting.

I believe you are following me all the days of my life,
    which I don't deserve.
If you really counted up all my selfishness,
    Lord, I would be so ashamed I couldn't keep going.
But instead you have chosen to forgive me, when I am truly sorry.
    Then you will turn me around so I will honor you...
    I will be a new person.

All of me is waiting for you ... listening ... and
    with your breath I dare to hope you will heal even me.
My self is longing to be right with you.
    Since midnight I have been awake praying that
        You will reach me soon,
    Like the way night people expectantly wait for the
        safety that the dawn's light brings.
    I have seen you before and you will come to me now!

Listen all of us in the beloved community! We can
    hope in the Lord. God cares about us, and has promised to
    always be there.
Indeed, She has the awesome power to forgive us and
    totally change our lives.
It is God who claims and renews us on our journeys beyond
    the grip of our secret dark places. I believe it!

# Psalm 131

*by Haru Akamatsu*
MINISTER'S WIFE

O Lord, my heart is humble
I turn away from arrogance
I do not seek things
beyond my ability
I have found serenity
like a child who finds
contentment in its
mother's arms. I am
at peace.

We must find hope
in God now and forever.

# Psalm 132

*by Sally J. Lemaire*
EXECUTIVE DIRECTOR, RETIRED


A Song of Ascents

Ascent:  The act of rising or mounting upward; climb; an advance in social status or reputation.

*—Webster's Seventh New Collegiate Dictionary*

To honor the Lord, I made a pledge: "I will find a home for you regardless of how long it takes or how hard the tasks. I will complete my pledge before I find my own place in the universe. No home shall welcome me, no bed be made for me, no peaceful sleep will I have until your dwelling place appears."

There are distant fields and towns to seek out as home, where we have the freedom to worship, freedom of movement and freedom to find joy in our lives. Come with me, Lord, as we search for a resting place for you and the ark with your cargo. Do not deny us. Do not turn away from the face of thy chosen one.

The Lord then swore to David an oath of commitment: to not turn back, to look to the future and teach his sons and daughters the covenant and testimonies, and to ensure his sons and daughters and their sons and daughters alike shall sit upon the throne.

The Lord in turn chose Zion for his throne and his eternal resting place. It is a place of bountiful provisions for oneself and to share with the poor. The priests' garments clothe the naked, and their horns celebrate the joy of music.

For my enemies, the unanointed, I shall cover them with shame. For you, the anointed, I shall give a crown of light and luster, to spread wherever your path leads.

AMEN.

# Psalm 133

*By Owen Green West*
STUDENT

People love being with other people.

Love is very precious to us all.

The Lord blesses us when we do good things.

# Psalm 134

*by Charles Kurose*
Student

These words were once spoken:

> Praise not the day until evening has come,
> A woman until she is burnt,
> A sword until it is tried,
> A maiden until she is married,
> Ice until it has been crossed,
> Beer until it has been drunk.

But it was a fool who spoke this, for we know that thankfulness and blessing are to be given in abundance and at all times.

The things worthy of our praise are active even as we slumber, and thus are worthy of our blessing every hour of the day.

# Psalm 135

*by Serious Play! Theatre Ensemble*

praise the lord

praise the name of the lord
what's the same as the lord
plays the game of the lord
moves in mysterious ways through
the maze of the lord
the sinner stays on the board while the winner
gains the reward never strays
from the lord or averts the gaze of the lord
it strikes a nerve in the lord
when you pervert the aim of the lord
so strike a phrase or a chord
The righteous man never weighs what he can afford
toward the price of the lord

The ice on your ring is too cold to feel the
blaze of the lord. It's all a device;
the bling doesn't matter as much as how you sing.

The idols of the nations are silver and gold
And idle corporations got you bought and sold
Midas always seems to want your hand to hold
But it's suicidal to always be controlled by the bridle
of culture. You worship posters of all of them
factory-produced celebrities
I condemn the machine that puts false hopes
And dreams on the screen
Too much fake gold will make your skin turn green
I've been thirteen, staring at the images of those
I'd like to adore, their brand-name clothes
they keep us begging for more
But if you go to the store and read the jackets
of albums you begin to see the racket
perpetrated by the higher bracket. What inspires
them is manufactured desire and the money
So isn't it odd how it seems every one of them
gives a shout-out to God?
See past the posters and the graven images
See past the boasters and clean-shaven visages
The stars are hollow as the producers who are hustlin' em
Like them be those who make them,
Yea, every one—who trusts in them.

# Psalm 136

## by Efraim Eisen
### SPIRITUAL LEADER OF TEMPLE ISRAEL

Thank God, who is so good and whose kindness is forever,
Who performs great wonders, and keeps the earth, the sun and the
      moon in
their perfect places in the heavens,
even as we spin at over a thousand miles per hour it is a wonder
That there is such stillness,
Give thanks to God for the waters, the lights and the great balance
      of the universe.

God's goodness is with us at all times,
Even when we are in the narrow places of our being,
The Holy One helps those who are near,
performing miracles and doing wonders,
God protects us from our enemies and helps us vanquish
Both our inner and outer foes,
God leads us on our journey through the wilderness,
And brings us to our Holy Land,
God remembers us when we are low and releases us
      from our tormentors,
God's kindness provides us with all we need
Praise the God of heaven whose kindness is forever.

# Psalm 137

*by Kelly Gallagher*
MINISTER

How shall I sing, God, of the music that flows within?
Shall I crash the cymbals of your righteousness?
Shall I hum the melody of your peace?
How shall I sing, Lord, of all harmony?
With tears on your gentle pools of sadness?
With screams in the nights of our darkness?
How, my God, do you wish me to sing?

"Sing," you might say, "with the promise of tomorrow.
Sing with the conviction that God is God, after all,
    And the song is one of many to be sung for your Lord."
"Sing," you say, "with words that do not dance on the lines of maybe...
Sing with words that evoke Truth and Understanding,
     No matter how unorthodox and painful those may be in
     this foreign land.
Sing, my children, so that the me in them will resonate and come alive.
So that I may come forth among you and call you my own.
Sing always with Hope—and know, too,
     My heart sings always with you."

# *Psalm 138*

### *by Sharon Washington*
#### College Administrator

I will praise you with my whole heart; before all prophets I sing praise to you.

I will pray in sacred places, and praise your name for your loving kindness and truth; for your words are magnified above all others.

When I cry you'll be there to strengthen my soul.

All people of the earth shall recognize your words and blessings and praise thee.

They will live in concert with your ways; for great is the glory of the Creator.

Though you are greater than all, you respect the common, and the prideful are bereft of your respect.

Even when I encounter difficulties, you sustain me and fight my enemies to save me.

I know that the Creator will hold precious my concerns, and your mercy will endure forever, never rejecting that which you have created.

# Psalm 139

## by Anita Magovern
CATHOLIC CHAPLAIN

O God, you know the inside and the outside of me.
You know every single secret of my heart,
You know my every spoken and unspoken thought and feeling.
Whatever paths I tread, through the tangled seaweed, the open
      meadows, or the darkness of my still uncharted waters, you
      know me and are with me.
Like the sea conch wraps the clam, so you too, my God, wrap me
      around and protect me.
Such fierce tenderness I have never known before.

Sometimes I want to flee from your constancy, but
      where would I hide and to whom would I turn?
If I run to the ocean's shores at dawn, you are there,
If I smell the fragrance from a nearby garden, I sense you with me.
If I scale the cliffs of Mount Kilimanjaro and find the darkest cave,
      you come and bring your light.
How is it that you are there in all these things that I love and care about?

O God, I know you have known me before my time began.
I am, because you have seen me and loved me into being.
I am, because you have spoken to me, and walked with me out into
      the days and nights.

O God, deepen my desire to want you.
Lead me into my heart where you dwell.
And then, lead me out to make a place for you,
      wherever you need to be.

# Psalm 140

## David Martin
### HEATING, VENTILATION AND AIR CONDITIONING TECHNICIAN

Dear God,

I recently became King of a small country, and I've been surrounded by conniving weasels ever since. I know, Lord, that You've looked out for me in the past, but things seem to be out of control. Everywhere I turn, people are trying to put me into a compromising position.

I'm surrounded by truly evil people, Lord. They dress up in their finest suits and hand-stitched Italian loafers. I don't think I'll ever see another expensive suit without thinking, "LIAR."

God, give me guidance. Almighty Lord, give me strength. Let me see through their evil plots before I wind up at war with the whole world. I know, God, that you bless the poor and helpless with justice. Good people are drawn to you. Where did I go wrong?

Sincerely,

David of Bethlehem

# Psalm 141

*by Margaret Riddle*
ELEMENTARY SCHOOL PRINCIPAL

When I reach out to you, O Lord, listen to me.
I honor you with my call for help.

Listen to my words and guide my decisions;
Let me not be tempted to pursue selfish goals;
Help me open my heart to those who challenge me.

If I keep trying to follow a path that is generous and not
      self-serving,
One day I will learn if my path was righteous.
One day I will learn if the choices of my life had meaning
      or were as useless as cracked vases.

Be with me when I reach out to you, O Lord.
Do not leave me alone.
Support me as I try to be the person I wish to be,
Free from temptation to be less.

# Psalm 142

### by Kim Bruce Abell
FAMILY DOCTOR


A Prayer for Help

The patient prays.
Every day she comes (or her sister, or one of her brothers)
        in need of help.
She tells me what is bothering her;
The Chief Complaint, the History of the Present Illness,
Past Medical History, the Review of Systems,
then the Physical Examination.
She has tried everything she could think of,
and still is not well; the pain is not going away.
She comes for diagnosis and treatment,
for an explanation,
to be taught, to be helped.
In the path of her life, illness and injury have befallen her,
and she feels very alone.

The doctor prays.
When treatment fails, or there is no satisfactory answer;
When he asks himself if this is all there is in life,
he cries "Let me believe!" and asks that God deliver him from his fear,
from the belief that the ills of our society will continue
        no matter what he says or does.

I pray.
Set free my soul from this cage of despair, that I may see your light
        in the makings of every day,
        and praise your name because you help me to see.

# *Psalm 143*

*by Sarah Pirtle*
ECO-PEACE EDUCATOR

I remember the days before
when it was easy and clear
to feel You right beside me,
a loving voice guiding my footsteps,
a beacon holding up a lantern
on every path, smooth or rocky.

But look—I have tumbled into a void,
and all the light you shine is lost
from me.

Believe I am faithful.

I am engulfed
by ones who no longer know the secret
that in Your light we make a constellation.

There are ones who do not hold
our Earth in caring hands,
and I am imprisoned with the neon glare
of those voices pursuing me.
They crush me, and my life spark is
ground down
until I cannot find myself,
which is Yourself singing,

I'm lost in the emptiness
between the worlds
where the living feel dead
because we can no longer blossom.

Trembling, I ask you, would you bring your hand
into this lost place and lift me back
before my spirit dies within me?

My heart is deadened,
confounded with anguish,

but my heart will start again
at the spark of Your heartbeat.
Do not judge me because I have lost
the thread of your voice
for none of us living knows how to keep
that fresh beat of spring always within us.

Let me see again Your face!
Even now I am hiding the depth of the horror from You,
as if it could hurt You to speak of it,
or push me further away from ever finding You again.

Some call to You to strike these people down,
but I will not do that
because I can feel it will just keep it going.

This "enemy" has invented the word enemy
to divide us. What is my name for their force?
Scatterer. Terror monger.
One who hides the face of Your light
for their own gain.

This is how it works. They show us
knives and we are scared,
and then bring out
something worse than knives.
When they use them on anyone anywhere
we fall into that void that knows You not.
Are you there?
Are You truly everywhere?

Give ear to my call.
I thirst for You in every pore.
I have so disappeared that in this place
I have forgotten that You hear every cry.

Once again I will call.
Once again I will look.
Turn me around so that I can see your sunrise.

# Psalm 144

*by Eric Foster-Moore*
<small>STUDENT</small>

Blessed be the Lord my Rock who traineth my hands for war, and my fingers for battle?

In you I take refuge, yet Your loving kindness has been perverted, and your fortress destroyed by the blood of my people who you subduest under me.

The Lord, what is man, that Thou takest knowledge of him? Or the son of man, that Thou makest account of him? And Man, what is the Lord, that He teaches us Peace and we take account of that? And that He teaches us war, and we take account of that also?

Man is like unto a breath; his days are as a shadow that passeth away, and each moment we spend with hate in our hearts the work of peace in our hands slips further from our grasp.

O the Lord, bow Thy heavens, and come down, condescend to our level and teach us peace; touch the mountains and all the people, that they may sing together.

Cast forth Your divine love, scatter it about the world; send out Thine radiance, that all may partake in your glory and be not discomfited by the world.

Stretch Thy hands from on high; rescue me, and deliver me out of many waters; by your way of love I shall arise from the hands of hate.

And we shall teach those whose mouths speaketh peace, and their message is peace, while their right hand is a right hand of violence and fury.

O God, I will sing a new song unto Thee, upon a psaltery of ten strings will I sing praises unto Thee; But hark! Hear my voice!

You who givest salvation unto Kings, who rescuest David Thy servant from the hurtful sword, yet let beggars die in the street and children collapse on their feet.

Rescue us, and deliver us out of the hands of hate and vileness, and we would have Your mouth speaketh peace, and Your right hand be not a right hand of wrath but one of love.

We whose sons are as plants grown up in their youth; whose daughters are as corner-pillars carved after the fashion of a palace; and together, though slight, we are a beautiful edifice on the earth;

Whose granaries are full and whose hearts are open; whose sheep increase by thousands and ten thousands in our fields; and whose fields are great expanses of love;

Whose oxen are well laden; with no breach, and no going forth, and no outcry in our broad places;

Happy are the people that are in such a place; happy are the people for whom God is the Lord. Yea, and happy are the people whose work is peace.

# Psalm 145

*by Noah Augarten*
Curative Educator

We will lift up the world to you!
For every action, we will have a reaction.
We will speak of your Glory Great.
We will tell stories and make predictions.
We will gather together and say that anything
      we can touch and
        feel
            bears the stamp of your make,
                our matter.

We will gather together and groan
                              and more
                    among us will
              stand up and
          cheer thy Mercy and
          more still, your Victory!
We are gathered here once more.
              To thy good or to thy
                    ill, we stand ready.
              We talk and speak amongst one another.
We are tuned in.
The message is, "when others
              would assault your name,
              we would stand firm,
              and repeat our stories."
You are the creation of poets!
              You live behind everything I believe in.
You are the satisfaction of madmen!
              Should I trust every word you might speak?
              Do I see you lifting those who are pushed down?
              or find you giving food to every man with eyes upon you?
I cannot see your hand,
              nor take from it,
              nor see any who are
              living do so.
Yet I know of justice
              and inertia.
We call your name.
              We see your traces in everything.
We grant mercy to those
              willing to put your name in their hearts
                    and we know that to behave terribly
                    may alter one's reality.
We sing of your grace and mercy.
              We see that your anger builds slowly
                    but your love flows forever.
We sing of your goodness, your compassion.
No doubt your name is in my mouth forever.

# Psalm 146

## by Wendy L. Williams
### SCHOOL BUS DRIVER

I will praise God with all of my soul.

I will praise him as long as I live and will sing praises to him while I'm alive.

Don't put your trust in a human prince because he won't help you. When he dies, he'll go back to earth and not to heaven. All of his plans will die with him.

The one who asks God for help will be happy. Have hope with God because he created the heavens and the earth and he will always keep his faith.

He is the one who gives justice to the oppressed and provides food for the hungry.

God sets prisoners free and gives sight to the blind. He lifts up the spirits of those who have troubles and loves those who are righteous. He looks out for travelers and widows with children.

If people are wicked, God will punish them and take away all that is theirs.

God will always be there for all of us.

Praise God!

# Psalm 147

*by Ron McMahon*
<small>GROUNDSKEEPER</small>

As I awake to a glorious sunrise I give thanks to the Lord for a new day to do my work.

Only God can complete the work I start each day with the sun and the rain from the heavens.

Through my work I am God's messenger.

By cultivating and nourishing what He has created, others may feel the carpet of grass under their bare feet and see the beauty of the flowers and trees that flourish around them on a summer day.

I toil not for corporate profit nor greed, but to preserve the gifts of the earth so that others may enjoy these blessings from the Lord.

# Psalm 148

*by Deborah Lubar*
ACTOR, WRITER, TEACHER

The earth and the sky are made of praise
Praise to the Great and Unfathomable Mystery—
Praise falling down from the tops of the mountains
Praise pouring out from the skies,
The Angels, the Sun and the Moon and the Stars of light—
Sing praise, praise to the unending Mystery.
May the heaven of heaven be a song of praise and
The waters of the world above heaven's own sky—
For out of the Great Spirit
All has been created
And, by divine promise,
sung into being forever.

From out of the earth praise grows up like vines,
From the giant-mouthed dragons of the deeps—praise.
From fire, hail, snow and thick mists,
From storm and wind—
For all these themselves are the language of Spirit—
The slow-breathing mountains and their mothers, the hills,
The fruit words of trees and sweet breath of cedar,
The myriad creatures that walk, crawl and fly,
And the people, all people, full-throated with praise:
The young and the old, the women and men,
Kings, queens and judges,
All made of praise,
Praise for the Great-hearted Mystery.

For the Spirit plays its music
for all of its beings,
all that are called "Israel"—
which means, after all,
"those who struggle-with-God."

# *Psalm 149*

## *by Julia Jean*
### Teacher, Researcher, Writer

Give praise to the Goddess within and without.
Sing unto our Lady a new song
      for we shall praise Her with our very presence.
Let the Universe rejoice in Her creations.
Let Her children be joyful as we praise Her names in the Great Dance.
We will play our heart drums and soul strings.
We will pluck the sinews of our skeletons.
We will merge in the Great Rite with equanimity and freedom
      in our stomping feet.

For She takes pleasure in Her devotees.
She clothes us in her radiant jewel strength.
All acts of love and pleasure are Her rituals.
We are joyful in Her glory.
We sing to Her in our beds, our lovemaking in Her honor.
We rejoice in Her edgeless luminosity.
We chant Her names in our waking and our sleeping,
      in our nakedness, fertility and death.

We lift Her praises as we whisper, sing, talk, eat, and kiss.
May She enter us with every breath, every motion, and every movement.
May our egos be sacrificed so we know each other more deeply
      through Her cruel compassion.
We humble ourselves so we may know the Truth
      and be released from the chains and fetters of illusion.
Then, the glistening radiance of Her wisdom will take us over completely.

When we surrender completely—in Truth—we lose only our smallness,
      not our power or our glory.
We step into Her: She of 108 names, 1008 names.
We become One.
We honorably install You in our hearts so that we might know
      the deepest truths, so that we might know ourselves as others.
And realize the blazing fires of the non-duality of all existence
      and non-existence.

# Psalm 150

## by Michelle Ames
PARENT

This is the day, this is the day that the Lord has made, that the Lord has made.
Let us rejoice, let us rejoice, and be glad in it and be glad in it.
This is the day that the Lord has made. Let us rejoice and be glad in it.
This is the day, this is the day that the Lord has made.

I start humming. I open my mouth and the humming escalates into song.
I can feel my body dancing happily with the rhythm of the tune.
As my young children come pouncing into the room,
they join in and are dancing merrily around the floor.
My heart wells with love and happiness as I watch them
proudly sing each word as loud as they can!
As we end the song with a great big hug, I can feel life
flowing through my body and life is good.

Praise you and thank you so much Lord,
for giving me so much of life in just the few happy moments of this song.
I think about all the things the Lord has given to us.
Praise the Lord for great and small, Praise the Lord for loving us all!
Praise the Lord both day and night, Praise the Lord for the endless fight!
Praise the Lord, strike up the bands, Praise the Lord for holding our hands!
Praise the Lord, let the angels help me to raise my children to know you,
love you and praise you!
God is good!
Praise the Lord!

*Postscript: About the Photos*

When I began experimenting with photography almost thirty years ago, I would sit in one place in my back yard, portrait lens on my camera, and watch as my children moved in and out of the frame. I loved how looking through the camera eliminated extraneous details and gave me a clear, uninterrupted view of my son and daughter.

One of the most important changes in how I see things, now that I have made thousands of portraits of children, families and community groups, is recognizing that by including the "extraneous details" a portrait can become more expressive and engaging. My children are grown now, and I still love the close up of their faces, but am more inclined to photograph them with their surroundings included. So too, for many of the Psalms photos.

For *Psalms In Ordinary Voices*, I worked with a traditional film camera, shooting in black and white. The majority of the images were taken in short, thirty-minute sessions at our contributors' homes or workplaces over a period of two years. A photographer's job is not only to snap the shutter at "the decisive moment," but also to help sitters shed their self-consciousness about being photographed, and to create a connection between photographer and subject. This relaxed, working relationship is essential to making intentional and successful portraits.

Including a photograph with each Psalm gives you, the reader, a much more complete picture of our writers. I hope you explore this book often and that the images will enhance your relationship to the 150 people who have generously contributed their interpretations of the Psalms.

Ellen Augarten
Northampton, MA

# Index of Names

*Acknowledgments*

Bringing *Psalms in Ordinary Voices* to the point of publication has been a long and convoluted journey. At some points during the last decade we were moving at high speed; there were also quiet and slow periods during which we waited, hoped and plodded forward. We are deeply grateful to the Psalm writers who made this book possible! And we are thankful for the many people who believed in this project and cheered us on—without their help and support, this book would not have reached publication. Our deepest gratitude to the following family members, friends, and colleagues who walked with us, with grace and faith, on this journey: Fred Ayvazian, Gloria Ayvazian, Ann Chiara, Faith Childs, Mark Dickstein, Sarah Grolnic-McClurg, Vicha Hajdamowicz, Sally Lemaire, Roxie Mack, Rebecca Neimark, Linda Roghaar, Jane Rohman, Steve Strimer, Karen Thatcher, and Emily Weir. Bless you all!

*Bill McKibben* is a writer and activist. His 1989 book, *The End of Nature*, was the first book on climate change for a general audience, and he has gone on to organize the largest international series of grassroots protests against global warming. His work appears regularly in periodicals from *Harpers* and *The New Yorker* to the *Christian Century*, and has been recently collected in *The Bill McKibben Reader*. McKibben's most recent book is *Eaarth: Making a Life on a Tough New Planet*.

*The Rev. Dr. Andrea Ayvazian* (*left*) is the senior pastor of the Haydenville Congregational Church, United Church of Christ, in Western Massachusetts. Andrea was formerly the dean of religious life at Mount Holyoke College. A long-time activist for peace and social justice, Andrea is an anti-racism educator, singer and poet. She lives in Northampton, Massachusetts, with her partner, Michael Klare. They have one grown son, Sasha.

*Ellen Augarten* (*right*) grew up in Queens, New York, and came in the mid-1970s to Western Massachusetts, where her career in portrait photography began and grew. She received her master of fine arts degree from Hartford Art School at the University of Hartford. An active community member, she lives in Northampton, Massachusetts, with her husband, Mark. They have two grown children, Libby and Noah.

*Psalms in Ordinary Voices*   *www.psalmsinordinaryvoices.com*

# EGYPT IN THE FUTURE TENSE

PUBLIC CULTURES OF THE MIDDLE EAST AND NORTH AFRICA

Paul A. Silverstein, Susan Slyomovics, and Ted Swedenburg, *editors*

# EGYPT IN THE FUTURE TENSE

*Hope, Frustration, and Ambivalence*
*before and after 2011*

Samuli Schielke

Indiana University Press

Bloomington and Indianapolis

This book is a publication of

Indiana University Press
Office of Scholarly Publishing
Herman B Wells Library 350
1320 East 10th Street
Bloomington, Indiana 47405 USA

iupress.indiana.edu

♾ The paper used in this publication meets the minimum requirements
of the American National Standard for Information Sciences—
Permanence of Paper for Printed Library Materials, ANSI Z39.48-1992.

Manufactured in the United States of America

Cataloging information is available from the Library of Congress.

ISBN 978-0-253-01584-6 (cloth)
ISBN 978-0-253-01587-7 (paperback)
ISBN 978-0-253-01589-1 (ebook)

1 2 3 4 5   20 19 18 17 16 15

*In memory of*
*Hazem Nasim al-Sabbagh*
*(1992–2009)*

*The discourse that makes people believe is the one that takes away what it urges them to believe in, or never delivers what it promises.*

—Michel de Certeau, *The Practice of Everyday Life*

*The more progress, the more boredom.*

—Tawfiq

# Contents

# Acknowledgments

ETHNOGRAPHY IS A collaborative enterprise, and so is anthropological theory. This book is the fruit of countless discussions, debates, and shared experiences with more people than I can in any way credit here.

Many of those to whom I owe the greatest debt do not appear in this book under their own names for the sake of privacy. But they will recognize themselves, and I hope that they find that I have made good use of the ideas I have either borrowed from them or developed in conversation with them.

Some of the best ideas in this book have grown out of my shared life and work with Daniela Swarowsky, without whose active participation, support, and critical questioning I could not imagine having written this book. Many parts of this book are also based on collaborative research with Mukhtar Saad Shehata, whose friendship, hospitality, and creative mind are another cornerstone of this work that I find difficult indeed to call mine.

I also owe great thanks for the support I have received from my parents Hannele Nätynki and Jürgen Schielke, the Shehata family, the people of Nazlat al-Rayyis, the "If you can, do like I do" group, the workers of G4S in Doha, Gudran Association for Arts and Culture in Alexandria, Studio El-Madina in Alexandria, and the Netherlands-Flemish Institute in Cairo. Thanks are equally due for the support, ideas, feedback, and critique I have received from Paola Abenante, Aymen Amer, Arthur Bueno, Daniele Cantini, Susanne Dahlgren, Abdalla Daif, Liza Debevec, Patrick Desplat, Kevin Eisenstadt, Ulrike Freitag, Omneya El-Gameel, Aliaa ElGready, Knut Graw, Sonja Hegazy, Abeer Hosny, Zaynab Hosni, Salwa Ismail, Harri Juntunen, Saad Kamel, Amr Khairy, Aymon Kreil, Kai Kresse, Jakob Lindfors, Kamal Aly Mahdy, Maged Makram, Maria Malmström, Annelies Moors, Shady Basiony Marei, Magnus Marsden, Omnia Mehanna, Laura Menin, Henri Onodera, Filippo Osella, Jennifer Peterson, Carl Rommel, Dorothea Schulz, Benjamin Soares, Aly Sobhi, Georg Stauth, Steffen Strohmenger, Gregory Starrett, Georg Stauth, Ted Swedenburg, Amira El Tahawy, Rebecca Tolen, Tea Virtanen, Mustafa Wafi, Jessica Winegar, and Ahmed Zayed. My sincere apologies are due to all those whom I have wrongfully forgotten.

Many of the theoretical insights of this book were shaped in conversation with students of courses I have taught while doing this research, especially Morality, Politics and Religion (University of Mainz 2007), Ethnographies of the Imaginary (Freie Universität Berlin 2009), Belief and Unbelief (University of Cologne 2010–2011), Capitalism as a Cultural Practice and Sensibility of Life (Freie

Universität Berlin 2011), and Is a Better World Possible? (Freie Universität Berlin 2013). I hope it has been as inspiring for them as it was for me.

The research for this book and writing of it were made possible by research positions and grants from a number of institutions and projects: the DFG (Deutsche Forschungsgemeinschaft) collaborative research center Cultural and Linguistic Contacts and the Department of Anthropology and African Studies at the Johannes Gutenberg University of Mainz, 2006–2007; the International Institute for the Study of Islam in the Modern World (ISIM) in Leiden, 2008; the research group What Makes a Good Muslim at the University of Eastern Finland, funded by the Academy of Finland, 2008; Zentrum Moderner Orient (ZMO), Berlin, 2009–2014; and the junior research group In Search of Europe at the ZMO, funded by the German Federal Ministry of Research and Education, 2010–2014.

Writing this book was greatly facilitated by the inspiring surroundings and friendly service provided by Zizo's Café in Cairo, Pâtisserie Délices in Alexandria, Westerpavilioen in Rotterdam, Café zur Rose in Berlin, Koskibaari in Siuro, Café Jelinek in Vienna, Zbojnická Chata in the High Tatras, and Deutsche Bahn.

Some of the material of this book has appeared in earlier publications in a different shape and at times with different conclusions. An earlier version of chapter 1 appeared in 2008 in *Contemporary Islam*. Chapter 2 includes some material that appeared in 2009 in *Journal of the Royal Anthropological Institute*. The first half of chapter 4 was published in Arabic translation in 2012 by the Bibliotheca Alexandrina. Chapter 5 is a heavily revised version of a chapter in the 2012 edited volume *Ordinary Lives and Grand Schemes*. A shorter version of chapter 7 appeared in the edited volume *The Global Horizon* in 2012. Many thanks are due to the editors and anonymous reviewers of these publications. I am furthermore grateful to Shaymaa Bakr, Shady Basiony Marei, Samia Jaheen, Muhammad Saad Shehata, and Mukhtar Saad Shehata for providing me the permission to use their copyrighted materials.

It has taken me more than eight years to come from a first idea to a finished book. It has not been an easy time for Egyptians to aspire for a better life—and I wonder if there ever has been an easy time for them to start with. The mood of those years, shifting between pressure, hope, frustration, enthusiasm, agitation, anxiety, and aggression, has left its mark on this book that also shifts between glimpses of hope and a sense of tragedy—and the tragic part prevails. With so much unrealized aspiration, so much wrong and oppression, so many struggles to make it better, and so much polarization and bloodshed, I feel that writing in a genre other than tragedy would be insincere. At the same time, I could not have done it without the friendship of all those who, despite everything, over and again have restored my faith in humanity and its capacity to strive for something better.

# Note on Transliteration
## of Arabic Terms

THE WAYS IN which Arabic is reproduced in Latin script vary greatly, and the systems preferred by Western scholars are very different from those used by most Arabic speakers for practical purposes. For proper names, the spelling used by the persons themselves or otherwise current in use is preferred. For other Arabic terms the simplified rules of *International Journal of Middle East Studies* are used.

This book makes use of expressions and words in three different forms of Arabic: classical Arabic; the form of Egyptian Arabic spoken in Cairo, Alexandria, and other cities; and the form of Egyptian Arabic spoken in the villages of the northern Nile Delta. I have tried to maintain this variety of forms in the transliteration of Arabic terms and expressions in this book. For the sake of clarity, however, the letter *qaf* (which is pronounced as *q*, a voiceless uvular stop, in classical Arabic, as *g* in rural regions of the Nile Delta, and as a glottal stop in Cairo and other cities) is transliterated with a *q* throughout, and the letter *ta' marbuta* at the end of a word (which is pronounced as *–a* in classical and Cairene Arabic and as *–e* or *–i* in the Nile Delta) is transliterated with an *a* throughout.

# EGYPT IN THE FUTURE TENSE

# Introduction

## A Moment in History

THE VILLAGE OF Nazlat al-Rayyis in northern Egypt, October 2009—in a café I ran into Saʿid, a soccer enthusiast whom I know from amateur soccer tournaments that take place every Ramadan. The global financial crisis was the talk of the day, and I asked him how the people in the village were affected by it. Saʿid said, "Here with the poor people, it's always crisis." The more he talked about it, the more upset he became:

> Here there is no middle, there are only poor people, and those who are well off are thieves. The country is divided in those who are honest and don't know how to steal, and those who are thieves and well-off. You know why I come here to watch soccer? I only watch soccer in order not to think. There are people who watch soccer because they really love it, I just don't want to think. Just like people who take pills and hashish—if you talk to one he is not there, he is happy and doesn't think about anything. And if his mother is sick or his family needs food he doesn't care. He could only care if he had power over his situation. But you can only have power over your situation if you have money.
>
> But one must thank God and be content. We accept what our Lord gives us, and it's good, no one can refuse to be content with the will of God.

SAMULI: But should one be content with oppression?

SAʿID: In Egypt the government is very content with oppression. They oppress and repress everybody. If someone reported me on what I tell you they would take me and arrest me—everybody is afraid and oppressed.

Saʿid interrupted his bitter lament of oppression and inequality for a moment when he resorted to piety as a way to remind me and himself that there is higher divine wisdom to the way the world is, and that a believer should always be content with the will of God. But how can one maintain that sense when one is expected to be wealthy, successful, and powerful while having no control over one's situation? For those without wealth or power, it is not always easy to distinguish contentedness from despair.

The key question that Saʿid takes up is how to have existential power over one's situation. He has two answers: contentedness with the will of God and money. But the question remains open, for Saʿid's contentedness is not of a lasting kind, and he does not have the means to make enough money.

## A Stormy Season

Saʿid narrated his lament in a historical moment that, in retrospect, appears as the eve of the January 25 revolution: a time marked by great expectations and deep frustrations, spectacular economic growth, an atmosphere of religious euphoria, a youth culture of romance and flirtation, a globally mediated sense of fantasy, dramatic economical and social inequality, a sense of moral crisis, an almost unbearable pressure to migrate, and a mixture of fear and hatred toward the government. For a moment in 2011, it appeared that this historical moment might be over, about to be replaced by something more harmonious and less troubling: a society in which Islamist politics and democracy would coexist, in which aspirations could be realized and people would have the power to change their condition. Like revolutions in general, the January 25 revolution was motivated not only by poverty and oppression but also, and more importantly, by hope and aspiration, strong and unfulfilled. The reality of postrevolutionary Egypt turned out to be troubling, however, and the great hopes associated with the uprising of 2011 have been replaced by equally great frustrations and anxieties—and terrible bloodshed.

The revolution began with bloodshed in late January and early February 2011, when around one thousand people were killed (most of them on January 28), most of them protesters who were facing the security forces of the falling regime of Hosni Mubarak.[1] During two and a half years of the not-so-peaceful revolutionary period that followed, protesters were killed by security forces, houses of Christians and other religious minorities were attacked by mobs, competing political groups staged street battles, and private conflicts were taken to the streets and settled with guns. The spiral of confrontation reached its peak on August 14, 2013, when supporters of deposed president Morsi were massacred by security forces in an act of violence that cost more than a thousand lives,[2] and that was expected and premeditated by everybody—the perpetrators, the victims, and those who wanted to have nothing to do with it. The unwillingness and inability to prevent that and other massacres from happening constitute a trauma marking Egyptians' relations with one another and their sense about hope, frustration, and possibility for decades to come. August 14, 2013, was the darkest hour of a period that some have called the Arab spring, but that I prefer to call a stormy season, in analogy to the Coptic month of Amshir (February 8 to March 9), which is characterized by stormy, unpredictable weather.[3] The one good thing about that day is that it made it impossible to write an enthusiastic story of the Egyptian revolution as the daybreak of a new, qualitatively different (i.e., better) era in the history of Egypt.

This book is in any case not a story of the revolution (if there was a revolution). It is the story of a longer trajectory of the pressing and often frustrating expectation of something more and better to come, of which the January 25 uprising was a part—an important part indeed, but only a part. An ambivalent unity of hope, frustration, anxiety, and struggle is characteristic not only of the revolution but in fact of all great expectations—religious, economical, moral, romantic, economical, political, or other—expressed by Egyptians in the current moment and the recent past. This book tells about those hopes; how they coexist in everyday lives; the paths people undertake to pursue them; and the frustrations, anxieties, and unintended consequences that accompany them.

Hope and trust in Egypt at the turn of the millennium have found their primary expression in religion. The previous four decades have witnessed a tremendous increase and a significant shift in religiosity among Egyptians, both Muslims and Christians.[4] Among the Muslim majority of the population, an Islamic revival has made a scripturally oriented and conservative sense of religiosity the most powerful source of moral certainty and existential hope. During the brief rule of the Muslim Brotherhood in 2012 and 2013, this revivalist sense of religion also gained political power. The polarization that marked that moment, however, also destabilized the power of religion as *the* source of moral certainty, and three years after the January 25 uprising, the consensus about the importance of piety among Muslim Egyptians has been shattered and replaced by a violent competition of militarist-nationalist, Islamist, revolutionary leftist, and other sources of moral certainty. And yet, also during the late years of the Mubarak regime, when there existed something like a consensus about the importance of fearing God, religiosity was neither a singular nor an uncontested source of hope and certainty. It was intertwined with and informed by other great promises and senses of hope—economical, romantic, community oriented, individualistic, political. The same people believe in the absolute truth of Islam, search for a base for sound moral conduct, desire and crave, fall in love, try to move up the social ladder, aspire to a life of comfortable middle-class consumerism, oppose the "system" of political economy, compare their situation with those in the wider world, believe in Egypt's supremacy over other nations, want to forget their worries and live in the moment, feel bored and frustrated, and do what they can to realize a life of dignity. What they can actually do, however, is only partially in their hands. They follow paths that are available and compelling, and the consequences of doing so, following paths unknown at the time they choose them, may be surprising, confusing, or disappointing. At rare moments, the decisions they make may shake the world.

This book explores the deep relationships between hope and frustration, ideals and experience, aims and consequences—under conditions of neoliberal capitalism, revivalist Islam, and political polarization. Rather than assuming Muslim religiosity to be irreducibly different from other great aspirations, however, this account explores the commonalities of those aspirations by focusing on the existential motivations and ambiguities of pursuing moral and spiritual perfection in an imperfect world. It is based on in-depth ethnographic study of social experience at a particular historical moment that is most dramatically marked by the stormy season of Arab uprisings between 2011 and 2013—but there are many other, more important stories to be told about that moment as well.

Grounded in a dialogic approach to ethnography and a view of anthropology as an open-ended conversation, rather than distanced observation, this book is not a detached one. It draws on diverse approaches. My narrative jumps from topic to topic, privileging contradictions and discontents. While it stands in a venerable tradition of ethnography as a way to provide a complex picture of multiple aspects of social experience, it is also a consciously partial narrative, and at times partisan. This is partly a matter of personal liking, the kind of story I am most comfortable telling. More important, though, it is a matter of the complexity and ambivalence at the heart of the reality I describe. Thus, although at times it may give the impression of being a subjective account, this book is in fact rather positivistic in its approach, committed to adjusting its narrative, style, and theory to the world it describes, and not vice versa.

## The Setting: Complex Realities and Grand Schemes

What kind of a world, what kind of a social experience, are we talking about, then? Where is it happening? Who is involved in it? This book is based on long-term ethnographic fieldwork among people who mostly could be described as lower middle class—poor but aspiring, educated but not well connected, usually hailing from provincial milieus—in the cities and villages of northern Egypt, Egypt's most populous region. Most of the people I write about come from one village near the Mediterranean coast, but many live in Alexandria and Cairo, Egypt's two largest cities. Among the people I write about, there are fewer women than men, and even fewer people from urban, bourgeois backgrounds. Almost all are Muslims. Most were between their teens and early thirties when I began my research, although they have grown older and many have married, so that this book is no longer about "the youth" per se.

In search of ways to grasp the many connections and trajectories of people's lives, I decided to return to the old-fashioned anthropological tradition of village ethnography. But villages are not what they used to be, and the same must count for village ethnography. While my ethnography has its focal point in a village, more of the ethnographic work has been actually conducted outside the village, in Alexandria, Cairo, and abroad.

The village of Nazlat al-Rayyis (not its real name, just as the people I write about do not appear here with their real names—with some exceptions[5]), the

Figure INT.1.  Village alleyway, Nazlat al-Rayyis, October 2007.

focal point of this book, is located between the Rosetta branch of the river Nile
and Lake Burullus, not far from the Mediterranean coast. First mentioned in medieval chronicles, it was originally a fishermen's harbor at the shores of the once
much-larger lake. Today, it is surrounded by fields on all sides, because much of
Lake Burullus has been drained for agricultural use in the past century. Like all
Egyptian villages built on cultivated land, Nazlat al-Rayyis is extremely densely
populated. With narrow unpaved alleys and small houses covered by rice straw
to heat ovens, it continues to give an impression of rurality, but it is deeply connected to the surrounding metropolises.[6]

In the 2000s, a shared understanding prevailed in Nazlat al-Rayyis that people have become more religious and that this is a good thing. People greet each
other with the Islamic greeting "peace be upon you" (*as-salamu 'alaykum*) rather

Figure INT.2. Construction of a new house on agricultural land on the outskirts of the village, Nazlat al-Rayyis, October 2010.

than with the religiously neutral "good morning" or "good evening." Construction of a lofty new mosque began in 2006 on the outskirts of the village (although this work was put on hold in 2009, rumored to be a result of losses during the global financial crisis). The village bar closed decades ago, and all adult women now wear the headscarf (*higab*), covering themselves so that only hands, feet, and face are visible.

Despite this increased religiosity, the inhabitants do not feel that their village has generally become a better place to live. Measured in terms of the quality of housing and the possession of consumer goods, the standard of living has risen significantly in the past decades, but so have economic pressures and frustration. There is a widespread sense of insecurity and moral alienation. Young people often express a nihilistic sense of boredom and frustration. As almost everywhere in Egypt, marijuana and hashish have swept over the black market in tremendous quantities and at low prices, and many young people have become habitual consumers.

A center of schools for surrounding villages, and less than five kilometers away from the nearby town, Nazlat al-Rayyis is well connected by rural standards. The village claims a high level of literacy and education by rural standards, and it has a history of political activism. It became a stronghold of the Wafd Party in the 1920s, and experienced a period of socialist and communist activity in the 1970s and 1980s. Since the beginning of the 1990s it has had a strong and active branch of the Muslim Brotherhood, and in 2011, a small but active circle of revolutionary activists formed in the village. According to information given on the phone by the district administration, the village had 12,800 inhabitants in the national census of 2006, but many live in cities or abroad, returning to the village only during vacations.

International migration is an important part of the economic and social life of the village, with waves of labor migration to Iraq in the 1970s and 1980s and to the Arab Gulf states since the 1990s. Many of the old two-story houses are making way for larger houses of up to four, even six, floors, built with the money of labor migrants. Aside from money earned through migration, the economy of the village relies mainly on fishing, farming, and public-sector jobs. While fishing has become less important and less lucrative as a result of pollution and land reclamation projects, it remains an important part of residents' identity (Tordhol 2014).

One of the descendants of fishermen with great expectations is Tawfiq, who appears frequently in this book. His grandfather, al-Hagg Mu'izz was a fisherman for most of his life, and his uncle Isma'il runs a small shop and struggles to find a regular position as a schoolteacher. Tawfiq is a civil servant in a local health center, but his work is so poorly paid that it does not even cover running expenses. His dream, when I met him, was to migrate abroad. By the time I finished writing this book, he had spent altogether more than four years working as a security guard in the Arab Gulf states. Tawfiq's family is connected through marriage to that of Abdelnaser and Muntasir, two brothers, also from a fisherman's family (they occasionally still work on fishing boats on the lake), who were running a successful shop in the village until the global rise in food prices forced them to close it in 2008. Since then, they, too, have been trying to provide income and save money for marriage by migrating to Saudi Arabia, but they have faced great adversity.

The vast majority of people who appear in this books are linked with Tawfiq by ties of family, work, passion for soccer, shared political commitment, or friendship. One of Tawfiq's closest friends is Mustafa. Unlike Tawfiq, Mustafa does not come from a family of fishermen, and both of his parents received some education. His material situation is slightly better than Tawfiq's, and his personal trajectory is in many ways different. He had been active in a Salafi group for a short period in 2006 when I first met him, and for a long time he felt disoriented, unlike Tawfiq, who had more clearly defined political and personal visions. While Tawfiq went for the career of a migrant worker, Mustafa chose the riskier path of making himself independent as a sales representative—with relatively good success.

These and other people who appear in this book come from a variety of different class positions in the village society, depending on their background, education, and livelihood. They mostly consider themselves to be middle class, although they often acknowledge that they are, in fact, relatively poor. From a metropolitan, bourgeois point of view, they would appear to be representatives of diffuse masses of rural poor people. And yet in reality, it is very difficult to tell who is rural and who is urban in today's Egypt, with the exception of a small segment of entirely urban bourgeoisie. Most rural people live or work in cities for longer or shorter periods of time, and they switch between rural and urban dialects as they move back and forth.[7]

From Nazlat al-Rayyis, it is a little more than an hour's minibus ride to Alexandria, Egypt's second-largest city. Because of its proximity, many villagers frequent Alexandria for work, study, medical care, and business. Some have moved permanently to the city but continue to visit the village on weekends.

Among them are the schoolteacher Fouad and his wife, Nazli. Fouad is a relative of Tawfiq and moved to the eastern outskirts of Alexandria in the mid-2000s. The family continues to move back and forth between the city and the village. Mustafa and his brother Salah moved to the western outskirts of Alexandria in 2009 but continue to visit the village where their mother lives almost every weekend. Even those who have lived in the city much longer, like Mukhtar Shehata (a relative of Fouad and, like him, a teacher), remain closely linked with the village, and in many ways the outskirts of Alexandria are also outskirts of the village.

People moving from the village to Alexandria usually settle in informal areas (*'ashwa'iyat*) in the far west or east of the city. One of those areas is the inland part of al-Mandara in eastern Alexandria, a district divided by the Abu Qir railway line into a relatively well-off seaside (*bahri*), where high-rise buildings, expensive cafés, restaurants, and night clubs line the seafront, and a low-income, "popular," informal housing area on the inland (*qibli*) side. Inland Mandara is crammed with apartment houses that, though often illegally built, often have more than ten floors, a result of the extreme congestion and high land prices. It is one of the places where people from the village are most likely to move for work and study, and like most of urban Egypt today, it is primarily dominated by descendants of migrants from the countryside. With its narrow but straight streets and its anonymous new buildings, its class and confessional divisions, as well as its location next to the Mediterranean Sea and, by extension, Europe, al-Mandara is a privileged place from which to understand the social dynamics of Egypt as part of a highly dynamic, unequal world.

Alexandria is also an important base of the Salafi movement in Egypt, to the extent that Salafism, which promotes a morally and ritually pure life based strictly on Islamic scripture, has come close to being the predominant form of Islam practiced in inland Mandara. The Salafi current is not an organization. It consists of several competing groups with key leading figures, in addition to individual Salafis who do not belong to any group. While the views of Salafis from different groups on ritual and moral life are often fairly similar, their position toward state and politics, as well as their social base, can be quite different. Throughout the city, buildings, public transportation, shops, and homes are covered by posters and stickers calling people to pray and fast, to bless the Prophet, to mind their manners and cultivate their characters, to fight the Jews and feed the poor. Women are called to cover their hair and bodies and men to teach Islam to their families. Until 2011, religious literature dominated the newsstands and bookstores. Broadcasts and recordings of the Qur'an and sermons are routinely played in cafés, buses, shops, and homes.

While various social niches have continued to cultivate worldviews and lifestyles that are at odds with the wave of Islamic revival, also those who do not support the Salafi movement generally show a strong emotional commitment to the religion of Islam. Until 2011, there was a very wide consensus that Muslims should fear God; fulfill their religious duties; shape their lives and societies according to Islamic principles; and defend their faith, the Prophet, and their Muslim brothers and sisters. One of the consequences of this consensus has been that the position of those who are not part of it has become increasingly precarious—a problem that particularly concerns Egypt's large Christian minority (between 5 percent and 10 percent of Egyptians), which is facing significant pressure and tensions in an atmosphere of heightened confessionalism. During the past decade, Alexandria has witnessed several anti-Christian clashes and a disastrous terror attack against a church (Heo 2013b).

At the same time, Alexandria is also an oppositional city. Because of its relative distance from the center of power, in Cairo, it has suffered from a certain neglect by the national government (albeit not nearly as grave as that experienced by other provincial cities). This neglect also provided grounds and spaces for a widespread oppositional attitude in the city during the Mubarak era. This made Alexandria one of the centers of the January 25 revolution. Islamist movements continue to form the best-organized political power in the city (except for the Armed Forces, of course), but the political landscape of the city is far from being under the control of any one of the parties involved. In the first round of the presidential elections in 2012, for example, the Nasserist socialist candidate Hamdeen Sabbahi was the clear winner in Alexandria, leaving Mohamed Morsi, the eventual winner of the race on the national level, far behind in fourth place (Schielke 2012b; Ali 2012).

One of the many currents that were involved in the political contestation in and of Alexandria between 2011 and 2013 was what was called the "revolutionary current," marked by the double rejection of the Mubarak system and Islamist politics. Among those revolutionaries are a few people who hail from the village, notably Fouad and Zaher. The latter currently lives between Alexandria and a satellite city, where he works in a private-sector company. But more prominent in this current are people like Rasha, whose families have lived in the city for a generation or longer and who are socialized in the milieu of the urban bourgeoisie. What brings these people together despite their different class backgrounds is their shared political commitment and the fact that they move in similar cultural circles.

Cairo, Egypt's gigantic capital, is unlike any other place in the country. Here the financial, political, and cultural elites of the country concentrate. For a visitor from the Egyptian province, the city is not only congested, loud, and chaotic; it is also fancy, cosmopolitan, and expensive. It is a place to make money, to make a career, to make things happen—it is a center of wealth, power, culture, and glamour. Cairo is the place to be, so to speak, in Egypt.

Fewer people from the village live in Cairo than in Alexandria. Cairo is farther away, and the cost of living there is prohibitive. Those who do occupy vastly divergent class positions in Cairene society. With the decline of fishing on Lake Burullus, some fishermen have moved to Cairo to work as doormen or garbage collectors. At the upper end of the social scale, a few university graduates have managed to make a middle-class living in the capital. Tawfiq's cousin Hilmi, who felt that he had been stuck in the village for many years, managed to find work in Cairo as a journalist in 2010, making him one the few people I know who has managed to move upward in the class structure of the capital. His friend Shady from the neighboring village managed to get a job at the Organization for Cultural Centers through another friend who worked there, but his income and living conditions are precarious at best. 'Abbas, who used to play soccer with Tawfiq in the village, studied in Cairo for some years and faced formidable economical hardship. Eventually, he had to return to the village, and later he migrated for work to the United Arab Emirates.

The path of social advancement in the capital is a difficult one, and many more would like to move to Cairo if only they could. But few in the village have *wasta*, or "a connection," in the form of relatives or useful contacts in the capital that would help them to make a start.

Making a career without *wasta* is a Herculean task in Egypt's highly stratified class society. The Mubarak era witnessed the development of the old social institution of *wasta* into the central principle of neoliberal governance. Everybody, from the poorest to the richest, has been compelled to do all they can to get the right connections. Knowing the right people helps one to get a job, to get promoted, to build a house, to start a company, to be released from police custody, and to be acquitted from criminal charges. Not knowing the right people, one has to expect to work in low-level positions for little or precarious pay, to see one's property destroyed, and to be arbitrarily arrested and tortured by the police.

This is just a short and superficial glimpse of three places and a few people in Egypt during and immediately after the Mubarak era. It is not a harmonious image. Some of the tensions and contradictions are troubling, oppressive, and violent. Others present themselves as a complex patchwork of different kinds of hope, different senses of living a good life. The same people who repent their sins and think about the afterworld also debate the previous evening's soccer match, tell jokes, feel bored, curse the old and new presidents, and glance at the opposite sex—all the while with religious stickers decorating the walls around them and the voice of the Qur'an in the background. They entertain ideals of obsessive romantic love that defies all norms. They search for a place in life, try to be responsible toward their families, and dream about new possibilities for themselves. They try to make money and to move up in society, often by any means possible. And in different moments, they hold different points of view and outlooks of life, arguing for them in very different tones.

Many of the things people pursue are absolute, perfectionist, and totalizing. Religion promises a good life in this world and the hereafter through total moral and spiritual commitment. Romantic love celebrates obsessive passion in spite of rational constraints. Making money by any means possible subjects everything to an economic calculus. How can we understand the coexistence of these ideas in a way that allows us to account for perfectionist promises and the inconsistencies of their coexistence in daily life?

Writing about sermons recorded and circulated on cassette tapes, Charles Hirschkind (2006a) fittingly described the ubiquitous presence of the recordings as an "ethical soundscape" that fills and structures the noisy and crowded spaces of Cairo. The sensory presence of Islam as an idiom of life, morality, and politics is formidable indeed. It is present in the sounds of prayer calls, sermons, and recitations; it is in the visual presence of religious decoration, graffiti, stickers, and the minarets that mark the skyline. It is present in the bodily moves of prayer and invocation; the strain of wearing covering dress in hot weather; the exchange of greetings, phrases, and handshakes; and the smell of certain perfumes preferred by Salafi activists. But this sensory presence is seldom clearly differentiated from other very different kinds of sounds, images, and sensory experiences that mark the everyday of the big city and provinces alike (see Ingold 2011: 136–139). Moving and interacting in the crowded spaces of Egypt's cities and villages requires commanding a wealth of gestures and affective and rhetorical styles, including the solemn and pious, the witty and humorous, the polite and considerate, and the rude and obscene (Elyachar 2011). Rather than a competition of pious and secular sensory regimes, an unpredictable coexistence of different nuances, moments, and registers characterizes daily life in Egypt (see Ghannam 2002: 181; 2013).

Speculative investment in mosques carries the double virtue of pious deed and tax benefits. Women's religious dress is a major fashion industry.

Advertisements, declarations of love, and competing political messages fill the walls in the cities and villages alike. The spread of private satellite channels has opened the way for Salafi-oriented religious channels teaching puritanical morals, highly sexualized video clips providing a fantasy world of fame, Turkish soap operas speaking to the hearts of women who want to be loved, and political talk shows of both the satirical and the serious kind into Egyptian living rooms, living rooms that have been furnished with much effort by aspiring Egyptian families to match a cosmopolitan lifestyle up to global standards.

On the seafront of Alexandria and on the Nile promenades of Cairo, lovers (*habbiba*) are everywhere. Pairs of young people walk or sit on the promenades, talking to each other, sometimes holding hands, always close together while keeping a polite distance from other couples. In a minibus driving up and down the seafront in Alexandria, religious stickers admonish young people about dating: "Didn't he know that God sees?" "Would you accept it for your sister?" Indeed, the idea of young unmarried people dating, sitting shoulder to shoulder, holding hands, and possibly kissing is a cause of considerable moral unease among Egyptians. But at the same time, the same Egyptians may consider the meetings of lovers a natural part of life, and they may write and consume love poetry and songs, celebrate Valentine's Day, and proudly identify themselves as romantic people (Kreil 2012). Some do decide to become "committed" and give up all the ambivalence, stop writing love letters and looking the other sex in the eyes, and instead dedicate themselves to the purpose of purified piety. But for many of them, this is a passing period in a complex biography. And for many more, one does not cancel out the other to start with. Also the very pious can fall madly in love, and when it comes to marriage, revivalist piety sometimes becomes an ally of romantic love in face of family interests.

It might seem as if different worlds stood here side by side: the world of Islam as a regime of divine protection, order, and justice; the world of global capitalism with its investment in financial schemes; the world of commercial media with its reliance on consumerism, advertisement, and desire; the world of romantic love with its celebration of passion. But these are not different worlds. They are constituents, parts, of people's lifeworlds—lifeworlds that can never be explained by any single principle but that must be understood in their complexity and openness, in their many hopes and frustrations. While the conservative ethics of the religious revival may appear completely opposed to, for example, the celebration of romance and sexuality in pop music, film, video clips, and youth culture, in fact one cannot be understood without the other, nor are they clearly distinct in people's lives. To understand what exactly is going on, we must take these different pursuits as elements of a complex and often contradictory subjective experience and practice that is guided by but never reduced to great promises and grand schemes (Schielke and Debevec 2012). By "grand schemes," I mean persons, ideas, and powers that are understood to be greater than one's ordinary life, located on a higher plane, distinct from everyday life, and yet relevant as models for living.

Grand schemes of this kind appear to be external and superior to everyday experience, a higher and reliable measure and guideline for living. What makes them so powerful is precisely the ambiguity that is central to their assumed externality. By virtue of their apparent perfection they can be called and acted upon, and yet the contradictions and setbacks of everyday experience seldom shake their credibility (see Simon 2009, 2012). Even if one's attempt to live a life guided by a grand scheme is frustrated by failures and tragedies, that grand scheme remains valid and credible. By virtue of their inherent ambiguity, appearing to be external to daily life and yet carrying existential significance for the everyday, such grand schemes can never be accounted for in isolation. They must always be understood as connected in at least two dimensions: first, in their relation to everyday concerns and experiences; and second, in their relation to other compelling grand schemes that promise to provide meaning and direction to those concerns and experiences.

Thinking about grand schemes and the promises and hopes they entail is to give priority to existential grounds of action and imagination over discursive rationality and cultural traditions. This means that rather than focusing on how exactly a specific discourse, idea, or rationality is articulated, legitimated, or defended, I ask what people try to accomplish by taking a discourse seriously, pursuing an idea, embodying a rationality, and with what consequences. Some attempts are more consistent than others. Some attempts actually help people to live a better life as they understand it. Others result in tragedy. Most are ambivalent, providing both satisfaction and suffering. Many attempts are short lived, and almost all of them are partial. In all cases, the grand schemes are forever unrealized, and yet always apparently within reach, promising a hold, a direction in a difficult, complex, and often frustrating life.

Such an approach involves a shift from a culturalist (looking at the shared specificities of a locality or a tradition) toward a more humanistic (addressing those specificities as constituents of human existence in general) take on anthropology.[8] And yet I do not think that the pursuit of particular grand schemes, promises, anxieties, trajectories, or moments of satisfaction and frustration is universally transferable across place and time. The pursuit of grand schemes is itself fundamentally shaped by (and shaping) the world in a particular place and time.

## The Age of Revivals and the Shape of the World

We live in a world in which there is great demand for knowledge about the history, institutions, and currents of Islam, as well as the religious views and lives of Muslims. The paradox is that while most anthropologists take explicitly anti-imperialist stances and sympathize with their Muslim interlocutors and at least some of their concerns, the availability of funding for research on Islam tends to respond to political demands for policing migrant populations, providing expert knowledge for trade and foreign policies, or winning wars (Sunier 2012; Johansen and Spielhaus 2012). Regardless of what the researcher's stance toward these policies may be, the politics of research have meant that recent anthropological study of the Middle East has been framed predominantly in relation to Islam, ignoring other dimensions of experience and broader human concerns. This is troubling, because the problems this book addresses are in no way unique to the followers of a particular religious tradition.

Between the early 1970s and the 2000s, there was a dramatic intensification of and shift in the attachment to Islam among Muslims worldwide, so also in Egypt. Islam has, of course, long been present in the lives of Egyptian Muslims who have spoken and acted in the name of God, marked their lives and expressed their feelings through prayers and invocations, cultivated an intimate attachment to the Prophet Muhammad, relied in their social interactions on Islamic traditions of legal and moral reasoning, and sought the help of Muslim "friends of God" or saints in times of trouble and sickness. This was a vision of a life based on the presence of God, the Prophet, and the friends of God in everyday life, at times reassuring and legitimizing, at times frightening and disciplining. Islam, in this sense, is an intimate relationship rather than a holistic system (for parallels in Roman Catholicism, see Orsi 2005). In contrast, the vision of Islam that has become prevalent in Egypt and much of the Muslim world today is that of a perfect system that is all-encompassing yet pure and distinct, somehow located outside and above everyday life. The demand and striving for knowing and practicing Islam properly that has characterized recent decades is a demand for a qualitatively different sense of being a Muslim, shifting the emphasis from living a life at times trusting and at times fearing God as a powerful but intimate master of life and world, to living a life "by the book," carefully distinguishing the Islamic and the un-Islamic. A prime example of this shift is the way the veneration of Muslim saints has lost its centrality at the core of Muslim spirituality while, at the same time, the study of religious texts and rulings has become more important (see Eickelman 1992; Schielke 2012a). This shift from a relational to an ideological sense of religiosity is a shift of emphasis, of course. Just as scriptural norms have always counted, intimate relationality continues to matter. But the order of priority has changed.

In English, this intensification and shift in religiosity has often been labeled "the Islamic revival" (a free translation of "the Islamic awakening," *al-sahwa al-islamiya*, the term of preference used by religious activists). I find that term rather fitting. There is a dynamic and creative moment implied in *revival*, and the Islamic revival is best understood as a historical event characterized by a turn to a specific kind of religiosity associated with strong hopes and anxieties, intimately linked to a shift in the shape of the world at large.

The Islamic revival is not the only religious revival gaining momentum, nor is the revivalist pursuit of clarity and purity necessarily linked with religious traditions. Evangelical and Pentecostal Christianity and Hindu nationalism are the best-known examples, but there is a vast variety of structurally similar revival and reform movements in different religious traditions, such as the Theravada Buddhist reform (Leve 2002), as well as African "animist" movements directed against the encroachment of Islam or Christianity (Bowie 2006). The way in which the new anti-immigrant populist nationalism in Western Europe addresses a sense of existential and societal anxiety and offers simple enemies, a plan of action, and a harmonious image of "our" good way of life shows striking similarities with religious revivals (Hage 2003). Importantly, the militarist nationalism that became the rallying ground of the new military regime lead by General Abdelfattah El-Sisi in the summer of 2013, is also a grand project of purity and clarity that promises to resolve the current anxieties and bring about a better future through the attachment to military leadership and values, paranoid anti-imperialism, and a strong friend-foe binary.

These religious and populist movements build on that which people already put faith in and identify themselves with, transforming those things into projects of national and global politics as well as of personal integrity and hope. They do so with a double move of emphatic attachment to a shared ground of truth and certainty, and a heightened anxiety and sensitivity toward those who do not share that firm ground. Such movements share a significant reinterpretation of religious and communal traditions; a strong emphasis on purity on various levels; the cultivation of a strong moral sentiment of righteous indignation; the mobilizing power of grassroots, political, and commercial groups; a heritage of modernism; an affinity to the commodity form and the pursuit of wealth; and last but not least, the striking simultaneity of the rise of religious and populist revivals with the rise of capitalist, consumption-oriented economy and neoliberal governance (see, e.g., de Boeck 2009; Eckert 2009; Smilde 2007).

We should therefore search for the grounds of such revivals less in the religious or political traditions themselves than in the general shape of the world that compels people to approach their religious scriptures and political histories with particular kinds of questions in mind (see, e.g., Piot 2010; Appadurai 2013). We cannot understand the significance of Islam in the contemporary world if we do not also understand the significance of modernist regimes of knowledge, the coexistence of different notions of morality and embodiment, the imaginaries of romantic love, the promises and menaces of global capitalism, the emotional attachment to nationalism, and the frustrations and dead ends involved in all ideals and promises of good life.

This is not to argue for a Marxist reduction of the spiritual and the moral to relations of production. Nor is it to argue for the Weberian counterpoint of tracing the origins of economic practices to spiritual dispositions. Instead, I try to think of the spiritual, the moral, and the economic as existing on the same plane to start with. I think of capitalist economy less as a relationship of production or a rationality of accumulation and more as a deeper sensibility of being in the world.

Distinctions such as religious and secular, moral and economic, and political and private often disguise underlying resonances between seemingly distinct practices, as well as contradictions within apparently consistent ones. Commodity exchange requires that morality appear to be separate from economy. The nation-state often requires religion to be subordinate to politics. Patriarchy depends on the naturalization of a gendered distribution of labor. However, actually living in a capitalist economy, a nation-state, or a patriarchal family requires an implicit and explicit practical knowledge that works on a different plane, a knowledge about how to make things happen, to find recognition and help, to survive. This underlying practical knowledge, the experience from which it arises and to which it contributes, is what phenomenology calls a lifeworld, or *Lebenswelt* (see Gadamer 1975: 229–250; Merleau-Ponty 1945: 403–425), a horizon of expectation and action that is existentially united but by no means smooth and consistent. It is therefore not on the level of political or intellectual discourses, with their preoccupation with putting things neatly in their place, but on the level of the lifeworlds of contemporary Egyptians where an ethnographic inquiry into the nexus of religiosity, economy, and other aspirational schemes needs to begin.

Thinking about the shape of the world from a phenomenological point of view of experience and existential pursuits echoes the observation by Michael Jackson (1996: 2) that "the knowledge whereby one lives is not necessarily identical with the knowledge whereby one explains life." This is by no means to argue that the people this book talks with would not be aware of what they are involved in, or not able or willing to articulate it. On the contrary, they are often very well aware of, and very good at articulating, their experiences and endeavors. Much of this book relies heavily on their own theorizing about their situation. What I want to draw attention to is, rather, that we need to resist the temptation to take the categories most visible in intellectual, legal, and political debates as those that matter most.

What does matter, then? This book has developed in an eclectic fashion from an attempt to account for some of the things that really matter for the people with whom I have worked. It is a very hopeful world, but that hope comes with a troubling dimension of pressure, uncertainty, and anxiety.

## Ethics, Ambivalence, and Anxiety

In early 2006, when I started to work on the research that resulted in this book, I felt the need to critically engage an emerging paradigm of anthropological study of Muslims' religious lives that focused on piety, ethics, people active in Salafi-oriented groups, and the juxtaposition of the religious to the secular. I wanted to look beyond this rather narrow focus and conduct an ethnography with people who were not actively involved in piety movements but nevertheless shared many of the views promoted by those movements. I tried to understand the place revivalist religious ideas and practices took in their ordinary lives. Over the course of years many other researchers have moved in a similar direction, providing rich, ethnographically based analyses of the ambiguities and struggles of religious lives (including but not restricted to lives of commitment); of the coming together of the Islamic revivalist, the liberal, the therapeutic, the romantic, and the mystical in the social and intimate lives of people; as well as of the nexus of aspiration, migration, consumption, and class with divination, destiny, gender, and charity.[9] Ambivalence has become an increasingly recognized starting point, and the existential grounds of people's various commitments an aspect worthy of consideration in current anthropological research be it on religious lives, migration, or intimacy. So the point about the ambiguity of grand schemes is not really new. In fact, it was not new even when I started my research, preceded as it was by the important works of Abu-Lughod (1992, 1996a), Meyer (1998), Ewing (1990), Marsden (2005), Ring (2006), and many others. Rather than saying something new, what I try to do is to put together bits and pieces of ordinary life, compelling ideologies, and historical transformations that are well known separately but are not well understood when it comes to the relations among them, their coexistence, contradictions, and consequences.

My way of addressing these issues stands in some contrast to a powerful paradigm of aspirational and moral being that has come to dominate the anthropological study of Islam and Muslim societies in particular: ethics. During the past decade, anthropology has witnessed a significant turn toward the study of morality and ethics as a conscious, embodied practice, importantly developed in the works of Michael Lambek (2000, 2002, 2010), James Laidlaw (2002, 2013), Joel Robbins (2004), Saba Mahmood (2003, 2005), Charles Hirschkind (2006a), and Jarret Zigon (2008), to name just few of those worth mentioning. Taking up and developing Aristotle's notions of reasoning and character, Michael Lambek in particular has shown that morality and ethics need to be taken seriously as a motivation not reducible to either power or desire (Lambek 2000). Along with a turn to Michel Foucault's (1984) later work on the subject and subjectivation, this Aristotelian turn has become something like a common ground in the anthropological study of Muslims' moral and religious trajectories and debates.

One of the most influential arguments in this direction is made in Saba Mahmood's (2005) *Politics of Piety*, which in a short time has become a standard reading on ethics and piety. Mahmood offers a brilliant critique of liberal feminist notions of subjectivity through the juxtaposition of these notions to the ways women in a revivalist piety movement in Cairo of the 1990s cultivated a docile, God-fearing character by means of the embodied practice of piety. Rather than romantically searching for moments of resistance inspired by liberal theory rather than anything else, Mahmood argues, we must take seriously the way these women embark on an ethical project in the Aristotelian (and Foucauldian) sense of crafting themselves as subjects through moral practice.

While Mahmood's critique of the search for empowerment is convincing, the alternative she proposes appears problematic. Mahmood emphasizes that activist women's pursuits are informed by an Islamic discursive tradition (Asad 1986) and posits them in distinct opposition to liberal notions of selfhood. Doing so, she takes their pursuit of perfection for granted and embeds it in a theoretical critique of Western liberalism and feminism. Now a pursuit of perfection does appear to be a central part of the appeal of revivalist piety and Islamist politics. But highlighting it can be problematic insofar as it risks taking this pursuit for granted, assuming that Muslims just want to be good Muslims and thus focusing on how they in practice try to negotiate situations in which the pressures of a secular state make it difficult to live out a committed Muslim life. This is a relevant concern but a shallow one. More is going on.

In this scholarly turn to ethics, we often see secular and pious subjects in a competition about the grounds and trajectories of the will, the body, the senses, and their overall purpose. We see them compete for space within a single culture (Mahmood 2005: 139), and as regimes of subjectivation we see them inform the subjectivities and choices of people even when they do not share the same principles (Fadil 2009). But they always remain clearly recognizable and allocated to specific traditions and regimes of power. But who are these subjects? Am I a secular subject? Are my friends and interlocutors in Egypt secular or pious subjects? Do Muslims really just want to be good Muslims? If they do, why?

The obvious reply to these questions is that we are not talking about A being a pious subject and B being a secular subject. We are talking about notions of subjectivity, the relationships of body, will, power, aspirations, and moral and other concerns that people hold. The subject, in this sense, is about the kind of ethical concepts people hold and pursue:

> An inquiry into ethics from this perspective requires that one examine not simply the values enshrined in moral codes, but the different ways in which people live these codes. Thus, what is relevant here is not so much whether people follow moral regulations or break them, but the relationships

they establish between the various constituent elements of the self (body, reason, volition, and so on) and a particular moral code or norm. (Mahmood 2003: 846)

This is a valid point. So let me try to rephrase my question. What do we actually want to know when we talk about ethics and subjectivity? An analysis built on the foundation outlined by Mahmood can tell us much about the intended outcomes of a particular ideal of personhood, as it can about the way it builds on a particular discursive tradition. But it can tell only a little about subjective experience. As Gary Gregg (2007: 297–298) points out, the fact that a person has fashioned a perfect identity "does not predict how consistently his or her experience will conform to its contours." This, however, means that to understand how "people live these codes," we do have to connect the notions of body, volition, and so on, with the issue of concrete experience and practice. In other words, the question of whether, and especially in which ways, people follow or break moral rules, and the question about their notions of selfhood are equally relevant. The two questions are best asked together. We need to be sensitive not only for the successful ordering of a social experience but also for ambivalence, contradictions, and experiences of failure (see Marsden 2005; Luhrmann 2006; Biehl, Good, and Kleinman 2007).

This is not obvious given our tendency (one that seems to be shared by scientific discourse in particular and human perception in general) to smooth out inconsistencies, to reconcile contradictions, to make things fit. However, our capacity to make things fit does not mean that things will actually fit. On the contrary, things in most cases do not even need to fit. A temporary illusion of consistency (Ewing 1990) may be better for everybody involved than an attempt to actually make things fit—an attempt that might require a great degree of force and violence. We should therefore be careful not to take narratives of perfection for granted and to view deviations from them as exceptions. On the contrary, we should take the less perfect stories very seriously, and claims to harmony, unity, and perfection should strike our curiosity and compel us to explore what such claims actually entail.

In a study of prayer in Indonesia, Gregory Simon (2009) argues that the practice of prayer is a way to address very complex moral tensions that will not (and need not) be solved by prayer as much as they are articulated and experienced through it (Simon 2009: 270). There is no guarantee that the practice of moral selfhood will actually help one to satisfy conflicting demands. The ways in which people try to live a good life under conditions of conflicting demands are ambiguous and often tragic in their outcomes. As Robert Orsi (2005) has shown in his work on American Catholicism, the same moments that provide hope, recognition, and inclusion can also be a source of frustration, intimidation, and exclusion. This ambiguity appears to be characteristic of our attempts to live good lives, and an anthropology committed to understanding the human condition is well advised to take it seriously.

Ambiguity is not necessarily troublesome. It can be rather comfortable, allowing people considerable leeway of action as long as they practice due consideration to avoid open conflicts and scandals. Far from being accidental, it is often skillfully cultivated (Marsden 2005). As I argue in chapter 2, this is the common way in which morality works. Ethics, as I understand it in this book, in contrast, is about reflecting on and discussing one's actions, character, and being in a more holistic fashion. It is not obvious to be involved in ethics, nor is it obvious for anthropologists to search for ethics among the people they study. Why, then, has it become so compelling to think especially about people's religious pursuits in terms of ethics?

An interesting clue about the existential grounds of ethics is offered by Carla Jones (2010) in her study of women's Islamic fashion in Indonesia. Focusing on the nexus of capitalist consumption and revivalist religious ethics, Jones argues that while pious fashion promises a solution to the troublesome and contradictory demands of virtue and fashion, it is a tragic attempt, because pious consumption actually reproduces precisely those anxieties about vanity and virtue that it promises to alleviate. Jones highlights that the self-reflective work of pious ethics is intimately related to the anxious work of fashion and consumption. Shared and cultivated by both capitalist consumption and revivalist piety, anxiety and reflectivity are individualizing practices of crafting one's sense of self and embodied dispositions. Ethics in this sense is individualizing not because it would marginalize the cultivation of community and relationality (in fact, pious ethics is very often about being good at fulfilling one's prescribed role in the family), but because it takes one's own proper being as the ground from which community and relationality are to be cultivated (Abenante 2014). Ethics, thus understood, is a reflective struggle with one's proper being.

Ethics as a quotidian practice and as a theoretical problem is part of a specific historical experience. Ethics is, of course, something humans have probably exercised at all times, be it in the practice of cultivating a good character on the basis of a known sense of the good or in struggles to make reflective decisions in moments when the problem one faces cannot be resolved or when one cannot rely on a given sense of good (Jackson 2011: 70; see also Zigon 2008). In the sense in which the contemporary study of revivalist religiosity has developed it, however, ethics appears as a totalizing endeavor, something that is needed all the time, a cumulative search for a sound moral base in shifting sands. From being something people need to do in times of personal formation and social becoming and in moments of decision, transition, and crisis, ethics transforms into a general and ideal way of aspirational and reflective being.[10]

Ethics in this sense is a specific necessity to reflect on one's proper attitudes, sensibilities, values, appearance, trajectory, relations, and reputation in a world in which these are constantly both appealed to and questioned. Not everybody faces this necessity, and those who do, do not face it to the same degree. In some social positions and periods of life, ethical reflection is more urgent, whereas in others it is much less so. There is much in life that is taken for granted, silenced, or stated as an irrevocable fact. Sometimes one has very little power to pursue the kind of ends that would require ethical reflection.

Could it be that the turn to ethics is also a reflection of the being-in-the-world of Anglophone academics? Would the turn to study Muslims' religious experience in terms of ethics be also based on the academics' own everyday experience of having to reflect and work upon themselves; their emotions; their skills; their performance as researchers, as friends, as teachers, as lovers, or as parents (see Bauman 2000)?

The turn to study ethics is grounded in the recognition, implicit or explicit, by anthropologists of their own predicament as one that is shared by others in spite of their evident difference. Doing so, they are holding high one of the more positive histories that anthropology can lay claim to: the history of a search for shared humanity against racist, colonial, and other prejudice. And yet the recognition of a shared condition in the practice of ethics can also imply a misrecognition of this practice as a universal and, even more problematic, a desirable one. Taking ethics as a universal category of moral subjectivity erases the social specificity and the historicity of the need to reflect about and work on one's proper shape and being in face of great promises and anxieties.

Instead of taking ethics as a starting point of my research, I therefore want to take up its underlying condition, the experience of living in a world that is not solid, in which things are not obvious, in which reflectivity is an essential survival skill for many (Bauman 2000). I also want to ask when and for whom this experience becomes important (or not). Neither the will to live virtuous lives, nor the will to freedom and autonomy, nor the dichotomy of secular and Islamic versions of personhood, can be taken for granted if we are to understand how people experience their lives in a time of religious revival, global fantasies, and frustrated aspirations. People not only argue for discipline at times, and for self-realization and freedom at others, but also live lives that often lack both.

## A Life in the Future Tense

Lack is not only a matter of scarcity and shortage. Rather, lack itself seems to be expansive in nature. One of the most curious features of the capitalist sensibility of being in the world is that under conditions of historically unprecedented (albeit very unequally distributed) abundance, the moral imperative of maximizing scarce resources has become more pervasive than ever.

In his provocative theory of general economy, George Bataille ([1949] 1991) argues that under normal conditions, any society produces more than it needs, and that the central problem of economy is not scarcity but the expenditure of surplus through feasts, nonreproductive sex, the arts, war, or growth. While Bataille's thesis in its original formulation is hyperbolic, to say the least, he offers the valid point that any economy has to give consideration to situations of both scarcity and abundance. Thinking with Bataille, what makes capitalism special is its way of dealing with abundance—even abundant expenditure, such as luxury or war—within the logic of scarcity, thus turning luxury into a service industry and war into an investment (meaning that only what can be produced and sold counts as luxury, and that only wars that are good for business are worth fighting). As less and less of the output of abundance is expended and more and more of it is reinvested, the only way to deal with excess is growth—up to a point at which the once-abundant resources of the planet itself become scarce.

Today, unlike in precapitalist economies, the surplus that any functioning economy produces can no longer be expended in an annual feast. It must be invested for future growth, and the worry about that future growth is a powerful emotional foundation for the ethos of scarcity. This sense of worry is paralleled by an important feature of revivalist religiosity. Although increasingly many Muslims have come to express outspoken pride and certainty about their religion, at the same time their religious practices, interactions, and cultivated affects reveal a constant worry about whether one has enough points of reward, whether God will accept one's prayer, whether this or that act is forbidden or permitted. A religious revival is essentially and centrally about not feeling entirely good about one's faith, just like capitalist consumption is essentially and centrally about not feeling good about what one already has.

Such concern with investment and growth carries a core emotional ambiguity because it is essentially located in the future. Aims and promises pursued within such a framework are fundamentally unrealized, not in the sense of being unreal, but in the sense of being always in the process, never complete. Unlike genuinely unrealized promises, they do provide actual gratification, turning desire into demand (Žižek 2006). But unlike ordinary promises that can and should be eventually kept, the gratification of cumulative promises lasts only as long as they grow, as long as there is more to come. The pursuit of religious commitment goes hand in hand with a cumulative increase in the sensitivity for religious shortcomings. The pursuit of middle-class respectability is always at least a step short of the upper classes. The pursuit of pure love thrives on separation. The hopes invested in the revolution have remained unrealized not just because the revolution eventually failed, but also because a revolutionary attitude is one of fundamental discontent and disagreement that will never be satisfied.

In his book on well-being in a world of limits, Michael Jackson (2011: xii) argues that the sense that "there is more to life than what exists for us in the here and now" is probably a universal constituent of a meaningful life. But there are differences regarding the extent, the speed, the intensity, the medium, the limits, and the materiality of that more that is yet to come. There is a specific quality to hope in the contemporary world, shared by revivalist religiosity, capitalist consumption, migration, love marriage, and the revolution. It is the temporality of the future under the conditions of a rapidly changing and expanding world that deprives people (especially, but not only, poor people) of many of the grounds of certainty that existed in a smaller and slower world. The turn to scripture as the means of a pious life has to do with a loss of God's certain presence in daily life. The pressure of migration that young men face has to do with the devaluation of paths of life that once were enough to make a man respectable. The search for moral perfection has to do with the shattering of comfortable moral ambiguity in a world where paths of survival and success are not only ambiguous but also blatantly immoral. The troublesome pursuit of love marriage has to do with a transformation of family life and livelihood in a way that makes family arrangements obsolete and inevitable at the same time. There is more to come, but what it will be and how one can secure it is an increasingly urgent, uncertain, and precarious question.

And yet this sense of worry does not deter people from embracing perfectionist promises in their lives. This is a powerful dynamic that depends on the constant production of both hope and anxiety. Promises of perfection are powerful as long as they are unfulfilled. Because they are unfulfilled, things can always be better, and reality will always fall short of expectations. This is an aspirational sense of existence, a life in the future tense where the state that one has reached is never sufficient, where one must always reach for more than one has, a sensibility that is essentially dependent on its being dynamic and growing.

To some degree, this is related to age and gender, and it is not a coincidence that most people who appear in this book are men, between the ages of eighteen and thirty-five when I met them. People who have moved past childhood but have not yet established themselves socially are most likely to articulate and feel the power of more to come, and men are more explicitly encouraged to act as the makers of their lives and families (see Ghannam 2013). However, I do not want to identify life in the future tense with youth and masculinity. Women often experience the pressures of more to come very strongly. Youth can also be a time with less responsibilities, and hence less pressure. The pressure that Egyptians feel so strongly really begins when one starts to think about marriage, and it is felt by men and women, albeit in different ways. And after marriage, one is constantly concerned with the health, education, marriage, and careers of one's children, and with the ability of one's children to in turn bear and educate and marry off their children. The power of future goes across gender and generations.

The linear outlook of expecting a better future is, of course, not the only temporality worth attention. There are other, nonlinear temporalities that structure people's lives, such as ritual prayer, the fasting month of Ramadan, and annual feasts and holidays. Just like the future tense is very present in daily life, so are various past tenses, such as the age of the Prophet, the Nasser era, and one's own childhood and youth, present as remembered and imagined pasts when things were so much better, even worse, or just different from now. These other times get their share of attention in the course of this book, but the main focus is on the experience of expectation—paired with the experience of facing the consequences.

This is often a tragic experience, and much of this book is devoted to situations in which things don't work out as expected, in which people have to find ways to make do with their dreams perpetually postponed, and in which people's attempts to do something about their condition reinforces that condition. There is a difference between hope and promises being ephemeral and their turning into an unbearable pressure. In terms of economic, political, and moral experience, that pressure had become terrible in Egypt before 2011. At the same time, this very sense of stalled expectation also becomes the site from which people continue to dream for a sound moral life and a better future. The January 25 revolution is a powerful reminder of the fact that while a life in the future tense is pervasive and compelling, it is never total and smooth, nor does it guarantee the power of those who most profit from it.

## Outline of Chapters

The structure of this book reflects the way I have come to recognize and address important issues step by step (not necessarily in the order in which I present them in the book). Wanting to study the morality and religiosity of not-very-committed people, I started doing fieldwork about Ramadan, a time of exceptional commitment, which motivated me to think about the way people speak about Islam as a perfect system of moral knowledge—but at the same time this also compelled me to study soccer. Soccer led me to the problem of boredom, and boredom made me look at love, consumption, and migration. Love compelled me to think about grand schemes beyond the framework of religious revivalism, thinking about consumption made me think about the cultivation of anxiety, and the issue of anxiety turned me to the experiences of those who try to replace anxiety with certainty of purpose in the Salafi movement. Migration compelled me to think about issues of imagination and the quest for conventional wealth, as well as political and existential freedom, which turned my focus toward the paradox of the perpetuation of oppression by the oppressed themselves—only to be reminded by the January 25 revolution that defiance, too, is an option, which took me finally to think about revolutionary commitment as another tragic grand scheme. What thus began as a critical contribution to the anthropology of Islam has become an ethnography of a life in which nothing ever quite works the way one hoped it would.

While undertaking this shift, I have come to appreciate the holistic ambitions of the early generations of anthropologists who saw it as their task to study the economy, agriculture, religion, literature, crafts, kinship, mores, and medicine of a society, even if afterward they might have focused on a specific aspect of these in their publications. It is, of course, impossible to know and tell about the totality of people's intimate, aesthetic, social, economic, and religious lives. Anthropologists are often terribly ignorant about the societies they write about. But rather than hiding our ignorance by defining our topics very clearly, we should face it by constantly looking beyond the limits of the defined topic. No matter what the specific subject of our inquiry, it is bound to be intertwined with countless other things, and paying attention to them makes a difference.

The structure of this book is grounded in the attempt to pursue that intertwining of things step by step, turning its attention first to the complexity of aims and ideals in daily life and then increasingly to the dialectics of aspiration and frustration, the tragic condition of trying to do something in a world where there is little one can do.

Chapter 1 opens the book by addressing the experience of boredom as an effect of the frustrated expectation that life should be meaningful and exciting, arguing that the nihilistic sense of pointlessness implied in boredom is both a problem and a motivation for perfectionist promises of commitment, and therefore a good starting point for thinking about grand schemes and great expectations. Chapter 2 develops the theme of different visions of a good life, which coexist as different registers of speech and action that imply different senses of embodiment and different ideals of being a good person expressed and embodied by the same people in different situations. Chapter 3 focuses on the issue of religious knowledge, looking at the relationship of a characteristically modern equation of religion and textbook knowledge with the ideal of moral perfection. Chapter 4 takes up romantic love as a powerful register of moral subjectivity that through its celebration of passion and obsession stands in a tense relationship with religion and family connectivity, leading to situations where no moral middle way is possible. Chapter 5 concludes the theme of ambiguity of grand schemes with an investigation of the alliance of religious revival and capitalist consumption that has made consumption a powerful strategy of religious proselytization and discipline, but at the same time also has turned considerations of investment, competition, and profit into a powerful sense of good life.

The second half of the book turns to attempts by people to come to terms with, to exploit, and to change the conditions described in the first part of the book. Chapter 6 pursues the question of doing something meaningful by following the trajectories of three persons who have tried to become committed Muslims in the Salafi fashion, highlighting the existential concerns that motivate such commitment, and its at times troubling and at times helpful consequences. Chapter 7 develops the themes of imagination and possibility by exploring the mediated presence of the wider world and the strong urge among young men to migrate, arguing that we need to take fantasy seriously as an endeavor to improve one's condition of life at home. Chapter 8 turns to the theme of governance, education, and work, showing how the political and economic system of Egypt has worked through the complicity of its subjects, who, by attempting to evade the system, have ended up giving it its particular shape. This everyday complicity eventually became a key emotional ground of anger for the 2011 revolution. And although the revolution eventually failed, it has contributed to a different, though not necessary new, sense of normality. Chapter 9 takes up a more specific consequence of 2011: the emergence of "the revolutionaries" as a political subjectivity and a sense of aspirational being that thrives on difference, critique, and struggle—even defeat and failure. While it is carried by a strong, albeit vague, vision of a better life in freedom and justice, being a revolutionary is first and foremost an emotional affect of rejection, combined with an at times outspoken tragic sensibility. Finally, the conclusion reconnects the different lines of inquiry through an engagement with the issues of freedom, destiny, and unintended consequences.

# 1 Boredom and Despair in Rural Egypt

In SPRING 2008, a pop song by Aamer Saeed caught the mood of the time: "The world's wrecked, there's no point" (*il-dinya kharbana mafish fayda*). It expressed a sensibility that young people in particular articulate as one of boredom (*malal*) and frustration (*ihbat*): it is all the same, it is not getting better, one's plans get thwarted—so what's the point?

Beginning an ethnography about hope and ambivalence with this sense of emptiness, boredom, even despair, helps us think about boredom as a condition in the lives of people who aim for a better life, a consequence as well as a grounding of aspiration. Moments of hope can be better accounted for if we first turn our attention to their flip side—despair, frustration, endless waiting, a sense of meaninglessness and lack of purpose. These negative sentiments come partly from dissatisfaction with unkept promises of improvement and progress, but also from expectation, which gives credibility to promises of purpose and hope. Boredom must therefore be taken seriously as an experience in its own right, because it points to a complex human condition that cannot be accounted for merely by reference to ideals, aims, and higher purposes. Instead, ideals are often discredited, aims frustrated, and life can seem to have no purpose.

Although this chapter deals with the sharply felt discrepancy between what might be and what is, politics is almost entirely absent from the discussion. This absence reflects the mood of the time.[1] As I started doing fieldwork in Nazlat al-Rayyis in 2006, people had a lot to say about boredom, as they did about religion, business, work, migration, marriage, love, and the difficulty of life. Politics, however, was tricky. People would speak about Iraq, the United States, and Israel. They would complain about the government and, in a less direct way, about the president. But even those who in the 1990s had been active in political movements of various kinds had abstained from political action for some time. There was little sense that collective action would be possible or meaningful. In the capital city, oppositional voices were growing louder already, and some years later, things looked very different in the village and the cities alike. In the final chapters of the book I turn to those later, highly politicized days of revolutionary hope and anxiety, but for now I focus on a different moment, one of dull emptiness, when hope, if it existed at all, was placed either in escape or in faith.

## Entertainment with and without a Purpose

While not a time of politics, it was a time when the idea of purposeful entertainment made the rounds, and new television formats and musical genres that
were explicitly identified as Islamic, morally committed, and purposeful gained
increasing popularity (van Nieuwkerk 2012, 2013; Tartoussieh 2007). In the long-
standing nationalist tradition of arts committed to the nation's development,
various religious actors entered the field of commercial entertainment through
media designed to serve a greater purpose by educating and guiding the masses
(as well as to generate). An emerging feature of Arab satellite television in the
first decade of the twenty-first century was the many religious video clips that
(copying the successful style of the British singer Sami Yusuf) praised Islam, the
Prophet Muhammad, and a happy, pious life to the tune of soft pop melodies.
Featuring beautiful young women wearing covering but elegant Islamic dress,
and handsome and smiling young men with trendy looks and high morals, this
genre of religious pop and video clips propagated a mixture of pious commitment and dreams of a life of wealth and excitement. The shift from the earlier
general distrust of Islamist and piety activists toward arts and entertainment to
the wave of religiously inspired pop music and TV series did not change this
primacy of purpose.

Developmentalist nationalism, on the one hand, and the ideal of purified
and virtuous religiosity, on the other hand, are both very important to young
people in the village. This, however, is only part of the story. Purpose, be it nationalist or religious, is not the primary way that young men in the village con-
ceive of the entertainment they consume and partake in. In fact, the very idea of
entertainment serving a purpose other than that of having a good time turns out
to be far from obvious.

In Anwar's café in the village of Nazlat al-Rayyis, the television is always on.
In the past, the café had a satellite dish of its own, but by 2007 it was connected
to the "central dish" (*al-dish al-markazi*) network, an illegal distributor of satellite television via cable. Run by two men with a rented room and a dozen satellite
receivers, the central dish network of the village was part of a nationwide wave
of countless small enterprises that brought satellite television into almost every
home in Egypt in the early 2000s. The TV set in the café sometimes it shows music channels with video clips of different kinds, both Islamic ones and those featuring lots of naked skin and lyrics that tell about love, desire, trust, and betrayal.
More often it shows movies, sometimes Egyptian ones but often also Hollywood
films. Since 2011, it sometimes shows news. Before 2011 and again after 2013, by far
the most popular thing on television has been soccer (the American name for the
sport that Egyptians know as *kurat al-qadam*, or football, or simply *il-kura*, the
ball).[2] For major matches between favorite teams, the café filled up with men—

Figure 1.1. Watching a soccer match in a café, Nazlat al-Rayyis, October 2007.

women never go to cafés in the village—watching the game in an atmosphere of intense concentration. If religious video clips have been successful on satellite television in the past few years, their success is minor in comparison to how the Champions League has swept Egypt since the establishment of central dish networks. Young men often wear jerseys of European teams, and everyone with the slightest interest in soccer has his or her favorite teams in both Egypt and abroad.

Soccer is not only big on television. Amateur soccer is a central part of the daily life of boys and young men, many of whom meet to play every afternoon in the school yards after they have emptied of pupils. In the month of Ramadan, an amateur tournament is held with approximately twenty teams from Nazlat al-Rayyis and neighboring villages and hamlets. I asked young fans and amateurs in autumn 2007 about what makes soccer so attractive, and their answers show a strikingly similar tone:

- "It makes time pass."
- "It's a good way to kill time."
- "Afternoon is an empty time, and soccer makes those hours pass quickly."
- "When you're a soccer fan you live much better than when you smoke marijuana or hashish."

Hashish is, in fact, soccer's most serious competitor as a pastime among young men. Walking through the cafés late in the evening, when older customers start leaving, one quickly notes the groups of young men who begin to gather in an atmosphere of nervous expectation. Hoping to escape the observing eyes of patriarchal authority, they meet up and hang around in the café, waiting for friends to show up, and some pay a visit to one of the many small-time dealers who work in the village. Finally, they get up and move to find a protected place to smoke—sometimes in a café, sometimes out in the fields, sometimes on the rooftop of a house. Beer was a common drink in Egypt until the 1970s and 1980s, but most Egyptian Muslims have stopped drinking beer in the course of the Islamic revival. Since then, the popularity of marijuana and hashish—which, unlike alcohol, are not explicitly forbidden in Islamic scripture—has skyrocketed. (For indirect evidence of a growing group of young habitual consumers of cannabis, see Higazi 2005, 32–34.)

Soccer and hashish offer young men in the village a very different framework of entertainment from that of nationalist melodrama (see Abu-Lughod 2005) and religious video clips. Like other forms of entertainment, such as television, cafés, music, weddings, joking, taking walks, flirting, Internet chats, and pornography, they are essentially seen as ways to escape boredom, and they are not measured by their purposefulness.

## Feeling Bored

Nazlat al-Rayyis is primarily a fishing village, and an important effect of fishing on the village is the large number of cafés. Fishermen meet at cafés to socialize, to hire labor, and to make contracts. Their irregular work hours mean that cafés are often open until late into the night. Even with the decline of fishing as a result of pollution and land reclamation projects, this aspect of fishery continues to mark male sociality. With its large size, its flourishing café culture, its amateur soccer tournaments, and its colorful festive culture that draws many visitors from nearby villages and hamlets, Nazlat al-Rayyis is a lively place by rural standards. And yet almost all young people whom I have asked find it dead boring.

Boredom, as was often pointed out to me, comes in different kinds. Young people suffer from it more than children and adults. It is different in the city and in the countryside, as well as in Egypt and in Europe. It comes in temporary and perpetual varieties. It is worst in the winter, when the nights are long, rain turns the alleys into mud, and power cut-offs are common. But even in the summer, even during holidays, even when one is having fun, boredom persists, as was argued by Faruq and Tawfiq, both in their early twenties at the time of this discussion and hanging out in the same clique (*shilla*) of friends:

> FARUQ: Boredom's everywhere. It's based on *routine* and *monotony*: Every day
> is predictable; there is no change. Everyone suffers from it—there is no one

here who is happy and satisfied. It is stronger at certain times—like in the hour before you sleep, when you lie in bed and start thinking.

TAWFIQ: That can also be positive, you can start thinking about ways to get out of the boredom.

F: Whatever you do, boredom's there with you. Boredom walks with us; it is part of us.

T: Boredom is like your shadow that never leaves you, day or night.

Young men from the village articulate an entire vernacular theory of boredom (*malal*). The theory describes boredom as a specific state of being, in many ways echoing the academic theories of boredom that have been developed in the fields of psychology, literature studies, philosophy, and more recently the social sciences (see, e.g., Revers 1949; Doehlemann 1991; Meyer Spacks 1995; Svendsen 2005; Matuschek 1999; Goodstein 2005; Mains 2007). The most explicit theorist of boredom I know is Tawfiq, a graduate with a two-year degree in public health. When I met him in 2007, he was in his early twenties. He argued to me that in the village, every day is a Saturday (since Friday is the main weekly day of rest in Egypt, Saturday is a very ordinary day, a day of no particular qualities):

> Every day here is like the other: I wake up, go to work, play soccer, eat, sleep, wake up, go to work, play soccer, eat, sleep, and so on and on and on. There is nothing new; every day is like the other. Assume that today is Saturday. Well, yesterday was Saturday, and tomorrow is Saturday, and every single day is a Saturday like the other. I want to get out of here, out of this boredom and lack of prospects, to see things change, to see the unexpected, to travel.

Tawfiq has a government job, something many other young men only dream of. Even though it is very badly paid, a government job implies health insurance and social recognition, and it is a major asset on the marriage market. But Tawfiq's job as a health inspector is not only badly paid; it is also completely pointless. In 2007, his work consisted of going every day to the same state-subsidized bakery, where he, with two other inspectors, wrote "condition: normal" in the inspection book and signed, no matter what the real condition of the bakery might be. Of all the boring routines that make every day a Saturday, Tawfiq hated his job most:

> Government employees must feel it stronger than all others: Every day you get up at the same hour in the same bed, take the same bus to the same work, do the same tasks at the same time, take the same bus back at the same time, sit at the same café with the same friends and talk about the same issues until you go back to the same home where you sleep in the same bed until you are woken up by the same alarm clock to a day that is just the same as the one before it. And you keep going on like that for sixty years. Imagine how many days exactly like the others that makes!

Tawfiq is not the only one describing the *routine* (a French and English loanword in colloquial Arabic) of every day being like the other—in fact, people brought up this topic over and again when I discussed the subject of boredom with them. They did bring in different nuances to the discussion, however. For Tawfiq, boredom is primarily characterized by the lack of new ideas and possibilities for expanding one's horizon. Nagib, like Tawfiq, an underpaid civil servant doing useless work in the public health administration, put more emphasis on economic frustration:

> NAGIB: "Our life is all about repetition and *routine*, and that *routine* causes boredom: things are the same, nothing changes. Every day is like the other. And you have to work a lot for little money, you work and work, but you cannot get forward because it is not enough. . . . That's why everyone wants to emigrate. They know that if I work in your country and spend ten euros for food and save twenty, in the end that's good money when I come back to Egypt, and I can build up a good life with it. It's all about economy. If they could, everybody here would leave, everybody. Nobody would stay. . . .
>
> SAMULI: So it's about being frustrated for lack of prospects?
>
> N: "Yes, it is frustration [*ihbat*] rather than boredom [*malal*]. Nothing changes. There is no improvement. You go to work in the morning, do the same stupid work, sit in the café every evening, and there is no change. Only on Friday it is a little different. Then I sleep long, go to the Friday prayer, and then hang around again.

These accounts highlight repetition and frustration as the key causes of boredom, and a perpetual sense of pointlessness and despair as its manifestation. The boredom people complain about is not the situational boredom that everyone experiences sometimes, such as when waiting for a bus, listening to an uninteresting lecture, or doing a repetitive and undemanding task at work. It is more an existential state of lacking of future and hope, which is intimately coupled with frustration and often close to despair. People often also see boredom and depression as related phenomena, and in one occasion people I talked with also associated boredom with the issue of suicide (see also Dabbagh 2005: 207–208, 218–220).

The young men do not attribute boredom to saturation by media, consumption, and a search for spectacular experiences, as some analyses of boredom in Euro-American societies do (e.g., Klapp 1986: 117–129). Their boredom (which they explicitly articulate as a rural one) is primarily framed as deprivation, not saturation. The only thing that is available in excess is time. Not only are the jobs young men have mostly either hard and unpleasant (e.g., fishing) or pointless and lacking challenge (e.g., government), they also spend relatively little time working. Men hardly ever participate in household work, which is done almost completely by women. So from early afternoon until late at night, young men mostly hang around, watch television, meet people, sit in cafés, or play soccer. Women, whose lives are much more confined to the realm of the house and whose options for leisure are much more limited (cafés are exclusively male, and so are sports and most cultural activities), nevertheless do not complain (at least not to me) about boredom the way young men do. Nazli, a mother of two in her midtwenties (in 2007), attributed this primarily to the extensive workload women have to handle:

> I think women have no time to get bored. They are busy all the time: make breakfast, dress the kids, school, private tutoring, clean, cook, wash, and at the end of the day you are so tired that you just fall in sleep. Their life may be boring and repetitive, with every day like the other, but they have no time to feel bored.

This is not to deny that women, too, may suffer from boredom and frustration. Often women feel less at ease openly exclaiming their dissatisfaction with their share in life, whereas for young men, complaining about boredom is often something like a performance of youthfulness. Men are encouraged to express a sense of general discontent with the world in a way that, if expressed by a woman, might compromise her reputation and virtues. But beyond this, the fact remains that women often do have more things to do that can be meaningful even if they are repetitive, wearing, and stressful. As Nazli points out, there is more to boredom than repetition and monotony. There is a difference between one's life being monotonous and the sense of boredom, an observation echoed by Tawfiq, who thinks that only people with the right mind-set are capable of being bored: "It's a matter of character. People can live in boredom without feeling it." In other words, boredom is an objective state of monotony, but being bored requires the capacity to aim for more and to become aware that there is an alternative to the monotony.

Boredom, as the young men of the village describe it, is indeed strongly related to aspiration and a progressive modality of time. Patricia Meyer Spacks (1995: 5, citing Fenichel 1953) argues that the very notion of boredom as a situation when "something expected does not occur" is an invention of early modernity intimately related to the linear concept of time (see also Matuschek 1999: 118–120, 132–133). In Arabic as well as in other languages, *boredom* is a relatively new term that has replaced notions of melancholy, weariness, sloth, and the like. These older notions do not carry the same sense of irritating disappointment about something not happening. Some, like melancholy (which approximately translates to the Arabic *shagan*), can even be poetically celebrated and, to a certain degree, enjoyed. In his study about young men in an Ethiopian city whose experience shows striking similarity to that of the men in the Egyptian village, Daniel Mains (2007: 664–667) argues for a connection between boredom and the frustrated expectation of progress (see also Hansen 2005). Elizabeth Goodstein (2005) convincingly describes boredom as a distinctively modern form of skepticism and discontent. But contrary to Goodstein's claim that "the bored subject . . . cannot perceive that this experience is peculiar to modernity" (18), the young men in Nazlat al-Rayyis are very explicit about their boredom being related to a progressive concept of time in which both human history and personal biography appear as processes of constant improvement. The expectation of a better future, they argue, is essential for the frustration at the repetitive nature of everyday experience. This is also the explanation al-Hagg Mu'izz, a retired fisherman in his late seventies, gave when I asked him whether he was bored as a young man:

> No, I was not bored. I had to work hard to make a living, from dawn to sunset, I would work long days at the lake, sometimes even fifteen days on a row. There was no time to get bored. But today there is so much more money in the village. When I was young, twenty pounds was a lot of money, but today a hundred pounds are not enough for anything. The people need more money, and want more money. And there is less work at the same time. When I was young we would work hard on the lake, and everyone had a clear line ahead of himself. Now the circumstances in the village have gotten much better, and the young people expect them to be even better. But when I was young one wouldn't know of better, one would just work on the line ahead of one.

Most older people tend to look back on their youth with nostalgia, and earlier generations may have in fact been bored. This definitely was the case with the emerging middle classes in the early twentieth century who described village life as boring and backward and, by doing so, gave contour to their own claims to being modern (Ryzova 2008). Theirs, however, was an experience of social mobility, quite unlike the pursuit of the given path ahead that was evoked by al-Hagg Mu'izz. His account is also supported by young men who also argue that boredom came to the village hand in hand with education, mass media, and mobility:

> FARUQ: The village has changed, the young people have progressed; they have a different look at the world. They see satellite television, and many people travel. They get a different idea.
>
> TAWFIQ: The more progress, the more boredom.

The calm, predictable rhythm of village life does not as such necessarily bore people. It turns into intense boredom and despair with the presence of strong but unfulfilled aspirations for a better, more exciting life. The increasing connectedness of the village with global media and migration flows offers imaginaries and prospects of a different and more exciting life, material wealth, and self-realization. Village life becomes measured against expectations that by far exceed anything the countryside or the nearby cities have to offer.

This is not something that is specific to an Egyptian village. A similar sentiment seems to prevail in cities and villages around the Global South. A similar sentiment also appears to have partly motivated the rapid urbanization of many European countries after the Industrial Revolution. The sense of existential boredom expressed by the young men in Nazlat al-Rayyis appears to be common to peripheral (thus not only rural) milieus around the world, particularly when they become more strongly connected to metropolitan flows of ideas, goods, and labor.[3] The sentiment that "here" there is "nothing," whereas somewhere "out there" time is not empty but full and everything is possible seems to be inherently related to the stark contrast of prospects and resources that young people at the periphery (be it in terms of geography, demography, or class) of great economic and social transformations and promises face.

A major outcome of globally mediated promises of a good life has been that people around the world perceive their immediate lifeworld as worthless and hopeless. As a consequence, "globalization is by many people primarily experienced in its absence, in the form of the non-arrival of change, unfulfilled promises and aspirations rather than in an actual increase of mobility or flux of goods" (Graw 2012: 32; see also Masquelier 2005; Ferguson 2006; Bordonaro 2010). Boredom is a key sentiment of the global province, grounded in a global political economy. From the point of view of those young men who suffer from boredom, there is almost nothing they can do to change the fundamental parameters of their situation. And yet they all try to solve their situation, or at least to cope with it in different ways. The question, then, is, what can you do if there is very little that you can do?

## Escape

Boredom is born of frustration with monotony, of there being no realistic prospect of progress. But where it leads to is a matter of individual assessment. Tawfiq argues that boredom is good because it compels one to sense the need for change and to work for it. But he acknowledges that boredom makes many others fall into a state of passivity, just killing time and letting the monotony take over their lives.

In 2007, Tawfiq, like most of the young men in the village, was sure that in the village he would have no chance to get an interesting job with better pay, or be able to experience a life that offered him new experiences, ideas, and horizons. In his view, the only solution was escape. Tawfiq pursued several plans at the same time, including finding work in the Persian Gulf or at a tourist resort on the Red Sea. In early 2008, he got a job in Qatar, where he worked as a guard for two years. He was very disillusioned about the situation in the Gulf but nevertheless determined to pursue his long-term plan to migrate to Europe or the United States.

Almost all young men in the village want to migrate, be it to the city, the Persian Gulf, or the West. For some people this is merely a dream they like to relish but do not actively pursue, but others are continuously busy with different plans to migrate. And with possibilities of legal migration to the West dramatically curtailed after September 11, 2001, most plans are illegal and dangerous. There is often a tone of despair and obsession in the way young men discuss over and over possible ways to migrate, with only a vague idea of what exactly they wish to make out of their lives once there, but a very strong sense that "here" there is nothing—no chances, no hope, no future:

> People are so desperate that they are ready to take the risk of dying to cross over the sea [illegally to Italy or Greece on fishing boats]. Their boredom, their unemployment, their lack of hope has gotten them so far. And the political pressure gives an additional share. In Egypt we have the worst government in the world, the worst! It gives the people no chance; instead, it puts more pressure on them. It pushes people so far that they, out of the emptiness [*faragh*] they are in, are ready to take the risk of dying on the way. (Ibrahim, a friend of Saʿid)

While few young people have had the chance to travel abroad, many have migrated temporarily or permanently to Alexandria and Cairo. And while living in the big city is expensive and advancement there is difficult, people who have lived in the city regularly argue that it is also more exciting. And yet the desire to migrate does not mean that people are not fond of their village. Mukhtar Shehata, a schoolteacher who lives in Alexandria but frequents his native village on weekends and holidays, expresses this fondness mixed with distance in a poem titled "I Love You Nazla":

> I love you Nazla, daughter of so-and-so
> I love you and I'll tell you why
> I love you, politics and culture
> religiosity and pious phrases
> I love you, your sons and the flowers of your youth
> who always bring you honor.
> I love you and fear only a handful of folks
> Of course, darling, you know whom:
> Those who stay up all night and don't care
> who on the day I first came to you
> were already high on the mix they smoke
> To whom can I complain, Nazla?
> I love you, Nazla of the good people
> party politicians, fanatics and extremists
> I love you, seeing you from afar

Your picture, Nazla, is in my house
in the black of my daughters eye, and in my son's laughter

In its ironic yet friendly way, this poem is telling of the attachment people express toward their home village even if they complain about the narrowness of its perspectives. The final lines of the poem point out at an ambivalence that is characteristic of most people who, periodically or permanently, have moved from the village to the city: they love the village best from a distance. When I noted this to Hilmi, who in 2007 was a university student and lived in the village even though he wanted to live in Cairo, he replied:

> The strange thing about this village is that when you leave it, you urgently long back, but when you're back you wonder why you returned, and just want to go.

Boring as it may be, village life does have many advantages. People who have moved away from the village point out that the closeness to relatives and friends, the low cost of living, and the stress-free pace of life all make the village a good place to live. The urge to escape does not rule out homesickness and love for one's place of origin. The biggest problem with escaping, however, lies in its inconclusive nature. For those who manage to get abroad, escape may be only the beginning of a new sense of being stuck, working to save money for a return that may never be realized. And for those who stay behind or return, the possibility of escape only aggravates the intensity of everyday despair and boredom. By subordinating all activities to merely waiting to get out, the aim of escape itself becomes a factor contributing to boredom.

## Killing Time

Bored by the monotony and hopelessness of everyday life as they perceive it, and focused on migration as the only real chance for improvement, most young men remain in a state of prolonged waiting. This sense of emptiness (*faragh*) also influences their approach to leisure and entertainment, which they often primarily see as a way to kill time, to fill the emptiness.

A range of entertainment and leisure activities is available in the village. Aside from playing or watching soccer, men often sit in their favorite café for several hours every evening, exchanging news, talking politics, telling jokes, and greeting passersby. Given their public nature, cafés are not suitable for private conversations, and a preferred way to meet people with more privacy is to take walks through the village and the surrounding fields.

Unlike sports, cafés, and taking walks, which are a male domain (women can go out for a walk just as men can, but they are expected to be going somewhere, whereas men can legitimately stroll around), television and music are available to practically everyone. Every house and café has a television set. In the early

2000s, the central dish network had provided wide and cheap access to satellite television, and by 2013, satellite dishes had become so cheap that the central dish networks with their more limited selection of channels were pushed out of business. There is also lively exchange of music, by 2007 still mainly on cassette tapes, meanwhile almost entirely via the Internet, flash drives, and mobile phones. And there is a rich fan culture focused mainly on Arabic singers but also on movie actors, both Egyptian and Western.

As soon as the Internet became available in the village in the mid-2000s, Internet cafés mushroomed. By February 2007, there were thirteen Internet cafés in Nazlat al-Rayyis, and two more were about to open. By 2010, private computers and Internet connections were rapidly spreading, and smartphones were making Internet access possible without a computer. The Internet is not exclusively about leisure, of course, but at least in the Internet cafés I visited in 2007, entertainment and socializing dominated, with music and movie downloading, computer games, religious knowledge, Internet chat, social networking, and sex sites allegedly the most popular features.

Nazlat al-Rayyis has also a rich culture of festive occasions that, unlike the male domains of cafés and sports, are also open to women. Once a year, a festive procession on the occasion of Mulid al-Nabi (the birthday of the Prophet

Figure 1.2. Celebration at the groom's house on the evening before a wedding in Nazlat al-Rayyis, November 2006.

Figure 1.3. Taking an evening walk in the outskirts of the village, Nazlat al-Rayyis, October 2007.

Muhammad) passes through the village, on the spring festival Shamm al-Nasim fishermen take their families on boats to the lake for a picnic, and during the canonical Islamic feasts, people visit one another and crowd the parks around the nearby Nile barrage. The most visible festive culture throughout the year, however, are weddings, with their atmosphere enveloping the groom's house for a week before the actual wedding day and mostly female friends and relatives crowding the inside of the house.

The variety of leisure activities does not seem too boring at a first sight. But the way people talk about killing time indicates that even though they sometimes have fun at a wedding, enjoy a good film, or become completely immersed in the excitement of a soccer match, in the end it is all the same anyway: there really is not much hope or point in all of it:

SAMULI: But people have different ways to kill time, what about them?

NAGIB: It's always the same: you sit in a café, you watch television, there is nothing more, that's it. . . .

S: So when you sit and watch television, what do you think?

N: Well, if I think at all, what do I think . . . [laughs, and does not tell what he thinks]

s: Still, I try to understand how people handle the situation of nothing changing, there being nothing new.

n: Well, they smoke hashish.

After this comment by Nagib, the discussion (which took place in a wedding)
swiftly moved to hashish, and the three men present started discussing different
new and old ways to smoke hashish, most of which involve collecting the smoke
in a glass, a bottle, a plastic bag, and the like. In fact, whenever I talked with
young men about boredom, they soon brought up hashish. Some stated its popularity as a fact, some emphasized that they did not smoke it, and others openly
praised its effects. One of the many hashish enthusiasts is Faruq, a man about
twenty years old who sports long hair (something that used to be out of the question but has recently become more common, even in the countryside) and wears
jeans, shirt, and a jacket in a style that clearly leans on global fashion. Around
2007, he and his friends met almost every evening either in Anwar's café, out in
the fields, or at one of the many weddings where it has become customary for the
groom to offer his male friends a treat of hashish and sometimes alcohol on the
eve of the wedding. Faruq subscribes wholeheartedly to the escape from reality
by means of hashish, into a temporary experience where things are meaningful,
conversations funny, and ideas flow freely:

> SAMULI: So what do you do, how do you kill time?
>
> FARUQ: The best way is with hashish. When you get high your worries fly away
> and are replaced by good thoughts. It's like living in two worlds, one where
> you have ideas, your thoughts run freely, you laugh and feel good, and this
> one we live in.
>     There are moments when time passes quickly, when you are with your
> friends, and moments when it doesn't pass—and it is then, when the time
> won't pass, when you want to smoke. Even just the things you need to do
> to get to smoke make time pass: you meet up people, you buy hashish, you
> find a place to smoke it—you don't want to smoke in front of people—that
> in itself already makes a couple of hours pass.

In a study on boredom and the experience of time among German youths, Ingo
Matuschek (1999: 388) observed a similar relation between boredom, leisure, and
drug consumption. For young people for whom leisure time was an occasion
for self-realization, there was no relation between boredom and drug experiments: "If, however, leisure time presents itself as escape from the everyday routine, boredom is experienced as distressing. In this situation drugs can become a
means of satisfaction, without which an acceptable leisure time no longer appears
as possible."

Leisure thus comes in different varieties with different emotional qualities.
Leisure as temporary escape from boredom remains dominated by killing time.

And killing time as an aim and a practice is not only escapist but also openly amoral. It does not defy moral or religious values, but it ignores them in stating that in the end, everything's just the same, quite meaningless and pointless. This nihilistic tone is best exemplified by the concept of *hiwar* (plural *hiwarat*, literally "dialogue" or "discussion"), youth slang for bluffing, cheating, and all the other performances of duplicity and deception that one undertakes to get money, kill time, solve problems, or move ahead.

> FARUQ: A *hiwar* would be, for example, if I have cheated you on sixty pounds, and when you come to claim it from me I manage to show that you have in turned cheated others for other sums of money and that way make your position difficult so that I can avoid paying. There are other, much bigger, and worse *hiwarat*, and I must admit that I have been doing some myself. But a *hiwar* is not only about making money; it is also a way to get good laughs.

> TAWFIQ: There are essentially three *hiwarat*: migration, hashish, and girls. But rather keep away from the girls. The problem with the girls is that they enter you into much more trouble than you can handle.

As Tawfiq notes, flirting is perhaps the riskiest of all the ways to make time pass. Making contact is tricky in itself given the strong social control over women's movement and contacts, and it can take a significant degree of "programming" to arrange just a phone call. More profoundly problematic, however, is the strong ambiguity of flirtation: something may remain on the level of flirtatious play, but it may also lead to serious—and often unhappy, as we will see in chapter 4—love stories. Finally, flirtation as a form of *hiwar* implies a significant amount of lying, cheating, and concealing. As such, it not only stands in opposition to the dominant sexual ethics of respect and honor but also can leave some of the parties involved (mainly the women) in a very difficult position.

The amoral tendency of killing time and the unsound nature of tricks and diversions do not, however, constitute open defiance of dominant moral standards. There is a tendency to keep killing time within minimal limits of religious and communal morality and respect. The preference for hashish rather than alcohol, and the attempt of smokers to avoid being seen by older men when smoking, are cases in point. Another illustrative case is the disappearance of pornography from the cafés. For a few years, cafés with a satellite dish were showing porn films late in the evening, but by 2007 I noticed that the cafés had shifted to showing soccer and Hollywood films instead. Asking Tawfiq's uncle Isma'il about this change, he gave the following explanation:

> From the event of the dish more than five years ago until the establishment of the central dish network, many cafés were showing sex films, mainly in winter evenings when people go to bed early and the streets are empty by eight

p.m. The café owner used to have a regular dish antenna and would buy the periodical card to decode the program, and the farmers from the nearby hamlets used to come by foot or by bicycle, pay fifty piastres entrance and double price for tea, and watch a sex film for an hour. The people called this charging [*shahn*], as they would afterward hurry home to their wives as quickly as possible. But since two years ago, the sex films in the cafés have come to an end for three reasons. First, the central dish has made European soccer available and extremely popular, and now all cafés show soccer, which draws a lot of public. Second, the sex films in the cafés became a well-known issue and drew negative attention to the cafés so they got a reputation as bad places. And the people were ashamed to face their older male relatives. European soccer offered a morally more acceptable alternative. Third, the decline of porn in the cafés happened at the same time as the rise of Internet cafes. Now the people can go to Internet cafés instead, where you have more privacy than in the café.

An important distinction must thus be made between entertainment with a moral purpose and entertainment within morally acceptable limits. It is the latter, not the former, that the bored young men of the village strive for. Even when they stretch the limits of minimal moral respectability, they do not want to do the wrong thing (see also Drieskens 2008). At the same time, I show in the following chapters, they are often working hard to be good, God-fearing people who know and do the right thing—but they don't do so all the time.

## Flights of Fantasy

It would be false to claim that all entertainment and diversion are purely escapist in nature. The same people who sometimes just want to kill time, at other times do take the nationalist and religious agendas of "entertainment with a purpose" that were mentioned at the beginning of this chapter quite seriously. More than that, they have their own particular agendas. The flight of fantasy that goes along with music, film, fan culture, poetry, and flirtation—and in some ways hashish—is also a site of constructive imagination. The state of waiting can also be a state of dreaming, as some people try to compensate for their physical and social immobility with movement on the plane of imagination.

Common sites of such imagination are soccer fan culture, youth fashion, film, the Internet, and literature. The two sources for ideas and imaginaries people most often mention are television and the Internet. While Arabic and Turkish TV series appear to be the most popular television programming, the young men I know show a great passion for Hollywood cinema. Action is the most popular genre of Hollywood films, but comedy, and especially romance, are enjoying great popularity as well. And if television and film can offer new horizons of imagination for those who are looking for them, the Internet also offers the possibility of interaction. Chat and social networks are high on the list of features people use on the Internet:

Buying a computer and getting connected to the Internet really has opened the world for me. I can read books online, I can meet people from around the world online, and I can play games. My favorite recently has been *Delta Force: Black Hawk Dawn*, where you can play in a Somali setting. You can also choose the Somali side to play against Americans, and every time in the past months when I felt upset about reading of George Bush in the news I would take pleasure in shooting and insulting the Americans in the game. (Fouad)

A much smaller group of young people is engaged with literature, especially poetry. While few people read fiction, surprisingly many write. When I noted this observation to Hilmi, a passionate reader of world literature and amateur writer of short stories, he commented: "Those who read are those who write." For those who are interested in literature, it is thus not only about consuming but also about creating literary imaginaries.

Writing is perhaps the most imaginative of the leisure forms available in the village. The relative popularity of writing also means that some people undertake imaginary travels by means of literary experiments. In 2007, Mukhtar Shehata (2010), the author of the poem cited earlier was about to finish the first draft of a novel whose hero is a man who, out of unhappiness, joins al-Qaeda and whose only true friends are the spies set after him by Arab and Western intelligence agencies, and he travels through much of the Middle East, Central Asia and Europe.

I was refused visa to Saudi Arabia where I was offered a job. Instead, I went there in my novel. And I went to Afghanistan, Chechnya, Russia, Poland, and Germany, I met bin Laden and fell in love with an American Iranian woman— all that I could do in my novel, but I couldn't have done it as a worker in Saudi Arabia.

I return to the constructive work of fantasy and Mukhtar Shehata's literary experiment in more detail in chapter 7. For the time being, I want to point out that there are more ways to approach leisure and entertainment than either revivalist or secular nationalist art with a purpose or nihilistic time killing time. Entertainment as an exercise of imagination differs from both of those in its emphasis on exploring the limits of what may be possible, what else one could do. And yet although the constructive fantasy of imagination can stand in contradiction to the pessimism and despair of escape and killing time, these two ways of dealing with the experience of boredom are by no means exclusive. The same people who claim that nothing has any point at other times can become very excited about something they have heard, seen, or thought of.

Boredom is not simply nihilistic; on the contrary, it is intimately related to the expectation that life be interesting and exciting, offer new perspectives and possibilities (Meyer Spacks 1995: 24). Young men like Faruq and Tawfiq do not simply state their boredom—they perform it. In their discussions boredom emerges as a distinctive ideology of youth that informs a critique of everyday life and values. As such, it carries a normative tenor of (frustrated) self-realization, a value that nevertheless does not stand in the way of their pursuit of communal ideals of respect and obligation and the revivalist ideal of a committed pious life.

## Hope?

Discussing my research on boredom with Hilmi's circle of friends, one of them pointed out that even if life sometimes gets boring, there definitely is hope: "You must pay attention to that we as Muslims do not feel so much boredom because when you pray regularly, it gives you hope again every time."

This is a hope that none of my friends in the village, not even those with openly secularist opinions, would call into question (not before 2011, that is). There is a real and powerful sense of hope and purpose involved in worship. And yet many of them also quote lines of poetry that present a rather more pessimistic view of existence, such as the following quatrain by Salah Jahin (1987: 29) in which the piety of Job (Ayyub), the Qur'anic and biblical hero of patience, is defeated by boredom:

> Destiny hit Job with all diseases
> Seven years sick and paralyzed
> Patience is good, Job's patience healed him
> But what irony, he died of boredom.
> How strange!

Hope is the solution to boredom and despair, and yet at the same time, existential boredom implies a denial of hope. It is based on discontentedness (*'adam al-rida*), whereas the promise of hope through piety posits contentedness (*rida*) as a key virtue of the believer.[4] This leads to contradictory promises and demands regarding the hope involved in religiosity. This is made explicit by Abdelnaser, a shopkeeper in his midtwenties who, at the time of the following discussion, did not find his life boring and did not want to emigrate: "I'm not bored because I have trust in God, and because I work all day and stay busy."

Abdelnaser's brother and partner in business Muntasir disagreed and said that religious people can also get bored sometimes, citing a friend of his whose motto is "there is nothing new under the sun." But Abdelnaser held to his point of view:

> The bored youths, they don't want to work. They sleep from dawn until afternoon, they don't work, they smoke hashish, and they have a mobile phone to call their girlfriend. If they would truly believe in God they would not be bored, because when you have certainty [*yaqin*] in God, you have hope and

you don't feel bored. I work and I thank God for my share [*rizq*] and know that today is better than yesterday.

But if Abdelnaser presents to us two mutually exclusive options—being bored and having trust in God—for most people the two cannot be separated. Abdelnaser himself later faced great difficulty in feeling optimistic after he and his brother were compelled by bad business (a result of the global rise in food prices in 2008) to close their shop and to migrate to Saudi Arabia, where unfortunate circumstances combined with an oppressive labor regime left them working under extremely exploitative and difficult conditions. For others, the tide has taken them into a brighter and more hopeful direction, and many more still are moving up and down.

Some of the bored young men who want to escape from reality in diversion and drugs at some point in their lives turn to religion in the search of a steady ground to stand on and a clear direction to follow. In particular, Salafi activism, a movement with some active followers and a lot of ideological influence in Nazlat al-Rayyis, strikingly often draws men who have gone through times of deviance and disorientation.

There was a time when Mustafa, a good friend of Tawfiq, after a period of personal crisis and in search of a clear orientation, let his beard grow and cut his trousers short in the distinctive fashion of committed Salafis. He tried to stop smoking, began praying regularly, and enthusiastically instructed anyone who was willing to listen about the Salafi "method" (*manhag*). After a few months, however, he shaved his beard again and returned to smoking cigarettes. While he still held to Salafi ideas about Islam, he no longer followed the rigorous discipline of being a Salafi. Sitting in a café together one evening, Tawfiq took this as an occasion to inquire, "When you were a sheikh, were you bored?"[5] To which Mustafa responded:

No, there was no time to be bored. My day was completely full: praying on time, waiting for the prayer, preparing, and after the prayer studying: Sheikh Salah gave lectures of Qur'an and Sunna, and I was studying some myself. I was busy all the time. And honestly, I was feeling more at peace [*bi-raha aktar*] then than now. Now my schedule is mixed up; I delay the prayers according to other things. Back then I was doing everything on time; it kept me busy all the time. And more than that: it was something I felt good doing. It is the same like when you do work you like: if you have an interesting, demanding work, you will be completely devoted to it; it will take all your time and you won't feel bored.

One might wonder, if Mustafa found his experience of intensive piety so fulfilling, what made him stop? I pursue this question in more detail in the chapter 6, where Mustafa features. What is important here is his observation about the kind of hope religiosity may offer.

Mustafa's comparison of intensive piety with demanding work highlights that the solution to boredom is doing something meaningful, an insight that is echoed also by Sa'id, a soccer enthusiast and wedding caterer:

> The only thing that really helps against boredom is work. But there is little work. My work is seasonal. I work two months a year—the rest of the time I'm unemployed.

Be it with work, religion, migration, or literature, there emerges an unsolved but dynamic relationship of hope and purpose, boredom and frustration. Boredom is fundamentally a state of aspiration in which one feels the need for such sense of direction but does not have it. Promises of greater purpose offer solutions to the sense of pointlessness, but at the same time that sense troubles those promises. Boredom is friend and foe at once of grand schemes, a shadow that follows them anywhere and everywhere, as Tawfiq put it.

# 2 An Hour for Your Heart and an Hour for Your Lord

ONE OF THE most important and powerful of hopes is the hope invested in the possibility of living a morally sound, good, and God-fearing life. While the moral aims that people strive for may appear clear, and even grand, the actual pursuit of those aims is far from straightforward. The same young men who think that hashish is the best way to escape boredom and who resort to shortcuts in order to kill time and make money also believe in revivalist Islam's promises of a meaningful life now and paradise in the hereafter, and they strive to act as respected and successful members of their family and society. As we look at the actual ways in which ideological grand schemes are made use of in everyday life, ambivalence is essential and often necessary. These uses may evoke a comprehensive discipline, whereas what they actually accomplish is something at once more complex and simple: an instantaneous sense of direction in a confusing and dull reality.

It is common knowledge that religious, moral, and other ideals are never fully realized in everyday life. A frequent explanation for this is the tension between moral ideals, on the one hand, and desire, interests, and power, on the other hand. In other words, people are either weak (from a more sympathetic perspective) or hypocritical (from a less sympathetic perspective). A more sophisticated version of this would point out that people are subjected to regimes of power that may contradict the ideals of moral personhood they hold, thereby leaving them suspended in between different moral traditions. In any version, this explanation is based on the assumption that people have a consistent idea on their own about what is good and right. This, however, is seldom the case in practice.

People commonly have clear and strong notions of what is good and right, but they are seldom consistent. In this chapter I propose an approach to morality that takes as its starting point this fundamental inconsistency. The unrealized—or temporarily realized—nature of moral and other ideals is not caused by a shortcoming in either the people who pursue them or the world they live in. It is grounded in the very way moral aims, discussions, reasoning, sentiments, embodiment, and practice are constituted. To understand how that works, I open this chapter with the case of Ramadan fasting, a time of exceptional morality and worship that, by definition, is framed by a the rest of the year when worship is less intense and morals less strict. Morality is not a single, overarching normative system or tradition but an incoherent conglomerate of different aims, ideals, boundaries, and senses of what is good, an ongoing dialogue of different moments, styles, and senses of personhood, embodiment, and belonging.

## Being Good in Ramadan

Ramadan is a blessed, holy month that constitutes a special period of piety that involves much more than just fasting. It is a time of increased social, moral, and pious commitment. In the evenings, mosques are often packed with believers participating in the voluntarily *tarawih* prayers in addition to canonical ritual daily prayers, which can extend more than an hour after the evening (*'isha'*) prayer. In the streets of the cities, wealthy citizens offer large-scale services of free food at fast-breaking time, known as "tables of the Merciful" (*mawa'id al-Rahman*). Arduous to maintain especially in summer heat, fasting is seen by many as a spiritual exercise in disciplining carnal desires. Furthermore, many people ascribe to the feeling of hunger a strong power in facilitating social responsibility toward the poor. The central and most important motivation for fasting, however, is the prospect of paradise. Ramadan is a time when God rewards believers most generously and forgives their sins. For the duration of Ramadan, "the gates of Paradise are open and the gates of Hell are closed."[1] According to a hadith (authoritative tradition) of the Prophet Muhammad, distributed as a poster by the local branch of the Muslim Brotherhood in 2006:

> Whoever fasts and stands for prayer in the month of Ramadan with faith and entrusting God with counting the reward, the sins he has previously committed are forgiven. And whoever stands for prayer in the Night of Destiny [Laylat al-Qadr, one of the last ten nights of Ramadan, when, according to Islamic belief, the revelation of the Qur'an to Muhammad began[2]] with faith and entrusting God with counting the reward, the sins he has previously committed are forgiven.[3]

Other traditions, quoted to me by people whom I asked about the significance of Ramadan, state that the obligatory prayer counts seventy times its value during Ramadan, that voluntary prayer gains the same reward as an obligatory one, and that a prayer in Laylat al-Qadr is better than that of a thousand months. In contrast, the consequences of not observing Ramadan are severe. Intentionally breaking the fast without a legitimate reason cannot be compensated by any other action, and both good and bad deeds count their double in reward and punishment during Ramadan.[4]

Not surprisingly, then, Ramadan is "the season of worship" (*musim al-'ibada*), a time when people try to be good—that is, observe religious commandments and moral virtues more rigorously than they usually do. People who otherwise rarely pray try to fulfill this obligation during the holy month, especially in the beginning of the month and around Laylat al-Qadr. Since it is believed that anger, curses, and insults break the fast, people attempt to avoid these during Ramadan, and in arguments (which are numerous in Ramadan, as people often have short nerves due to fasting), people often use the phrase "Oh God, I'm fasting!" (*Allahumma ana sayim*) to avoid using foul language but also to call upon oneself and others to calm down. Similarly, bystanders appeal to people involved in an argument with the phrase "Because you're fasting" (*'ashan inta sayim*).

This focus on reward and piety is framed, however, by a general sense of gathering, joy, and entertainment. Streets are decorated with flags, colorful strips of paper, lights, and lanterns. A month of fasting, Ramadan is also a privileged time of eating, as people compensate for fasting in daytime with special delicacies in the evening. The consumption of meat and sugar skyrockets. Special television programs and, in the cities, cultural events in theaters and public spaces offer a variety of Ramadan entertainment. In the evenings—especially toward the end of Ramadan—people invite over friends and relatives; the cafés are full; and in the cities, a veritable season of cultural events characterizes the second half of the month. People generally spend more money than usual during Ramadan, and toward the end of the month, with 'Id al-Fitr (the feast of breaking the fast) approaching, consumption reaches an intensity similar to that of Christmas in the West.

Yet as festive as they are, Ramadan gatherings still express a spirit of religious and moral discipline. During the holy month, one must abstain from all the other misdeeds—minor and major—that may be forgivable at other times. If God's reward and blessings are very close during Ramadan, so are God's wrath and punishment. Forms of entertainment deemed immoral—flirting, consuming alcohol and cannabis, pornography—largely stop during Ramadan. In the cities, bars are closed. In the villages, Internet cafés are empty. The trade in cannabis that otherwise flourishes in cities and villages alike reaches a seasonal low. Other forms of entertainment that are not considered immoral in themselves are suspended in Ramadan because they have no place in the rigid schedule of fasting. For example, saints' festivals (*mulids*) and weddings are not celebrated during Ramadan.

For the young men with whom I have spent much of the time in Ramadan in the village of Nazlat al-Rayyis, these forms of entertainment, temporarily unavailable during the holy month, are partly replaced by soccer. Every afternoon before fast-breaking time, young men gather to play at school yards or other open spaces. At the secondary school, a Ramadan tournament of local amateur clubs attracts up to a hundred spectators, who sit from early afternoon until shortly before sunset in the shade, watching the usually two or three consecutive matches that take place in an afternoon. Soccer is seen as a form of the sociality (*lamma*) and amusement (*tasliya*) that characterize Ramadan in Egypt as much as fasting and prayer, but it also is a form of amusement deemed in accordance with the spirit of Ramadan. "The soccer matches," my friend Isma'il argued, "are for the youths a way to compensate for not being able to go after girls, smoke marijuana, and drink beer. It's a way to fill the emptiness that they otherwise fill with immoral entertainment."

Ramadan soccer is an ambivalent exercise. It is one of the gatherings so characteristic of the sense of community that prevails in the month of fasting, and it is a way to kill time that is not deemed immoral or un-Islamic. But at the same time it points to an ambivalent understanding of religion and morality. Not only does it mix ascetic discipline with fun and entertainment; it is also part of a time of exceptional morality that, by its nature, will last only as long as Ramadan lasts. The rigor of worship and the fullness of sociability during Ramadan are exceptional by definition, and this exceptional nature indirectly legitimizes less consistent approaches to religion and morality for the rest of the year.

Both the "Christmatization of Ramadan," as it has been called by Walter Armbrust (2002), and the character of Ramadan as a time of exceptional morality have been regularly subjected to criticism both by religious authorities and by ordinary citizens who feel that the "true" spirit of Ramadan is lost in the midst of all this. They argue that Ramadan should be a time of spirituality and moral cultivation that helps create a committed Muslim personality and society free of vices and unnecessary spending, oriented toward individual and collective self-improvement (al-Shurbasi 2006: 1428–1431; Sha'ban 2006: 4; Abu l-Ma'ati 2006: 7; al-Khashshab 2006: 7; Matar 2006: 23–24).

The practice of Ramadan, however, in both its ascetic and its festive variations, does not necessarily focus on the progressive improvement of society and self. Firmly based on the authoritative sources of Islam but with a different emphasis than that offered by the discourse on *iltizam* and cultivation of character, its focus is explicitly on reward (*thawab*), the forgiving of sins, and the ultimate aim of entering paradise in the afterlife. This does not mean that the common practice of Ramadan and the publicly proclaimed ideas of Ramadan are opposed to each other—on the contrary, the strong focus on reward and the afterlife is a key moment of the entire Islamic revival and is intimately related to the notion of cultivating a committed character always aware of the prospect of death. And the revivalist turn to a constant presence of the afterworld no doubt also informs the practice of Ramadan, though in ways that depart from the proclaimed ideal of perfectionist commitment. During Ramadan, people frequently discuss in detail the correct form of voluntary prayers and the exact details of fasting so as to maximize the reward of praying and fasting. By doing so, they also—implicitly or explicitly—establish Ramadan as a moral and pious exception from not-so-perfect everyday life. If Ramadan is a time of exceptional reward when God forgives one's previous sins, one may commit some sins and slip a little from one's obligations during the rest of the year—in a year's time, after all, it will be Ramadan again.

Ramadan as a time of exceptional morality demonstrates and enforces the supremacy of God's commands by constituting a time in which morality is not ambiguous but categorical, and in which religious obligations *must* be fulfilled. But in the end, it is precisely the temporary rigor of the holy month that establishes and legitimizes the flexible and ambiguous nature of norms and ethics for the rest of the year. This can be best seen in the time of the feast of fast-breaking ('Id al-Fitr) that marks the end of Ramadan. In line with the established traditions of ritual law, Muslims take the feast as an occasion to reward themselves for withstanding the test of fasting. But the extent and ways in which they do so can significantly depart from individual and collective self-improvement and reform. The feast marks not only a reward for fasting but also the return to a normal order of affairs. On the first Friday after Ramadan, the sermons at the congregational Friday noon (*gum'a*) prayer invariably circle around one issue: reminding believers that they must follow the commandments of their creed not only during Ramadan but also for all of the year; the feast does not mean that one is allowed to fall back to one's bad habits. And yet every year when Ramadan soccer gives way to other forms of entertainment, the same young men who pray and fast during Ramadan celebrate in ways that would have been out of the question a few days earlier. These ways sometimes also include outbreaks of aggressive sexual harassment (*Malcolm X* 2006; *Manal and Alaa's Bit Bucket* 2006; Schielke 2009a).

But the power of the moral shift of the feast lies not simply in the falling back to bad habits. More important, it marks the shift from a period of observance during which the sins of the previous year are erased to a more complex order of morality. The alternative to being good in the pious sense of Ramadan is not simply being bad, although that is, of course, part of the story. The more central alternative is a complexity of different modes of being good, different situational senses of personhood, embodiment, and action.

## Senses of Right and Good

The moral universe in which Ramadan morality is embedded is characterized by a profound ambivalence that not only is a coincidental result of circumstances but also actually provides the foundation of situational moral action and subjectivity that are based on various coexisting motivations, aims, and identities that can and often do conflict but do not constitute exclusive opposites. Young people in the village generally share the revivalist understanding of religion as a clear, exact set of commandments and prohibitions that leave no or little space for different interpretations or negotiation. But they also express other ideals that may take very different directions from their religious discourse.

To understand morality in everyday life, it is therefore not sufficient to look at religious discourse. While the young people of Nazlat al-Rayyis do study the Qur'an, listen to sermons (mainly in the mosque and on television), and discuss the correct application of religion, they also subscribe to political movements of a different color; save money for a wedding; dream of migrating to Europe or the United States (as they imagine them from cinema and the habitus of returning migrants); appreciate and criticize the character and career of their friends on different grounds in different situations; try to make some money to make theirs a metropolitan and comfortable, middle-class lifestyle; read poetry (and less often novels); watch Egyptian, Indian, and Hollywood films; and listen to and comment upon the romantic love songs of their favorite singers. Especially women—who spend more of their free time watching television than men, who have the option of sitting in cafés and strolling around—often have an encyclopedic knowledge of films and actors. Popular cultural imagination is an extension of people's everyday experience, a source of citations, discussions, and fantasies. It provides models for identities and styles and inspires discourses and imaginaries of love, excitement, and success that, while seldom posited in an open opposition to religion, do present their own particular modes of being good.

In everyday situations, discussions, and moral performances, notions of rigid sexual morality coexist and compete with the imaginaries and experiments of romance and sex, wishes of self-realization with concerns for family connectivity and communal reputation, ideals of moral integrity with the aim of material well-being. In fact, people often speak in very different tones and with very different arguments and styles about different topics. While young men often ridicule Salafi activists, with their long beards, short-hemmed *gallabiyyas*, and painstakingly precise ritualism, at the same time their idea of a profoundly religious person is often identical to the image of the Salafi. People can argue for very conservative and strict standards of gender relations at one time but express rather liberal ideals of romantic love at other times.

These different moments of moral reasoning and practice are not just an expression of hypocrisy, as some Egyptians argue. Magnus Marsden (2010), writing about Afghanistan and northwestern Pakistan, argues that hypocrisy in the sense of living according to double or multiple standards is not necessarily a fault in people's moral integrity. More often, it is the necessary condition of moral action whereby one has to take into consideration that what is right in one occasion can be wrong in another, and that exposing this contradiction can do more damage than tacitly accepting it. In this sense, criticizing hypocrisy is a moralizing strategy aimed to discredit certain (but never all) forms of complexity and duplicity, or certain persons involved in it. Rather than hypocrisy, I thus suggest that we talk about the complexity involved in moral action.

Complexity is the normal way morality works: as a loose and unsystematic dialogue of different modalities, or registers, of normative action and speech. Each in turn, such registers offer a temporary solid foundation for reasoning and action, thus allowing for both some clear directions and some space for ambiguity to navigate a complicated life. In her ethnography of the invisible in Cairo, Barbara Drieskens (2008: 37) argues that this flexibility of temporary solidities is the necessary condition that makes life livable:

> Shifting truths and the constant adaptation of appearances, and the trans-formations a person undergoes moving from one place to another, from one encounter to another, are at the core of daily life in Cairo, and constitute the flexibility and livability of everyday events.

Speaking of normative registers, I thus try to account for the way people can ar-gue for very coherent and clear moral claims without systematically subscribing to or living according to a coherent system of values and aims. In short, morality is not a coherent system but an incoherent and unsystematic dialogue of different moral voices that exist parallel to and at times contradict one another.

It would be a fallacy, however, to understand these moral voices or regis-ters as neatly ordered drawers from which one can choose a moral judgment. We need to keep in mind the communicative, dialogic, and pragmatic aspect of morality, always related to oneself and others, and often in need of thinking, questioning, or explanation, as Jarret Zigon (2008: 155) reminds us:

> Morality is better thought of as a continuous dialogical process during which people are in constant interaction with their world and the persons in that world, rather than as a set category of beliefs from which one picks appropriate responses according to particular situations.

These communications and interactions that make up morality as a part of the social world commonly aim for coherence and consistency. But that coherence appears to be often of a more temporary, situational nature, whereas people's character, life experience, and expectations remain complex and inconsistent. This is what Catherine Ewing (1990) has described as the "illusion of wholeness," people's ability to shift between contradictory sets of views without being trou-bled by them. With the notion of moral registers—inspired by a long tradition of the anthropology of morality, identity, and subjectivity (see, e.g., Abu-Lughod 1996b; Robbins 2004; Zigon 2008; Stephan 2010)—I try to account for that essen-tial ambiguity of moral action and discourse. On one level that ambiguity offers a solid ground and clear framework for action, while on another level it allows for the coexistence of different moral, and to a certain degree amoral, aims (e.g., piety, respect, friendship, family, success, wealth, love, self-realization), which in a given situation may (but do not have to) have different consequences.

Speaking of registers rather than systems, discourses, or traditions highlights the performative, situational, and dialogic character of norms. A normative register is a way of speaking about a specific range of topics with a specific style of argumentation, embodying a specific emotional tone, acting in specific ways. It contains not only a set of arguments and affects but also an implicit ontology of the subject matter: the kind of categories in which it can be described and the kind of actions that are possible. The choice of the register in which a subject is described and discussed is, in itself, a key form of normative debate. To declare an issue a religious matter, or to discuss it in the registers of, say, romantic love, or social justice and rights, is also to draw different conclusions about it, to suggest different paths of action.

What, then, are these registers or modes of morality? What do they contain? In an earlier study I compared them to a mosaic (Schielke 2009b), but I now think that even the metaphor of a mosaic is too rigid to make sense of the inherent fluidity of moral certainty. In the following, I try to give an overview of some of the moral registers that I have encountered in Egypt, but already the attempt to turn them from practical knowledge into a catalog is problematic. Every "register" could be separated into smaller parts, specific styles, even common expressions and arguments that carry a specific logic. At the same time, they all come together in people's lives and character in ways that are not distinct the way the stones of a mosaic are. The following list, therefore, should be understood as an impressionistic and incomplete account of some important moments of moral action, each involving characteristic ontologies, topics, and understandings of embodiment and personhood, rather than as any definite pieces in a mosaic.

First of the key modalities of morality is, not surprisingly, religion (*din*), understood most importantly—but not only—as an objective set of rules based on the Qur'an and the Sunna that provide guidelines for a good life and the key to paradise. Evocations of "Islam" and "religion" are not identical, however, with arguments on the basis of evidence drawn from the Qur'an and the Sunna. For example, when it comes to questions of gender relations, the need to control women is identified with Islam without any further reference to commandments and prohibitions in the scripture. Furthermore, religion cannot, of course, be restricted to its normative significance. Beyond its moral and political significance, religion is—perhaps most fundamentally and unanimously—an overarching emotional and metaphysical order that gives life and the world structure and significance in ways that go far beyond the focus on the ethical and the moral.

Equally central for everyday moral actions and judgments, and in many key points intertwined with religion, is the register of respect (*ihtiram*), referring to one's social standing in the community, good behavior, responsibility for one's family, and wealth. Respect is embodied by persons but always collective, in the sense that it is shared by families and social groups. Most important, it is essentially intersubjective, a performance of relations between people. The notion of respect is also strongly gendered, especially in the way a young woman's respectability is key to her standing as a person and chances for marriage. This gendered aspect of respect bears resemblance to the "honor-shame complex" that has often been mentioned as a core moral sentiment in ethnographies of the Middle East. Articulated as jealousy and protection a man should feel toward his wife and female kin, and as modesty (*hiya'*), which "good" (*kwayyisa*) girls and women are expected to perform, this gendered aspect of respect is indeed very closely related to the honor-shame complex. Yet in my fieldwork I have found the notion of respect to be more central, and notions of honor and shame often secondary to it. Respect and the lack of it can involve different moments of honor and pride, shame and scandal, not all of which are gendered, or they are not gendered in the same way. Compare, for example, the notion of *sharaf*, male-dominated honor related to the sexuality of female kin, with that of *karama*, more general human dignity (Drieskens 2008: 27–29).

Very closely related to respect are the ways people understand family and kinship (articulated in taxonomies like that of home or household, or *bayt*; nuclear family, or *usra*; extended family, or *'ayla*; and patronymic group, or *jama'a*),[5] describing the intimate relations of spouses, children, and relatives and the recognition of patriarchal and maternal authorities. There is an important emotional dimension to family and kinship that cannot be reduced to respect: the sense of being and belonging together, which has been fittingly described by Suad Joseph (1999) as "connectivity." Connectivity is a very important moral category because of the ontology of the acting subject involved: it is about being part of an emotionally bounded unit and acting together as one. It would be a fallacy, however, to conclude that Egyptians are generally "collectivist," as the language of political liberalism would put it. While people can be very much oriented toward connectivity and act as parts of a collective when it comes to being a member of a family, they can be very individualistic in other situations. And in most cases their identities, lives, and horizons of action involve both individual and collective aspects, as well as different senses of the individual and the collective.

Respect and family, in turn, are complemented but also countered by a register of good character, expressed in qualities such as being *tayyib* (kind and friendly) or *gada'* (noble, courageous, and capable).[6] With different emphases, the focus of the different notions that describe good character is on an idea of underlying traits that are expressed in readiness to help even at one's personal risk; avoidance of conflicts; and a general sense of joviality, friendship, and sympathy. Good character involves a much more individualistic sense of morality than do the intersubjectivity that is inherent to respect and the connectivity that is key to family. While good character is essentially relational—it is measured by actions toward others—it cannot be had or lost collectively the way that the respectability of a family can. Significantly, it is also, to a certain degree, independent from issues of religion and respect, as was pointed out to me by a friend who, discussing the vices and virtues of another mutual friend, pointed out to me that however many his faults may be, he is a very kind (*tayyib*) person, something that makes him worthy of friendship regardless of his other qualities.

Social justice and rights are the most important ways people deal with the economic and power relationships among people and address (often with socialist overtones) issues such as corruption, privatization of public-sector enterprises, nepotism, authoritarian rule, and lack of opportunities. The register of social justice is very complex in itself, inspired by Nasserist socialism, Islamic notions of justice (especially in regard to charity and the prohibition of interest), and the liberal and neoliberal notions of human rights and good governance that have become increasingly important to the vocabulary of discussing justice and society after the 1990s. Social justice and rights, though often formulated in the language of law, politics, and economy, have important links with other, more subjective moral notions. The best cases in point are dignity (*karama*) and freedom (*hurriya*), which became the powerful demands of the 2011 revolution, capable of uniting people of different political orientations because they articulated a commonsensical moral outrage rather than a specific political agenda.

Last but not least come registers that I will dwell on in some detail later: love, celebrating passion and emotional commitment and describing "pure love" as an all-sacrificing obsession that disregards both self-interest and communal respect; and wealth, success, and self-realization, expressed in the aim of finding wealth and a place in life and, less outspokenly, of broadening one's horizons of experience.

Morality in this sense is not only situational, unsystematic, and ambiguous; it also does not have clear boundaries. It is not possible to draw a neat distinction between morality and politics, morality and kinship, morality and economy, or morality and religion. There is no definite moment in which issues of marriage, family relations, religious rites, social status, and political conviction do or do not concern the cultivation of an embodied sense of good personhood, social practice, and communal belonging. Morality is not a field but an aspect of human life. An issue *can*—but does not have to—become a moral one when it is addressed from the point of view of good personhood, practice, and belonging. Not everything is moral—or immoral (which would imply a recognition of the moral relevance of an action). People have interests, worries, and desires that they do not articulate as moral ones. Much of life is not characterized by moral concerns, and sometimes people quite consciously avoid considering a possible moral aspect of their actions.

These modes of action and discourse are not isolated fragments, nor do they constitute a coherent system. Different normative voices (both collective and individual) that make sense of the everyday are commonly united—take, for example, religion, respect and family, good character and love, or religion and social justice, which in a given situation might be identical. But sometimes they clash, and oftentimes the registers themselves are complex. Respect is sometimes doubted, which implies that intentions may matter after all. Good character can be measured by different criteria. Religiosity as collecting reward may differ from religiosity as self-formation, and religiosity as comprehensive commitment may differ from religion as an overarching metaphysical and moral framework, without being exclusive opposites.

Different moral registers are not necessarily unresolvably opposite or even clearly distinct—in most cases they are not, and they commonly go perfectly together. But sometimes they do not. In those cases we should resist the temptation to analytically resolve all contradictions as only apparent ones. Some contradictions are resolved, others are not, yet others never should be (Girke 2008). This is not to ignore that there are spaces of negotiation. But not everything is negotiated, and not everything needs to be negotiated. *Negotiation*, a market metaphor that evokes the idea of eventually striking a bargain somewhere in the middle,[7] has become a highly used term in anthropology to explain how people are able to live "in between" different demands and expectations. While in some cases negotiation is what is going on, in other cases, negotiation evokes a misleading image of people generally reconciling things to make them fit. In practice, they more often than not live a life of many ambiguities, shifting between at times opposed moments and outlooks of life, being firmly something at one time and strictly something else at another time, rather than looking for compromises.

## Situational Logics

In their ethnographies of the Islamic revival, Saba Mahmood (2005) and Charles Hirschkind (2006a) argue, with different emphases, that there is a strong Western liberal, Protestant tradition of seeing the ethical as a matter of disembodied arguments and deliberation rather than bodily practice. They contrast this bias on inner rationality and spirituality to the ways the Islamic tradition and the current Islamic revival cultivate bodily practice (be it styles of speech and audition, prayer, or weeping) as a constituent of ethical states. This may be something of a caricature of Western traditions of ethics, which, after all, have often placed enormous emphasis on the cultivation of character through practice, and in doing so have also influenced contemporary Egyptian understandings of ethics and religion (see, e.g., Demolins 1897, 1911; Umar 1902; Starrett 1998). Nevertheless, their point is helpful for interrogating the unquestioned common sense of objectivity that is attached to some notions of embodiment over others. The relationship of morality and embodiment is key if we want to understand the different senses and moments of moral action.

To do so, however, we need not only to give up the idea of ethics as generally located "inside," that is, the idea that one's true personality and choices should be located "inside" oneself. We have to go further and question the very duality of inner states and outward appearances. The question regarding morality and embodiment is not simply one of whether bodily acts form or express inner states. Different notions of embodiment and morality actually entail different ontologies of the acting subject, some of which work with a duality of the inner and the outer, whereas some of them do without (see also Mittermaier 2011).

Furthermore, the kind of relationship cannot be distinguished from the specific acts involved. That is, a sense of morality cannot be separated from its contents. A logic of action is, strictly speaking, not a logic at all if we take logic to be the formal reasoning on which mathematic calculations and scientific arguments are based. Unlike proper, formal logic, a "logic" of moral action is a sense of acting in certain possible ways in regard to certain problems and things. Such "logic" is by default situational, not universal. As such, it is also contingent, that is, not necessary. It is always possible to follow a different way of reasoning and feeling, a different line of action.

Take, for example, the register of respect. How to deal with other people depending on their standing, how to have a standing toward others, and how to deal with situations in which people's actions may lead to a conflict of standing and reputation—respect is the most explicitly outward and visible modality of moral action. Respect is essentially about meaningful and proper performance that neither can be seen as merely external nor fits the notion of crafting inner states through visible practices (or their expression through visible practices), because acts of respect do not refer to anything "inside"—they refer to one's relations to others.

The issue of smoking illustrates the performativity of respect. In Egypt, most men smoke cigarettes, but not everybody can smoke anytime with everybody. (Women smoke much less often, and when they do, it is often considered improper.) Young men do not smoke in front of their fathers, and they avoid smoking in front of other older relatives, as well as older men in general. Youngest sons often do not smoke in front of their older brothers. This does not mean that they would smoke secretly. Their fathers and older relatives know perfectly well that they smoke and do not necessarily object to it. But it would be disrespectful to smoke in front of one's father because smoking as a social practice is characterized by a sense of camaraderie, such as between friends, peers, colleagues, cousins, and the like. Smoking in front of one's father is disrespectful in that the father is being treated as an equal. When a youngest brother manages to make his older brothers accept that he smokes in their company, this means that he is—to some degree at least—accepted as their peer. Hiding one's cigarette when one's father enters is a moral performance of respect toward patriarchal authority. Its value lies in the performance itself, in the social relationship it affirms, and cannot be seen as either a cover for something else (which it might be if one smoked in secret) or an ethical practice in the Aristotelian sense (which it might be if one tried to give up smoking).

The point I am trying to make goes beyond the issue of smoking, and beyond the issue of respect. What I want to make clear is that different modalities of moral action entail different modes of embodiment and different concepts of moral personhood. Respect is about a performance that in itself is meaningful for social relations and hierarchies. Good character, in contrast, is about fundamental traits expressed in and measured by actions but that essentially come "from inside" (*min guwwa*). Religiosity, in turn, is a moral-ethical practice that consists of actions and expressions that are considered both formative and expressive of a deeper (which is not the same as inner) disposition.

Different ways of embodiment and situations thus entail rather different senses of normative practice. Some emphasize discipline and vigilance; others, unconditional recognition and help. But when to follow which sense?

This question was decided very spontaneously by passengers on a minibus I was riding in Alexandria in the spring of 2008. As the minibus stopped to let a passenger out, a teenage girl in an immodest dress by Egyptian standards was trying to run away from a man on the street. She escaped into the minibus, followed by a man who shouted at her and tried to slap and hit her. He declared himself as a police officer and said the girl was trying to stop cars on the street, so he would arrest her and take her to the Sidi Bishr police station. "No! Not to Sidi Bishr station! To Muntazah!" (names of different police districts), the girl cried. The passengers immediately turned to help. A young woman sitting behind her helped her to the backseat while the passengers started to argue with him. The police officer claimed that she belonged to a gang of girls who get picked up in cars and then rob the drivers, but passengers were completely unmoved by this and continued to argue with him. When the policeman got out of the car (possibly to get assistance), the passengers immediately closed the door and shouted, "Drive! Drive!" After a short moment of hesitation, the driver left, leaving the police officer behind. The girl was hysterically crying, and passengers tried to calm her down. She said she had been waiting for her fiancé. "Call your fiancé and let him come and pick you up," the passengers suggested. At the same time her phone rang. Still crying, she told to the person at the other end of the line that she was not coming to the rendezvous, got out, and hailed a taxi. A discussion evolved among the passengers, who all agreed that the police officer had no right to arrest her. The female passenger who had previously helped the girl argued, "Even if she was at fault, he had no right!"

The people on the minibus who spontaneously came to the girl's help at an other moment might have criticized her for her dress and argued for the importance of modesty and parental control for young women. Such views are commonplace in Egypt, and it is rare for anybody to seriously contest them. Also, the policeman claimed that the girl was involved in illegal and immoral activities. And yet the minibus passengers did not for a moment hesitate to unconditionally defend her from the police. The young female passenger in fact argued that the policeman had no right "even if she was at fault," that is, even if she really were a thief or a prostitute. In this moment, two sensibilities overruled the issues of sexual morality and law in a way that made the situation subject to a completely different kind of logic, one where the question of the girl's moral or legal innocence did not arise.

Just two days earlier, Fouad had showed me on his mobile phone a film, recorded secretly on a phone and circulated on the Internet, showing a plain-clothes vice police officer beating and shouting at a suspected prostitute arrested in an apartment in Alexandria. Such films showing police officers assaulting arrested people, especially women, circulated widely in Egypt in the years before 2011. They touched two very important sensibilities. The first is many Egyptians' deep distrust of and hatred toward the police force, which in the course of its increasing brutality and informal privatization had become a de facto criminal organization. A second moral sensibility, strongly provoked by images of helpless women being beaten by police officers, was the moral sense of obligation to protect and help people in a weak position.

These two sensibilities were the basis for the passengers' spontaneous and unconditional performance of gad'ana ("courage," "willingness to help," and in other contexts also "youthful manliness"; see Ghannam [2013: 121–125]). But while it was unconditional in that situation, this does not mean that it would be in others. No modality of reasoning or action is a priori obvious, nor are its consequences. There exists no clear hierarchy for determining when exactly one should act according to which "logic." Helping the weak can override considerations of respect and control over women's bodies, motivating passengers of a minibus to rescue a girl from very likely abuse at the hands of the police. But if the person running after the girl would have been her father, a different dynamic might have evolved in favor of moral virtues that foreground discipline and control. Sometimes, helping the weak can also take violent forms that victimize others—as, for example, in mob attacks on churches incited by rumors claiming that women who had converted to Islam were being held captive inside. Much is due to the spontaneous dynamic of a situation and the combination of the sensibilities it evokes.

This does not mean, however, that I advocate reducing morality and moral action to specific moments and situations. Morality is not just as an issue of obeying or disobeying norms; it is a question of cultivating a character and a habitus, of imagining and leading a good life. This turns us to the key question of doing the right thing not just as something bound to a specific moment but also concerning the trajectory of a person's life.[8]

## Ambivalence and Integrity

When I asked Abdelnaser, a young shopkeeper in the village about what he considered a good life, he replied without hesitating that it would be simply "living according to the Qur'an and the Sunna." Having said that, he immediately added that unfortunately, the way things are, with people being driven by greed and materialism, this is at the moment impossible. Such comments, contrasting high ideals and a much more cynical view of reality, constitute a central topos of moral discourse. The basic claim of this very common critique is that "in this village" or "in our society" all that really counts is money, and true moral values have no importance anymore. This is a form of moral critique that at once establishes a value and offers an excuse. By insinuating that if it weren't for all this money and materialism, people really would be able to live happy, God-fearing lives in justice and harmony, the critique of materialism at once establishes important moral sentiments and ideals, and explains why it is not possible to live according to them. Doing so, it allows one to leave moral maxims unrealized, and so those maxims remain perfect, free of conflicts and contradictions. Such forms of moral critique and protest are thus not simply expressions of discontent and disagreement. More important, they are expressions of the essentially ambivalent and ambiguous nature of moral discourses and practices. The critique of materialism is a way *not* to negotiate moral aims with other aims, both moral and amoral. It is a way to hold high the perfection of a moral ideal in face of a complicated and troublesome life. The explicit rigor of a moral aim is not a proof of moral rigor in practice, and at times it may even indicate the opposite.

Although Abdelnaser immediately relativized his assertion that a good life would be one lived "by the book," his critique of materialism was not only an excuse. He was seriously concerned with finding a reasonable middle ground amid the ambivalence of everyday morality and amorality. By referring to the ideal foundation of life in the Qur'an and the Sunna, and by contrasting it to the amorality of daily life, Abdelnaser tried to communicate to me his understanding of moral integrity in a complex life: holding to the true word of God as a guideline while living among greedy and materialistic people.

The moral world that I have tried to sketch here in a very rudimentary fashion is often a very oppressive one, inspiring not only trust and sympathy but also distrust and anxiety. There is much trouble, fear, and anxiety involved in knowing to judge a situation appropriately, worrying about one's reputation, and making at times difficult choices. Morality, especially in terms of respect and reputation, often takes the shape of predatory moralism, of crediting and discrediting people according to their perceived qualities and shortcomings. Many everyday interactions, be they trade, friendship, marriage, or hospitality, involve different kinds of obligations and considerations, and failing to take them into account can easily lead to a scandal. Especially in a rural community a scandal can seriously damage one's respect, and in turn the marriageability of one's children and one's access to resources and services. In consequence, silence, double standards, and dishonesty are not just coincidental; they are an absolutely necessary element of living a good life as an individual, a family member, and a neighborhood or village resident.

It is from this background that we have to approach the striving for moral integrity that people often express and appreciate. The criticism of materialism and hypocrisy (*nifaq*) is telling of a genuine concern for moral integrity in a world where such integrity is difficult to have.

The registers of moral speech and action that I have tried to develop here are not just senses of instantaneous action. They offer specific senses of embodiment and personhood, and also specific ways to think about moral integrity: being kind (*tayyib*), being courageous and manly (*jada'*), being respectable (*muhtaram*), being religious (*mutadayyin*), being a good mother or a good father. Ideally one should embody all of these moments, but in practice one is not expected to embody them all at the same time. This sense of essential and legitimate ambivalence is often expressed in colloquial proverbs, most fittingly in one that states, "There is an hour for your heart and an hour for your Lord" (*sa'a l-qalbak w-sa'a l-rabbak*). In other words, there are times to see after different obligations, aims, and desires. This is not just a question of a degree of ambiguity to allow for leeway. In my view, it is a question of a fundamental moment of human condition: while moral discourses and the strive for moral integrity can be inspired by an ideal of a complete, overarching set of embodiment, moral aims, and character, in practice humans do not have just one sense of embodiment, one simple basis of character, nor do they have one single set of aims (see Gregg 2007). And nor is moral integrity in practice an issue of following one consistent line of cultivation. Rather, different lines of integrity and consistency emerge (see Kaya 2010), some parallel and some crossing, some dynamic and some frustrated. The power of moral discourses and sentiments lies less in their factual unity and consistency and more in the way they offer a sense of consistency and direction without necessarily excluding other senses, other directions.

Herein lies the most attractive and yet most troubling power of the Islamic revival. Unlike all other moral registers, religion in its revivalist sense of living according to the Qur'an and the Sunna is often argued for in the sense of a genuinely comprehensive and holistic commitment to pious personhood and social relations. To be "committed" (*multazim*), in the dictionary of revivalist Islam, is not just to obey God's commands. It is to develop a character completely devoted to God's commands in every respect and every moment. It is to overcome all ambivalence and to form a comprehensive and consistent God-fearing personality.

We face two different senses of moral integrity here. One, based on the recognition of ambivalence as a key condition of life, is about living up to specific demands and ideals at appropriate moments. Another, based on the revivalist promise of perfection, is about doing away with ambivalence for good and replacing it with meticulous clarity. This difference has a history.

The religious promise of clarity and perfection has not always been around with the same power of persuasion. While the religion of Islam has always offered a key idiom of morality, good life, and personhood, earlier periods have often been dominated by ideals of piety that have centered less on the issue of ritual and moral rigor. This is clearly the case with Sufism (Islamic mysticism), which until the twentieth century formed the most important sense of religiosity throughout Egypt and most of the Muslim world. The emphasis on spiritual union with God and the hierarchies of sainthood and grace never replaced the importance of ritual practice and ideals of obedience (*ta'a*) to God. But they did provide notions of religiosity that focus on help and comfort rather than the perfection of normative knowledge and practice (Schielke 2012a). These mystical notions have been increasingly marginalized by the pursuits of clarity, positive knowledge, and moral perfection. These pursuits are not the exclusive privilege of revivalist (especially Salafi) religiosity, however. They are closely connected with the ideology of developmentalist nationalism, which posits the ideal of a rational, committed, and disciplined citizen who, much like the ideal Salafi believer, has "awareness" (*wa'y*), that is, clear and authoritative knowledge, and a correspondingly sound ethical disposition. This is a notion of society, religion, and the subject that, in its secular and Islamist varieties alike, centers on discipline, clarity, and consistency in service of a grand purpose (see Schielke 2007, 2012b; Winegar 2008).

Yet although developmentalist modernism and revivalist religiosity are strongly motivated by the hope to overcome hypocrisy and ambivalence, they more often than not become part of, or even contribute to, new contradictions that in turn prompt people to a critique of hypocrisy. In this tone Fouad, a schoolteacher, complained to me about his colleagues. After I had once visited his workplace in eastern Alexandria, he had faced questions by his colleagues that he found outrageous:

> At the school people come up with stupid questions about you, like one guy who came and asked, "Why don't you try to make him [Samuli] convert to Islam?" I told him that the man has studied our religion and knows it well enough to make his own decision, it's his choice and none of my business. His next question was: "Well, did he then at least bring you a sex video?" That's a

total contradiction; one question cancels the other, you cannot ask them from the same person!

For Fouad, inquiring about conversion to Islam and sex videos from the same person in the same conversation not was not only a sign of hypocrisy and stupidity but also an insult to his own sense of moral integrity. His annoyance was not only directed at the obviously ambivalent concerns expressed by his colleague—Fouad willingly admits to being a complex person with at times contradictory expectations for life and himself. What Fouad really criticizes about his colleagues is his lack of practical judgment (in Fouad's words, his "stupidity") to make sense of the situation, the person one speaks with, and the consequences implied in one's words and deeds. This is an important nuance. There is a fine but significant difference between the idea of moral integrity in the sense of consistently following a clear path laid out ahead of one by a corpus of objective knowledge, and moral integrity in the sense of thinking and acting responsibly as a complex person in a complex world. If the first is what people in Egypt often openly proclaim and aim for, the latter is what is often required from them in their lives.

# 3 Knowing Islam

More often than not, the demand for clear commitment and consistency does not replace the ambivalence and ambiguity of living "an hour for your heart and an hour for your Lord." Still, it is a very compelling and attractive demand, which raises the question, if the promise of pious moral perfection does not deliver pious moral perfection, what does it deliver? To answer that, this chapter looks at the emotional tone and underlying concerns of the pursuit to know one's religion. Even if evidently unrealized, the pursuit of serious truth can provide moments of firm hold that are urgently needed in a not-so-perfect, not-so-serious life.

## A Moment of Truth

One evening in late 2008, I was sitting with a small group of young men in one of the many cafés in the village. As was often the case, this informal gathering of men (only men—women never attend cafés in the village) was characterized by an ongoing discussion flowing from one topic to another, from the global economic crisis to the prospects and perils of migration; to the Iraqi journalist Muntazar al-Zaydi, who two days earlier had thrown his shoes at George W. Bush at a press conference; to a variety of jokes and anecdotes. In the course of the discussion, someone's very religious uncle was mentioned. A bricklayer by profession, the uncle was known to be not only very pious but also a very slow worker. Someone commented: "He recites the Fatiha (the first chapter of the Qur'an) for every brick he lays!" Laughter followed. Someone else was inspired to tell of how he witnessed at a funeral a woman expressing her emotions very loudly. Her brother came to her and tried to make her calm down by asking her to recite the Fatiha, to which she replied, "I don't remember it!"

This story caused general amusement over the idea that someone could be so uneducated that she wouldn't even know the Fatiha (which is very short and memorized by practically everybody) by heart. It prompted Hilmi—Tawfiq's uncle who is only two years his senior—who was at that time a student of English literature at a provincial university not far from the village, to tell another funeral anecdote about a man who insisted on receiving his father's body in the grave. The man descended into the grave backward (which, Hilmi pointed out to me, and here for the first time his tone of speech took a more serious note, is how it should be, according to Islamic law) but forgot that another person was still inside the grave digging it. That person grabbed his ankle and the man was so shocked that he fainted. One of the men didn't get the joke, so Hilmi told it again, and everybody laughed about the shock of someone grabbing your ankle from the grave. At this moment Hilmi, now much more serious and calm, moved on to argue that the act of receiving the body in the grave should, "in Islamic law" (*fi al-shar'*), be done by a family member, just as washing the body, and that the event of funeral should be calm and consist of reading the Fatiha, and there should be no loud emotions or noise, because that is "of course forbidden" (*tab'an haram*).

Others listened calmly and seriously. But the talk took a different turn again. One of the people present took the theme of death and funeral as an occasion to tell a ghost story about a printer at the university that started working on its own account. Sheets of paper were printed, lifted to the air, and piled in rapid tempo as if by an invisible hand, but when security arrived, the sheets of paper were back in the box and blank. This inspired others to tell more ghost stories, but also to raise doubts and discuss whether they could be true, and from there, someone started telling stories about children who were dressing up as ghosts to scare people at night. By this time, everyone was back laughing and joking.

Among the people I know in the village of Nazlat al-Rayyis, Hilmi is a consistently religious person by conventional standards. As long as I have known him, he has kept his daily prayers. He is quite knowledgeable about religious debates and judgments. Unlike most men of his age whom I know, he does not smoke cannabis, and he is generally considered a responsible person in his interactions with others. Although he is opposed to Islamist politics and has never been an active member of any religious group, his views of ritual practice during this time did come close to the Salafi reformism that, by the first decade of the twenty-first century, had become one of the most powerful religious currents in Egypt and much of the Muslim world (see Meijer 2009). Yet this is only one side of him. Notorious for his irregular sleeping hours, Hilmi was a talented yet extremely undisciplined student when this discussion took place, and very unhappy about his life in a village that, he felt, was choking his aspirations, which were mainly artistic in nature. A fan of Arab pop music and Hollywood films, and a passionate reader of world literature, Hilmi would spend much of his time deciphering the plot conventions of American cinema, reading novels, and improvising songs and satirical plays with his friends. He also has an encyclopedic knowledge of jokes, riddles, and anecdotes, which he also stores on his mobile phone and exchanges with his friends.

Hilmi was, during that period in his life, part of a powerful cultural mainstream in Egypt, one in which cultural production has a high status, in which the cultivation of humor is highly valued as a crucial part of everyday interactions, and in which being a good and responsible person is closely connected with command of religious knowledge. It is a mainstream of different parallel currents that often do not fit together, but also do not cancel each other out. When Hilmi spoke about funerals, he sounded very much like the pious activist Muslims who aim to shape life and society according to a conservative vision of God-fearing perfection. Yet while he agreed with a Salafi-inspired understanding of proper ritual practice (where preventing expressive mourning by women is a major concern—see Becker [2013]), he did not pursue a life of religious commitment (*iltizam*), and his views of life and society are heavily at odds with those promoted by Salafi and other Islamic activists. His love for arts and literature were not at all framed by the aim to Islamize arts and entertainment, which had gained increasing popularity in Egypt (see Winegar 2008; van Nieuwkerk 2008, 2013). He was interested in *ibda'* (creativity, cultural production) for its own sake, for the sake of broadening his horizons of ideas and expectations. When he spoke about music and cinema, one could equally well mistake him for a "secular subject" along the lines of the nationalist modernism disseminated by many institutions of the Egyptian state. And when he was depressed and could not wake up to a day that once again would provide nothing new, theories of revivalist piety and secular subjectivation equally fail to tell what he was up to.

How, then, are we going to understand his convincing certainty and seriousness when he, in the middle of a gathering of jokes and funny stories at the café, carefully details the requirements for the discipline of emotions at a funeral? It would be mistaken to think that the complexity of the situation and his character would somehow make banal or invalidate this moment. It certainly does not. The moment he speaks about Islam as a Muslim with the authority of textual knowledge and ritual practice, Islam indeed is a consistent, perfect, and accessible ground for moral action. Its perfection, however, lies less in its capacity to determine an entire life and character—which it rarely does—than in its peculiarly fleeting nature, accessible anytime but seldom realized. (Religion in its revivalist modality of moral perfectionism is, more than anything else, a promise) As a promise, it is always available (but also at times avoidable), it provides a ground for an ongoing striving (Khan 2013), it is pure and untainted (Simon 2009), and it is also elusive.

Looking at the religious practice of Muslims who have come to embrace revivalist ideals of religiosity around the world, what quickly stands out is their strong emphasis on knowledge. In different parts of the globe, people establish reading groups, attend lectures and conferences, read booklets and online fatwas, memorize the Qur'an and study the Sunna (the authoritative tradition of the Prophet Muhammad). This was also the situation in Egypt in the years before 2011. In a country where the market for books is generally small, the market for religious books flourishes. Religious satellite television channels providing religious explanations, answers, and debates on a vast variety of issues have become very popular in just a short period of time (see Maguire 2009). People who own computers often engage in an extensive exchange of religious texts. The motivation of these practices is frequently framed as a pursuit to "know one's religion." Of course, acquiring knowledge in this way is not the only important form of religious discourse. The study of religious texts (including visual and audio texts) has by no means excluded other forms of mediation, such as charismatic preaching (Hirschkind 2006b) or dream visions (Mittermaier 2011). But textual knowledge has become a paradigmatic path to and marker of religiosity, and the most dynamic one. This begs the following question: In what sense have Muslims previously not known their religion? In other words, what kind of knowledge is at stake? Why is all this knowledge so important?

The questions and debates at stake have a primarily moral focus and generally deal with the proper normative conduct and character of Muslims. And this clearly is a key preoccupation involved in religious knowledge. But identifying the pursuit of religious knowledge as moral or ethical does not yet allow us to understand the grounds that make it credible and compelling. The questions that arise, then, are, What are the existential concerns involved in this ethical project? What exactly do people want to know about Islam? The question that concerns me here is the relation between existential concerns, moral pursuits, and the paradigm of knowledge involved.

## Salafism and the De-traditionalization of Islam

The contemporary urge to know one's religion is intimately related to the emergence and successful spread of a religious current that has a very special place in the Islamic revival: Salafism (*Salafiyya*), a religious reform movement that emerged in the early twentieth century and has become a serious contestant for theological hegemony in the early twenty-first century (Meijer 2009; Gauvain 2012). The age of the Islamic revival is crowded with different movements and groups that share the aim of making religion the central source of moral, social, and political life—such as the Muslim Brotherhood, various Sufi groups, countless urban mosque and reading groups, conservative preachers like Muhammad Mutawalli al-Sha'rawi (see Chih and Mayeur-Jaouen 2002), global media muftis like Yusuf al-Qaradawi (Gräf and Skovgaard-Petersen 2009), and neoliberal piety counselors like 'Amr Khaled and others with the habitus of the new upper middle classes (Lutfi 2009). But it is the Salafis who during the past ten years have most successfully set the tone and terms of religious knowledge in working-class and lower-middle-class milieus in Cairo and northern Egypt, the most populous part of Egypt (Gauvain 2012).

Salafism has its roots in an intellectual movement of Muslim religious experts in Syria and Egypt who, over several generations, moved from a tradition of scholarly Sufi reformism to a new hermeneutics that criticized the dominance of the four Sunni traditions (*madhhab*) of law and demanded that rather than sticking to the tradition of a chain of scholarly authorities, Islamic legal and theological reasoning have more space for *ijtihad*, direct engagement with the Qur'an and the Sunna (Weismann 2001; Hudson 2004). This movement, which took on the name Salafism only in the 1920s (Lauzière 2010), was in many ways inspired by the "Wahhabi" movement (called such only by its opponents[1]) that had emerged in Najd in the eighteenth century and came to dominate the Arabian Peninsula after its conquest by the Sa'ud family after World War I. Today, the difference between Salafism and Wahhabism is fluid, to say the least. The oil-based wealth of Saudi Arabia and the returning migrants and students who were inspired by Wahhabi Islam have turned the Wahhabiya from an obscure sect into a serious contender for worldwide religious hegemony. In Egypt, Salafism has transformed from an intellectual project to a popular piety movement—and since 2011, a serious contender for political power.

During the 1990s and 2000s, Islamist movements that challenged the power of the state faced repeated waves of heavy-handed repression. It was a golden hour for the Salafi movement, which (at that time) highlighted private piety and morality, and therefore gained tacit approval of the government. This does not mean that Salafism of the Mubarak years was not political. Puritan piety

Figure 3.1. Salafi men with books at the Cairo International Book Fair, February 2006.

involves a distinct and radical vision of society. But not posing any challenge to the Mubarak regime was the condition under which the thriving network of Salafi preaching, teaching, and media were able and allowed to act.² In this period, Salafism gained much ground with the help of satellite television and an extensive network of mosques, and at the expense of established religious institutions such as the Azhar, Sufi orders, and the Muslim Brotherhood. Salafism has also significantly influenced the religious common sense of those who do not belong to or even support the Salafi current. Committed (*multazim*) Salafi activists are distinctly recognizable by their style of dress, which they believe to be an imitation of the Prophet Muhammad and his companions: men with long beards but shaved moustaches, and short-hemmed *gallabiya*s or trousers, and women with full face veils. While their numbers are relatively small, a much larger part of Muslims commonly subscribe to some Salafi doctrines and view committed Salafis as truly religious people.

The key feature of the contemporary Salafi movement is its demand that the Qur'an and the Sunna can and must be made the direct source of all aspects of life. There is, of course, nothing new about the idea that the Qur'an and the Sunna should guide the life of Muslims—this is a view that has been commonly held throughout the history of Islam. What is novel about Salafism, however, is the idea that Islam is a simple, clear, and coherent system that everybody with basic literary and language skills can and must access directly.

This direct access should not be confused with democratic notions of pluralism and deliberation. Salafis and other Muslims have repeatedly reminded me that Islam is not a matter of opinion. It is something that exists independently of the opinions and acts of Muslims. This is mirrored in common parlance, where Islam—rather than God—commands, prohibits, states, knows, and guides. Egyptians' increasing turn to Salafi-inspired piety is therefore not so much about people becoming religious—most of them have been religious already. Rather, there is a shift from a presence of God, the Prophet Muhammad, and Muslim saints (the last are categorically rejected by Salafis) in everyday life into the study and application of Islam an external, independent, and factual system, crystallized as common sense in the expression *id-din keda*, "it's like that in religion."

What is the ground of the common sense with which Muslims today grant "Islam" and "religion" such factuality, even something like a will of their own? The Salafi revivalist paradigm of religious knowledge has two distinctive and explicit key premises (I take up some implicit ones later). The first is that the Qur'an and Sunna are the sole and in every way sufficient source of religious knowledge. The second is that Islam is a coherent system of commandments, prohibitions, and metaphysics that can be rationally discovered by means of studying scripture (see, e.g., al-'Uthaymayn 1998). This is very strongly mirrored in the vast market for religious texts that share a manual-like approach. Most of them are modern works organized as accessible catalogs of commandments and regulations. There is a strong tendency to present and to study Islam in the form of a science textbook or a manual that contains a systematic and detailed overview of possible problems and solutions, always carefully documenting the evidence at hand (Becker 2009).

This is by no means obvious, given the heterogeneous and unsystematic nature of the authoritative texts of Islam. The Qur'an, which Muslims—with very few exceptions—believe to be the exact and unchanging word of God, does not have a clear narrative structure but consists of a complex array of verses with changing topics. Rather than coming together as a coherent whole, many verses actually contradict each other, which has compelled generations of Muslim scholars to try to establish their exact order of revelation, on the basis of the premise that those which are last in order of revelation are the authoritative ones. The situation is even more complex with the Sunna, which consists of a very large number of hadiths, reports about the Prophet Muhammad's and his companions' sayings and deeds. The body of hadiths is vast and contains a very wide range of topics. For one thing, Sunni and Shia Muslims have significantly different collections of hadiths. More crucially, also the numerous collections recognized as authoritative by Sunni Muslims only partly overlap, containing as they do very different, often contradicting and contested hadiths. And unlike the Qur'an, which stands beyond doubt, the authenticity and reliability of specific hadiths is subject to continuous debate and contestation.

Partly because of this complexity, Muslim traditions of scholarship and law have until recently been highly pluralistic and only accessible to trained experts.[3] There are four Sunni traditions of law, each with a different approach on a number of key issues, all recognized as correct and authoritative. Until the nineteenth century, Islamic learning and spirituality were based on chains of transmission: textual transmission of the Qur'an and the tradition of the Prophet, transmission of religious sciences from teacher to student, genealogical transmission of prophetic descent, and spiritual transmission of sainthood from spiritual guide to disciple (Eickelman 1992; Reichmuth 2009). In this period, Islam was indeed a tradition in the sense of being personally connected to the Prophet Muhammad by an ongoing chain of transmission.[4] This is powerfully expressed in the way a hadith by the Prophet Muhammad: "Who shakes my hand, or shakes the hand of who shook my hand enters paradise" is transferred from the teacher to the pupil by a handshake.[5] Like the hadith itself, this handshake has gone down along the entire line of transmission. Through a chain of transmission, the receiver of the handshake receives (and eventually will pass on) the Prophet Muhammad's proper handshake.

Today, the Prophet's handshake has given way to much more textbook-like manuals of religious conduct. An intimate personal veneration of the Prophet remains the focal point of Muslim religious devotion, but the nature of this relationship has shifted. The most important success of reformist revivalism in the twentieth century has been the gradual replacement of this tradition-based mode of transmission and authority by one based on the direct reference to the text. It is not a depersonalized one, however, and the scholarly and spiritual authority of the teacher-sheikh is crucial for Salafism today (see Gauvain 2012). But the emphasis has shifted. The knowledge of Islam has become to a certain degree de-traditionalized, transforming from the command of chains of transmission based on a strong sense of history and personal links to a search for the pure, original truth underneath the potentially corrupting layers of history. It is thus not the revival of a tradition of religiosity against a secular regime of power but the articulation of new religiosity based on a common sense that has been significantly informed by the ideologies, aspirations, and vocabularies of nationalism, progress, capitalist consumption, and positivist reason (Hafez 2011).

## The Hermeneutics of Facts

The image we gain from this short exploration of religious knowledge is puzzling. There is a powerful sense of there being one objective doctrine of Islam that is not only true but also simple, clear, coherent, and accessible. But this sense is built up on a textual basis that is complex, contested, and contradictory. From where, then, does its air of objective clarity emerge? To answer this question, we need to take a slight detour through modern intellectual history.

The Salafi sense of religion as the discovery of objective facts shows a striking similarity to the nineteenth- and twentieth-century philosophical and intellectual movement of positivism. Three assumptions mark the common ground shared by most, if not all, currents of positivism. First, knowledge can be based only on experience. Statements that cannot be reduced to experience are "senseless," that is, not proper statements. Second, knowledge is by definition nominalistic; that is, it offers only generalizations and abstractions on the basis of empirical data but does not add any new content to those. Third, value judgments and normative statements lack the empirical content that could qualify them as knowledge (Stöltzner and Uebel 2006: 11–17; Bryant 1985: 2–6). The key concern of positivism in philosophy and the natural and social sciences has been to enable the collection of data that are unmediated and uninfluenced by normative expectations or theoretical biases, and to articulate theories that are empirical and universal.

As a philosophical epistemology and a theory of science, positivism was largely discredited and abandoned by the 1970s and 1980s (see Kuhn 1996; Lakatos and Musgrave 1970), but it continues to exert great influence in the form of a banal common sense conveyed by textbooks and popularized science. There is a great aesthetic attraction to the idea that it is possible to get down to the basic facts and use them to carefully build an objective model free of ideology and personal opinion.

The hermeneutics of the Islamic revival are not positivist in the sense that they would privilege empirical observation. But they do make a very similar distinction between observation statements (i.e., statements that have empirical content) and opinions and speculation that do not qualify as knowledge. Where positivism celebrated empirical observation, Salafi and other revivalist hermeneutics celebrate the Qur'an and the Sunna as the irreducible unmediated bases of knowledge. Religious knowledge, in this view, consists only of generalized commandments and doctrines that are extracted from that textual base in a rational, logical way without adding anything—very much in line with the positivist postulate of nominalism. Importantly, although religious knowledge is essentially normative, it is emphatically different from opinions. Right and wrong, in this hermeneutics of facts, are not about making up one's mind; they can and must be based on observable religious facts (see Becker 2009; Meijer 2009).

The similarity of positivism with this religious hermeneutics of getting down to the facts is anything but coincidental. I cannot claim a cause-effect relation in favor of one or the other. But there certainly is a shared genealogy in the form of a banal positivist common sense disseminated by administrative practices, schoolbooks, and science curricula, and the rise of a religious hermeneutics of direct access to scripture, both emerging and establishing themselves in the nineteenth and twentieth centuries. Ever since the colonial period, Muslims in Egypt—and all over the world—have shown a striking urge to argue that their religion is rational. But why should a religion be rational? This question did not arise, at least not with any urgency, until the emergence of European colonial hegemony of power and knowledge. A key part of this hegemony was a discourse that described "the Orient" and consequently also Islam as deeply backward and irrational in contradistinction from the alleged rationality and superiority of European science and virtues. In response, intellectual elites of Egypt and other Muslim countries put a lot of effort into reformulating Islam as something rational and functional—a prime case of how hegemonic power works (Mitchell 1988; Starrett 1995a; Schielke 2007).

Positivism not only had great intellectual appeal—it also became associated with high social status as the kind of knowledge involved in the work of scientists, engineers, and doctors (El Shakry 2007: 10–11; Bryant 1985: 11–33). In the past fifty years, more and more people have had access to various levels of state education—an education that, especially in the fields of natural sciences, engineering, and medicine, is heavily influenced by a commonsense positivism of objective facts and universal knowledge. It is not a coincidence that the Islamic revival as a whole has been primarily driven by the middle classes that emerged in the twentieth century, and that the militant Islamist groups of the 1970s to 1990s mainly recruited among students of agriculture, medicine, engineering, and sciences—upwardly mobile people equipped with a simple and compelling paradigm of objective, universally applicable knowledge. These modes of learning were also involved in religious school education: "'Knowing' Islam means being able to articulate the religion as a defined set of beliefs such as those set down in textbook presentations" (Starrett 1998: 9; see also Eickelman 1992).

A shift in hermeneutics involves also a shift in the sense of religious and moral conduct. In the *Book of Disciplining the Soul*, one of the volumes of his extremely influential treatise *Ihya' 'ulum ad-din*, the mediaeval Muslim thinker Abu Hamid al-Ghazali (d. AD 1111) presents a wealth of anecdotal evidence to argue that good character (*akhlaq*—the same word also translates as "morality" and "ethics" in contemporary Arabic) is more important than ritual obligations and legal norms (al-Ghazali 1995: 3–50). Such valorization of good character as something that can be separated from ritual obligations and adherence to legal norms is largely absent in the contemporary revivalist ideal of moral personhood as expressed in the ideal of *iltizam*, the commitment to religion as a complete set of norms, practices, sentiments, and will. By conflating the ethical and emotional with the textually normative, this ideal defines textual knowledge as essentially marked by a specific emotional tone and a specific moral orientation.

We can see this well in Hilmi's change of tone when he took the anecdote about the man fainting at a funeral as an occasion to lecture on the proper emotional tone of funerals. An emotional tone of stern solemnity characterised his speech on two levels: on the level of a discipline of emotions that, he argued, is "of course" commanded by religion; and on the level of the emotional tone that himself—temporarily—embodied while making his argument. On both levels, to know Islam is to cultivate an emotional disposition of solemnity, discipline, and vigilance.

In a study of the transformation of Orthodox Judaism, Haym Soloveitchik (1994) argues that there is an intrinsic relationship between vigilance and the turn to text as the key medium of religious faith. According to Soloveitchik, the destruction of traditional European Jewish community life in the Holocaust and the integration of American Jewry into middle-class white society from the 1960s on marked a point of transformation of Jewish Orthodoxy whereby the central locus of learning to live a religious life shifted from the household and community to text and scholarly authority. This turn to text has created a sheer endless need for ever more detailed regulations, because, unlike learning by doing from one's family and neighbors, learning to do something well by the means of a manual is a tricky task indeed, requiring ever more detailed advice and constant vigilance. The point is not that textual religious knowledge is disembodied. Revivalist learning to know Islam is all about learning to embody a set of attitudes and sensibilities (Mahmood 2005). But compared to an earlier tradition of learning by doing, in which the role of religious text is ritual and protective more than disciplining and guiding (Fawzi 1992; Starrett 1995b; Schielke 2006), learning from text is a rather different—by nature more meticulous, more systematic, and more inflationary—work of embodiment.

As Soloveitchik (1994) points out, the turn to text does not come from out of nowhere. It emerges from a historical condition, from an experienced need to know. What, then, are the underlying reasons to learn to know Islam?

## Reasons to Know

The power of the hermeneutics of facts lies in the manner in which it makes it possible to express and reinforce specific existential and moral concerns by presenting them as positive and universal facts.

Muntasir, brother and business partner of Abdelnaser (see chapters 1 and 2), is a great fan of the Salafi television preacher Abu Ishaq al-Huwayni, who has a daily lecture on the al-Nas channel, which, along with a number of others of its like, broadcasts exclusively religious programming with a distinct Salafi approach. Abu Ishaq presents himself as a learned scholar of hadith, the most valued form of religious knowledge for Salafi hermeneutics. As a virtuoso, he combines these scholarly credentials with a strongly colloquial, personal style of discourse and an argumentation that relies heavily on a characteristically Egyptian sense of wit and friendly and sympathetic conversation.

I went to visit Muntasir one afternoon in 2009, soon after he and his brother had given up their shop and his brother had migrated to Saudi Arabia for work. Muntasir had recently broken off his engagement to a girl from the village after a disagreement about money between them. He was now waiting for a visa to follow his brother, and having no bride, no work, and no money, he had much free time. As I arrived, I met him watching a lecture by Sheikh Abu Ishaq, who was discussing the issues of *niqab* (women's full face veil) and the circumcision of girls, both practices that had been recently condemned by Muhammad Sayyid Tantawi, at the time president of the Islamic al-Azhar University and generally considered Egypt's highest religious authority. In response, Abu Ishaq and other Salafi preachers had started an intensive campaign against Tantawi, insisting that even if niqab and the cutting of girls' genitals may not be explicitly sanctioned by Islamic scripture, in light of the "current moral crisis," they were obligatory for Muslims. Muntasir followed the sermon with a high degree of concentration, and every once in a while he emphatically nodded or expressed his agreement. What Sheikh Abu Ishaq had to say about the need to control women's bodies greatly appealed to Muntasir. I saw things differently and expressed my disagreement to Muntasir. He insisted that he agrees with Abu Ishaq because "he's a great scholar of hadith, and religion is knowledge or science (*il-din 'ilm*). He commands the whole field of religious knowledge. [. . .] I may not understand things as well, I don't command a good knowledge, but I can follow him as an expert in knowledge." I challenged Muntasir's trust in his television sheikh by pointing out that different sheikhs often seriously disagree, but this did not deter him: "I love him, that is why I believe him rather than anybody else."

While Sheikh Abu Ishaq's credentials are based on his status as a scholar of hadith, his appeal is of a more emotional nature. He appears to be a fatherly, friendly, witty, trustworthy figure who offers the promise of a good, happy, conservative Muslim life in following the guidance that comes from the knowledge he has mastered. For Muntasir, his appeal does not lie in the specific arguments he makes, nor in the project of perfectionist commitment that Abu Ishaq and other such preachers promote. While Muntasir sees himself as religious, he does not try to become a committed (*multazim*) Muslim devoted to a life of pious, God-fearing perfection. What attracts him to Abu Ishaq's message is a mixture of his personal charisma and his morally conservative vision of a society in which things have their proper place, wives obey their husbands, people greet one another politely, and debts are paid on time but without interest.

To observe and to know anything, one needs some kind of a framework that makes it possible to expect which kind of things can be known and what is worth knowing. In other words, knowledge requires a bias, a "knowledge-constitutive interest" (*erkenntnisleitendes Interesse*; see Habermas [1969: 261]), that directs the questions one asks and the solutions one tries to find. Looking at knowledge-constitutive interests that inform the hermeneutics of the Islamic revival, three issues quickly stand out.

One of those issues is the preoccupation with a male-dominated conservative moral discipline, especially but not only in regard to sexuality, gender, and social reproduction (the passing on of social mores and class from generation to another; see Bourdieu 1984) in a way that maintains an unambiguous and solid moral order in which men and women, parents and children, all know their place and duties, generally to the advantage of patriarchal authority (i.e., men and parents), and always in a disciplined and legally correct manner. Second, and related to the first, is a concern with purity and boundaries, expressed in the great emphasis on establishing clear, unambiguous, and hierarchical difference between men and women, Muslims and Christians, Islamic and un-Islamic ideas, permitted (*halal*) and prohibited (*haram*) acts, committed Muslims and God-less secularists. A third (and this list is not exhaustive) key knowledge-constitutive interest of this hermeneutics of facts is an intensive concern with death and the afterlife. It is not a coincidence that hell and the punishment of the grave (*'idhab al-qabr*, which is crudely translatable as an Islamic equivalent of purgatory) have become some of the most recurring and emotionally powerful themes of Islamic sermons that rely on and foster the sense that the primary, if not sole, purpose of pious and moral action in this world is to avoid the ever-looming prospect of punishment (and to maximize the prospect of eternal reward) in the afterlife.

Thus, what on the surface of the argument is an insistence on reason and facts is actually an insistence on a specific kind of sentiment, an emotional and aesthetic disposition that is based on the cultivation of key anxieties and sensibilities, aligned with the promise that cultivating these sensibilities will offer one a firm hold, a clear guideline, a sense of trust and hope. Charles Hirschkind (2006b) points out that the emotions evoked by an Islamic sermon are commonly judged by both preachers and listeners as more crucial than the specific arguments involved. Thus, while the *credibility* of the hermeneutics of facts is in part (but only in part—consider Muntasir's insistence that it is love that makes him believe the words of Sheikh Abu Ishaq) due to the high social prestige and dynamic character of science textbook knowledge, its underlying *concern* is the ability to judge clearly between right and wrong, friend and foe; to keep society and family together under male and parental authority; and to achieve a sense of hope in regard to death and afterlife.

The issue of the head scarf (*higab*) and especially the debate on the face veil (*niqab*) taken up by Sheikh Abu Ishaq, are telling examples. The issue of scriptural fundament otherwise so central to the Salafi hermeneutics is marginal in discussions about *higab*, and in regard to *niqab*, its scriptural basis (or rather its lack of scriptural basis) is only taken up only by those who oppose it.[6] The numerous religious posters and stickers that admonish women to cover their hair never quote the rather complex passages on the subject from the Qur'an or the Sunna; instead, they state it in a much clearer and more categorical way: "*Higab* before

Figure 3.2. Stickers sold in front of a mosque in Cairo in April 2008. Messages from top right to bottom left: "The higab before Judgment Day"; "The higab before the Day of Regret"; "My higab—my paradise"; "Why don't you wear the higab?"; "Sister, the higab is the dress of modesty. Why do you not wear the dress of modesty?"; "Why don't you wear the higab?"

Judgment Day" or "The *higab* is an obligation like the prayer." Such admonitions appeal to a moral gut feeling about *higab* being a very important thing in religion. They refer either to a sense of gendered modesty or Judgment Day and the terrible punishments that await those women who fail to cover themselves. But they do not need to argue for the textual justification of the head scarf, because it is taken for granted, thanks to a shared firm conviction that control over women's bodies is an essential constituent of Islam.

Such admonitions would not be very compelling, however, if it weren't for the sense of urgency they are associated with. The image of Egypt drawn by Sheikh Abu Ishaq when he argues for *niqab* and the circumcision of girls is that of a nation in a moral crisis, a society in the grips of rampaging secularization and Godlessness. This vision stands in rather puzzling contrast to the increasing religiosity of Egyptians in the previous decades (Starrett 2010). Sheikh Abu Ishaq and other preachers make very competent use of this trope of moral crisis to promote an expansive set of conservative sensibilities and rules. There will always be a moral crisis, and Egypt will always be haunted by secularization. This is a strategy of proselytization that makes powerful use of the very anxieties it promises to solve. People will never be pious enough. Yet more than a trope in service of proselytization, the sense of Egyptians being a God-less nation in the grips of secularization is a more widespread and diffuse structure of feeling (Williams 1969), a sense that something is wrong in the society. In this light, claims of moral crisis and secularization appear as an expression of the experienced fact that despite people becoming increasingly religious, things are still not all right in Egypt. There is some underlying moral trouble that is addressed by, but not fully solved by, the promise of good life and the afterlife through knowing Islam.

The pursuit of conservative moral truth and the hermeneutics of facts are not opposed to a changing world. They are part and parcel of it. For example, the moral grounding of positivist hermeneutics and its emphasis on the discipline and control of gender, sexuality, and social reproduction are not identical with an unchanging conservative patriarchal normality. On the contrary, they are an effect and an element of the shattering of patriarchal normality. While the Islamic revival is characterised by a sexually anxious concern over dress, coeducation, and sociability, it also stands very much in the tradition of conscious attempts to craft a modernist and class-conscious habitus suited for women in a nationalist public sphere. The urge to accumulate conservative religious knowledge is not so much opposed to as intertwined with this move to the public (Najmabadi 1993; Abu-Lughod 1998; Reuter 1999; Moors 2006; Hafez 2011).

Herein emerges a key shift in the way moral personhood is implicated in the revivalist focus on gendered morality. In many (but not all) passages in the Qur'an and the Sunna, as well as in the conventional ways in which family relations and responsibility have been understood in Egypt, women appear as extensions of men's moral responsibility, and less commonly as moral agents in their own right. The drive to "know Islam" as the path to paradise, however, contains an important emphasis on personal moral responsibility. From this background, the heavy emphasis on women's sexual morality makes women appear much more strongly as moral subjects in their own right (Karlsson Minganti 2007, 2008; Schulz 2011).

This shift from discipline to self-discipline shows a striking resonance with the neoliberal shift of governance from public responsibility to self-responsibility and self-care (Abenante 2014). An emphasis on ethics and self-reflection has become a key mode of searching for moral certainty not only in Western Europe and North America but also among the new upper middle classes that have emerged in the wake of neoliberal reforms worldwide (Spronk 2009; Pahwa 2010). Obviously, the revivalist hermeneutics of facts involves a very different ideal of moral being than the Euro-American valorization of self-realization and freedom. Rather than freedom, the effort of deliberation, consideration, and reflection is directed at fearing God and reinforcing a conservative and hierarchical (most explicitly so in regard to gender and confession) social existence (Mahmood 2005). And yet rather than being categorically "nonliberal," the revivalist ethics of self-discipline shares a common ground with the preoccupation with self-realization: the shift from morality as the pursuit of the known good to ethics as the individualizing and reflective work on oneself, motivated by a lived experience in which neither good nor the ways to attain it are solid. The specific answers offered are different, but the condition they address is a similar one, and so are some of the techniques employed, best exemplified by the recent spread of counseling groups and online forums that discuss marital, sexual, and romantic problems in the revivalist framework of pious work of self-improvement (Mehanna 2010; Kreil 2012).

This does not mean that the hermeneutics of facts and the pursuit of conservative moral certainty are mere effects of material conditions. Material conditions that give people more or less control (and different forms of control) over their existence are certainly important. But the urge to know one's religion and the moral concerns associated with this pursuit also constitute a social dynamic in their own right, and in today's Egypt, they have become compelling partly because of the power of their prevalence. People who might otherwise care little about religious knowledge face the need to think more, and more actively, about their faith.

While the ideological aim of the hermeneutics of facts is one of uncompromising purity and clarity, in practice it accomplishes for most people something else: temporary recourse to the seriousness and clarity of religious facts is a powerful and compelling site at which one can come to terms with contradictory and at times troubling lived experience (Pandolfo 2007). And yet the turn to learning one's religion better is also constitutive of contradictions and anxieties. It offers a clear and solid foundation for moral being and action in a world that is otherwise neither clear nor solid. But it also depends on the reproduction of a sense of moral crisis and shortcoming, and the cultivation of an anxious vigilance toward anything that could relativize the certainty of religion as an absolute truth above all interpretation, negotiation, and reconciliation.

## A Shifting Firm Hold

Hilmi is a great narrator of jokes and funny stories. Like many Egyptians, he has cultivated a fine sense of humor. A good joke at the appropriate moment can take a person a long way in Egypt. And yet there is a striking absence of humor in the tone of truth that Hilmi embodied during his short lecture on funerals.[7] Although much of the conversation was very funny, and humor the leading tone of most of the discussion that evening, when it came to the proper expression of emotions at funerals, there was much less place for it. This is not to deny that Islamic religious discourse can be very funny at times. Especially Sheikh 'Abd al-Hamid Kishk (1933–1996; see Hirschkind [2006b: 58–59]), the most important voice of the Islamic revival in the 1970s and 1980s, was famous for the often hilarious jokes and comments he made in his sermons. But his humor was aimed at those he wanted to criticize or admonish. Humor in the sense of ambivalent laughter at both oneself and another (see Bakhtin 1968) is less often present in this moment of serious truth. Ambivalence would be badly out of place there because what this kind of religious knowledge is about is the opposite of ambivalence: certainty and perfection, not as a holistic project but as the cultivated emotional tone of a passing moment of eternal truth, a sense of solemn perfection in an imperfect life, at once sincere and halfhearted.

Five years later, however, something had changed. By 2013, Hilmi had become much more irreverent, and so had many of his friends. It had become common in his social circles to poke fun not only at religious people but also at current religious ideas and beliefs. Hilmi continues to express faith in the truth of Islam, but the topics that compel him to adapt a tone of certainty, seriousness, and urgency are different now.

For Hilmi in 2013, living in Cairo and active in the revolutionary movement, his political antagonism against Islamist movements would weigh much heavier than what remains of his agreement with them on ritual matters. Since 2011, different Salafi groups had entered the stage of party politics and become prominent actors in the general political and spiritual polarization. At the same time, Hilmi and others who previously had rather vague political views had come to develop more pronounced secularist visions. In consequence, Ṣalafi-inspired hermeneutics became less consensual than they used to be, and a tone of irreverence in discussions about religious matters also had become more common.

On a visit to the home of one of Hilmi's in-laws, Fouad, who moves in the same circles and shares similar views as Hilmi, began to explain his theory that before creation, God was lonely and longing for creatures, because just like humans experience a spiritual longing for the Creator, God can also experience loneliness and longing for the company of God's creatures. One of the guests, a man known for both his learnedness and his irreverence, countered that the sense of longing and loneliness are not part of our God-bound spirit (*ruh*) but are part of our bodily sensibilities that experience the sense of longing toward the spirit and, by extension, God. He then returned to the issue of creation and added, "And for all I know, we could just as well be God's dream, he is dreaming about us." To which Fouad replied, "Then give me quickly a cigarette before he wakes up!" Everybody present broke out in laughter.

In this discussion, complex theological speculation was mixed with irreverent laughter that cheerfully involved the Creator. This exercise in the "play of the mind" (Marsden 2005: 85–212) was not anti-religious, however. Irreverence does not mean that people partaking in it would have stopped putting their faith in Islam (although their Islamist counterparts might like to argue so). Rather, they approach the truth of Islam with a different knowledge constitutive interest.

A tone of seriousness is more likely go along with things that are at risk and need to be protected and guarded, whereas irreverent laughter at oneself and the world goes along with the need to explore ideas and certainties, to play around with them to see what they might be good for. The tone of serious truth linked with knowing Islam is a tone of urgency: a need to have a clear, single, firm hold in a world with little firm hold available. The tone of irreverent play of mind, in contrast, is a tone of exploration in a situation where one does have a sufficiently firm hold of certainty available. To doubt and question something, one needs certainties that are not questioned (Wittgenstein 1969). In the revolutionary situation after 2011 and among people like Hilmi and Fouad, that other firm hold was partly ideological, related to nationalism, to liberal and leftist visions of freedom, and to the valorization of confrontation and struggle. Perhaps even more, it was related to a general sense of emboldening, whereby it was more likely to simply take one's own interests and points of view as the grounds of certainty.

Just like the tone of religious truth, if studied out of context, might seem to imply a stern and devoted life in piety, bare of humor and ambivalence, also the tone of irreverence might be mistaken for a rejection of religious truth. But the very brevity of Hilmi's discussion of funerals (so brief that one person kept laughing about the joke and missed the change of tone) shows how close this tone of piety is to other, rather different emotional tones. Fouad's joke, in turn, was part of a philosophical discussion about the relationship of humans and God. Fouad explained to me on another occasion that he considers joking and laughing a privileged medium of critical knowledge. For the participants in such a gathering, he explained, poking fun and laughing was like the protective layer around an underground electric cable; it creates a space for a critical discussion that might be impossible to conduct in a serious tone.

# 4   Love Troubles

In present-day Egypt, love is everywhere. There is no film without a love story; most commercial pop songs talk of love; hearts and "I love you" signs decorate shops and houses; lovers' graffiti covers bridges and walls in cities and villages alike; and online networks and satellite channels are crowded with romantic messages featuring hearts, declarations of love, and aphorisms about what it means to be in love. Parks, promenades, and bridges are frequented by couples, dating and courting are common among young people in the cities, and most young Egyptians hope to marry a person they love. Love is a moral value in its own right, a promise of a better kind of being, a grand scheme that people put enormous faith in. And as is the way of grand schemes, love is mostly unrealized and often unhappy.

The strong presence of love wherever young people express themselves in poems, graffiti, on the Internet, and in everyday discussions, stands in a striking contrast to the equally strong presence of a morally conservative interpretation of religion that not only has a strong focus on confining all forms of heterosexual intimacy to marriage (and banning homosexual forms) but also includes a generally reserved attitude toward passion. There is a formidable tradition of Arabic love poetry, and love has a long tradition in Muslim religiosity as well. In Sufi spirituality, and when Muslims express their attachment to the Prophet Muhammad (as they have done very vocally in the wake of the Danish caricature affair of 2005 and 2006), the notion of unconditional love and devotion is very central (Schielke 2008; Mahmood 2009). And yet love has a troubled position in the contemporary religious discourse on morality. When it comes to the central grounds of anxiety—gender, sexuality, and social reproduction—that motivate the turn to religious knowledge in search for a good life, love is often (but not uniformly; see Kreil [2012: 209]) viewed with significant suspicion as an amoral desire that threatens the values of female sexual inexperience, gendered hierarchies, and gender segregation. Conventional ideals of marriage, respectability, and gender hierarchy also have little space for love, concerned as they are with establishing bonds between families and conditions for material welfare rather than with aiding people in reaching emotional fulfillment.

This does not mean that love, piety, and respect are inherently at war with one another; on the contrary, love as Egyptians commonly describe it is very much formed by its coexistence with other concerns. But at certain moments—

Figure 4.1. Lovers on Qasr al-Nil bridge in central Cairo, April 2008.

typically in relation to marriage—love conflicts with other concerns in ways that can be very troublesome for the people involved.

The anthropology of gender, family, and sexuality has witnessed an increasing interest in the affective dimension of gender, sexual, and marital relations.[1] The general tone of these studies is that romantic love is not simply a modern, Western invention that is entering the rest of the world through modernity and globalization. Instead, it seems that romantic love has long been known around the world, but it has taken on a new quality through the promises of modernity, whereby romantic love and the ideal of a love-based nuclear family emerge as an element of a modern subjectivity as well as practices of consumption that in turn create new practices of courtship and marriage, and a shift in the experience of desire.

While romance has always been present in Arabic literature, the ways people in Egypt today articulate love is an eclectic combination of different ideals of love, which incorporate a classical Arabic tradition of impossible love—with its paradigmatic lovesick hero Majnun, the melodrama of Arab soap operas, Hollywood romance, Valentine's Day, and modernist ideals of the monogamous nuclear family—to make sense of frequently contradictory experiences of passion and attachment. These ideal images and personal experiences and experiments of love articulate a narrative of subjectivity that is explicitly associated with individual fulfillment, modernity, and monogamous love marriage. And yet the issue of marriage especially often turns out to be very difficult to combine with romantic love.

The encounter of love with marriage is one of those moments when the multitude of aims people entertain collapse into a moment in which a decision must be made. It is one of the key moments in which people in Egypt are compelled to engage in intensive ethical reflection. However, the framework of ethics goes only so far in helping us understand the trouble of love. Love is often experienced as madness and marriage as destiny, and contrary to the notion of ethics that is built on the fundamental premises of freedom and the capacity to act of one's own accord, madness and destiny are not.

## Pure Passion

Love (*hubb*) is a layered and polyvalent concept in contemporary Egypt (as it probably is everywhere). It is a very central notion for people describing their and other people's motivations and characters, and it carries a general, albeit not unconditional, tone of positive valorization (Inhorn 2007: 142). *Hubb* can mean romantic and erotic attraction, sexual intimacy, obsessive longing, sympathy and liking, companionate marriage, parental and family affection, friendship, religious devotion, and a general sense of human compassion. The verb *yihibb* means both "to love" and "to make love." There is an elaborate and historically rooted language of love that describes these different feelings and expressions of love in more detail (Strohmenger 1996), but the overarching notion of *hubb* remains vast and inclusive.

In many of the love stories I know, both fictional and real, the perhaps most outstanding sentiment is that of burning, obsessive passion, which people who experience it often willingly acknowledge as a form of madness. Men describe it more openly, whereas women, whose respectability can be seriously damaged by their past love stories, tell about it only under conditions of strict confidentiality. Because retelling such stories would involve some very private knowledge about my friends and interlocutors, the following is a fictional account similar to many real stories:

> M, a young man from northern Egypt, met L, a girl from the neighboring town during their studies at a medium-level institute. They fell in love and spent much time together during their studies. After she completed her studies, they met less frequently but spoke often on the phone. M, in his early twenties, had not yet saved the funds necessary for marriage, but nevertheless he went to L's father to ask for her hand. L's father refused because L did not have property, a permanent job, or a good family line to prove that he would be a reliable and respectable husband for his daughter. M and L, determined to marry, continued to put pressure on L's parents, but without success. In the end, M gave up

and L consented to marry a suitor who was more acceptable to her parents. M is still unmarried and works to save funds for a future marriage. He continues to feel strongly for L and carries her picture in his wallet. Although he has not met her for more than two years, he frequents places where they spent time together. He now works in the same city where L lives, and he usually takes a detour on his way from work at least once a week to walk past her house. He willingly acknowledges that his behavior is "mad," but he seems either unable or unwilling to give up his madness for her. L, meanwhile, has never told her husband about her love for M (although he probably does know or at least has a hunch about it). Although she is not unhappy with her husband, she continues to have strong feelings for M, and she named her recently born son after him.

This is perhaps a very dramatic version of the story of romantic obsession. In other versions, the couple may successfully marry, either with the consent of or in spite of their families. Or only one party in the story is madly in love, while the other is more distant. In yet other versions, the burning passion is transient, and the people involved afterward look back on it, wondering what kind of "sickness" had hit them. What all these different variants do share, however, is the centrality, and the celebration, of the passionate longing of one lover toward another. While love may be mutual, it does not need to be. Unanswered love appears to be equal to, if not even greater than, a love that is fulfilled.

Everyone who has been in love can probably recognize such passionate, even obsessive longing for another. But many Egyptians, both young and old, not only experience romantic obsession—they actively perform and celebrate it as a key moment of true love. Arabic literature, poetry, and popular culture are full of loving characters and love stories, but one character stands out as the obsessive lover above all others: Majnun Layla, literally "the madman for Layla." Majnun is the pen name of Qays ibn Mulawwah al-'Ameri (died AD 688), the hero and reputed author of a collection of Arabic love poems. There are different variants of the story, but they all share the same basic setting: Qays (i.e., Majnun) and Layla know each other from childhood and fall in love. Majnun cannot marry Layla, and her father has promised her to another man. Layla travels with her new husband to his hometown, where she falls ill and dies. Majnun, left behind, reaches a state of madness; lives in the desert with the animals there; and speaks in verse of his burning, absolute longing for Layla (Majnun 2003).

The poems attributed to Majnun belong to the genre of 'udhri (virgin) love poetry, which has been popular in the Middle East since the Middle Ages, a genre that has also influenced European courtly romance and finds its echo in, among other things, Shakespeare's *Romeo and Juliet* (Andrews 1985; Scott Meisami 1987; Andrews and Kalpakli 2005). In the twelfth century, the poems were rewritten by the Persian poet Nezami in the spirit of Islamic mysticism (see Seyed-Gohrab 2003), in which the unconditional and absolute love of Majnun comes to symbolize the experience of mystical spirituality. In the twentieth century, the Egyptian poet Ahmed Shawki wrote a modernized play on the basis of the story (Shawki 1933), and contemporary poets continue to make use of the character of Majnun as the paradigmatic lover.

The most characteristic features of *'udhri* romances are their unfulfilled and tragic nature, and the simultaneous celebration of purity and madness. Love, in the way it is embodied by Majnun and Layla, is pure for two reasons: because it is absolute, and because it is unrealized. Although it is dramatically at odds with social mores of respect and parental authority, it does not present a practical alternative to it (the practical alternative would be to elope; see Marsden [2007b]). This gives the romantic obsession embodied by Majnun a peculiar ambiguity, oscillating between the willingness to do anything for the sake of one's beloved and the rather prude opposition of ideal love and actual intimacy. The point around which this ambiguity develops is the recurring theme of sacrifice, the idea of love as giving without asking anything in return.

'Abbas, a student from the village who was living in Cairo, had a girlfriend of a year or two but had split up with her. When I met him in Cairo in the spring of 2008, he expressed a critical and disillusioned view of love. He argued that true love for the sake of another person exists only in movies and books, and that what people call love is just sexual instinct. But while he in one moment criticized the young couples who crowd the bridges and promenades of the capital for "running after an illusionary desire," he was also courting a new girlfriend. He said that he did "not love her very much," nor did he know whether his courtship with this girl would later lead to marriage. He also emphasized that he knows many girls and is good friends with them, and they often ask him to go for a walk with them for the sake of an outing. But he also was emphatic that he wants their relationship to remain pure:

> You see the people on the bridges leaning on each other and touching each other. I never touched my first girlfriend, I never kissed her. It would have been against my love. It may be backward, but for me it would be out of the question to do so with my girlfriend—and if she would allow that, it would make her unacceptable for my love.

Chaste as it is, this ideal of pure love expressed by 'Abbas is at the same time highly passionate. For 'Abbas, true love is foremost about the willingness to make another person the single most important thing in one's life, regardless of everything else:

> I know someone who is plays in the junior selection of al-Ahly soccer club. He told me once: "There is this girl who loves me to the degree of madness, so much that she has to see me every day." I think this may be the closest thing to true love. He told me that once he refused to see her after a dispute between

them, and she tried to get hit by a driving car. . . . I met her and asked her: "Is this really what happened?" She said: "Yes, this is what happened. I felt that if he is angry at me, there is no point for me to live." I said: "Wow! That's a *love story*, I would like to meet a girl like that!" She said, this is exactly what she said: "When you feel that in the whole life there is nothing else than the person you love, you can do something like that." . . . That is true love.

The way 'Abbas tells about true love, commitment to a degree of madness comes together with a valorization of virginity and female inexperience such that a girl who actually agrees to intimate contacts proves herself as unworthy of love. But it would be a mistake to reduce romantic obsession to a cult of virginity. While "true love" in 'Abbas' view is somehow "opposed" to sex, it is nevertheless not disciplined or responsible (nor is it consistent, as we will see later). The valorization of obsessive, violently jealous, or self-destructive passion establishes love as a value in pure form, an ability to feel and to suffer for the sake of another. As such, love is a moral value that stands in a tense relationship with other, more responsible moral considerations such as family connectedness and reputation. This becomes especially clear when we look at the celebration of first love, which many Egyptians see as the most authentic experience of love.

'Arabi, a man in his sixties from a small town in northern Egypt, ascribes this partly to human psychology and partly also to the "constraints" (*quyud*) of Arab society that contribute to the impossible and unhappy nature of love:

> The first love is the most enduring one. The first love one has at the age of prep school, in the beginning of adolescence, is a pure, spontaneous emotion. It has nothing to do with reason and logic—it comes spontaneously. But when you grow older, you start to think about marriage, whether she is a good wife, your thinking becomes wider, you start thinking more rationally. But the first love leaves its strongest, lasting trace. It's like if you make a line on an empty paper, whatever lines you draw on it afterward will not remove the first line. . . . In Arab society there are many constraints around love. I can go and say to a woman that I hate her, that's considered acceptable, but I can't say to her that I love her—although the latter should be a better thing to say to someone. But we also say that "the forbidden is desired."[2] The deprivation created by the constraints also makes love more intensive. This love from one side that is based on pain is also described in many love stories, like Majnun Layla, 'Antara [the hero of an Arabian epic who died in the attempt to gain his tribe's approval to marry his beloved 'Abla; see Heath (1996) and 'Antara (1998)], and others, or also in European literature, like Romeo and Juliet. True love is sacrifice.

In 'Arabi's interpretation, the valorization of first love, pain, and sacrifice is not simply an extension of a patriarchal gender order; instead, it is a universal human emotion—the universality of which 'Arabi underlines through the reference to European romance side by side with Arabic poetry and epics—people cultivate love despite social constraints, but it is also shaped by them. The adolescent first love, in this view, is a pure, spontaneous emotion that has not yet been disciplined by the "constraints" of reason and social conventions—a process that in 'Arabi's view is necessary and unfortunate at once.

## Discrete Struggles

While both young and old Egyptians continue to recognize themselves in Majnun, there is still more to their love stories. Half a year later when I met 'Abbas again, he spoke in a very different tone. The previous time we met, he had done his best to present a credible, correct understanding of love, presenting himself as a capable man who knows how to talk to girls but also knows to do the right thing. This time, the tone of his talk was closer to a confession. He was missing his old love very much and told me that he could not stop thinking about her, that he kept reminiscing about the moments when he was walking with her, holding her hand, and kissing her. No talk about purity this time, and no bragging about his conquests either, but a troubled longing for a love that for a while was realized.

In the first version of 'Abbas's unhappy love story, in which he would have never kissed his girlfriend, love had to remain pure and mindful of gendered modesty. In the second, in which he reminisces about the moments he kissed her, it is inseparable from intimacy. Which one of the two versions of the story is true, I cannot tell. In any case, it may be less an issue of truth and falsehood and more a matter of different registers of speaking about love and sexuality (Kreil 2012). Majnun and Layla provide one very powerful register of love—a full-fledged theory of love, in fact—but it is not the only one, paralleled and reshaped as it is by others in which fulfillment and intimacy play a much greater role.

Looking back at the fictional account of love I presented earlier, it is worth pointing out that unlike Majnun and Layla, the contemporary lovers M and L did actually have a period, possibly a long one, of courting and dating. This period may have involved a great degree of intimacy, even sex, possibly under the cover of a secret *'urfi* marriage.[3] In any case, much love in Egypt does not remain entirely unrealized, even if it does not lead to marriage. And even when Egyptians often agree that the first cut is the deepest, this also implies that after adolescent first love, there may be other loves.

There exists, in fact, a flourishing, albeit precarious, culture of flirting, courting, dating, and secret affairs in the cities and, to a more limited degree, in the countryside. Furthermore, some Egyptians actually do manage to marry the person they love, and at least in urban northern Egypt a love match with the consent of one's parents is commonly considered the ideal form of marriage. Both the culture of courting and the daily life of love marriages imply a practice of love that is inspired by, but in important ways different from, the Majnunian ideal of pure passion. This, together with new models of love offered by the media, has contributed to a subtle shift in the way young Egyptians articulate love as an experience and a mode of subjectivity.

The most important day for lovers in Egypt—and like them others around the world—is Valentine's Day, in Arabic 'Id al-Hubb (Love Day).[4] A celebration of European and American origin (Schmidt 1993), the day is the paradigmatic moment of the culture of dating, love letters, and lighthearted romance that has become associated with being "modern" in opposition to the stereotype of a materialistic and antiromantic "backward" or "Eastern" (*sharqi*) character. On Valentine's Day, shops run a good business with small gifts that often feature red hearts and English messages such as "I love you." But many, if not most, of the celebrations of Valentine's Day take place in secrecy via text messages, phone calls, online chats, and discretely passed letters. A degree of secrecy is perhaps the most striking feature of courting and dating in Egypt, especially in the countryside, where the possibilities for young men and women to meet are heavily circumscribed by considerations of respect and reputation.

Secrecy is, in fact, the other key characteristic of love, in addition to romantic obsession. But unlike madness, which, in the Majnunian variant at least, is one sided and unrealized, secrecy is the condition in which two sides can come together and love can gain the character of mutual intimacy. Secrecy and discretion are needed every step of the way: to obtain a phone number, to make a call, to arrange a meeting, to meet again, and to mobilize relatives in support of a marriage. Online media and mobile phones have proved extremely useful for this kind of communication. Secrecy does not mean defiance of parental authority, however, but rather it is a way to protect that authority by avoiding situations in which it would be compromised or challenged (Bochow 2008; Drieskens 2006). And as Hakim, an unmarried man from the village in his midthirties, argues, with secrecy you can do what you want:

> In Europe, you can have a relationship if you want; it's easy. Here you can have a sexual relationship, too, but you are worried about respect, about religious values, about what people say, about committing adultery [*zina*]. You do it anyway, but you do it secretly.

Unlike unconditional commitment, secrecy is not a virtue in its own right. At the same time, it is more than just a necessary precaution. Practicing secrecy when appropriate is a secondary virtue that one must command in order to avoid moral conflicts and scandals.

The secret love messages and red hearts of Valentine's Day, as well as the equally secret (i.e., secret from one's relatives—especially in the mixed space of universities, where there is much space for relatively open dating; see Kreil [2012: 69]) meetings, affairs, and arrangements imply a shift in the focus of love on two levels. On one level, there is something like a widespread culture of easy romance that does not require passionate commitment but can remain on the level of pleasant play and flirtation with the condition of appropriate discretion. On another level, however, the association of love and romance with the ideal of monogamous marriage moves the focus of what is considered true love more toward a possibly successful struggle for the sake of a love marriage.

Nagat is the daughter of a family committed to Sufism (Islamic mysticism) from a village in the central Nile Delta. She spent the better part of her twenties searching for a suitable, marriageable partner, which she found excessively difficult. In her early twenties, after she had been engaged twice and both times publicly left the decision to her parents while being active in organizing things behind the scenes, she argued that while adolescent first love is a naive, lighthearted age of rosy dreams, real love is about struggle:

> When people are sixteen they want to feel that they are in love, write love letters, to live in the feeling. But later they start to think about marriage, about making sacrifices, about struggling to marry the man they love.

This is a different sense of sacrifice than that articulated earlier by 'Arabi. Nagat argues for love as sacrifice for the sake of something, not just for its own sake. While her version of love still implies the valorization of suffering and sacrifice, it also implies a demand for fulfillment. This demand, in turn, is closely associated with the outspokenly modernist ideals of love marriage and a nuclear family living in an apartment of its own that have come to saturate, rather than replace, the practice of collectively arranged marriage as a union of two families (Hart 2007).

Just as the literary heritage of Majnun has offered countless generations of lovers a model of and for their emotions, globally mediated popular culture has become an important source for the articulation of this subtle shift in the focus of love (see Larkin 1997; Marsden 2007b: 104). One such source—albeit by no means the only one (on the equally if not more important Arabic films and TV series, see Abu-Lughod 2005)—is Hollywood cinema. American films have long been popular in Egypt, and they are now more accessible than ever because of Arab satellite channels that specialize in Hollywood films and series. While among women Turkish soap operas (which swept the Arabic market around 2009 and successfully challenged the dominance of Egyptian productions) have become an extremely popular source for ideas about love and emotions, men often prefer American films, such as Tawfiq and Faruq from Nazlat al-Rayyis (see chapter 1). These films, they say, are changing the outlook they have on their lives by offering a greater variety of models for emotion and action:

> TAWFIQ: The media have very much influence on the people's ideas about love. You watch films and they give you ideas.

SAMULI: Does that mean that the stories and characters of films are examples of what kind of things are possible?

TAWFIQ AND FARUQ: Yes.

FARUQ: . . . There's one film in particular that I really liked, that gave a very strong idea of love: . . . *City of Angels*. It's a really, really strong film. In it an angel gives up his immortality and his place in heaven and goes to live on the earth as a mortal because he has fallen in love with a woman. But one day later she dies in a car crash. Imagine that sacrifice! He gives up his eternal life because all he wants to is to touch her hair. As an angel he could only see her.

Both Faruq and Tawfiq were fascinated by the tragic quality and the overwhelming power of love presented by *City of Angels* (1998), a Hollywood remake of Wim Wenders's *Wings of Desire* (1987). They found the love story of the film powerful because it was neither entirely familiar nor fully foreign; it touched known literary conventions and personal experiences but showed them from a new, unfamiliar perspective.

What makes *City of Angels* "strong" from its Egyptian viewers' perspective is the way it connects an ideal of true love as the willingness to sacrifice anything for the sake of love with the idea of fulfillment as the result of a struggle for the sake of something—even if it is just a short moment of fulfillment. The hero of the film turns from an angel into a mortal for the sake of one day and one night with his beloved, a luxury that was not granted to Majnun.

One of the most striking features of Hollywood cinema is the way it has made the gratification of desire—a key power of the consumerist age in general (see Žižek 2006)—into a cinematic principle, building a narrative world of happy endings against the odds that is rather different from the narrative world of classical tragedy. This is a shift that can also be observed in the ways young Egyptians link romantic obsession with the struggle for fulfillment. Unlike with Majnun, who had to go mad, or with Romeo and Juliet, who had to die, the love stories of today's romantic fantasy are increasingly expected to have a happy ending.

The shift from unrealized love to struggle for the sake of fulfillment does not diminish the appeal of romantic obsession—it only gains a different direction, a point made explicit by Muhammad Sa'd Shehata, a poet and journalist who moved from the village to Cairo in the 1990s, in a poem written during his early years in Cairo, "A Greeting Due to Majnun Layla":

My friend
You were great when you loved her
And Layla was generous with you
She allowed her image—every night
to visit your dreams

She gave you from her smiles
the letters of your poems
How many did you write to sweeten your loneliness?
My friend
You were truly great
when you—despite all the obstacles
saw her
And spoke to her with all you have
all you know
And now
After so many years have passed
The deserts have changed a lot
Others live there now
But your great love
—representing all lovers—
continues to sing:
"Oh Lord, bring close the houses of lovers." (Shehata 2002: 36–38)

Instead of highlighting purity and separation, Muhammad Shehata interprets Majnun's obsessive love with Layla as a union, a passionate struggle that bears fruit in moments of seeing and speaking to each other, even if only in dreams.

This moment of union that brings together romantic obsession and the struggle for fulfilled love comes along with a shift in regard to the pain of love. Resonating with the intertwining logics of capitalist consumption as a call to enjoyment (Žižek 2006) and the gratification of desire involved in Hollywood romance, love becomes linked, even if only partly, with its fulfillment. Fulfillment was rather absent in the emotional tone of *shagan*, a sense of ever-lasting melancholic longing that has long characterised Arabic songs and poetry.[5] Appreciating the story of Majnun often carries this emotional note of *shagan*, which implies a sense of pain that is valuable in itself and does not call for resolution. But with the emergence of new forms of sociability and family, *shagan* has been complemented and complicated by a more anxious sense of pain and a struggle for resolution.

## Marriage, Destiny, and the Limits of Ethics

Love has evidently counternormative dimensions. Madness is by definition the opposition of responsible, rational action. Lovers often end up doing things that bring them into various kinds of trouble. At the same time, the Egyptian lovers quoted earlier quite clearly articulate love as a matter of being a good human being toward others and oneself. To be able to love, they argue, is a virtue in its own right, something that not only is part of human nature but also is a moral quality worth cultivating. As such, it is a grand scheme not less compelling than piety and consumption. And like all grand schemes, love also is located in the ambivalent nexus between a forever-unfulfilled perfectionist promise and actual attempts to live a life guided by it.

As a grand scheme, love does not need to be fully realized in people's lives. Both the valorization of the pure unrealized first love and the secrecy of romantic encounters as they actually happen help one evade the conflicts that might emerge between love and other, often very different ideals of what it means to be a human being to oneself and others. But the conflicts are not resolved, and usually they need not be resolved. Love, just like piety, is powerful partly as an experience and partly as a promise, and although as a promise it can take the form of a supreme power that overwhelms everything else, as an experience it usually exists in a complex and often tense coexistence along with everything else. But sometimes conflicts cannot be evaded and decisions must be made. And nowhere else are the conflicts and contradictions of romantic love, sexual mores, respect, and family connectivity as strong and as urgent as they are in the struggles to bring love and marriage together.

When thinking about marriage, passion faces the formidable forces of reason, reputation, and destiny. This could be interpreted to mean that love is not a real value for people in the Middle East, because when it comes to marriage, they sacrifice it all too easily for the sake of safeguarding material interests, family alliances, and parental authority. At least in rural milieus, in most marriages, love indeed comes second, if at all, after considerations of reputation, descent, class, money, and complex arrangements between families. But this is not because people do not try to find love, or do not think highly of love. It just really is very difficult.

Lila Abu-Lughod (1996a: 258), in her groundbreaking study of Bedouin poetry in northern Egypt, points out that while an ideology of dispassionate honor is the most visible face of Bedouin society, the poetry of love and passion that people recite offers another, very different face, and it is neither possible nor meaningful to determine one of those two faces as truer or more essential than the other:

> Rather than positing one monolithic cultural ideology that determines experience, it is probably fair to say that there are at least two ideologies in Bedouin culture, each providing models of and for different types of experiences. [. . . T]hese discourses are not templates, but rather languages that people can use to express themselves.

When love comes together with marriage, different languages of expression, to follow Abu-Lughod's terms, come together, intersect, and clash. The attempt to combine love and marriage in the rural milieu is an attempt to combine two languages that not only follow different grammars but also communicate different things.

Marriage is the paramount social institution in Egypt and the Arab world. With the exception of some very specific and limited social milieus, it is impossible for unmarried couples to live together in public. Getting married is expected, encouraged, demanded, and often also enforced. Offspring are essential, and a newlywed wife must get pregnant as soon as possible after the wedding. Pregnancy without marriage, in contrast, comes with extreme social stigma and severe consequences for the mother and the children (much less so for the father), ranging from social exclusion to even murder. To get married, the couple must have an apartment (in the countryside, it should be privately owned, not rented) and furniture; the groom must provide the bride and her family with gold, presents, and money; and the bride must bring kitchen utensils for the new home. There is tremendous concern about the reputation (good or bad) that women bring upon the entire family and of the possibilities of social ascent and fears of social descent through marriage. Getting married is expensive, time consuming, and difficult; many people are involved; and it is urgently necessary.

With all these great anxieties and expectations invested in marriage, the arrangement of marriages follows a peculiar double logic. On the one hand, marriage is a highly rational, strategic business in which the people involved (including not just the groom and the bride but also parents, uncles, aunts, siblings, and friends) try to check every eventuality; consider each plus and minus; and maximize the chances of making the union a profitable, successful, and stable step in the reproduction of a family's intimate belonging, reputation, property, and status. On the other hand, it is generally and widely agreed that it is impossible to anticipate whom one will eventually marry, how life with that person will be, and whether it will work out at all. The process of marriage may be highly strategic, but its outcome is understood to lie in the realm of *nasib*, or "destiny." In the complex Arabic vocabulary of destiny, *nasib* is "destiny-as-fortune," the unpredictable turns in life or the unpredictable outcome of a course of action that one can accept and deal with but not choose or even anticipate. Of course, recourse to *nasib* is also a way to slip out of responsibility. When a marriage deal does not work out, the polite way to break the bad news is to acknowledge *mafish nasib*, "there is no luck this time." Women who are unhappy, neglected, or abused in their marriages are often encouraged by others to just try to cope with it, because it is one's *nasib*. But in addition to this evasive aspect, the language of *nasib* is also an expression of the recognition that no matter how well one plans it, marriage is a life-changing step into the unknown, a step one takes while being subject to powers that are greater than one's expectations and desires, and one can never know what really awaits.

The language of *nasib* tells that it is better to accept the fact that what comes is not in one's own hands. The language of love, in contrast, often tells of moments of pain that happen when passion meets destiny. But painful as the encounter is, it also creates new dimensions, new languages, as the thrust of love shifts from Majnunian passion to discrete struggles for the sake of something, as when marriage arrangements based on a rational recognition of destiny become instilled with expectations of romance and companionship. When people try to bring love and marriage together, as they often do, there opens a space of ethical reflection, consideration about the grounds of one's actions and possible alternatives. It is in this moment that the issue of freedom, which is absent in the language of both madness and destiny, emerges.

Magnus Marsden (2007b), in his study of love and elopement in Chitral (northwestern Pakistan), argues that idioms of love and passion are not only a language parallel to an idiom of honor and hierarchies; they form part of the complex reasoning and discussions people engage in about their situation. Marsden (2007b: 92) emphasizes that "the theoretical importance of recognizing the diversity of ways in which Chitralis themselves actively reflect upon their conceptions and experiences of the emotions." This, in fact, is also what many Egyptians are engaged in. They do not simply experience love, religion, or any other of the things important to them; they are actively engaged in trying to make sense of them, and often their attempts involve subtle shifts and redefinitions of the issue at hand.

In this sense, the encounter of love and marriage is a privileged moment of practical ethics in the sense outlined by Michael Lambek (2010), Michael Jackson (2011), Jarrett Zigon (2008), and others, the moment in which one has to reflect about one's aims, how embodied actions relate to moral ideals, what those actions and ideals are good for, and what one should do in a situation when it is not clear what one should do. Returning to the question I posed in the introduction to this book about when and why people are compelled to engage in ethics, part of the answer is that it is because they try to find space for both passion and strategic considerations when they get married. But as already mentioned, it is really very difficult.

To start with, there exists no clear distinction between a love marriage and an arranged marriage. Almost any marriage is a family arrangement to a large degree, with parents and relatives intensively involved, contracts and arrangements made, and the engagement period with its many rites of passage serving as an occasion to establish relations and obligations between families. This is also emphasized by the way an Islamic marriage contract is usually made, namely by two male guardians (usually fathers or uncles) of the groom and bride. Also, as a motivation, love is rarely the exclusive reason for marriage. While there are cases in which a couple marries out of love and against the will of their families, and others in which a couple is married by their families in the absence of any romantic attachment, or even against their will, much more often a combination of romance, interest, and arrangement is involved (see Hart 2007). Most Egyptians continue to see marriage as the union of two families rather than just two individuals. Therefore, in marriages that are motivated by a preceding romantic attachment, issues of class, reputation, descent, income, alliances, and enmities between families, furniture, housing, religiosity, and political views matter very much. Usually a marriage is a complex combination of different considerations, further complicated by the degree of necessary concealment (such as keeping a preceding romantic involvement secret) and fiction (such as doing as if the groom had come to ask for the bride's hand from her father without knowing her previously, although everybody knows that they already were in love) involved. In some cases I know, a marriage was motivated by a love relationship but it was imperative to maintain the fiction of what is called a "traditional marriage," an interest-based marriage arrangement with no romantic history.

A contemporary middle-class ideal of marriage, as propagated by Arabic films and television series, is a love match between partners from the same social class in consensus with and under the guidance of both partners' families. In practice, however, love can be both a driving force for and an obstacle to a marriage.

In the complex interplay of different moral considerations around love, sexuality, and marriage, young men have much more space in which to manoeuver than women do. While men can more easily balance different ideals of personhood, women experience much more pressure to fulfill conflicting ideals of modesty and attractiveness. Young men expect girls to be attractive and willing to meet them in cafeterias, promenades, and other such spaces that have become preferred sites for (potential) couples to meet, lest they risk being seen as "backward" (*mutakhallifa*). At the same time, however, young women's status of being respectable (*muhtarama*)—a key condition for marriage—is essentially linked to the virtues of virginity and seclusion, with the result that romantic love itself can become an obstacle in the way of marriage. In the countryside, a girl who goes out with boys is "bad" (*wihsha*) and not respectable (regardless of her virginity), and thence not suitable for marriage in the eyes of young men and their families. Or, as a friend of mine put it, "The girls you go out with are not the girls you marry." Girls who do go out with boys therefore often end up marrying from outside the village. This does not mean that young men simply take advantage of young women. Many do, and there is a predatory aspect to the way young men enter into affairs with young women (Kreil 2012: 67). Others, however, are seriously troubled and heartbroken when it turns out that considerations of descent, class, and respect make the girl they love unsuitable for marriage. This is what happened to Mustafa, a man from the village, in his early twenties when I first met him in 2006. He and his friend Tawfiq retell his story, trying to make sense of his unhappy love from the point of view of religious legitimacy of a relationship, communal reputation and respect, and family connectivity:

MUSTAFA: When I was at secondary school I met a girl. . . . I knew her a long time, full three years, and I was together with her when we were students. I was either with her in Damanhur [a provincial capital some fifty kilometers from the village], or she was with me in Alexandria, where I studied. It was all really wild and crazy, and a lot of problems happened. After that I was surprised to realize that she isn't the person that suits me, she isn't the one who should be in house, she isn't the one to bring up my children.

Here at home, I spoke to my mother, too, about marrying her. My mother of course rejected her completely. There is one more thing: descent [*nasab*]. Her descent's not good for us. I talked about it with my mother at home, I talked about it with my uncle [but they refused]. There [with her family] the matter was clear, they wanted me to come and ask for her hand, to make things clear: you know her for three years and she knows you, that's not good, there are circumstances and customs, there's a scandal about to happen.

From inside me, there are of course other things. Although my feelings toward her might have become even stronger in the meantime, in life itself, in this life we live in, is she suitable to be a wife?

TAWFIQ: Look, marriage is not just about the bed, it's about being a nuclear family [*usra*]. How can you build a marriage on the base of an illegitimate [*batil*] relationship and with people talking about you?

M: I started feeling other things. I started feeling constant doubt. How come did she get to know me this way? Couldn't somebody else just take my place with her? I started to fear her. When she would be away from me for two or three days I would call for her to talk with me. She got used to this from me; she was always telling me what she'd done in the past three days. That was the main reason inside me, she did not sense it, that I was doubting her, thinking that she could meet someone else.

SAMULI: But you, too, could meet someone else?

MUSTAFA: Inside me, I'm an Egyptian, Oriental [*sharqi*] guy, I was educated that way.

T: Here the guy can know many girls, but the girl can't know any guys.

M: As for marriage itself; if a man and a woman agree on marrying, there is a new woman entering the extended family ['*ayla*]—my mother will be her mother and my father will be her father.[6] . . . After the first experiment, I realized that there were things that I had completely forgotten and hadn't thought of: how do I find one that suits my mother and her character? I have to see what my mother wants, too. I have to find a girl whom my mother accepts.

т: You have to think about marriage from the side of religion, and from the side of material wealth and money, and from the side of education, from a lot of sides. Maybe the descent of the girl's family is not good and spoils the whole marriage. And there can be a girl who's beautiful and from good family and has money, but if she's not respectable [*muhtarama*] it's not good, it has to be all four together.

The complex moral reasoning undertaken by Mustafa and Tawfiq is telling of the difficult choices and inner conflicts young people experience. They offer a good case of the sense of ethics that Michael Lambek (2002, 2007) has developed through the concept of *phronesis*, or "practical reasoning." This kind of moral reasoning is not only about making a practical decision and weighing the different elements and requirements of a situation—it is about deciding, in the moment, who you want to be (see also Zigon 2008).

And yet the reflective moment of ethics and the practical reason of *phronesis* take us only so far. The discussion between Mustafa and Tawfiq could be interpreted as a case of practical reasoning, in which Mustafa was convinced by the argumentative power of tradition and familiar connectedness to pursue out of his own accord a conventional ideal of marriage. But two things complicate this ethics-oriented interpretation of the power of convention. For one thing, Mustafa was deeply unhappy about how it all went. Furthermore, as years passed and he started to think about marriage again, he got into conflicts with conventional expectations once more.

In the autumn of 2011, by then approaching the age of thirty, Mustafa told me that he felt that it would be time to get married. He had reached an age during which there is significant pressure on men to marry. He was not after a wild and crazy love story this time, but a marriage in the conventional framework of a family arrangement. Aware of the importance of families, reputations, and class, he was searching for a good young woman with a good reputation from a good family, preferably with roots in the village. Whenever he heard that there was a marriageable young woman in the village who fit that description, he went to visit her family as a suitor, which at times resulted in comic and painful situations when one or both parties were uninterested but found no polite way to express it. (For more marriage comedy, see Abdel Aal 2010).

In the neighborhood where he lives in Alexandria, Mustafa came to know a young woman who lived nearby and whom he found very pretty. When he first asked people about her, he was told that she was married. But later, a neighbor acting on behalf of her parents asked him if he would want to marry her. It turned out that she had been divorced after less than one year of marriage by an abusive or negligent husband. She returned to her parents' house with a baby son, and her parents were trying to find her a new husband (which is very difficult). Mustafa told me that he never had even thought about marrying a divorced woman because in the village, and often also in the cities, men are expected to marry virgins. He was well aware that divorce comes with a big stigma for divorced women. But he thought that it might not do justice to them:

> At my work there is a woman, the sister of a colleague. She got divorced by her husband, she smokes cigarettes, for a while she was wearing a *higab* and then she took of her *higab*, and people think that she is crazy and must have been a bad wife and responsible for the divorce. But who am I to judge her?

And unlike his colleague, the neighbor woman had the reputation of being modest, and he knew her family. As he thought about it, he told me, it seemed to be not such a bad idea. He took up the issue with his mother.

He in fact took it up at least twice. The second time, I happened to be present. Her reply was clear and simple:

> MOTHER: No! No way! Absolutely not! Divorcées are for men who are themselves divorced or widowed or old or poor. You marry a virgin girl. Is she is divorced she must have done something wrong and you may not be happy with her. You don't know her.
>
> MUSTAFA: But if I marry a girl from the village I also don't know her, and she might turn out to be bad.
>
> MOTHER: Then it's destiny and fortune [*qisma w-nasib*], and you make do [*titsarraf*] with it.
>
> MUSTAFA: But with the divorced girl, it would be *nasib* as well.
>
> MOTHER: No! You don't marry her! I would feel no joy in the marriage. And what would people say?

Mustafa's mother laughed, made jokes, and remained completely unimpressed by Mustafa's attempts to question why there should be anything wrong about marrying a previously married woman, especially one with a good reputation from a good family. For her, a marriage with a divorced woman would be a second-grade marriage, something that would cause embarrassment and worry instead of joy (thus foregrounding emotionality rather than rationality). He tried to engage his mother in a reflection about what the foundation of a happy marriage should be and about what counts as destiny that one accepts and what not—and run against a wall of concrete.

For Egyptian men, it is very difficult to defy the will of their mothers. Mustafa told me that he still does not see what the problem is, and continued to think about a solution, a way to marry her with his mother's consent after all. But it wasn't possible.

A year and a half later Mustafa finally did get married—and quite happily so—with another young woman, one who did bring his mother joy. It was an arranged match with a good deal of mutual affection, a good marriage by all standards.⁷ But can it be considered the outcome of ethical choices by Mustafa?

A good degree of reflection about ends and means has certainly been involved over the years as Mustafa's thinking about the marital union has shifted from wild and crazy passion to the recognition of conventional marriage and then the search for a synthesis of affection and arrangement, companionship and conventional roles. But along the way, there were also countless moments when there was no real choice, moments when he could reflect but not decide, and others when he could decide but not know what that decision really meant. Ethics was involved, but overall, it was *nasib*.

While some theories of ethics explicitly distance themselves from freedom in the sense of autonomy, they do in one way or another assume that people are capable of consciously doing something. Saba Mahmood (2005), for example, provides a convincing critique of autonomy but implicitly grants the protagonists of her book the freedom of actively pursuing the path of piety, rather than being just thrown into it. Without such more existential sense of freedom (which is not quite the same as agency; see Laidlaw [2002, 2013]), there would be little point to ethics in the sense of reflecting on the relationship of bodily acts and moral values. If one is not capable of doing—or not doing—something, or if one has no power over the consequences, what is the point of reflection and cultivation?

Both love and marriage, in their conventional form, are subject to logics that are structurally opposite to ethics and freedom. Love is associated with madness, which is the very opposite of the capacity to reflection and reasonable, responsible behavior. With all the strategic consideration involved in initiating a marriage, in the end destiny decides whom one actually marries and what the consequences are. One could of course try to develop something like a theory of the ethics of living a life that is ruled by destiny, and in fact I try to do that in the conclusion of this book. But for the moment I find it necessary to insist that people do crazy and stupid things, refuse to listen to reflection and arguments, and face situations in which decisions are made for them and not by them. Ethics would be an inadequate and misleading way to understand these situations.

Situations in which ethics is an adequate approach indeed are those in which the question of freedom arises in one way or another (see Laidlaw 2002, 2013). While both love and marriage as such have little to do with freedom (a person is usually neither free to choose whom to love nor whom to marry), when they come together, the question of freedom arises in a forceful way: "I want to marry the person I feel passionate about, why can't I?" Mustafa repeatedly sought a space of freedom in his marriage plans, but he faced powers too great to overcome. Others at times manage to actually turn such questions into more or less successful paths of action. But more often than not, some things are simply not possible, and others are very difficult.

## Freedom of the Heart

I return several times in the course of this book to the issue of freedom as something that is not absolute, but that emerges in face of specific forms of unfreedom. I also return in the conclusion to the issue of destiny, an existentially true and heuristically useful concept to understand what it means to act in a world of overwhelming powers and unknown consequences. However, for the moment, I take up one specific space of freedom that is opened up at the intersection of love and marriage. The shift of the language of love from pure passion to struggle for the sake of something is a part of this opening. Another part of this opening is the development of a psychological expert language of emotions and intimacy that is disseminated by radio programs and counseling groups alike, often combining therapeutic discourse and techniques of Western import, ideas of self-realization, and religious arguments about proper heteronormative gender roles in syncretistic and at times contradictory combinations (Kreil 2012). A third part, which I take up here, is the way the search for love-as-fulfillment and the reflection about love and marriage emerge as a political and social critique.

In her ethnography of love, intimacy, and friendship among young women in Morocco, Laura Menin (2012: 223) argues that in the milieu of her research, the demand for "true love" was a political demand indeed, a demand for a world built on "fidelity, equality and care." A male interlocutor of Menin's goes a step further: "Talking of love is talking of power. It's a political issue because you attack . . . you touch on the King, religion, the system" (Menin 2012: 233). Such a view of love as not just the romantic other of the powers that make society but as a power that can challenge other social powers is also shared by some of the Egyptian lovers I have spoken with.

In the spring of 2011, when freedom was being widely evoked in the wake of the revolution, Nagat asked me:

> With the freedom that we have gained with the revolution, are we now really free to say what is in our minds, or are our hearts still chained? In our Oriental society [*mugtama' sharqi*] we keep so much to ourselves and don't talk about it. Shortly before the revolution I was with my brother in Cairo and spoke long about it with him. Why is it that he can call a female friend on the phone and I can know it, but if I have a male friend, even if there is no romance in it, I have to hide it from him?

Searching for freedom to express one's feelings and concerns and to build social relationships without fear and secrecy, Nagat demands that freedom should not be just political freedom, but freedom of the heart. Importantly, she does not articulate this demand in the language of liberal or feminist ideology. Rather than being a demand against family connectivity, parental consent over marriage, or religious ideas of female respectability, Nagat's question is articulated from a conservative, rural lifeworld by a person who is part of that world but has some means to search for openings within and beyond it. In this regard, Nagat's demand for freedom of the heart shares a common ground and thrust with Mustafa's attempt to change the rules of a conventional marriage.

Sometimes, destiny is on the side of lovers and it all goes well—or so it seems. Fouad, a man from the village who moved to the Alexandria, where he works as a teacher, and Nazli, a woman from the same village, fell in love and got married. They faced no resistance from their families. The need to save the necessary money delayed the marriage by a year or two, but compared to many other people, they got married easily. Their struggle has been of a different kind. Some five years into their marriage, Fouad said:

> Being married with the woman you love puts a big strain on love: You want to cherish your beloved, keep that image of the pure perfect love for her, but you are married with her in all the troubles and banalities of everyday life. You live with two women: a beloved and a wife. And usually the wife is the stronger of the two when the troubles of the everyday make you think about material issues. But actually poverty does not make love weaker. It may even make it stronger. I need moments of feeling emotionally close, just lying together with her without sex. I need moments where she is weak when otherwise she as wife and mother needs to be strong, where I am soft when otherwise to get along in life I need to be tough.

Fouad and his wife, Nazli, have lived a married life of many ups and downs, busy with paying the rent and educating their children, working to establish an emotional bond, and also frequently facing serious conflicts. Both Fouad and Nazli expect from married life something more than just a shared household and social reproduction. They both have expectations of companionship, self-realization, creativity, and participation in urban life. But at the same time, the means to live a married life they have learned, the social roles they are able to play well, are those of a traditional marriage. In good times, there is a degree of mutual understanding, a kind of complicity, even happiness between them, which makes the hardship of ordinary life much less grave. But in difficult times, there is a sense of looming crisis and potential breakup. For Fouad and Nazli, marriage for love has been a roller coaster. And yet they have been lucky compared to some others whose marriages have failed when the idealized love of the period of engagement (sometimes ironically called "the period of lying") has turned into the everyday of marriage. It is much easier to demand a life of equality, fidelity, and care, and much more difficult to live one in a world where numerous other powers push one in a different direction.[8]

Fragility has been a price of the love match around the world, visible in high rates of divorce (Wardlow and Hirsch 2006: 25). In a society like Egypt where an ideal of pure passion and a practice of secrecy inform people's expectations and practices of romantic love, the contrast of expectations and experience is especially troubling. Love in the sense of mutual intimacy in the middle of a prosaic life, which Fouad describes as "feeling emotionally close," is something Egyptians often find themselves unprepared for when they finally manage to get married. Loving one's wife or husband involves a kind of love that is very different from that evoked by Majnun's passion and Valentine's Day, and uniting the two is a formidable problem. Many do not even try, and especially for people who live in marriages where there never was much mutual passion to start with, secret romantic friendships and affairs become spaces for experiencing a sense of emotional connection that marriage so often does not provide.

While love is easy to have as an unrealized grand scheme of absolute passion and sacrifice, as a practical guideline of life and marriage it is confined to the volatile realm of the reflective, ethical, and experimental. The conventional ways of romantic love and married life, in contrast, come with a force of unquestionability, be it in the shape of madness or destiny. Love as a struggle for the sake of something is in a position of severe structural disadvantage with respect to other considerations and greater powers. This is why love so often is at the losing end of life-changing decisions. In the face of such formidable powers, however, the fact that people nevertheless try, and at times even succeed, to take steps in their lives that are motivated by passion and romantic longing, tells how very important it is for them.

# 5   Capitalist Ethics?

Although people understand grand schemes as being located outside the ordinary world, they do have material form and shape. And most often in the early twenty-first century, that form is of a commodity.

Commodity and consumption have become a ubiquitous part of life in Egypt. Being a respectable person largely depends on one's capacity to buy consumer goods. Love is transformed through the consumerist principle of gratification. Religious proselytization is a lucrative trade. This shared sense of existence is in the focus of this chapter. Capitalism is not only a configuration of relations of production and consumption but also a sensibility of existence inherently accompanied by an ideology, promises, and ends of its own. And while Islam may appear to be the moral counterpart to capitalist economy, the Islamic revival has brought key anxieties to the forefront of people's religious consciousness that resonate with capitalist modes of production and rationality in peculiar ways. Capitalism and religious revival share a sense of temporality that connects the two in complex and unpredictable ways. It is the temporality of a life in the future tense.

This may seem counterintuitive, given the tendency to see the economic realm as separate from the spiritual, romantic, or moral one. Such separation is fundamental to the capitalist exchange of goods that, unlike the exchange of gifts and favors, is not bound with moral reciprocity (Mauss [1924] 2007)—but it is a separation that is never complete. In real practice the exchange of goods comes with a morality of its own, and moral and spiritual ends are pursued through economic means and logics.

In cultural and social anthropology, this link has become the focus of a tremendous amount of research around the keyword *neoliberalism*. I am somewhat undecided, however, as to whether to speak about capitalism or neoliberalism. To speak about neoliberalism is to highlight issues of governance and subjectivity, whereas to speak about capitalism is to emphasize issues of production and exchange. Academic debates on neoliberalism often address the ways in which is our lives, our governments, our loves, and our faiths become saturated (however unevenly, partially, and imperfectly) by a neoliberal logic of capitalism-as-government that governs people by making them the agents responsible for their own exploitation and policing (see, e.g., Elyachar 2005; Shever 2008; Shore 2008). And although much of what I address in this chapter could be well described in those terms as neoliberal, I prefer to speak about capitalism, in order to emphasize more the things one can and must buy, the ways to earn the money to do so, and the sensibilities toward one's future and present being that one gains while trying to earn that money and buy those things. In the world this book tells about, it is a largely capitalist business of buying industrially produced and commercially distributed goods with money earned or borrowed under the conditions of a market of labor, financing, and services. It is not a textbook case of capitalism, though: the markets are usually not free, the money is sometimes borrowed without interest, and much of the labor is organized according to socialist principles. Instead, it is what I would describe as actually existing capitalism: a process (rather than a system) of relationships and transactions characterized by the expansive creation of markets; a valorization of competition; an increasing monetization of social relationships and obligations; and perhaps most important, a strong future orientation created by constant economic growth through the reinvestment of surplus that is at once a structural necessity and a moral imperative. As a process capitalism is neither systematic nor necessarily rational (Miller 2012). And it does not exist in a pure form except in textbooks.

In referring in the title of this chapter, "Capitalist Ethics?" to Weber's (1992) seminal study *The Protestant Ethic and the Spirit of Capitalism*, I do not intend to understand the contemporary transformations of Islam in analogy with the Christian Reformation (e.g., Loimeier 2005; Browers and Kurzman 2004; Eickelman 1998). Rather, I am critical of many of these attempts, which in my view fall prey to the anachronism of cross-historical analogy. Instead, I want to take up Weber's counter-Marxist question about how ideologies inform the very relations of production that Marx took to be irreducible. I want to turn this question around once more and look at the shared existential grounds of the economic, spiritual, and moral. In particular, I try to address the complications that result from living under conditions in which capitalism provides a key sense of livelihood and a better future and revivalist Islam provides a key promise of moral righteousness and existential trust. Central to these complications are the countless and often unpredictable daily moves, uses, and adaptations of people who try to make a living, to do the right thing, and to gain salvation. People's moves and uses should therefore also be the analytical starting point of our inquiry. Following Daniel Miller's (2012) suggestion that we should see capitalism as the outcome rather than the cause of our actions, I try to think about both capitalism and Islam not as things substantial and given but rather as things that emerge in daily interactions.

## Faces of Capitalism

Since the 1970s, Egyptian society has been transforming from an economy based on the nation-state, with strong socialist leanings, to a globally oriented capitalist one with strong pious overtones. Mass-produced and mass-mediated consumer goods such as television sets, satellite dishes, and computers have become a main aim of people's aspirations, as well as a central medium of religious messages. In the public sector, a planned socialist economy has become informally privatized, as civil servants' income derives mainly from privately selling public services (also known as corruption). There have been major, successful efforts to create (niches of) Islamic markets and finances. And so also has the logic of markets, financing, production, profit, and consumption become a part of Muslims' religious experience and beliefs.

One feature of capitalism that has made it so successful and dynamic around the world (aside from, of course, its exceptional capability to generate and reinvest surplus) is its peculiar dual face of a value-neutral, even amoral technology that can and must be "filled" with moral content, and of a moral order that privileges innovation, initiative, self-responsibility, enjoyment, competition, success, and freedom as core characteristics of a good human being.[1] The first face makes capitalism and movements of religious revival natural allies, as proselytization can become a profitable way to make a living, consumption an ethical means to achieve a religious purpose, and a religiously inspired notion of morally responsible action the normative framework to guide the search for profit. At the same time, this alliance has a deeper layer of mutual resonance that is related to the second face of capitalism as an ideologically grounded practice that carries notions of morality and humanity of its own, paradigms of human action with a powerful dynamic to transform all social practices—including religious ones—according to a logic of investment, profit, and consumption.

Here, caution is needed, because one part of the power of the metaphors of capitalism is that "capitalism" appears to be something clear, solid, globally unified, whereas in reality it, too, is complex, dynamic, and embedded in idiosyncrasies and cultural specificities (Tsing 2000: 340; see also Ho 2005; Kingfisher and Maskovsky 2008). So rather than looking at the abstract, systemic faces of capitalism as a technique and an ideology, it is more helpful to look at the more individual, human faces of capitalism in Egypt and the specific capitalist niches those faces represent.

A list of the most (in)famous individual faces of capitalism in Egypt in recent years would include (but not be restricted to) the following: Ahmad Ezz was a steel monopolist and a leading figure of Mubarak's National Democratic Party in the 2000s. He was sentenced to a long prison sentence in 2013 but has since been released and found not guilty of the corruption charges he faced. Naguib Sawiras is head of a Christian family clan with numerous enterprises in telecommunications, media, and import-export trade, and a prominent sponsor of liberal political movements. After 2011 he was a favorite figure for Islamists to hate, and in 2013 he was a main sponsor of the Tamarrud campaign against

Morsi's presidency. He has proved a reliable ally of the El-Sisi regime since 2013. Khayrat al-Shater is owner of numerous supermarket and retail chains—or he was, because much of his property was confiscated in 2014. He serves as deputy supreme guide of the Muslim Brotherhood. After 2011 he was the favorite figure to hate of the leftist and liberal opposition. During Morsi's presidency al-Shater was one of the most powerful men in Egypt; he was imprisoned in July 2013 along with the entire leadership of the Muslim Brotherhood. Last but not least is the Armed Forces, which owns and runs numerous businesses, including agricultural and industrial production, as well as health care and retail trade. The Armed Forces has received the lion's share of public infrastructures projects since 2013 and was busy expanding its retail and consumer goods sectors significantly in 2014.

These faces not only are involved in ongoing struggles with shifting fortunes that concern who controls Egypt's economy but also stand for characteristic ways of doing capitalism that emerged during Egypt's transition from Arab socialism to a new era of capitalism.

In the 1950s, Egypt's growing sector of private industry and trade, largely owned by foreign nationals residing in Egypt, was mostly nationalized in the course of the Gamal Abdel Nasser's socialist experiment. In the 1970s, his successor, Anwar al-Sadat, initiated the *infitah* (open door) policy of gradual privatization and economic liberalization. In the 2000s, under the influence of Gamal Mubarak (Hosni Mubarak's son and by that time his expected successor) this liberalization developed into a system of governance that united the neoliberal utopia of entrepreneurial spirit and wealth with a systematically nepotistic way of producing and distributing that wealth.

Ahmad Ezz was one of the architects and primary profiteers of this era, but the Sawiras family, Khayrat al-Shater, and the Armed Forces all got their share of the profits as well. Policies of trade liberalization created a situation in which industrial production stood in an increasingly disadvantaged position with respect to European and Asian competition, and more and more profits could be made by import-export and retail trade. This shift bred a generation of successful entrepreneurial families who often made significant profits and turnovers while employing a relatively small workforce. Naguib Sawiras and Khayrat al-Shater may stand at different ends of the Muslim-Christian confessional split and the political spectrum, but they are sons of the same economic process, and together they represent one face of capitalism, oriented toward services, media, real estate, and retail trade; organized through family clans; and having a clear preference for import trade and services over industrial production. This tendency is not restricted to the big players. It also extends to small entrepreneurs who in previous decades have largely shifted from artisanal and industrial production to import and retail trade (Ismail 2013; Mitchell 2002).

In contrast, the Armed Forces—the main profiteers of which are established officer families, who also control the recruitment of new professional officers, most of whom come from officer families—built its economic power largely as a side effect of structural adjustment policies dictated by the International Monetary Fund. In the 1980s and 1990s Egypt decreased its public sector not only by selling public-sector companies but also by turning civil bodies into military ones. The Armed Forces also had the unique advantage of free labor in the form of conscripts at its disposal. In contrast to Sawiras and Shater, however, the Armed Forces put much more emphasis on industrial production, infrastructure, and construction, such that "made by the army" has become a mark of quality for everything from foodstuffs to street repairs (Abul-Magd 2011).

These different faces continue to coexist, but their fortunes keep shifting. In 2012, many considered Khayrat al-Shater to be the real leader of Egypt; in any case he was one of the most powerful people in the country. The economic experience he and his fellow Muslim Brothers have gained also informed the economical policies they tried to pursue—oriented toward ongoing trade liberalization, reducing subsidies, and turning public services into public-private partnerships. This is an economic policy with real estate developments, malls, and hypermarkets as both a marker of success and a template for what a successful economy is about. It is a vision of economy that is flashy yet conservative, providing hedonistic pleasure but selling no alcohol, distributing charity but fighting trade unions. At the time this books went to press, al-Shater was in prison and his businesses were being confiscated. It was a golden hour for the Armed Forces—and for Naguib Sawiras, who was under much pressure during Morsi's presidency. But just as Khayrat al-Shater compels one to think about revivalist ethics of piety and supermarket chains, so Naguib Sawiras makes one wonder about commercial media and real estate together with liberal politics and confessional tensions, and the Armed Forces inspires one to reflect about road construction and industrial production in relation to militarist nationalism.

## Living Capitalism

And yet these faces do not yet provide a satisfactory account of what capitalism is like in post-Nasserist Egypt. What is it like to make a living, to work, consume, and to invest under the conditions described here? To make sense of the experiential side of living capitalism, I elaborate six crucial moments: socialist structures, debt, class, marriage, informal privatization, and last but not least a sense of increasing pressure.

First, a key feature of capitalism at the turn of millennial Egypt is the uneasy coexistence of elements of Arab socialism with neoliberal structural adjustment. Although state subsidies have been dramatically reduced and many state-owned companies sold (often under questionable circumstances), rent income from oil, gas, the Suez Canal, and political alliances has allowed the Egyptian state to maintain some of its socialist structures, notably a very large and unproductive public-sector workforce. Despite poor salaries, people with lower incomes especially rely on public-sector jobs because of the security and social status they continue to be associated with, not to mention their social insurance and pension benefits. Despite the neoliberal policies of privatizing—formally and informally—the functions of the state, an Arab socialist image of the public sector prevails, in which it is responsible for solving societal and economic issues of all kinds.

Second, there is the increasing prevalence of debt as a mode of finance. Much of the expansion of investment and consumption since the 1990s have been made possible by generous credits, be it in the shape of companies financing their investment on credit or consumers buying on installments, with the result that both individuals and companies base their spending on large-scale debt. This is congruent with worldwide economic policies, as the International Monetary Fund has offered loans to governments and microloans to the poor, turning debt into one of the most pervasive forms of power worldwide, both coercively and subtly (see Elyachar 2005; High 2012). In rural and popular milieus in Egypt, however, people have also gone into debt without much input from international agencies. Instead, the need to finance growing consumption and to overcome critical urgencies (such as sickness) has led to a proliferation of payment in installments and mutual credit. Even the lowest levels of economic transactions in small village shops are based on installment payments, often guaranteed by blank checks. Loans exchanged at weddings have grown from a way to finance weddings to an expanding form of mutual credit. Going into debt has lost much of the stigma it used to have, and some forms of debt have even become associated with a certain prestige.[2]

Such reliance on debt is essential to the future-oriented and growth-driven process of capitalism, producing as it does both the financial means to invest in future growth and the necessity to realize that growth in order to pay back what one owes. This "commodification of the future" (Appadurai 1996: 66–85), implied in the way investment and consumption are made possible by credit and installment payments, has become necessary for the growth and expansion of a capitalist economy. From a practical, everyday perspective this means that the pressure of debts and installment payments has become one of the most present issues in people's lives as they accumulate consumer goods—apartments, furniture, televisions, satellite dishes, mobile telephones, computers, and fashionable clothing—with money they yet have to earn.

However, not all debt has the same effect. Tawfiq's uncle Isma'il, a shopkeeper selling clothes to the poorest inhabitants of Nazlat al-Rayyis, rarely receives the

Figure 5.1. Collecting wedding loans, Nazlat al-Rayyis, November 2006.

price of his goods at once in cash. He sells even shirts and socks on installments. For his customers this means a constant pressure of debt, but for him the situation is hardly any better, because most of his capital is actually bound up in unpaid, interest-free installments, and if people are late with their payments, he cannot force them to pay.[3] It is different when a person owes money to a bank or a traditional moneylender, of course. The point, though, is that although there is a strong historical relation betweeen monetary debt and violence (see Graeber 2011), debt is not a uniformly coercive form of power. It is, however, an almost uniformly future-oriented one, leaving transactions and obligations ever incomplete, yet to be fulfilled.

Third (following socialist structures and debt as the first two moments of living under actually existing capitalism), the future orientation is also visible in the way being middle class has become an ideal of social normality. People ranging from very poor to very wealthy have come to see themselves as middle class. "The middle classes" of Egypt consist of people very far apart in terms of income, education, livelihood, and habitus, from executive employees in international companies who hold an English-medium university degree and live in privileged neighborhoods of Cairo or Alexandria, to civil servants who have almost no formal income and a devalued, low-quality state education, living in informal areas of the cities, small towns, and villages. This expansion of the middle classes is a generic feature of the consumerist stage of the capitalist process, in which established class boundaries of earlier times are downplayed while new social inequalities are created (Heiman, Freeman, and Liechty 2012).

Where, then, is the real middle in a society so carefully stratified by descent, income, education, and housing, and at the same time so united in the desire to belong to the middle class? Trying to pinpoint this is a futile task, because the "middle" of the middle class is not a place but a direction. The "middle" of the middle class denotes aspiration for inclusion in the nation and the world, grounded in the awareness that there are others whose inclusion is more perfect and marked by attempts to distinguish oneself from the poor and the ignorant. "Middle" as a reality is forever elusive. But as a direction, an imagined site of "good" social normality (Fehérváry 2013; Yeh 2009), it is very powerful.

The rapid expansion of consumption, the commodification of the future, and the social utopia of a middle-class existence are driven by high expectations of a good life. In this sense, these things can be considered aspirational, even utopian in some instances. The question, however, is to what degree people can pursue these expectations at will, and to what degree they experience them as pressing necessities.

This leads us to the fourth (following socialist structures, debt, and class) moment of living in actually existing capitalism in Egypt: marriage. Marriage for most Egyptians is the largest economic investment of their lifetime. It is a nodal point of consumption and a key occasion to go to debt. Strategic choice of marital partners is the primary means to ensure that one's children and children's children belong to the same or higher social class. One of the greatest paradoxes of life in contemporary Egypt is that in a society where marriage is considered a self-evident, destiny-like necessity (see chapter 4), it has become increasingly difficult to get married.

The primary reason for that difficulty is the rising cost of marriage. A standard marriage arrangement in the village involves not only a bride-price of gold, cash, and presents but also an apartment, a bedroom set, the furniture either for a combined living room and *salon* (room where guests are received) or for two separate rooms if possible, linens, a television set, possibly a computer, a dining table, a bathroom with toilet, shower, washtub and a boiler, a kitchen with furniture, cookware and dishes, refrigerator, gas stove, and possibly a washing machine. Most items are for daily use, but there are also items that are intended to be looked at but not used, such as silverware and glassware displayed in a purpose-built cupboard and practically never used. On top of all these investments comes the cost of a usually lavish wedding party. The bride and her family cover some of these items, but the groom carries the bulk of the expense. Who buys what is subject to a written agreement. The actual cost of marriage varies according to income, place of residence, and social class, but as a rule of thumb a marriage should cost slightly more than one can afford. Some of the rising cost of

Figure 5.2. A bride and a groom buying clothes for their marriage,
Alexandria 2003.

marriage is caused by the increasing cost of housing, a result of real estate specu-lation and shifting prices of globally traded goods like steel (needed for building houses) and gold (needed for the bride-price). But most of it is an effect of com-petitive conspicuous consumption. As families try to negotiate the best possible terms to marry off their daughters, prospective grooms try to outbid one another in the cost of their contribution. Isma'il, whose shop also finances the purchase of brides' contributions to the marital household (he provides the complete con-ventional package and receives payments in installments), says that it is almost impossible to know how much marriages really cost, because all parties involved tend to exaggerate the price of the goods they buy:

> A groom may buy furniture for 12,000 Egyptian pounds but tell the bride's father that it cost 18,000 in order to make himself look more generous and capable. The father's neighbor will hear about it, and he will tell the young man who comes to ask for his daughter's hand that he should bring furniture worth of 20,000 pounds, because he doesn't want his daughter to appear lesser than the neighbor's.

A paradoxical dynamic of marriage-as-investment thus emerges: because people consider marriage a singularly important form of social becoming, and because of the availability of more and more consumer goods, better housing conditions, and the income and/or credit to finance them, the cost of marriage is constantly magnified, to the degree that people can barely afford it and so end up waiting much longer than previously was common to get married.

A fifth and paradoxical moment of what it is like to live under capitalism in Egypt (the first four being socialist structures, debt, class, and marriage) is that government policies, laws, and international agreements highlight transparency and rationality, but in practice almost nothing is what it seems. The actual work-ings of educational, administrative, and economic institutions differ systemati-cally from their official, legal form. These fields are governed by informal logics and structures so that in most cases "other considerations" (*hisabat taniya*) based on family relations and clientelist allegiances (*wasta*), bribes, and other informal transactions bypass formal qualifications and legal entitlements (see Rabo 2006). Also the socialist sectors of the economy have been transformed by an informal version of the privatization of public services. School diplomas with high grades are almost impossible to get without private tutoring, which in turn can be a very lucrative business for teachers who officially are very poorly paid. Govern-ment jobs that include the possibility of significant income in bribes are either distributed on the basis of *wasta* or sold for high prices. The police can be hired to extract private debts. Largely because of these clientelist relations, in the early twenty-first century Egypt has emerged as a highly stratified class society in which paths to success are extremely dependent on family background and the ability to pay for private, high-quality (preferably English-medium) education

(A. de Koning 2009), and in which for every law there is an established way to circumvent it (I return to this point in more detail in chapter 8).

Sixth and last (following socialist structures, debt, class, marriage, and informal privatization), the overall image of lived capitalism in Egypt reveals a fundamental contradiction between expectations and experience that Egyptians describe as pressure (*daght*). Even in a rural location like Nazlat al-Rayyis, there is some work available, people have enough to eat, and child mortality and illiteracy rates have dropped while the standard of housing has dramatically risen and people have many more things than they did just few decades earlier. At the same time, everybody complains about the unbearable economic pressure of rising prices, consumer debts, housing, marriage, education, private tutoring, and so on. While the standard of living in the village has risen somewhat, it is still dramatically lower than that of wealthier Egyptians living in the urban centers—a difference that people are acutely aware of. Expectations have grown much faster than the resources to fulfill them. And while most Egyptians can now buy many more things than they could twenty or fifty years ago, buying those things is not something one can choose to do—in most cases, they are things one must buy, even if they may seem a dispensable luxury to an outsider. Dining tables, glasses, and coffee sets, which have little practical use in a rural Egyptian household, must be part of the apartment of a newlywed couple. Color television sets, mobile phones, and computers must be bought. Egyptians often find it strange that I do not have a car even though I could afford one. If you can afford a car, you buy one. Consumption is not a choice. It is a necessity.

## Any Means Possible

Given the pressure of consumption and the simultaneous scarcity of reliable legal paths to success, immoral, illegal, or quasi-legal means to success appear as necessary and even acceptable in the face of the idea that anyone who has money must be a thief anyway, or the heir to a thief. Although people often stress the legality and legitimacy of income (especially in the religious sense of that income being *halal*), economic practices have not been influenced by the Islamic revival in the way in which, say, gender relations, dress, and drinking practices have been. More than that, the moral thrust of Egyptian Muslims trying to know their religion better for the sake of living a morally sound life is not primarily directed at economic practices (with the exception of Islamic banking). Women's dress and behavior; prayer and repentance; paradise and hell; abstinence from tobacco, alcohol, and drugs; fighting Israel—all these form the basic stock of religious admonitions that as stickers and graffiti have covered the walls of homes, shops, and public transportation in the 2000s. Only after the revolution in 2011 did such issues as taking and paying bribes emerge as a theme of stickers and graffiti in public space. The wave of fashionable piety that went through the upper middle classes in the early 2000s in the wake of the former accountant and now preacher 'Amr Khaled was accompanied by an enormous concern for charity as a way to do good with one's money, especially during Ramadan, but by much less concern with the source of that money (Lutfi 2009; Sobhy 2009; Saad 2010).

The expectation that Muslims, by virtue of their faith, would be more moral and responsible economic actors stands in a strange tension with everyday economic practice in Egypt. On one level, the morality of economic practice is constantly addressed and questioned in what Salwa Ismail (2013) calls an "ethics of transaction." At the same time, however, the revivalist project of a sound moral conduct is widely pursued by people whose livelihood is based on various tricks, shady deals, exploitation, bribes, swindle, and outright theft. Even interest or usury (*riba*), the most central issue of contemporary Islamic economics, is far from absent in the Egyptian economy. While traditional moneylenders have come to face significant opposition in their communities for religious reasons (and probably because they have never been very much liked in the first place), installment payments routinely involve interest, as do bank accounts, which are becoming increasingly popular especially among small entrepreneurs.

This is a reality that is widely acknowledged. It is subject to a constant moral critique that often centers on the notion of respect, a key interpersonal register of moral action that is closely connected with material well-being and the ability to act generously. Respect is heavily dependent on the ability to consume conspicuous goods and to pay back one's debts, which also makes respect very powerful and very controversial. People take respect seriously, harshly judging those who fail to meet the (rapidly growing) economic obligations involved in performing respect. At the same time, they routinely complain that respect has become an empty virtue based entirely on money:

> ISMA'IL: One wants to live as a respected [*muhtaram*] person one day, to plan for the future so as to have a decent and respected life when one is forty. The older one grows, the stronger the pressure. And when one has lived in poverty, it is very important.
>
> SAMULI: What makes one respected in the village?
>
> I: That it is primarily measured by wealth. Having stable income, money, a good house, and so on.
>
> S: Is respect not measured by friendship, love, moral integrity, religiosity, and so on?
>
> I: No, all that really matters is wealth. People respect my cousin because they think he is a millionaire because he works in the Gulf since fifteen years, invites everyone in the café, and lives lavishly, not because of his personal qualities.
>
> S: What if one's wealth is based on bribes or drug trafficking?

I: It has become irrelevant, it no longer matters where your money comes from as long as you have it.

Isma'il presents a highly critical vision of a society in which moral values are mere appearances and all that matters is money. At the same time, he works hard himself in order to become respected on these terms. He carefully manages the meager capital of his shop by participating in numerous saving associations and wedding-loan exchanges, and he is very good at discovering niches to make a little bit more money in his trade as well as in his other job as a teacher. With the best of his efforts, his economic situation remains precarious, but he is helpful and generous to friends and family in need. He is a vocal critic of materialism, and yet he spends most of his time trying to make more money, reminding his customers to pay their installments, negotiating a better deal in buying a house, purchasing new goods, and mediating relatives' marriage arrangements. His critique of materialism should thus be understood not so much as opposition to the promises and pressures entailed in consumption but rather as an expression of the ambivalence they create. The ability to spend money on conspicuous commodities is a virtue in itself, and even when people express their discontent about it being so, in their daily judgments about the qualities of other people as respectable or disrespectable, it counts. This is a real and serious pressure of at once moral and economic kind.

Isma'il sees himself as a socialist and is not very pious. He thinks that the turn to revivalist piety under these conditions is insincere, and he points out that shops owned by Muslim Brothers in the village charge the highest interests rates on their installment plans. However, people can be quite sincere about wanting to live "according to the Qur'an and the Sunna" while reckoning with what they deem economic necessity. This was the case with two other small shopkeepers from the village, the brothers Muntasir and Abdelnaser (see chapters 1 and 3). In 2007, they argued to me that they would want to live and do their business according to the law of God and the example of the Prophet, but they added that as materialistic as their society was, this was not possible. By 2009 they were forced to close their shop because of increased prices of foodstuffs, and they went to work as migrant workers in Saudi Arabia, where they faced highly exploitative conditions. By 2011, Abdelnaser was back in Egypt trying to find work there (unsuccessfully, it turned out), and when I asked him what kind of work he was searching for, he answered: "The kind of work doesn't matter. The money matters."

## Profit and Reward

There is widespread moral trouble with a life in which money matters so much. It is a problem, however, that also comes with a sense of direction.

There has been much research on pious capitalism and spiritual economies. Most of that research has foregrounded the attempt of pious entrepreneurs to instill capitalism with religious-moral values (e.g., trading in *halal* products, giving money for charities), or to use capitalist means of training and distribution for pious ends, such as combining management training and *da'wa* ("call" to Islam, that is, proselytization and preaching), developing Islamic entertainment, and clothing fashions (see, e.g., Osella and Osella 2009; Rudnyckyj 2009; Jones 2010). As the focus of those works is often mainly on the ethical aspect of the encounter between piety and business, there has emerged a lacuna regarding its unethical aspects (but see Ghannam 2002: 179–181). Capitalist production, accumulation, and exchange often create moments of severe moral disturbance: the rising cost of marriage undermines gender ideals; the opacity of the process makes it difficult to distinguish right and wrong; the pressure to marry, to build a middle-class existence, and to pay back debts compels one to resort to any means necessary. Exploitative working conditions in the private sector and the destruction of welfare guarantees in the public sector through structural adjustment generate a sense of grave injustice. In this situation the revivalist turn to religion as a grand promise of clarity has a curious double role. One the one hand, it appears as a site of moral certainty necessary to fill the moral vacuums of capitalism. On the other hand, it promotes an affective sense of being that strongly resonates with a sense of affective being that is central to the experience of capitalism. That is, revivalist Islam and actually existing capitalism share key moral anxieties as well as certainties that are taken for granted.

There are, of course, Islamist voices who raise fundamental questions about the logic of consumption, fashion, and the pursuit of worldly profit. But they are not the ones who gather mass followings. The *higab* may have been anti-fashion when it first became part of the dress of middle- and working-class women, but it could become the dominant form of Muslim women's dress only as a consumable fashion item (MacLeod 1991; Hoofdar 1999: 197; Moors 2009; Ahmed 2011). The power of Islamist movements relies heavily on their promotion of and reliance on retail trade and consumerist lifestyles. And no matter how ambivalent, demoralizing, and troubling the experience of living capitalism may be, even for people who hold to a socialist views of economy or who end up being at the losing end of the redistribution of wealth, capitalism is never merely a menace. It is also a key source of hope.

Wealth, which today is measured primarily by the ability to consume, equals a promise of good life and happiness, and it is the issue people I know spend the most energy and time on. As Isma'il pointed out, conditions of poverty make this promise of wealth only stronger. Wealth is a matter of having the resources to live a humane existence in command of dignity and respect. In other words, wealth is about existential comfort. As Sa'id pointed out at the opening of this book, wealth is a means to have existential power over one's condition (see also Jackson 2011: 156). This is not in any way new, of course. The pursuit of wealth predates capitalism by millennia at least. Capitalism is not the cause of people's pursuit of wealth—it is better described as the processual outcome of an increasingly systematic pursuit of wealth (Miller 2012). However, in the course of this process, the existential comfort of having a little more than one needs has transformed into something more peculiar: an anxious combination of pressure and aspiration to realize a constantly better life by accumulating more wealth. Rapid economic growth has made it possible for many people to have more—even a lot more. And yet many among those people do not experience growth as a comfortable margin of surplus. Instead, they experience it as pressing scarcity, because the installments for the goods that were bought are yet to be paid, because others already have even more, because the children need to be educated to keep up with the competition.

Predictably, this causes anxiety, which is further amplified by the notorious precariousness of most Egyptian livelihoods. In such an unpredictable mixture of dramatic hardship, grand promises, increasing wealth, and shady deals, religion can appear to be precisely the kind of firm hold and straight path needed to make things a little clearer. But that is easier said than done. Revivalist Islam is neither an alternative to nor a corrective for capitalism. Rather, it is an especially compelling way to live capitalism, and vice versa.

In the course of the parallel processes of economic liberalization and religious revival, consumption has emerged as a key strategy of proselytization and an important means of living a religious life (women's *higab* being a strong case in point). But consumption is never simply a neutral means for the ends of an ideological project, as Martin Stokes (2002: 331) reminds us: "Consumption-based strategies can never take everything into account. The commodity form is never simply amendable to ideological control. The commodity fetish, as Marx constantly reminds us, leads its own life—it 'thinks us,' no matter how much we like to believe we are capable of 'thinking it.'"

That is, when a religious movement makes use of the commodity form—which the Islamic revival has done in numerous ways, be it in Islamic fashion, mass-produced religious objects, or the linkage of supermarkets and Islamist proselytization—the commodity form also leaves its mark on the movement in unpredictable ways. However, this is not to assume the materialist causality of commodification. Even when businessmen become preachers, Islam has not become business. In his work on consumption, Daniel Miller (1993, 2008) argues that consumption and commodities are not something external that take over our lives. Rather than being something done to us, consumption is something we do, and when we buy and use things, we de-alienate them; that is, we transform them from commodities that are produced and sold under conditions of alienation into relational objects that may embody intimate emotional value. The intertwining between religiosity and capitalism is not simply about religiosity being shaped by capitalism. Instead, what is at hand is a resonance, a mutual relationship between the process of commodity exchange and the work of de-alienation.

The resonance between monetary profit and reward in the afterworld is a case in point. While the religious discourse of the Islamic revival promotes the ideal of *iltizam*, or the commitment to a pious and moral discipline of willing and holistic obedience to God, this project is not one of selfless devotion. The ideal of commitment is linked with concerns over collecting rewards (*thawab*) for the afterworld, which can be obtained by praying, fasting, invoking God, doing pious and good deeds, and the like. Preachers of the Islamic revival have very successfully mobilized the afterworld, especially people's fear of hell and punishment of the grave as a key religious sentiment.[4] Cultivating the daily worry about punishment and reward is a central part of pursuing the path of revivalist piety (Mahmood 2005: 140–145; Hirschkind 2006b). Booklets and sermons that detail the terrible tortures of punishment of the grave are among the most widely circulated. While the pursuit of reward is typically aligned with the ideal of commitment, the aim of commitment and the concern for reward do not always sit comfortably together. They present somewhat different emphases of religiosity: one based on a holistic discipline, and the other focused on maximizing divine reward for the sake of maximal pleasure in the afterworld.

The concern with reward and punishment, paradise and hell, positive and negative points (*hasanat* and *sayyi'at*) in one's account for Judgment Day, is as old as Islam itself. It is a recurring subject in the Qur'an, and it has a firm place in Islamic eschatology. However, concern for the fine details of maximizing reward has not been quite as central in other times as it is now. In my earlier fieldwork in the Sufi milieu (Sufi ways of devotion were hegemonic in Egypt until recently), I never encountered people discussing the issue of reward in such an explicit and elaborate manner. Reward in the afterworld for good and pious deeds committed in this world was taken up from time to time, but generally Sufi Muslims were more concerned with searching for assistance from the "friends of God" (i.e., Muslim saints) in this-worldly problems and with discussing the spiritual progress to higher states of religious experience.

The way a middle-class urban mother who had come to the *mulid* festival of as-Sayyid al-Badawi in Tanta in 2006 to take her children to see the rides and the fairgrounds interpreted the meaning of a Sufi gathering is telling of the shift. She argued that the Sufis who were engaged in an ecstatic *dhikr* (collective meditation in tune of music) were misguided in their attempt to gain reward that way. I had actually never heard followers of mystical Islam claim that reward was the primary motivation for participating in a gathering, but unlike the Sufis, this mother articulated reward as the paradigmatic, if not the only, motivation of a religious ritual.

The privileging of reward is related to a more general vision of the human condition that also privileges profit as a paradigmatic motivation and outcome of action. Take, for example, the countless small prayers and invocations that circulated on the Internet by the end of the 2000s, invariably carrying some variation of the promise that they would bring huge "mountains of *hasanat*" (reward points) to whoever would read, speak, and forward them. One such invocation that circulated on Facebook in 2008 declared:

> Send this to 15 [others]—in an hour you will have gained [the reward equaling that of] 15 million blessings for the Prophet in your accounts, God willing. Don't be arrogant towards God by saying you don't have time. This is a million points of reward which you certainly need.[5]

Such hyperbolic promises of millions of points of reward and thousands of angels praying for a person are very common, and very telling of a rather utilitarian notion of worship in which saying a prayer and forwarding it to friends is an easy, accessible way to balance one's account: everybody certainly needs a million points. The issue of religious commitment is not absent; it is present through the very fear and anxiety that make people so eager to circulate such messages. But the hyperbolic promises of easy reward are motivated by a sensibility that does not require one to enter the path of committed personality. In the prayer posts on the Internet, reward (and punishment) is concrete and immediate. It does not require (though it may imply) elaborate work on the self. And that reward is just a click away.

Such messages, in handy posts and pictures, often written in an informal colloquial style similar to that of advertisements, are one of the many successful means of a religious revival initiated but no longer controlled by groups of religious activists. By virtue of the life experience and the horizon of expectation of the people who write and read them, the rhetoric of persuasion they employ, and the sensibilities they appeal to, they also resonate with ideals and logics other than the one they were ostensibly designed to proliferate. They bring together concern for reward and punishment after death with concern for profit, success, and consumption in this world.

This was first pointed out to me by Layla, a Cairene woman in her midtwenties who, in the spring of 2008, was working as a consultant for an international company—a very exclusive social milieu where the Islamic revival only became tangibly felt after 2000. She complained about one of her colleagues, a very religious person who prayed regularly. She said that she ended up doing much of his work because he, rather than praying in the office or at the mosque next door, would always walk to a mosque further away because every step he took to walk to a mosque for prayer would bring him more reward:

I think it is something similar with the work itself. At my job, we work by the hour. The hour is paid well in dollars, and it means that I have a very high pressure to optimize my use of time, to work as much and as efficiently I can in that hour. My colleague does the same in religion. Just like I count at work: "How much have I done in my working time?" he thinks, "How much reward have I gathered, how many points do I have, am I falling behind in points?" He thinks about religion exactly the same way he thinks about money and work. And religion for him is not about peace of mind, about the feeling in his heart; it's all about gathering points. All life shrinks to just making profit for the afterworld. The women with *higab* really suffer in hot weather under their clothes, but they say, "It's OK, I do it all for the afterlife." They think about religion in a completely capitalist way.

This is evidently the point of view of a person who finds collecting reward a misguided form of religiosity. Layla probably underestimates the peace of mind and sense of direction that intense involvement in ritual practice may offer. Furthermore, while her colleague may have had a capitalist approach to worship, he did not seem to have a capitalist approach to capitalism, at least not in Weberian terms. His concern with prayer went at the cost of productivity and efficiency, and at least in Layla's account, this did not seem to cause him much concern.

There is a similarity, even an affinity, between the capitalist logic of profit and the revivalist logic of reward. But this similarity is not based on one colonizing the other. Revivalist religion gains a flavor of capitalism, but capitalism also gets its share of destiny and miracles. Importantly, the focus on wealth and profit in Egypt does not necessarily mean a Protestant work ethic (Weber 1992)—on the contrary, the unpredictable and chaotic nature of global capitalism in a dependent, postsocialist economy makes both wealth and poverty often appear sudden, unpredictable, and even miraculous.[6] The resonance lies less on the side of rational calculus and more on the side of the promise of miraculous abundance (see Mittermaier 2013). In fact, very much like the Internet posts that promise huge rewards (even more than those entailed in performing major religious obligations like pilgrimage to Mecca) for reading a short prayer, so also stories of dramatic and sudden wealth due to successful migration, lucky breaks, shady deals, rags-to-riches careers, and dark alliances of politics and trade monopolies circulate among Egyptians from less privileged milieus. Rather than being a transparent outcome of rational economic actions, profit has much affinity with the logic of *nasib*, or unpredictable strikes of destiny. In the complex Arabic vocabulary of destiny, *nasib* comes close to *fortune*. It is destiny as it hits one in decisive moments: marriage, children, profits and losses, accidents, illness and healing. One can make the best out of one's *nasib*, but one cannot plan or choose it.

This is a significantly different sense of capitalism from that described by Weber (1992) in his *Protestant Ethics*, but it carries a similar dialectic. Weber

famously argued that in a cosmology in which one's fate is irreversibly prede-
termined by God, uncertainty about one's share in the afterworld turned wealth
from something one should spend to please God (and the church) into an indication of one's belonging to those whose souls are saved. In combination with an
austere approach to life that rejected feasting and other ways of expenditure, this
cosmology laid the groundwork for an economic practice oriented toward investment and accumulation. Weber describes a world of unknown salvation and
transparent wealth. In the current stage of capitalism, in contrast, the origins of
wealth and the means to gain it are often highly opaque, not transparent. Despite
the emphasis of neoliberal governmental discourses on transparency, the actual
practice of accumulation under conditions of neoliberal government—especially
so in dependent economies—relies on processes that are too complex for the un-
initiated to grasp and on ways of operating that are rejected by the ideology of
good governance as "corruption" or "nepotism" but nevertheless instrumental
for making anything happen, and therefore made invisible (see chapter 8; see
also Shever 2008; Sanders 2009, Comaroff and Comaroff 1999). At the same time,
salvation emerges as accessible, transparent, to some degree even calculable. This
is notably the case with two of the most successful religious movements in this
age, revivalist Islam and Evangelical Christianity, the first with its preoccupation
with maximizing points of reward, the latter with its promise of a tangible and
definitive guarantee of salvation by means of rebirth through Christ.[7]

This is not a matter of simple causality. For one thing, it is very difficult to
determine which side of this dialectic relationship comes first, whether religious
practices give contours to economic beliefs, or vice versa. In the final instance
both Islam and capitalism are processes and outcomes of human action, and
as such they cannot be ascribed causality in any direct way. Neither revivalist
religion nor global capitalism exist as conclusive systemic wholes but rather as
complex everyday practices and discourses that partly influence and partly contradict each other—not to mention the multitude of other practices and pursuits
that cannot be reduced to these two things. What we have at hand are affinities
or resonances between different practices undertaken by people who "share a
spiritual disposition to existence" (Connolly 2008: 42). The notion of points of reward and punishment has long tradition in Islam, as do trade and profit. But the
particular contemporary capitalist shape of consumption and profit—especially
sudden, abundant profits—resonates with notions of religiosity that highlight reward, because they appeal to key sensibilities that have developed into master
metaphors of subjectivity and social practice in the course of the reintroduction
of capitalism in Egypt: the capability to consume as a key to happiness and social
being (thus not really a choice, though it is commonly framed in terms of choice),
measurable profit as the main aim and motivation of action, and the often sudden
and miraculous appearance of profit and conspicuous consumption.

## Contentedness and Anxiety

Despite its well-known discontents, capitalism offers perhaps the most powerful social utopia of our time, grounded in its capacity to actually provide fulfillment in the shape of material goods and services. The evident inequality of the distribution of that fulfillment does not make the promise any less attractive. On the contrary—poor people around the world have come to invest enormous hopes in the capitalist utopia of wealth and freedom. The trouble with this vision is not only its inequality but also its elusive temporality. The fulfillment offered by capitalism is ephemeral, and bound to debt, investment, and continuous expansion (see, e.g., Appadurai 1996; Žižek 2006). Of course, consumption is not always ephemeral. Through the way people make things part of their life consumption also provides moments of lasting memory and emotional bond. Such "comfort of things," as Daniel Miller (2008) has phrased it, is the ground of the emotional gratification capitalism offers. This power of durable comfort is paralleled and made problematic, however, by the power of the future, the pressure resulting from a dramatic gap between expectations and actual resources in a world where expectations are fulfilled and expanded at the same time. Under conditions of that pressure, there is no option for stability and satisfaction, even if the things themselves have the potential to provide them.

In this situation of elusive gratification, Islam offers a powerful site of emotional stability, hope that is most pointedly expressed in the ideal of contentedness (*rida*, or *qanaʻa*) with the will of God. Muslims often emphasize that, in the end, praise is to God in good and bad times alike because contentedness with the will of God at all times is one of the virtues of a believer, and the preachers of the Islamic revival have put a lot of effort into motivating people to cultivate this attitude. At the same time, expressions of contentedness with the will of God are often made in the middle of bitter complaints and agitated anxieties about one's share in life. And the heavy emphasis of revivalist sermons on cultivating anxiety about one's share in the afterlife does not make things easier. Rather than simply becoming content, Muslims who embrace the promises of the Islamic revival are called to cultivate the two contrary affects of contentedness with the present and anxiety about the future.

Mustafa had been bothered by this for a few days when we met in a café in downtown Alexandria in 2009. He had recently started his career as a salesman in an import-export company, and he was making good progress establishing business contacts, but he could still sense nothing but pressure to go ahead:

> It's a strange thought I have had in the last days. I think that contentedness [*qanaʻa*] is all a lie. Everybody talks about it, but nobody is really content. Sure, faith [*iman*] should be about contentedness with what our Lord gives us. I'm sure that in the age of the Prophet people were content. When you read the

Qur'an it praises the grain, the dates—but it doesn't talk about chicken or meat. In those days people could be content with the simple gift [*ni'ma*] our Lord gave them. But I don't see anybody today really having that, everybody is under pressure, never content, always looking for something better. You can never stop and be happy with what you have reached. If I make 700 pounds [at that time about US$140], I am already worried about where I can get more. The only way you can stop and be content is to surrender like a beggar, stretch out your hand and let things happen to you.

This combined sense of religiosity and aspiration shares a key sense of temporality with capitalist production and consumption: both are based on a constant sense of shortcoming, of a perpetually underfulfilled aspiration. It is a sensibility of living in the future tense, which exerts continuous pressure and anxiety for the present moment, and posits fulfillment always in the future, almost but not yet within reach. The actual moments of satisfaction they do provide—the sense of peace and certainty that religious practice often offers, the sense of satisfaction that the successful acquisition of goods often brings along—are characteristically transient. The moment after the prayer is one before the next prayer, and with life being full of small and large shortcomings, there is no certainty of one's status of reward. After new goods have been bought, the installments are yet to be paid. And as soon as they are paid—or even before—newer, better goods have to be purchased.

This state of anxiety (*qalaq*) is not simply the raw opposite of well-cultivated contentedness. Anxiety, too, is often cultivated. The most powerful form of cultivated anxiety is the religious virtue of fear (*khuf*) of God, the dialectic counterpart of contentedness with God's will. Saba Mahmood (2005: 140–145) offers an insightful analysis of fear as a religious sentiment. For women in the piety movement, she argues, fear is not simply a motivation to follow commandments and prohibitions; it is most importantly an ethical faculty. Learning to be pious is learning to fear God, and cultivating this fear is a way to cultivate vigilance of oneself and become willing to make the commandments of religion a part of one's life. Developing Mahmood's idea further, I argue that the capacity to fear is more than an ethical capacity to distinguish right from wrong paths. It is an emotional state of constant shortcoming that is central to the historical nexus of capitalism, religious revival, and neoliberal rule. It is visible in the intense piety of Ramadan, in the troubled ambivalence of conflicting moral aims, in the millions of points of reward promised in Internet posts and in the need to buy more and better things. The key emotional basis of both capitalism and religious revival is the cultivation of constant anxiety. In a somewhat different mode, that anxiety is also what characterizes the shift in love from the emotional note of *shagan* (melancholy) to that of struggle for the sake of fulfillment that I took up in the previous chapter.

Conversely, the greatest counterweight to religious revival would be the sentiment that actually one is a good-enough Muslim, that following some basic moral rules will do just fine, and that "our Lord's mercy is vast" (an Arabic proverb), just like the greatest counterweight to the capitalist process of expansion would be a sense of accomplished satisfaction, a sense that one's material needs are satisfied, and that any eventual surplus no longer needs to be invested for future maximization. Both counterweights seem unlikely to ever fully prevail given the apparently universal capacity of humans to imagine and to expect more than they need for survival (Jackson 2011: 196–197). But the balance between the powers of satisfaction (or contentedness) and the powers of anxiety (or hope) is a shifting one, and it has clearly been in favor of the latter in the past decades.

No wonder, then, that Mustafa had come to see contentedness as a lie. It is a sensibility that under conditions of constant pressure, cumulative growth, and shortcoming becomes very attractive but very difficult to attain because the means to pursue contentedness are saturated by the cultivation of anxiety.

I do not, however, aim to argue that people would be victims of structural constraints under which both their religious and worldly aspirations offer little more than false comfort. Critically appropriating the approach of Michel de Certeau (1984; see also Mitchell 2007) on the tactics of the weak versus the strategies of the powerful, I instead argue that the power of both capitalism and the Islamic revival is at once established and circumvented through everyday tactics as people try to make the best out of the powers, expectations, and pressures they face (see also Jackson 1998: 26–27; Schielke and Debevec 2012). Rather than as a duality of the powerful and the powerless, I suggest that we should understand these tactics as the very condition under which people live their lives while at times trying to develop and enforce theoretical, ideological, and theological grand strategies. Just as tactics are not necessarily of the weak, strategies are not necessarily of the strong. The articulations of perfectionist religious ideology is a case in point of a grand strategy undertaken by people in marginal and precarious situations. The complex workings of economic desires, pressures, transactions, tricks, and detours are a tactical business in which the elites are involved as much as the poor are. This is not to overlook that there are winners and losers, powerful and weak. But to understand what it means to act and live under given circumstances, it is important to avoid too much dualism and instead highlight the general, existential concerns that motivate people's acts.

The race to build better homes on credit and the hope invested in a prayer that makes one's afterlife "account" overflow with reward points are both practices that allow people to make their life bearable, manageable, and hopeful. The tragic catch of these attempts is that they also constitute the pressures and powers that people face when every potential groom tries to outbid others in standards of housing and every attempt to strive for reward reminds one of the punishments that await around every corner. This is a power that no grand strategy could ever accomplish. At the same time, this power is never absolute, always the outcome of particular actions that can be changed, oftentimes slightly, sometimes dramatically.

This power of capitalism and religious revivals as processes that are made by people who at the same time are subject to them raises two final questions, only one of which can be answered here. The second takes up the second half of this book.

The first question has to do with the ethicality of capitalism. I titled this chapter with an inversion of Weber's famous thesis on the role of Protestant ethics in the genealogy of capitalism, with the intention of developing a nondichotomous view of living revivalist Islam and consumption-oriented capitalism—a view in which economy and religion belong to the same world, and in which economic processes and moral and spiritual pursuits share a resonance, a "disposition to existence" (Connolly 2008). But is *ethics* the right term? When we look at the pressure of the future and the increasing uncertainty and insufficiency of life trajectories people experience even though they have more things than before (things that ought to bring existential comfort), and how that experience compels people like Mustafa to wonder how one could possibly live by the Qur'anic attitude toward God's grace today, then the reflective moment of the ethical mode is certainly there. But it is often not there when people borrow more money to cover growing consumption and cost of weddings, or when people try to maximize their reward in the afterworld by sharing a link on social media, or when certain issues and problems of moral relevance are systematically *not* scrutinized. In short, the processes of capitalist consumption and expansion, and the revivalist moral scrutiny of ritual, gender, confession, and the affective relationship with God, do create new and increasing uncertainties and thus also the need to reflect and wonder about what is right and wrong and what one should do about it. But they also create certainties, things that are taken for granted, necessities that defy reflective critique, affects that are cultivated not so consciously, as well as contradictions and wrongs that need to be evaded or silenced. Perhaps the better term, then, is *ethos,* the actually existing affective disposition to existence, self and relationality, which may or may not be part of an aspirational project of active self-making, and which may or may not be actively reflected upon.

This is as far as the engagement with grand schemes, their ambiguous coexistence, and their yet-to-be-realized nature can take us. From here, we need to shift our focus to the second question raised in this chapter, a question about the actual paths people take and their consequences. If the pursuit of grand schemes is inseparable from the pursuit of tactical advances, this means that we must turn our attention to specific trajectories of action that people actually realize under such conditions. It is to such paths and their winding trajectories that we now turn.

# 6   I Want to Be Committed

WITHIN A FEW months' time in 2009, three friends told me independently of one another that they "wanted to be committed" (*'ayiz* or *'ayza altazim*) but found it surprisingly difficult and frustrating. They all share an experience that in the first decade of the twenty-first century became a paradigmatic case of intense spiritual and moral dedication: Salafi activism. Of the various movements and currents that characterize the Islamic revival, Salafism emerged in the first decade of the twenty-first century as one of the most powerful in setting the tone of what it means to be truly religious. And "commitment" (*iltizam*) has become a very compelling keyword for discussing and describing what it means to be a good Muslim.

Why is it difficult to be committed? Difficulty is definitely not the impression one gets from the sermons of preachers who emphasize the ease and simplicity of Islam as a comprehensive guide to life. Much of the attraction of the revivalist turn to textual knowledge and moral perfection in general, and Salafi Islam in particular, lies in its apparent simplicity and straightforwardness, typically expressed in ritual and moral rigor, a quest to leave no gray areas, the world neatly divided into the permitted and the prohibited. And yet most of those who sympathize with the idea of commitment do not try to turn it into reality. And many of those who do try (and increasingly many do, as Salafi preachers have been gaining more ground as representatives of the correct, standard Islam) eventually find their activist drive inexplicably receding, face problems in living a committed life, and discover more and more contradictions in the teachings and teachers they follow. When people try to be perfect, there is trouble involved.

To understand a specific path of commitment and dedication, it is necessary to pay attention to existential pursuits, historical conditions, and unexpected consequences. Striving for perfection is a paradoxical path in a life in the future tense that may fail to accomplish a pious formation of the self, and yet it always transforms those who try—only it does so in unpredictable ways.

In circumstances where all promises of a good life are in some ways troubled, religion offers a powerful promise of hope, happiness, and clarity. This probably has always been so, and for most of the young men and women I know, religion is an important part of their lives and imaginations, a source and an element of a good life. For them, religion is a framework of subjectivity and action that is neither exclusive nor exhaustive and that, precisely because of the flexibility in its practice, can maintain its perfection in theory (see also Simon 2009; Schielke and Debevec 2012). But for various reasons, some of the people I know have come to a point at which they have wanted to go further, to turn the idea of perfection into a perfect life. And yet their activist commitment has been problematic in different ways. The outcomes of their attempts to overcome the disturbing ambiguity of everyday life have been ambiguous most of the time, and tragic sometimes.

Wanting to be committed is by no means something Muslims have always wanted. There is no doubt that deep and consistent religious devotion has a long history in Egypt and elsewhere. But the specific way of being religious involved in "commitment" is distinctively modern—even the word *iltizam* itself is borrowed from nationalist discourse, where it originally was used to translate the French literary-political notion of *engagement* (Klemm 2000; Sartre 1949). There is a characteristically factual and systemic sense to *iltizam* that distinguishes it from earlier notions of piety: its focus is less on tradition, communal belonging, and personal devotion to the Prophet and Muslim saints, and more on the meticulous work on oneself through a constant comparison of one's actions and feelings with normative texts.

Embracing a Salafi understanding of religiosity and morality is not necessarily the same thing as becoming a committed Salafi, however. In the words of the Egyptian journalist Husam Tammam, Salafism in Egypt is less about strictly following a Salafi path and more about cultivating a Salafi "mood" (*mazag*), a way to think about the power of God in daily life that embraces the creed but not necessarily the consequent path of perfection (Tammam and Kreil 2010; Peterson 2012). Within this mood, there is much space for different paths, from unveiled young women listening to Salafi sermons to men with long beards citing love poetry. But it is also a mood that opens a particularly compelling path of dedication to those who, for various reasons, search for a more comprehensive certainty, a more certain sense of purpose, a more unambiguous way to tell right from wrong.

Commitment as the ideal of a religious life is intertwined with the pursuit of knowing Islam as a foundation of moral practice and being. At the same time, the Salafi path of commitment is rather different from the "Salafi mood" of a life guided by a textual positivist ideal of religiosity. The latter is about living a complex life in the guidance of moments of firm hold, whereas the former is about overcoming complexity for the sake of a single, exclusive sense of purpose.

This is why I insist on using the notion of commitment (*iltizam*) that is current in Egypt rather than the notion of piety, which has lately become so popular in the anthropology of Islam. Looking at the emotional, spiritual, and societal grounds and consequences of religious commitment, I argue that trajectories of commitment may be more telling of the nature of activist dedication than of piety in general. Taking into account the specific character of given activist movements as well as the personal idiosyncrasies and comparative moments of activist dedication, we will be able to understand Salafi commitment better, both in its specific shape and in its relation to more general human pursuits.

The question, then, is why Salafi commitment is so compelling, and what kind of experience and what kind of emotional and practical consequences are involved in it. This is a question that requires a biographical approach to account for the emergence and changes of people's pursuits in life. While I have met and interviewed many people who are or have been involved in the pursuit of Salafi commitment, this chapter focuses on the stories of three people whom I have known over a long time: Mustafa, whom I met in early 2006 and who joined a rural Salafi group in search of a solid moral ground amid a personal crisis; Fouad, whom I have known since 1998 and who has gone through several short periods of intensive *iltizam* but has generally kept a distance from Salafi organizations; and Nagat, whom I have known since 2003 and whose spiritual search led her to a short-lived experiment with Salafism.

## Solving a Crisis

When I first met Mustafa in early 2006 in his native village of Nazlat al-Rayyis, he had just gone through very difficult times. His father, with whom he had been very close, had died three years earlier. This left him seriously disoriented, and to make things worse, he had become the senior male in his family, loaded with responsibilities but lacking the experience to handle them. In this situation he fell into what he describes as bad company and started smoking hashish on a regular basis and getting into various kinds of trouble. His habit of smoking hashish ended up costing him a sizable part of the inheritance his father had left him, until his mother and uncle intervened. The unhappy end of his love relationship (see chapter 4) also took place in this period. After a while he gave up his consumption of hashish and started to look for a principle to tell right from wrong, a principle that he found in Salafi piety. He started praying in a Salafi mosque, grew his beard long, shortened the hems of his trousers in the Salafi manner, and tried to stop smoking cigarettes (Salafis hold that smoking is *haram*). He demanded that his mother (who until then had dressed in the colorful combination of long gown and headscarf common in the countryside) to wear the full face veil called *niqab*, which she refused, and they settled for a single-color *khimar*, which is plainer than standard dress but does not cover the face. He removed all pictures from his home, except for the photograph of his late father, which he did not have the heart to remove. Months of intensive piety and worship followed, a period that he describes as a very happy time in his life. But bit by bit, practical problems came up: he was compelled to shave his beard when he was about to be conscripted, he felt the drive of piety slowing down, he started smoking cigarettes again, and he became less dedicated in his observance of ritual obligations. Still holding to Salafi ideas of piety but not finding the energy to enact them, he began to suffer from feelings of guilt and failure.

This was the state he was in when I met him again in the autumn of 2006. In a matter of few months he had gained the reputation of being an enthusiastic Salafi proselytizer, and although he no longer sported a Salafi beard and dress code, young men continued to ask him for Salafi literature, which he got from his sheikh. And yet he was deeply shattered. He was troubled by his quite inexplicable inability to maintain the rigorous ritual schedule of Salafism, which in addition to the obligatory five daily prayers, contains an extensive program of voluntary prayers and lectures. He felt that he had found the correct, true Islam but had failed to live it out. He had been happy, but now he was troubled.

His friend Tawfiq, who had not gone through such intense crises as Mustafa, described Mustafa's move to religious commitment as a sudden and surprising transformation, and he suggested that those who have gone seriously astray in their lives are the ones who become very strict when religious. He argued that Mustafa might have gone too far and put himself under so much strain that he was suffering a backlash.

Like Mustafa, Tawfiq adheres to notions of ritual practice close to the Salafi movement. He does not, for example, pray in the main mosque of the village because it was built next to the tomb of the local Muslim saint. But Tawfiq has never been attracted by the idea of becoming *multazim* (committed) in a religious sense. He has been following other compelling pursuits (e.g., migration, revolution) with great determination, but his religiosity meets the bare minimum by conventional standards. While Tawfiq and Mustafa thus share a similar religious doctrine, their paths of religious practice have been very different. Both give the same answer to the question as to what motivated Mustafa's Salafi turn: an urgent personal crisis experienced as a moral vacuum. In Mustafa's words, it was a matter of urgently wanting to be able to "know right from wrong."

By late 2006, it looked like Mustafa's attempt to find a moral ground of certainty had failed and taken him from one crisis to another. But he had little time to dwell in this situation; he was conscripted. In Egypt military service is usually associated with extreme physical and emotional hardship: bad food, lack of sleep, and continuous humiliation. According to Mustafa, few soldiers keep their prayers, and even fewer fast during Ramadan. In the hardship of the army, all other considerations come second to the crucial issues of friendship and material conditions that allow one to stay healthy and sane. As I met Mustafa during holidays, he would still occasionally discuss his trouble with *iltizam*, but it bothered him less. The military service kept him busy, and in a peculiar fashion it offered him something of the same thing he had been searching for in Salafism. During a holiday shortly before his release from the army in 2008, he told me:

> I feel relaxed (at peace) [*mirtah*] in the army. Since a few months ago, although it's difficult and there is a lot of humiliation and trouble [*bahdala*], I feel at peace because everything has a clear structure, you don't have to think for yourself—I take care of my things, see that my stuff is OK in case of inspection so that I don't get punished, and everything follows a clear routine.

After his release he again told me that despite having had a tough time in the beginning, he eventually found military service to be the best time in his life. Military service gave him discipline and order—very similar, he said, to what he was looking for among the Salafis. It was this sense of a clear schedule and structure that he felt he had been lacking, and which he was beginning to gain bit by bit. He appeared less anxious, and although he occasionally smoked a joint again, he did not return to the excessive consumption of hashish that had previously messed up his life. He was pursuing various plans to find work, and he eventually found reasonable, if not perfect, work as a salesman for an import-export company.

Although Mustafa has since faced new troubles and tragedies in his life, he has not been drawn to Salafi commitment again. When I met him in Alexandria in the spring of 2010, months after his brother was killed in a car accident, he was still recovering from the shock and sorrow of the accident, but he did not express a sense of a loss of direction. On the contrary, he said that the sudden tragedy had made him acutely aware of his obligations to his mother.

In the course of our discussion, Mustafa asked me where I stood with my research, and this turned the talk back to his Salafi experiment four years earlier. I started by telling him that I had been looking at the way people hold ideas of perfection, not just about religion but also about love and material welfare, without it having to mean that their lives look like that. Instead, I explained, I thought that people search for a firm hold in perfectionist ideas to find a way in life. Mustafa agreed and related this idea to his own experience of commitment. He described his trajectory as a path curving left and right from "the straight path" (*as-sirat al-mustaqim*) but approximately following its course. He drew this with his finger on the table: a straight line and a curving line following it:

> I still sometimes feel that I want to be committed [*'ayiz altazim*], but I find myself unable to return to it. When I pray, I may manage the noon prayer but I forget the afternoon prayer and lose the rhythm again.

I suggested that the reason he became a committed Salafi might be because he was experiencing a personal crisis that he urgently wanted to solve and that gave him the drive, desperately searching as he was for a way to tell right from wrong.

But when his crisis was solved, he gradually came to stand on his feet through a long process in which the Salafi period and the time in the army were key experiences. Standing on his feet and being again able to instinctively tell right from wrong, knowing which way to go, he no longer had the need or the urge for *iltizam*, I suggested. He responded:

> That is true, although I find it difficult to admit it to myself. But when I hear it from someone else, it is absolutely true. But the beliefs I took on then have become rooted in me. They stick also when I do not follow them. Praying, for example. I know I should do it even if I find it difficult to keep up with it. Or *sadaqa* [voluntary alms]. Sometimes I give generous alms to a beggar willingly and with ease. But at other times I think about the bills to pay and the economic pressure I'm in and I reluctantly give fifty piasters.

Developing this thought, Mustafa again drew the straight path and the curving path with his finger on the table.

For Mustafa, his Salafi activism has done two kinds of an emotional work. For one thing, it was part of his own troubled search for firm ground. Salafism did not actually provide an answer to this search; it was not the solution he was looking for, or else his period of commitment would have been longer. But just like the army, it helped him find clues that eventually led him to the moral ground he was looking for. Part of this ground is the Islamic notion of the straight path (*al-sirat al-mustaqim*), which he acquired during his Salafi period. Another part was his recognition of his need for structure and discipline, which he acquired during military service. This acquiring of notions that in combination could become constituents of a moral ground was the second kind of emotional work involved in his activist period. And yet although he continues to adhere to Salafi notions of good ritual and a moral life, his vision of the straight path is quite different from the Salafi ideal of wholehearted and uncompromising commitment, just like it is quite different from military discipline. In Islamic eschatological tradition, from where the notion of the straight path has been developed into a principle of righteous life, *al-sirat al-mustaqim* is a bridge as narrow as a knife's blade that people must pass to enter paradise. Those misguided fall to hell; those rightly guided enter Paradise. There is no space for missteps. Mustafa, however, borrows from common wisdom the idea of approximation, of a life drifting at times to the left and at times to the right but more or less maintaining the right direction. It is also worth noting that the kind of religious values Mustafa entertains are colored by his personal preferences. Prayer and charity are what concerns him most. In regard to gender relations he is more ambiguous. And although he did vote for the Salafi Nour Party in the 2011 elections (because he considered the Salafis the only political force capable of restoring law and order), he does not generally support Islamist political movements.

## Unresolved Struggles

What made the pursuit of Salafism so attractive to Mustafa, and why did he stop? This was a question that Mustafa, Fouad, and I were pondering while taking a walk in the fields during a holiday from his military service in the autumn of 2007. Speaking from his own experience with short periods of *iltizam*, Fouad offered a basically psychological explanation:

> The search for *iltizam* is a way to give oneself peace: to concentrate on worship and to thank God for whatever the circumstances are. That makes it a way to handle the pressures and troubles, but they will later appear again, and people's commitment will recede, and that causes often even greater pressure than one experienced before the period of commitment. One misses the feeling of being included in God's mercy and the happiness about being committed, and at the same time one has developed a more intense feeling of guilt [*zanb*] for anything sinful.

In Fouad's interpretation there emerges a contrast between the ideal and the actual motivations and experience of pious commitment. Determined, all-encompassing pious commitment remains for him the real, ideal way of being a good Muslim. In his view, *iltizam* is something that Muslims should strive for at all times, and what really counts is developing a profound, even if not visible, religious character. But at the same time he argues that actually the psychological reason for pious commitment is that one wants to find peace. Only afterward does one actually confront the details of obligations involved in a committed Salafi life. Mustafa confirmed this from his own experience: "I was first asking: how can I find peace [*artah*]; the rest followed."

Fouad's psychological interpretation of the consequences of *iltizam* is not a consistent one, either. It contains two parallel, partly contradictory versions. In one version, a person becomes *multazim* in an attempt to escape inner conflicts and problems, but those will still follow, which is why the pursuit of pious commitment motivated by personal trouble is likely to be unsuccessful. In another version, Fouad points out that Mustafa, who was a real troublemaker before, did profit from his period of commitment by becoming a calmer and more responsible person. In one version, Salafi religiosity is an escape from one's inner struggles, not a real solution, because it does not solve one's inner struggles. In another, Salafi-style religiosity as a period in one's life can help break a personal crisis or a life of deviance and lead to a more balanced life.

In both Fouad's and Mustafa's accounts, a vision of commitment as the true, proper sense of being Muslim is intertwined with psychological and moral urgencies. When Fouad speaks about commitment as an ideal way of being Muslim, he sounds very much like the sermons and religious slogans that present commitment as a cumulative path of perfection, and also like some of the ethnographies that develop a theory of Islamic ethics and piety as an aspirational project of self-formation. And yet when he speaks about the actual experience of commitment, it appears to be a much more fragile and troubled business. This is immediately related to his own experience as a committed Salafi Muslim.

Fouad has gone through at least four periods of Salafi commitment, one in his youth and three in his adult age, the last in 2010. These periods have been short, possibly because the very perfectionism of being committed stands in too stark a contrast to his playful and willingly ambiguous character. By 2011, he turned quite radically against Salafism and became involved in revolutionary politics and liberal hermeneutics, which gives his trajectory a particular twist.

Since his marriage in 2003, Fouad has become generally more religious than he was before, but he has also enthusiastically pursued artistic and literary pursuits and visions of life and society that he describes as leftist. He never tried to reconcile these pursuits with his religious trajectory, which in Egyptian parlance would best described as nonmovement (*ghayr haraki*) Salafism, focused on the pursuit of *iltizam* but not aligned with any particular group or leader. He willingly admits to being "a person of extraordinary contradictions." (This may also be why he is likely to articulate a psychological explanation of his and others' trajectories.) But at times, the contradictions and pressures of life have become too much for him. His periods of Salafi commitment appear to be an attempt to come to terms with some especially troubling pressures and contradictions in his life by trying to make one principle prevail over all others—an attempt that he recognizes as an antagonistic one: "It's as if there were two of me, each trying to kill the other." Being "committed" for him has been related to being mentally in a bad shape, and becoming "moderate" again has been part of a general improvement in his emotional situation.

In this sense, there is a tragic moment in Fouad's strive for commitment. Unlike with Mustafa, for whom the end of his Salafi period was a painful but eventually fruitful experience, Fouad's relation with *iltizam* has often been inherently troublesome as he has been repeatedly trying to overcome feelings of guilt and conflict in ways that have actually increased his sense of guilt and his moments of conflict—and he is the first one to admit it. The promise of happiness through perfection became a measuring stick that provided him with impossible demands and troubling, even destructive, solutions. For most of the time between 2003 and 2010, he did not pursue these solutions, and the perfectionist demands to which he adhered offered him a sense of spiritual and moral certainty. But in moments when he did pursue the path of perfection, the results were ambiguous.

If Fouad's trajectory with *iltizam* was marked by antagonism and impulsiveness, so was its end in January 2011. A long-standing opponent of the Mubarak regime, Fouad participated in demonstrations against the government in Alexandria almost daily in January and February 2011. In this time, he became enraged about the support of the regime by Salafi organizations that in Alexandria distributed leaflets reading that demonstrating against the government is forbidden to Muslims. On one occasion, he witnessed how the sheikh of a Salafi mosque he knew locked the doors to demonstrators who tried to take a wounded man to the mosque. He became founding member of a left-wing political activist circle in his native village in the spring of 2011 and a regular demonstrator against the military government, and later the Muslim Brotherhood. After 2011, Fouad has become not only a fervent supporter of the revolution but also a sharp critic of Salafi sheikhs and organizations. He has also turned away from the textual hermeneutics of facts to instead appropriate a humanistic or Sufi vision of Islam that revolves around the idea of a loving God and reading of holy texts as a creative act. But while he has turned from *iltizam* and the struggle with himself to a struggle with society, antagonism remains a key trait of his life—but the thrust and scope of the struggle have shifted.

## Searching for Perfection

It would be mistaken, however, to claim that the turn to Salafi commitment is generally motivated by personal crises and struggles. The search for peace through clarity and rigorous perfection does emerge as a core motivation for religious commitment, as does a discomfort with ambiguity. But this search can be grounded in quite different life experiences and expectations. This has been the case in the spiritual search of Nagat, an unmarried woman in her midtwenties (at the time of her experiment with Salafi commitment) from a village in the central Delta province of Sharqiyya.

Nagat comes from a devout Sufi (Islamic mystic) family. Her late father was the sheikh of a small Sufi group, and since her childhood she had been traveling with her family to several *mulid*s (Muslim saint-day festivals; see Schielke 2012a) around the country, where they organize a service of free food and a celebration with a religious singer at night. Through her socialization in the culture of *mulid*s she knows a considerably broader range of people, points of view, and ways of life than most of her female age-mates in her village.

As long as I have known Nagat she has been very religious by any standards. She fasts two days a week, prays regularly, and shows great interest in religious matters. However, Nagat's religious interests have developed in a way that has made her look beyond the devout but unintellectual traditions of spirituality in her family. In the course of this process, she became increasingly interested in the scripturalist ideals of normative religious behavior that have gained currency in Egypt in the past decades. In 2006 she shifted her style of clothing from a colorful head scarf, blouse, and skirt to a long black *khimar*, which reveals only her face. In 2008 she started attending Qur'an classes in a neighboring village. These classes, like so many others around the country, were organized by a Salafi group. Nagat quickly became more drawn to the teachings of her sheikh, a schoolteacher in his late twenties who provided her with books by Muhammad Nasiruddin al-Albani, Muhammad ibn Baz, and other modern Salafi and Wahhabi authorities. By the end of 2008 she had stopped traveling to *mulid*s with her family, following the Salafi view of Muslim saint veneration as idolatry. She stopped watching soap operas, films, and video clips, and instead had the television set turned to religious programming, except when her brother insisted on watching a movie. She also wanted to start wearing the full face veil (*niqab*), but her family refused her this. As I discussed her Salafi turn with her during this time, she was very enthusiastic about it but insisted that she was not following the Salafi teachings but quite generic Islamic views. In her family, this predictably caused conflicts, and especially her older brother was very upset but unable to make her change her mind.

Yet when I returned to Egypt in the autumn of 2009, she asked me to join her family to a *mulid*. Her Salafi turn was over and she was back to the Sufi devotion of her family. She was also back to watching soap operas, films, and game shows on television. I may have not been entirely uninvolved in this because I had sent with her brother a selection of books representing contemporary Islamic discourses ranging from the Muslim Brotherhood over Sufism to liberal Islamic thought. When we met again, she thanked me for the books, especially for one by Gamal al-Banna, an influential thinker of a liberal current in the Islamist milieu that others have called "post-Islamism" (Roy 1999). But more important than the books were her own experiences in the Salafi milieu that had compelled her to go on with her spiritual search:

> I want to be committed ['*ayza akun multazima*], and I search for perfection. But wherever I look for it, in the end I find contradictions. The sheikh whose Qur'an course I attended last winter, turned out to act contrary to his own teachings. He was teaching that the mixing of sexes is strictly forbidden [*haram*], but he was teaching women! And he was telling that music and television are *haram*, but he was having a song as a ring tone on his phone and watching movies. In the beginning, I completely adored the sheikh and his teachings, but in the end, he fell completely. After that I followed for some time the preachers on television. I called them on the phone many times but found that also they contradicted themselves.

What troubles Nagat most in Salafism is the way Salafi men relate to women. She describes them as having a tense, unnatural relationship to the opposite sex:

> In the village quite a few young men have recently let their beards grow and go to pray in a mosque in al-Mahalla al-Kubra [an industrial city in the central Delta region]. They have become very strict and committed, and keep saying

"it is not allowed in Islamic law" [*la yaguz shar'an*] to everything, although just shortly before they were ordinary youths who would flirt with girls. But now they make a big curve around women and look away as if we were something filthy.

A friend of mine has a cousin who joined the Salafis and let his beard grow long. When he met her again he started to admonish her. He told her that she must wear a face veil [*niqab*[ and that she will be going to hell. The poor girl got so upset that she started crying and finally shouted at him: "What's the matter with you? Wasn't it you who used to be looking at me through the window and sending me love letters!?"

The image of the letter-writing young man suddenly turning into a preaching and admonishing sheikh emerges as the central moment of Nagat's critique of the perfectionism of committed Salafis. For her, there is something insincere and suspect in the young men's sudden zeal for gender segregation. And she also sees it as unfair toward women. For Nagat the Salafi pursuit of perfection has discredited itself through its inherent contradictions, which women feel more severely than men.

After leaving behind both the village Salafi group and the Salafi preachers on television, Nagat identified herself with the Sufi devotion of her family again. But she continued searching. In the spring of 2009 she told me that he path of perfection continued to attract her, but the closer she looked, the more she was puzzled by the answers, for example regarding the difference of the Sunna and Shia branches of Islam. Having taken a look at both, she came to the conclusion that they both have a point of view that is logical in itself and confirms its own rightness. How can she tell which one of them is right?

Telling this to me, she expressed her puzzlement: Why is the pursuit of perfection so contradictory? Why is it so difficult to be committed? As she asked me for my opinion, I answered that in my personal view, to be a good person, one needs to listen to one's heart and to give space for the different movements and moments in oneself. She recognized herself in my point of view and said that she tries to be perfect, but at the same time she does things every day that she decides not to do again and then does them again the next day.

Writing about Dutch Salafis, Martijn de Koning (2009, 2013) has shown that contradictions are inherent to the search for moral clarity and perfection but do not necessarily compromise the project of activist commitment. Rather, the repeated experience of imperfection is a major motivation for the further pursuit of perfection (see also Beekers 2014). Navida Khan, in her work on Pakistan, points out that there is a search for perfection grounded in the specific history of Pakistan as a Muslim nation. It is an open-ended, striving perfection, however, which has no end or finite state of accomplishment. Instead, it gives rise to spiritual experimentation and striving, a "doing and redoing of known forms" (Khan 2013: 7).

There is an ambiguity between perfection as a concrete promise and as an open-ended quest, and that ambiguity can be motivating as well as troubling. Different people draw different conclusions from the experience of that ambiguity, depending on their social and intellectual resources, families and friendships, and personal temperament.

While Nagat was disappointed about the reality of Salafi activism, she remained more than a little ambivalent about the issue of perfection. In one moment she held up the idea of perfection, lamenting the Salafi sheikhs not for their teachings but for their own weakness when it comes to living as they teach. In another moment she distanced herself from the very pursuit of perfection and commented that people keep wanting to see everything as black and white, but that there must also be something in the middle.

Unlike Mustafa, who for a long time saw the end of his Salafi period as a failure, Nagat could see her return from the Salafi path of commitment largely as an accomplishment. It endowed her with significantly increased trust in her own judgment, which she has since demonstrated in articulating and insisting on her point of view when discussing with her family her plans for marriage. Importantly, this emphasis on one's own moral judgment and capacity to act of one's own accord is not simply a consequence of her break with Salafism; it was already part of her embracing it, individual moral responsibility being ingrained to the very project of commitment, with often contradictory outcomes (Abu-Lughod 1996b; Reuter 1999; Karlsson Minganti 2008; Schulz 2011; Abenante 2014). This does not necessarily mean that she would have started to pursue feminist notions of gender equality. She searches for a space of action, mastery over her life and the ability to speak her feelings within a conservative and pious framework.

Through her serious engagement with the idea of perfection, Nagat displays a much stronger sensibility and dislike for contradictions than that displayed by Mustafa and Fouad. At the same time, there is less sense of an existential crisis in her account. Nagat's Salafi experiment was motivated by a longer-lasting spiritual search in which serious and wholehearted dedication play a key role. While Nagat has become critical about the perfectionist, black-and-white ideal of commitment, her short-lived period of Salafi activist commitment did not give way to noncommitment, as was the case with Mustafa. Instead, it was followed by a new—in a way much more radical—commitment. She became a Shiite.

One of the paradoxical consequences of the spread of Salafi Islam is that by demonizing other traditions of Muslim piety, most importantly Sufism, and polemically associating them with Shia Islam—which in the Salafi view is not Islam at all—Salafis have compelled many Egyptian Muslims to develop an increased interest in Shiism, among them Nagat and her brother. In a matter of few years, a small but thriving community of Egyptian Shia Muslims has come into existence. It is a very precarious existence, because following Shia Islam is de facto illegal in Egypt, and people have been convicted to prison sentences for publicly identifying themselves as Shia Muslims.

For Nagat, joining the Shia branch of Islam was a way to link her Sufi devotion with a strongly mediatic movement and a powerful religious doctrine in which devotion for the family of the Prophet Muhammad had a central place. But it was also a clear gesture of opposition to Salafism and the Muslim Brotherhood, and since 2011 her embracing of Shiism also has gone hand in hand with a firm political opposition to the Muslim Brotherhood, which she expresses and communicates with like-minded people, mainly by means of social media and Internet fora. Perhaps because Shia Islam in Egypt is by default minoritarian and oppositional, she does not experience it as contradicting her search for a space of independent action and expression the way Salafism did, nor does she search for perfection in purity the way she did as a Salafi—for example, she has no problem combining her Shiite devotion with her love for Turkish soap operas.

Nagat is a person for whom it is important to do something right and good, and if possible, to do it 100 percent. Unlike for Fouad and Mustafa, who became committed not only to be better Muslims but also to solve problems they suffered from, for Nagat commitment is something she pursues for the sake of being committed. With this temperament of hers, she might be drawn to some sort of activist commitment regardless of the circumstances. This raises the question of the degree to which the power of Salafi commitment lies in the tradition of piety evoked by Salafi preachers and teachers, and the degree to which it is related to more general (and more idiosyncratic) human pursuits. How can we understand the appeal and consequences of Salafism as a model of and for dedication and activist commitment in more general terms and in a historical moment when a reflective struggle with the self is a powerful paradigm of doing the right thing?

## The Grounds of Dedication

Throughout this book I have argued that we should take seriously the ambiguous coexistence of different aims that characterize people's moral, religious, and aspirational lives. In the previous chapters, I have made that argument primarily in relation to a vast majority of people who are not committed activists. But committed activists are not a different species of people, and just as they should not be made paradigmatic representatives of religious and other experience, they should not be excluded from it either. The question, then, is how to account for the specificity of activist commitment while recognizing its embeddedness in more complex life trajectories, general societal sensibilities, and historical constellations. If not only the everyday lives of people who are not very committed but also the experience of people who do want to be committed are characterized by ambivalence and trouble, then it is not sufficient to expand our vision of religiosity from dedicated activists to include the not-so-dedicated majority. We need an approach that helps us look at the existential grounds and consequences involved in following an activist trajectory.

This is, in fact, an issue that has been taken up in a number of recent studies on Muslim religious activism that, instead of taking the activist paths for granted, specifically inquire about the underlying concerns, complex paths, and consequences of activist trajectories in a way that is open to their specificity as well as their connectedness to wider social experience (M. de Koning 2009; Hafez 2011; Schulz 2011; Gauvain 2012; Janson 2013; Abenante 2014). For my part, I build on this body of work but want to specifically add two dimensions to the inquiry. One is the importance of looking at the trajectories of people whose activist commitment is either short (as with Mustafa) or shifting (as with Fouad and Nagat). The other is a theoretical approach that takes as its starting point the primacy of existential concerns and pragmatic considerations of living a life, people's attempts to have power over their own condition—along with their often unpredictable and contradictory consequences (Jackson 2005; Orsi 2005).

In the end, this is more than a theoretical problem: it is a matter of an emotional commitment to anthropology as a dialogue and an encounter. This is why I have tried to build this chapter on the reflections I have undertaken together with my interlocutors more than on current theoretical models. But this does not mean that I advocate an ethnographic isolationism and refuse a comparative theoretical perspective. On the contrary, I believe that taking seriously the existential concerns and individual idiosyncrasies of activist commitment helps us also better understand both the specific appeal of Salafi Islam and the general pursuit of dedication.

The first step of an activist path is preceded and directed by a mood (*mazag*; see Tammam and Kreil 2010); a diffuse structure of feeling (Williams 1969); a set of powerful pressures, anxieties, promises, and hopes—and it is here that we must search for the particular appeal and dynamics of Salafi commitment. Contrary to some other researchers in the field (e.g., Mahmood 2005; Hirschkind 2006b; Caeiro 2006; Anjum 2007), I do not think that this diffuse mood is best approached in the framework of a discursive tradition of Islam. Explaining the grounds and shapes of contemporary transformations of Islamic religiosity in general and activist commitment in particular through a more or less given discursive tradition involves the risk of taking the emotional dynamics of a global wave of economic and religious transformation for granted instead of inquiring into exactly what is going on. Muslims do not simply want to be good Muslims. They face a dynamic historical process in which some aims emerge as especially compelling, and pursuing those aims in turn has consequences that change the ways people view themselves, the world in which they live, and the future they expect.

The appeal of being committed has specific grounds and motivations. In my encounters with Mustafa, Fouad, and Nagat, three motivations feature centrally. One is the search for an immediate solution for an acute personal crisis; another is an ongoing struggle with conflicting pressures and pursuits; and a third is the desire to find something truly important to pursue in a way that gives one's life a clear and permanent purpose. All appear to be quite general human pursuits, but they are also specific to the life situations of each person, their temperaments, and the promises and pressures that prevail in the world they are located in.

Some of the questions that arise from these three encounters, are, What makes a specific direction of activism attractive in a specific situation? What are the anxieties people try to overcome and what are the promises they are offered? What does their actual work of dedication look like? What consequences does it have? How do the experiments of activist dedication, which are often temporary, become a part of people's biographies?

To pursue these questions, it is important to be open to the generally human as well as the historically and culturally specific, and the individually idiosyncratic (while recognizing that one can seldom if ever clearly distinguish one from the other). For the sake of illustration, I return to Mustafa's account once more. To understand his trajectory, it is first necessary—but not sufficient—to look at the success of Salafi Islam in gaining a near-hegemonic position as the most powerful religious voice in many parts of Egypt. According to Mustafa, he faced three choices in his search for a base to know right and wrong: the Sufis, the Muslim Brotherhood, and the Salafis. Having been socialized with a vague reformist sense of Islam, like many from his generation, for him the Sufis were already disqualified. The Islamist political activism of the Muslim Brothers did not attract him. The Salafis, with their intense and detailed program of personal commitment, appeared to him to be the right choice.

Mustafa explicitly phrases his turn to the Salafi path as a choice. This is not obvious—choice has not always been important in the society he was born into, but it has become increasingly so, resonating with the paradigmatic role choice has for capitalist consumption and for (neo)liberal visions of individual responsibility that have become increasingly influential in Egypt in the course of the reintroduction of capitalism (Saad 2010; Pahwa 2010; Abenante 2014). And yet it is clear that his choice was extremely limited from the start. None of the many other currents of Islamic piety and practice was on his list of options. More important, all the options were explicitly Islamic. Again, this is not obvious. There is a much wider variety of forms of social and moral engagement that might have also provided a way to know right from wrong. And yet in the first decade of the twenty-first century, under the conditions of depoliticized social life during the Mubarak regime and the rise of the revivalist ideal of piety to hegemonic power, religious paths of dedication became extremely compelling to the degree of marginalizing other paths.

In a time during which religion understood as a system of facts emerged as the most dynamic, albeit by no means only, source of moral and existential trust, and during which most political paths to gaining some power over one's situation had become very difficult and frustrating to pursue, some few paths of dedication thus became extremely compelling. In most cases, and definitely so in rural contexts, there is much choice regarding to whether and to which degree one may pursue such highly compelling pursuits, but there is much less choice between different pursuits. The attraction of Salafi Islam as a path of perfection is thus twofold. On one level, it presents a promise of clarity, happiness, and hope through rigid perfection, which is very compelling in itself in a world that is experienced as chaotic and troubling. On another level, however, the gradual success of Salafism and other movements in turning the counterdiscourse of the Islamic revival into a social hegemony also means that the Salafi path of perfection has become more and more compelling simply by virtue of its strong presence, of the normality of committed religiosity as the ideal type of moral integrity. This hegemony is associated with a paradoxical sense of increasing moral chaos so that regardless of the increasing degree of religiosity, social life is depicted as more sinful than ever. From the background of this perpetual sense of moral crisis, a determined and complete turn to religious commitment is a very compelling solution. Whoever was searching for a path of determined dedication in Egypt before 2011 would thus find Salafism a very likely path, and the number of those taking the path of commitment has been on the rise for many years.

Under these circumstances, Salafi commitment was the obvious answer for Mustafa's search for a way to know right from wrong. From there, Mustafa's dedication took a specific direction with emphasis on gender segregation; male control over women; abstinence from alcohol, drugs, and cigarettes; and a view of life as the systematic application of divine law. This had very specific consequences for the way he dealt, for example, with his mother and some of his friends. It continues to have consequences for the way he understands worship and moral action and the way he thinks about what it means to be a good person. In this sense, Mustafa's activist path as a Salafi had a specific shape and specific consequences, quite different from, for example, what would have been involved in becoming the follower of a Sufi sheikh, which was a likely thing to do in similar circumstances in the Middle East for centuries until quite recently (see Gilsenan 2000), or in joining a political or social movement that does not articulate its concerns in primarily religious terms, which was a major option in his village just two decades earlier and became so again in 2011.

And yet the emotional work involved in Mustafa's Salafi experiment was also of a more general nature: Mustafa at different times has compared it with an interesting work and with his time in the army. To understand his account, we therefore also need to take seriously his idiosyncratic experience, his family history, and the characteristic way he sometimes marches and sometimes stumbles through life. And considering this idiosyncratic level also helps make intelligible some more generally human features of his quest.

Take, for the sake of comparison, the way Mustafa in an interview in 2006 described his motivations to become a Salafi and the way John Steinbeck ([1936] 1961: 6) lets the literary figure of Jim Nolan, in *In Dubious Battle*, describe his decision to join the Communist Party:

> Nilson touched the desk here and there with is fingertips. "Even the people you're trying to help will hate you most of the time. Do you know that?"
> "Yes."
> "Well, why do you want to join, then?"
> Jim's eyes half closed in perplexity. At last he said, "In the Jail there were some Party men. They talked to me. Everything's been a mess, all my life. Their lives weren't messes. They were working toward something. I want to work toward something. I feel dead. I thought I might get alive again."

Mustafa, on his side, told me:

> In the time when I started to get back to myself I had lost many things. I started to search. Where is the right way? . . . I didn't have a basic method that I could follow to solve my problems and to face the world. I had no principle to follow. I had no law that I could apply and that would allow me to tell right from wrong. . . . I took to asking about everything in my life: is it *halal* or *haram*? Even if I didn't have awareness about it, no clear textual proof. But my feeling was, if I could only know whether this is *haram* or *halal*?. . . For a while I lived a better life like I hadn't lived it since the death of my father. It was even better. I got to know a lot of people, and I felt that the life I live is good.

Would Mustafa have been attracted to communism instead of Salafism if he had lived in a different time? The question is not as unlikely as it may sound. Mustafa's father left him a copy of *Das Kapital*, by Karl Marx, in Arabic translation. Until the 1980s, socialism and communism were big in many parts of Egypt, and some middle-age men in Nazlat al-Rayyis still know their Marx and Lenin inside out. In 2011, following the political shockwave of the January 25 Revolution, a number of young men in the village who until then had sported vague left-wing sympathies became politically active and linked socialist ideas and symbols with a commitment to revolutionary struggle against "the system"—among them Mustafa's good friend Tawfiq and his brother Salah.

But with respect to Mustafa, the answer is probably no. Communism and prerevolutionary Salafism are different solutions, not because they stand on different sides of a secular-Islamic divide but because they appeal to slightly different kinds of sensibility. Both the real person Mustafa and the literary figure Jim Nolan search for a way to feel alive, to do something meaningful, to have a basis and direction of life. But while the communist creed that provides the sense of existential hope on the pages of *In Dubious Battle* is oriented toward a struggle against someone, a search for meaningful existence through collective action, the Salafi creed that provided Mustafa a temporary firm hold in a time of crisis was heavily focused on individual discipline and salvation.

Today, that Salafi creed has transformed into something else. When I wrote the first version of this chapter in 2010, I thought of Salafism as inherently prioritizing a concern with the self and communism as inherently collective-political. Since 2011, various Salafi groups are heavily involved in postrevolutionary politics and the project of purity now also involves the laws and institutions of the state. The Salafism to which Mustafa, Fouad, and Nagat were drawn to between 2006 and 2010 was part of the privatization of the political in the late Mubarak years. In those days, Salafism was about the radical purist transformation of one's intimate and family life, partly because Salafi organizations were obliged to stay out of politics (in the narrow sense of contestation for state power) to be allowed to act. Today, the aim of purifying one's intimate life has become linked with the aim of purifying the whole society, by persuasion if possible and by force if necessary. At the same time, the heritage of communism has been revived by left-wing revolutionaries, among them Fouad and Tawfiq, who aim to transform state and society, but in actual fact are changing themselves more than anything else. The historical conditions of activist paths have shifted, and in this sense, the Salafism of the late Mubarak years no longer existed after 2011. In 2006, Mustafa was in search of something to fix his self, and Salafism offered exactly that. Now that the path of Salafism has become an openly political one and there is a different choice of paths of commitment, it would be very difficult to guess which way Mustafa would go now, because the choice he would face would pose itself in a different way.

An existential view of commitment that looks at its motivating grounds, available paths, and consequences should not be mistaken for a functionalist explanation. A path of commitment can have different grounds of urgency, and its outcomes are unpredictable, unlikely to fit into a simple functional explanation of ends and means. It should also not be mistaken for a story of false consciousness. People who enter a path of commitment tend to know quite well what they are doing even if they cannot anticipate the consequences.

## Transience and Transformation

In her work on the women's piety movement in Egypt, Saba Mahmood (2005) points out that the intense work of learning, prayer, and weeping undertaken by the female piety activists is understood by them as an ethical project of developing a submissive, willingly God-fearing character through pious practice. My exploration of the motivations and experience of commitment offers a somewhat different picture. While the formation of a committed self certainly is something many Muslims aim for, the experience of activist religiosity appears to be different from that aim.

The very brevity of the periods of Salafi commitment by Mustafa, Fouad, and Nagat indicate that something more complex than ethical formation is going on. Of course, not all experiments with Salafi (or other) commitment are transient. Many people join the movement and stay for the rest of their life, and there are Salafi families keen to pass the tradition of activist rigor from generation to generation, with varying success. And giving up the dedication of an activist life does not yet mean giving up the Salafi creed. But the outcomes are not obvious.

The experience of commitment, even if relatively brief, leaves a lasting trace on one, often in the form of beliefs and sensibilities that "become deeply rooted" to borrow Mustafa's words. In some ways, activist commitment thus appears to be very formative indeed. At the same time, the particular emotional state of commitment, like the sense of immediate purpose and spiritual purity that is so central to Salafi activism, is often very transient, like Mustafa's euphoric sense of happiness associated with intensive worship that left him and never returned. The reason for this difference of lasting and transient effects lies in the difference of two forms of cultivation: cultivation of specific affects and attitudes, and cultivation of a complete, unambiguous sense of purpose-driven personality. The first is something that is probably involved in all forms of education and socialization all the time. The second is characteristic of activist commitment and is more suggestive than formative in character. It is also a feature of a life in the future tense that resonates with a capitalist process of constant expansion, growth, and pressure.

Key religious practices, notably ritual prayer and sermons, have a strongly suggestive character. By their repetitive and often cathartic nature, they over and again temporarily establish clear hierarchies, clarity, and certainty. It is no coincidence that the careful observance of not only the obligatory prayers but also a number of voluntary prayers (*sunna* and *nawafil*) is central to Salafi piety. A constant schedule of ritual work directs one's attention toward God and, when successful, offers a fulfilling spiritual experience. This is not specific to either Salafism in particular or Muslim rituals in general. Other religious practices, as well as many forms of political and social activism, often have a similar character, providing a fulfilling and full schedule that allows one to constantly refocus oneself, to overcome doubts, and to feel that things are meaningful and right.

But if the drive of ritual work recedes, the entire sense of commitment is in danger. This was made explicit by Mustafa in the autumn of 2006 when he, looking back on his earlier, almost euphoric sense of piety and commitment, was troubled by the state of his heart:

Yesterday I heard a sermon on the computer that made me think about my priorities. You have to be self-vigilant and repent every day to our Sublime and Exalted Lord, and renew your promises to our Lord. I felt a state of lethargy. When I heard the same tape earlier I cried. So why didn't I cry yesterday? Because my heart is black. Why am I like this? I remember an example Sheikh Salah told me: Let's assume that next to the chimney of an oven there is a freshly painted wall. What will happen to that wall? On the first day it blackens a little. On the next day it blackens more. On the third day it blackens more, and so on. The same thing in the heart, which stays polished and clean with the obedience to Sublime and Exalted God. When you give up worship ['*ibadat*] the heart keeps being blackened by dirt.

In this account pious commitment emerges as a fragile form of continuous self-suggestion rather than cumulative self-perfection. It is fundamentally transient, lasting only when actively maintained. This is not to deny the crucial role of habit for moral and religious practice—the embodied sense of ease and embarrassment that guides so many everyday moral practices such as greetings, movement in gendered spaces, prayer, and offering and accepting hospitality are strong cases for the formative power of habit. But we must distinguish between the formation of specific dispositions and senses of proper behavior, and the enactment of a complete personality ruled by one overarching principle. The latter, unlike the former, takes place in competition and conflict with other elements of one's personality in a way that is inherently unstable because it includes the attempt to impose on oneself a way of being that stands in contradiction with the way human personality and subjectivity actually work: as a dialogue of "a dynamic multiplicity of I-positions" (Meijl 2007: 929). Human experience cannot simply be melded to a shape postulated by a normative ideal—especially if that ideal aims a harmonious unity and clarity that, in practice, is opposite to the ambivalent character of human experience. To keep up this normative ideal, what may aim to be sustainable self-formation in practice takes the form of fragile and transient self-suggestion.

The stories of Salafi Muslim activists may therefore tell more about the nature of activist dedication in a specific historical moment than about the nature of Muslim religiosity. When we look at Salafi—or any other—activism, it is important not to just study the aims and claims of a particular activist movement. The study of activist lives must also be sensitive to idiosyncratic and comparative dimensions. It must be grounded in an understanding of the existential grounds of dedication as well as its shifting historical conditions and complex outcomes. And it must account for the diffuse common sense about what dedication is like that the people involved share. Activist commitment addresses quite fundamental and generic problems of human condition, but at the same time, the urgency of specific problems, the ways of addressing them, the solutions offered, and the consequences involved—these are historically unique and dynamic.

One of the most interesting questions regarding that dynamic is this: what happens when people give up a particular sense of commitment? The turn to revivalist religiosity in Egypt in the 1970s and 1980s was influenced by former socialists and communists who had grown disillusioned with the promise of socialist progress (Aishima and Salvatore 2009). What might be the role of former Salafis in future Egypt?

As I have tried to show here, the actual experience of commitment can be full of contradictions and requires constant work of suggestion and dedication. That work of dedication may not be formative in the sense of establishing a stable pious personhood, but it is transformative, though often in ways not originally intended. Such unintended transformation is evidently most pronounced among those for whom Salafi commitment is a period in their lives, not a lasting condition. The work of dedication has helped Mustafa become a more responsible person, although it also subjected him to a long period of troubling uncertainty after the transient experience of happiness. Part of her longer trajectory of religious dedication and spiritual search, Nagat's period of Salafi commitment has motivated her to see herself increasingly as the active agent of her life. It also provided directions for the further course of her spiritual search. The work of dedication at least temporarily sharpened the antagonistic traits of Fouad's struggle with himself, but it has compelled him to enter into struggles of a different kind. As a part-time Salafi, Fouad was torn between the pious and the creative parts of himself. As a revolutionary, he is less at war with himself but is involved in equally troubling conflicts with the social world around him.

In this sense, by looking at Salafi activism not only as a period of activism in a not-so-activist life, but also as a particular moment in a longer and more complex career of commitments, we see that the work of suggestion and dedication, though fragile and transient, has a permanence in people's lives insofar as it marks significant turning points in their biographies, moments of rethinking, changes in perspective, different feelings about the world. Such turning points may not directly produce what they promise—Salafism may not actually deliver peace of mind, just as a revolution may not actually deliver freedom and dignity—or they may deliver those things only for a short while. But such moments do produce something more complicated: a "parallactic shift," to borrow Slavoj Žižek's (2006) terminology, a change in the way of understanding one's condition in the world whereby questions about peace of mind and freedom and dignity arise differently than they would have before.

# 7 Longing for the World

## An Intersection of Possibilities

Mukhtar Shehata, a frustrated and underpaid teacher in an informal area (*'ashwa'iya*, an area that has been built without a master plan and proper permits, sometimes also referred to as "slum," although the ten-story buildings of reinforced concrete and red brick in an Egyptian *'ashwa'iya* hardly conform with the stereotypical image of a third-world slum) in eastern Alexandria is one of the many sons of the village who have moved to the city in search of work and a better life. He lives just a block inland from the Abu Qir suburban train track that divides the upmarket seaside from the "popular" (*sha'bi*) inland of the city. Unlike in Cairo, where upmarket districts are increasingly physically apart from the rest of the city, many of Alexandria's upmarket districts are within everybody's reach,[1] given the double role of the seafront Corniche Road as a main area for middle-class outings (the true elites are drawn to the more exclusive resorts to the east and west of the city) and as the city's main thoroughfare.

The Corniche is a peculiar place, an intersection of very different things and people who otherwise might not come together in Egypt. The beach is covered by cafés and clubs, some accessible at a price that is neither cheap nor exclusive, and others are for hotel guests or members only. There are very few public beaches that are free of charge, and those are crowded to the limit in the summer vacation, when people from other parts of Egypt come to spend a vacation in Alexandria. On the other side of the road, high-rise buildings house cafés and restaurants catering to the upper middle classes. Not many people actually live on the seafront, where the salt blown in by the sea rapidly damages facades beyond repair. Many of the flats overlooking the sea are furnished holiday apartments, some of which are used by one family over years, whereas others are rented by the month, day, or hour. The part of the Corniche that is truly accessible for all is the wide sidewalk between the road and the beach. It is a place where families go for a stroll, where lovers meet, where minibuses stop, and where one can look at the sea and—so people say—see the lights of Cyprus at night.[2]

Mukhtar and his family live less than half a mile from the Corniche, and he sometimes jokingly claims that he lives "next to the Sheraton." There are some sites accessible to him and his family, such as the Fathallah supermarket, which offers a sense of global consumerism at very competitive prices. But in general, his very modest, lower-middle-class standard of living is precarious at best, and the other side of the railway track is his for walking and window-shopping only (see Abaza 2006: 258). And as for so many other people in Alexandria, walking along the waterfront and dreaming is one of Mukhtar's favorite pastimes.

> When I sit on the seafront, it depends on my mood which way I look. When I'm in an optimistic mood I look away from the sea towards the high-rise buildings and think about the life of the people who live in them. When I'm depressed I look at the sea and think about the other side. And I imagine that on the other side there is someone who, miserable and depressed just like me, looks across the sea and dreams of the other side.

On the waterfront in Alexandria different promises of a good life come closer together than anywhere else in Egypt. One is the wealth and comfort of affluent Egyptians who spend weekends and vacations in holiday apartments overlooking the sea in Alexandria. Another is travel across the sea as a migrant worker, a prospect of which the Mediterranean Sea is a constant reminder. In January and February 2011, a third quite suddenly entered the scene, as the Corniche became the site of huge demonstrations demanding the removal of president Hosni Mubarak and the system of corruption and oppression associated with him. During those short and intense days, Mukhtar, his wife, and their two children were among the hundreds of thousands of demonstrators who turned the waterfront

Figure 7.1. The Corniche at Raml Station, October 2011.

Figure 7.2. Mukhtar Shehata and his children on the waterfront, April 2012.

Figure 7.3. Upmarket housing on the Corniche in seaside al-Mandara, November 2011.

Figure 7.4. Al-Mallaha Street in inland al-Mandara, March 2010.

of Alexandria into one of the key sites of Egypt's revolution, a political space for a better future.

As an intersection of aspirations and possible paths of action, Alexandria's waterfront offers a starting point for thinking about aspiration, fantasy, and people's relationship with the wider world in a time when labor migration has become *the* way to connect one's life with the possibilities and promises of globalization. Expectations, plans, and to a lesser extent experiences of migration play an important role. The urge to migrate serves as an entry point to thinking about the aspiration for a good life at home, embedded in a vision of a wider world—a state of "dreaming of the other side," to borrow Mukhtar's words.

If I use *dream* and *aspiration* almost synonymously, this reflects the colloquial Egyptian usage of the word *hilm*, "dream." To have a dream is to have guiding, driving ideas, something to pursue. Dreaming, then, is not only something that happens inside one's head. It is a tangible and intersubjective business of telling stories, plotting plans, studying, furnishing living rooms, window-shopping, strolling. Dreams in this sense of something to pursue raise the question of their realization. Unlike nighttime dreams (see Mittermaier 2011) or even daydreaming, such aspirational dreams can be more or less realistic (see Bloch [1959] 1980). However, there is a peculiar logic of imagination and action that greatly complicates the relationship of dreams and reality. Whether a dream can be acted out is one thing. What is actually accomplished through the act of pursuing a dream can be quite a different thing (see Jackson 1996: 34).[3]

## Cosmopolitanism as a Longing

The gaze toward the other shore encompasses at once a vision of a world made up of different, interconnected parts, and the recognition that the relationship between those parts is marked by inequality and exclusion. Grounded as it is in an imagined world of possibilities and promises, it is an example of the social practice of imagination (Appadurai 1996) that shapes the scope of possible actions and trajectories. In today's Egypt possible actions and trajectories are saturated by globally marketed and mediated commodities, promises of middle-class prosperity and a good life, and various kinds of traveling theories (Said 1983) that once emerged in a different context and are today cited by Egyptians to explain their condition. Globally mediated and circulated things and ideas are everywhere—in new houses built with migrant remittances; in furniture modeled after European styles (even if unpractical for Egyptian ways of dwelling); in youth fashion oriented toward global tastes; in the spread of Salafi-inspired religiosity; in the fan culture around Lebanese singers, Egyptian and Hollywood movie stars, and European soccer players; in the Turkish television series, Saudi Arabian sermons, and Egyptian and American films through which people narrate their lives. And yet Egypt has not become like Italy, Saudi Arabia, United States, or Turkey. Rather than a direct emulation of these goods and ideas, what appears to be going on are attempts by people to transform their own world to make it seem valuable in face of these powers and promises (see Weiss 2009: 36).

There is a growing current in contemporary anthropology studying this condition as a cosmopolitan one, in order to account for the fact that not only the wealthy and intellectual but also people of very modest means live lives that exceed the limits of what earlier generations of anthropologists called indigenous, traditional, or local. They aspire to make global modernity their own, without becoming homogenized or fully connected in the sense evoked by globalization.[4] Cosmopolitanism, in this sense, is about versatility in and belonging to "the world," of "ways of living at home abroad or abroad at home—ways of inhabiting multiple places at once, of being different beings simultaneously, of seeing the larger picture stereoscopically with the smaller" (Pollock 2002: 11). As such, cosmopolitanism is a modality of both action and imagination. It is not only about life trajectories that exceed borders but also about expectations that exceed borders.

"Cosmopolitanism" has a flavor of being a privilege of the global elites (Ekholm Friedman and Friedman 2011), and in Egypt, too, it makes most sense in regard to the wealthy classes that can successfully afford and master a sense of global connectedness (Peterson 2011; A. de Koning 2009). But when looked at from the point of view of the practice of "open-ended subjectivities" (Marsden 2007a, 2008: 215), cosmopolitanism certainly has to do with class, and yet it is not the privilege of any particular class or place in the world, nor is it detached from particularistic local identities and hierarchies. Heba Elsayed (2010), working with lower-middle-class youth in Cairo, argues that cosmopolitanism is something that is in fact characteristic of poorer but aspiring people in an urban setting. Unlike the elites who usually can rely on a specific social milieu, the lower-middle-class youth Elsayed writes about need to master a large variety of social idioms, milieus, and ways of relating to the world (see also Tuominen 2013). Brad Weiss, in his study of hip-hop barbershops in Tanzania, points out that the absence of material means of advancements gives gazing out to the world particular urgency. It is a situation in which the people involved "are both able to recognize the values of a wider world they find uniquely compelling and yet feel almost completely incapable of realizing the potential of those values in their lives" (Weiss 2009: 14).

Thus, the notion of cosmopolitanism, although properly speaking a privilege of intellectual and economical elites, is also useful for understanding what it means to have a horizon of expectation that is global but means of movement and advancement that are much more limited. The world evoked by cosmopolitanism in this sense is not a world without borders, but a world full of borders, inhabited by people who try to cross them.

There is good reason, then, to think of Mukhtar's stroll on the waterfront of Alexandria as a cosmopolitan one. With its intersection of different milieus of a stratified class society, and with the Mediterranean Sea a reminder of the presence of what lies overseas, beyond the horizon, the Corniche is a cosmopolitan site par excellence. Crucially, Mukhtar also describes the experience of walking along the waterfront as one that often comes with depression and frustration. The longing for a world of material comfort and money and a life of dignity and freedom (I come back to the details of this a little later) is an unfulfilled one in most cases, and even moments of modest material success are usually relativized by the undiminished sense of pressure that comes with the race for material improvement. A world of fantastic promises is also a world of deep disappointments.

## Sites of Possibility

Like Mukhtar's visions at the Corniche, the different moments and sites of aspiration together make up a bigger picture of the world of possibilities. In Nazlat al-Rayyis, as in much of Egypt, the years before 2011 were a time in which sustained economical growth filled the cities' streets fill with private cars and new red-brick buildings of up to six floors transformed the appearance of villages. But it was also a time when almost everybody bitterly complained about increasing economic pressure, corruption and nepotism, and deepening social divisions. During this time, three sites stood out when people imagined and discussed the world and the possibilities it offered: Cairo and Egypt's upper classes, the Arab Gulf states, and Europe and North America.

The first of these sites include the wealthy strata of class society in Egypt, the imagined and actual lifestyles of the Egyptian upper and upper middle classes, which are omnipresent in advertisements, cinema, television, popular culture, and the notions of wealth and happiness evoked in them. This is a fancy world of upmarket shopping malls, air-conditioned coffee shops, exclusive social clubs, and gated communities, and yet the actual dreams of a good life these things inspire are not extravagant. The stereotypical dream of a comfortable life that people whom I know express consists of marriage, children, a reasonably large and well-equipped apartment, and a private car—a decidedly middle-class fantasy. As I have already argued, one of the particular features of contemporary consumer-oriented capitalism is that while it produces striking inequalities, the social utopia of a good life it offers is that of the middle class, *middle* evoking a sense of being at the center of society as one of the good, decent people. What is important about this dream beyond its resonance with a worldwide capitalist sensibility, however, is that even in a time of an omnipresent pressure to migrate, the dream is primarily located in Egypt. The most important kind of social movement that people with such modest middle-class aspirations expect is a movement upward (or perhaps from the margins toward the middle), toward the lifestyle and standard of living of affluent Egyptians.

And yet precisely this movement appears to be the most difficult of all. Egypt experienced a period of relatively high social mobility through the socialist policies of the 1950s and 1960s, and many of the current promises of social advancement still draw upon that era. The economic liberalization has been often blamed for halting social mobility, but in my experience this appears to be only partly true. While the economic liberalization has strongly favored the existing elites, it has also assisted many small entrepreneurs in accumulating reasonable amounts of money (although economic mobility does not automatically translate into social mobility in a class society; see Ismail 2013). But for those people whose income and status depend on agricultural and industrial labor or public-sector jobs, the path of upward economic or social mobility has become extremely narrow (for agricultural work, see Tordhol 2014). The heritage of Arab socialism, the system of state education and public-sector jobs continues to be the main hope for people of lower-middle-class background or aspiration. At the same time, however, all possible paths of advancement to the more privileged positions of the public sector have become regulated by *wasta*, networks of nepotistic and clientelist dependency. Without *wasta*, one has no hope of entering anything except the lowest jobs in the public sector. In the private sector the situation is slightly less dominated by *wasta*, and more so by the educational capital of having attended the right schools. People with degrees from government schools have little to no hope of entering good private-sector careers. In the 1970s, economic liberalization and currency deregulation made mass migration abroad for work both possible and attractive. But only more recently has migration become so compelling as to make other paths seem worthless. It was only when people's main aim was to build a comfortable middle-class life in Egypt, but when the means to reach that aim at home were increasingly socially exclusive, that migration came to appear as *the* solution over all others.

When Egyptians think about migration abroad, they think essentially about two sites: the West (i.e., Europe and North America) and the Arab Gulf states. Both sites are associated with complex expectations, promises, and perils. The Gulf is perhaps the most common site of migration for Egyptians. It has always been and continues to be more accessible for Egyptians to migrate to, although the highly exploitative contracts of labor agents significantly diminish the profits of migrants. The Gulf, and especially Dubai, is not just a goal for labor migrants. It has gradually gained a hegemonic status as a central site of modernity in the Middle East. If the urban planners of Cairo in the early twentieth century used to look at Paris as the paradigmatic metropolis, today's urban planning has been busy with making Cairo look and feel like Dubai, as the life of the affluent classes moves more and more to exclusive suburbs, malls, campuses, and compounds built around the Ring Road. The Gulf is not only about money—it is about lifestyle, and its cultural influence on all levels of Egyptian society can hardly be underestimated, be it in terms of migrant remittances, urban planning, religiosity, or styles of consumption. The first world to which Egyptians hope to belong has long ceased to be identical with Europe and the United States. Today, Dubai and Doha feature along with Paris, London, and New York as the magic names of global modernity.

The Gulf is a site associated with highly contradictory sentiments. It is an Arab and Muslim place, and this gives it an aura of proximity and familiarity. Especially Saudi Arabia enjoys a bright aura of Islam thanks to its privileged position as the country of the holiest places of Islam and as a globally successful center of the Salafi current of Islam. This is clearly reflected in the way women's migration is primarily directed to the Gulf states, which are considered more appropriate for women than the culturally more different and morally more liberal, or decadent, Western countries. But the positive aspects of the Gulf as a familiar Muslim, Arab place are countered by a very negative image of the Gulf as an uncivilized place of arrogant and immoral hypocrites, and ruthless exploitation of workers, and therefore also perilous to women. If most Egyptians see

Europeans and Americans as irresponsibly materialistic and individualistic, their view of the Gulf Arabs is hardly better—often, it is worse. This negative stereotype is partly the result of a historical competition about who presents the cultural center of modernity in the Arab world. More immediately, perhaps, it is a result of the actual experiences of Egyptian migrant workers, who often face extreme exploitation and humiliation, further aggravated by the cultural familiarity and shared religion that would make one expect better treatment.

Europe and North America, in turn, stand for a different, equally complex and contradictory set of promises and concerns. While perhaps less accessible than the promises of the Gulf, those of North America and Europe are in many ways even more attractive and present in the lives of Egyptians. The increasing sense of nationalist and religious confrontation and paranoia that marked the first decade of the twenty-first century has not diminished the appeal of a Western (i.e., mainly American) way of life. The same people who in different combinations hold militantly nationalist, anti-American, anti-Jewish, and Islamist views of world politics can also be enthusiastic consumers of Hollywood fiction, as well as global brands of consumer goods, American fast food, and European soccer. They identify with the global fan community of Real Madrid, refer to Hollywood plots to make sense of their own life, argue that the world is driven to ruin by an American-Zionist conspiracy, express solidarity with the global community of Muslims, and look up to Western industrial nations as examples of social and political progress.

It is the nature of hegemony that certain powers and places cannot be ignored, whether one likes it or not. As an Egyptian from the provinces, it is very difficult to think about social mobility without reckoning with the wealth and possibilities of Cairo. And as an Egyptian from anywhere, it is very difficult to think about a better life without reckoning with the Gulf, Europe, and the United States. The very power of these sites to determine possible paths of progress makes the ways people engage them necessarily differentiated and complex. Therefore, more fruitful than looking for moments of rejection or affirmation is looking at some of the specific desires and concerns that people express when they think about their prospects in relation to places like "Cairo," "the West," and "the Gulf." In the following I take up two issues closely related to migration and that, simple as they seem, evoke quite complex frameworks of aspiration for good life: money and freedom.

## Money and Freedom

In December 2009, I showed the documentary film *Messages from Paradise #1* (Swarowsky and Schielke 2009) to Mustafa, his mother, and his brothers in their house in Nazlat al-Rayyis. The family had just invested its modest but well-managed savings to build a house on the outskirts of Alexandria. The widowed mother of the three sons hoped that her youngest son would be able to make career as a doctor in Egypt, but she encouraged the older two, Mustafa and Salah, to think about migration. Both Salah and Mustafa were in fact seriously thinking about it at the time, albeit in somewhat different ways from their mother. Watching the film, which begins in Egypt and then moves on to show the stories of Egyptian migrants in Vienna, one scene in particular caught their attention. In that scene Magdi, a former boxer and now civil servant in Vienna, declares that his entire life is now in Vienna and that he does not want to return to Egypt except on holiday. He even wants to be buried in Austria (most Egyptian migrants, even if they never return, hope to be buried at "home"). Their mother expressed her discontent with the idea and saw it as a kind of failure, even a betrayal of what in her view was the proper meaning of migration: to go abroad with á clear plan, realize it, and return. Salah contradicted her: "No, he's right." His view of migration, too, was about making money to build a life, but he also looked forward to the idea of building a life in Europe.

After seeing the film, the three brothers, two other friends, and I went to a café in the village, where we continued to discuss motivations and plans for migration in more detail. In the course of the discussion, they developed money and freedom as the two essential motivations to migrate—they are not exclusive, but complementary. Those who just want money, they argued, are more likely to go to the Gulf states, which are more accessible but also less attractive to live in. In any case, they said, the plan of the Gulf-bound is always clear and simple: go abroad and collect money to "build a life" at home. In contrast, they argued, those who also want freedom are more likely to want to go to Europe or, even better, North America, where they can live a life free of the constraints and oppression they experience in Egypt.

The way these men, and many others like them, used *money* and *freedom* as evident shorthand terms for entire sets of aspirations and subjectivities, makes it necessary to take a closer look at the two notions. They are not only more complex than they may seem; they also express the sensibility of a particular historical moment, a conjunction of political and economic experience. And they are particularly gender-sensitive labels that can mean very different things for men and women.

Following conventional anthropological wisdom, money and freedom could seem to be one and the same thing. In Georg Simmel's ([1900] 1989) seminal interpretation, money *is* freedom, insofar it leads to increasing abstraction and objectification of human relationships, so that while people in a monetary society are increasingly interdependent in abstract terms, they are less dependent on each other on a personal level—a form of freedom that comes at the cost of alienation. While Simmel's vision of the world-changing dynamics of money continues to have much currency, it does not seem to be the whole story. Bill Maurer (2006:

17) has pointed out that there is a discrepancy between anthropological theories of money, which often build on Simmel's vision, and ethnographic analyses of money, which often show that money continues to be grounded in "moral, embedded, and special-purpose functions"—an insight that is echoed by the young men in the café when they explicitly distinguished money and freedom as different sets of aspiration.

"Money," to start with, is not just about getting money. It is very strongly associated with the specific things money is needed for, commonly expressed in the phrase "building a life." For a man, building a life implies all the conventional responsibilities and assets that make a respectable man: marriage, an apartment or house (a necessary precondition for marriage) built of reinforced concrete and red brick, and a reasonable standard of living—the most important marker of which at the moment is a private car (and which most Egyptians cannot afford). All this, in the imaginary evoked by "money," is to take place in or near one's place of origin, be it in a new floor over one's parental house, a new house in the fields outside the village, or an apartment in a nearby city. "Money" thus evokes an ideal of establishing oneself as a respected and wealthy man in the already-existing web of family relations, moving upward while remaining connected (Ghannam 2002: 148), which also, significantly, involves willing financial assistance to less well-off relatives.

While there is some money to be earned even for the poor in Egypt, it is hardly ever enough to qualify as "money" in this sense of sufficient resources for social advancement. Yet at the same time, money is absolutely indispensable in an informally privatized economy where *wasta* and bribes are the only paths to good jobs in the public sector. It is this situation—in which to move upward, one first needs to have money—that migration appears as the path over all others to a middle class existence.

"Freedom," in turn, is not quite what Europeans often assume it to imply for people from the Middle East. While the Western popular political imagination associates freedom with an individualistic sense of a freedom of choice—of lifestyle, partner, sexual orientation, and the like (which is very much freedom in the sense evoked by Simmel in his theory of money), freedom as for young Egyptians is a more complex notion and less exclusively centered on choice. Choice certainly is an issue, notably so in regard to sexual freedom, an issue that at once greatly animates the fantasies of young men but also appears to be something dangerous, especially in regard to women (in the sense both that men's sexual freedom can endanger women and that women's sexual freedom is considered dangerous). But while freedom of choice is an ambiguous issue, another sense of freedom is almost unanimously phrased as positive: having rights.

Mustafa argued on another occasion that migration to Europe is, of course, about money, but it is also about enjoying a degree of freedom and rights. When

I commented that it is no fun to be an Arab Muslim in Europe at the moment, he replied: "Even if the law discriminates me as a Muslim and an Arab, I will know where the law stands and where I stand." A similar idea was put forward by Tawfiq, who was pursuing several plans to migrate when we interviewed him for *Messages from Paradise #1* in the autumn of 2007:

> My uncle told me that once a friend of his sent him a letter from America. He wrote: I am in a country where five garbage men can demonstrate in front of the White House and return to their homes safely. Here it could never happen. Here the judges get beaten up. Imagine what would happen if the garbage men tried to demonstrate here.

This view of the United States may appear excessively optimistic in light of the many civil rights violations that the past decade has witnessed. But in light of the routine and haphazard brutality of the Egyptian state, Tawfiq's appraisal of the garbage collectors' demonstration and Mustafa's hyperbolic claim that it is better to be discriminated by a rule of law than to be subject to a state of lawlessness, are telling of a longing for freedom that is about predictable justice and, most fundamentally, human dignity in the face of a brutal and demoralizing social and political reality. And just like the idea of migration for the sake of money is really about living a better life at home, so the idea of migration for the sake of freedom in the sense of rights is very much about the frustrating injustice, humiliation, and inequality at home.

Eventually, freedom (*hurriya*) and dignity (*karama*) were to become two key demands of the January 25 revolution, so evidently interconnected that one couldn't be thought without the other. Also in the way developed here by Mustafa and Tawfiq, the demand for freedom is a demand for dignity, directed against the same sense of oppression, humiliation, and economical pressure. Importantly, Tawfiq eventually joined the very first demonstration in Tahrir Square on January 25, 2011. That event puts the relationship of migration and freedom in a somewhat different light, and I get back to his story toward the end of this chapter.

But there is also another, more individualistic and escapist sense of freedom that is not about changing things at home but about getting away from them. This is a sense of freedom that is very typical for the life situation of young, unmarried men. Not coincidentally, marriage to a European woman—financially accessible, sexually exciting, and accompanied by a visa—is the paradigmatic path to this kind of freedom. It implies the escape from the often heavy financial burdens involved in being a respected man—often phrased as "constraints" (*quyud*)—such as the high cost of marriage and the class-based limitations on the choice of a partner. This, however, is often seen in a significantly different way by women whose rights often are based on precisely those obligations that some young men view as constraints: the financial transactions from groom to bride (and her family) involved in an Islamic marriage and the proximity and good contacts between their families. This is not to say that family arrangements and economic transactions generally favor women. They are a formidable obstacle in the way of any attempt to marry the partner of one's choice, and as such they make life difficult for Egypt's lovers, men and women alike. But they also involve bonds of security and connectedness that can be experienced as constraints by men but safety nets by women.

It is in this sense that Nagat argued that a marriage organized by the families to a man working in Europe is the safest way for a young woman to go to Europe. With few exceptions, Nagat said, this is also the only reason for women from her milieu to migrate to the West:

> A woman from the village who marries an Egyptian in Italy goes on in living there just as she does here. If she has a problem with her husband in Italy, she can call her mother, who goes to his mother, who calls him and settles the problem. But if she marries a stranger abroad, she has nobody to rely on.

In much, if not most, of Egypt, such social networks of kinship remain the most significant guarantee for the modest rights of a married woman. To migrate alone or to marry a foreigner would imply losing these rights. Migration to the West, in Nagat's perspective, is not associated with more rights for women the way it is associated with more rights from the perspective of young men.

This is not to say that freedom would not be a concern to Nagat—on the contrary, she articulates quite radical views about the freedom to express one's feelings and concerns and to build social relationships without fear and secrecy. Rather, Nagat's point is that freedom can be quite a different thing for young men and women, and something that for men means freedom may mean unfreedom for women.

Nagat's thoughts about freedom are not connected to migration the way men's freedom is—in both its political and its escapist dimensions—because of the different gendered roles involved in migration. For a woman who is after freedom in the sense of choice and rights, Nagat points out, metropolitan Cairo has a lot more to offer than becoming the wife of a migrant worker in Italy.

From the perspective of the things money must buy and the different gendered senses of freedom, it becomes clearer why Salah's mother insisted that men who migrate have to stick to their plan. Certainly women's views about migration are also significantly influenced by common ideas about what is suitable for a woman to do and to desire. Even when those women I know who have migrated to the Gulf or to Europe speak about their experience in generally positive tones, the aspiration for financial and personal independence and a full possession of rights is not something women in rural and provincial milieus are comfortable expressing. But there is more to women's different outlook on migration. For men migration opens a potential door to escape heavy social obligations, but women are those who generally profit from such obligations. Men's migration, in this light, thus offers most women both uncertainties and hopes.

## The Two Powers of Imagination

So far I have spoken about the world, and being included in it by means of social advancement and migration, as an expectation, a potentiality. But how does this potentiality connect with action?

Really migrating is the most obvious kind of action involved. But the tragic twist of migration as practice is that while it seems to be about widening one's scope of action and imagination, the actual experience of migration may narrow one's horizon of expectation. When one is there, abroad, working in a restaurant in Italy, selling newspapers in Vienna, or guarding a bank in Doha, life is utterly monotonous and boring, completely ruled by very few questions: "How much money can I save this month?" "Do I have enough to get engaged on my next holiday?"

For Tawfiq, who dreamed of migrating for both money and freedom, this was a very disheartening experience. In early 2008, he got a two-year contract as a guard with an international security company in Doha, Qatar. Although the Gulf was not where he really wanted to go, he was hopeful that going there would open new possibilities to move ahead. In October 2009 I went to Doha and met him there. He was living an utterly monotonous life between the bank where he worked and a worker's hostel on the outskirts of the city. He was very disillusioned about his situation, which, he said, brought him some useful experience, but a lot less money than he hoped and a life under conditions of virtual slavery. Back in 2007 when I had asked him whether he would return if he could leave Egypt, he had replied: "If you would be released from prison, would you want to return?" In Doha, I asked him what he thought about it now. He responded:

> It turned out to be a bigger prison. The problem is how to know the borders of your prison. It's a prison of many walls. After crossing one wall you find another wall. It's like you're in the beginning in the innermost circle, and when you jump the wall you find yourself only in the next circle of the prison. You have to know where the borders of your prison are so that you know how to jump all the way over the outermost wall. But how to know which wall is the outermost? That's the problem.

Tawfiq's reply is a philosophical reflection about the condition of people who try to cross borders in a world full of borders (and there never may be that outermost wall). His colleague Abdelwahhab adds a more explicit complaint about the narrowness of migratory paths in the Arab world (as he explicitly frames it):

Figure 7.5. Lunch break in Doha, Qatar, November 2009.

What exactly is it that you are after in your research? After the hopes, aspirations, and frustrations of each one of us? The individual ideas of everyone are different, and people from the city and from the countryside have different contexts of life, different costs and standards of living and housing that they can hardly catch up with—but the shared thing that moves everybody in Egypt to migration is the need to get married, and the cost it involves. . . . Money for marriage is the one single thing that everybody has to be after. There is no choice.

Abdelwahhab explicitly juxtaposes the things money must buy to freedom (this time explicitly in terms of choice). The problem he has with migration, however, is that while it has offered him the possibility of meeting people from different parts of the world and learning different ways and ideas (something that is, in fact, rather uncommon among migrant workers, who usually prefer to stick to their compatriots' company), it has not offered him any practical means to pursue different trajectories of life. On the contrary, the centrality of money—salary, cost of living, savings, remittances, presents—in the everyday life of migrant workers means that "money" in the sense of the conventional things money must buy becomes only more powerful. And the biggest problem is that the little money migrant workers do earn is usually always much less than they hoped for. Rather than returning home with a fortune to "build a life," they more often than not end up living in a more or less permanent state of migration to sustain that life.

The trouble of migration as practice, then, is even bigger than the lack of freedom outlined by Tawfiq and Abdelwahhab. Even if one were only and exclusively after "money," the problem is that migration troubles, even breaks, precisely that sense of connectedness so central to the social imaginary of the things money must buy. To build a life, they find themselves living in a shadow existence of overcrowded accommodations, alienated work, and general monotony that feels less than real and lacks all those things that makes up a life in its moral and connective sense. Migrants end up living far from their families, and instead of helping to live out a conservative social ideal, their economic profit often comes at the cost of alienation (see Jackson 2009).

This tragic side of migration is the subject of many songs, proverbs, films, and stories about *ghurba*, the loneliness and disconnection of being abroad and outside one's familiar networks. Yet at the same time, young men and their parents are often hesitant to believe migrants when (if ever) they tell about

Figure 7.6. Workers' accommodation in Doha, Qatar, November 2009.

the specific hardship they experience. The systemic price of migrant money is known in general terms but silenced when it comes to individual experience. There is an enormous pressure to believe in the dream of migration, and migrants, too, do their best to serve that dream, performing as they do a sense of success and well-being through presents and generosity when they return home on holiday, leaving it to the songs and proverbs to say how high the price of that generosity is.

This is the first of the two powers of imagination, the power of dreams that are so compelling that they become almost inescapable. In this regard, the expectation of migration as an imaginative, world-making practice (Graw and Schielke 2012) is a tragic one, because the imaginaries of the proper social roles of the migrant and the dynamics of migrant labor compel people to pursue dreams that greatly limit their capacity to dream. Because it can be acted out, and because there is some real money to be earned abroad, actual migration is a realistic dream. But what it accomplishes is often a troubling limbo, where precisely those good things in life, which migrants so urgently dream of attaining, keep eluding them.

Tawfiq returned from Qatar exactly two years after his departure, without extending his contract. It was a difficult decision, because by staying he could have saved at least some money, whereas back at home his meager civil servant's salary does not even cover running expenses. Back in Egypt, he told me that reading Paulo Coelho's 1988 (1996) novel *The Alchemist* in Arabic translation several times over during his time in Doha was what gave him the strength to return. *The Alchemist* is a parable of explicit symbolism; a story of winding paths to the fulfillment of a dream; and a plea for a life of individual self-realization guided by one's unique, true potential. If reading this novel could be powerful enough to help a person take a step against the compelling stream of migration, then this certainly raises a question about the power of imagination not only to create paths so compelling that other paths become almost impossible, but also to create alternative paths in spite of their apparent impossibility.

The "realistic" (in the sense of the socially accepted plan evoked by Mustafa's mother) dreams of migration often end up limiting one's horizon of fantasy. Unrealistic dreams, in contrast, have the advantage that their practical relevance is not bound to their practicability. Mukhtar Shehata, whose stroll at the waterfront in Alexandria opened this chapter, is one of the most unrealistic dreamers I know in Egypt, and his own experiments in the relationship of dreams and practice offer some important insights about this second power of the imagination.

## Now, You Are the Other Side

Mukhtar has often considered migrating, and on two occasions he tried to get a visa to work in the Gulf states but without success. At the same time, he preferred to see migration for money as secondary to travel for widening one's horizons, as he explained in an interview for *Messages from Paradise #1* in 2007:

> It wasn't my dream to marry and have children, a house, a family. But it was my dream to go abroad. I didn't want to migrate to change my situation here. I wanted to migrate to find other dreams.

As Tawfiq's account reminds us, migration can be a disappointing way to search for other dreams. Yet Mukhtar, unable to migrate even to the Gulf, turned to fantasy as a means of imaginary travel. In 2007 he started to write a novel, the plot of which he explained to me on one of our strolls on the Corniche. After many difficulties (publishing a book costs money in Egypt), he finally managed to get it published in the spring of 2010. Titled *No to Alexandria* (Mukhtar Shehata 2010), it is the puzzlelike story of Saʿid (Arabic for "happy"), a deeply unhappy man who reacts to a personal tragedy by emigrating, a journey that leads him from Egypt through Saudi Arabia and Afghanistan to Germany, with his only true friends being the spies set after him by Arab and Western intelligence agencies. A psychological novel in the guise of a spy story, *No to Alexandria* turns the themes of migration and global politics into broader engagement with the Other, an issue that is central to Mukhtar's creative work.

Pursuing the theme of the Other, Mukhtar began to write a second novel; this one, located in Alexandria and the United States, tells the story of the fraught relationship between Christians and Muslims in Alexandria. It is also a story of the city and the class boundaries that divide it, and the Abu Qir railroad plays a major role. In the summer of 2009, in discussing my research about migration and his ideas about the railroad and the Other, we decided to produce together an experimental short film on the topic(s).

The film, *The Other Side* (Shehata and Schielke 2010), tells in nine minutes the absurd story of a man with extremist looks (played by Mukhtar himself) who at first seems to plan a suicide attack at the Abu Qir railroad but turns out to pursue quite different objectives, ones that appear related to an unhappy love story across class boundaries. Finally, the hero finds himself on the waterfront, expressing the very thoughts about the seafront quoted at the beginning of this chapter. And in the film there is indeed an Other across the sea, longing for the other side just like the hero. The film ends with a leap of both the hero and his counterpart toward the sea, leaving open whether or not this border can be overcome.

Both the novel and the film develop the theme of migration through the ideas of unfulfilled search and the engagement with the Other. Both look at situations in which migration appears to be the only possible choice after other choices have become impossible in the eyes of the characters. These works leave their protagonists in a state of never arriving, always about to take yet another step ahead. This turns hope and loss into an intimate pair, with the characters

Figure 7.7. Film still from *The Other Side*, directed by Mukhtar Shehata and Samuli Schielke.

repeatedly finding themselves in situations in which they desperately hold on to the dreams that once motivated them, but those dreams are now there to overcome their experience of exile. In this moment, the dream itself becomes the homeland they long for.⁵

Mukhtar's work, which also crosses the boundaries that usually differentiate anthropologists and their interlocutors, is interesting in several respects. First of all, as I have tried to show here, it is interesting because of what it says. At another level, it is interesting because of what writing and publishing a novel and producing a short film has helped Mukhtar accomplish. For one thing, it gave him the opportunity to visit Germany and Mali as an author and filmmaker to present his vision. In this regard, my collaboration with him has been instrumental. But of course, most people who enter creative practice do not collaborate with anthropologists, and there is a reason Mukhtar's literary and cinematic work is relevant beyond our encounter.

Mukhtar's literary work is part of a new wave of writing that emerged in Egypt in the first decade of the twenty-first century. After a long period of readership of literature stagnating, the 2000s witnessed the rise of new, accessible styles of novels (see, e.g., al-Aswany 2002; al-ʿAydi 2003) and colloquial poetry (e.g., Salama 2007; Saʿid Shehata 2010; al-Jakh 2010), as well as an entirely new genre of sarcastic observations about daily life (e.g., Fadl 2005; al-Khamisi 2006; Ez El-Din 2010). These forms of writing, which are often published online before they appear in print (if they do at all), share a stylistic proximity to colloquial Arabic, distribution beyond and past literary circles, and a strong focus on critical social commentary. In the years before 2011 when politics was a sometimes dangerous and usually frustrating terrain, this social commentary developed into an important channel of critical political imagination.[6] Eventually, many writers of this wave turned out to be among the most enthusiastic revolutionaries in the spring of 2011.

This is not to say, of course, that becoming a writer is the solution to the problems of frustrated young men and women in Egypt. Writing involves a good amount of social distinction and privilege, requiring education, peer support and access to media where literary texts circulate. Few people are talented and obsessed enough to enter literary circles without the necessary social capital. In any case, literary writing is almost never a way to make money. And the biggest problems in the lives of young Egyptians are economic in one way or another. Yet the rare occurrence of a revolution makes dramatically visible what the imaginative search for alternative paths usually accomplishes in undramatic, less visible ways. One's horizon of expectation and action is determined not only by the landscape of structures, powers, and promises one looks at but also by one's way of looking at them (Merleau-Ponty 2005; Graw and Schielke 2012). What the practice of imagination can accomplish in favorable conditions is a change in the way the world appears to a person, and thus a change in that person's possible paths of action. The power of flights of fantasy lies in their ability to give birth to new dreams (see also Masquelier 2009).

In a way, writing did to a certain section of young Egyptians what reading Coelho did to Tawfiq: it opened up unlikely paths of action despite the odds. But they remain difficult and uncertain paths. Tawfiq, back in Egypt from Qatar, turned into a very capable political activist in his village in the months after the revolution. But in May 2011, he left for the Gulf again for a new two-year contract. Although this was a time when Egyptians were more hopeful than I had ever seen, the pressure to migrate had only grown because of the difficult economic situation in the middle of revolutionary turmoil. But there was a different tone to migration now. When Tawfiq first migrated to the Gulf in 2008, he was a bored young man completely disillusioned with his society, looking forward to leave for no return. When he went the second time, he was still a young man, but one extremely politicized and experienced in running a revolutionary movement in his village, as well as compelled to be realistic about the need to save some cash to overcome the difficult years and to get married.

Tawfiq's trajectory is telling of the dialectic relationship between the capacity to generate new dreams and the recognition of the sturdy power of political economy. Just as it would be mistaken to assume that people are simply determined by the conditions to which they are subjected, it would be also illusory to assume that they could simply change those conditions by choosing to think and act otherwise. However, even this is only a partial picture. People do not face abstract conditions. They face other people, material objects, and technologies, and these encounters—be they immediate, virtual, or imagined—are the conditions under which we all live. There is thus a third, relational aspect to this relationship of imagination and the material world that takes us back to the moment of gazing at the other side.

In 2011, the practical relevance of cosmopolitan imagination became very tangible around the Mediterranean. For a rare and exceptional moment, ordinary Egyptians were not compelled to compare themselves with Europe, North America, or the Gulf, but occupied the center stage of history as protest movements in Bahrain, the United States, Spain, and France emulated the tactics of peaceful resistance developed in Tunisia and Egypt. Egypt itself became a site of possibility. In this spirit, I was inspired to comment to Mukhtar: "Now, you are the other side." And this is, of course, what the idea of gazing across the sea is all about. The idea that also on the opposite shore there is someone longing for the other side crystallizes the moral implicit in cosmopolitan longing. As Eric Gable (2010) has pointed out, it is not only about wanting to be like (or equal to) the wider world; it is also about expecting the wider world to be like oneself. That expectation may be factually false, and gazing at Egypt from Italy is not like gazing at Italy from Egypt. But more important than the factual accuracy of this vision is the gesture of mutuality it embodies. This sense of "moral mutuality" (Gable 2010: 89) is an important part of what a cosmopolitan horizon is about: being able to see one's predicament as one that others share. In this sense, gazing at the other side on the Alexandria waterfront involves not only a demand for inclusion (see Ferguson 2006) but also the more fundamental questions of why the world is full of borders and what can be done about it.

# 8 Condition: Normal

ONE OF THE formidable problems of aspiring to a better life is that the world is structured in a way that allows one's aspirations to be realized, if at all, at the price of severe compromises. This creates discontent, more so when those compromises are oppressive and morally troubling. But what can one do? As people from the village have pursued education and work and have sought to gain a degree of what they see as a life in human dignity in the face of an oppressive system, they have resorted to subversive diversion at times, and to direct defiance at other times, with different consequences. One consequence was the longevity of the Mubarak regime. Another was the January 25 revolution, a dramatic and exceptional moment when everything seemed possible. But was there really a revolution? If there was one, what did it accomplish? And what, in a historical perspective, is the normal condition, and what is exceptional?

January 25, 2011, certainly felt exceptional. On the evening of that day I wrote the following note in my research diary:

> 25.1. midnight. Big day of demonstrations in Egypt, on massive scale, all over the country, demanding Mubarak and his system to go. Amazing. I wish I were there. Following the news and footage uploaded by the people on the net much of the evening. . . .
>
> How much this changes everything. How completely a day like this can change the image I have been drawing lately of people stuck in the circle of living in a frustrating system that turns every promise into pressure and every subversion of the system into a part of the system. There is a moment when they glimpse hope, the impossible suddenly appears in a hand's reach, a different step can be taken than could be taken just weeks and days ago, and the world changes a little.
>
> Even if this revolution will be crushed (but I am optimistic), this glimpse of hope, this moment in which a path opens where a wall just stood, is something to hold. Chatted with Tawfiq who just came back from the demonstration. Here an excerpt:
>
> TAWFIQ: This is a joyful thing. This is a day one can rarely see.
>
> I ask on the police.
>
> TAWFIQ: Really, they were brutal, but in a wicked way.
>
> SAMULI: How?

T: They let the big demonstration run and arrested people in the narrow side streets. And the mobile phone networks are offline. . . . They threw light-bulbs on the demonstrators from the roofs, and beat up people in the side streets, and arrested them."

S: But you went out, and in big numbers all over the country. That didn't happen since 1919.[1]

T: Yes. The people want to do something real [*ta'mil haga bi-gadd*]. Instead of letting Police Day be a day of rest to celebrate the police, the people decided that it would be a day the police never forgets.[2] Really, I was happy that I participated in something like this. Because maybe it won't happen again in my lifetime.

Tawfiq had returned only a few months earlier from a two-year contract as a migrant worker in Qatar. It had been a dull and demotivating job, but the work he had in Egypt was no better, only much worse paid. Before and after his contract in Qatar, he worked in the health administration of the district to which his village belongs.[3] In the autumn of 2007, his job had consisted of going to a state-subsidized bakery once a day, collecting a pile of bread without having to wait in the line, and signing in the inspection book: "Condition: normal." On that occasion, Tawfiq pointed out that this doesn't indicate whether the condition is good or not, only that it is the way it is. In the autumn of 2009, I met Tawfiq in Doha, Qatar, where he was working as a security guard. At the desk of one of his colleagues, he showed me the inspection book. With minor differences in the formulation, every entry had the same content:

26-10 13:20. I am [name] # [number]. Take over my duty from outgoing (A) shift by normal conditions.

21:20. I am [name] # [number]. Hand over my duty to incoming (C) shift by normal conditions.

And so on. I suggested to Tawfiq that I should write an article with the title "Condition: Normal." He found it a very good idea and suggested that I take a photo of the shift book, which we did in the bathroom because of closed-circuit TV cameras installed every other place in the building.

In that article, I wanted to write about the demoralizing experience of finding lofty promises of development and progress surrounded by a maze of nepotism and corruption, and high aspirations of personal advancement countered by repeated frustration. In the intervening years, I have become rather critical of the Foucauldian approach of looking at religion, morality, government, and secularity, from the point of view of governmentality and the production of affects and subjects (Foucault 2007), because I have sensed that these approaches do not explain how it is to live under the conditions they describe. In the article

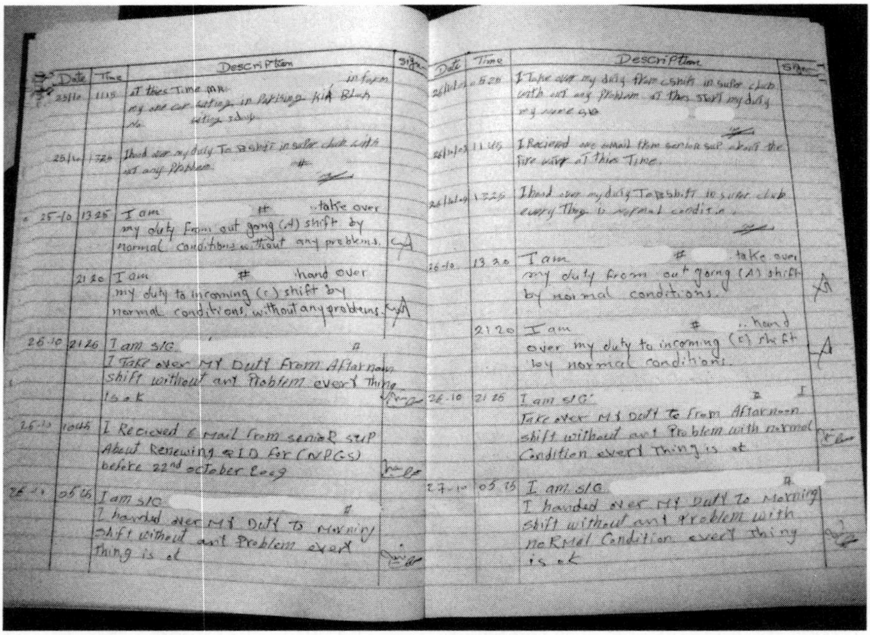

Figure 8.1. The shift book, Doha, Qatar, November 2009.

I was going to write, I wanted to look at everyday tactics of evasion (see de Certeau 1984) that people undertake to find a minimal degree of human dignity in a world that denies them that. This was a tragic undertaking, I wanted to argue, because it was those very tactics of evasion that, at the same time, constituted the system of corruption, nepotism, and shady businesses people tried to evade. My prediction would be that this was a very stable system and most unlikely to change anytime soon.

I was wrong about the stability. Suddenly and surprisingly—not only to foreign observers but also to Egyptians themselves—a vast part of the population went out to the streets and claimed their human dignity by demanding the overthrow of the entire "system" (*nizam*)—a system to which they all, in one way or another, belonged.

What I had not taken into account was that the demoralizing experience of being forced to become a part of a corrupt system in order to survive its pressures, had become the breeding ground for a growing sense of anger and an urgent desire to live in a different world—a sense that needed only the revolution of Tunisia as an example to transform to the realization that rather than coping with the condition of normality, it is, after all, possible to change that condition.

What made the world seem so normal for such a long time, and what made it seem that it was possible to make a difference after all? And who says that it was really possible to make a difference? Has that condition actually changed?

## Discontent and Diversion

Tawfiq had entered the path of migration in large part because of disillusionment with the reality of education and work at home in Egypt. This is, in fact, the field where the modernist great promise of progress is at its most attractive to young Egyptians: the promise of social and personal advancement in the shape of education and cultivation, salaried work, and middle-class comfort and status. It is the promise of a life in relative comfort that Egyptians often describe as "humane" (*hayat bani adamin*), implying that a life that falls short of a certain material and emotional standards and securities is lacking in human dignity. In the previous chapter I took up the urgency and power of migration as a tragic path toward such humane existence. But although there is at least one migrant in almost every family, most Egyptians do not migrate abroad but search to build a humane life through education, a professional career, and business. It is possible, but tricky.

Mustafa and his two younger brothers, Salah and Kamel, were all busy pursuing their education and careers during my fieldwork. Salah, second of the three, is streetwise, witty, and pragmatic, a person with a critical mind and the wits to manage in a less-than-ideal world. At one of our first encounters in 2008, during his final year at the university, Salah and I had a long conversation about education. It began with him asking me what Egyptians can profit from my studies. He took up the problem that academic studies are not distributed to a wider reading public, and that in Egypt even students and researchers don't bother to read them. The newest references to foreign studies he got to read at the university were from the 1980s. Standing in front of a barbershop in the village square late in the evening, he then told me the story of his studies:

> Originally I wanted to study engineering, but I didn't get good enough marks at school, so I had to study something else—you know how it is here, people study something at the faculty of letters just to get the degree, and even the degree is not much worth because a degree in, say, psychology, doesn't really open you any jobs except perhaps teaching. My family said: just do a *ma'had* (two-year applied education) degree; it's enough if you just get a degree of some kind. I chose social service [*khidma igtima'iya*, applied social sciences for public administration—one of the least valued academic degrees in Egypt] and thought, "Maybe after two years of *ma'had* I can continue on university level." I found social service extremely interesting. In the beginning I would go to all lectures and read very intensively—I found it fascinating because it was about the life I experienced and knew, but looking at it from a general,

scientific perspective. So I got good marks on the medium level and decided to continue on university level for a baccalaureate degree. And I decided to study in Alexandria because it's a decent university, and it looks better to have studied in Alexandria than in a province university like Kafr al-Shaykh. And of course there was the reason that, like you said, it's Alexandria, you know, I don't deny it [we had previously talked about the importance of universities as a place to meet the opposite sex]. There I soon got a close circle of friends who were not-so-enthusiastic students, and I started falling behind with my studies. When I would want to go to a lecture, they would say, "Oh, come on, what's the point." And there was lots of boredom and frustration. I saw many boring lectures and stupid professors. And other students would belittle the value of studying with comments like, "The son of a doctor is a doctor." That's an extremely frustrating thing to hear. And you could pass easily without really studying: you just buy the examination book, you don't even have to learn it by heart, you just answer as much as you understood about it in the examination, and you pass.[4] I lost my motivation. . . . I do want to complete my studies—not that it would matter too much for the sake of the studies. I already have a degree. But there are other reasons: it will make my military service shorter. With a university degree I only need to go to the army for one year [instead of one and a half for people with a *ma'had* degree.] . . . When I have a baccalaureate I can marry a girl who is educated (intellectual) [*muthaqqafa*] and has a baccalaureate.

With a degree of bitterness and frustration, Salah had settled with appreciating the university system for what it did accomplish: flirt, shorter military service, and a better position on the marriage market. He no longer expected his education to be of any use for a career, and he lived from odd jobs as an electrician.

Even more frustrated than Salah was his younger brother, Kamel, whom I met for the last time in the autumn of 2009, soon after he and his brothers had moved to a modest but pleasant house they had built with the family's savings in the inland part of 'Agami in western Alexandria, far from the city center and the sea, but an inexpensive spot to build and live. He had just began his studies in Alexandria, and he was already very frustrated. The youngest and most talented of the three brothers, Kamel was the greatest source of hope for their mother, who invested enormously in his school education.

Entry to university education in Egypt is by aggregate grade (*magmu'a*) of the secondary school final examination, and Kamel had worked hard to get the best possible grades that would allow him to study medicine. On the final examination in 2009 there were six questions in biology that Kamel answered correctly but not with the exact phrase from the book. Those six answers were graded as wrong, which was enough to make his *magmu'a* fall below the very high entry level required for medicine. With his still exceptionally high *magmu'a*, he faced the choice of studying either sciences or nursing (a BA level for leading positions). He went for nursing, partly because it has the reputation of offering good work chances, and because it still kept him closer to his dream of becoming a doctor:

> Becoming a doctor has always been my goal, nothing else has attracted me. Even when most people would study anything that brings money I just want to become a doctor.

He was putting his hopes into getting a scholarship to study medicine abroad, and he interrogated me intensively about any opportunities I knew of. We discussed the advantages and disadvantages of studying abroad—Kamel was worried that an education abroad might deprive him of entitlement to a public-sector job in Egypt—and this turned the discussion to the different university selection procedures in different countries. I mentioned the entry examinations that some countries have, and Kamel replied:

> They will introduce that in Egypt too, but it will be a disaster. Why? It may be a good idea elsewhere, but here it will become subverted by diversions [*thagharat*]. The professors will choose people by money and *wasta*, and in the end the old *magmu'a* system will be better.
>
> If you look at the system here in Egypt, it's actually perfect. In theory, we have a very good education and health-care system, it can compare with any country. But the Egyptians introduce all those diversions that will spoil it and turn it into something completely different.

Kamel ascribed to Egyptians the strong propensity to subvert regulations, to divert public property to their own advantage, to abuse and manipulate even the best systems beyond recognition. This is a very fitting description of the lived reality of neoliberal governance—not only in Egypt but across the world. Based on the promise of efficiency, rationality, competition, and transparency as the key to growth, wealth, and social well-being (eloquently summarized as "good governance"), neoliberal government stands out for its strikingly contradictory nature. The promise of efficient government and less public spending means, in practice, a shift (even an increase) in public spending in favor of privileged groups. The promise of less bureaucracy means, in practice, an overwhelming load of auditing, reporting, and controlling. The promise of transparency means, in practice, the production of public performances of success in the shape of brochures, advertisements, reports, model projects, and so on, that may conceal more than they reveal. What makes such form of government actually work are invisible practices of support, affect, favoring, finance, and diversion—practices that in public discourse are condoned and fought as corruption and nepotism.[5] And yet they were so deeply intertwined into the economical and political system of the Mubarak era that one could not be thought of without the other.

The fancy appearance of Egyptian universities as shown in official government policies and English-language brochures could not have existed in any other way than blatant contradiction to a reality of diversions. With professors' salaries so low that they do not cover monthly rent, with a growing pressure on university employees at all levels to earn more money and guarantee the future of their children, with institutional pressure to perform excellence in order to gain international funding while offering an education to millions, there are no resources to actually have a "properly" functioning university in the sense entailed in the promise. Corruption does not subvert international investments and university reforms. It is the condition under which investments take place and universities work. Without diversions, the whole system would collapse.

Less than a month after this meeting with Kamel, the news reached me that he had died in a car accident. I never got to know the exact circumstances of the accident, but I do know that traffic rules are nearly absent, driver's licenses can be received through connections without having to take a single driving lesson, and the proliferation of private cars and motorcycles has been accompanied by a dramatic increase in accidents. Hazardous traffic is one part of the system of diversions Kamel described.

Life had to go on. Mustafa, the oldest of the three, gave up his plans of trying to migrate to Europe illegally on a fishing boat. He could not put his mother at the risk of losing another son. He now put all his effort in the job he had found in Alexandria earlier the same year. He had tried many jobs, all of which fell short of his expectations, and argued:

> Only in the cinema, during the illusion of two hours we spend in a film, do people actually work in jobs that they dream of and which they believe in. In reality people end up just doing whatever can bring them money, no matter if legal or not, *halal* or not.

In the spring of 2009, Mustafa had worked as a sales representative for a brand of American-style bread that was sold at very good profit to shops in Alexandria. At first he found it very difficult to make money. After every round there were goods missing. Then he found out that the driver was stealing bread and selling it on his own account:

> Little by little I realized that the whole business depended on theft by everybody involved. Everybody preys on each other [*il-kull biyakul fi ba'd*]. I understood how the system worked, and I started to earn good money, but I felt guilty every day I came home: my income was *haram*, based on stealing. Every day I thought that I can't go on like this. There was an older engineer who used work in another company but was laid off and who had a family to take care of. He also felt very guilty about the work but he couldn't give it up. Everyone in the system was involved in it.

Mustafa eventually left that job, and by 2010 he was working as a sales representative in an import-export business, a job that included no outright stealing and still offered an acceptable income. But while he was getting better at his job, he was also becoming disillusioned. Reminiscing about his period of Salafi activism some years earlier, he commented:

> I think I was a much better person back then because I would see the world in a rosy way. I was younger and more naive. Meanwhile I have had to learn how to get along [*atsarraf*] in the world, and in order to get along, you must sometimes be tough and exploit the situation.

Saying this, he made the gesture of a vampire's teeth with his fingers.

The mastery of immoral and dubious things like stealing, diverting, cheating, and favoring and getting favored has become a necessary practical skill in Egypt in the past decades. It is a skill that has come at a price. It has shifted moral pressure to areas in which one can do something—family, gender, symbolic politics. But the possibility of cultivating moral concerns in some areas did not remove the original sense of moral trouble involved in a life built on an unsound foundation. Egypt during the Mubarak era was not simply divided into oppressors and oppressed. As Mustafa points out, everybody was involved. The system of governing Egypt in the Mubarak era relied on the complicity of its subjects on every step, even when they were struggling against it.[6]

Isma'il received his teacher's diploma in 2003 and tried to get a civil servant's position as a teacher, with no success until 2011. Throughout that time, his main income was from the shop owned by his father, which he was running with considerable skill. But he never lost sight of his desired public-sector job, with its security, status, and income opportunities from private tutoring. In the meantime, he had various short-term contracts and advanced training. A key task was to remain working at a school on temporary contracts in order to be eligible for a regular position. One of these contracts involved a posting to develop the teaching equipment of a school in a village, a job about which Isma'il told a group of men at a wedding in Nazlat al-Rayyis in October 2009. He had nothing to do there, he said. He spent a month just waiting to meet the director, playing computer games in the office, staying for an hour a day at the most. At the end of the term and with the end of his contract approaching, he was finally assigned a room in the basement as a technician, but he refused and pointed out that he is a teacher, not a technician. With pride, he told us: "Until today I don't know where the door to that room is."

The point of the whole enterprise, Isma'il explained, was just to remain officially employed by the Ministry of Education. He took pride in his ability to do so while avoiding actually doing any work, especially any work that would be below his level. Telling this story to entertain wedding guests, he was not so much complaining about the injustice or inefficiency of the system. He was bragging about his ability to outwit it.

The way Isma'il tells it, it is a story of him facing an unjust and stupid system made up of incapable and arrogant people, an encounter in which he manages to manipulate the situation to his best advantage, to maintain his dignity, and even to gain a symbolic victory. Later I spoke with Isma'il about my research and told him that at that moment I was researching what people do when there is very little they can do, how people try to maintain their dignity in the face of unacceptable situations. He immediately recognized himself in this description. This was exactly what he was trying to accomplish.

In his book *The Practice of Everyday Life* Michel de Certeau (1984) takes up the mundane ways of doing things, the ways in which people make do with and manipulate the structures and powers they face in often unpredictable ways. Relating to Foucault's (1977) *Discipline and Punish*, de Certeau (1984: xiv) argues that Foucault's insight about the workings of disciplinary power begs the question about its efficacy and responses to it:

> If it is true that the grid of "discipline" is everywhere becoming clearer and more extensive, it is all the more urgent to discover how an entire society resists being reduced to it, what popular procedures (also "minuscule" and quotidian) manipulate the mechanisms of discipline and conform to them only in order to evade them, and finally, what "ways of operating" form the counterpart, on the consumer's (or "dominee's") side, of the mute processes that organize the establishment of socioeconomic order.

If Foucault offers us a theory of *strategies* of forming subjects through discourse, discipline, and—in his later work—cultivation, de Certeau offers a theory, or perhaps rather a theology,[7] of the *tactics* needed to live under the conditions shaped by those strategies. Yet although the image of everyday life in Egypt drawn by Tawfiq, Sa'id, Salah, Kamel, Mustafa, and Isma'il clearly does not conform to the rather neat image of disciplinary power as drawn by Foucault, it does cast a different light on de Certeau's analysis of the potential of antidiscipline involved in everyday usages and the tactics of the weak. The tactics of making do may be less antidisciplinary than intended by those involved, or than seen by de Certeau. Looking at the tactical diversions that made life livable under conditions of the neoliberal-clientelistic rule of the Mubarak era, it turns out that those diversions were in fact instrumental to the efficacy of that form of government.

While struggling to maintain his dignity in face of a frustrating system, Isma'il also took part in a different accomplishment: the constitution of a public sector in which employment is primarily an entitlement and a privilege, one in which positions are distributed to those who have the best connections and the best skills in manipulating the formal structure to their own ends. The oppressive institutional world of endless diversions described by Kamel is the outcome of attempts to carve a space for dignity and capacity to act within a system. Not only did people feel oppressed and dispossessed by class divisions, political and trade oligarchies, and police brutality; they also were themselves part of the very system they suffered from, making money through illegal and immoral schemes, favoring their relatives, stealing and diverting public and private property. As people struggled to have at least some power over their situation, they participated in producing the very conditions against which they struggled.

This is not to deny the importance of more brute forms of power that relied on fear and violence in the shape of a brutal police force, an omnipresent apparatus of the State Security, and the practice of contracting thugs to intimidate opposition and to guarantee desired results in elections ('Abd al-'Aziz 2013). On the contrary, these forms of violent government were inseparable from more subtle forms of power, and instrumental in channeling discontent and resistance to tactics of diversion that allowed people to "walk by the side of the wall" [*yimshi ganb il-hit*], that is, to go after one's interests while keeping low profile and avoiding head-on confrontation (Tordhol 2014: 16). But it worked only as long as very few people seriously tried to face the system head-on.

This would have been the ending point of an article to be titled "Condition: Normal." But this condition turned out to be less stable than I and a few others had thought. Diversion as an attempt to have power over one's life ends up producing the very system people try to divert. But it is a frustrating and morally troubling experience. It makes people angry. When diversion becomes the invisible work needed to maintain the face of perfectionist promises of sound moral life, efficient production of wealth, and transparent governance, it may generate more discontent than it can channel. It becomes the breeding ground for even graver discontent.

## A Leap of Action

On January 31, 2011, a friend of mine from Nazlat al-Rayyis and I were walking back to his apartment in Giza from Tahrir Square, where the sit-in that would eventually result in Hosni Mubarak's fall had started three nights earlier. There was a curfew and much fear of looting, and the otherwise busy streets of Cairo were almost completely empty, except for people returning from the demonstration and the popular committees (*ligan sha'biya*) guarding the streets. We walked through the empty streets with a small group of demonstrators, shouting slogans against the system and calling people to a peaceful "march of a million people" (*masira milyuniya*).[8] The conditions were not normal any more.

There were a few people on the streets but much discussion going on. A young man who walked with us all the way to Giza was very excited about the new situation. He said that he had not at first believed in the demonstrations of January 25—he went there not believing that others would go. He described the feeling: "Until few days ago I felt that I live in a nightmare, and suddenly I could dream freely." My friend added, "Things became possible that I couldn't have imagined. Suddenly we can make a difference." The next day, an old friend of mine whom I met by chance during the demonstration in downtown Cairo echoed the same experience: "This is more than I could have ever dreamed of."

What made it possible to make the difference? Much has been said and written about new political discourses, social critique, literary imagination, oppositional activism, tactics of protest, and social media that made it possible to spread the word and to organize a wave of protest big enough to force the political and economical elites of Egypt to regroup and take the demands of ordinary Egyptians and political activists seriously.[9] And yet the element of surprise remains central. Not only was Egypt's political leadership surprised and overwhelmed by the events, so were the revolutionaries. What made the revolution initially successful was the realization by a significant part of Egyptians that it was possible, after all, to face the system head-on. It was a realization grounded in moral trouble and anger, and fed by a language of political discontent and a fantasy for a better life. But in the actual event of revolution, its nature was not ideological, intellectual, or imaginative, but physical and emotional. Being part of it in whatever way—going to a demonstration, guarding a neighborhood, cooking and caring for others—was an embodied act of doing something that could make a difference. Committing that act of doing constituted something like a leap of action, a physical move that made the world appear in a different light.

The uprising was a golden hour of poetry and songs (both old and new) that expressed the spirit of defiance and faith in a different life. It was not a moment for the sophisticated work of fantasy, however, because reality itself, for a few short weeks, was more fantastic (or more nightmarish, depending on one's point of view) than anything that one could think up. A revolution is in itself a poetic event insofar as it is about taking the ordinary things, otherwise evident and transparent, like the words of prose, and playing with them, wondering about them, not taking them for granted, putting them together in a new configuration (Sartre 1947). It is a moment in which things appear in a different light, and the walls on which one had, metaphorically speaking, sprayed one's commentary through the work of fantasy, are crumbling and falling, opening up new fantastic horizons of action and imagination. If in ordinary days the work of fantasy precedes action by opening up the space to think of alternatives, in the time of a revolution, action runs ahead of imagination and forms it. This was the original revolutionary moment: the birth of a sense that something previously unimaginable is in the process of being realized—hence the element of surprise.

But what exactly was being realized? Did the leap of action really make a difference? If so, what kind of a difference? The answer cannot be found in Tahrir Square.

On January 28, 2011, one of the bloodiest days of the revolutionary period and a turning point that ultimately destabilized the rule of the Mubarak clan,

Mustafa slept late. He had followed the events of the previous days on the news but did not expect that the announced "Day of Anger" would make a difference. Internet and mobile phones had been disconnected by the government, and having neither a landline phone nor satellite television in his new apartment in 'Agami in Alexandria, he was cut off from news. As he finally left his apartment in the early afternoon, he came across two neighbors carrying a pair of metal doors. Arriving at the main street he found the 'Agami police station on fire and people looting it (which is how his neighbors had gotten hold of the doors). Shortly before his arrival there had been a confrontation between demonstrators and police. Four protesters had been shot dead, the police had retreated, and four police trucks and the police station had been set on fire. Now there were increasing numbers of people gathering on the street. Mustafa, who at first could not believe his eyes, joined the protesters who were ready to die and waiting for the police to return. But the police did not return. Only slowly did they begin to receive news that similar clashes had taken place across the country and that the police had withdrawn everywhere. Mustafa described to me the contradictory feelings he had:

> I felt that it was like a dream, that after we had been so long being treated like chicken, Egypt will be a paradise tomorrow. But at the same time I asked: "Why burn the police station?" It will be rebuilt with our money.

January 28, 2011, today remembered as the "Friday of Anger," was one of the most cathartic and ambiguous moments of the revolution, a disturbing victory that Mustafa remembered with a mixture of hope, bewilderment, and ambivalence. In mid-March 2011, when he recounted this experience to me, the aspect of hope was already dwindling. He told me that he had been really happy since that day. Recently, however, he had started to feel that the army wasn't much of an expert in managing the country, that many things would not change, and that there would still be bribes to be paid and politicians stealing from the people.

Mustafa's increasing doubts were not his alone. As the euphoria of the initial moment passed, it became clear that much had been destroyed but that it was very unclear what, if anything, was being built in its place.

During the days immediately following Mubarak's resignation on February 11, a sense of cathartic transformation prevailed. For a while, almost nobody dared to either pay or accept bribes. The relative rarity of sexual harassment during the demonstrations and the effort that demonstrators and inhabitants of residential areas put into cleaning the streets led some to assume that a new Egypt would emerge where people would be cooperative and responsible, where one could go to a government office without having to know the right people or pay bribes, where women could walk along clean and orderly streets without being troubled. It was a cathartic moment, and as is in the nature of catharsis, it couldn't last. People still depended on bribes for their livelihood. The streets got dirty again. Women were still harassed—at times even worse than before. Instead of a cathartic transformation, the spring of 2011 was the beginning of a stormy season marked by an increasingly polarized and violent struggle with changing alliances among the Muslim Brotherhood, Salafis and other Islamist fractions, cadres of the old system, the military elite, and a radical revolutionary current, as well as a wave of strikes, repeated new uprisings and outbreaks of violence, a worsening economic situation, and a dramatic growth in street crime. Amid this ongoing political struggle and uncertainty, people continued to search for work, make a living, get married, and have some power over their situation.

It is important to remember that most Egyptians did not partake in the leap of action. For a lot of people, including many who were very discontent with the way things had been, the revolution was a disconcerting and frightening experience. Rather than giving them the power to change the world, it deprived them of their power to do anything about their situation. Many women did not dare to go out or were not allowed to. People making their living in retail trade, informal jobs, and services had no income. Especially in wealthy neighborhoods people lived in fear of looting and robbery. People who had become good at using their connections to help themselves and others experienced a condition of chaos. As time passed, this sense of disorientation and disempowerment was further magnified by an ongoing sense of insecurity and chaos. In her account of the revolution from the point of view of mothers staying home with children, Jessica Winegar (2012) has pointed out how much the capacity to participate in the revolution, and in consequence the emotions invested in the events, depended on gender, class, and geographic location. Women staying inside, fearing for their own safety and that of their husbands and children, and left with neither income nor freedom to move safely would find it difficult to support a long struggle. They would rather hope that it would all be over quickly. Just like the leap of action was a physical one, so also the point of view and the emotional response one would have toward the events was related to one's physical place of being and scope of movement.

These different experiences are an important ground for divergent ways of trying to do something about one's condition postrevolutionary Egypt. "The system"—that is, the way of governing and being governed that characterized the Mubarak era—fell in Egypt in January and February 2011 insofar people found new effective ways of dealing with their condition that were products of a different kind of normality. However, many of the ways of governing that were successful in the Mubarak era continued to be successful, with certain modifications. Much of what has been described here in the past tense did not change and will still be valid in the future. The leap of action that was the January 25 revolution was neither a complete nor a final one. It was transient, it was not shared by all, and in the end it failed catastrophically.

### There Was a Revolution?

Especially (but not only) those who actively participated in street protests in 2011 soon came to express a frustrated and skeptical vision of the situation. Baybars, a man in his late twenties whose first experience of street protests was in the uprising of Mohamed Mahmoud Street in November 2011 (see Ryzova 2012), commented bitterly some months later:

> Was the revolution successful, or did it fail? The problem is that it was neither successful nor did it fail. Was there a revolution in the first place? If there was one, it was stolen.

A fitting description of the revolution's failure to be one is offered by Shaymaa Bakr, a teacher and poet from Alexandria. In her poem "I Say," written in the autumn of 2011 and revised in late 2012, the wrong of the past is too great to be corrected, the revolutionary spirit not radical enough to make a chance, and the bitterness of daily life unchanged:

. . . . . . . . . . . . . . . .
We had to grab for the wind
The sheep had to reject being skinned
after it was slaughtered
Brothers of ours had to die . . .
            so that the open graves . . .
can promise to us that we haven't died yet
that there is a killing that does not kill us
But we should not have
raised our ambition so that it can devour us
We had to set in fire
            all the dry wood
without afterward demanding from time
that it may turn the earth green again
Who would trust his feet if he staggers
            if one step
tries to change its pace
on the same futile road

Those are our zeroes[10] . . . glimmering on the face of the river
But the stars . . . disappeared
            —as they do—
                        in haze
and we returned to the vocabulary of hell
(which we knew word by word)

Time won't pass
Our dirty chairs by the side of the cafés
Playing with half a cigarette
When pretty women pass by, our gaze
with straying eyes

The strenuous sleeping pills
deadly if required

The tormenting pain in grandmother's breast
after standing in a punishment drill for the old
in the free clinic
The medicine leaves the disease at ease
        in her breast
while she finds no rest.
So even medicine brings pain?

The children want things . . . but we say:
—"By the end of the month"[11]
—"So many ends of the month"—they reply—
"The month has lost its beginning!"
(We are cheap in this regard)

An empty fridge and empty shelves
We envied the plants wholeheartedly
when poverty almost compelled us
to photosynthesis

The debts, the debts!
So, we need to live
on two cents a day
through the coming year

Then, a widow knocks on the door
—to console a neighbor's loneliness—
and leaves his apartment crying

The suspicious paleness on our neighbours' faces
when we meet in the morning by chance:
"Who will pay for the repair of . . ."
And the storm of locusts
at the busy popular bakery[12]
The crowds or the bakery
—Who wins the prize?

If there was no revolution, then what was there? What happened? And how can we relate the sense of disappointment that prevailed in 2012 with the nationalist enthusiasm and extreme violence that followed in the summer of 2013?

Michel Foucault famously argued that his way of thinking about power by no means excludes resistance, but every form of power is met by its own particular form of resistance. Toward the end of the 1970s, Foucault became increasingly interested in the "counterconducts" of resistance and revolt, and in his 1977–1978 lectures *Security, Territory, Population* (Foucault 2007) he develops the theme of counterconducts at some length. He recognizes the "immediate and founding correlation between conduct and counter-conduct" (196) but insists on the "non-autonomous specificity of these resistances" (197). At other times, Foucault seems to have had put more hopes into the autonomous capacity of resistance, but in either case, the implicit hierarchy remains of power as a relationship of dominant strategies (i.e., conducts) and resistance (i.e., counterconducts), whereby the second is dependent on and directed at the first.

Both the normality of discontent and diversions as well as the January 25 uprising compel me, therefore, to turn Foucault's idea of power and resistances around. I suggest thinking about "resistances" as the primary "conducts," to borrow Foucault's terminology. Before the revolution, "the system" actually consisted largely of the people's attempts to carve spaces within it, which also gave the system its particularly wicked and demoralizing form (see Hibou 2011; Bayat 2010; Ghannam 2002). By reckoning with that which they considered inevitable, and acting in accordance with that reckoning, they were participating in creating that which they expected—even if it was detrimental to their own living conditions (Tordhol 2014: 39–40).[13] After the revolution, Egypt remained in a chaotic state because a new state of "as if" (Wedeen 1999) was not yet there.[14] Different people based their actions on highly different understandings of what was going on in the first place. Various forms of paranoid fear toward political opponents, different assessments of what could and what could not be done, of right and wrong, and a collapse of social taboos and inhibitions created a situation that was confusing, to say the least. The haphazard, inconsistent, and often clearly ill-conceived policies of the first military rule (2011–2012), the short-lived government of the Muslim Brotherhood (2012–2013) and the El-Sisi regime as it established itself in 2013 and 2014 were not just due to the incompetence of these old and new ruling elites (although that cannot be entirely ruled out either). They were the reflection of an attempt to govern a population that did not display an established pattern of being governed. Any system of political economy is not just a structure laid down by constitutions, elections, laws, elites, and contracts. It is the outcome of the ways in which people act in anticipation of such structures. In a reversal of Foucault's thesis, the Egyptian revolution shows that every form of resistance also produces its own particular form of power (see also Hardt and Negri 2000).

What can be said, then, about the arts of being governed (the ways and techniques of facing a government's power, as opposed to the "arts of government") in the first years after 2011? How different were they from the past normality? And which past counts as the measure of normality?

Much remained the same. When anti-Brotherhood protesters stormed numerous offices of the Muslim Brotherhood's political wing, the Freedom and Justice Party, during protests in late 2012 and early 2013, they found documents in which party members and others asked for (and received) preferential treatment in regard to employment, housing, and military posts. Party members paid reduced electricity bills while the government was cutting subsidies, and they enjoyed other privileges that were rather similar to those associated with membership in Mubarak's dissolved National Democratic Party (Abou-El-Fadl 2013).

In the summer of 2011, Isma'il finally received a permanent teacher's position in the course of a major wave of public spending aimed at appeasing popular discontent. He became feverishly busy trying to move from the technical position he had to a teaching position. He told me why:

> The Muslim Brotherhood, as soon as they form a government, will set on a reform project of the educational system that will remain superficial and fail to address the underlying structural problems. Criminalizing private tutoring will be a cornerstone of this program, and it means that the prices for private tutoring will skyrocket.

Isma'il's calculus didn't turn out to be accurate, at least not in the short term. During the one year of its rule, the Muslim Brotherhood was too busy trying to stay in power, and not even a superficial reform project was initiated, aside from the ideological modification of textbooks. The Muslim Brotherhood's declared aim was to build a well-functioning neoliberalism with conservative social and educational policies (as opposed to the corrupt neoliberalism in the name of enlightenment of the Mubarak era; see Abaza 2010). But already in its first steps, it became involved in the same kind of clientelistic politics of intransparency, favors, unequal access, and repression as its predecessors. It turned out to be a way of running things that still worked as long as people continued to play along, ask for favors, divert reforms to their private ends, and bandwagon with those in power.

It did not work sufficiently well, however. In the summer of 2013 the Muslim Brotherhood was removed from power by an unlikely alliance of the military, the Ministry of the Interior, old system loyalists, liberal media, and radical revolutionaries. In a chain of events more violent and bloodthirsty than anything seen in Egypt since the revolution of 1919, a new military regime with formal civil leadership was established, and the Muslim Brotherhood and its supporters brutally repressed in the name of "fighting terrorism" and "continuing the revolution," or, as Mubarak loyalists preferred to put it, a "corrective revolution." Supporters of deposed president Morsi unsurprisingly saw the events as a military coup, and much of the international media and scholarship have agreed that it was a coup indeed. Although technically the overthrow of Morsi certainly was a coup d'état, the question of whether what happened was a coup or a revolution is primarily one of moral positioning: coup is bad, revolution is good. This is why it is a misleading question when one tries to understand *what* actually happened.

To start with, it is important to realize that Egypt was not made up of solid political blocs at the time. People changed their views and visions constantly. These shifts also reflected the shifting fortunes of those struggling for political power. When I met Mustafa in March 2011, he was not only skeptical about the military's ability to rule the country; he was also very worried about the Salafi movement's forceful entry to the political arena, and he expected them to inflict their too-strict, rigid vision on the country. In November of the same year, he was excited and enthusiastic about the first parliamentary elections, and he gave his vote to the Salafi Nour Party, because he believed that they would be the only ones able to establish law and order. The following spring, he told me that he had grown skeptical of Parliament but did think that the president of the National Assembly Saad al-Katatni (from the Muslim Brotherhood) was doing a good job. He especially mentioned how al-Katatni interrupted a Salafi member of Parliament who called for prayer in a parliamentary session. By the winter of 2012–2013, he had reached a different conclusion. He then thought that the president should come "from within the army" because it was the one and only patriotic, powerful, and organized institution able to run the country and promote its interests. When in spring 2013 the Tamarrud campaign began collecting signatures for a popular impeachment of Morsi and the Muslim Brotherhood, he, too, signed. When I met Mustafa in October 2013, he—knowing my point of view—asked me not to take up the theme of the military and the Rabea al-'Adawiya massacre, saying that he gets "very upset when someone criticizes the army and talks about those killed in Rabea." For two and a half years, Mustafa had always thought of himself as being on the side of the revolution, even when political instability meant that business was bad over long periods of time. But aside from his preference for law and order, what and who has represented the revolution for him has constantly shifted.

Tactics of diversion and adaptation are not a privilege of the weak. Mustafa was not making tactical shifts of allegiance; he was simply changing his mind about who was trustworthy and able to realize what he hoped from the revolution. The most important tactical moves were undertaken by those who saw their position and power threatened by the revolution. Just like people in different positions of power diverted "the system" to make life livable, they also diverted the revolution to carve a space of acceptable living within it. In the spring of 2011, within a short time, almost everybody in Egypt claimed to speak in the name of the revolution, although the revolutionary movement enjoyed the support only of a minority. Painting patriotic slogans in national colors over anti-Mubarak graffiti, supporting the military in the name of the revolution, waving the Egyptian flag in the name of a quick return to stability—people who were at least ambivalent about the revolution and institutions that were keen to guard their power and privileges turned the revolution into something other than what it was on the evening of January 25.

In a situation where the accustomed means of government had become ineffective, where a large part of the population acted in ways that no longer reproduced the anticipation of a stable system, revolution became the new condition of "as if" (Wedeen 1999), a structuring fiction that is powerful because people act in accordance with it, regardless of whether they believe in it. Revolution as the "as if" condition means not so much the establishment of a new order after a full rotation, as in the French etymology of the English term, as an ongoing state of uprising and revolt, as in the Arabic word for revolution, *thawra*. That condition brought along a sense of boldness that is expressed in revolutionary opposition (more about which in the next chapter), artistic production, and street crime, a sense of the right and the need for confrontation for one's rights, perhaps best expressed in the wave of small-scale (and often successful) strikes around the country.

At first, evoking revolution for the sake of stability remained a relatively ineffective tactic, because it made reference to revolutionary symbols but could not tap into revolutionary anger and defiance. Governing Egypt in the name of a happy revolution where everybody participated and nobody was at fault did not work well for a population that was likely to strike, demonstrate, and sabotage the functions of the state. The situation changed, however, with the rise to power of the Muslim Brotherhood in the summer of 2012 and the Brotherhood's inability (or unwillingness) to form alliances outside the Islamist current. Nationalism emerged as a positive shared ground of anti-Islamist sentiment that could unite people with otherwise entirely opposed views and interests. The symbolic language of revolution in combination with the sentiment of anger and defiance could now work against those who had gained power through revolution—and who, in turn, had to rely on a language of unity and electoral legitimacy that had little credibility in an increasingly polarized atmosphere. This was the mobilizing ground of the mass demonstrations of June 30, 2013. This made the consequent establishment of the new military regime in the name of the revolution possible and successful.

Paradoxically enough, then, there has been a revolution in Egypt, but not of a kind that fits into the binary of good revolution versus bad coup. Instead,

revolutionary energy was popularized and reappropriated to new ends in a counterrevolution. The July 2013 counterrevolution was successful because it was able
to appropriate the chaotic energy of defiance against one single enemy—the Muslim Brotherhood—and because it could link that energy with the grand scheme
of nationalism and the glorification of the army. Last but not least, it made uncompromising use of a powerful technique of revolutionary government that
once was called terror but today goes by the name "war against terrorism" (see
Camus 1991; Schielke 2014).

## Back to Normal

For Tawfiq (and for me), the end of January 2011 was a once-in-a-lifetime experience, a singular moment that seemed to be radically different from all social
normality. Talking about this with Tawfiq online on the evening of January 25, I
mistakenly claimed that this was the first time something like this had happened
since 1919, and he did not correct me.

Until 2011, Egypt as I knew it was that of the late Mubarak era, one of the
most depoliticized times in Egypt's contemporary history. I first arrived in Egypt
in the late 1990s, a time when the de facto civil war between the Mubarak regime and "Islamic groups" (al-Gama'at al-Islamiya) in southern Egypt was ending with bloody defeat for the Islamist militants. The 1990s until 2010 was a time
when everybody in Egypt, including Islamists, were compelled to *yikabbar*, that
is, to mind their own business and not get involved with politics. In retrospect,
however, the Mubarak era that was Egypt as I knew it appears to be exceptional,
an interruption in a long history of revolutions and uprisings in Egypt since the
nineteenth century.

The history of modern Egypt is a history of popular uprisings, student and
strike movements, riots, and full-fledged revolutions. It begins in the nineteenth
century and continues throughout the twentieth century, with the 1919 revolution
against British colonial rule, student protests in 1935, student and labor protests
in 1946, the military coup of 1952 and the following revolutionary reorganization
of political and economic power, strikes and demonstrations in the late 1960s and
early 1970s, and the so-called bread riots of January 1977 (a wide-scale protest
movement involving workers, students, and political activists of different color-
ings against Anwar al-Sadat's policies of economic liberalization). The 1990s witnessed the uprising of al-Gama'at al-Islamiya, and the second half of the 2000s
was marked by a series of major strikes as well as street protests of more limited
scale. Most of these different protest movements and uprisings share a number
of important features: a key role played by young people (especially students, and
since the 1940s industrial workers), significant participation across political and
party lines, large-scale demonstrations often focused on Tahrir Square (formerly

Isma'iliya Square) in Cairo, a visible role played by women, and an at best moderate degree of success in realizing the protesters' demands (Diyab 2011).

The moment of revolution carries an experienced singularity of a once-in-a-lifetime event that, because of its singularity, exceeds the imaginable. The January 25 revolution was not a singular event, however. It stands in a tradition, and without repeating history, it builds on its predecessors and paves the way for struggles to come. At the time this book goes to press, a street movement of Muslim Brotherhood supporters and other smaller factions that struggled against the El-Sisi regime for more than half a year appears to be defeated and the new regime firmly established. It looks like the stormy season of revolution has ended with a victory for the army. However, while a new regime is establishing itself, the seeds of the next storm are being sown, and the songs that will be sung in the next uprising may already be written.

Historically speaking, this is the normal condition. The long years of calm are not more normal than the stormy years of uprising and turmoil. This doesn't tell whether or not the condition is good, only that it is the condition of a society with deep unsolved conflicts and mutually irreconcilable powers. January 25, 2011, was not the opening of a new era in Egypt. It was the return to the historical normality of a nation in revolt, the continuation of a state of uprising that began in 1919, or perhaps already in the Orabi Rebellion of 1881, and that is bound to continue. I am not sure whether this is a cause for optimism or a pessimism, however. The continuation and repetition of oppositional movements and uprisings means that there is a strong social current of defiance that repeatedly surfaces at moments of urgency and opportunity, enforcing a shift in the exercise of power (echoing the vision of Hardt and Negri 2000). But it also means that the current of defiance repeatedly fails to overcome a powerful logic of exploitation, oppression, and humiliation that, by virtue of its ability to adapt to and appropriate the energy of rebellion, continues to make new uprisings necessary.

# 9 Those Who Said No

ONE OF THE most tangible outcomes of the stormy season that began in January 2011 was the emergence of a new kind of political subjectivity among an active and visible minority of people who would often call themselves "revolutionaries" (implying that others speaking in the name of the revolution were not). This active minority participated in the ongoing protests against the Mubarak system, then against the military rule, then against the Muslim Brotherhood, and then finally broke up into mutually hostile camps after the establishment of the El-Sisi regime and the violent oppression of the Muslim Brotherhood in the summer of 2013. In ideological terms, they have been variously described as liberal, leftist, secular, and a gang of thugs. In practice, they had neither a clear ideology nor organization (in fact, they were and remain severely disorganized). Rather than being united by an ideology or organization, the revolutionaries were united by a common struggle and a shared affect of rejection.

That struggle and this affect are the topic of this final chapter of a book, on the ambiguity and consequences of great expectations. Although oppositional by definition and exceptional in many ways, the revolutionaries' commitment to saying no is by no means opposed to the more general shape of a life in the future tense. On the contrary, their outlook on the world is built on an especially radical sense of futurity. And like no others, they embody the tragic quality of expecting and demanding something more and better.

## The Village Revolutionaries

The revolutionary current is something I would never have thought of writing about before 2011, because it was limited to small circles mainly in the capital (Onodera 2009), and the people with whom I did my research rarely, if ever, took part in any explicitly political action even though they often had strong political opinions.[1] If they did become active for the sake of something other than building a conventional life, they either would join the Salafi movement to reach peace of mind and a sense of purpose through perfectionist religious commitment, or they would write poetry and prose for the sake of an imaginative way out of the ordinary.

However, following the uprising of 2011, there was a wave of politicization, with people participating in protests, joining and leaving movements, and taking parts in actions. This wave was at its strongest in the cities, but it was also felt in villages like Nazlat al-Rayyis. Some people joined the many old and new Islamist movements and supported the rise to power of the Muslim Brotherhood. Others sided with continuity and stability and fought against those who fought for a change, of whatever kind. Some went for the radical antisystem path of the revolutionaries. Others still preferred to wait and see. Street battles and the mutual demonization of competing factions created a dramatic sense of polarization, antagonism, and hatred. Friendships were strained and broke; families became arenas of political struggle. Social circles became increasingly politically exclusive, people stopped speaking with one another, and not speaking about politics was rarely an option. In this new situation, I felt that it was necessary to return to the existential grounds and consequences of activism that I had previously taken up in regard to Salafi commitment before 2011. If before 2011 one was well advised to work on oneself rather than aiming to change state and society, then in 2011, many feasible paths of political and social commitment became available. These merit a comparative look at the trajectories of people in different groups and movements. But in the years immediately after 2011, such a comparative look was not really an option for me. I, too, had to choose sides. I chose the side of those who called themselves revolutionaries.

Who are—or were—the revolutionaries? In demographic terms, supporters of an ongoing revolution between 2011 and 2013 were most likely to be found in the big cities of northern Egypt: Cairo, Alexandria, Port Said, al-Mahalla al-Kubra, al-Mansura. The smaller the place, or the further from the Mediterranean coast and the Suez Canal one goes, the fewer the revolutionaries, and the stronger the power of either Islamist movements or functionaries of the Mubarak system. In a city like Alexandria, protests by the "civil forces" (*al-quwa al-madaniya*)—*civil* in the sense of neither theocratic nor military—as they at times called themselves, were often dominated by mostly young men and fewer women with distinctively middle-class urban styles of dress. In the elections and referenda the central urban districts of big cities were those most likely to vote for a revolutionary candidate or to vote no on a constitutional proposal backed by the army and/or the Islamists in the two constitutional referenda of 2011 and 2012 (Schielke 2012b; Ali 2012). However, support for the revolutionary current is by no means limited to this urban middle-class constituency, and in all major events, people from poorer backgrounds have made up the bulk of participants (as well as the majority of protesters killed). And there were (and remain) revolutionary groups active in the countryside. One such group was established in the village of Nazlat al-Rayyis in 2011, and as it happened, several of the people with whom I had been doing fieldwork were involved in it.

Before 2011, ideological positioning was not a matter of urgency except in small activist circles. In a place like Nazlat al-Rayyis, there was a broad social consensus of Islam as a shared moral idiom (albeit with different visions of its political relevance) and a sense of the government as immoral, even infidel. In 2011, this consensus broke down, and ideological and political positioning became an important issue. There has been a lot talk about ideological orientations, such as leftist (*yasari*), socialist (*ishtiraki*), secularist (*'almani*), civil (*madani*), liberal (*laybirali*), Islamist (*tayyar islami* or *islamiyin*), Salafi, Muslim Brotherhood (*ikhwan*), jihadist (*gihadi*), and the like. *Liberal*, in particular, which hardly existed in the political dictionary before 2011, has become a catchall term, similar to its use in the United States. Islamists usually positively identify themselves as Islamists, but among others, there is often remarkable unease when it comes to identifying oneself with any ideological labels, and many people avoid identifying themselves ideologically at all; instead, they define themselves with more generic self-identifications such as revolutionaries (*thuwwar*) or youth (*shabab*). And many of the most powerful identifications are polemic ones that are used against others along current political conflict lines, such as ancien régime (*filul*); infidels (*kuffar*); secularists (*'almaniyin*); beards (*duqun*, referring to the beards which many Islamists sport); those who do business with religion (*tuggar bi-d-din*); thugs (*baltagiya*); good-for-nothing troublemakers (*siyya'*); and most recently, terrorists (*irhabiyin*) and slaves of the military boot (*'abid al-biyada*).

In February 2013, I asked people who belonged to a circle of revolutionaries in Nazlat al-Rayyis how they would define themselves politically. Baybars, son of a fisherman and himself a self-learned taught computer technician making a living from odd jobs, answered as follows:[2]

BAYBARS: I'm neither for the bad nor for the worse. I'm against the Brotherhood and against the National Democratic Party [Mubarak's now-dissolved ruling party].

SAMULI: But what do you stand for, what do you support?

B: I would want one those who started the revolution on January 25 to lead us.

S: But what ideas do you support?

B: I would like to see one like Nasser, one who cares for the poor. That's why I support Hamdeen Sabbahi.

I asked him if this would make him a socialist. Baybars agreed, but without emphasis. His answer was a telling one, starting as he did with a double negation and only hesitantly formulating a positive stance. In a coffeehouse in the village some days later, I asked the same question from others from the same circle. Saleh, a teacher living in the village, explained:

We may personally agree with one or the other of these titles. Most of us are leftists, but there is one among us who says that he is a liberal and not a leftist. But in the end the difference of liberal, left, or secular is not important. What unites us is that we all want good for the country, whatever title you give it—

unlike the Muslim Brothers and Salafis, or anybody from the Islamist current, who just reiterate whatever their leaders tell you. You can have a good discussion with one of them today but tomorrow he says again what his sheikh says, and it may be completely different from what his sheikh said yesterday.

Saleh emphatically drew a distinction between people who want good for the country and do so out of their own accord and by using their own mind, and people who in his view only want good only for a specific group and divide the country into Muslims and Christians, believers and infidels. Another young man in the group seconded, "Rather than leftist, secular, or liberal, I see myself as somebody who wants to change the society." Yet another participant in the discussion came up with a more specific vision:

> I want a state that is neutral, that provides the same legal framework and security to a mosque, a church, and a nightclub. The stones of which this mosque [the café where we were sitting was next to the wall of a mosque] are not more Islamic than the stones of any other building. If I want to buy a T-shirt, I don't want a T-shirt made by a Muslim, but a good one, or a cheap one. I want the state to be inclusive for all, and I don't want it to be based on any ideology, but on *'ilm* [meaning both science and knowledge]."

Although the others agreed with him about the importance (and current lack) of science or knowledge, his view was fiercely challenged, and a heated debate evolved about how exactly science, faith, and ideology relate to one another, whether the early Islamic caliphate was a religious or a knowledge-based state, whether there are contradictions between scientific knowledge and Islam, and if so then how to solve them. After much arguing and shouting, they finally agreed that with the help of hermeneutical interpretation and adaptation to the change of times, faith would in fact turn out to be commensurable with science.

On the basis of their standpoints, is it reasonable to describe these men as leftists or secularists? To varying degrees, these two stances in fact play a formative role for them, and yet neither one (and also not the two together) amounts to that which they actually put their faith in, and they explicitly distance themselves from being reduced to one label or another.[3] When it comes to leftism, many of these young men (as well as some of their female kin, who cannot join them in the café but share their stance) stand in the footsteps of an important local tradition: communism. Their village, as well as the entire region, has a history of communist activism that was at its strongest in the 1970s and 1980s, but since the 1990s gradually declined to near insignificance. Some (but not most) village revolutionaries hail from families with a history of communist activism, and many of the older village revolutionaries once were or still are members of the Egyptian Communist Party. The younger generation, in contrast, often expresses a general distrust toward political parties, and if they support or join a party at all, it is most likely to be either the Constitution Party of Mohamed ElBaradei or the Egyptian Popular Current movement of Hamdeen Sabbahi. Actual communists are extremely few among the young generation, and the ecumenical approach the young men have toward any kind of ideology would not fit well with the doctrinal rigor of Marxism-Leninism. The communist heritage and the older men who carry it are an important source of inspiration for the new generation of revolutionaries, but when they define themselves as leftist, they are after something else, something less doctrinal and clear, a critical attitude rather than a Marxist utopia. And when it comes to more specific socialist visions and realities, Nasser is more relevant than Marx and Lenin.

As for secularism, it is a stance taken less explicitly by village revolutionaries because it is so easily employed by their Islamist competitors to accuse them of being not religious, and perhaps not even Muslim. The revolutionaries in the village all consider themselves Muslim, and some of them are quite religious by conventional standards (measured mainly by regular prayer). The accusation of not being proper Muslims seriously troubles them. At the same time, they not only advocate the vision of a religiously neutral state but also often entertain quite irreverent discussions about religion, God, and the hereafter. At times they even appropriate the accusation of being infidels (*kuffar*) as an ironic self-description. They spend much time arguing what in their view is a true, universal, and humanist Islam and how it differs from both Islamist politics and from conservative social conventions. Rather than being "secular," however, they would prefer to be appreciated on their own terms as people who care for their country and think for themselves.

Not only the village revolutionaries have problems with the label "secularism." It has also become a fraught category in academia, invested as it has become with somewhat mystifying theorization (Asad 2003; Asad et al. 2009). The perhaps most sophisticated and interesting contribution to the theory of the secular from this direction has been offered by Hussein Agrama (2012), who follows Talal Asad in understanding the secular as essentially and fundamentally a quality of state power, and adds that rather than being a set of doctrines or principles, secularism is a problem space that imposes certain questions and anxieties about the relationship of law, politics, religion, and the dividing line between the religious and the secular. Agrama points out that the question of secularity became an urgent one in Egypt at the moment that Islamism arose as a major political force. Following Agrama's reasoning, Egypt of the Nasserist or royal eras, although in many ways less religious, was actually not nearly as secular as the Mubarak regime, the latter constantly busy with determining what could and could not be said in the name of Islam.

A conclusion that Agrama does not draw but that in my view is quite pressing is that secularism or the secular is not a force or a logic of governmentality in its own right but a tactical position in a social and political conflict in which one of the most powerful currents makes highly contested claims in the name of the religion shared by the majority of the population. Because it is difficult to deny the religious source of those claims, the wisest tactical move is to limit their scope and deny their political validity, with the result that the question about where to draw the boundary of that limited validity becomes a main focus of political contestation. Following this logic, the village revolutionaries also would be secular insofar as they act and react against a powerful social and political current that makes contested claims in the name of a shared religion. But the struggle they are involved in is not restricted to those claims. More is at stake. Just as it would be a mistake to reduce the revolutionaries to their leftist or communist heritage, it would also be a mistake to reduce their struggle to their opposition to the Muslim Brotherhood and Salafis.

If they are irreverent toward and critical of political Islam, it is because they are generally irreverent toward and critical of many things. If they adapt the accusation of unbelief in irony, it is because they also adapt other accusatory terms ironically, such as *infiltrators* (*mundassin*) or *thugs* (*baltagiya*). Rather than longing for a clear ideological doctrine, they celebrate difference and disagreement. Their constant disunity and disorganized nature is a crucial weakness in political struggle, but it is also a matter of principle and one exercised with certain pride. Their vision of themselves as people who think for themselves should not be taken for granted, of course, for the revolutionaries regularly accept ideas because others accept them, just as Islamists and supporters of the old system regularly think for themselves. But we should take their claim of thinking for themselves seriously as a strongly held value. What marked being a revolutionary between 2011 and 2013 was not a fixed ideology but an affect of critique and rejection (a double rejection, in fact, aimed at the old system and Islamist politics), combined with rather diffuse ideals of patriotism, the common good, redistribution of wealth, independent thought and social change, and the nation as the key framework of action.

But is such an affect of critique a fundamental one, or is it shaped by one's specific position in a political struggle? The events of the summer of 2013 became a practical test for that question. The original revolutionary coalition that went across the political spectrum had already broken up in 2011 when Islamist movements proved themselves more capable of pragmatic electoral politics and worked to secure a share of power, and many others found themselves in a position of fundamental opposition. By the time the Muslim Brotherhood officially gained power in 2012, most leftist and liberal revolutionaries no longer saw them as revolutionary allies but as traitors to the cause. The spring and early summer of 2013 witnessed an unprecedented coalition of the most unlikely allies, bringing together revolutionaries and supporters of the old system under the umbrella of nationalism against the rule of the Muslim Brotherhood (which, its opponents claimed, was not only incompetent and authoritarian but also, and most important, unpatriotic). This movement, which culminated in large-scale protests on June 30 and the military overthrow of Morsi's presidency on July 3, for a short moment suspended the antagonism between revolutionaries and old system loyalists, only to give birth to a split among the revolutionaries themselves, who had become divided about their stance toward the military and the issue of violence. Many of those who had said no previously now emphatically said yes to the leadership of General Abdelfattah El-Sisi (later promoted to field marshal and then elected president) and the "war against terror" he declared on supporters of the Muslim Brotherhood. A unity of the military and the nation, in combination with extreme rejection of the slightest sympathy for the Muslim Brotherhood, became their rallying ground. Others—fewer in numbers—who had participated in the June 30 protests became at first skeptical and then horrified about what had come in place of the Islamist rule they had so fiercely fought against.

For the village revolutionaries at least, a key breaking point was the so-called popular mandate (*tafwid*) for a war against terror that El-Sisi called for in the form of mass demonstrations on July 26, 2013. Those who joined the popular mandate viewed those who didn't as traitors. Those who said no to the mandate saw themselves as the true revolutionaries but found themselves marginalized, unwilling to join either the army's war on terror in the name of the nation or the Muslim Brotherhood's anti-coup campaign in the name of electoral legitimacy. Along with this political split, the social circle of the village revolutionaries also broke up. Baybars, for instance, refused to participate in the popular mandate, arguing that he did not want to write a blank check for bloodshed. Saleh, in contrast, joined the military nationalist camp along with others who believed that leftist, civil politics could be realized only within a strong nationalist vision and with military leadership powerful enough to defeat the Islamists. A series of fierce debates in one of the village cafés ended in angry mutual accusations, and those who had once been the revolutionaries became two separate, mutually antagonistic social circles. When they met by chance (which happens often in a village), people from different sides of the split would greet each other according to the requirements of polite conduct, but they no longer sat and talked together.

Those who still said no in July 2013—that is, said no to the new regime instead of collecting the fruits of victory by joining the wave of military nationalism— are few, but they are worth taking seriously. Theirs is an attitude that is oppositional not just by the circumstance of their party not being in power but also in essence: prioritizing critique, change, and difference.

Where does such attitude of fundamental opposition come from? How did discontent with the way things are transform for some people into a general ethos of rejection, critique, and difference? In the following, I return to the time before

June 2013 and look at three important moments, each of which provides parts of an answer: the sense of antagonism and anger from repeated setbacks; the sense of a better world realized in moments of struggle; and the way revolutionary politics is embedded to intimate, imaginative, and social lives marked by nonconformity, critique, and a search for distinction.

## Why Don't the Motherfuckers Die?

Antagonism was an elementary part of the stormy season of revolution from the beginning, but immediately after Mubarak stepped down, it looked like the nation could be united for the sake of building a new Egypt. In this spirit, a group of men, most but not all of them young, from Nazlat al-Rayyis (some of them lived in the village, and others worked or studied in the cities and had come to their village for an extended holiday, since schools and universities were closed and tourist destinations deserted) decided to bring the revolution to the countryside.

Following the example set in the cities (Winegar 2011), they started a cleanup campaign to vacate the streets and alleys of the village from the great amount of litter that covered them. But their aim was greater than this: they wanted to change local politics and spread a new political consciousness in the village.

Figure 9.1. The third and last cleanup campaign in the village, Nazlat al-Rayyis, March 2011.

Emboldened by two successful cleanup campaigns in three days, they arranged a meeting with the mayor of the nearby district capital. He arrived to the meeting two hours late and sharply refused to apologize for being late. Indignant, the group staged a sit-in at the city hall demanding the mayor's resignation. After hearing rumors about thugs coming to burn the city council, the group members settled for a compromise. In a chaotic meeting at the end of the day, the mayor, with a State Security agent and a former member of Parliament of the district from the Muslim Brotherhood sitting with him at his side of the table, offered his apologies but remained in office. Two weeks later, the group organized a third cleanup campaign but with diminished numbers. A fourth was announced but never took place. The same week, they organized a large public gathering with the village mayor (who was more cooperative) on reforming local public services, starting with street cleaning and electricity bills (see figure 9.2). The gathered men (no women), however, wanted to speak about the distribution of subsidized bread, an issue that made tempers rise dramatically. What the group of revolutionaries had hoped to be a constructive meeting to plan a better future turned into an occasion to express anger and grievances. Voices got louder, tempers rose, and people stopped listening to each other. In the end, some decisions were made

Figure 9.2. Public gathering in the village youth center,
Nazlat al-Rayyis, March 2011.

but never implemented, and a meeting was scheduled for the following month. It did not take place. The revolutionaries held a private meeting (figure 9.3) in which they argued that it was necessary to vote no in the referendum over a preliminary constitution, but they and many others across the nation who called people to vote no failed to make a difference in the popular vote.[4]

What happened in Nazlat al-Rayyis and other villages was in many ways a miniature of what happened in the capital, where it turned out that the temporary military government pursued a quite different agenda from promoting revolutionary change. The honeymoon between the revolutionaries and the military ended in no more than two months, and since the summer of 2011, anti-military protestors repeatedly occupied public places. The military rulers replied with a great degree of violence and repression. Maspero (where a largely Christian protest was bloodily crushed, and dozens of people died), Mohamed Mahmoud Street (where a violent storming of Tahrir Square cost tens of lives and resulted in a week of street fighting), Port Said stadium (where tens of supporters of Ahly soccer club were killed with at least tacit support of security forces), and Abbasiya (where this time tens of supporters of the disqualified Salafi presidential hopeful Hazem Abu Ismail were killed) are some of the landmarks of the short, bloody

Figure 9.3. Debating the constitution in the home of one of the village revolutionaries, Nazlat al-Rayyis, March 2011.

history of direct military rule from February 2011 to June 2012. At the same time, the Salafi Nour Party emerged as a political force on the side of the Muslim Brotherhood, and the two competing Islamist movements entered a more pragmatic struggle for political power through shifting alliances and highly successful electoral mobilization, winning elections while the revolutionaries were fighting the army on the streets.

During the presidential elections in the summer of 2012, it again looked like the revolutionaries might seize the day after all. Military rule had been badly discredited in little more than a year, and the Muslim Brotherhood was losing some of its aura of piety and competence as the National Assembly (dominated by the Brotherhood) failed to make change for the better. During the presidential race, the village revolutionaries became active again and participated in a highly successful campaign for the Nasserist candidate Hamdeen Sabbahi, who came in third nationwide but won the province of Kafr al-Shaykh and the village of Nazlat al-Rayyis in a landslide. It was a big success, and there was a sense that the village revolutionaries were capable of making change after all. But then, nothing happened. In the second round of elections, the revolutionaries sympathized with neither of the two remaining candidates, although some voted for Morsi, considering him the lesser evil over Shafiq, Mubarak's last prime minister. Summer vacations began, people who lived in the city were back in the village again, but with no urgent issues at hand, no new actions took place, and life returned to its ordinary course.

After four months of cautious expectation, unrest broke out again after a new preliminary constitutional declaration by Morsi that made his decrees immune to lawsuits (the background was a battle by the Muslim Brotherhood to establish control over the judicial system, which in turn fought to sabotage the Brotherhood's grip on power). New mass protests took place in the cities, at times peaceful, at times leading to street clashes whenever competing groups met at the same time and in the same place. Numerous offices of the Freedom and Justice Party were stormed, and more than ten people were killed, mostly under unclear circumstances. Again, the village revolutionaries became active, organizing a well-attended protest march against the constitutional declaration and a campaign to vote no in the constitutional referendum of December 2012. The no vote in the village was nearly 50 percent, extremely high for the countryside. But the total no vote was only 36 percent nationwide, and the constitution, which began as a compromise of different political forces but was completed by Islamists largely among themselves, was ratified. Not long after, the second anniversary of the revolution on January 25, 2013, marked a new moment of escalation, with new and ongoing street battles, a harder hand by the police, more aggressive tactics by the protesters, again tens of people killed, and Morsi and the Muslim Brotherhood still in power.

The history of the first two years of the revolutionaries' struggle can be told as a history of repeated setbacks and failures. The short moment of euphoria in the spring of 2011 quickly passed and was replaced by bewilderment and doubt, and then anger, bitterness, frustration, and eventually an increasing loss of faith in peaceful action. Soon after the Maspiro massacre in October 2011, the Alexandrian satirical writer Galal 'Amer expressed this sentiment in a one-liner that was to become a widely cited motto: "Li-madha la yamut wlad il-wiskha?" Or in idiomatic translation, "Why don't the motherfuckers die?"[5]

With its mixture of anger, bewilderment, and frustration, expressed in the kind of explicit language that had become much more prevalent after 2011 (Colla 2012; Mehrez 2012), this phrase might seem an unlikely slogan for a revolutionary struggle, for it does not express any concrete hope or demands. And yet it has been written on banners and walls as an expression of ongoing defiance ever since.

The repeated failures of the revolutionary movement might provide an occasion to question their tactics, search for a way to overcome their disunity, or find ways to win elections rather than fighting street battles. Such advice is easily given but much harder to follow. Repeated defeats are bitter, but without an

Figure 9.4. A protester in the Abbasiya clashes in Cairo, May 2012, holds a sign asking, "Why don't the motherfuckers die?" Photo by Shady Basiony.

organization with a command structure and members who actually would be willing to follow orders, anger is the best thing that makes people move. As the struggle of the revolutionaries against changing faces of the system perpetuated itself, that struggle turned into something that has inherent value even in the absence of victory.

And when victory finally came (or what most revolutionaries for a moment thought was victory), it turned out to be more terrible and devastating than any of the many preceding defeats. Powered by the increasing unpopularity of the Muslim Brotherhood and organized around the Tamarrud campaign (meaning "rebellion," "insurgency," "insubordination") that in spring 2013 collected signatures to withdraw trust from Morsi, an unlikely alliance of old regime loyalists, revolutionaries, and powerful institutions of the state (especially police, judiciary, military) was able to seize the day. During May and June 2013, the Tamarrud campaign gave the village revolutionaries a renewed sense of energy and optimism. They were successful. Morsi and the Muslim Brotherhood were overthrown, a nominally civilian government under the de facto leadership of the minister of defense seized power, and that was the end of the revolutionary current as it had emerged in 2011. What remained were scattered groups and individuals with different stances and visions about what was going on and what was to be done in the midst of the most severe polarization and violence that Egypt had seen in a century. This time, the street battles, bloodier than ever, were fought by supporters of the Muslim Brotherhood who, as they lost power over the state, gained back the power of principled resistance and martyrdom.

Paradoxically, the one thing that could still unite those among the revolutionaries who said no to El-Sisi in July 2013 was bitterness and frustration. But they had no struggle in which they could turn that sentiment into action. Those revolutionaries who did not join the military nationalist euphoria were pushed to a position of silence in a situation where their hatred of Islamist politics was too great to allow for any alliance with the Muslim Brotherhood against the El-Sisi regime. Only in November 2013, after the Muslim Brotherhood's organizational capacity had been largely destroyed and its supporters had faced numerous massacres and mass arrests, did some from the former revolutionary current—now also known as the "third current"—manage to mobilize for a limited confrontation with the new military rule.

## Longing for the Smell of Tear Gas

Bitterness and frustration is only half the story of the revolutionaries' struggle. It is a meaningful struggle for them, an accomplishment in itself. Hilmi, who had a year earlier moved from the village to Cairo, where he got a job as a journalist, participated in a demonstration for the first time in his life on January 28, 2011, at Giza Square, where he was half reporting, half protesting. When I met him in Cairo three days later, he was still very excited about that day:

> This feeling of dignity was something I wanted to write about to everybody on Friday, but there was no Internet. That was the first day in my life I felt that I live a natural human life. I got up, I had breakfast, I prayed, I went out to the demonstration and said, "No!" even though I got beaten up, I called my sweetheart, I went home and slept. This was the first day in my life that I had nothing missing.

Hilmi's narrative, told at a moment when the further course of the struggle was still completely unknown, is a story of being alive in the extended, moral sense of the word. It tells of a "leap of action," as I mentioned in the previous chapter, but it is not a story about how the ordinary world changes through one's discovery of the path of defiance. It is a story of the moment of defiance itself as one that makes it possible to live a full life with nothing missing.

What happened in the revolutionary squares in January and February 2011 was not just a protest against an oppressive regime and a demand for freedom. In itself, it was freedom. It was a real, actual lived moment of the freedom and dignity that so many people had felt deprived of in the preceding years. As such, it was bound to be transient, doomed to pass in favor of party politics, fractional struggles, compromises and tactics, and a return to the ordinary course of daily life. Ever since the first big protests in Tahrir Square ended after February 11, 2011, one of the key occupations of the revolutionary current has been to over and again re-create the fantastic moment of feeling fully alive in a meaningful struggle.

One of those moments was in Alexandria on January 25, 2013, the second anniversary of the revolution. It was expected to be a tense day, and in the previous days many people expressed fear (and some hope) that there would be clashes. Some saw it as a necessity. Rasha, a thirty-year-old woman from Alexandria, was employed in changing jobs in the cultural sector and had been an active participant in demonstrations since the spring of 2011. Anticipating the coming anniversary, although she had never actively participated in street fighting, such as throwing stones or the like, she said:

> I don't go to a demonstration when there is no fighting [*darb*]. I don't like the people who put on perfume to go to a demonstration and when any trouble happens they are the first to run away and leave us standing.

Fighting street battles with the police is often seen as young men's prerogative, an expression of the virtue of *gad'ana* (meaning "courage," "nobility," or "youthful manliness"; see Ghannam 2013: 121–125). But the active presence of some women among the revolutionary activists is a reminder that *gad'ana* is not a consistently gendered virtue. Rasha is an experienced protester who in clashes usually adapted the role of first-aid provider, equipped with micro-gel spray for the effects of tear gas and other medicines. She is not a member of any organized group. Until the summer of 2013, she went to every demonstration, and all her best friends were revolutionaries like her.

On January 25 at noon, I ran into Rasha at Raml Station, where a large (but not huge—the fear of violence had an impact on the numbers) crowd of protesters was gathering and marches were starting in various directions. Rasha was there with a group of other young women and told that they were going to the City Council "to see if there is fighting." Many other people were also heading to the City Council, and I followed them. Arriving there, I found a police line blocking the entrance to the street, and hundreds of protesters standing directly in front of them. This was a crowd characteristic of the active revolutionaries of the city: They were mostly young, mainly but not only middle class, many of them wearing Palestinian *kufiyas* and masks for protection against tear gas, and there were many women among them. They had headed for the place where it was most likely that troubles would happen. And very soon, they happened.

Just weeks earlier, "black blocks" had been established in Egypt following the example set by the autonomous radical left in Europe (LeVine 2013).[6] They arrived on the scene in a moment when tempers were already rising after a protester had ripped off a part of the sign of the city council. Heading a march arriving at the site, some tens of young people, dressed in black and carrying a large flag, arrived right in front of the police cordon and tried to push forward. Seconds later, tear gas was shot from the side of the police, and stones were flying from the side of the protesters. A street fight evolved, and while I moved away from the scene and more tear gas entered the street, bit by bit more people entered the street to aid the protesters. The numbers of people in the square increased, the activists with their *kufiyas* were joined by young men from popular quarters on motorcycles and armed with wooden sticks, as well as a big and mixed crowd of protesters, some of whom headed forward to face the police, while others stayed back to chant slogans against the government, and yet others carried spray bottles with medicine to treat the effects of tear gas. The fighting quickly took on a repetitive pattern: people would arrive on the square and push toward the police, tear gas was fired (from quite some distance), and people were forced to retreat to breath freely—but as soon as the air was clean again, they would push forward again. It went on until late at night.

By the time I was leaving, I ran into Rasha again in the company of other protesters. She was just returning to the demonstration because the tear gas used that day was fresh and sharp, and she had inhaled so much of it that she almost passed out and had to leave. She managed to stay on her feet: "I don't like to be carried by people." Fearing that there would be arrests of activists at their homes

Figure 9.5. Protesters in Alexandria, January 25, 2013.

in the night, she didn't dare to go home but stayed with her sister. As I met her again for an interview a day later, she was still sick from the effects of tear gas and skeptical, wondering, "Have we accomplished anything?" But she was already making phone calls for the next protest that night. She said that she draws her energy from the action, from "the pleasure of seeing the stubbornness and stead-fastness of the youth."

CS gas, commonly known as tear gas, is a usually nonlethal chemical weapon. It was employed in vast quantities by changing Egyptian governments against protesters since January 2011. Because tear gas incapacitates only for a short moment, and afterward makes people only angrier, it is an inefficient means of crowd control. In contrast to the live ammunition that was used by security forces occasionally throughout the revolution and systematically in the summer and fall of 2013,[7] the use of tear gas usually results in lengthy street battles in which the gas forces protesters to stay at a distance from police forces but does not disperse them. For those who frequented protests from 2011 to 2013, tear gas became the olfactory metaphor for revolutionary struggle.

Esam, a musician from Alexandria, was among those on the front line of the street battle in Alexandria on January 25, 2013. I offered him a sandwich left over from my lunch, but he replied, "No thanks, I'm getting high [*sharib*] on tear gas." Ashraf, a teacher and poet from Alexandria, was also a regular protester but resented excessive polarization and sought for constructive solutions.[8] On that same day, he found that things were going the wrong way, and he argued that the escalation of the protests had made protestors less able to gather mass support. And yet he, too, described the inhalation of tear gas as an indication of oppositional attitude: "My friend and I went as far into the gas as we hated Morsi. I hate him 75 percent, so I only went so far; my friend hates him 200 percent, so he went further ahead." Both those who still searched for a common ground, as well as those who no longer believed in peaceful action, were inhaling tear gas on that day, and they described their doing so as meaningful, even exciting. "Egyptians have become addicted to tear gas" was a running joke between 2011 and 2013.

Inhaling tear gas is very unpleasant. One's eyes and face burn, one starts to cough heavily, and it becomes difficult to breathe and see. All these unpleasant sensations are combined with a general sense of confusion as people start to run away to avoid the gas cloud, and one has to run along while coughing and trying to keep one's eyes open. Heavy exposure to tear gas makes one faint, and continued exposure can be lethal (Carron and Yersin 2009). How could a person become addicted to something so unpleasant?

Of course, it is not the gas that people are addicted to. When I showed her an early draft of this chapter, Rasha commented that tear gas is a metaphor "for that something which we cannot name" in protests and fighting. There is a sensual and spiritual quality to protests and clashes that attracts and transforms people. Getting exposed to tear gas without being defeated by it is part of the formative experience of protesters for whom demonstrations, sit-ins, and clashes are among the most beautiful and meaningful moments of their life. The people at the protest on January 25, 2013, were angry and upset, but they were not frustrated, depressed, or cynical. They knew that they were struggling for a good cause, and they were surrounded by friends and like-minded people. While the protesters moved back and forth toward the police and then away from the gas, they were at the same time involved in countless warmhearted encounters with friends, shaking hands and hugging, joking and exchanging news. Coming together in struggle makes life full and meaningful; it is the better world that the revolutionaries strive for, over and again temporarily created in passing moments of a shared act of defiance.

Struggles like that in Alexandria on the second anniversary of the revolution are a continuation and reinforcement of the by now proverbial "breaking of fear," a sense of assertiveness and boldness, a willingness to say no and to enter confrontations rather than avoid them. The breaking of fear has been widely cited as one of the few true accomplishments of the revolution. Between 2011 and 2013, a part of the revolutionaries grew quite fearless, not only in demonstrations but also in their own lives. Many of them started to live much less conventional lives

Figure 9.6. Protesters running away from a cloud of tear gas in Alexandria, January 25, 2013.

and have stopped worrying about what others say. But I also know of people who turned violent in their domestic lives. And there can be a lot of trauma underlying the loss of fear.

Mukhtar Shehata (2013) argues that what has happened is something more complicated than simple loss of fear:

> The truth is that neither has fear been broken, nor have any other emotions been removed. Rather, these are new emotions born out of the preceding chaos of emotions. . . . Thus the emotion of natural, immediate fear is replaced by an entirely new emotion which we do not know but we call it 'the broken fear.'"

Thus, rather than an overcoming of fear, broken fear is an emotional or affective complex in its own right that involves anxiety, excitement, terror, boldness, courage, unrest, and hope. This was the prevalent mood that marked the stormy season of revolution in Egypt. In more specific terms for the revolutionaries, broken fear has been linked with an affect of rejection that is about not just uttering a specific no on a specific matter but also cultivating rejection and struggle as a way of experiencing freedom and dignity. Rather than indicating the lack of a positive political agenda, the affect of rejection is a positive program of its own kind. Both the celebration of debate and difference as well as the insistence on

ongoing struggle despite defeats are ways to valorize and produce shared moments of what, with some reservations, may be described as autonomy and self-
determination. It is important to emphasize that these are shared moments. They
are not individualistic, and it would in fact be impossible to have them alone.
Their location is in shared struggle, in coming together in debate and action, in
feeling and acting as part of the revolution. An emphasis on individuality and idiosyncratic difference is part of it, but it is not the whole story. Rather, revolutionary struggle creates an autonomy of a more relational and collective—also more
combatant and antagonistic—kind, established and measured in confrontation
with its enemies. It is a struggle that is centered on the ability to desire something
different as an aim in its own right.

That ability to desire is grounded in specific struggles with concrete enemies,
however. This may be one reason so many among the revolutionaries who were or
became skeptical about the El-Sisi regime found it impossible to express sympathy or support for the Muslim Brotherhood's supporters in the months following
June 30, 2013. Not only was there an extreme wave of hatred and incitement against
the Brotherhood and its supporters, which provided the emotional groundwork
for the Rabea al-'Adawiya massacre on August 14, 2013, when the police stormed
protest camps of Morsi supporters, killing possibly as many as one thousand
people; there was also more particular emotional work going on among those
few who were (or slowly became) opposed to the new military rule and its "war on
terror": while speaking out in general terms against bloodshed, they emphatically
refused to recognize the experience of the protesters supporting Morsi as similar
to their own. When in late August 2013, the Rabea sign (a hand showing four
fingers in reference to the meaning of the word *rabi'a*, "fourth") was released as
the "symbol of steadfastness" of the struggle of the Brotherhood and Morsi supporters, it was quickly countered by claims that the Rabea protesters were merely
following orders and knew nothing of the true steadfastness and spirit shown in
the battle of Muhammad Mahmoud Street in November 2011, the "best battle," as
one of the older village revolutionaries described it, because it took place against
military rule and without the participation of the Muslim Brotherhood. In their
search for a third position through a gesture of double rejection—crystallized in
the mythologization of Mohamed Mahmoud Street—they were able to claim a
moral high ground over all others, but by doing so they condemned themselves
to passivity and failed to act according to their own principle of steadfastness,
which until then had granted them the moral authority they had had.

## Radical Future

Saying no is not a little thing. Sixty years earlier, this was well captured by the
poet Amal Dunqul in his much-quoted poem "Last Words of Spartacus" ([1962]
2005; here in the translation of Sumeela Mubayi [Dunqul 2012]), in which

Spartacus speaks to his countrymen from the gallows and gives a bitter account of the consequences of defiance. The poem opens:

> Glory to Satan—god of the winds
> who said "no" in the face of those who said "yes"
> who taught humans to tear apart nothingness
> He who said no—thus did not die
> And remained a soul eternally in pain

In the poem, there is no hope of final victory. Spartacus encourages his countrymen to look up at him so that they will have raised their heads at least once before it is their turn to hang on the gallows. But he does not promise them anything but tears, nor does he wish his son to follow in his footsteps. Parts of this poem have been frequently quoted in the course of the revolutionary struggle. In autumn of 2010, at several spots on the Alexandria waterfront a graffiti artist sprayed the following lines (in my translation) from the poem:

> Do not dream of a happy world
> After every emperor who dies
> There is a new emperor

Before the constitutional referendum in 2012, several people who supported voting no cited the opening lines of the poem on social media (sometimes with, sometimes without a mention of Satan). They expected that they would not win.

What, then, is the point in insisting on saying no? Just as I have asked why somebody would actually follow the Salafi path of commitment for the sake of purity, I also find it necessary to ask why somebody would enter the revolutionary path of struggle for the sake of being steadfast in saying no, and with what consequences? After all, most people do not. Many people participated in protests once or twice, and left it at that. Others were happy to see the Muslim Brothers seize the day. Yet others were happy to join the terrible victory of the army over the Muslim Brothers. Why would some return to the struggle against changing faces of "the system" again and again? Partly, this is, of course, a circumstantial consequence of some people finding themselves over and again on the losing side. In other circumstances, they might have been willing and able to say yes. But the biographies of many revolutionaries also show an undercurrent of difference, defiance, and nonconformity that cannot be reduced to the circumstance of shifting fortunes.

Although the circle of revolutionaries in Nazlat al-Rayyis counted its numbers in the tens at the best, it is big and strong on rural standards. The relative successes of the Hamdeen Sabbahi campaign in the presidential elections and the campaign to vote no in the 2012 constitutional referendum showed that the revolutionaries actually were able to win over a significant part of the population in their village, even if only conditionally. And yet Baybars, who was active in both campaigns, was far from satisfied with the outcome of the no campaign in the village. It could have been much better, he said, if it hadn't been for the women.

Baybars volunteered as an observer at the referendum ballot box in a local school, and told that there had been three distinct waves of voters: Muslim Brothers and Salafis arrived with their families in the morning, all voting yes. Then at noon came students and civil servants voting mainly no. Then towards the evening came what he described as a wave of uneducated people, mainly women. They mostly voted yes, according to Baybars, "because the Muslim Brothers had told them that it would please God, and because they were not used to saying no." For Baybars, this pointed out a fundamental problem:

> Our problem in the village is that we don't have girls among the revolutionaries. We are only guys, and we don't reach the women in the village. In the village society, I cannot talk with women who are not my relatives.

The Muslim Brotherhood, in contrast, masterfully mobilized the female vote in the 2012 referendum (incidentally, also the military relied strongly on women's votes in the presidential elections of 2014). Wives and daughters of Brotherhood families went from house to house on friendly visits, and then took up the issue of the constitutional referendum, arguing that voting yes for the constitution was voting yes for Islam, stability, a better economy, and the accomplishment of the goals of the revolution. The revolutionaries, in contrast, had a huge problem in mobilizing and reaching women. As I raised this question in the circle gathered in the café in February 2013, Saleh challenged the others: "Name three leftist women in the village!" Fouad named his wife, and the mother and sister of one of the village revolutionaries. Saleh pointed out that they are from the village, but they all live in Alexandria. One of the others present added, "Here, the women are simply not allowed to."

Fouad's wife, Nazli, has several times gone to demonstrations with her husband, describes herself as liberal, and has adapted explicitly feminist views since 2011. She is one of the few women from the village with an outspoken revolutionary attitude, which she has also come to cultivate in her family life. In an interview in the spring of 2012 she said: "They say that we did the revolution so that our children will live in freedom one day. But I don't want freedom just for my children. I want it for me." It has been a difficult struggle—but most important, it has taken place mainly in Alexandria, where she and her husband live. She took no part in the public actions of the revolutionaries in the village itself.

One of the great paradoxes of the revolutionary current is that although gender equality and a socialist redistribution of wealth rank high on its agenda, there are many more men than women, and more people with higher education and a middle-class family background than poor and uneducated people among those who call themselves the revolutionaries. They speak out loud in the name of equality and inclusion, but becoming and being a revolutionary is not equally accessible, nor is it equally attractive for everybody.

The gender divide in the village is an especially instructive case in understanding who would, and who would not, be drawn to the politics of saying no. (This gender gap is less grave in the cities, but it exists also there.) Men are allowed (even encouraged) to express discontent, ambivalence, and anger about their situation. They are also expected to show *gad'ana*, manly courage, and stand up and fight if necessary. Men also enjoy vastly greater freedom of movement. And the key gathering space of the village revolutionaries is the cafés, which in the countryside are strictly off-limits for women. Women, in contrast, easily risk scandalizing themselves and their marital prospects with open displays of discontent and ambivalence. The struggles they fight, less visible to public sight, are often deeper and harder than those fought by men, and the pressures and contradictory expectations put upon them are often unbearable. And yet many fewer of them react to this condition by a public display of rejection and nonconformity. A search for harmony and fit, combined with manipulative and tactical moves, is a much more accessible path for them. A pursuit of constructive values such as family, religion, and patriotism is much more respectable, acceptable, and rewarding for a woman from a village than being a leftist revolutionary ever could be (unless one happens to be born or married into a revolutionary family, and even then it is difficult).[9] A path of religious commitment, for example, is one of submission and assertion at once—submission to a conservative or ultraconservative role of gendered piety, combined with the assertiveness and authority of being the responsible agent of one's piety. A path of revolutionary critique, on the contrary, is one of more general insubordination. To pursue it, it helps to have already reached a degree of empowerment, to have accomplished some freedom and dignity in order to claim more of it.

There is no general recipe, however, to determine who would and who would not become a revolutionary after 2011, and what stance they would take in the summer of 2013. Position in class society and gender hierarchy, education, friends, family—all these make a difference. But there is no determinism. As with those who follow the Salafi path of commitment, for those who entered the path of revolutionary opposition (and some did both), personal idiosyncrasies and life situations were as important as class and socialization. Nazli and Baybars, for example, are both somewhat unlikely revolutionaries—Nazli because she is a woman from a village, Baybars because he has neither higher education nor a family history of leftist politics. For Nazli, the circumstance of her husband joining the revolutionaries came together with a lifelong sense of not quite fitting, not wanting to belong to any group, and being dissatisfied with her lot in life as a woman. For Baybars, the circumstance of some of the revolutionaries being cousins and good friends of his came together with a strong sense of injustice and an outspokenly black-and-white vision of right and wrong, a sense that was further radicalized after his participation in the battle of Mohamed Mahmoud Street in November 2011.

These two themes—not conforming to conventional roles and a black-and-white sense of right and wrong—are common among the revolutionaries. Among them, there are not only many people from aspiring middle classes, but strikingly, there are also many writers, artists, and all kinds of people who in one way or another do not fit the conventional ways of living. They are often people who are not good at saying yes, who experience difference as an important condition of their existence, and who express strong anger and outrage about what they see as systemic moral wrongs. While often highly skeptical about any organized movements, they search for the company of others, with whom they can cultivate and celebrate difference and moral anger.

A paradoxical consequence of this underlying thrust of difference and moral anger is that although the revolutionaries claim to speak in the name of "the people," they in practice often argue and act against society. In the spring of 2012, Zaher, who works as a white-collar employee in a private industrial company and frequents the village during vacations and weekends, confronted me with a self-critique of the revolutionaries' isolation: "We are so good at arguing, and understand the situation and can analyze it well, but why are we not able to convince ordinary people although they otherwise seem so easily influenced?" The campaign in the village in the spring of 2011 failed, he said, because the activists were not able to gain a wide popular base. Zaher, too, lives in Alexandria and comes to the village only on weekends. Relating to the downtown cultural scene of Alexandria, which he occasionally frequents, he wondered why it is that a leftist political attitude so often also comes along with a *style* (he used the English word): guys with beard and long hair, girls smoking imported rolling tobacco, and people wearing Palestinian *kufiyas* when going to a demonstration. "What do long hair, rolling tobacco, and *kufiyas* have to do with being revolutionary? And yet I, too, put on a *kufiya* when I go to a demonstration." The revolutionary movement of 2011–2013 was accompanied by a much-celebrated spread of styles of music, dress, media formats, and visual aesthetics that before 2011 were limited to much smaller circles. But for Zaher, the development of a revolutionary attitude hand in hand with a revolutionary habitus and jargon were problematic and isolating because they were becoming markers of distinction—very much in the sense of Bourdieu's (1984) theory of habitus, taste, and distinction—and as such, exclusive by their very nature. The problem Zaher addresses is not exclusive to the revolutionaries of Egypt, of course. It is a common predicament of the New Left around the world, largely disconnected from workers' movements and instead focused on radical critique and distinctive lifestyles.

The alternative to that predicament, however, turned out not to be less problematic. The June 30 movement claimed a patriotic unity of "the people" (*al-sha'b*) that appeared to offer the revolutionary movement a unique chance to reconnect with society in its entirety. It was a unity that also prominently included the army and the police, and many of those who only a year and a half earlier had been protesting against military rule now had come to see the army as a powerful patriotic institution that could save Egypt from the Muslim Brotherhood's rule. The power of the counterrevolution born on June 30, 2013, was that it connected dramatic polarization against Islamist politics with the framework of the nation and with the army as the nation's protector. For many, if not most, of the revolutionaries, it was a moment when they could feel that they were struggling not only for the people but also with the people against what they saw as Islamist fascism and terrorism. Those from the revolutionary current who sided with military nationalism in the summer of 2013 saw it not as a change of mind but as a continuation of their struggle (see Schielke 2014).

Both for those who joined the alliance of military nationalism and for those who sooner or later grew skeptical of it and searched for an alternative, third position, the price was very high. For the former, it was the paradoxical price of victory, the loss of the moral authority of a critical stance, which they exchanged for a sense of being on the side of the people and the nation, whatever the cost. For the latter, it was the frustrating price of powerlessness upon realizing that they had been pawns in a battle that was not theirs and then finding no struggle that could be theirs.

When Amal Dunqul predicted eternal torment as the destiny of those who say no, he was writing in the middle of the Nasserist repression of all political opposition. At the time this book went to press, the situation was in many ways even more severe than it was in Nasser's time. Yet so far, those who have remained among the revolutionaries have been only a secondary target of a wave of repression primarily aimed at destroying the Muslim Brotherhood.

But Dunqul's poetic insight has a wider reach. Saying no belongs to the genre of tragedy.

The politics of rejection has been fundamental to and necessary for the uprising and political and social shifts since 2011. But it also carried the seeds of its own failure. The valorization of critique and difference makes it difficult to formulate positive plans of action. It is not a likely way to gain a significant foothold of power in parliaments and political institutions—in fact, it has often turned out to work unintentionally in favor of other currents, ones that go on to win elections and take over institutions in the name of stability, unity, and the people.

However, while the revolutionary current has without doubt either failed (for those who said no to El-Sisi in July 2013) or allowed itself to be co-opted (for those who said yes), it has not remained without success.

By making the revolution something greater and purer than politics, a vision of uncompromising freedom in struggle, the revolutionaries transformed it from a historical rupture into a grand scheme: an ideal that is larger than life, unrealizable yet calling for its realization, pure yet capable of providing a firm hold in an uncertain world. What as a historical event has been a confusing moment of hope, anger, anxiety, boldness, and violence as a grand scheme has developed a more peculiar dynamic, elevating rejection to a sort of moral principle. At the time this book went to press in the summer of 2014, this was the only thing left of the revolutionary movement—but it is not a little thing.

There is a strong link between the affect of rejection and the sense of living in the future tense. It is no coincidence that revolutionaries commonly come from families and social milieus in which also the aspiration for a middle-class life, the impact of the Islamic revival, the remaking of livelihoods through migration and education, and the need to engage in constant ethical reflection have been at their strongest in the past decades. The fact that so many of the people I did my research with since 2006 joined the liberal-leftist revolutionary current in 2011 is more than a coincidence. Perhaps the urgency of frustrated aspiration for a better life in every respect that I encountered among them was not shared with the same intensity by all people across Egypt, nor was the sense of hope and determination they invested in the prospect of revolutionary change. Whatever the demographics may be, joining the revolution was not a way to overcome the troubling pressure of a better future. On the contrary, it has only aggravated that pressure. Although often anticapitalist in theory, the revolutionaries actually practice and promote a radical and compelling version of the capitalist-revivalist ethos of futurity by singling out the capacity to desire, hope, and demand something more and something else, and claiming that that capacity itself is the thing most worth desiring, hoping for, and demanding.

# Conclusion

## *On Freedom, Destiny, and Consequences*

IN A LIFE that is guided but not determined by grand schemes such as following Muhammad's message, searching for a life in better material conditions, longing for romantic love, and demanding political change—a life that is hopeful and meaningful but also confusing, frustrating, and boring—how can one have existential power over one's situation? Or is such power only God's?

This was the question posed by Sa'id in the opening of this book. He was bitter and angry about the oppression and economic inequality he faced. He tried to forget about it by escaping into the leisurely excitement of sports. He argued that money was the only way to have power over one's situation, and he pointed out that such power is only God's, and one should always be content and grateful. Despairing in one moment and trusting in God seconds later, he offered a preliminary answer that I have tried to elaborate on and flesh out in the course of this book.

In this conclusion, I try to reach a sort of synthesis by thinking about the general problem of hope in an uncertain and unpredictable world. I approach this conclusive question through three concepts: freedom, which is an urgent issue for many people in Egypt but not necessarily linked with autonomy; destiny, which not only is a crucial part of a Muslim lifeworld but also is quite a useful concept of acting in a world of greater powers; and especially unintended consequences, for which we do not yet have a satisfactory anthropological theory. To do so, I borrow some theories that friends and interlocutors have been citing and developing in conversation with me, to make sense of their situation. Incidentally, their theories draw upon an Islamic theology of action and predestination. However, their significance is wider, for they provide parts of an answer to a problem that has concerned, and continues to concern, humanity in various places and times: how to act in a world that is not of one's own making.

## Consequences

Although it has not always been explicitly stated, every chapter of this book is about hope: hope for a morally sound life with space for various incompatible aims and without conflicts or scandals; hope for a firm grounding in truth through religious knowledge; hope for true love that will allow one to live a passionate and happy life, for wealth and salvation that will relieve one from pressure and anxiety, for excitement and something meaningful to do; hope for one clear path of committed life that will overcome ambivalence, ambiguity, and boredom; hope for a life of broader horizons; hope for a political system that treats one as a human being and in which things are really what they seem; and finally, hope invested in hope itself as the capacity and energy to demand a better world.

When people have hope, it means that things are not as well as they might ← be. It also means that they might never be well, but perhaps they will. The only certainty of hope is the nonreality of that which is hoped for. The thrust of hope, however, is that one does want something to become real.[1] Which brings us to the question of consequences. The question of how to have existential power over one's condition is also a question of what works, and if it works, how it works.

Most good ethnographies say something about consequences. They do not just cite the aims of people or describe how things are. Instead, they look at dynamics of relationships; chains of events; trajectories of persons, families, institutions, and communities. Their accounts of consequences are typically after the fact, often telling about surprises and adaptations in the process when things gained a different dynamic than either the people involved or the researcher expected. The longer the time frame of the research, the better such after-the-fact accounts usually are—for example, the consequences of Mustafa's short-lived Salafi experiment looked quite different to me in 2006 and in hindsight. In opposition to the great number of good after-the-fact accounts, however, stands the generally highly unreliable nature of social scientific predictions. Very often there is just no way to tell beforehand what the consequences of a project, an idea, an event, a decision, will be. Some things are so routinized and well explored that we can expect the outcome with some reliability, but as soon as some circumstance changes or a person's intentions shift, the element of surprise returns. The surprise effect of January 25, 2011, is a case in point.

And yet much of current and classical anthropological theory leaves little space for the uncertainty of the unintended. Theoretical approaches inspired by the work of Michel Foucault, in particular, tend to focus on discourses, strategies, and the cultivation of a governmental rationality or an ethical sensibility in a way that often ends up highlighting strategies over battles, aims over accomplishments, and questions over answers. In his later work, Foucault (2007) himself became interested in resistance, but the hierarchy of "conducts" and "counterconducts" he develops still depicts counterconducts as dependent, and he does not raise the question of efficacy.

Michel de Certeau (1984: 91–97), in contrast, does raise the question of efficacy, calling us to think about the tactics of making do with the conditions created by strategies and *dispositifs* of power. In his famous essay on walking in the city, he juxtaposes the bird's-eye view over New York from the World Trade Center to the actual steps people take on the streets of the city, pointing out that the actual ways of doing things appropriate structures in an unpredictable way, accomplishing small tactical victories in an unequal struggle. However, de Certeau paradoxically assumes that these tactics of making do are successful. In a passage where the political thrust of his work becomes most evident, he points out how the indigenous people of South America adopted the religion of the colonial rulers but transformed, adapted, and subverted it to fit their own ends (de Certeau 1984: 31–32). But what if it was precisely this transformation, adaptation, and subversion that enabled the spread of Christianity across the continent? While de Certeau questions the efficacy of grand strategies, he does not consider how tactics of making do fail, backfire, or end up constituting that against which they are directed.

A more classical anthropological theory offers an explanation of how actions bring about something other than their explicit aim. Structural functionalism—for decades in the mid-twentieth century the standard theory of British anthropology in particular—had its main focus on the production of social stability and cohesion. A key premise of structural functionalism is that people may think that they are doing one thing, but actually they are accomplishing something else. For example, Max Gluckman, in his interpretation of festive rites of reversal in which social authority and mores are temporarily inverted, mocked, or suspended, argues that while such rites may appear to be counternormative and directed against the cohesion of the society, what they actually do is strengthening social norms and boundaries through their symbolic but always temporary inversion (Gluckman 1995). Structural functionalism was eventually abandoned, largely because it explains stability so well that it becomes quite useless in a rapidly changing world. Furthermore, and most important for my purposes, structural functionalism does not actually address the problem of unintended consequences, because it does not pay attention to intention in the first place. In a functionalist world, things do not go wrong, and the issues of hope, frustration, and despair do not arise.

Eliminating the question of intention is something that structural functionalism incidentally shares with two of the great economic theories of the modern era: (neo)classical economics and Marxist political economy. The "invisible hand" attributed to Adam Smith is a theory in which the attempt of some to maximize their private profit ends up producing wealth for all. Marx ([1852] 2006) stated, "Men make their own history, but they do not make it as they please," and develops a dialectic model of historical progression through the dynamics of relations of production. Both theories have undeniable specific valence, but they both fall short of explaining how things go wrong, partly because they either exclude the question of intention (as in Marxist theory, where material conditions define consciousness) or presume a given intention (as in neoclassical economics, where profit maximization is the only valid assumption). In the end, both are theories of logical, abstract forces. They do not explain how things don't work, how they work in a paradoxical fashion, how the working class gets deradicalized as it transforms into a middle class in a consumer society (Heiman, Freeman, and Liechty 2012), or how the allegedly natural force of the free market actually is the outcome of planning (Polanyi [1944] 2001).

The problem has to do with our expectations on social scientific theory. We want theories that predict, that tell what is going to happen, that give us a sense that we grasp what is going on. I, in contrast, am concerned with finding a theory that accounts for the sense of not grasping what is going on, one that describes how people face the unpredictable.

Some social theoreticians have offered useful directions for such a theory. Karl Popper, who in his later work spent considerable effort fighting what he saw as the totalitarian tendency of almost all utopian thinking and holistic theory (he singled out Plato and Marx in particular), argued that complex social processes are unpredictable and that we do not know what is going to happen. As a solution, he proposed "piecemeal social engineering," doing things in small steps to avoid the likely catastrophe that will result from the inevitably unpredictable and uncontrollable dynamics of a holistic change (Popper [1957] 2002). Popper's point is helpful, but not sufficient. As busy as he is saving the Western World from the communist totalitarian experiment, Popper is concerned with regaining control and minimizing, if not avoiding, the unpredictable. A more productive theory of acting in an unpredictable world has been suggested by James Scott (1998), in his history of failed high-modernist projects of the twentieth century. Rather than rational central planning, Scott argues, what people actually need and employ to make things work is *mêtis*, a Greek term that translates approximately as "cunning," the skill to solve various kind of problems in the face of greater powers (Detienne and Vernant [1974] 1991). As does Popper, Scott also offers a practical theory of how to get something done successfully in a world that thwarts master plans. I want to think one step further, however, and search for a theory that accounts for how things do not work, the experience of seeing one's plans thwarted despite all the care and cunning one has employed.

In his work in Gambia on men's search for income and fortune through diamond mining, migration, and other promising yet precarious schemes, Paolo Gaibazzi (2013) draws our attention to the concept of luck, which in Gambia is a thoroughly religious concept related to Islamic notions of destiny and *rizq*, the worldly income provided by God. Because God has predestined everyone's luck (or *rizq*) and fate, God alone knows where one's luck lies and when one will find it. But one needs to actively search for one's luck. Thus, rather than promoting fatalism, "destiny and luck are ways of reckoning with forces that lie beyond human control" (Gaibazzi 2013) Luck, fortune, destiny—these notions are not part of the standard vocabulary of social sciences. But perhaps they should be, for they are extremely useful when it comes to developing an understanding of living in an uncertain world.

## Destiny

Also in Egypt, destiny is the most accessible theory for not being certain about the outcomes of an action. Christian and Islamic theories of destiny are current in Egypt, but for my purposes, I focus on the Islamic theory. Islamic destiny (*qadar*) is grounded in the numerous Qur'anic assertions about God's omnipotence, all things in the universe happening through God's will and foresight, irrevocably written (*maktub*) by God at the beginning of time. At a first glance, destiny appears to be not a theory of action at all, since it might be understood as attributing all power to God and none to humans. However, the more specific vocabulary of destiny, the way people employ the notion in their lives, and the way it has been developed by Muslim theologians all tell a different story.

To start with, destiny has different aspects. There are absolute aspects, such as *qada'*, or "fate," the written hour of one's death, which one can neither know nor change. There are more pragmatic aspects like *nasib*, or "fortune," which one cannot plan but can and should make do with (*yitsarraf*—a concept quite similar to *metis*) in order to make the best of it. More important, people speak about destiny but at the same time consider themselves and one another to be responsible agents who can and should be advised, helped, hindered, thanked, or blamed. Knowing that one's date of death is irrevocably written does not hinder one from searching out all possible medical and spiritual aid in the case of illness, for example. God willing, it may help. Knowing that God alone knows whether one's search for success and fortune is successful does not prevent one from searching—on the contrary, it can motivate one to search for success, to be prepared for surprises, and to pray for God's help while doing so (see also Gaibazzi 2013).

In principle, everything that happens is destiny written by God. But in practice, people do not apply destiny consistently as a general rule, but rather in a more specific manner and with a specific intention: to recognize that while one should try one's best, one cannot tell how things will turn out in the end. The moral thrust of evocations of destiny is variable, however. It can mean praying that the will of God is on the side of one's plans. It can mean searching for one's fortune while acknowledging that God alone knows whether and where one will find it. It can mean encouraging people to accept a life of poverty and oppression as the will of God. It can mean insisting on a struggle for a better world because fighting for it is written by God as one's destiny.

The way *destiny* is used in everyday speech, it emerges as one of the two key elements of a partly explicit, partly implicit theory of action and consequences in which the notions of freedom (or human power) and destiny (or divine power) can be drawn upon for different uses and situations.[2] Destiny, therefore, does not exclude freedom. To speak of freedom, choice, responsibility, and human power is to say that decisions must be made, things changed, action taken. To speak about destiny, fortune, and the will of God is to say that greater powers are at play, that after one does what one can, the further course of things is beyond one's power, that contentedness with one's share is the proper attitude to cultivate. However, the evocation of destiny usually also involves taking action, often phrased with the word *yitsarraf*, "to make the best out of one's circumstances."

Most of the time, people refer to freedom and destiny separately, shifting seamlessly between one and the other, depending on what they want to emphasize. But occasionally, they take the time to sit down and debate how exactly the two come together. Sometimes people do so in situations where the moral tension between one's own powers and greater powers becomes too troubling to overlook, and one has to reflect about their relation in more detail. Sometimes they also do so because of the pleasure involved in an intricate theological and philosophical debate. And sometimes they address the relationship of destiny and freedom with a political intention.

In the summer of 2011, when freedom was the talk of the day, Safwat Hegazy, a leading figure in the Muslim Brotherhood, coined the slogan "God alone brought down the system." According to Hegazy, Egyptians went to the streets to protest not out of their own accord but by the power of God. The rhetorical intention of this slogan was that if the revolution was the will of God, then Egypt's political future must be Islamic (it was explained to me in exactly this way by an Islamist sympathizer at a demonstration on Tahrir Square in the autumn of 2011). Shady, an active supporter of continuing revolution from a village near Nazlat al-Rayyis, socialist by conviction and a firm opponent of Islamist movements, unsurprisingly did not agree with Sawfat Hegazy. But he could not simply ignore his claim, because he, too, believed that the revolution was the will of God. But he had a different theory.

Shady and I met in a café in Alexandria on October 10, 2011, one day after the massacre at Maspero during which the Egyptian army killed almost thirty mainly Christian protesters and then blamed them for attacking the army. Shady and I were in a gloomy mood, and Shady explained to me that, in his view, the revolution had failed, nothing good was to be expected from either the army or the Islamists, and the liberal and leftist revolutionary current was not able to contest the power of religious political discourse. Only when he started reminiscing about the first days of the revolution did his tone change. No matter how bleak the situation appeared to us then, those first days had been the happiest moments of his life. He started to reminisce about some narrow escapes from death, injury, and arrest:

> I lived, and for me the fact that I lived means that I'm not done, that I have a mission [*risala*] to complete. The protests on January 25 began with a shared sentiment of us all being so upset that we were ready to die. When we decided to go to protest on the Twenty-fifth, each of us felt that we were alone. But we became hundreds, then thousands. After feeling powerless and alone, we felt a sense of power in the moment when we were able to do something together. The Muslim Brothers claim that God moved the revolutionaries in spite of themselves [*ghasban 'anhum*]. But that is not true. We did it ourselves, with the will of God [*bi-mashi'at Allah*]. From my religious belief, I believe that everything that happens to me is written. What happens to me is destiny determined by God. But it doesn't mean that I'm not free. It's like in the script of a film. When you watch a film, you don't think that the characters just do what is written in the script: you see them acting in freedom, making choices, turning left or right. God is the director, but the characters act their roles in freedom. I don't know what my destiny is. I fulfill it without knowing what it will be.

Shady did not invent this theory himself. It is a theory with a remarkable history that goes back to debates among early scholars of Islam about whether humans are capable of choice (*mukhayyar*) or are predestined (*musayyar*). The canonical sources of Islam do not offer a univocal answer. The Qur'an states that everything happens by the will of God, and God alone makes people believers and infidels. The Qur'an also addresses believers and infidels alike as agents who can make up their minds, decide and act accordingly, and are held accountable for their deeds. The best-remembered (although in the end not victorious) party in this debate was the intellectual movement of the Mu'tazila, who favored a rationalist approach, argued that predestination contradicts moral responsibility and divine justice, and came to the conclusion that humans were free and not predestined (Vasalou 2008). The Mu'tazila continue to inspire intellectuals who search for alternative formulations of an Islamic faith. But a different theory eventually became the standard view of freedom and destiny. It is associated with Imam Abu al-Hasan al-Ash'ari (d. 324 AH, AD 936) the founding figure of the Ash'ari school of theology, which marked a departure from the rationalist tendencies of earlier centuries. According to the Ash'ari theory, humans are both capable of choice and predestined. People do out of their own accord that which God has predestined for them. We fulfill our written destiny in freedom.

From a philosophical and logical point of view, it could be argued that while the Mu'tazilite theory is sound, the Ash'arite theory is unsound because it does not solve the paradox of reward and punishment in a world where one could not have acted otherwise. And yet the logical contradiction of the Ash'arite theory should not make us overlook its existential truth. One does not have to believe that an omnipotent God has written our destiny for us to consider this a useful theory insofar as it describes what it means to act out of one's own accord in a world that is not of one's own making and in which one does not have the power to determine the consequences of one's actions. To develop a materialistic reading of al-Ashʿari's theistic theory, one could argue that destiny is nothing else than the sum of all consequences. All acts inevitably have consequences. We do not know them, but we turn them into irrevocable reality. Although it appears external to our will, we participate in making it happen, and yet that reality is not in our hands.

By insisting that he and his comrades acted out of their own accord as actors in God's masterpiece, with a mission to fulfill, Shady makes explicit the implicit entanglement of destiny and freedom, of being part of a great divine chain of events that is not of one's making and the course of which is unknown while also being able and responsible to make decisions and act, trying to make a difference while knowing that one's effort is part of a bigger picture that is beyond one's powers.

Shady takes up the issue of destiny frequently and with various people. He has a political reason to do so. He argues as an explicit philosophy of life what most people do implicitly, and by making it explicit, he gives it a twist. He insists that we should be consistent about the unity of destiny and freedom: The revolution was an act of God, but so was the Mubarak regime. If we thank God for the fact that somebody is a Muslim, we should also thank God for the fact that somebody is a Christian or an atheist. We are taught to accept poverty and oppression as God-given destiny, but when we struggle to change those things, we do so with the will of God. Underlying Shady's insistence on consistency regarding destiny is, not surprisingly, a revolutionary politics of freedom (see chapter 9)—a politics that, according to Shady, is a mission, a destiny written for him.[3]

Even when people do evoke destiny to deny freedom, it is a specific, contextual denial, not a general one. It may be phrased in a general way, but its asserted validity is in practice about putting one's trust in God for a moment, much in the way Saʿid argued for contentedness with the will of God in the middle of an angry complaint about the difficulty of having power over one's condition. It seems that speaking about destiny, the unpredictable yet inevitable consequences of what we do with the will of God, in fact systematically invites the question of intentionality and freedom, the power to do something of one's own accord. The question of what it means to act while not knowing how well those actions will work is also a question of what it means to act and to have aims in the first place.

## Freedom

Even in very averse situations, there is usually some limited space of freedom in the manipulative tactics of making do with the inevitable. Just like destiny is specific, one aspect of a dialogical relationship, so also freedom always exists in relation to the inevitable, the given, the obligatory. This echoes Maurice Merleau-Ponty's ([1945] 2005: 504–530) thesis that freedom is never absolute, but always a limited freedom, a specific range of possibilities within the limits of the world. However, this is not quite what people in Egypt mean when they speak about freedom.

There was a time in academia when freedom seemed like a simple matter, a time when anthropologists felt more at ease to talk about freedom and empowerment, oppressed people's (especially women's) search for self-determination (for a critique, see, e.g., Spyer 1997). It was not a detached vision, grounded as it was in a moral commitment to support the struggles of people with whom the researchers often greatly sympathized. Those who did not seem to search for self-determination or freedom, or even were opposed it, understandably received many fewer charitable interpretations. Saba Mahmood (2005) offers an important attempt to provide that missing charitable reading for a group of people who, rather than aiming for freedom, try to be good at submitting themselves to the will of God. Mahmood argues that it is a mistake to assume a priori that people want freedom: the question of what they really want is an empirical one, and the answer depends on the authoritative traditions they draw upon. Far from being universal, Mahmood argues, the pursuit of freedom in fact conceals a particularly Western, liberal concept of individual autonomy that has a specific cultural history of its own and cannot be taken as a starting point of a research about, for example, pious Muslim women.

But what do when a pious Muslim woman like Nagat (in chapter 4) speaks out in the name of freedom? I agree with Mahmood that we should not take freedom as a starting point. It is always better to ask what people want and what they, in a given historical and social context, can want in the first place than to assume what they should want. However, just as there is no reason to assume a priori that people want freedom, there is no reason to assume a priori that freedom means individual autonomy. Autonomy is one particular sense of freedom, embedded in a cultural fiction that is very powerful in a place like the United States but less so (albeit not irrelevant) in a place like Egypt.

So what do people in Egypt mean when they demand or deny freedom? At several occasions in the course of this book, freedom has emerged in the sense of choice, such as choosing whom to marry, a consumer's choice in everyday capitalism, or Mustafa's choice for Salafism as a path of commitment. In each case, the choice is one that is limited, a choice from a finite range of possible options. This is a rather conservative sense of freedom, but occasionally it is also articulated in a more radical way, as when people are discontent with the choice they have and desire to have other things to choose from, "to find other dreams," as Mukhtar put it in chapter 7. Even in its conservative sense, and certainly in its radical sense, freedom of choice can become a dangerous freedom of license, the possibility of making immoral or irresponsible choices. Especially when it comes to gender relations, sex, and religious creed, this is a highly sensitive matter. The ideas that Muslims could be free to change their religion or that women could be free to act without male guardians go severely against the grain of conservative moral sentiment that the Islamic revival draws upon and reproduces. Even the most liberal-minded men easily turn into enemies of freedom when their female relatives try to have it.

However, choice is just one sense of freedom among many. In chapter 4, Nagat articulated freedom in an expressive sense as the ability to speak out about one's feelings and pursue their fulfillment. In chapter 7, the people who thought about freedom as a motivation for migration described freedom not only in terms of choice but also in terms of having rights, of facing a predictable and just legal and political system. In chapter 9, the revolutionaries lived out freedom in union with dignity through the utopian space of demonstrations and struggle, and they built their affect of rejection on a spirit of (collective) self-determination as the key quality of a better world.

Together, these visions of freedom involve a demand for relative autonomy, a space wherein one can act without being hindered or forced. But the actual demands for freedom are too specific, too evidently related to specific moments of force and necessity to fit into the abstraction of capital-*A* autonomy of liberal theory. Furthermore, the actual demands for freedom often contradict the premise of individuality that is usually associated with freedom-as-autonomy. Take, for example, the way freedom arises as an issue when love meets marriage. Rather than posing the individual against the collective, the struggles to unite love and marriage are about a better relationality in which shared emotions and desires of the marital partners are not sacrificed for the sake of those of their parents and relatives. Rather than being associated with freedom, individuality is in fact often associated with loneliness, isolation, and lack of power—a condition that was instrumental to the sense of fear that prevailed before 2011 (Hibou 2011). Importantly, the freedom-as-experience of the revolutionaries that had the "breaking of fear" as its starting point is indeed associated with autonomy—but not an autonomy of the individual kind. While the revolutionaries celebrate difference of lives and lifestyles and the individualistic moment of thinking for oneself, the autonomy they strive for is a collective autonomy against "the system." Loneliness is defeat, and freedom the outcome of coming together in struggle, as Shady pointed out earlier. Freedom emerges always as relational and relative: choosing from among options, wanting to have options other than those available, claiming rights to the state and social authorities, fighting the system, voicing one's feelings toward people who may not want to hear them.

This is in no way surprising—after all, autonomy is a social and cultural fiction, accomplished by making invisible the relational and institutional preconditions of a self-determined life in relative material security. Also, in a place like, for example, London, what people would describe as a happy, full life is made up of fulfilling and constructive relationality more than individuality (Miller 2008: 285–287). The invisibility of the material and relational preconditions of freedom may be easier to maintain in Western Europe and North America, but in Egypt they are all too visible and hard to overlook: they have to do with class, education, citizenship, demography, family traditions, gender, clientelistic relations, religious commitments, political allegiances, and money—especially money. The power to speak out, to claim rights, to make choices, to act together—these are not freely available. That power is grounded in a highly gendered and class-conscious economy of what Arjun Appadurai (2013: 188) has called the "capacity to aspire." There is a lot of destiny involved in having the means to search for freedom.

This brings us back to our original theme: having existential power over one's condition, something that, according to Sa'id, is possible only when one has money. Is that power the same as freedom? Was Sa'id actually lamenting the lack of freedom in his life? In terms of the political freedoms of having rights and being able to express oneself, it seems that he did speak about a lack of freedom. But with respect to the ability to have power over one's condition, he was addressing a wider issue. Using the verb *yiqdar*, "to have power," or "to be able to accomplish something," Sa'id spoke about the capacity to act at all, the power to make any difference. Freedom, in contrast, appears to be a more specific case of that capacity to act.

Being able to do something is generally considered a necessary and a good thing. Freedom, in contrast, is desired but also feared. Freedom means taking a transgressive approach toward specific limits of the possible (e.g., what one can imagine, what one can do, what one can get away with). With the exception of freedom in the conservative sense of choice from a limited range of options, freedom as Egyptians speak about it is not unlimited, but it also does not take place within limits. It goes against limits.

In his book *Life within Limits*, Michael Jackson (2011) points out that more often than not, people struggle to make their best out of that which they take for given. Rather than trying to go beyond the limits of the given, which often would be exceedingly difficult indeed, they take them for granted as the framework of their struggle. This is very much in line with what I described as "reckoning with the inevitable" in chapter 8. It is important to hold that most of the time, people take the structural conditions of their world as given, and rather than changing them, they try to be as good as they can in mastering those conditions. However, over and again in the course of this book we have also seen people trying to gently push the limits of the given and inevitable, and at times they have even dared to pick a fight.

This is not to conclude that there is an authentic human desire for freedom after all. Rather, I would agree with Saʻid and Michael Jackson that having power over one's condition, being able to do something in a world of overwhelming powers and unpredictable destiny, is an authentic human desire. But whether people develop that desire within limits or against them is an open question. Often, a life in and for freedom is precarious, dangerous, and confusing, whereas trying to master one's moves within the inevitable can be more fulfilling and bring more recognition and comfort.

## The Trouble of Grand Schemes

If only it were that easy. Living a life within limits may be what many, if not most, people around the world would happily settle with most of the time. However, the shape of the world pushes them into a different direction.

There is a tragic aspect to the pursuit of existential power through grand schemes, ambivalent commitments, and daily diversions and defiance alike. Because we are we always somewhere in between the power to act of our own accord and the destiny of facing the unpredictable consequences of our own and others' acts, the promises that provide hope and the actions taken to realize that hope are also often the same things that generate the anxieties and the limits of the inevitable within which, or against which, people try to live their lives (see Orsi 2005; Scott 2004).

This is a tragedy well described in ancient myths and poems, and it can be told about a solid and eternal world as well as about a fluid and changing one. The trouble this book describes, however, is more specific. It is the trouble with a changing world in which one is constantly promised more and new things. There really are more and new things, lots of them in fact. But they come at a price, they are not enough, and they are not quite what was promised. This is the genius of the capitalist process: by actually providing goods and gratification on the condition of constant growth, capitalism constantly raises expectations, undermines lives and livelihoods that once were safe and certain, and creates pressures and promises that once would have been unimaginable. These pressures are troublesome even under conditions of relative wealth. Under conditions of poverty—the condition in which most people who appeared in this book live—they are extreme.

This is a revolutionary process in a double sense. For one thing, it puts things into movement, compelling people to reconsider, rethink, or reinforce certainties that once could be taken for granted, and at times to search for new ones. Furthermore, it raises questions and doubts in a way that makes answers and certainties seem available, if not now, then in the near future. It provokes discontent and rebellion. The outcome is an increasingly sharp tension between what is and what could be, a tension that is expressed in the proliferation, success, and radicalization of what I call grand schemes: ideas that people understand as larger than life, unrealizable yet calling for their realization, pure yet capable of providing a firm hold in an uncertain world.

I have no doubt that people have always put their faith in someone or something that is greater, wiser, and more powerful than they themselves are. There can be no better example of that faith than the monotheism of Abrahamic religions. But I am hesitant to call Islam a grand scheme. The Islam of Muhammad's revelation as I read it (I make no pretensions for an objective reading) is a relationship, an act of worship and submission by believers toward God, and an act of revelation and power by God toward humans. This relational ground of faith remains central today, and in fact it seems central to most religious traditions, as well as to much of our political and personal hopes, which we invest in friends, comrades, parents and parental figures, heroes, ancestors, leaders, saints, prophets, saviors, and gods (see, e.g., Orsi 2005). Schemes, in contrast, have something impersonal, systematic, abstract to them. They are related to the fact that we live in ever-larger communities, our horizons ever wider (or at least geographically broader), and some (but never all) of our social relations increasingly abstract, functionalized, monetized. Most important, however, they are related to the concept of progress, the idea that there is more to come in the future, and that already today, one can anticipate the shape, if not the details, of that more that is to come. Grandness is not new, but what is new, is the way it is attributed not only to persons and powers but also more and more to ideas, systems, and plans.

Grand schemes, thus, are a feature of a world that is rapidly changing, one in which the expectation of more to come is linked to the undermining of certainties. The trouble of love emerges at the moment when the institution of family-arranged marriage is in the process of being transformed but also fiercely defended. The pursuit to know Islam as an objective set of truth emerges in a moment when the everyday presence of God, the Prophet, and the saints becomes elusive or even rejected. Young people suffer intensely from boredom because they put great faith in progress. The drive to be a committed Muslim fully devoted to God's commandments becomes compelling when the contradictions of living a devout but ambivalent life become unbearable.

This is undoubtedly an account of the temporality of the future from the point of view of mostly poor people in a relatively poor and conservative place. It is not the vision of a postmodern society of abundant choice and moral relativism, with autonomous agents designing their lives. (And perhaps the postmodern vision is not really that true of the wealthy postindustrial nations either—see Miller [2008].) Defying common sociological evocations of modernity, the vision this book offers is very much what modernity looks for the majority of the world's inhabitants (see also Piot 2010; Appadurai 2013): God-fearing, consumerist, poor but aspiring, romantic, debt financed, violent, authoritarian, gender anxious, worldly, nationalist, overcrowded, polluted, heteronormative, constantly short of cash, guided by unrealized grand schemes, unpredictable, partly subject to ethical reflection and purposeful action, partly given and inevitable—and always saturated by hope, anxiety, pressure, and frustration.

In an optimistic vision, the sense that there is more to come is a good thing. It means that our minds will be more open, our material conditions more comfortable, our world more just and better organized. Alternatively, in a dystopian vision, "more to come" is the looming disaster, the loss of all that made up our lives and societies, the collapse of all that was good. In Egypt at least, both visions apply, but neither offers a sufficient account. Where there is hope, there is trouble—not just because the misery of the world compels us to hope for a better world, as Ernst Bloch ([1959] 1980) argued, but also because the consequences of our hoping can unsettle the limits of the given and compel us to aspire beyond limits, which is troublesome.

This is the most fundamental ambiguity of grand schemes: in the course of this book I have elaborated at length how people pursue different grand schemes at once in a way that is both sincere and halfhearted, and how people's specific trajectories always oscillate through moments of hope, determination, boredom, and frustration. Grand schemes and great expectations seem to systematically bring something other than people hoped that they would. The best available theory to explain this is destiny. But there is a crux. Just like thinking about destiny often compels one to think about freedom, so pursuing grand schemes and trying to be good at mastering a known good (such as love, religion, wealth, or building a life) often compels one to think and act beyond limits. Grand schemes and compelling pursuits like revivalist piety, capitalist profit, romantic love, and migration for the sake of money as such are not schemes of freedom. (In this regard, Mahmood was quite right in removing freedom from the vocabulary of her analysis of the piety movement.) But in the way they put people under pressure and force them to try to navigate a confusing reality, they draw the framework and limits of action into question.

Revivalist ideals of moral consistency, religious knowledge, and commitment raise the issue of moral responsibility and shift the focus from the community to the self. The capitalist ethos of profit and future growth requires wits, reflectivity, and adaptation as structural conditions of a functioning economy. Love turns from passionate but unrealized obsession into a struggle for the sake of emotional fulfillment when it crash-lands on the destiny- and strategy-driven logic of arranged marriage. Migration for the sake of building a life reduces one's scope of fantasy to making money, thus making migrants acutely aware of the unfreedom of their condition while also allowing them to perceive the world of vaster opportunities that surrounds them. These and other grand schemes and lived trajectories repeatedly raise the question of freedom, or more specifically, the question of existential power in spite of and beyond the limitations one faces. But more often than not, the answer to that question is no.

# Notes

## Introduction

1. "Hasr qatla al-18 yawm al-ula min al-thawra tafsiliyan," *WikiThawra* (blog), 2013, http://wikithawra.wordpress.com/2013/10/23/25jan18dayscasualities/ (accessed 29 December 2013).

2. The figures on the death toll of August 14, 2013, vary greatly, and violent events spread across the country and continued for several days. Especially in southern Egypt churches and police stations were attacked in retaliation. According to the Ministry of Health, the nationwide death toll on August 14, 2013, was 638, including 43 police officers. According to the documentation of *WikiThawra* ("Hasr qatla fadd i'tisamay Rabi'a wa al-Nahda wa-tawabi'iha," https://docs.google.com/spreadsheet/ccc?key=0ApHKfHFs3JYxdFBfWVUySk4ySUJLQk EzV3VsdnIzT2c#gid=0 [accessed December 29, 2013]), in contrast, the nationwide death toll on that day was 1,385 (among them 52 policemen and conscripts) and 399 more (including 48 policemen and conscripts) were killed during the following five days. According to the same source, the storming of the Rabea al-'Adawiya sit-in alone cost 904 lives, among them 7 policemen.

3. In Egypt, the Gregorian solar calendar is used for administrative and for most practical purposes; the Islamic lunar calendar serves Muslim ritual and festive use, and the Coptic solar calendar is used in agriculture and traditional wisdom about seasonal weather changes; as well as in Christian ritual use.

4. The hopes invested by Christian Egyptians into Christianity are not part of this book, which is based on fieldwork with Muslims. Compared to the long history and continued strong presence of Christianity in Egypt, there is strikingly little literature focusing on how it is like to live as a Christian in Egypt—but see Assad (2009); Shenoda (2010); Mahmood (2012); Heo (2013a, 2013b); Elsässer (2014).

5. Authors of poetry and prose appear with their own names to give them credit for their literary works. Some people who are quoted in Chapter 9 and the conclusion insisted on appearing with their real names to hold on record their political engagement for future readers.

6. For rural Egypt and its connections with the world, see also Weyland (1993); Hopkins and Westergaard (1998); Abu-Lughod (2005); Stauth (2010); Abaza (2013).

7. In rural regions and small towns of the Nile Delta, a variety of Egyptian Arabic known as Fallahi is spoken. Fallahi is quite distinct from the Egyptian Arabic spoken in Cairo and Alexandria.

8. For why many anthropologists have called into question a humanistic approach, and what it can nevertheless accomplish, see Abu-Lughod (1992: 28–29).

9. On religious ambiguities and struggles, see Beekers (2014); Martijn de Koning (2009, 2013); Abenante (2014); Schulz (2011); Oustinova-Stjepanovic (2011); Simon (2009, 2012); Khan (2013). On the coming together of different ideals and techniques, see Deeb (2006); Meyer and Moors (2006); Masquelier (2007, 2009); Hafez (2011); Mittermaier (2011); Kreil (2012); Menin (2012). On their coming together in the making of masculinity in particular, see Ghannam

(2013). On the nexus of the economic and the spiritual, see Gaibazzi (2013); Graw (2012); Jones (2010); Rudnyckyj (2009); Osella and Osella (2009); Moors (2009).

10. Michael Lambek (2010) and James Laidlaw (2013) argue that ethics needs to be understood in a wider sense that encompasses the entire evaluative dimension of social life, all considerations about right and good. In contrast, I argue that the evaluative aspect that is intrinsic to human interaction is best called moral, whereas ethics is a more specific work of reflection on the values involved. While Lambek posits the ordinariness of ethics, I emphasize the specificity (situational and historical) of conditions that compel people to engage in a reflective questioning about their proper being and possible values and actions. See Chapter 4 for an elaboration of this point.

## 1. Boredom and Despair in Rural Egypt

1. Lori Allen's (2008) work on how Palestinians grew bored and indifferent to violence during the Second Intifada provides an interesting comparison and a reminder that just because people in a given moment are frustrated and indifferent about politics does not mean that there are no political dynamics at play.

2. During the first decade of the twenty-first century, the Egyptian state invested enormously in sports as a means of promoting success, patriotism, and belonging. The enthusiasm for international soccer was linked with a series of victories of the national team and the Al-Ahly Club in African competitions. Following the revolution, interest in soccer dipped dramatically, and after the Port Said stadium massacre on February 1, 2012, which cost more than seventy lives, and the consequent cancellation of the national league, soccer almost disappeared entirely from public interest, only to return with some vigor in autumn 2013 under the El-Sisi regime (see Rommel 2013).

3. For a historical parallel from nineteenth-century Great Britain, see Lecky ([1896] 1903: 1:319); for the contemporary Global South, see Verkaaik (2004); Hansen (2005); Mains (2007); Jeffrey (2010); Masquelier (2013).

4. I'm indebted to Ayman 'Amer for this point. See also Dabbagh (2005: 81).

5. Colloquial expression for a Salafi. Depending on the context, calling a Salafi a sheikh can be both respectful and ironic.

## 2. An Hour for Your Heart and an Hour for Your Lord

1. al-Bukhari: Sahih, book of fasting (al-sawm), chapter 5; at-Tirmidhi: al-Jami' al-sahih, book of fasting (al-sawm), chapter 1, hadith 682. Because of the great variety of different print and electronic editions of the Sunnite hadith collections, I refer to them by chapters rather than page numbers.

2. The exact date of Laylat al-Qadr is not known, but it is commonly celebrated on the night before the Twenty-seventh of Ramadan.

3. Reported in slightly different versions by ad-Darimi: Sunan, book of fasting (al-sawm), chapter 54 (Fadl qiyam shahr Ramadan); at-Tirmidhi: al-Jami' al-sahih, book of fasting (al-sawm), chapter 1, hadith 683; al-Bukhari: Sahih, book of fasting: chapter 6.

4. For Laylat al-Qadr, see Malik ibn Anas: al-Muwatta', book of retreat in the mosque (al-i'tikaf), chapter 6 (ma ja' fi laylat al-qadr), hadith 15; for intentionally breaking the fast, see al-Bukhari: Sahih, book of fasting (al-sawm): chapter 29; for double reward, see Muslim: Sahih, book of fasting (al-siyam): chapter of the merit of fasting (fadl al-siyam), hadith 164.

5. This is the taxonomy as I know it from northern Egypt, where tribal affiliations are of little or no importance and the level of patronymic group (*jama'a*) does not include any actual institutional hierarchies, only a more diffuse sense of solidarity. In southern Egypt, where tribal (*qabali*) identity is central to social organization, the terminology and taxonomy of family and kinship are different.

6. The female forms of these words are created by adding a *ta' marbuta* at the end of the word: *tayyiba*, *gada'a*, and so on.

7. I am indebted to Filippo Osella for this point.

8. See, e.g., Foucault (1984); Laidlaw (2002); Lambek (2000, 2002, 2007); Robbins (2004); Mahmood (2005); Zigon (2008); Simon (2009); Schulz (2011).

## 3. Knowing Islam

1. Strictly speaking, only critics of the Wahhabiyya call the movement so, after its founder Muhammad ibn 'Abd al-Wahhab. Followers of the movement call themselves *muwahhidun*, or "monotheists," implying that others are not.

2. The rapid spread of the Salafis in the 2000s appears to have been enabled by a deal with the State Security, Egypt's secret police, whereby the Salafis were allowed to compete with the Muslim Brotherhood on the condition of abstaining from oppositional politics. By 2010, the Salafis' success had become so striking, however, that steps were taken to limit their influence. One important step to reinforce an anti-Salafi religious establishment was notably the appointment by President Mubarak of Ahmad al-Tayyib, a Sufi and determined anti-Salafi as the sheikh of the al-Azhar University, Egypt's leading Islamic institution, in 2010. Nevertheless, most (but not all) Salafi groups abided by the deal, under which they were allowed to act, and so remained loyal to the Mubarak regime during the revolution in 2011. The Salafi Nour Party (established in 2011), which represents some of the most powerful Salafi groups, also sided with El-Sisi's military rule in 2013.

3. *Law* is a poor translation for the notion of *shar'* or *shari'a*, which implies a much wider array of norms and procedures than the secular notion of law (see Asad 2003).

4. By the end of eighteenth century, a hadith known by a religious specialist would be preceded by a list of transmission of approximately twenty persons, and the study of religious knowledge included the study and memorization of those chains of transmission. Today, in contrast, hadiths are usually quoted only with a chain that ends with one of the canonical collections or entirely without the chain of transmission (see Reichmuth 2009: 19–20).

5. For a practical demonstration, see "al-Hadith al-musalsal bi-l-musafaha wa-l-mushabaka," posted by mostafaalazhary, July 21, 2011, http://www.youtube.com/watch?v=13WQH_nf7Rk.

6. Two Qur'anic verses are commonly mentioned as proof for the obligation of Muslim women to cover their body and hair. The first (24:31) calls women to cover their beauty or private parts from men, excepting their close relatives and slaves. But while the verse is very detailed in defining to whom women may show their beauty, it does not specify which body parts or which kind of covering are involved. The other (33:53) calls Muslims who visit the house of the Prophet Muhammad to address his wives "from behind a veil" (*hijab*). This verse has provided the name for Muslim women's head scarf, but this interpretation has been challenged because it explicitly speaks about the Prophet's wives and because it is not clear what *hijab* means here.

7. I am indebted to Irfan Ahmad for reminding me about the significance of humor.

## 4. Love Troubles

1. For anthropological contributions to the theme of love, see Abu-Lughod (1992, 1996a); Strohmenger (1996); Joseph (1999); Fortier (2004); Masquelier (2005, 2009); Wardlow and Hirsch (2006); Ring (2006); Hart (2007); Padilla et al. (2007); Marsden (2007b); Bochow (2008); Cole and Thomas (2009); Kreil (2012); Menin (2012).

2. This is a proverb frequently cited by Egyptians in relation to love and sexuality.

3. *'Urfi* marriage is a form of temporary marriage that young people often use as a way to have a sexual relationship with a minimal degree of religious legitimacy. It is also commonly a cover for prostitution. It does not involve any of the guarantees for the wife that are involved in a regular *shar'i* marriage, and children who result from an *'urfi* marriage may be considered illegitimate, which in Egypt is a very serious problem for the mother and the child.

4. See Tammam and Kreil (2010); Kreil and Schielke (2012). In addition to Valentine's Day, there is also National Love Day, 'Id al-Hubb al-Qawmi that is celebrated on November 4.

5. I'm indebted to Saad Kamel for this point.

6. Since Mustafa's father had died a few years earlier, it is evident that he is quoting common wisdom here rather than talking about his father in particular.

7. Eventually, also the divorced woman from the neighborhood remarried.

8. For a rich and nuanced account of the expectations and experience of marital life, see Farha Ghannam's (2013) work on masculinity in Cairo.

## 5. Capitalist Ethics?

1. This moral ontology and the utopian spirit of capitalism have been perhaps most powerfully expressed by Milton Friedman (1962).

2. This is the case especially in regard to *nuqta*, an interest-free mutual credit that is exchanged at weddings and family occasions. Unlike wedding gifts in many other societies, *nuqta* is explicitly considered a loan, not a gift. At a wedding a guest who owes, for example, fifty pounds, will pay one hundred pounds to the host so that the host now owes the guest fifty pounds. All this is recorded in an accounting book. No interest is paid, but the host serves a meat lunch to his guests who come to pay *nuqta*. Payment is enforced by social pressure. Participation in *nuqta* exchange is voluntary, but withdrawing from it is difficult, because the exchange of loans is associated with prestige, family connections, and friendship. Although formally a loan, *nuqta* is also an act of generosity and confirmation of mutual respect and relatedness (which makes it an interesting inversion of the classical anthropological theory of the gift). Additionally, *nuqta* has become a common way to finance all kinds of investments and consumption. According to people who participate in the *nuqta* exchange, its volume and frequency have significantly expanded in past decades. There are some cases of people driven to ruins by conspicuously collecting *nuqta* that they couldn't repay. Unable to pay from their own funds, they were forced to borrow from moneylenders with a high interest rate and eventually to sell their houses.

3. "Interest-free" in the sense that there is no interest that accumulates over time. But the price of goods bought on installments is higher than goods bought in cash.

4. Analogous to the Christian belief in purgatory, punishment of the grave is understood as punishment that believers must undergo for their sins before they are granted entrance to paradise.

5. Such feeds were in active circulation especially between 2008 and 2010. But by 2014, their URL addresses were no longer active or not available to me.

6. I am indebted to Jan Beek for this point (see also Comaroff and Comaroff 1999; Sanders 2009).

7. Daromir Rudnyckyj (2009: 130) has argued in regard to neoliberal training programs that combine management training and Islamic piety that, in contrast to "prosperity religions" that promise followers profit (e.g., some Pentecostal groups do so very explicitly), Islam in the neoliberal age appears instead as a "spiritual economy" that is about developing the ethical capacities needed for success in the business world. However, both typologies presented by Rudnyckyj are about this worldly profit. He mentions reward in the afterworld only in passing; in contrast, here it is my main concern.

## 7. Longing for the World

1. Not all, however. Some of the most thriving upmarket areas, like the suburb King Maryut and the City Center commercial district, are further away from informal areas and difficult to access without a private car.

2. Cyprus being some 300 miles from Alexandria, it is more than unlikely that the visible lights are those of Cyprus and not of fishing boats or gas platforms. But adapting such an unromantic interpretation would not do justice to the emotions and imaginations involved in looking at the sea by night.

3. The ideas I present in this chapter are strongly indebted to my shared work with Daniela Swarowsky on her documentary film project *Messages from Paradise*, the first part of which we shot in Egypt and with Egyptians in Austria (Swarowsky and Schielke 2009), and with Mukhtar Shehata, who has been my host in Alexandria and with whom I have developed many ideas together. Inspired to such a high degree by shared work and thinking, this chapter is to an important degree also theirs.

4. See Rouch (1958); Larkin (1997); Piot (1999); Behrend (2002); Weiss (2009); A. de Koning (2009); Elsayed (2010); Gable (2010).

5. This paragraph is partly an adaptation of an Arabic abstract about the novel and the film by Mukhtar Shehata.

6. Blogs and bloggers are the internationally best-known and best-studied part of this writing trend, but the phenomenon is wider, blogs being only one aspect of it (see Onodera 2009; Jurkiewicz 2011; Hirschkind 2011; Pepe 2014).

## 8. Condition: Normal

1. Actually, it had happened much more often, most recently in 1977. But at the moment of this conversation I did not remember that, which is also telling of what I took to be Egypt's normal condition. For the history of the many rebellions in twentieth-century Egypt, see the end of this chapter and Diyab (2011).

2. Since 2009, January 25 has been a public holiday dedicated to the police in commemoration of the defense of the Isma'iliya police station against the British Army on January 25, 1952.

3. As a civil servant, Tawfiq did not lose his job but returned to work in the health administration, responsible for taking test samples of groceries offered for sale and spending most of his time playing computer games in the village health clinic.

4. Buying the textbook is often the key requirement for passing an examination. Textbooks are an important source of income for professors whose official salaries are very low.

5. For the different aspects of the contradictory nature of neoliberal government, see, e.g., Armbrust (2011); Shever (2008); Shore (2008); Šynková (2010).

6. For important parallels with Tunisia and Syria, see Hibou (2011); Wedeen (1999).

7. De Certeau's work is grounded in an outspokenly emancipatory vision, which is why Jon Mitchell (2007) has suggested that de Certeau offers a theology rather than a theory of action. This becomes visible, for example, in de Certeau's (1984) assumption that tactics of diversion actually help the weak to create non-autonomous but real space of freedom.

8. The first large, undisturbed demonstration held on Tahrir Square on February 1 is remembered as al-Masira al-Milyuniya (Million-Person March), a rather ingenious propaganda trick by the revolutionaries, since the mere name laid claim to huge numbers even before the demonstration began. Whether it actually gathered a million, or a little more, or a little less, is unclear. After the revolution, various groups have tried to call for *milyuniyas* in a rather inflammatory fashion, and most of these demonstrations have gathered tens of thousands rather than a million.

9. So much so, in fact, that it is impossible to produce a review of relevant literature. On the beginnings of this development, however, see, e.g., Fadl (2007); Onodera (2009); Hirschkind (2011).

10. The number zero in Arabic has the shape of a dot. In the poem, the dots one took for stars turn out to be nothing, just zeroes.

11. Civil servants receive their salaries on the last workday of the month.

12. Because of a shortage of subsidized bread, there are usually long queues in front of bakeries that sell subsidized bread, and sometimes fights or stampedes occur in the crowd of people trying to get bread.

13. For the concept of reckoning, see Winegar (2006).

14. I am indebted to Danielle Kuzmanovic for drawing my attention to Lisa Wedeen's (1999) notion of acting "as if" as an instrumental part of the Asad regime in in Syria.

## 9. Those Who Said No

1. Distinguishing currents from movements, I follow Arabic usage, in which broad social movements (e.g., Islamism) often go by the term *current (tayyar)*, whereas the term *movement (haraka)* tends to be used for movements that have a more distinct group identity, ideology, and perhaps also membership and leadership.

2. A peculiar feature of the political landscape of Nazlat al-Rayyis is that in a village that is approximately equally divided into families of fishermen and farmers (although most young people no longer work in these trades except seasonally), the clear majority of supporters of the revolutionary spectrum are from families of fishermen.

3. Despite these village revolutionaries' strict opposition to the Muslim Brotherhood and Salafis, not all supporters of the revolutionary current are actually opposed to Islamist visions in general. Salah, for example, who joined the village revolutionaries in the spring of 2011, shifted back and forth between socialist and Salafi sympathies in the following two years. There is a whole history of the Islamists who said no that is yet to be written: the story of those individuals with Islamist visions and smaller Islamist groups whose understanding of an Islamic society was at odds with the reality of Muslim Brotherhood government (as well as with the opportunistic tactics of the Salafi Nour Party), and who took a critical distance toward the Muslim Brotherhood in 2012 but joined its protest against military rule in the summer and autumn of 2013.

4. These events are shown in more detail in the documentary *The Secret Capital* (Shehata and Schielke 2013).

5. The one-liner, which shifts in the middle of the sentence from polite classical Arabic (in literal translation) "Why do not die . . ." (*li-madha la yamut*) to the offensive colloquial "dirty mother's sons" (*wlad il-wiskha*), does not lend itself to a direct translation without losing its shift of register and offensive language. The word *wiskha* is common in street talk but routinely censored on television and in printed publications. For this reason, the one-liner is also conspicuously absent from the collected work of 'Amer's (2012) latest writings.

6. "Black blocks" are originally a tactic of organized street fighting against the police developed by the radical left in Europe, called so by the black clothes worn by the members of a block among the demonstrations that would spearhead confrontations with the police.

7. Events with a heavy death toll among protesters were always related to the use of live ammunition by security forces. During July and August 2013, the security forces also systematically employed snipers against pro-Morsi protesters. The deadliest events during the revolutionary period were Friday of Anger, on January 28, 2011, with up to one thousand people killed nationwide, and the storming of the Rabea al-'Adawiya and the Nahda sit-ins on August 15, 2013, with officially more than six hundred—but probably more than one thousand—people killed. For an estimate of the death toll and forms of injuries, see "Hasr qatla fadd i'tisamay Rabi'a wa al-Nahda wa-tawabi'iha," WikiThawra, 2013, https://docs.google.com/spread sheet/ccc?key=0ApHKfHFs3JYxdFBfWVUySk4ySUJLQkEzV3VsdnIzT2c#gid=0; and "Egypt: Security Forces Used Excessive Lethal Force: Worst Mass Unlawful Killings in Country's Modern History," Human Rights Watch, 2013, www.hrw.org/news/2013/08/19/egypt-security -forces-used-excessive-lethal-force.

8. Which is also why in the following summer, he and some of his friends were among those few who opposed Islamist politics but did not support the June 30 uprising.

9. Families with a history of leftist and revolutionary stances in the village have brought up some women (a few more than the three named by Fouad, in fact) with an outspoken, oppositional consciousness. But also in those families, women's social lives are usually quite separate from men's gatherings and discussions. Furthermore, leftist families do not exert an ideological power of conformity on their female members—partly because it is against their ideals, but perhaps more so because in their domestic lives, leftist men act very much according to the logic of patriarchal family, let women take care of the household, and reinforce conventional female roles of domesticity and invisibility.

## Conclusion

1. For elaborations on hope, see Bloch ([1959] 1980); Hage (2002); Miyazaki (2006); Berlant (2011).

2. I do not equate freedom with agency here. Destiny and freedom are both parts of a broader notion of what, for the lack of a better term, can be called agency, in the sense of having the power to make a difference. Destiny implies that such power is God's but may be embodied and exerted by humans. The assumption of causal efficacy of human acts from the social scientist's point of view, criticized by Laidlaw (2002, 2013), whose fundamental misgivings about the concept of agency I share, is not part of this theory, which describes acting in a world ruled by greater powers and which leaves open the question who possesses the power of efficacy.

3. However, Shady is not quite consequent when it comes to freedom and destiny. Most of the time he speaks about himself in a way such that freedom is the implicit underlying condition of his actions: he decides, he is responsible, he accomplishes. But when death comes into the discussion or when the yet-unknown outcomes of his revolutionary mission come up, he becomes aware of destiny and is compelled or inspired to explain his specific take on it.

# References

Abaza, Mona. 2006. *The Changing Consumer Cultures of Modern Egypt: Cairo's Urban Reshaping*. Cairo: American University in Cairo Press.

———. 2010. "The trafficking with tanwir (enlightenment)." *Comparative Studies of South Asia, Africa and the Middle East* 30, 1: 32–46.

———. 2013. *The Cotton Plantation Remembered: An Egyptian Family Story*. Cairo: The American University in Cairo Press.

'Abd al-'Aziz, Basma. 2013. *Ighra' al-sulta al-mutlaqa: Masar al-'unf fi 'alaqat al-shurta bi-l-muwatin 'abr al-tarikh*. Giza: Sefsafa Publishing.

Abdel Aal, Ghada. 2010. *I Want to Get Married! One Wannabe Bride's Misadventures with Handsome Houdinis, Technicolor Grooms, Morality Police, and Other Mr. Not-Quite-Rights*. Trans. Nora Eltahawy. Austin: University of Texas Press.

Abenante, Paola. 2014. "The ambiguity of virtue: Expectations and experiences of piety in the life of a young Egyptian woman." *Ricerca Folklorica* 69.

Abou-El-Fadl, Reem. 2013. "Mohamed Morsi Mubarak: The myth of Egypt's democratic transition." *Jadaliyya*, February 11. http://www.jadaliyya.com/pages/index/10119 /mohamed-morsi-mubarak_the-myth-of-egypts-democrati (accessed May 12, 2013).

Abu-Lughod, Lila. 1992. *Writing Women's Worlds: Bedouin Stories*. Berkeley: University of California Press.

———. 1996a. *Veiled Sentiments: Honour and Poetry in a Bedouin Society*. Cairo: American University of Cairo Press.

———. 1996b. "Honor and shame." In Michael Jackson (ed.), *Things as They Are: New Directions in Phenomenological Anthropology*, 51–69. Bloomington: Indiana University Press.

———. 1998. "Feminist longings and postcolonial conditions." In Lila Abu-Lughod (ed.), *Remaking Women: Feminism and Modernity in the Middle East*, 3–31. Princeton, NJ: Princeton University Press.

———. 2005. *Dramas of Nationhood: The Politics of Television in Egypt*. Cairo: American University in Cairo Press.

Abu l-Ma'ati, 'A. 2006. "Min khawatir al-Sha'rawi ar-ramadaniya: Hikmat al-siyam fi ramadan." *al-Akhbar* (Cairo), September 28: 7.

Abul-Magd, Zeinab. 2011. "The army and the economy in Egypt." *Jadaliyya*, December 23. http://www.jadaliyya.com/pages/index/3732/the-army-and-the-economy -in-egypt (accessed May 12, 2013).

Agrama, Hussein. 2012. *Questioning Secularism: Islam, Sovereignty, and the Rule of Law in Modern Egypt*. Chicago: University of Chicago Press.

Ahmed, Leila. 2011. *A Quiet Revolution: The Veil's Resurgence, from the Middle East to America*. New Haven, CT: Yale University Press.

Aishima, Hatsuki, and Armando Salvatore. 2009. "Doubt, faith, and knowledge: The reconfiguration of the intellectual field in post-Nasserist Cairo." *Journal of the Royal Anthropological Institute* 15, S1: S39–S53.

Ali, Amro. 2012. "Sons of beaches: How Alexandria's ideological battles shape Egypt." *Jadaliyya*, December 29. http://www.jadaliyya.com/pages/index/9311/sons-of -beaches_how-alexandrias-ideological-battle (accessed June 9, 2013).

Allen, Lori. 2008. "Getting by the occupation: How violence became normal during the Second Palestinian Intifada." *Cultural Anthropology* 23, 3: 453–487.

'Amer, Galal. 2012. *Qusr al-Kalam*. Cairo: Shorouk.

Andrews, Walter G. 1985. *Poetry's Voice, Society's Song: Ottoman Lyric Poetry*. Seattle: University of Washington Press.

Andrews, Walter G., and Mehmet Kalpakli. 2005. *The Age of Beloveds: Love and the Beloved in Early-Modern Ottoman and European Culture and Society*. Durham, NC: Duke University Press.

Anjum, Ovamir. 2007. "Islam as a discursive tradition: Talal Asad and his interlocutors." *Comparative Studies of South Asia, Africa and the Middle East* 27, 3: 656–672.

'Antara ibn Shaddad. 1998. "The Poem of Antar." In Paul Halsall (ed.), *Medieval Sourcebook: Pre-Islamic Arabia: The Hanged Poems, before 622 CE*. http://www.fordham .edu/halsall/source/640hangedpoems.asp (accessed July 24, 2014).

Appadurai, Arjun. 1996. *Modernity at Large: Cultural Dimensions of Globalization*. Minneapolis: University of Minnesota Press.

———. 2013. *The Future as Cultural Fact: Essays on the Global Condition*. London: Verso.

Armbrust, Walter. 2002. "The riddle of Ramadan: Media, consumer culture, and the 'Christmasization' of a Muslim holiday." In D. Bowen and E. Early (eds.), *Everyday Life in the Middle East*, 335–348. Bloomington: Indiana University Press.

———. 2011. "The revolution against neoliberalism." *Jadaliyya*, February 23. http://www .jadaliyya.com/pages/index/717/the-revolution-against-neoliberalism (accessed February 24, 2011).

Asad, Talal. 1986. "The idea of an anthropology of Islam." Occasional Papers Series. Washington, DC: Center for Contemporary Arab Studies, Georgetown University.

———. 2003. *Formations of the Secular: Christianity, Islam, Modernity*. Stanford, CA: Stanford University Press.

Asad, Talal, Wendy Brown, Judith Butler, and Saba Mahmood. 2009. "Is critique secular? Blasphemy, injury, and free speech." Townsend Papers in Humanities No. 2. http://escholarship.org/uc/item/84q9c6ft (accessed September 11, 2009).

Assad, Shamei. 2009. *Harat al-nasara*. Cairo: Dar Dawwin.

al-Aswany, Alaa. 2002. *'Imarat Ya'qubiyan*. Cairo: Maktabat Madbuli.

al-'Aydi, Ahmad. 2003. *An takun 'Abbas al-'Abd*. Cairo: Merit.

Bakhtin, Mikhail. 1968. *Rabelais and His World*. Cambridge, MA: MIT Press.

Bataille, Georges. [1949] 1991. *The Accursed Share*. Vol. 1, *Consumption*. Trans. Robert Hurley. New York: Zone Books.

Bauman, Zygmunt. 2000. *Liquid Modernity*. Cambridge, UK: Polity Press.

Bayat, Asef. 2010. *Life as Politics: How Ordinary People Change the Middle East*. Stanford, CA: Stanford University Press.

Becker, Carmen. 2009. "'Gaining knowledge': Salafi activism in German and Dutch online forums." *Masaryk University Journal of Law and Technology* 3, 1: 79–98.

Becker, Felicitas. 2013. "Religious anxieties in two marginal regions: Reformist debates on funerary ritual among Tanzanian and Acehnese Muslims in the twentieth century." *Comparative Studies of South Asia, Africa and the Middle East* 33, 1: 102–116.

Beekers, Daan. 2014. "Pedagogies of piety: Comparing young observant Muslims and Christians in the Netherlands." *Culture and Religion* 15, 1: 72–99.

Behrend, Heike. 2002. "'I am like a movie star in my street': Photographic self-creation in postcolonial Kenya." In Richard Werbner (ed.), *Postcolonial Subjectivities in Africa*, 44–62. London: Zed Books.

Berlant, Laurent. 2011. *Cruel Optimism*. Durham, NC: Duke University Press.

Biehl, João, Byron Good, and Arthur Kleinman (eds.). 2007. *Subjectivity: Ethnographic Investigations*. Berkeley: University of California Press.

Bloch, Ernst. [1959] 1980. *Das Prinzip Hoffnung*. Frankfurt: Suhrkamp.

Bochow, Astrid. 2008. "Valentine's Day in Ghana: Youth, sex and secrets." In Erdmute Alber, Sjaak van der Geest, and Susan R. Whyte (eds.), *Generations in Africa*, 418–429. Hamburg: LIT Verlag.

Bordonaro, Leonardo. 2010. "Modernity as marginality: The making and the experience of peripherality in the Bijagó Islands (Guinea Bissau)." *Cadernos de Estudos Africanos* 18–19: 117–137.

Bourdieu, Pierre. 1984. *Distinction: A Social Critique of the Judgement of Taste*. London: Routledge.

Bowie, Fiona. 2006. *The Anthropology of Religion: An Introduction*. Oxford, UK: Blackwell.

Browers, Michaelle, and Charles Kurzman (eds.). 2004. *An Islamic Reformation?* Lanham, MD: Lexington Books.

Bryant, Christopher G. A. 1985. *Positivism in Social Theory and Research*. London: Macmillan.

Caeiro, Alexandre. 2006. "The shifting moral universes of the Islamic tradition of *ifta*': A diachronic study of four adab al-fatwa manuals." *Muslim World* 19: 661–685.

Camus, Albert. [1951] 1991. *The Rebel: An Essay on Man in Revolt*. Trans. Anthony Bower. New York: Vintage Books.

Carron, Pierre-Nicolas, and Bertrand Yersin. 2009. "Management of the effects of exposure to tear gas." *British Medical Journal* 338: 1554.

Chih, Rachida, and Catherine Mayeur-Jaouen. 2002. "Le cheikh Sha'râwî et la télévision: L'homme qui a donné un visage au Coran." In Catherine Mayeur-Jaouen (ed.), *Saints et héros du Moyen-Orient contemporain*, 189–209. Paris: Maisonneuve et Larose.

Coelho, Paolo. [1988] 1996. *Al-Khaymiya'i* [The Alchemist]. Trans. Bahaa Taher. Cairo: Dar al-Hilal.

Cole, Jennifer, and Lynn Thomas (eds.). 2009. *Love in Africa*. Chicago: University of Chicago Press.

Colla, Elliot. 2012. "In praise of the insult." Presentation at the annual meeting of the American Anthropological Association, San Francisco, November 17.

Comaroff, Jean, and John L. Comaroff. 1999. "Occult economies and the violence of abstraction: Notes from the South African postcolony." *American Ethnologist* 26, 2: 279–303.

Connolly, William E. 2008. *Capitalism and Christianity, American Style*. Durham, NC: Duke University Press.

Dabbagh, Nadia Taysir. 2005. *Suicide in Palestine: Narratives of Despair*. Northampton, MA: Olive Branch Press.

de Boeck, Filip. 2009. "Re/proselytizing in the (post-)colonial city: Kinshasa/Brussel." Public lecture at the conference "Global Prayers to Go: Erlösung und Befreiung in den Megastädten der Welt," Berlin, June 2.

de Certeau, Michel. 1984. *The Practice of Everyday Life*. Trans. Steven Rendall. Berkeley: University of California Press.

de Koning, Anouk. 2009. *Global Dreams: Class, Gender and Public Space in Cosmopolitan Cairo*. Cairo: American University in Cairo Press.

de Koning, Martijn. 2009. "Changing worldviews and friendship: An exploration of the life stories of two female Salafis in the Netherlands." In Roel Meijer (ed.), *Global Salafism: Islam's New Religious Movement*, 404–423. London: Hurst.

———. 2013. "The moral maze: Dutch Salafis and the construction of a moral community of the faithful." *Contemporary Islam* 7, 1: 71–83.

Deeb, Lara. 2006. *An Enchanted Modern: Gender and Public Piety in Shi'i Lebanon*. Princeton, NJ: Princeton University Press.

Demolins, Edmond. 1897. *À quoi tient la supériorité des Anglo-Saxons*. 5th ed. Paris: Maison Didot.

Demolins, Edmond (Idmun Dimulan). 1911. *Sirr taqaddum al-injiliz as-saksuniyin*, Trans. Ahmad Fathi Zaghlul. Cairo: Matba'at al-Gammaliyya.

Detienne, Marcel, and Jean-Pierre Vernant. [1974] 1991. *Cunning Intelligence in Greek Culture and Society*. Trans. Janet Lloyd. Chicago: University of Chicago Press.

Diyab, Muhammad Hafez. 2011. *Intifadat am thawrat fi tarikh Misr al-hadith*. Cairo: Shorouk.

Doehlemann, Martin. 1991. *Langeweile? Deutung eines verbreiteten Phänomens*. Frankfurt am Main: Suhrkamp.

Drieskens, Barbara. 2006. "Spaces of seduction." Unpublished manuscript.

———. 2008. *Living with Jinns: Understanding and Dealing with the Invisible in Cairo*. London: Saqi.

Dunqul, Amal. [1962] 2005. "Kalimat Spartacus al-akhira." In *Al-a'mal al-kamila*, 91–97. Cairo: Maktabat Madbuli.

———. 2012. "Spartacus' Last Words." Trans. by Sumeela Mubayi. *Jadaliyya*, August 23. http://www.jadaliyya.com/pages/index/6998/amal-dunqul_spartacus-last-words (accessed July 27, 2014).

Eckert, Julia. 2009. "The social dynamics of communal violence in India." *International Journal of Conflict and Violence* 3, 2: 172–187.

Eickelman, Dale. 1992. "Mass higher education and the religious imagination in contemporary Arab societies." *American Ethnologist* 9, 4: 643–655.

———. 1998. "Inside the Islamic reformation." *Wilson Quarterly* 22, 1: 80–89.

Ekholm Friedman, Kajsa, and Jonathan Friedman. 2011. *Modernities, Class, and the Contradictions of Globalization: The Anthropology of Global Systems*. Walnut Creek, CA: Altamira Press.

El Shakry, Omnia. 2007. *The Great Social Laboratory: Subjects of Knowledge in Colonial and Postcolonial Egypt*. Stanford, CA: Stanford University Press.

Elsässer, Sebastian. 2014. *The Coptic Question in the Mubarak Era*. Oxford: Oxford University Press.

Elsayed, Heba. 2010. "The unlikely young cosmopolitans of Cairo." *Arab Media and Society* 12. http://www.arabmediasociety.com/?article=760 (accessed June 6, 2011).

Elyachar, Julia. 2005. *Markets of Dispossession: NGOs, Economic Development, and the State in Cairo*. Durham, NC: Duke University Press.

———. 2011. "The political economy of movement and gesture in Cairo." *Journal of the Royal Anthropological Institute* 17: 82–99.

Ewing, Catherine. 1990. "The illusion of wholeness: Culture, self, and the experience of inconsistency." *Ethos* 18: 251–278.

Ez El-Din, Amr. 2010. *Khaltabita: Kuktil misri sakhir.* Cairo: Dar Layla.

Fadil, Nadia. 2009. "Managing affects and sensibilities: The case of not-handshaking and not-fasting." *Social Anthropology* 17, 4: 439–454.

Fadl, Bilal. 2005. *Bani Bajam.* Cairo: Merit.

Fawzi, Esam. 1992. "Anmat at-tadayyun fi Misr: Madkhal li-fahm at-tafkir al-sha'bi hawl ad-din." In *Ishkaliyat at-takwin al-ijtima'i wa-l-fikriyat al-sha'biya fi Misr*, 214–248. Nicosia: Mu'assasat 'Ibal li-al-dirasat wa-al-nashr.

Fehérvary, Krisztina. 2013. *Politics in Color and Concrete: Socialist Materialities and the Middle Class in Hungary.* Bloomington: Indiana University Press.

Fenichel, Otto. 1953. "The psychology of boredom." In *The Collected Papers of Otto Fenichel*, 292–302. New York: Norton.

Ferguson, James. 2006. *Global Shadows: Africa in the Neoliberal World Order.* Durham, NC: Duke University Press.

Fortier, Corinne. 2004. "Séduction, jalousie et défi entre hommes: Chorégraphie des affects et des corps dans la société maure." In Françoise Héritier and Margarita Xanthakou (eds.), *Corps et affects*, 237–254. Paris: Odile Jacob.

Foucault, Michel. 1977. *Discipline and Punish: The Birth of Prison.* New York: Pantheon Books.

———. 1984. *L'usage des plaisirs.* Vol. 2 of *Histoire de la sexualité*. Paris: Gallimard.

———. 2007. *Security, Territory, Population: Lectures at the Collège de France 1977–1978.* Ed. Michel Senellart, trans. by Graham Burchell. London: Palgrave Macmillan.

Friedman, Milton. 1962. *Capitalism and Freedom.* Chicago: University of Chicago Press.

Gable, Eric. 2010. "Worldliness in out of the way places." *Cadernos de Estudos Africanos* 18–19: 75–90.

Gadamer, Hans-Georg. 1975. *Wahrheit und Methode: Grundzüge einer philosophischen Hermeneutik.* 4th ed. Tübingen: J. C. B. Mohr (Paul Siebeck).

Gaibazzi, Paolo. 2013. "In search of luck: Destiny, work and the unexpected in Muslim Gambia." Presentation at the staff seminar of Zentrum Moderner Orient, Berlin, April 18.

Gauvain, Richard. 2012. *Salafi Ritual Purity: In the Presence of God.* London: Routledge.

Ghannam, Farha. 2002. *Remaking the Modern: Space, Relocation, and the Politics of Identity in a Global Cairo.* Berkeley: University of California Press.

———. 2013. *Live and Die Like a Man: Gender Dynamics in Urban Egypt.* Stanford, CA: Stanford University Press.

al-Ghazali, Abu Hamid. 1995 [d. 1111]. *On Disciplining the Soul and on Breaking the Two Desires, Books XXII and XXIII of The Revival of the Religious Sciences.* Trans. T. J. Winter. Cambridge, UK: Islamic Texts Society.

Gilsenan, Michael. 2000. *Recognizing Islam: Religion and Society in the Modern Middle East.* Rev. ed. London: I. B. Tauris.

Girke, Felix. 2008. "For an anti-literalist anthropology." Presentation at the EASA biannual conference, Ljubljana, August 28.

Gluckman, Max. 1995. *Custom and Conflict in Africa.* Oxford, UK: Blackwell.

Goodstein, Elizabeth. 2005. *Experience without Qualities: Boredom and Modernity.* Stanford, CA: Stanford University Press.

Graeber, David. 2011. *Debt: The First 5,000 Years.* New York: Melville House.

Gräf, Bettina, and Jakob Skovgaard-Petersen (eds.). 2009. *The Global Mufti: The Phenomenon of Yusuf al-Qaradawi*. London: Hurst.

Graw, Knut. 2012. "On the cause of migration: Being and nothingness in the African-European border zone." In Knut Graw and Samuli Schielke (eds.), *The Global Horizon: Expectations of Migration in Africa and the Middle East*, 23–42. Leuven: Leuven University Press.

Graw, Knut, and Samuli Schielke (eds.). 2012. *The Global Horizon: Expectations of Migration in Africa and the Middle East*. Leuven: Leuven University Press.

Gregg, Gary S. 2007. *Culture and Identity in a Muslim Society*. Oxford: Oxford University Press.

Habermas, Jürgen. 1969. "Gegen einen positivistisch halbierten Rationalismus." In Theodor Adorno, Hans Albert, Ralf Dahrendorf, Jürgen Habermas, Harald Pilot, and Karl Popper (eds.), *Der Positivismusstreit in der deutschen Soziologie*, 235–266. Neuwied, West Germany: Luchterhand.

Hafez, Sherine. 2011. *An Islam of Her Own: Reconsidering Religion and Secularism in Women's Islamic Movements*. New York: New York University Press.

Hage, Ghassan. 2002. "'On the side of life'—Joy and the capacity of being" (interview by Mary Zournazi). In Mary Zournazi, *Hope: New Philosophies for Change*, 150–171. Sydney: Pluto Press.

———. 2003. *Against Paranoid Nationalism: Searching for Hope in a Shrinking Society*. Sydney: Pluto Press.

Hansen, Karen Tranberg. 2005. "Getting stuck in the compound: Some odds against social adulthood in Lusaka, Zambia." *Africa Today* 51: 3–16.

Hardt, Michael, and Antonio Negri. 2000. *Empire*. Cambridge, MA: Harvard University Press.

Hart, Kimberly. 2007. "Love by arrangement: The ambiguity of 'spousal choice' in a Turkish village." *Journal of the Royal Anthropological Institute* 13: 345–362.

Heath, Peter. 1996. *Sirat Antar and the Arabic Popular Epic*. Salt Lake City: University of Utah Press.

Heiman, Rachel, Carla Freeman, and Mark Liechty (eds.). 2012. *The Global Middle Classes*. Santa Fe, NM: School for Advanced Research Press.

Heo, Angie. 2013a. "The bodily threat of miracles: Security, sacramentality, and the Egyptian politics of public order." *American Ethnologist* 40, 1: 149–163.

———. 2013b. "Saints, media and minority cultures: On Coptic cults of Egyptian revolution from Alexandria to Maspero." In Andreas Bandak and Mikkel Bille (eds.), *Politics of Worship in the Contemporary Middle East: Sainthood in Fragile States*, 53–71. Leiden: Brill.

Hibou, Beatrix. 2011. *The Force of Obedience: The Political Economy of Repression in Tunisia*. Trans. Andrew Brown. Cambridge, UK: Polity Press.

Higazi, Ahmad Magdi. 2005. *al-Mukhaddirat wa-l-azma al-rahina lil-shabab al-misri*. Cairo: Markaz al-buhuth wa-l-dirasat al-ijtima'iya, Faculty of Letters, Cairo University.

High, Holly (ed.). 2012. Special issue of *Social Anthropology* 20, 4.

Hirschkind, Charles. 2006a. "Cassette ethics: Public piety and popular media in Egypt." In Birgit Meyer and Annelies Moors (eds.), *Religion, Media, and the Public Sphere*, 29–51. Bloomington: Indiana University Press.

———. 2006b. *The Ethical Soundscape: Cassette Sermons and Islamic Counter-Publics.* New York: Columbia University Press.

———. 2011. "The road to Tahrir." *The Immanent Frame*, February 9. http://blogs.ssrc .org/tif/2011/02/09/the-road-to-tahrir/ (accessed June 27, 2011).

Ho, Karen. 2005. "Situating global capitalisms: A view from Wall Street investment banks." *Cultural Anthropology* 20, 1: 68–96.

Hoofdar, Homa. 1999. *Between Marriage and the Market: Intimate Politics and Survival in Cairo.* Cairo: American University in Cairo Press.

Hopkins, Nicholas S., and Kirsten Westergaard. 1998. *Directions of Change in Rural Egypt.* Cairo: American University in Cairo Press.

Hudson, Leila. 2004. "Reading al-Sha'rani: The Sufi genealogy of Islamic modernism in late Ottoman Damascus." *Journal of Islamic Studies* 15, 1: 39–68.

Ingold, Tim. 2011. *Being Alive: Essays on Movement, Knowledge and Description.* London: Routledge.

Inhorn, Marcia. 2007. "Loving your infertile Muslim spouse: Notes on the globalization of IVF and its romantic commitments in Sunni Egypt and Shi'ite Lebanon." In Mark B. Padilla, Jennifer S. Hirsch, Miguel Muñoz-Laboy, Robert Sember, and Richard G. Parker (eds.), *Love and Globalization: Transformations of Intimacy in the Contemporary World*, 139–160. Nashville, TN: Vanderbilt University Press.

Ismail, Salwa. 2013. "Piety, profit and the market in Cairo: A political economy of Islamisation." *Contemporary Islam* 7: 107–128.

Jackson, Michael (ed.). 1996. *Things as They Are: New Directions in Phenomenological Anthropology.* Bloomington: Indiana University Press.

Jackson, Michael. 1998. *Minima ethnographica: Intersubjectivity and the Anthropological Project.* Chicago: University of Chicago Press.

———. 2005. *Existential Anthropology: Events, Exigencies and Effects.* Oxford, UK: Berghahn Books.

———. 2009. "The shock of the new: On migrant imaginaries and critical transitions." *Ethnos* 73, 1: 57–72.

———. 2011. *Life within Limits: Well-Being in a World of Want.* Durham, NC: Duke University Press.

Jahin, Salah. 1987. *Ruba'iyat.* Cairo: Markaz al-Ahram li-t-tarjama wa-l-nashr.

al-Jakh, Hisham. 2010. *Juha* (video). http://www.youtube.com/watch?v=27jVymklmtU (accessed June 27, 2011).

Janson, Marloes. 2013. *Islam, Youth, and Modernity in the Gambia: The Tablighi Jama'at.* Cambridge: Cambridge University Press, International African Library.

Jeffrey, Craig. 2010. *Timepass: Youth, Class, and the Politics of Waiting in India.* Stanford, CA: Stanford University Press.

Johansen, Birgitte, and Riem Spielhaus. 2012. "Counting deviance: Revisiting a decade's production of surveys among Muslims in Western Europe." *Journal of Muslims in Europe* 1: 81–112.

Jones, Carla. 2010. "Materializing piety: Gendered anxieties about faithful consumption in contemporary urban Indonesia." *American Ethnologist* 38, 1: 58–72.

Joseph, Suad (ed.). 1999. *Intimate Selving in Arab Families: Gender, Self and Identity.* Syracuse, NY: Syracuse University Press.

Jurkiewicz, Sarah. 2011. "Blogging as counterpublic? The Lebanese and the Egyptian blogosphere in comparison." In Nadja-Christina Schneider and Bettina Gräf (eds.), *Social Dynamics 2.0: Researching Change in Times of Media Convergence*, 27–47. Berlin: Frank & Timme.

Karlsson Minganti, Pia. 2007. "Muslima: Islamisk väckelse och unga kvinnors förhandlingar om genus i det samtida Sverige." PhD diss., Stockholms Universitet, Stockholm.

———. 2008. "Becoming a 'practicing' Muslim—Reflections on gender, racism and religious identity in a Swedish Muslim youth organisation." *Elore* 15, 1: 1–16. http://www.elore.fi/arkisto/1_08/kam1_08.pdf (accessed July 27, 2014).

Kaya, Laura Pearl. 2010. "The criterion of consistency: Women's self-presentation at Yarmouk University, Jordan." *American Ethnologist* 37, 3: 526–538.

al-Khamisi, Khalid. 2006. *Taxi*. Cairo: Shorouk.

Khan, Navida. 2013. *Muslim Becoming: Aspiration and Scepticism in Pakistan*. Durham, NC: Duke University Press.

al-Khashshab, 'Umar. 2006. "Fi multaqa l-fikr al-islami: al-intisar 'ala shahawat an-nafs tadrib lil-intisar fi ma'arik al-hayat." *al-Akhbar*, September 28: 7.

Kingfisher, Catherine, and Jeff Maskovsky. 2008. "The limits of neoliberalism." *Critique of Anthropology* 28, 2: 115–126.

Klapp, Orin E. 1986. *Overload and Boredom: Essays on the Quality of Life in the Information Society*. New York: Greenwood Press.

Klemm, Verena. 2000. "Different notions of commitment (iltizam) and committed literature (al-adab al-multazim) in the literary circles of the Mashriq." *Middle Eastern Literatures* 3, 1: 51–62.

Kreil, Aymon. 2012. "Du rapport au dire: Sexe, amour et discours d'expertise au Caire." PhD diss., École des hautes études en sciences sociales (Paris) and Université de Neuchâtel.

Kuhn, Thomas. 1996. *The Structure of Scientific Revolutions*. 3rd ed. Chicago: University of Chicago Press.

Laidlaw, James. 2002. "For an anthropology of ethics and freedom." *Journal of the Royal Anthropological Institute* 8, 2: 311–332.

———. 2013. *The Subject of Virtue: An Anthropology of Ethics and Freedom*. Cambridge: Cambridge University Press.

Lakatos, Imre, and Alan Musgrave (eds.). 1970. *Criticism and the Growth of Knowledge: Proceedings of the International Colloquium in the Philosophy of Science*. Cambridge: Cambridge University Press.

Lambek, Michael. 2000. "The anthropology of religion and the quarrel between poetry and philosophy." *Current Anthropology* 41, 3: 309–320.

———. 2002. "Nuriaty, the saint, and the sultan: Virtuous subject and subjective virtuoso of the postmodern colony." In Richard Webner (ed.), *Postcolonial Subjectivities in Africa*, 25–43. London: Zed Books.

———. 2007. "Sacrifice and the problem of beginning: Meditations from Sakalava mythopraxis." *Journal of the Royal Anthropological Institute* 13: 19–38.

——— (ed.). 2010. *Ordinary Ethics: Anthropology, Language, and Action*. New York: Fordham University Press.

Larkin, Brian. 1997. "Indian films and Nigerian lovers: Media and the creation of parallel modernities." *Africa* 67: 406–440.

Lauzière, Henri. 2010. "The construction of Salafiyya: Reconsidering Salafism from the perspective of conceptual history." *International Journal for Middle East Studies* 42: 369–389.

Lecky, William Edward Hartpole. [1896] 1903. *Democracy and Liberty*. 2 vols. New York: Longman, Green & Co. http://www.archive.org/details/democracyandlibe01 leckiala (accessed September 7, 2008).

Leve, Lauren G. 2002. "Subjects, selves, and the politics of personhood in Theravada Buddhism in Nepal." *Journal of Asian Studies* 61, 3: 833–860.

LeVine, Mark. 2013. "The revolution, back in black." *Aljazeera* (English), February 2. http://www.aljazeera.com/indepth/opinion/2013/02/201322103219816676.html (accessed June 9, 2013).

Loimeier, Roman. 2005. "Is there something like 'Protestant Islam'?" *Die Welt des Islams* 45, 2: 216–254.

Luhrmann, Tanya M. 2006. "Subjectivity." *Anthropological Theory* 6: 345–361.

Lutfi, Wa'il. 2009. *Zahirat al-du'at al-judud*. 2nd ed. Cairo: Dar al-'Ayn li-l-nashr.

Macleod, Arlene Elowe. 1991. *Accommodating Protest: Working Women, the New Veiling, and Change in Cairo*. New York: Columbia University Press.

Maguire, Thomas E. R. 2009. "'A light in every home': Huda TV's articulation of Orthodox Sunni Islam in the global mediascape." PhD diss., University of Texas at Austin.

Mahmood, Saba. 2003. "Ethical formation and politics of individual autonomy in contemporary Egypt." *Social Research* 70, 3: 837–866.

———. 2005. *Politics of Piety: The Islamic Revival and the Feminist Subject*. Princeton, NJ: Princeton University Press.

———. 2009. "Religious reason and secular affect: An incommensurable divide?" In Talal Asad, Wendy Brown, Judith Butler, and Saba Mahmood, *Is Critique Secular? Blasphemy, Injury, and Free Speech* (Townsend Papers in Humanities; 2), 64–100. http://escholarship.org/uc/item/84q9c6ft (accessed September 11, 2009).

———. 2012. "Sectarian conflict and family law in Egypt." *American Ethnologist* 39, 1: 54–62.

Mains, Daniel. 2007. "Neoliberal times: Progress, boredom, and shame among young men in urban Ethiopia." *American Ethnologist* 34: 659–673.

Majnun. 2003. *Le fou de Layla: Le diwan de Majnun*. Ed. and trans. André Miquel. Arles, France: Sindbad and Actes Sud.

*Malcolm X* (blog). "Su'ar Wasat al-madina al-jinsi." October 25, 2006. http://malek-x.net /node/268 (accessed June 25, 2007).

*Manal and Alaa's Bit Bucket* (blog). "Kull sana wa-antum tayyibin bada' 'id hatk al-'ard bidayatan muwaffaqa." October 25, 2006. http://www.manalaa.net/sexual _harrasement_and_eid (accessed June 25, 2007).

Marsden, Magnus. 2005. *Living Islam: Muslim Religious Experience in Pakistan's North-West Frontier*. Cambridge: Cambridge University Press.

———. 2007a. "Cosmopolitanism on Pakistan's frontier." *ISIM Review* 19: 6–7.

———. 2007b. "Love and elopement in northern Pakistan." *Journal of the Royal Anthropological Institute* 13: 91–108.

———. 2008. "Muslim cosmopolitans? Transnational life in northern Pakistan." *Journal of Asian Studies* 67, 1: 213–247.

———. 2010. "Cultivating a complex character." Public lecture at Zentrum Moderner Orient, Berlin, November 25.

Marx, Karl. [1852] 2006. *The Eighteenth Brumaire of Louis Napoleon.* http://www.marx ists.org/archive/marx/works/1852/18th-brumaire/ (accessed June 9, 2013).

Masquelier, Adeline. 2005. "The scorpion's sting: Youth, marriage and the struggle for social maturity in Niger." *Journal of the Royal Anthropological Institute* 11: 59–83.

———. 2007. "Negotiating futures: Islam, youth, and the state in Niger." In Benjamin F. Soares and Rene Otayek (eds.), *Islam and Muslim Politics in Africa*, 243–262. New York: Palgrave Macmillan.

———. 2009. "Lessons from Rubí: Love, poverty, and the educational value of televised dramas in Niger." In Jennifer Cole and Lynn Thomas (eds.), *Love in Africa*, 204–228. Chicago: University of Chicago Press.

———. 2013. "Teatime: Boredom and the temporalities of young men in Niger." *Africa* 83, 3: 385–402.

Matar, Iman. 2006. "Ukaziyun al-maghfara." *Ruz al-Yusuf*, September 29: 23–24.

Matuschek, Ingo. 1999. "Zeit und Devianz: Zeitorientierung, Langeweile und abweichendes Verhalten bei Jugendlichen." PhD diss., Humbold-Universität Berlin.

Maurer, Bill. 2006. "The anthropology of money." *Annual Review of Anthropology*, 35: 15–36.

Mauss, Marcel. [1924] 2007. *Essai sur le don: Forme et raison de l'échange dans les sociétés archaïques.* Paris: Quadrige and puf.

Mehanna, Omnia. 2010. "Sexuality online: Obtaining knowledge and counseling through a faith-based website in Egypt." In Oka Obono (ed.), *A Tapestry of Human Sexuality in Africa*, 119–136. Johannesburg: Jacana Media.

Mehrez, Samia (ed.). 2012. *Translating the Egyptian Revolution: The Language of Tahrir.* Cairo: American University in Cairo Press.

Meijer, Roel (ed.). 2009. *Global Salafism: Islam's New Religious Movement.* London: Hurst.

Meijl, Toon van. 2006. "Multiple identifications and the dialogical self: Urban Maori youngsters and the cultural renaissance." *Journal of the Royal Anthropological Institute* 12: 917–933.

Menin, Laura. 2012. "Crafting lives, negotiating ambivalence: Love, friendship and intimacy amongst Moroccan young women." PhD diss., University of Milano-Bicocca, Italy.

Merleau-Ponty, Maurice. [1945] 2005. *Phenomenology of Perception.* Trans. Colin Smith. London: Routledge.

Meyer, Birgit. 1998. "'Make a complete break with the past': Memory and post-colonial modernity in Ghanaian Pentecostalist discourse." *Journal of Religion in Africa* 28, 3: 316–349.

Meyer, Birgit, and Annelies Moors (eds.). 2006. *Religion, Media, and the Public Sphere.* Bloomington: Indiana University Press.

Meyer Spacks, Patricia. 1995. *Boredom: The Literary History of a State of Mind.* Chicago: University of Chicago Press.

Miller, Daniel. [1987] 1993. *Material Culture and Mass Consumption.* 2nd ed. Oxford, UK: Blackwell.

———. 2008. *The Comfort of Things*. Cambridge, UK: Polity Press.

———. 2012. *Consumption and Its Consequences*. Cambridge, UK: Polity Press.

Mitchell, Jon. 2007. "A fourth critic of the Enlightenment: Michel Certeau and the ethnography of subjectivity." *Social Anthropology* 15, 1: 89–106.

Mitchell, Timothy. 1988. *Colonising Egypt*. Cambridge: Cambridge University Press.

———. 2002. *Rule of Experts: Egypt, Techno-politics, Modernity*. Berkeley: University of California Press.

Mittermaier, Amira. 2011. *Dreams That Matter: Egyptian Landscapes of the Imagination*. Berkeley: University of California Press.

Miyazaki, Hirokazu. 2006. "Economy of dreams: Hope in global capitalism and its critiques." *Cultural Anthropology* 21, 2: 147–172.

Moors, Annelies. 2006. "Representing family law debates: Gender and the politics of presence." In Birgit Meyer and Annelies Moors (eds.), *Media, Religion and the Public Sphere*, 115–131. Bloomington: Indiana University Press.

———. 2009. "'Islamic fashion' in Europe: Religious conviction, authentic style, and creative consumption." *Encounters* 1, 1: 175–199.

Najmabadi, Afsaneh. 1993. "Veiled discourse—Unveiled bodies." *Feminist Studies* 19, 3: 487–518.

Onodera, Henri. 2009. "The Kifaya generation: Politics of change among youth in Egypt." *Suomen Antropologi: Journal of the Finnish Anthropological Society* 34, 4: 44–64.

Orsi, Robert. A. 2005. *Between Heaven and Earth: The Religious Worlds People Make and the Scholars Who Study Them*. Princeton, NJ: Princeton University Press.

Osella, Filippo, and Caroline Osella. 2009. "Muslim entrepreneurs in public life between India and the Gulf: Making good and doing good." *Journal of the Royal Anthropological Institute* 15, S1: S194–S212.

Oustinova-Stjepanovic, Galina. 2011. "Performative failure among Islamic mystics in urban Macedonia." PhD diss., University College London.

Padilla, Mark B., Jennifer S. Hirsch, Miguel Muñoz-Laboy, Robert Sember, and Richard G. Parker. 2007. "Introduction: Cross-cultural reflections on an intimate intersection." In Mark B. Padilla, Jennifer S. Hirsch, Miguel Muñoz-Laboy, Robert Sember, and Richard G. Parker (eds.), *Love and Globalization: Transformations of Intimacy in the Contemporary World*, ix–xxxi. Nashville, TN: Vanderbilt University Press.

Pahwa, Sonali. 2010. "Culturing the self: The privatization of personal development in neoliberal Egypt." Public lecture at Centrum für Nah- und Mitteloststudien, Philipps-Universität Marburg, Germany, April 27.

Pandolfo, Stefania. 2007. "'The burning': Finitude and the politico-theological imagination of illegal migration." *Anthropological Theory* 7, 3: 329–363.

Pepe, Teresa. 2014. *Fictionalized Identities in the Egyptian Blogosphere*. PhD diss., University of Oslo.

Peterson, Jennifer. 2012. "Going to the mulid: Street-smart spirituality in Egypt." In Samuli Schielke and Liza Debevec (eds.), *Ordinary Lives and Grand Schemes: An Anthropology of Everyday Religion*. New York: Berghahn Books.

Peterson, Mark Allen. 2011. *Connected in Cairo: Growing Up Cosmopolitan in the Modern Middle East*. Bloomington: Indiana University Press.

Piot, Charles. 1999. *Remotely Global: Village Modernity in West Africa*. Chicago: University of Chicago Press.

———. 2010. *Nostalgia for the Future: West Africa after the Cold War*. Chicago: University of Chicago Press.

Polanyi, Karl. [1944] 2001. *The Great Transformation: The Political and Economic Origins of Our Time*. Boston: Beacon Press.

Pollock, Sheldon. 2002. "Cosmopolitan and vernacular in history." In Sheldon Pollock, Homi K. Bhabha, Carol A. Breckenridge, and Dipesh Chakrabarty (eds.), *Cosmopolitanism*, 15–53. Durham, NC: Duke University Press.

Popper, Karl. [1957] 2002. *The Poverty of Historicism*. London: Routledge.

Rabo, Aannika. 2006. "Aleppo traders and the Syrian state." In A. Rabo and B. Utas (eds.), *The Role of the State in West Asia*, 115–127. Swedish Research Institute in Istanbul, Transactions, No. 14. London: I. B. Tauris.

Reichmuth, Stefan. 2009. *The World of Murtada al-Zabidi (1732–91): Life, Networks and Writings*. Cambridge, UK: E. J. W. Gibb Memorial Trust.

Reuter, Bärbel. 1999. *Gelebte Religion: Religiöse Praxis junger Islamistinnen in Kairo*. Würzburg: Ergon Verlag.

Revers, Wilhelm Josef. 1949. *Psychologie der Langeweile*. Meisenheim, West Germany: Westkulturverlag Anton Hain.

Ring, Laura. 2006. *Zenana: Everyday Peace in a Karachi Apartment Building*. Bloomington: Indiana University Press.

Robbins, Joel. 2004. *Becoming Sinners: Christianity and Moral Torment in a Papua New Guinea Society*. Berkeley: University of California Press.

Rommel, Carl. 2013. "When affect is no more: Exploring alterations in football's ability to affect from the late Mubarak era until the present." Presentation at the workshop "Affective Politics in Transitional North Africa: Imagining the Future," Swedish Institute in Alexandria, May 27–28.

Rouch, Jean. 1958. *Moi, un noir (Treichville)*. Documentary film. France: Films de la Pléiade.

Roy, Olivier. 1999. "Le post-islamisme." *Revue des mondes musulmans et de la Méditerraée* 85–86: 11–30.

Rudnyckyj, Daromir. 2009. "Spiritual economies: Islam and neoliberalism in contemporary Indonesia." *Cultural Anthropology* 24, 1: 104–141.

Ryzova, Lucie. 2008. "Efendification: The rise of middle class culture in modern Egypt." PhD diss., University of Oxford.

———. 2012. "The battle of Cairo's Muhammad Mahmoud Street." *Aljazeera*, November 29. http://www.aljazeera.com/indepth/opinion/2011/11/20111288494638419.html (accessed July 27, 2014).

Saad, Nirvana. 2010. "Ramadan culture in modern Cairo: Young females' leisure patterns and the politics of piety, unity and authenticity." PhD diss., Rijksuniversiteit Groningen, Netherlands.

Said, Edward. 1983. *The World, the Text, and the Critic*. Cambridge, MA.: Harvard University Press.

Salama, Ali. 2007. *'Ala bab sifarit Canada* (video). http://www.youtube.com/watch?v= vh8qFVFnfVw (accessed June 27, 2011).

Sanders, Todd. 2009. "Invisible hands and visible goods: Revealed and concealed economies in millenial Tanzania." In Liv Haram and C. Bawa Yamba (eds.),

*Dealing with Uncertainty in Contemporary African Lives*, 91–117. Uppsala, Sweden: Nordiska Afrikainstitutet.

Sartre, Jean-Paul. 1949. *What Is Literature?* Trans. Bernard Frechtman. New York: Philosophical Library. https://archive.org/details/whatisliterature030271mbp (accessed July 27, 2014).

Schielke, Samuli. 2006. "Sakralisierung des Alltags und Banalisierung des Heiligen: Religion und Konsum in Ägypten." Working Paper No. 69, Department of Anthropology and African Studies of Johannes Gutenberg University of Mainz. http://www.ifeas.uni-mainz.de/workingpapers/AP69.pdf (accessed July 27, 2014).

———. 2007. "Hegemonic encounters: Criticism of saints-day festivals and the formation of modern Islam in late 19th and early 20th-century Egypt." *Die Welt des Islams* 47, 3–4: 319–355.

———. 2008. "Mystic states, motherly virtues: Female participation and leadership in an Egyptian Sufi milieu." *Journal for Islamic Studies* (Capetown) 28: 94–126.

———. 2009a. "Ambivalent commitments: Troubles of morality, religiosity and aspiration among young Egyptians." *Journal of Religion in Africa* 39, 2: 158–185.

———. 2009b. "Being good in Ramadan: Ambivalence, fragmentation and the moral self in the lives of young Egyptians." *Journal of the Royal Anthropological Institute* 15, S1: S23–S38.

———. 2012a. *The Perils of Joy: Contesting Mulid Festivals in Contemporary Egypt.* Syracuse, NY: Syracuse University Press.

———. 2012b. "Some social science of the presidential elections." *You'll Be Late for the Revolution: An Anthropologist's Diary of the Egyptian Revolution and What Followed* (blog), May 25. http://samuliegypt.blogspot.de/2012/05/some-social-science-of-presidential.html (accessed June 9, 2013).

———. 2014. "There will be blood: Expecting violence in Egypt, 2011–2013." *You'll Be Late for the Revolution: An Anthropologist's Diary of the Egyptian Revolution and What Followed* (blog). http://samuliegypt.blogspot.de/2014/06/there-will-be-blood.html (accessed July 27, 2014).

Schielke, Samuli, and Liza Debevec (eds.). 2012. *Ordinary Lives and Grand Schemes: An Anthropology of Everyday Religion.* New York: Berghahn Books.

Schmidt, Leigh Eric. 1993. "The fashioning of a modern holiday: St. Valentine's Day, 1840–1870." *Winterthur Portfolio* 28, 4: 209–245.

Schulz, Dorothea. 2011. "Renewal and enlightenment: Muslim women's biographic narratives of personal reform in Mali." *Journal of Religion in Africa* 41: 93–123.

Scott, David. 2004. *Conscripts of Modernity: The Tragedy of Colonial Enlightenment.* Durham, NC: Duke University Press.

Scott, James C. 1998. *Seeing Like a State: How Certain Schemes to Improve the Human Condition Have Failed.* New Haven, CT: Yale University Press.

Scott Meisami, Julie. 1987. *Medieval Persian Court Poetry.* Princeton, NJ: Princeton University Press.

Seyed-Gohrab, Ali Asghar. 2003. *Layli and Majnun: Love, Madness and Mystic Longing in Nizami's Epic Romance.* Leiden: Brill, 2003.

Sha'ban, Khalid. 2006. "al-Siyam wa-l-shabab." *al-Akhbar* (Cairo), October 9: 4.

Shawki, Ahmed. 1933. *Majnun Layla: A Poetical Drama in Five Acts.* Trans. Arthur John Arberry. Cairo: A. Lencioni.

Shehata, Muhammad Saad. 2002. *Hawamish kharij al-matn: Shiʻr.* Cairo: al-Hayʻa al-misriyya al-ʻamma li-l-kitab.

Shehata, Mukhtar Saad. 2010. *La li-l-Iskandariya.* Cairo: Arabesque.

———. 2013. "Al-ʻatifa wa al-siyasa." *al-Hiwar al-Mutamaddin,* June 18. http://www.ahewar.org/debat/show.art.asp?aid=364672 (accessed November 29, 2013).

Shehata, Mukhtar Saad, and Samuli Schielke. 2010. *Al-Nahya al-tanya [The Other Side].* Short film, Egypt and the Netherlands.

———. 2013. *Al-ʻAsima al-sirriya [The Secret Capital].* Documentary film, Egypt.

Shehata, Saʻid. 2010. *Halimt bih. wi-nsit: Ashʻar bi al-ʻammiya al-misriya.* Cairo: Kitab al-Yawm/al-Qiraʾa li al-gamiʾ.

Shenoda, Anthony. 2010. "Cultivating mystery: Miracles and a Coptic moral imaginary." PhD diss., Harvard University, Cambridge, MA.

Shever, Elana. 2008. "Neoliberal associations: Property, company, and family in the Argentine oil fields." *American Ethnologist* 35, 4: 701–716.

Shore, Cris. 2008. "Audit culture and illiberal governance." *Anthropological Theory* 8, 3: 278–298.

al-Shurbasi, Ahmad. 2006. "al-Sawm madrasat tahdhib." *al-Azhar* 79, 9: 1428–1431.

Simmel, Georg. [1900] 1989. *Philosophie des Geldes.* Frankfurt: Suhrkamp.

Simon, Gregory. 2009. "The soul freed of cares? Islamic prayer, subjectivity, and the contradictions of moral selfhood in Minangkabau, Indonesia." *American Ethnologist* 36, 2: 258–275.

———. 2012. "Conviction without being convinced: Maintaining Islamic certainty in Minangkabau, Indonesia." *Ethos* 40, 3: 237–257.

Smilde, David. 2007. *Reason to Believe: Cultural Agency in Latin American Evangelicalism.* Berkeley: University of California Press.

Smith, Adam. [1776] 2005. *An Inquiry into the Nature and Causes of the Wealth of Nations.* Electronics Classics Series, Pennsylvania State University. http://www2.hn.psu.edu/faculty/jmanis/adam-smith/wealth-nations.pdf (accessed June 9, 2013).

Sobhy, Hania. 2009. "Amr Khaled and young muslim elites: Islamism and the consolidation of mainstream Muslim piety in Egypt." In Diane Singermann (ed.), *Cairo Contested: Governance, Urban Space, and Global Modernity,* 414–454. Cairo: American University in Cairo Press.

Soloveitchik, Haym. 1994. "Rupture and reconstruction: The transformation of contemporary orthodoxy." *Tradition* 28, 4: 64–130.

Spronk, Rachel. 2009. "Media and the therapeutic ethos of romantic love in middle-class Nairobi." In Jennifer Cole and Lynn M. Thomas (eds.), *Love in Africa,* 181–203. Chicago: University of Chicago Press.

Spyer, Patricia. 1997. "The eroticism of debt: Pearl divers, traders, and sea wives in the Ary Islands, eastern Indonesia." *American Ethnologist* 24, 3: 515–538.

Starrett, Gregory. 1995a. "The hexis of interpretation: Islam and the body in the Egyptian popular school." *American Ethnologist* 22, 4: 953–969.

———. 1995b. "The political economy of religious commodities in Cairo." *American Anthropologist* 97: 51–68.

———. 1998. *Putting Islam to Work: Education, Politics, and Religious Transformation in Egypt.* Berkeley: University of California Press. http://ark.cdlib.org/ark:/13030/ft4q2nb3gp/ (accessed November 2, 2008).

———. 2010. "The varieties of secular experience." *Comparative Studies in Society and History* 52, 3: 626–651.

Stauth, Georg. 2010. *Herausforderung Ägypten: Religion und Authentizität in der globalen Moderne*. Bielefeld: Transcript Verlag.

Steinbeck, John. [1936] 1961. *In Dubious Battle*. New York: Bantam Books.

Stephan, Manja. 2010. *Das Bedürfnis nach Ausgewogenheit: Moralerziehung, Islam und Muslimsein in Tadschikistan zwischen Säkularisierung und religiöser Rückbesinnung*. Würzburg: Ergon Verlag.

Stokes, Martin. 2002. "Afterword: Recognizing the everyday." In D. Kandiyoti and A. Saktanber (eds.), *Fragments of Culture: The Everyday of Modern Turkey*, 322–338. London: I. B. Tauris.

Stöltzner, Michael, and Thomas Uebel (eds.). 2006. *Wiener Kreis. Texte zur wissenschaftlichen Weltauffassung von Rudolf Carnap, Otto Neurath, Moritz Schlick, Philipp Frank, Hans Hahn, Kerl Menger, Edgar Zilsel und Gustav Bergmann*. Hamburg: Felix Meiner Verlag.

Strohmenger, Steffen. 1996. *Kairo: Gespräche über Liebe*. Wuppertal, Germany: Peter Hammer/Trickster.

Sunier, Thijl. 2012. "Domesticating Islam: Exploring academic knowledge production on Islam and Muslims in European societies." *Ethnic and Racial Studies*. doi: 10.1080/01419870.2012.753151.

Svendsen, Lars. 2005. *A Philosophy of Boredom*. London: Reaktion Books.

Swarowsky, Daniela, and Samuli Schielke. 2009. *Messages from Paradise #1: Egypt-Austria: About the Permanent Longing for Elsewhere*. Documentary film, Stichting ZiM, Austria and the Netherlands.

Synková, Hana. 2010. "Claiming legitimacy in/of a Romany NGO." In Michael Stewart and Márton Rövid (eds.), *Multidisciplinary Approaches to Romany Studies*, 280–291. Budapest: Central European University Press.

Tammam, Husam, and Aymon Kreil. 2010. "'Id al-hubb: qira'a fi al-gadal al-thaqafi wa-l-dini bi-Misr." Public lecture at CEDEJ (Centre d'Études et de Documentation Économiques, Juridiques et Sociales), Cairo, February 23.

Tartoussieh, Karim. 2007. "Pious stardom: Cinema and the Islamic revival in Egypt." *Arab Studies Journal* 15, 1: 30–43.

Tordhol, Tor Håkon. 2014. "Dialectics of protest: Political mobilisation in the Egyptian countryside." MA thesis, Department of Culture Studies and Oriental Languages, University of Oslo.

Tsing, Anna. 2000. "The global situation." *Cultural Anthropology* 15, 3: 327–360.

Tuominen, Pekka. 2013. "The clash of values across symbolic boundaries: Claims of urban space in contemporary Istanbul." *Contemporary Islam* 7, 1: 33–51.

Umar, Muhammad. 1902. *Hadir al-misriyin aw sirr ta'akhkhurihim*. Cairo: Maba'at al-Muqtataf.

al-'Uthaymayn, Muhammad b. Salih. 1998. *al-Ibda' fi kamal al-shar' wa-khata' al-ibtida'*. Cairo: Maktabat al-'ilm.

van Nieuwkerk, Karin. 2008. "'Repentant' artists in Egypt: Debating gender, performing arts and religion." *Contemporary Islam* 2: 191–210.

——— (ed.). 2012. *Muslim Rap, Halal Soaps, and Revolutionary Theater: Artistic Developments in the Muslim World*. Austin: University of Texas Press.

———. 2013. *Performing Piety: Singers and Actors in Egypt's Islamic Revival*. Austin: University of Texas Press.

Vasalou, Sophia. 2008. *Moral Agents and Their Deserts: The Character of Muʿtazilite Ethics*. Princeton, NJ: Princeton University Press.

Verkaaik, Oskar. 2004. *Migrants and Militants: Fun and Urban Violence in Pakistan*. Princeton, NJ: Princeton University Press.

Wardlow, Holly, and Jennifer S. Hirsch. 2006. Introduction to Jennifer S. Hirsch and Holly Wardlow (eds.), *Modern Loves: The Anthropology of Romantic Courtship and Companionate Marriage*, 1–34. Ann Arbor: University of Michigan Press.

Weber, Max. [1930] 1992. *The Protestant Ethic and the Spirit of Capitalism*. Trans. Talcott Parsons. London: Routledge.

Wedeen, Lisa. 1999. *Ambiguities of Domination: Politics, Rhetoric, and Symbols in Contemporary Syria*. Chicago: University of Chicago Press.

Weismann, Itzchak. 2001. *Taste of Modernity: Sufism, Salafiyya, and Arabism in Late Ottoman Damascus*. Leiden: Brill.

Weiss, Brad. 2009. *Street Dreams & Hip Hop Barbershops: Global Fantasy in Urban Tanzania*. Bloomington: Indiana University Press.

Weyland, Petra. 1993. *Inside the Third World Village*. London: Routledge.

Williams, Raymond. 1969. *Marxism and Literature*. Oxford: Oxford University Press.

Winegar, Jessica. 2006. *Creative Reckonings: The Politics of Art and Culture in Contemporary Egypt*. Stanford, CA: Stanford University Press.

———. 2008. "Bringing culture to the Muslim masses: Egyptian state anxieties and the instrumentalization of high culture." *ISIM Review* 22: 28–29.

———. 2011. "Taking out the trash: Youth clean up after Mubarak." *Middle East Report* 259: 32–35.

———. 2012. "The privilege of revolution: Gender, class, space, and affect in Cairo." *American Ethnologist* 39, 1: 67–70.

Wittgenstein, Ludwig. 1969. *On Certainty*. Ed. G. E. M. Anscombe and G. H. von Wright, trans. Denis Paul and G. E. M. Anscombe. Oxford, UK: Blackwell.

Yeh, Rihan. 2009. "Passing: An ethnography of status, self and the public in a Mexican border city." PhD diss., University of Chicago.

Zigon, Jarrett. 2008. *Morality: An Anthropological Perspective*. Oxford, UK: Berg.

Žižek, Slavoj. 2006. *The Parallax View*. Cambridge, MA: MIT Press.

# Index

SAMULI SCHIELKE is a research fellow at Zentrum Moderner Orient (ZMO) and an external lecturer at the Free University of Berlin. He is author of *The Perils of Joy: Contesting Mulid Festivals in Contemporary Egypt,* and editor (with Knut Graw) of *The Global Horizon: Expectations of Migration in Africa and the Middle East* and (with Liza Debevec) of *Ordinary Lives and Grand Schemes: An Anthropology of Everyday Religion.*

# GENO

## THE LIFE AND MISSION OF GENO BARONI

**\*\*\*\*\*\*\*\*\*\***

## Lawrence M. O'Rourke

PAULIST PRESS

NEW YORK    MAHWAH

BX
4705
.B1958
O 76
1991

BOOK DESIGN BY THERESA M. SPARACIO.

Library of Congress Cataloging-in-Publication Data

O'Rourke, Lawrence M.
    Geno : the life and mission of Geno Baroni / by Lawrence M. O'Rourke.
      p.  cm.
    Includes index.
    ISBN 0-8091-3274-5
    1. Baroni, Geno C. (Geno Charles), 1930–  .  2. Catholic Church—United States—Clergy—Biography.  3. Cabinet officers—United States—Biography.  4. Church work with minorities—United States.  5. Church work with minorities—Catholic Church.  6. Church and social problems—United States.  7. Church and social problems—Catholic Church.  8. United States—Politics and government—1945–  I. Title.
BX4705.B1958O76    1991
282'.092—dc20
[B]                                                  90-28934
                                                  CIP

Published by Paulist Press
997 Macarthur Boulevard
Mahwah, New Jersey 07430

Printed and bound in the
United States of America

# Contents

# Foreword

On an April evening in 1981, Geno Baroni telephoned me. He had a simple proposal: that I write his biography.

"I have cancer, you know," he said. The stark statement implied that he did not know how much longer he had to live, but was anticipating death.

We arranged to have lunch in the DuPont Circle Hotel, which turned out to be just the first of several negotiating meetings we held before I said yes to his proposal.

Geno and I had known each other for 15 years. I had been introduced to him in the mid-60s when he was a curate at Sts. Paul and Augustine parish in northwest Washington. I was a newspaperman, as I am today.

Patricia Coe was a volunteer tutor in Geno's V Street Center. At least one night a week she either went to the Center or had a youngster from the Center meet her elsewhere to get help with schoolwork. I was dating Pat (and we went on to marry in 1967). Pat said I had to meet this wonderful priest who was doing such great work. We met over dinner in Pat's apartment. After Pat and I were married, Geno occasionally came to our home for dinner, and we saw him at the movies, the theater and at other gatherings. Geno and I became friends. I also considered him as an excellent source of information for what was going on within the civil rights movement, the District of Columbia, the Democratic Party, and the progressive wing of the Catholic Church.

When he left Sts. Paul and Augustine to work, first at the U.S. Catholic Conference and later at the National Center for Urban Ethnic Affairs, Geno and I fell into a pattern of lunch every other month. I

1

once did a column on his views of ethnicity for my newspaper, the now-dead *Philadelphia Bulletin*, but usually I treated the information from Geno as background. Certainly he was very helpful with his insights during the 1976 Gerald R. Ford-Jimmy Carter campaign. After he joined the Carter administration as assistant Secretary of Housing and Urban Development in 1977, he asked if I wanted a job on his staff. I told him no. We then for three years saw one another every few months on the same basis as before. Of course, I followed his activities through the newspapers.

I joined the Carter administration in 1980 as a deputy assistant Secretary of Education for policy and planning and Geno and I then ran into each other frequently at government meetings. He lamented the inability of the Carter administration to pull itself together politically. He was right, of course.

After the people in November, 1980, voted the Carter administration out of office, I practiced law and wrote on the new Reagan administration. That is what I was doing when Geno and I negotiated over his biography in the spring of 1981. I was reluctant to take it on, since I knew him to be incredibly disorganized and nonspecific. As a test, I pushed him for details over significant events in his life, and he responded with unrelated anecdotes, but few facts on point.

I kept asking Geno why he wanted me to be his biographer. He tossed back something about the garrulous Irish or our common experiences in government or our shared belief that the Catholic Church had to address social problems and the most effective way to do that was through a political process which required compromises.

Beyond worrying about Geno's ability to deliver the goods for his biography, I worried about how he and his friends would react to a critical evaluation. We kept tossing back and forth the words "honest biography." Geno said that's what he wanted and that's one of the reasons why he asked me to write it. He said he would open his records to me, undergo whatever interviews I needed, and would urge his friends to cooperate fully.

On that basis, I agreed, and we began. I interviewed Geno for more than 200 hours during the next 18 months. I traveled with him to some old haunts—I went to Acosta to spend a day with his mother, to Somerset for several days to talk with Geno's school friends, and to Arco in northern Italy to dig into Geno's roots.

I began writing in late 1982 and provided first drafts to Geno as I went along. He always said they were fine, but I had the feeling that he never read them. I had the sense that to him the process was the important thing. In fact, he told me repeatedly that I, through my questions, forced him to think about things he had not thought about for years. Often he would tell me I was helping him with his "life review."

As I suspected, Geno was a hard man to draw specifics from. Many of my questions he answered with his all-purpose stories which he told as if I had never heard them before, although they were on tape several times.

At best, this book is only a partial review of Geno Baroni's life. He was an enormously complex man, too complex and elusive to capture on paper. "I am not a linear person," he sometimes joked when he could not find the right words to explain his role in an event that in some mysterious way occurred because of him. He was a man of vision and ennobling spirit. He was also often a star-crossed and lonely human being. This book is an attempt to tell part of Geno's story.

\* \* \*

Geno Baroni served as a young priest in a city parish in a neighborhood known to police as a center for prostitution, drug dealing, and violent crime. Refusing to hide in a rectory and pray in a church building while the world outside resembled hell, he launched a series of programs—pre-school for children, summer recreation for young people, tutoring, a medical clinic—that became foundation stones for the nation's historic effort of the 1960s to build a Great Society, to win a war against poverty, and to transform millions of Americans from consumers of public welfare to producers of public good.

Geno saw the Catholic Church, which he served as an ordained priest, as not doing enough of the right things to change victimization of the poor in America. It was no longer enough, he said, to respond with charity to appeals for a food basket, the month's rent, or a bag of used underwear. The problems were too big for charity alone. Charity maintained people, but did not alter the system which locked them in their dismal place and exploited their weakness. Baroni set out to change the institutional church's mission to the poor. In so doing, he started a campaign which revolutionized the church in America, reshaped its social objectives and prodded its bishops to speak out forcefully for government policies of social justice and eventually against the nuclear arms race.

Geno Baroni, a loyal priest in the Catholic faith, saw that his church in America too often refused to recognize values in other religious faiths. He saw the potential strength of concerned people sapped by unnecessary and self-destroying religious differences. Confident of his own religious heritage, but not triumphant or absolutist, he reached across confessional barriers to grasp in common purpose the hand of the Protestant Christian, the Jew, the Muslim, and those who doubt the existence of a god. He thus broke new pathways to cooperative social justice that even cardinals and bishops of his faith would follow.

Geno Baroni stood at the jagged edges of church and the world, at those irregular and dangerous points which often slash and cut in conflict, rather than fit together in smooth harmonious purposefulness. Honestly assessing the strengths and weaknesses of church and world, Baroni sought to ease them toward a conciliation that would allow all men and women, wherever they may be on the jagged edge, to share and follow the Inaugural prayer of John F. Kennedy that in this world "God's work must truly be our own."

He looked at America's cities and saw them torn by hatred and tension between blacks and whites. He saw deteriorating neighborhoods, politicians and experts making matters worse, people misunderstanding each other, many fleeing cities in anger and intent on vengeance. Geno Baroni shaped a new approach to rebuild and revitalize America's urban ethnic neighborhoods. In so doing, he became leader and spokesman for millions of people in neighborhoods, brought their legitimate concerns and fears to national attention, and built coalitions of poor that transcended race and ethnic heritage.

Designing a new vision of ethnicity, Geno deliberately and provocatively pitted the nation's best-known Polish-American political leader, the senior United States senator from Maine and future secretary of state, Edmund S. Muskie, in an argument with an unknown Baltimore social worker and street-smart organizer, Barbara Mikulski. They debated whether the United States should be portrayed as a melting pot for immigrants or whether that was a flawed image which robbed immigrants of their vital identities without providing a replacement. By giving importance to honoring and understanding the strengths of ethnicity, Geno Baroni started a movement that was to sweep across the nation's big cities.

Sensitive to the strains as well as the strengths within the ethnic movement, he set out in 1976 to make the nation's bicentennial celebration of its independence a time for rejoicing in the diversity and ethnic pluralism which identify the United States. He had not anticipated opposition from George Bush, then the chairman of the Republican National Committee. Bush described Baroni as a representative of the "more radical ethnic people" and sought to toss him out as a bicentennial celebration leader. Baroni fought back and defeated Bush. Steady on course, Baroni helped the bicentennial celebration to recognize the ethnic heritage of America.

An astute political analyst, Geno advised presidents and had a major role in the election of one. In 1976, he saw Jimmy Carter's campaign in disarray because it did not know how to deal with the nation's Catholic voters and their bishops on the politically explosive issue of abortion. Baroni reworked Carter's campaign strategy, forced him onto Polish Hill in Pittsburgh to campaign among urban ethnic Catholics, and told him what to say to those voters. He thus opened for himself a new career as an advisor on national urban policy by accepting appointment to a sensitive political position within the Carter administration. Baroni became the highest ranked Catholic priest ever to serve in the U.S. government's executive branch.

In and out of government, Geno disdained simple answers to complex problems. He rejected what others saw as traditional thinking and inescapable conclusions. For Baroni, politics and government were meant to serve, not to constrict, public endeavor. Well ahead of others, he created a vision of cooperation in America among government, business and voluntary sectors that would forge new public policies and innovative approaches for the relief of human misery and injustice. He filled blackboards, tablecloths and scraps of paper with drawings of connected triangles and circles. His initial explanations of his theories often confused his listeners, and some never did understand. But by doing this, Baroni challenged audiences of one to thousands to remove the barnacles from their thinking and to search creatively within themselves and their neighborhoods for new ways to lift the human condition and spirit.

Geno Baroni believed in democracy and its institutions for self-government. He rejected the oft-held belief of Catholics and ethnic Americans that politics is a dirty business best left to others. He loved politics and those who practiced it. While working to raise the art of politics to the highest level of service, he drew toward it men and women who shared precious values of family, culture and community, which profoundly influenced elections for the White House, Congress and state and local government offices across the land.

He struggled all his life against his internal devils. He was burdened by self-doubt, pains of inadequacy, fear of authority, and an inability to confront directly those he believed to be wrong and to have wronged him. Recognizing his human frailties, he was not afraid to seek counseling from psychiatrists and therapists who forced him to answer basic questions about his personality, life and purpose. In so doing, he searched through self-confessed weakness and in the process encouraged others to face their failures and fears with courage and hope.

Geno Baroni suffered through more than his share of physical pain as well. Aware that death would come to him long before he completed his earthly agenda, he converted his personal tragedy into a ministry for others equally marked for early death. Experiencing the human emotions of anger, rejection, quiet desperation and futility, he turned to his own beliefs and came to understand that he had fought life's battles as well as he could, that a merciful and loving God would welcome him to an eternity of justice, peace, good friends and fettuccine. As he saw the approach of death and said his last goodbyes, he gave, by example, his final instruction and gift—how to die in dignity and peace.

*        *        *

I want to acknowledge with gratitude those who helped make this book possible. Father William J. Byron, S.J., president of The Catholic University of America, provided constant assistance. John A. Kromkowski read the many versions and offered constructive criticism as well as support. Mary Anne McNerney typed transcripts for hundreds of hours. Jo Dunne provided wise and solicitous counsel. Dorianne Perrucci gave careful and helpful editing. Patricia Coe O'Rourke completed the final editing. Margaret Higgins O'Rourke performed valuable research. Timothy E. O'Rourke typed the final manuscript. If I name more, I shall certainly forget others. Suffice it to say, Geno's family and friends provided information and encouragement.

I could not have put in the many years of labor on this book without support and love from my family, who bore patiently with me on weekends, evenings and through several summer vacations and leaves of absence from my work as a newspaperman to complete this book. So to Trish, and to Chris and Katie, and Jenny and Timmy, my love and hope that in this book you find enough to justify your faith and endurance.

Chevy Chase, Maryland
June, 1990

# 1

## A New Beginning

Geno Baroni nervously tucked in his black shirt, squared his black hat, adjusted his white clerical collar, and climbed the stone steps. He came to the front door of St. Augustine's parish rectory in northwest Washington.

It was a little after 11 in the morning of Wednesday, October 12, 1960. Baroni pushed the doorbell and waited. There was no answer. Filled with anxiety, he rocked from foot to foot on the top step. Had he come on the wrong day? Was he at the right place? He pushed the doorbell again. Still no answer. With hesitation, he knocked on the wooden door.

The door was opened suddenly by a stocky, white-haired, middle-aged man in clerical garb. "Monsignor Gingras?" Baroni asked. "Yes," Gingras replied, "and you must be Father Baroni."

For the first time the two men came face-to-face—Gingras, a member of the inner circle of Archbishop Patrick A. O'Boyle of the Roman Catholic Archdiocese of Washington, and Baroni, a self-professed failure as a young priest ordained for the diocese of Johnstown-Altoona in Pennsylvania. They shook hands warmly.

"Come into the parlor," Gingras said with a reassuring smile. Baroni took off his hat and entered the rectory. Light came through the lace curtains. Gingras took a chair behind the desk and peered over a pile of paper. Baroni sat on a stiff-backed chair in front of him, his hands twisting in his lap and darting to his face.

They began to talk. They exchanged words of appreciation for Monsignor George Higgins, a staff member at the U.S. Catholic Conference, who had arranged the meeting. Baroni explained the purpose of his visit. He had been a priest for four years and was interested in

7

leaving central Pennsylvania and coming to Washington, where he thought he might do parish work while studying at the Catholic University of America. He explained how he had an interest in urban parish life, though no experience at any place like St. Augustine's.

Baroni did not tell Gingras all that he had heard about St. Augustine's: that it served many of the poorest of the black people of Washington, how the neighborhood was better known for prostitution than for piety, nor did he repeat to Gingras another thing told to him about St. Augustine's—"It's a colored parish, but the priests are OK."

As Baroni held back, so did Gingras. He knew more about young Father Baroni than he cared to lay on the desk at that first meeting. Gingras knew that Baroni was in Washington to visit St. Augustine's with a one-day pass in his pocket from the Seton Institute outside Baltimore. Baroni had lived there for several months, recovering from an emotional collapse. In fact, he had been committed to the Seton Institute by a Pennsylvania psychiatrist who had been treating him for severe depression. Baroni was a troubled young priest and he was looking for a fresh start.

Gingras also knew that St. Augustine's was a hard place for any young priest to work. It had few social amenities. Only a few dollars came in each week in the collection basket. The parish was not only behind in its mandatory payments to the archdiocese, but it often had to borrow money to pay the energy bills. Gingras also knew that it was tough to get young white priests of the archdiocese to come voluntarily to St. Augustine's as curates. They could be forced there, of course. If Archbishop O'Boyle assigned a young priest to St. Augustine's, the young priest had better obediently pack and move on schedule. But O'Boyle was reluctant to send people, even young priests, to places where they might not fit in. Gingras was a special kind of priest. He never expressed an ambition to be pastor of a rich suburban white parish. He seemed to have no difficulty in working in a desperately poor parish made up almost entirely of blacks.

As Gingras looked at Baroni across his cluttered desk in the parlor that Columbus Day, he sensed a little of himself in the young priest, somebody who reveled a bit in being different from his colleagues. "Yes," said Gingras to Baroni, "you might like it here."

At those words, Baroni's face lit up and he seemed to sit up straighter in his chair. "Then can I come?" Baroni asked. "There are formalities," Gingras said, "but I think it can be arranged."

"You understand, Father," said Gingras, "that we are a poor parish with few frills." Baroni would get $30 a month in pocket money. There would be no fancy weddings, but plenty of beggars at the kitchen door.

Geno would have little time off and would be expected to stay in the rectory many days by himself as Gingras went to meetings in his capacity as O'Boyle's representative to the black community.

They made a few arrangements, and Baroni left. He was elated. He felt his heart pumping. He had been afraid of rejection, but he had not been rejected. He had been accepted, a rare moment, as young Geno saw it, of acceptance in his life. Baroni had gotten to St. Augustine's from Union Station by bus. Now he decided that in getting back across the city to the railroad station for his return trip to the Seton Institute, he would walk.

He got directions from Gingras for a circuitous route—down 18th Street to DuPont Circle, and from there down Connecticut Avenue to the White House. Baroni stopped on the sidewalk in front of the mansion at 1600 Pennsylvania Avenue and, peering through the iron fence across the lawn, he mused about its occupant, President Dwight D. Eisenhower, and the election campaign then under way. It was John F. Kennedy against Richard M. Nixon. Baroni wanted Kennedy to win, though he was not confident it would happen. But wouldn't it be wonderful, Baroni said to himself, if he and Kennedy arrived in Washington at the same time. What a great new beginning that would be for the two young Catholic men.

Kennedy was in New York City that day, telling a conference that America needed a strong economy not only to sustain defense but also to demonstrate U.S. resolve to other nations, particularly those "wavering between our system and the communists, that the way to freedom is the way to strength and security, that their future lies with us and not with the Soviet Union." Richard Nixon spent that day in Los Angeles, filming campaign ads and telling a rally that the Democrats were the "war party" and that Kennedy's position on Quemoy and Matsu, islands off the east coast of China, reminded him of British Prime Minister Neville Chamberlain's appeasement of Adolf Hitler at Munich. Kennedy and Nixon bitterly assailed each other as they prepared for their third campaign debate.

Baroni followed each detail of the campaign in the newspapers. Back in Pennsylvania that summer, and after that in Seton Institute, Baroni talked up Kennedy's election. He was jubilant that the polls showed Kennedy running ahead of Nixon, inspired by the thought that Kennedy could become the nation's first Catholic president.

Now on Pennsylvania Avenue in front of the White House, Baroni felt a surge of excitement as he thought about the future. He thought about Kennedy and the country, but mostly about his own future. Geno Baroni was heading for a new life, a fresh start, in Washington.

# 2

# The Weight of the World

A week later, the young priest came back to St. Augustine's, this time, though he didn't know it, to begin a lifetime of service on behalf of people who live in America's cities. He carried all his worldly possessions in one old suitcase. Geno could not help but think back four years to his arrival as a newly-ordained priest to his first parish, Sacred Heart in Altoona, Pennsylvania.

He had been surprised at the Altoona assignment. Sacred Heart parish was considered one of the most comfortable parishes in the diocese of Johnstown-Altoona.

The Catholic faith came to central Pennsylvania in the eighteenth century. As the mines and factories attracted thousands of immigrants in the latter part of the next century, the U.S. Catholic population grew. By the time of Baroni's ordination in 1956, there were more than 600,000 residents within the combined Johnstown-Altoona diocese. About a quarter of them were Catholic. The diocese was also large geographically, covering 6,674 square miles and including Bedford, Blair, Cambria, Centre, Clinton, Fulton, Huntingdon and Somerset counties. Baroni came from Somerset County, where his Italian-immigrant parents, Guido and Giuseppina, still lived in their small frame house in Acosta.

Baroni was aware of the ethnic polarization in Altoona, focused around the ethnic Catholic parishes. He knew that as a young Italian priest he should—by tradition—have been assigned to an Italian parish. By the conventional thinking of the era, Baroni would be more effective and comfortable with Italians than with the Poles, Greeks, Hungarians and Germans who claimed ethnic parishes. On the other hand, he also shared to some extent the conventional view of the Irish. They were thought to be more open than other ethnic groups to a priest from another ethnic background. Baroni suspected that the real reason he was not assigned to an Italian parish was that the main Italian parish in Altoona was run by the Franciscans and Geno was ineligible for assignment there.

He was naturally nervous as he embarked on his first assignment, and his confidence wasn't helped by the fact that the pastor at Sacred Heart, Monsignor Joseph O'Leary, ran a tight ship. There were fixed meal hours, visiting hours, and lights-out hours, and O'Leary wanted them all punctiliously observed. During Baroni's masses and homilies, O'Leary stood in the sacristy, listening and taking mental notes. In the privacy of the rectory, O'Leary gave his critique of Baroni's style and message. "You talked too long this morning, Geno," O'Leary often said.

In other ways, Sacred Heart was an uncomfortable place for the young priest. Sacred Heart, besides being Irish, was a parish for the Altoona establishment—for families like the O'Learys. O'Leary had a brother who was a priest and two sisters who were nuns. Another brother was a lawyer, and another a physician. Baroni doubted that as a coal miner's son, born in a shack in Acosta, he would be accepted as an equal by the sophisticates of Altoona. He felt inadequate.

The overly sensitive Baroni, stung by O'Leary's critiques and an apparent lack of response from the congregation, began to believe that he wasn't a good homilist. Just knowing that O'Leary was listening from the sacristy added to his worry. On O'Leary's advice, he kept his homilies brief. O'Leary also said not to talk about controversial dogmatic and theological topics, but Baroni did not always comply. He suggested in one homily, for instance, that he leaned toward the idea of policemen and firemen in Altoona having a union. That issue was controversial in the city at the time. City authorities, some of whom were members of Sacred Heart parish, resisted police and fire unions. The parties decided to go to arbitration. The city picked its arbitrator, the police and fire representatives picked theirs, and the two arbitrators came to Baroni: Would he serve as neutral arbitrator? Baroni checked with O'Leary. The pastor was less than pleased about the development. Stick to the church, not politics, O'Leary ordered. Fortunately for Baroni, the parties settled their strike without his involvement. But the chastisement he got from O'Leary bothered Geno and clung to him.

O'Leary said that if Baroni wanted to be kept busy, he would oblige. "I'm appointing you moderator for the Holy Name Society and the Sodality," O'Leary told Baroni. The appointment expanded Baroni's contacts. He got to meet parishioners informally and, in time, to hear their complaints. He met a woman in the parish who worked for a local finance company. She told him of how many Sacred Heart parishioners who appeared to be so comfortable financially were over their heads in debt. Baroni had read in the seminary about the Antigonish movement in Nova Scotia, where the church worked with local Catholics to establish a credit union. One night at a meeting with Holy Name Society officers, Baroni casually mentioned that it was a shame that Sacred Heart parishioners were forced to pay high interest rates to banks and finance companies. If the parish had a credit union, said Baroni, it could charge lower loan rates and use profits to help people in need.

Several Holy Name officers, including a few themselves in hock to the finance company, liked the idea. The next week, they had a proposal. "We want you to set up a credit union here at Sacred Heart, Father." Baroni went to O'Leary. The pastor hesitated. He thought it was the idea of this young inexperienced priest who had never managed money and did not even have a savings account. But when support for the idea developed within the parish, O'Leary agreed that the credit union plan could continue, but with conditions. Baroni could play an active role, but not the leading public role. O'Leary reserved the right to pick the treasurer. Baroni wrote for credit union material, pulled a local lawyer into the effort, and created a board of directors, with himself as a member, though not as chairman.

Some parishioners resisted, asserting that the parish was entering a minefield of potential disaster. Others said that if the parish were going to do it, it had to be done by the rectory. This was the first time that Baroni encountered the problem of lay people looking to the clergy for expertise that the priests, in fact, lacked and for decisions they were not trained to make.

With Baroni's support, the credit union got started, and by the 1980s had 7,000 members, and assets of more than $9 million. Baroni was to consider it one of his greatest accomplishments. But he could not tell the story of the credit union without adding a detail: O'Leary's hand-picked treasurer, a pillar of the parish, a solid member of the community, absconded with credit union funds. Insurance covered the loss. Baroni always noted that he had nothing to do with the selection of the treasurer.

In 1957, Baroni had another idea that illustrated the sensitivity of the young priest to linkages between the parish and the world beyond the church grounds. He went to O'Leary with an idea to hold a special mass for workers on Labor Day. Such masses were becoming custom in working-class neighborhoods across the country, and the idea fit in with Baroni's idea of what the church should be doing. But there was resistance to the idea of a Labor Day mass from those who saw it as a gesture of support for unions. To Baroni's surprise and to the dismay of some members of the parish, the pastor accepted Baroni's suggestion. Geno was the principal celebrant at the first Labor Day mass in Sacred Heart parish in Altoona.

One of young Father Baroni's major responsibilities was the hearing and absolution of sins in the sacrament of penance. Saturday afternoons and evenings, he sat in the dark confessional box, hearing first from one booth, then from another, the recounting of violations against the laws of God and church.

"I was not prepared for it," Baroni said. "In the seminary we received instruction on the rules of moral dogma and theology and the roles and teaching of the church, but that was in the abstract." Here he came up against real problems of human beings, and he was overwhelmed by them.

Many of the recited confessions were routine, quickly said by men, women and children who expected a quick assignment of prayers called penance. Geno Baroni didn't operate that way. He wanted to talk to people in the box, not just to move them along with a formula response. Some of the topics, especially those dealing with sex, embarrassed Baroni. He heard details of private intimate relations that had not been on the seminary's agenda. Baroni said the formulations of the seminary sometimes sounded hollow when applied to the actual people kneeling before him.

Many confessions dealt with artificial contraception. Men and women confessed practicing birth control. Why? Baroni asked them. Because we already have more children than we can support, but we want to engage in sexual relations, they responded.

What did you tell them? Baroni was asked three decades later.

"To keep trying," he said.

Least of what Baroni liked were the questions. I did this or that, Father, said the penitent. Was it a sin? Baroni was non-judgmental, non-directive. Besides, he reasoned, sin is for the individual conscience to determine. He would not make decisions for others. He sensed that many people left his confessional box irritated at the failure of the priest to make their moral decisions for them. Yet he also felt that he should be more authoritative, but that some inherent defect held him back. His feelings of inadequacy grew.

Baroni began to see a slice of humanity that his sheltered boyhood years in Acosta and his protected seminary days in Mount St. Mary's Seminary had left unexplored. He became a bundle of nerves in the

confessional. He dreaded the four or more hours every Saturday afternoon and evening that he was assigned confessions.

He developed the nervous habit of breaking off little pieces of the
asbestos soundboard that lined the confessional box. He chewed and
swallowed the asbestos.

Baroni's problems with distressed parishioners went beyond the
confessional box, though. He didn't have it any easier in the front parlor
of the rectory. Another assistant priest was assigned by O'Leary to deal
with young people. But many young people arrived at the door and
asked for Father Baroni. Protocol or not, Geno was not about to turn
them away. He said that he could understand and sympathize with most
of the troubled young people of Sacred Heart. After all, he was not
many years away from having many of those problems himself. Many
young people couldn't find jobs. They lacked goals in their lives. They
couldn't get by solely on what the church was able to offer them; it was
irrelevant to their immediate needs, yet they sought the counsel of its
priest.

Baroni said later that the standard view of too many churchmen in
the late 1950s was that the laity's role was to "pray, pay and obey."
Baroni found that unacceptable. He believed that the church had to
address directly the worldly concerns of its lay people. Thoughts like
that began to creep into his Sunday homilies. One day O'Leary called
him aside and said, "Geno, you're causing a lot of trouble with that kind
of talk. You're never going to make bishop that way." Baroni took the
pastor's remark as a criticism and a suggestion that he was out of step
with the church. O'Leary's words carried great weight with the young
priest. "I was scared silly of him," Baroni said. "Part of me said that I
was getting good at being a parish priest. But mostly I still felt like a
shy, backward coal miner's son. O'Leary reminded me of my father. He
was very strict. But I remember how pleased I was on those mornings
when he said, 'good sermon.' "

Baroni said he was often thrust into situations he felt inexperienced
to handle. One such situation brought him reproach from O'Leary. A
battered woman arrived at the rectory and was ushered into the parlor
to see Baroni. "What can I do, Father?" she asked. "My husband beats
me. He drinks too much. He's either out of work or has some terrible
job."

Baroni mulled it over, and said he did not see that much could be
done with the abusing husband or to improve the marriage. "Leave
him," Baroni advised the woman.

"Leave him?" responded the woman. "Leave him? He's my husband. I can't leave him."

Baroni said he really wanted to tell the woman to see a psychiatrist, but he knew that would get even a worse reception than the advice to leave her husband. The woman told other people of Baroni's advice and soon O'Leary got wind of it. He called Baroni onto the carpet. "You cannot give advice like that," O'Leary told Baroni.

Though Baroni had his difficulties with O'Leary, the Irish monsignor was considered progressive for the times. He brought the English Jesuit, Clifford Howe, to Sacred Heart to conduct a week-long program for lay people on their mission in the church. That was considered avant garde for the 1950s. O'Leary was also open intellectually to reforms in the liturgy, though he warned Baroni not to try anything fancy from the altar.

O'Leary was aware of the social justice movements taking place in the Catholic Church and spoke approvingly about many of them to Baroni. O'Leary encouraged Baroni to assist in expansion of the Christian Family Movement and Young Christian Workers' Movement in the parish.

In time, Baroni would acknowledge that he was overly sensitive to O'Leary's criticism and supervision, and conceded that he may have bruised too easily at O'Leary's advice and corrections. O'Leary certainly seemed gracious to young Baroni. One day O'Leary learned through a friend about a used car available in Toledo, Ohio. Would Baroni be interested? Baroni, who had never owned a car and had rarely driven one, said yes. O'Leary drove himself and Geno more than seven hours from Altoona to Toledo, where Baroni bought his first car with money from his family and a loan from O'Leary.

Though settling in slowly into life as a young parish priest at Sacred Heart, Baroni was still restless. He applied for and received appointment as a part-time religion teacher at Altoona Catholic High School. The rector, Father Vincent Luther, was a church traditionalist. He wanted Baroni to do things the way they had always been done. Baroni had a different approach. Another priest in the diocese said that Baroni "drove the poor man Luther up the wall. He didn't know how to cope with Geno. Geno was into contemporary theology, political action and the liturgical movement."

The approved class text called for Baroni to talk about sexual petting, attendance at Sunday mass and support for the church, and other individual issues and church rules. Instead, Baroni talked about a major role for government in providing shelter, medical care, education, food and justice for the poor. Geno raised questions about why the Catholic Church in the United States wasn't doing more to promote justice in civil affairs.

Baroni brought *Jubilee* magazine, a journal of progressive Catholic thought, local newspapers and *The New York Times* into the classroom and used them rather than the books assigned by the diocese as texts. He raised provocative questions about civil rights activities in the U.S. South, union organizing in Pennsylvania and the growth of the American military complex.

When some parents learned of Baroni's approach, they protested to Luther. Luther and Baroni exchanged words over what material was appropriate for Altoona Catholic High School juniors. Baroni was instructed to return to the established texts and leave the newspapers outside the classroom. He continued to urge students to read newspapers and magazines for examples of how ethical values are tested. But the teacher had little confidence that the students did anything more than study the books enough to get passing grades.

In 1958, after two years at Sacred Heart, Baroni was transferred to St. Leo's Parish in Altoona. Baroni was not happy to learn that Luther, the high school rector, lived in the St. Leo's rectory. The St. Leo's pastor was Father John Manning. Baroni recalled Manning warning that the singing of Protestant hymns and the recitation of the Protestant version of the Lord's Prayer at such events as public high school graduations were potentially sinful. Baroni knew of those experiences firsthand. He had attended Somerset High School, where Protestant variations of hymns and prayers were proclaimed.

Manning was proud of his New York education. He was an outspoken political and church conservative. He spoke coldly of labor unions, social welfare programs administered by government, and the doctrinal, structural and liturgical reforms bubbling to the surface in the Catholic Church. Manning avidly read William F. Buckley's *National Review* and gave Baroni the magazine with suggestions that he read it carefully to change his views about unions and government. "Monsignor O'Leary was strict. Father Manning was far right," Baroni said.

At St. Leo's, it was Manning and Luther against Baroni day and night. The two older priests worked steadily to convince Baroni to back away from his unorthodox views. To escape the rectory, Baroni volunteered for more than his share of hospital visits. His only friend in Altoona among the priests was Father Robert (later Kevin) Seasoltz, who had studied at the North American College in Rome and whose family in Sacred Heart Parish had befriended Baroni. But then Seasoltz left Altoona to become a Benedictine monk, and Baroni was then without a priest friend or any friends at all of his own age.

Reaching out for a friend, Baroni contacted priests who had gone through the seminary with him and who worked in Altoona, but they had their own parish activities. A few suggested to Geno that he join them for a round of golf, but he did not play the game and chose not to try. A couple of priests had dinner with Baroni, but they did not call for a return event. Baroni acknowledged that he was not the most cheerful guy to be around, and that he didn't do well in conversations about sports or diocesan gossip. His interests were the social justice movement and changes in the church, and he could speak of little else.

More and more, Baroni drew into himself. He spent nights reading, attending movies, or walking through Altoona. He escaped whenever he could to nearby Seven Springs, Pennsylvania, where the Dupre family was developing a resort. Geno had gone through elementary and high school with Phillip Dupre. Baroni didn't go to Seven Springs for the skiing, but for the solitude and the chance to talk with Philip, who didn't harass him for reading *The New York Times* or *Time* magazine.

As Geno's alienation from his pastor grew, and the sense of his inadequacies festered, he became a tense and highly-strung young man who seethed inwardly against what he saw as injustice and rebelled against unnecessary and improper restrictions on his activities. Outwardly, however, he looked placid and unaffected by pressure. "I was certainly not the kind of guy who exploded in anger or frustration and let the hurt escape," Baroni said. "I held it in and it began to gnaw at me."

He didn't know how to deal with his anger, and was "scared silly" of his superiors, all the while aware of their faults and limitations. Geno said his style, learned while dealing with his old-world authoritarian father, Guido, was non-confrontational. He wanted to speak out, to fight back, but he could not bring himself to do it.

Ironically, adding to the pressure, Baroni became known in the parish as a priest who listened sympathetically to people's problems. "I started to get all the problems," Baroni said. "I really attracted them. And the only thing I had in my favor was time. I could sit with them for long periods because I had nothing else to do. Time and patience. I sure didn't have any answers. I started looking around and reading books. I remember a book by a Dr. Cavanaugh on psychiatry and mental health. Thomas Verner Moore wrote a book on psychiatry which I read. But Fulton J. Sheen was preaching against it. He was saying, 'Go to confession.' He was getting hot on television by then."

Geno suggested to Manning and Luther over the dinner table at St. Leo's that some troubled parishioners should be encouraged to seek professional psychiatric care. The two priests rejected the idea and told Baroni to forget it.

In the late 1950s the Catholic Church in Altoona and most other places was a conservative institution which preached strict orthodoxy and manifested skepticism about ideas that human beings could resolve the earthly problems of poverty and injustice individually or through collective action. It was a time, Baroni said, for bigger church buildings and seminaries. It was a boom period, with 46,000 seminarians, plenty of nuns to teach in Catholic elementary schools, and expanding Catholic colleges. "They were bragging about how big the parishes were and how many priests the bishops had," Baroni said. "Catholics had the feeling they were moving into power. They were going to make it, no matter what. Within this big powerful church, there wasn't room for any problems."

Baroni felt trapped in this setting. He enjoyed the privileges of the priesthood, but felt himself somewhat unworthy of them. He felt closer to the people than to the pastor. He shared the people's legitimate concerns, and wanted to join them in their search for relief from their problems, but felt himself held back.

By 1959, after three years as a parish priest, Baroni felt he was miscast, yet could not walk way from his priesthood, because he was overwhelmed and afraid. He was often depressed, and began to diagnose himself as at risk of a nervous breakdown. He summoned the courage to write the bishop and ask for a new assignment. "I can't deal with Father Manning. I am afraid of him," Baroni wrote. The bishop agreed to reassign Baroni. Geno moved to St. Columba's Parish in Johnstown. It was not a good idea.

In good moments, the pastor at St. Columba's was witty and charming. Baroni, especially sensitive to the issue of ethnicity, got the sense that the pastor considered the Irish a superior breed of humanity to the Italians. From the pastor, Baroni learned Irish history and Gaelic symbolism. The pastor was not fond of the works of James Joyce, the one Irish writer Geno had read. The pastor lumped Joyce with "atheists and heretics" who lured the Irish people away from loyalty to the Roman Catholic Church. Baroni quickly learned that he could not argue the merits of Joyce, nor anything else, with this pastor. When family and friends asked Baroni how he was getting along with his new pastor, he said, "Father is a gifted and learned priest and I am learning a great deal from him." He was afraid to say what he really felt.

Baroni was most concerned by the pastor's mood swings. At breakfast and lunch, the pastor treated Geno graciously. Evening supper was different. The pastor railed against the world's stupidities, including those committed by his young assistant. Baroni, for the most part, sat through the tirades in silence. He was afraid of the pastor, and did not argue back.

More and more, Baroni became convinced that his stress would lead to a nervous breakdown. He had often recommended to others that they seek professional psychiatric help, but for now he could not look for it himself. Instead, he turned to a friend from high school and college days, a young Italian lawyer in Somerset, Nat Barbera.

Not that Barbera and Baroni were ideological kindred spirits. "We had differing points of view and Geno found it stimulating to talk to me about my point of view which was much more conservative than his," Barbera said. They thrashed out opposing ideas on labor, capitalism, philosophy and Catholicism. Barbera described himself as "a conservative in the sense that I felt anyone who had talents had the responsibility to develop them and the reward would correspond, depending upon the effort put forth. Geno felt there were so many people who were downtrodden and had so many problems and so many artificial shortcomings in the sense of environment, background and so forth, that they had to be helped to get there." The Baroni-Barbera debates were good-natured. They had a running argument over right-to-work laws which Barbera favored for Pennsylvania, and Baroni opposed.

"What are you, a commie or what?" Barbera challenged Baroni.

"There's nothing wrong with communism except it's godless," Baroni replied.

Barbera, like Baroni, came from a poor immigrant Italian family. Barbera's father was a shoemaker and after class at Somerset High School, he had to rush home to help in the family business. But there was a distinction in high school between the two boys. Barbera was a fighter and often in trouble. Geno, he said, was "a shy young man who did not express his feelings very well generally."

Now, as Baroni tried to deal with his domineering pastor and his crisis of confidence in Johnstown, he was once again avoiding confrontation with authority, swallowing his anger, and tearing himself apart, Barbera observed.

Baroni and Barbera talked as they fished for trout on Laurel Hill Creek or from the dock at Seven Springs. "I knew Geno wasn't happy," Barbera said. "He was torn inside. Geno would fume and would vow he would change things. I wanted to change things individually. He wanted to change things socially." Later, Baroni would say of this period of his life: "I had gone through a couple of difficult pastors. I didn't know if it was my fault or theirs, but I was blaming myself."

With Baroni sliding into depression, a crisis in the parish provided his first direct contact with a psychiatrist. A young woman scheduled to be married at St. Columba's cracked under pressure the week before the wedding. She and her family asked Geno for advice. He advised them to seek psychiatric help. The psychiatrist contacted Baroni for more information and during the conversation, Geno asked if he could drop by to talk about himself.

The psychiatrist encouraged Baroni to enter therapy. He agreed with Baroni that the situation at St. Columba's was unworkable and agreed to support any moves that Baroni would work out. Baroni set about finding an escape, and asked Bishop Howard J. Carroll for an appointment. The bishop told the nervous young priest that he was working too hard and worrying too much, and needed a vacation. "Take $200 and get away for a week," Carroll told Baroni.

Baroni was grateful for the offer, but he wanted more. "I've been thinking I need psychiatric help," Baroni told the bishop. Carroll thought it was unnecessary. To Baroni, Carroll sounded contemptuous of the idea of a priest going into therapy. That only made things worse. "I began to realize how neurotic I was," Baroni said. "I realized that much of my problem came from the fact that I had a lot of conflict with authority. I felt I was a disaster case."

With the $200, Baroni drove to Combermere in Ontario, Canada, to a retreat house built by Baroness Catherine de Hueck, founder of the Friendship House Movement. That was the beginning of Baroni's life-long association with the Friendship House Movement and an offshoot, Madonna House. Many times through the years Baroni fled to their houses in moments of personal crisis.

He had a restful week in Canada, but when he returned to Johnstown, he told the bishop that he could not go back to St. Columba's because of his conflicts with the pastor. Baroni also revealed that he had written to The Catholic University of America in Washington for admission as a scholarship student in political science, and to Monsignor George Higgins asking for help in relocating to Washington. Geno needed the bishop's approval. Because he needed Geno in the diocese, Carroll was reluctant to grant it. Baroni went back to his psychiatrist and outlined his plan. The psychiatrist said that the move might help, but that first Baroni needed an additional period of rest and care. To this, the bishop agreed and Baroni made his way to the Seton Institute as a patient committed for care after suffering a nervous breakdown.

In the late spring of 1960, Baroni arrived at the suburban Baltimore facility. "I felt a failure," he said. "My name was mud in the diocese." For a few weeks he was restricted to the institute grounds. He spent days in individual and group therapy. In time, he was permitted to leave the grounds to attend movies, take walks and meet friends. He told his family where he was living, but did not explain why. It was only many years later that family members learned of Geno's bout with depression.

Years later, Baroni talked freely for this biography about his history of emotional problems. He estimated that he counseled hundreds of people throughout his life to seek therapy. Baroni himself was in individual or group therapy almost constantly from his beginning at the Seton Institute to his final days. He had mixed feelings about therapy. On one level, he saw it as an admission of failure to solve his personal problems unaided. On the other, it was a sign that he had emotionally matured to the point where he could be honest with his emotions, no longer concealing and submerging the currents of fear and rage which ran deep within him.

# 3

## Standing on the Jagged Edge

When Baroni arrived at St. Augustine's in the fall of 1960, it was the closest thing black Catholics of Washington had to a mother church. That was both a blessing and a mark of shame. In truth, the hospitality toward blacks at St. Augustine's served to keep blacks out of churches with white congregations. The few blacks who did live in Washington's white neighborhoods felt discouraged from attending services at their local churches, so they went to where they felt wanted. St. Augustine's was founded during the Civil War as the District of Columbia's first church for "colored Catholics." The parish founders, most of them former slaves, raised start-up money through a strawberry festival on the White House grounds on July 4, 1864. President and Mrs. Abraham Lincoln attended.

For the black Catholics trying to build their church, it was slow and rough going. It was not until 1874 that the black parishioners acquired a plot of land at 15th and L Streets in the northwest quadrant of the District of Columbia and began construction. Parishioners themselves excavated and built the church to save money. The brick building, topped by two 60-foot-high Gothic spires, was dedicated on Trinity Sunday in 1876. It seated 1,500 people.

For 75 years, black Catholics at St. Augustine's struggled to preserve their faith in a city that treated them, at best, with indifference. Though the blacks built the church entirely with their own money, they were required by church rules to turn over the title to the bishop. So in 1948 the archdiocese had the proper authority when it ordered the parish closed, the church building razed, and the land sold. The property sold for $300,000. In a compromise, the black congregation was

22

authorized to move to a vacant church a dozen blocks north of the first site, transferring the location of St. Augustine's parish church while keeping the name. The new church building lacked the comfortable feeling and enriching history of old St. Augustine's. Within a week of his arrival, Baroni learned about this bitter history which was still resented by many black Catholics in Washington.

In the fall of 1960, the nearest Catholic Church to St. Augustine's was St. Paul's, and it was just around the corner. But the gap was more than a city block or century long. It symbolized the divided nation and the racial segregation within the Catholic community. St. Paul's was known as a church for whites only. It was as segregated as a Southern lunch counter or Northern executive suite. In its heyday, prior to the 1950s, St. Paul's was a rich thriving parish, serving Roman Catholics from the embassies on 16th Street. St. Paul's had a private school that included among its graduates many daughters of world leaders. Its most famous graduate was actress Helen Hayes. Baroni arrived at St. Augustine's at the end of a period during which the surrounding neighborhood changed racially and economically. Embassies moved west to Massachusetts Avenue. Their staffs went to the suburbs. Contributions fell. The parish needed a subsidy from the archdiocese to pay bills. It had a declining white congregation. St. Augustine's had a small black congregation. They were in the same boat. Few blacks entered St. Paul's. Those who did, mostly chauffeurs and maids, were by custom required to sit on benches at the rear of the church. Where the forward benches for the whites were polished and comfortably curved with padded kneelers, benches for the blacks were uncomfortably straight-seated. When black chauffeurs and maids knelt in prayer, their knees were right on wood, not on the pads reserved for whites. Some blacks remembered being asked to leave St. Paul's Church if they broke the rule and moved toward the front of the congregation. A few recalled being told at St. Paul's that they could not confess their sins to the priest there, but would have to go to the "colored church." With two churches, the failing, costly—and empty—St. Paul's, and the poor, black—and empty—St. Augustine's just around the corner from one another, something had to give.

As Baroni arrived, black parishioners of St. Augustine's picked up the rumor that their church would be closed, for the second time in its history, and they would be assumed into St. Paul's. They were furious. "A lot of good people were so mad they said, 'To hell with it. We're not going to church anymore,' " Baroni said.

The decision to close and sell the St. Augustine's church building a second time was made public a few weeks after Baroni's arrival at the parish. Fulfilling the fears of the black parishioners, Archbishop O'Boyle decided to close St. Augustine's as an independent parish and to merge it with St. Paul's as Sts. Paul and Augustine Parish. For the first few months on his new job, Baroni kept his head down while controversy swirled about him. He behaved circumspectly as a young parish priest, celebrating mass in Latin, hearing confessions, but avoiding the controversy. When he met parishioners and visitors in the St. Augustine's rectory, it was his introduction to black people. Back in Acosta where he grew up, there was only one black family, and it kept apart from the whites. Nor did young Baroni ever meet the few blacks in Somerset where he went to high school or the handful in Johnstown and Altoona. They were not in Baroni's parishes. He had read about blacks and understood their problems—now he was priest to a black congregation.

Many of the black Catholics Geno met during his first months in Washington were hard-working, proud, dignified people, including several prosperous professionals and merchants. They came to Sunday mass at St. Augustine's from neighborhoods around the city. Baroni was struck by how quiet and conservative most of them seemed to be. From his reading, Baroni knew of the rising movements for change in the church. Many Catholics wanted liturgies in their own languages and more participation by the laity in liturgies and parish management. But the first blacks Baroni met at St. Augustine's treated him deferentially. Hearing their confessions, he was struck by their strict consciences. They did not advocate change in the church. In fact, they were agitated by it, especially when it meant their loss of identity. They wanted their mass in Latin, their hymns from the same books used by their white brethren.

Geno soon discovered that life as a parish priest in the nation's capital had very exciting moments. On January 21, 1961, Geno walked three miles through snow from the rectory to Capitol Hill to view John F. Kennedy's inauguration. Gingras' sister, a reporter, got two guest tickets for the Inaugural. The tickets were numbered and coded, but neither Gingras nor Baroni knew what the information meant. Gingras gave Baroni one ticket and kept the other for himself. Baroni arrived at the Capitol grounds and was ushered forward, past one security check after another. At high noon, as President Dwight D. Eisenhower and his young successor, John Fitzgerald Kennedy, arrived on the Inaugural platform, Geno was close enough to see every frosty breath. By accident, Geno had gotten the better of the two tickets.

Back at the rectory that evening, Baroni said, "Thank you, Monsignor, for that ticket. I had an excellent view."

"I'm glad you did, boy," said Gingras. "I was a quarter mile away at the Library of Congress and I couldn't see a damned thing."

Baroni found Gingras a pleasant change from his pastors in Pennsylvania. "George was a very decent human being and a wonderful priest," Baroni said in later years. "He was patient. He worked hard. At night he'd sit there and have a Scotch and tell me how the parish and diocese worked. I was finally getting an education in how to be a parish priest. George should have been a bishop." In public and private in those formative years, Baroni called his pastor "Monsignor." In the rectory, Gingras called his young priest "boy," rarely calling him Geno. Baroni took the "boy" tag as a mark of affection.

In the fall of 1961, despite the bitter objections from many blacks, St. Paul's and St. Augustine's formally merged. (Two decades later, the parish reverted to the name St. Augustine's.) St. Augustine's church building was torn down and the St. Paul's church building became the church for the merged parish. Baroni and Gingras moved to the St. Paul's rectory in the 1400 block of V Street. The physical plant at the new Sts. Paul and Augustine was rundown. But more importantly to Baroni, the parish community was dispirited. Encouraged by Gingras, Baroni set out to revive the parish. But first he felt he must find out what made the neighborhood around the church tick.

Geno found that one of Washington's worst slums began at the edge of the church's property. Nearby 14th Street was notorious as a center for prostitution. While widespread use of narcotics had not yet swept across Washington's black community, the 14th and U Streets corner was cited by police as a primary drug distribution center. Bars and liquor stores on 14th Street left indelible marks on the neighborhood and the parish.

Talking to people, Baroni found another cause for outrage. Landlords charged exorbitant rents, but failed to provide heat or sanitation. When pipes broke, the landlords were in no hurry to fix them. The city, run by an appointed panel of commissioners, made sure trash and garbage were collected on schedule in Spring Valley, Georgetown and other white neighborhoods, but neglected such service for Cardozo, Shaw and other black neighborhoods.

Horrible stories of human misery abounded. One afternoon nuns found a dead newly-born baby stuffed into a pillowcase in the convent garbage pail. Baroni baptized the baby while the nuns notified police. More than half the children dropped out of high school before graduation. The neighborhood had the city's highest crime and alcoholism rates.

Yet Baroni found in his parishioners "a kind of grace and glory no one ever talks about at the penthouse conferences on poverty." He saw decency in women who begged for money to help fend off the landlord and feed their families. The parish had little money. Instead, Baroni spent hours on the phone each week pleading with landlords to give them another month, or another two weeks. "I knew that most of the time the people wouldn't be able to come up with the rent, no matter how long they were given. But I figured if I bought them any time, I had accomplished something."

Geno found dignity in the alcoholics who begged at the rectory door for a sandwich or a dime. Baroni was non-judgmental. When he had money, either parish funds or his own, he gave. He called a classmate from Mount St. Mary's College, Edward Eagen, a Washington native. "Ed, we're having some terrible problems in this parish. Could you round up some graduates from the Mount and see if they could chip in a few bucks to help us out?"

Eagen did better. He gathered larger sums and brought an envelope of cash to the rectory. He passed a line of men and women waiting to see Geno in the parlor. It was clear to Eagen that his classmate had found a unique mission in serving the poor of the nation's capital. Eagen didn't understand it at all, but he sure admired what Geno was doing. The truth was, Geno didn't understand it at all either, but he didn't tell his friend that. The question about what the church should do to relieve this situation began to obsess him.

Sometimes, teaching a class in government at Mackin High School in Washington, Baroni would startle the students by asking them to help him answer questions he was confronting on a daily basis at Sts. Paul and Augustine. Once he put these problems to his students:

"Theresa S. has 4 children. Her husband is a prisoner in Cuba. She works 2 days a week as a maid to support her children. Because of her poor health she is not able to find a permanent job. What kind of assistance should a democratic society give to this family?

"Clyde B. has a family of 5 children. He is unskilled and untrained and now works as a dishwasher in Arlington for $1.00 an hour. He often works 7 days a week and sometimes works as many as 90 hours per week. Yet he is only paid for 8 hours a day. What can be done about this injustice? What can society do to protect the poor and unskilled individual?"

Baroni's questions were drawn from real-life situations he encountered in the rectory. He said that through these examples he hoped to impress on the young minds in his care the problems of poverty and the duty of a caring society to solve them.

Often after midnight, Baroni closed his book or magazine in his room at Sts. Paul and Augustine and went for a walk. In his Roman collar he became a familiar figure at that hour to the alcoholics, pimps and prostitutes, drug dealers and junkies on 14th Street. He knew the location of shooting galleries where addicts mainlined heroin. He knew about sleazy hotels where prostitutes serviced their johns. He could say where white alcohol could be purchased in a jelly glass.

Baroni said he didn't take to the streets after midnight to kibbitz with the characters of the underworld, although he did some of that. His excuse for late night walks was to buy the first edition of the *Washington Post*. On most nights he was the only white man to buy a newspaper at 14th and U Streets. He chatted with the news vendor and everybody else and got plugged into the neighborhood news that didn't make the papers. Many nights Geno stopped in a late-hours grocery store to get a piece of watermelon or other fruit, which he ate as he walked along. Police warned Baroni several times that he courted disaster by walking unarmed through the streets of the crime-ridden neighborhood. Baroni thanked them for their advice and kept on walking.

Sometimes, though, he slowed down to talk with homeless people he met seeking shelter for the night. He escorted many to a policeman with the request that they be taken to a city shelter. Often, when the homeless person was a woman, and he couldn't find a police officer, Baroni brought her to the home of someone in the parish who offered emergency shelter. Frequently he came across people evicted from their rental units for nonpayment of rent. There were as many as sixty evictions a day in Cardozo. With anger, Geno spoke of a city that was efficient in throwing people out of their homes, but incapable of finding them shelter. The District's welfare system at the time operated under a man-in-the-house rule. Sen. Robert C. Byrd, West Virginia Democrat who was the Senate's czar over the District government, was the principal author of this legislation. It cut off welfare payments to families when a man was living in the house. The senator said the man should work and provide for the family.

Baroni saw the man-in-the-house rule as a government policy that split families and gave a cash incentive to fathers for deserting children. Women and children were pushed onto the streets of the nation's capital every day because a welfare worker spotted a man in their apartment.

Geno, meanwhile, had embarked on a major project back in the parish. When St. Paul's and St. Augustine's merged, the cloistered community of French nuns who had served as St. Paul's parish school teachers for decades moved away. This left the convent on V Street vacant and in the care of Gingras as the pastor of the new parish. The cloister was a forbidding place, where high walls were topped with jagged glass to prevent intruders. Reasonable though that may have once seemed to the nuns, the glass-topped walls stood symbolically as an insurmountable barrier between the Catholic Church of Washington and the neighborhood it purported to serve. "The convent was a perfectly good building," Baroni said. "A little seedy inside maybe, but certainly better than almost all the other buildings in the neighborhood, and nobody could figure out what to do with it. Somebody down at the chancery suggested we tear it down and have ourselves a parking lot."

Baroni had other plans. "I didn't have any credentials," he said, "but I had ideas." He proposed to Gingras that the parish turn the building into a service center for the entire community, since he knew there weren't enough Catholics to justify a service center just for Catholics. "I'm talking about a place for all the people who live around here," Geno said. Gingras counseled Baroni to curb his enthusiasm. He agreed that a service center open to all comers would serve the neighborhood's interests, but said the chancery would never go for it.

Baroni knew from his contacts on the streets and his growing numbers of friends among other clergy in the area that the city's welfare agencies were noticeably absent from the neighborhood. Those who sought government benefits had to go downtown, to wait in long lines for surly service from clerks who often were white and who lived outside the city. "This city is run like a plantation," Geno said.

His vision of a service center included offices for government, school, welfare and housing agencies. Sensitive to the diocesan ledger watchers, Baroni talked about the parish renting space in the proposed center to government agencies. He said that the St. Vincent de Paul Society and the parish credit union could operate out of the service center.

Baroni finally persuaded Gingras that the idea had merit. "It took a long time for George to buy the idea because he didn't trust me," Geno said. "I didn't have any credentials. I was an outsider to Washington, a vagabond." Gingras then went ahead and convinced O'Boyle and chancery officials that turning the convent into a service center was not only right for the parish and neighborhood, but good public relations for the Washington Catholic archdiocese. The idea caught O'Boyle's fancy.

Patrick Cardinal O'Boyle, though a conservative inside the church, was in many respects a risk taker, and Baroni admired him for it. In 1953, seven years before Baroni's arrival in Washington, O'Boyle desegregated the Catholic schools. He acted a year before the U.S. Supreme Court ruled that segregated schools were inherently unequal and in violation of the U.S. Constitution.

O'Boyle's decision to allow the new Sts. Paul and Augustine Parish to convert the convent into the V Street Center gave Baroni an independent base for his activities and the freedom to move out of the traditional role as a parish priest. With Geno taking advantage of the opening, lines of responsibility merged. Gingras was pastor of the parish. He dealt with Downtown—the church bureaucrats. Gingras had the legitimacy and history within the Washington church that Geno lacked. Gingras was an effective church politician who knew the rules and stayed within them. Gingras had the title from O'Boyle as Secretary for Human Relations, and was the priest most often invited to pray at meetings of blacks. He was the archbishop's official contact with the House and Senate District Committees and the D.C. Board of Commissioners.

But now with the V Street Center, Baroni had a base from which to operate. The center was under the institutional church's umbrella. He served there as priest of the archdiocese, but running the Center created a special distinction for him apart from the church and the parish. The form and function of the V Street Center gave a unique identity to Baroni. Simultaneously, he had the security of the church and the flexibility of a quasi-independent private entity. It was a combination that Geno would search for and construct throughout his ministry as a priest. He learned on V Street how to stand on the jagged edges where the church and the world met.

Baroni had the vision to see in the abandoned and rundown convent a facility that would be filled with vitality and public service, but he also knew that he could not manage the place. He looked for a manager, and he found Mary Houston. She was the first of many Baroni recruits and disciples. One mark of Baroni's genius was his ability to spot talented people and to bring them to convince themselves that they should follow him. The story of Mary Houston is also the story of U.S. Senator Barbara Mikulski, a Maryland Democrat, and U.S. Representative Marcy Kaptur, an Ohio Democrat, and scores of others whom Baroni encouraged into public service.

A social worker from the District of Columbia, Mary Houston was an experienced and competent bureaucrat who was a committed Christian.

"She was the key to this place," Baroni said. "Mary was one of those women who came out of Berkeley, of all places, and joined Dorothy Day and Catherine de Hueck. She had been in the Catholic Worker, Friendship House crowd, and belonged to a lay secular French group that reported to the bishop.

"She was working for the welfare department and I coaxed her to come out. She had to make a living. All her time was voluntary. I didn't know where the hell we were going to get the money to pay her or keep her because the pastor didn't have it. Mary came out and lived here as director."

Baroni named himself the assistant director, and he was the first priest in the history of the archdiocese to work, on paper at least, as a subordinate to a woman.

Mary Houston moved into one of the cells in the abandoned convent and began to organize the V Street Center. "The building is a mess," Baroni told her. "I had the building inspector come in on the q.t. and check it out. We have no certificates of occupancy. The building has old wiring."

Baroni sometimes worried about what he had done. "I used to wake up in a cold sweat in the middle of the night and wonder if the place would burn down," he said.

The extraordinary Mary Houston was just right for the times. The Catholic Church in the United States in the early 1960s luxuriated in a new vitality. Kennedy's election and performance in the White House encouraged young Catholics to enter public service. It was Baroni's fortune to be alive at the moment in history when American Catholics were ready and willing to live out their principles of social justice. The spirit of volunteerism exemplified by Mary Houston was matched by the Peace Corps, which offered idealistic Americans the opportunity to serve the poor in foreign countries. Thousands volunteered. Under the leadership of R. Sargent Shriver, Kennedy's brother-in-law, the Peace Corps dramatized the spirit of a can-do nation. Baroni was of the same stripe.

Young Catholics were heading for the action. Whether it was the Peace Corps or local politics, Catholics as a class responded in large numbers for the first time in the nation's peacetime history to the public service call. Kennedy's election roughly coincided with the election of another John—Pope John XXIII. Initially dismissed as an elderly caretaker guided by the Vatican bureaucracy, John XXIII opened the doors and windows of the Catholic Church. He demystified the liturgy and the priesthood. The ordained and laity now had an example in Rome of a man who served the poorest of the poor. The church moved from being an institution which strove on earth not merely to provide charity, but to change the system. Baroni saw himself doing what the pope invited Catholics to do, what Kennedy showed Catholics they could do. It was also what Baroni wanted to do.

As altars were turned around to create community, and as the Latin mass was replaced by the vernacular to promote participation, parish priests like Baroni searched for new formulas and mechanisms for the church and world to engage in the building of the Kingdom on earth.

"Ask not what your country can do for you; ask what you can do for your country," Kennedy said in his Inaugural Address. Baroni often repeated those words and others from Kennedy: Remember that on this earth, God's work must truly be our own.

Under the Houston-Baroni leadership team, the V Street Center acquired a reputation as a place where people in need of assistance or just friendly conversation could drop by without being hassled. Among the occasional visitors in the early 1960s were two men who were later to achieve fame as civil rights activists, H. Rap Brown and Stokely Carmichael. Another occasional visitor was Marion Barry, then a civil rights activist, later the mayor of the District of Columbia.

Carmichael was a student at Howard University with a fascination for religion and theology that he explored with Peter Hinde, a young Carmelite volunteer at the Center. To Baroni, Carmichael was a gentle and decent kid, bright and ambitious, increasingly radicalized by the conditions he witnessed in Baroni's neighborhood. As a firebrand civil rights leader later, Carmichael sadly and bitterly remembered how few whites there were like Baroni and his V Street Center band.

Students from Japan, India, Mexico, South Africa and Jamaica arrived. Mary Houston was housemother for the women, who took rooms in the upper two floors at the V Street Center. The men ate their meals on V Street and were housed elsewhere.

The Center became what Baroni envisioned when he saw an empty convent. Community service agencies found Baroni willing to accommodate them. Alcoholics Anonymous and TOPS (Take Off Pounds Sensibly) got space. The Catholic Inter-Racial Council and the Educational Inter-Racial Home-Visit Office hung shingles. Baroni recruited young Catholics to tutor schoolchildren. Later his operations were studied when the federal government created War on Poverty programs.

A group of doctors from Georgetown University Hospital wanted to set up a pre-natal and infant care clinic in the basement. Baroni suspected some of the doctors might urge their patients to practice birth control and explain to them how to do it. He was nervous about that, because he knew the position of the church on birth control and he knew O'Boyle would enforce it. Baroni found a solution—he would ignore what was going on at the clinic.

Baroni also got to work on the outside of the building. He ordered the jagged glass removed from the convent walls, and arranged that the yard behind the glass become an outdoor recreation and rest center. He built a basketball court to which neighborhood youngsters were welcomed. He recruited Carl Linn, professor of architecture at the University of Pennsylvania and a well-known landscaper, and Vincent de

Forest, an urban design student, to create a shaded quiet zone for the elderly, a play area for young children, and a small theater for backyard summer stock. Neighborhood youngsters performed Lorraine Hansberry's *A Raisin in the Sun*.

Vincent de Forest was a young black Catholic on his way from his home in Cleveland to a Peace Corps assignment in Tunisia. He stopped in Washington for a physical examination. Doctors found an nonrepairable hernia and struck him from the Peace Corps list. One summer evening in 1963, de Forest, running out of money and unable to find a job, walked at 15th and V Streets. He passed the open front doors of Sts. Paul and Augustine Church, but did not enter. He was angry at the Catholic Church. It had refused a funeral mass for his father because his father had not registered in a Catholic parish. Cleveland church authorities said the senior Mr. de Forest could be buried in a Catholic cemetery, but his grave would not be marked by a tombstone.

Walking through the neighborhood that night, Vincent de Forest was not sure he wanted anything more to do with the Catholic Church. But on his third trip past the door, he stepped inside. He saw Baroni standing by the altar. The two men talked, de Forest telling Baroni of the Peace Corps rejection and his financial plight. "Let's go to the rectory and I'll see what I can do," Baroni said. Geno telephoned Martin Alexander, who lived near the church, and asked him to take in de Forest temporarily. Alexander agreed. Within a few months, de Forest landed a job and Baroni had a new disciple.

During a visit to the Center, de Forest learned of Baroni's plan to remake the backyard of the former convent into a neighborhood gathering place, an idea promoted by Linn. "I'd like to help," de Forest said. Using scrap materials, borrowed tools, help from the neighborhood's retired stonemasons, strong-backed young men as laborers, unemployed painters and carpenters, they built the V Street Center Neighborhood Commons, a gathering place for all people. De Forest's proudest contribution was a sandbox which attracted hundreds of children.

Behind all these activities, Baroni was the driving force. He was constantly on the phone. On a typical day, he got 200 calls or messages. The rectory phone had three incoming lines and sometimes Baroni juggled conversations on all of them. Yet he always seemed to find time for the parishioners or volunteers to talk. Never did he seem too rushed for them.

Late one night the phone rang in the rectory. It was Sister Mary Leo Vincellete. She had found a mother and four young children wandering near the Capitol. They had no money and no place to go for the night. Baroni called back a little later. He had been unable to secure help, and advised Sister Mary to contact the Salvation Army. It was the best he could do, he apologized.

But instead the nun took the mother and children to the convent and put them up for the night. Sister Mary and the other nuns spent nine hours on the telephone the next day trying to find help for the family. They were unsuccessful and finally called the police. Officers took the mother to D.C. General Hospital. Split from her husband and now her children, her mental condition deteriorated. For days, she repeatedly mumbled, "services, agencies, services, agencies." Then she died.

Slowly the details became known, and with each mention of the case, Baroni grew sadder and more determined to do something about it. He gathered the facts. John and Mary Ethridge were a young black couple with five children aged four months to eight years. They came to Washington from the country and were unprepared for city living. John Ethridge drank too much and had difficulty holding a job. He wanted to remain with his family, but was trapped by Senator Byrd's man-in-the-house rule. Ethridge was spotted by a social worker in the same house as his wife and children. Welfare payments to the family stopped. The Ethridges were evicted. With emergency funds from the government, Mrs. Ethridge rented a single room for herself and the children for $12 a week. John Ethridge moved elsewhere. The family disintegrated. In April, the landlord took Mrs. Ethridge to the Women's Bureau. He felt she was not mentally competent to handle responsibility for the children. But she was allowed to return home. But then they lost the $12 apartment and wandered through the streets.

The case touched the conscience of Washington. Baroni talked about it to his newspaper friends and urged them to write up this tragedy. Prodded by the Johnson Administration, the city government said it would open an emergency shelter. But weeks passed and there was no shelter.

Baroni and several Protestant ministers decided to dramatize the impact of Senator Byrd's man-in-the-house rule and the failure of the city to open a shelter for families like the Ethridges. Baroni and his colleagues carried a black wooden coffin to the Senate steps and placed on it a sign saying, "Is there a man in Byrd's house?" Police ordered the coffin removed and did not arrest the clergymen. But the rule was soon repealed and shelters were opened.

Baroni's role in the Capitol Hill protest got into the newspapers and some officials at the chancery were angry. They said that although he was not arrested, he broke the law and brought scandal to the church. But Baroni suspected that the unforgivable sin was that he was edging closer and closer to working with the Protestants.

# 4

# Bridging the Gap

When Geno Baroni came to Washington in 1960, there were scores of churches and clerics within easy walking distance of the St. Paul's and St. Augustine's neighborhood. But as far as Cardinal O'Boyle, Monsignor Gingras and young Father Baroni were concerned, those churches and clerics might as well have been on different planets. While clergymen of other denominations banded together for social activism, members of the Roman Catholic hierarchy and priesthood generally stayed separate.

With a characteristic laugh, Baroni said, "A Protestant minister or rabbi could say grace before meals and the cardinal or another Catholic priest could say grace after meals, but that was about as close as the two got." Within the Catholic Church was a well-established tradition of working for social justice, but that effort was not shared cooperatively with other religious faith communities. The Catholic Church's description of itself as the "one, holy, catholic and apostolic church" served to work against interdenominational activities. Protestants could work together and Protestants and Jews were linked in social justice activities in Washington. But Catholics worked alone.

Baroni was only in Washington a few months when he realized that Protestant and Jewish clerics were far more involved than his brother Catholic priests in practical applications of the scriptural mandate to work for material improvements in the lot of the poor. Baroni did not suddenly reach a decision to join with non-Catholic clerics.

Baroni had become close friends and comrade-in-arms with the Rev. William Wendt, an Episcopal priest and pastor at St. Stephen's and the Incarnation Church, and the Rev. Philip Newell, a Presbyterian minister assigned to direct his denomination's social ministry program.

Wendt was one of the first to see a brother in Baroni. In many ways, Wendt's story is similar to Baroni's. Wendt was assigned to St. Stephen's and the Incarnation Episcopal parish by his bishop in the early 1960s to deal with a rapid social, economic, and racial transition in the 16th Street neighborhood and to save the parish. In about a year, the 1,000-member St. Stephen's congregation had dropped to 200. "My first job was to break down the barriers in the parish to allow the neighborhood to come in and make the church useful to the neighborhood," Wendt said. "Not by getting membership in, but to start social service programs that were the name of the game that day."

Wendt heard that there was a nearby Catholic parish that was facing the same problems as his church and that a young priest named Geno Baroni was trying some creative efforts, and was a decent and unpretentious fellow to boot. But frankly, Wendt didn't expect much from a Catholic priest.

"I had hard times with Roman Catholics in New York City," he said. "Things happening like children being ripped out of my arms literally by nuns who told the children they were going to the devil if they weren't part of the Catholic Church."

And so when Wendt and Baroni met at a neighborhood event, the Episcopal priest was skeptical that anything would come of it. Instead, he found Baroni to be a "breath of fresh air." It was "absolutely delightful" for Wendt to find in Baroni and Gingras a pair of Roman Catholic priests willing to work with Protestant clergymen on an apparently equal basis.

Wendt and the Rev. James Reeb, pastor of All Souls Unitarian Church in the same neighborhood, set out to woo Baroni toward membership in clerical alliances. Reeb knew the history of Roman Catholic Church involvement in social action programs, but was not encouraged about an inter-faith effort. However, he recognized that not only was the Catholic Church the largest Christian denomination, it was also the only one with a member who happened to be President of the United States.

The Capitol Hill protest after the Ethridge family case illustrated how Baroni and the Protestants were able to work together. The event itself contributed to their bonding. Wendt and Newell were the principal Protestant conspirators in carrying the coffin to Capitol Hill.

"Somebody got the idea that we could show the horror that hit the Ethridge family and embarrass Byrd by taking a coffin up to the Hill," Baroni said. Baroni joined this criminal conspiracy rather nervously. He

had never knowingly violated the law. He didn't know what his ecclesiastical superiors would think about it. He was not anxious to get arrested. But there was an unspoken pressure on him from Wendt and
Newell to act. Baroni liked being regarded as a social activist. Now he
had to prove it.

After notifying the press, Baroni, Wendt and Newell toted their
large empty wooden box to the Capitol steps. They fastened a sign
indicating their desire that the man-in-the-house rule be given a decent
burial and stepped aside. Reporters and photographers recorded the
event for history. The Capitol police stood by the side and watched.
Then they said the demonstration had gone on long enough. The three
clerics picked up their coffin and left. The event was an item in the
newspapers and got mentioned on radio and television. It was not a
major protest as those things went in the 1960s, but it was a big event
for Baroni.

A couple of days later, Baroni got a call from the cardinal's office.
He was read a message from the cardinal—"The next time somebody
suggests to you that you deposit a coffin on the Capitol steps, say that's
something that Protestants do, but not Catholics."

Despite the reprimand, however, Baroni was learning that
O'Boyle's rules could be stretched. Through the clerical grapevine to
which he was increasingly a contributor as well as a gatherer, Baroni
learned that there was to be a civil rights demonstration in the church
of the young black preacher, the Rev. Walter Fauntroy, a Baptist pro-
tégé of the Rev. Dr. Martin Luther King, Jr. Dressed in clerical black
Baroni, after Sunday morning mass and lunch, walked to Fauntroy's
church and took a seat in the balcony to view the civil rights rally.
Fauntroy delivered an impassioned address which ended with a call for
all assembled to march down Pennsylvania Avenue past the White
House where John F. Kennedy lived. The march was to be a show of
support for civil rights demonstrators in the South. It was time, Fauntroy told his listeners, to show whether you're for us or against us,
whether you're with Martin Luther King or George C. Wallace and
Ross Barnett.

Then and there, Baroni decided that he would join the marchers.
He was recognized and invited to the front ranks. A *Washington Post*
photographer snapped the marchers with the White House in the background. The next morning, on the breakfast tables of O'Boyle and Auxiliary Bishops Philip A. Hannan and John Spence was the picture,
showing Baroni, quite distinct in his Roman collar, black suit and black
hat, walking arm in arm with other clergymen in a civil rights demonstration.

Baroni was barely finished with his breakfast when the Sts. Paul and Augustine rectory phone rang. It was the cardinal's office. Father Baroni was instructed to come by for a visit with the cardinal. That afternoon the young priest stood before the prelate who could decide, without explanation or notice, to toss Baroni out of his job and the rectory and back to central Pennsylvania. Still without official papers, Baroni feared as he stood there that he might be expelled from the Archdiocese of Washington. "I was very afraid," Baroni said.

He stood nervously before O'Boyle's desk. The cardinal had the *Washington Post* spread out before him. His finger at the picture, O'Boyle asked, "Is that you, Father Baroni?"

"Yes, your eminence," replied Baroni.

"What were you doing there?"

Baroni explained how he had come to march at the front of a civil rights demonstration past John F. Kennedy's residence in the White House.

"All right, Father," said O'Boyle after hearing Baroni's explanation. "By the way, I was pleased to see in this picture you had your hat on. That's the way I like my priests to appear in public. You can go now."

That was it, no chastisement, no one-way to Altoona. Baroni told his friends of his ordeal and explained it as a signal sent by O'Boyle that there were acceptable as well as unacceptable ways for priests to engage in civil rights activities, and that the march past the White House was acceptable. The word spread through the Washington clerical networks that O'Boyle had allowed one of his priests to march in a civil rights demonstration.

Maybe, Wendt, Newell and Reeb agreed, this fellow Baroni could help them out. The Protestants saw Baroni as a useful opening to the strength of the Catholic Church in Washington. These were hard times and they were engaged in serious battles. They needed all the political muscle they could gather. They saw Baroni as a way to O'Boyle's heart and clout.

Wendt said he detected that Baroni, even as he came to meetings with Protestant clergymen, was trying to maintain some distance between their churches. "There was still that conflict," Wendt said. "I felt it. But it was part mine, too. There was a little touchiness, some wariness of compromising yourself as a priest in the old areas of dispute between the churches." Wendt said Baroni "had this understanding concern for people rather than the institution. That was remarkable. He was really more concerned about peoples' lives and their welfare and making the world a better place to live in."

Like victims in a storm, Wendt and Baroni sought one another's advice, comfort and assistance. Newell was the third major figure. He was a clerical heavyweight as assistant pastor at the large downtown New York Avenue Presbyterian Church. Baroni, Wendt and Newell became the core of just about every white clerical group formed around social action issues in northwest Washington between 1962 and 1968. Often working with them were several rising young black clergymen, among them Fauntroy, the Rev. Channing Phillips of the United Church of Christ, and the Rev. Ernest Gibson, later president of the Baptist Ministers' Conference, an organization that included 350 black Baptist clergymen who met weekly and whose president was an automatic member of the city's power structure.

Baroni, Wendt and Newell, drawn increasingly to the same issues, realized that they could offer each other psychological support and dressings for wounds incurred in the line of battle. "I had a Protestant game I was playing and Geno had a Catholic game and we put together an ecumenical game," Newell said. "We were trying to organize the city and to impact the political system." They were in daily contact. In fact, during those years the first phone call for Newell and Baroni in the morning was to each other and the same held true for their final phone call at night.

The two men, uncomfortable with their institutional arrangements, established a weekly breakfast meeting which came to be called the Tuesday Morning Breakfast Club. Newell and Baroni set the agenda, giving them effective control over projects that might be undertaken. Bishop Moore and Wendt attended most of the meetings. The breakfasts were held on the grounds of the Episcopal Cathedral on St. Alban's Hill in upper northwest Washington. Baroni spent more time in those years with Protestant clergymen than he did with fellow Catholic priests.

No binding decisions were ever made for their denominations at the Tuesday breakfasts. The men used the sessions to develop strategies to deal with their own church leaders.

Reaching beyond the Christian faiths, Baroni and Newell formed an alliance with Dr. Isaac Franck, executive vice president of the Jewish Community Council of Greater Washington. Baroni, Newell and Franck came to be known as The Holy Trinity. The three men made appointments together with city officials and members of Congress. They testified as a unit on Capitol Hill. "The joke about us was who is the Father, who is the Son, and who is the Holy Spirit," Franck said years later during an interview in his office on the Georgetown University campus.

Franck said that the Catholic Church in Washington got a bum rap and that, contrary to the image that the Catholic Church was prone to lay back from active involvement in social issues, the record was much more positive. "Cardinal O'Boyle was thought of as a conservative, a reactionary, by many," Franck said. "But on race relations and civil rights, he had an immovable sense of justice." O'Boyle had organized and chaired the Interreligious Committee on Race Relations in the late 1950s. He testified on behalf of fair housing legislation before the District of Columbia Board of Commissioners. That was thought to be the first time in the history of the United States that a Roman Catholic prelate had testified in support of fair housing legislation. He also moved aggressively to desegregate the Catholic schools of the Washington archdiocese in the early 1950s, before the Supreme Court in its 1954 *Brown v. Board of Education* decision ruled that segregated schools were inherently unequal. O'Boyle's action was considered progressive for its time.

Until Baroni's arrival, Gingras had served as O'Boyle's point man on race relations and inner-city work. He spoke for the archdiocese of Washington on those matters in political forums and the press. O'Boyle did not get along with the press, especially the *Washington Post*, the city's major liberal opinion-leading newspaper, but he welcomed favorable news stories. But O'Boyle would not give press conferences or respond to reporters' calls. One result of this was that reporters tried to go around O'Boyle to someone with whom they could have a friendly give and take.

Such a person was Baroni. He was a news junkie who had caught the bug while listening to radio reports of World War II. As a high school boy in Somerset, he preferred to spend afternoons in the Somerset public library reading magazines rather than assigned textbooks. While studying for the priesthood, Baroni virtually ignored the theological library on the first floor of the seminary building, and instead spent free hours with secular works in the Mount St. Mary's College library. The seminary librarian, Father Hugh J. Phillips, often spotted Baroni behind *The New York Times* or *Time* magazine and asked him, "What are you reading that stuff for?"

Baroni's heroes were John L. Lewis, Franklin Delano Roosevelt, Philip Murray, labor leaders and politicians of all kinds. He was especially fascinated by Senator Joseph McCarthy of Wisconsin and Baroni closely followed the right-wing senator's attacks on Harry Truman and his hounding of the State Department. Though Baroni did not claim expertise in foreign policy, he had some sympathy as a young man for McCarthy's anti-communism.

To Baroni, events did not happen until they were duly reported in the newspapers, preferably *The New York Times*. He always had a skepticism about news on television. He liked the feel and durability of newsprint. To Baroni, a tree that fell in an empty forest didn't make any noise since nobody heard it. Public figures could only be successful, as Baroni saw it, if they were able to get their message across to the public, and the main way to do that was through the press.

So it was natural that when reporters came around in the 1960s asking for information about civil rights, Washington's inner-city and the Catholic Church, they found a source in Geno Baroni.

Two years after his 1960 arrival in Washington, Baroni began to cultivate reporters. He invited them to visit his parish and to write about his V Street Center. He sought out reporters at meetings, and was always patient with them, answering seriously and completely even the most naive questions of the young reporters assigned to neighborhood meetings, police reporting and the religious beat. He became a tipster for reporters on what was going on in the inner-city. Reporters promised to protect his identity as the source of material. He was a source for Robert Woodward and Carl Bernstein as young *Washington Post* reporters, long before they found their "deep throat" and broke the Watergate scandal in 1972–1974. On and off the record, Baroni spoke nothing but praise for O'Boyle. About some of the other hierarchy he was less flattering.

Baroni was quotable. He had an ear for newspaper vocabulary: nothing too pedantic, colorful language, bright anecdotes, profound and complicated points briefly summarized. From the reporters' point of view, Baroni's most endearing characteristics were his willingness to return telephone calls and to be quoted on the record.

By the mid-1960s, thanks to the press, Baroni was without doubt the best known parish priest in Washington and his name and reputation were becoming known across the country. If Baroni had a union, one Washington columnist wrote, "It would be called something like the Amalgamated Association of Low-Income Families."

Baroni cultivated the press to further his social justice objectives. He spelled those objectives out this way:

> For the American Christian, the greatest challenge is to overcome the racism and impoverishment in our center cities. Pope John said that man has human rights, and that he has a duty to claim these rights. By coming together at the same time, the civil rights movement and the ecumenical movement have

brought the churches together in civil rights and in the community. Probably the highlight is that the churches are cooperating together in the neighborhoods, not so much on dogmatic and liturgical differences, but on community problems. The churches can't be absent from the same type of movement that brought us to effective labor and civil rights legislation. The poverty program isn't going to be sufficient. We have to go further.

For Geno, attainment by minorities of their civil rights and the alleviation of poverty were critical aspects of the social justice to which he was dedicating his life.

In 1964, as the U.S. Senate debated President Lyndon B. Johnson's civil rights legislation O'Boyle, urged by Baroni, appeared at a rally in McDonough Gymnasium on the Georgetown University campus. O'Boyle joined others in calling on Congress to enact strong, effective civil rights laws. O'Boyle was considered to be considerably more progressive on racial issues than his auxiliary bishops, Philip Hannan and John Spence. As Baroni stepped further out on civil rights and other social issues, he said later, he was confident that O'Boyle supported him, but concerned that Hannan and Spence were undercutting him. Within the archdiocese, Baroni was described, sometimes in praise, sometimes in derision, as "O'Boyle's boy."

Baroni lobbied Capitol Hill for passage of the civil rights legislation. In a Christmas, 1964, letter to family and friends, Baroni wrote that "the first order of business of the past year was the Civil Rights Act. For the first time clergymen of all faiths joined forces to work for the passage of the new Civil Rights Act. It was a sight never before witnessed in Washington. I recall stalking the halls of Congress in search of those uncommitted congressmen. I recall visiting the office of Congressman Lesinski of Michigan with clergymen from Detroit. He didn't see the moral side of the issue and was willing to take his stand on the political knowledge of his district. I nearly fell off my gallery seat on that great day when the House passed the bill but the Michigan congressman voted 'no.' It was only a bit of sweet revenge when he lost his bid for reelection in November."

The Civil Rights Act of 1964 had great importance for people in his neighborhood, Baroni wrote. "Even the youngest of children knew what was happening. One remarked, 'Maybe when I grow up I might be able to get a good job.' Parents found new hope for their aspirations for the future life of their children. However, the movement for human dignity has gone beyond the law. It is true—where justice is not evident—the law must take its stand. But we have debts to pay and each day's delay in the lack of equal opportunity spells increased difficulty for the months ahead."

Difficulty in the months ahead. Baroni didn't know how prophetic he was.

# 5

# "No Turning Back: The March to Selma"

Geno Baroni was in the Sts. Paul and Augustine rectory, watching television, on the evening of Sunday, March 7, 1965. Like millions of other Americans, he was viewing the movie, *Judgment at Nuremberg*, which ridiculed the Nazi defenses: "I didn't know about it" and "I was only taking orders." The movie was interrupted to show vivid footage of that day's events in Selma, Alabama. Some 525 marchers left Brown Chapel on Sylvan Street that day and crossed the Edmund Pettis Bridge. Their goal was to march from Selma to Montgomery in a civil rights demonstration. The Rev. Dr. Martin Luther King, who was in Atlanta to preach at the Ebenezer Baptist Church, reluctantly agreed that the march could begin that Sunday without him. King wanted to lead it, but that would have forced delay. The marchers were ready. At the front of the column were Hosea Williams, a King lieutenant, and John Lewis, of the more militant Student Nonviolent Coordinating Committee.

They crossed the Pettis Bridge to find officers of the Alabama highway patrol three deep across the four lanes of Highway 80. The state police wore blue hard hats and gas masks and carried wooden truncheons. An officer shouted over a bullhorn to the marchers to turn back to Brown Chapel. The marchers did not turn back and the police charged, striking with their billy clubs. Men and women were knocked to the ground, some seriously hurt. Lewis' skull was fractured. The police fired cannisters of tear gas into the crowd. Choking, screaming, the marchers turned and ran back toward the church.

43

From in-between buildings off the highway, Sheriff James G. Clark's deputies charged on horseback. Swinging bullwhips and rubber tubing, some wrapped in barbed wire, they rode into the crowd of blacks. Many were struck and knocked to the ground. In shock they continued to stumble toward Brown Chapel. Clark's force followed the blacks into the black section. Some sought refuge in the nearest church. The state police followed them inside. When it ended, seventy blacks were hospitalized with injuries and more than 70 others were treated for injuries.

Baroni watched the film accounts of these events on television during the break in *Judgment at Nuremberg*. "I thought, 'My God, this is my country, in my time.' I couldn't look the other way as the Nazis did in Germany. I wanted to cry. I wanted to scream. I know I had to do something."

In Atlanta, King moved to action. He often complained before that Sunday about the failure of clergymen to join in his demonstrations at the beginning, when the outcome was uncertain and the situation dangerous. He noted that clergymen tended to wait until the dust settled, the battle had been won, and violence unlikely, and then participated. Here was a chance, King said, for clergymen to put their bodies on the line.

King sent telegrams to religious leaders across the nation to join him in Selma for a "ministers' march to Montgomery" the following Tuesday. Baroni did not get a telegram. In fact, very few Roman Catholic priests did. King knew that the Catholic hierarchy frowned on its priests and nuns joining in demonstrations, and few did. There were a few sisters in Alabama, but they were looked on by their superiors as rebels clearly outside the church mainstream.

Baroni walked down the hall to the room of his pastor, Monsignor Gingras, and alerted him to the situation in Selma and King's appeal. Gingras had seen the television footage and was outraged. Baroni said that the archdiocese should act immediately and that the appropriate person to go was Gingras, O'Boyle's representative and adviser on racial issues. Gingras said he didn't want to go, and that, at any rate, O'Boyle would never allow it. It was not that O'Boyle did not support the right of blacks to vote, Gingras said. Had not O'Boyle desegregated Washington's parochial schools and insisted on equal treatment of black physicians and patients at Washington's Providence Hospital? The question for O'Boyle was simply whether priests and nuns for whom he was responsible should be demonstrating. Gingras reminded Baroni that O'Boyle had on previous occasions ordered nuns to stay home from demonstrations and had advised priests to do the same. Gingras shared these views. Geno recognized that Gingras was not the demonstration-type.

"George was a good priest, a fine human being," said Baroni. "He was not the same type as I am. He didn't walk the streets at night. He didn't know the characters in the parish. He was much more familiar with people in the business community and city government who could find some money for a project or some jobs. He did it the old way of calling on the phone and saying, 'This is Father Gingras and can you do a favor for some people.' "

Unable to move Gingras to instant action, Baroni telephoned his Italian sidekick at the chancery, Floyd H. Agostinelli, who was in his northeast Washington home also thinking about the day's events and the right response. Agostinelli was very much the firebrand. "I liked to see myself as the constant thorn in O'Boyle's side," said Agostinelli. O'Boyle in 1960 hired Agostinelli to be the first lay person with any authority and access in the chancery. After Baroni came to Washington in 1960, he and Agostinelli became fast friends. "The fact that we were both Italians in the world of Irish bishops and priests drew us together," said Agostinelli. So did the fact that both men were the rough-hewn type. They much preferred a glass of earthy red wine and a night of swapping gossip to tea cups and polite conversation. Baroni often sought friendly advice from Agostinelli. They shared conspiratorial tendencies.

"Did you see the television?" Baroni asked Agostinelli. "What the hell can we do to get O'Boyle to send someone to Selma?"

"Nothing. But let's try," Agostinelli said.

"O'Boyle was liberal in the morning, conservative in the afternoon, and reactionary at night," Agostinelli recalled later. He told Baroni, "Let's get together for coffee at your rectory first thing in the morning and see if we can figure out what to do."

Baroni had a call later that evening from Wendt. One of Wendt's parishioners, Marjorie Gumble, had been so outraged by events at Selma, Wendt said, that she was arranging to charter an airplane to fly Washington clergymen to Selma. Would any priest from the archdiocese be permitted to go, Wendt asked.

"I don't think so," Baroni said, "but Floyd and I are working on it. I'll get back to you."

Baroni said the 7:30 mass the next morning and afterward found Agostinelli in the kitchen. Gingras joined them. The NBC morning program "Today" ran the footage of Selma. The *Washington Post*, lying on the kitchen table, had pictures and stories, including one on King's appeal for support from the ministry.

Contrary to Baroni's expectations, Gingras that morning was convinced that the Catholic archdiocese of Washington should be represented in Selma. He was image conscious, and when Baroni told him about the delegation Wendt was forming, Gingras decided that it would not look good for O'Boyle and the church in Washington if the Catholics stayed home.

Agostinelli had a proposal. "Get an appointment with O'Boyle this morning, George, and ask him if you can go."

"Not me," said Gingras. "I don't want to go. How about you, Geno?"

"Well, I would like to go," said Baroni. "But I think others should go too."

Gingras called O'Boyle's office on Rhode Island Avenue in downtown Washington and asked for an early morning appointment. Then Baroni called Wendt and said, "See what you can do to get one of your bishops to put some pressure on O'Boyle." Wendt said he would try.

Wendt said later he was "very happily surprised" by the possibility that a Catholic would fly with the Protestant clergy to Selma.

Wendt telephoned his religious superior, Bishop Paul Moore. Within the past 18 months, Moore and O'Boyle had gotten to know one another through their support for inner-city work in Washington. Before that, the Catholic bishop and the Episcopal bishop might see one another at a dinner or an inauguration when they would be present to offer a benediction. They would nod to each other like ships passing in the night and have nothing to say to each other. The ice broke in Washington with the Coalition of Conscience, an interreligious group formed initially by the major Protestant denominations to deal with poverty, hunger, poor housing and schools, in the capital. Jewish groups joined and then O'Boyle agreed to participate. Usually he sent Gingras as his representative at Coalition meetings. But the cardinal did attend a few sessions where he met Moore and other Protestant leaders. "O'Boyle never let his guard down, but he was more gracious and less majestic than we expected," one Protestant leader said.

Wendt talked with Moore about the delegation formed for Selma. Moore agreed to call O'Boyle and press for a Catholic representative. Meanwhile, Agostinelli was at his office arranging to see O'Boyle. "The old boy had an uncanny sense of what was going on," Agostinelli said. "I felt he could almost read what I was about to say before I said it. I was beginning to read him too, and I had the feeling that morning that I could get him to say yes."

Agostinelli opened the meeting by discussing the events in Selma the previous day. O'Boyle said it was a disgrace to the nation. Agostinelli mentioned King's call for clergy to come to Selma. O'Boyle said he had heard about that.

"Wouldn't it be a good idea if somebody from this diocese went?" Agostinelli said.

"Would you like to go, Floyd?"

"No, it should be a priest. The whole idea is to have clergy in the march and then see what the cops will do."

"Who do you have in mind, Floyd?" O'Boyle asked. Agostinelli felt that O'Boyle was teasing a bit. O'Boyle had a quick wit and a talent for deviousness. "Well, I was thinking about a number of priests."

Agostinelli was not above a bit of droll humor. "Perhaps Bishop Hannan or Bishop Spence would like to go." John S. Spence was an auxiliary bishop of Washington and an adviser to O'Boyle. "But if they can't go," said Agostinelli, "Monsignor Gingras or Father Baroni could go."

O'Boyle then made it evident that he had been thinking about allowing diocesan representation on the plane. He spelled out his conditions for Agostinelli. There were to be no more than four. All had to be priests. Absolutely no nuns. They were to wear clerical black garb with Roman collars. They were not to look for trouble. He did not want martyrs. They were to do it quietly. O'Boyle had one more condition: "Clear it with Bishop Toolen in Mobile." Bishop Thomas J. Toolen headed the diocese of Mobile from 1927 to 1969.

"You know, Floyd, that ecclesiastical protocol requires that before a priest of this diocese goes into the diocese of another bishop, you have to have permission from that bishop."

Now it was time for Agostinelli to be disingenuous. "God was on our side because Bishop Toolen wasn't in his chancery," said Agostinelli. He was not in Mobile. In fact, Agostinelli knew that Toolen was in Washington attending a meeting at the U.S. Catholic Conference. Agostinelli enlisted his secretary, Joan Briscoe, in the conspiracy. He asked her to try to contact Toolen in Mobile.

Agostinelli telephoned Gingras. "George, the cardinal says you and Geno and two other priests can go." Gingras called two other priests in the archdiocese who agreed to go. Baroni and Gingras hastily packed overnight bags. "Geno and I were trying to hurry Monsignor Gingras out because I think George was getting nervous about going and was starting to drag his feet. Geno and I were worried we were going to get called back and I think that Gingras was hoping that would happen."

Gingras wanted to take his hat with the red tassle. "I think it will be more impressive if they know a monsignor is there," Gingras said. But he couldn't locate it.

"To hell with it," Baroni said. "Just grab anything and let's go."

Agostinelli drove them south on 14th Street and across the Potomac River to Washington National Airport and the Page Terminal where the chartered plane was being prepared. A small crowd had already gathered. It was still two hours before the scheduled departure. Baroni was impatient. He wanted to get out of Washington as quickly as possible.

For good reason. Spence learned quickly through friends in O'Boyle's office that the cardinal had granted permission to Baroni, subject to approval from Toolen. He also learned that Agostinelli had stuck his head into O'Boyle's office several times with the same message: "I can't reach Bishop Toolen in Mobile."

Spence knew that Toolen was not in Mobile, but in Washington. So he called Toolen at the national Catholic offices and reached him there. Toolen told Spence that as the bishop of the diocese which included Selma, he opposed the presence of any outside priests. He wanted this conveyed to O'Boyle, and then to Baroni.

Agostinelli, no slouch at developing his own intelligence network, learned that Spence had reached Toolen, so he made a quick exit from his office, and did not inform his secretary, Joan Briscoe, where he was going.

Spence moved quickly to contact O'Boyle, but Agostinelli was faster. O'Boyle's secretary called down to Briscoe: "The cardinal wants Floyd." Briscoe said he was out and she didn't know where he was and when he would return. The cardinal's secretary called every 15 minutes. Briscoe gave the same message.

Spence then arrived in Agostinelli's office. He suspected that Agostinelli was with Baroni and Gingras. "Where are they getting the plane to Selma?" he asked. Briscoe said she didn't know for sure, but she thought it might be Dulles Airport. Nearly thirty miles separate Dulles from National. Dulles is southwest of Washington in Fairfax County. It is a modern airport with runways long enough to accommodate the largest passenger airplanes flying in 1965, the Boeing 707. National's shorter runways and noise restrictions prevented 707 flights there. It could have been a natural mistake on Briscoe's part to confuse Dulles with National.

Spence, through O'Boyle's secretary, called Dulles and began to page Baroni. At that moment, Baroni was talking with reporters at National, declaring himself a representative of the cardinal and asserting that his presence was an expression of the support by O'Boyle and the Roman Catholic Church in Washington for King and those in Selma demonstrating for civil rights.

There was a great deal of excitement at National Airport. Television and still photographers recorded the scene. Baroni played his presence as a most natural and not unexpected development. Among the arriving Protestant clergymen, the presence of a Roman Catholic priest was epochal.

Agostinelli did not tell Baroni of the effort to jettison the trip. Agostinelli kept looking at his watch, hoping that the plane would soon take off. He wanted to get back to his office without being missed, though he recognized that chances were slight. The question in Agostinelli's mind was whether the plane or Spence would win.

Departure was delayed for the arrival of Methodist Bishop John Lord. He came to the airport to personally endorse the journey of his representatives. Lord decided on the spur of a moment to get on the plane and go to Selma. Spotting Agostinelli, whom he knew from committee work, he said, "Floyd, please call my wife and tell her I'm going with them."

Finally, with a great sense of relief, Agostinelli said goodbye to Baroni and watched his friend climb up the steps into the airplane. A few minutes later, the plane was flying south toward Selma.

Agostinelli called the office and Ruby Smith, the switchboard operator answered. "Do you know the cardinal and Bishop Spence are looking for you?" Ruby Smith said.

"Put me through to Joan and don't tell anybody I called," Agostinelli said.

"Where are you?" Briscoe said.

"At National Airport."

"This place is burning. Spence is phoning me every other minute to know if I got hold of you."

"What did you tell him?" Agostinelli said.

"That I keep trying to get you at Dulles Airport, but nobody there can find you. They want Geno and the others off the plane."

"It's too late now," said Agostinelli.

"The next day O'Boyle gave me hell for being gone from the office so long without telling anybody where I was going," Agostinelli said. "But I had the feeling he didn't really mean it." Agostinelli also told O'Boyle how fine it was that Bishop Lord, the Methodist, had gone to Selma. "Wouldn't it be great if Bishop Hannan would go?" Agostinelli said to O'Boyle. The cardinal growled.

Aboard the plane, Baroni and the other clergymen got instructions. Marjorie Gumble offered some advice. "Roll up a newspaper and put it in your hat, so that if you get hit on the head by a billy club, your skull won't be fractured."

Baroni had his breviary, a book of daily required readings for Roman Catholic priests. "I'm going to put my breviary in my hat instead of newspapers," he said. In years to come, Baroni was to tell audiences: "I marched at Selma with my breviary in my hat."

A veteran of civil rights demonstrations in the South had other advice. "Pay attention to the direction the wind's blowing. If they fire tear gas, try to get upwind." Another said, "Absolutely wear clerical garb. A Roman collar is your best insurance against getting hit by a cop. If you are going to get hit, protect your head."

For Baroni, and for most clergy on the plane, Selma was to be their first "real" civil rights demonstration. Like soldiers going off to combat, they bonded themselves to the group and to one another in ways unimaginable not long before. Baroni walked the aisles of the airplane, gladhanding everyone. He played it straight about O'Boyle. "The cardinal wanted somebody to come," he said.

That same message, meanwhile, was being spread across the country from Chicago by Matthew H. Ahmann, secretary of the Catholic Inter-Racial Conference. He was advised of O'Boyle's decision almost immediately through the Catholic civil rights grapevine. Agostinelli called Father John Cronin, a civil rights advocate at the National Catholic Welfare Conference in Washington. "Tell Matt Ahmann that O'Boyle says Baroni could go to Selma," Agostinelli told Cronin.

When Ahmann received the message, he got on the phone. To other Inter-Racial Conference contacts around the nation he said, "Cardinal O'Boyle has agreed to let his priests march in Selma. Tell your bishop that O'Boyle has done it, and that now it's all right for them to do it too." Some priests skipped the procedure, heading directly for Selma, prepared to defend themselves later with the line "Cardinal O'Boyle let his priests go. I assumed you would too."

Ahmann said the initial O'Boyle decision was the key to releasing several dozen priests and nuns to travel to Selma on that day and following days. "For the first time, priests with authorization from their bishops marched in their clerical garb in civil rights demonstrations," said Ahmann. "I give Baroni's trip full credit for that."

Bishops later credited themselves for sending priests to Selma and building political support for the Voting Rights Act. "They forgot," said Agostinelli, "they had to be dragged into it."

Ahmann continued his calls for demonstrators in Selma over several days, each time citing O'Boyle's permission. He learned subsequently of O'Boyle's change of mind, but didn't choose to give much weight to it.

In Selma, before the day was over, about 400 ministers, rabbis, priests, nuns and lay people were on hand to walk with King. Wallace's lawyers went to U.S. District Court in Birmingham that afternoon for an injunction restraining Tuesday's march. King was not worried. The judge was Frank M. Johnson who had the best civil rights record of any Federal judge in the Deep South. Johnson, as King hoped, refused to issue the injunction, but he asked King to postpone the march until after a hearing Tuesday. King agreed.

But King changed his mind when he reached Selma. Baroni was in Brown Chapel that evening when King arrived to address the clergy and other demonstrators. "Emotions were high. I was ready. I hadn't gone there to wait for a few days while the judge thought about it and Wallace and his people came up with some way to beat Martin Luther King," Baroni said. King, finding a mood to march, decided to break his commitment to Johnson. "We've gone too far to turn back now," he told a rally in Brown Chapel. "We must let them know that nothing can stop us, not even death itself."

Baroni joined arms and hands with others and they rose to their feet singing the civil rights movement anthem, "We Shall Overcome." "Tears were on everybody's face," said Baroni. "I was scared silly, but I was going to march."

He, Gingras and Wendt had dinner that evening in a Selma restaurant. They talked during it with James Reeb, Boston Unitarian minister who had previously worked with them along Washington's 14th Street corridor. When they said goodbye to Reeb, Baroni added, "See you tomorrow, Jim."

Baroni and Gingras spent the night in a local rectory and as was often the case, Baroni could not sleep. He prowled through the rectory during the middle of the night looking for newspapers, magazines, books, anything he could read.

As Baroni and others headed the next day for Brown Chapel and the beginning of the march, they learned that Judge Johnson that morning had issued an order barring the march. King was in a dilemma. He had 400 clergymen ready to march. They had come here at his invitation for a march. Many told him they had to go back to their own work. Perhaps never again would he have so many members of the clergy ready to walk at his side. Losing them would be a victory for Wallace. Baroni and other clergymen were aware, too, that in the black district of Selma, emotions were rising. King had to respond. There were others far more militant than he ready to seize the movement and steer it away from the nonviolence he preached.

It was a "painful and difficult decision," King told the clergymen in Brown Chapel that afternoon. But he had decided to defy Judge Johnson and to march. King was also turning down President Johnson, whose representative in Selma, LeRoy Collins, director of the U.S. Community Relations Service, asked King to wait until another day. Collins was meanwhile negotiating with Lingo and Clark. The two police officers finally agreed that they would hold back their men as long as King's marchers went only as far as the marchers had gone on Sunday.

Baroni, his breviary under his hat, listened as King said in Brown Chapel: "I do not know what lies ahead of us. There may be beatings, jailings and tear gas. But I would rather die on the highways of Alabama than make a butchery of my conscience. There is nothing more tragic in all this world than to know right and not do it. I cannot stand in the midst of all these glaring evils and not take a stand."

Baroni walked with Gingras as the marchers, two abreast, left Brown Chapel and headed toward the police line. King stopped at Pettis Bridge where a U.S. marshal read Judge Johnson's restraining order. They continued on. When they reached Jefferson Davis Highway, the road to Montgomery, state police again barred the way. King called on his followers to kneel and pray. They did.

King's lieutenant, the Rev. Ralph David Abernathy, said a prayer. Then Bishop Lord prayed. He recalled the Israelites fleeing in Egypt from the Pharaoh and God opening the Red Sea for them to cross to safety.

As if on cue, the state troopers stepped aside, leaving the road to Montgomery open. But King, uncertain over the meaning of the move, ordered the marchers back to Brown Chapel. Baroni was both relieved and disappointed. "I was not looking to be a hero with my head busted," he said. "But I thought we hadn't accomplished anything." But King saw it differently.

He said it was a victory, and that his followers would someday reach Montgomery. He was right in that. The march did go on. And so did Congressional action on the Voting Rights Act. President Johnson signed it into law that summer.

Baroni and Gingras flew aboard the chartered plane back to Washington that evening. There was a feeling among the Washingtonians that they had made history, that they shared in a common experience that would affect their lives forever.

Their elation was cut short by a tragedy that affected many of them, particularly Wendt and Baroni. For years, neither man could speak of Jim Reeb without a choking pause. While the Washington contingent flew home that evening, Reeb went to dinner at a cafe in Selma. Reeb and two fellow white ministers walked after dinner to the Southern Christian Leadership Conference headquarters in Selma. As they passed the Silver Moon Cafe, someone inside shouted, "Hey, you niggers." Four young white men emerged from the cafe. One struck Reeb on the head with a baseball bat.

As the Washington contingent landed at National Airport, Reeb was rushed to a hospital in Birmingham. He lay in a coma until Thursday. Then he died. Johnson sent Air Force One to Alabama to fly Mrs. Reeb and the body of her husband home.

The journey to Selma left an indelible mark on Geno Baroni's record. It also helped change his self-image. It was a rare time in his life when he openly confronted authority. The bravery he showed in the shadow of the Alabama state troopers sparked him to other risks. Suddenly, Baroni discovered strength that he had not felt before.

His credentials in the world of Washington's urban activists were now well-established. Like a veteran of combat, he enjoyed the special common bond of those who defy death and rise above their fears. That bond was strengthened in the weeks ahead when friends of Jim Reeb in Washington attended a memorial service in a Washington church. Baroni was there, as a friend and as the archdiocesean representative.

Baroni's friends saw changes in him after his journey to Selma. "He was talking more in his own name than in the name of the cardinal," one said. "I have a feeling that Geno saw himself much differently after Selma, that he had taken a giant step beyond his brother priests in Washington."

But Geno Baroni had many more giant steps to take as he continued his own march.

# 6

# The Walls
# Come Tumbling Down

Geno Baroni chaired a meeting in the basement of Sts. Paul and Augustine Church between police community relations representatives and Cardozo residents on April 4, 1968. The residents complained of harassment, including unprovoked violence against blacks by police. Baroni set up the meeting to air the issue.

Geno was called away to take a telephone call. Police Commissioner Patrick Murphy was on the line. "Dr. King has been killed," Murphy said. An assassin had cut down Martin Luther King, Jr., while he was standing on the balcony of a hotel in Memphis. Murphy told Baroni: "We're expecting trouble when the word gets around. If you can help, fine. But be careful in that neighborhood."

Four hundred yards from the Sts. Paul and Augustine rectory, at 14th and U Streets, stood the Washington headquarters of the Student Non-Violent Coordinating Committee, SNCC. Baroni knew that Stokeley Carmichael, who two years earlier at Sts. Paul and Augustine had discussed theology and politics and tutored children, had become a radical leader of the militant SNCC. Geno knew that another sometime V Street Center visitor, H. Rap Brown, who had recently given a speech in Washington that many saw as threatening, also hung out occasionally at SNCC headquarters. This was one place in the neighborhood where Geno was not welcomed. Baroni understood. He could talk to Carmichael on the street, but not in the building.

For years, Baroni, Wendt and Newell had anticipated the day that Washington would burn in a riot. "It wasn't a matter of 'if'. It was a

54

matter of 'when,' " Baroni said. "We knew a riot was inevitable. The police knew. Nobody wanted to talk about it publicly for fear of feeding it. But as I walked the streets and talked to people, I could feel the tension building." Baroni often used the imagery of the first play that Marlene Hoffman had directed in his Neighborhood Commons, Lorraine Hansberry's *A Raisin in the Sun*. A grape left lying in the sun, Baroni said, will burst. He predicted the same bursting forth of violence on Washington's streets. He felt growing tension in the black community. "Its legitimate needs were not being met," Baroni said. "There were thousands of unemployed. They lived in rotten housing. Their kids weren't learning anything in school. All around there was violence. It was a tinderbox. All that was needed was for somebody to strike the match."

After the earlier riots in Watts and Newark, Protestant clerics across the country established an informal communications "hot-line" to keep one another abreast of developments in their cities. Newell passed on alarming reports from the Protestant network to Baroni. Tuesday Morning Breakfast Club members talked about what they would do when the Washington riot erupted.

The members had faith in their own abilities to survive on the streets. Not only did they wear religious garb, they were familiar white faces on the street. Wendt at St. Stephen's and the Incarnation, Baroni at the V Street Center and Newell out of a storefront church on upper 14th Street were visible and non-threatening. They had white skin, but they had black suits and white collars. Baroni made certain that clerics who lacked austere clerical garb could count on him for an extra Roman collar and black cloth vest that identified the clergy. He acquired a few extra outfits from other priests and kept them ready in his closet at Sts. Paul and Augustine.

In anticipation of street violence, police issued special identity cards to Newell, Baroni, Wendt, Moore and others whose influence was thought to have potential for calming tense situations. Newell was the official contact for the religious community at the command post set up by Mayor Walter W. Washington and the U.S. Justice Department on E Street downtown. Though only Newell, with card number 92, was officially to be admitted to the command post, he took Baroni there, before and during the riot.

When Baroni, Newell and Wendt got the message that King had been slain, they donned clerical garb and headed for 14th and U Streets. Baroni saw a large crowd gathered around SNCC headquarters. He circulated, nodded and chatted, deplored the violence, offered agreement at the horror of the assassination of King and consolation to the people there. Then a delegation appeared from the SNCC office. A few words were spoken. Young blacks began to move north and south along 14th Street and east along U Street, smashing windows, stopping cars, yelling for others to join them. "It's time for me to get out of here," Baroni said to himself.

He went back to Sts. Paul and Augustine, and telephoned Newell, the Chancery and officials at the U.S. Catholic Conference at 14th and Massachusetts Avenues. The USCC building is a long walk from 14th and U, but as it turned out, not far from the southernmost border of the 14th Street riot corridor. Baroni instructed white workers and volunteers at the V Street Center to leave the building immediately. Most had cars. He told them to drive on V Street to 15th Street, away from the disturbance, and to head west and north. Baroni knew that the rioters were not likely to come down V Street. There were no stores there and the occupants of the houses across from the church were black. Beyond the church were residential neighborhoods. Nonetheless, as the sirens began to wail, amid the sounds of wild shouting and glass smashing, Baroni set to work in his Center office. He cancelled religious services for that Easter weekend.

Radio and television kept him informed of the outside view of what was happening inside the ghetto. He talked through the night with clergy, reporters, government officials and friends across the country. Uncomfortable and potentially dangerous as it was, Baroni experienced excitement and a sense of destiny as he sat in the middle of the action. At that moment, he said later, he began to realize that for the last few years he had been part of an epoch in American history. As the rage swirled about him, however, he began to wonder whether his time as a street priest had come and passed. "I knew immediately that the riot in Washington was not going to be forgotten quickly and that I was going to have to do things differently," he said.

Baroni was afraid, but that did not prevent him the next morning from walking to 14th Street to view the devastation. He sensed immediately that it was a lull in the storm, that the anger had not burned itself away. There were crowds of angry blacks, but no police. Baroni, hoping he was protected by his clerical garb, walked among them, assessing the damage. He immediately saw there were no remaining operating stores. The big food stores, including a Safeway Supermarket, had been looted and burned. Even if food could come into the area, there was no conventional way to stock and distribute it. Baroni noted the destruction of the People's Drug Store where he bought his newspapers. No newspaper trucks ventured up 14th Street that morning. In the middle of the biggest story of his life, Baroni couldn't read about it.

Back at the rectory, Baroni called Newell. They agreed to set in motion a planned food distribution system. Baroni, turning his Center office into a riot response center, called priests and ministers throughout the area, asking them to honor previously-made commitments to convert their churches and meeting halls into refuges and food stations. Newell and Wendt went about the same task.

Months before, Tuesday Morning Breakfast Club members talked with supermarket executives about what to do if a riot came. Baroni was impressed with the promised cooperation of Joseph Danzansky, head of the Washington-based Giant food chain. That morning Baroni confirmed with Danzansky that the Giant warehouses had food at the ready and trucks prepared to haul it. But not yet, came the word from the E Street command center. We're only had day one, they said. There's likely to be more trouble. They warned against unarmed and unguarded trucks entering the riot zone. Police were not able or willing yet to ride shotgun for a bread and milk run.

The police who predicted more rioting were correct. Once again Baroni sat for most of the night in his office as the rioters surged up and down 14th Street. The smoke from nearby fires drifted into his office, and he smelled tear gas. Standing in the Neighborhood Commons, his specially-designed playground, theater and gathering place behind the Center, he looked up and saw helicopters. "It was like a war zone," Baroni said.

O'Boyle and other religious leaders were invited to the command center. Baroni, hearing from Newell, drove to the Cathedral office and briefed O'Boyle on the purposes of the meeting. Not only did officials want a call from the religious leaders for calm and reason, they needed a way to deal with frightened businessmen who were demanding that the police, the National Guard, and elite airborne Army units, called to Washington by President Johnson, shoot to kill. The business executives pointed out that Johnson created a fortress with city buses bumper to bumper around the White House and Executive Office Building, that National Guardsmen were bivouaced on the White House grounds, but their stores had no such protection. "Kill the looters," the businessmen said.

The executives said, accurately to a great extent, that the police had decided to let the riot burn itself out. Baroni told O'Boyle that the shoot-to-kill request would be discussed at the command center. "You'll be asked to take a position on that, your eminence," Baroni told the cardinal. Asked for his opinion, Baroni said the cardinal should oppose any such orders, because not only would such shooting claim many lives, including the innocent, it would also prolong and perhaps worsen the riot. Whether Baroni's advice played a pivotal role is unclear, but O'Boyle argued at the meeting against shoot-to-kill orders. Mayor Washington, Murphy and Justice Department officials turned down the business executives' request.

Another night of rioting followed. By now, however, police and Guardsmen circled the riot corridors. Again Baroni was awake all night, talking by telephone from his own command post and occasionally walking over to 14th Street, disregarding his own analysis that a stroll through the riot zone was foolhardy.

By the next morning, the situation had stabilized so that the food plan could begin. Under armed guard, trucks moved into the neighborhoods. One stopped at Sts. Paul and Augustine and from the church basement, volunteers began to distribute food.

During the following days, ordinary life returned slowly to the riot-torn city. As shops reopened, the Sts. Paul and Augustine food system shut down. Baroni then had another idea, and broached it to Gingras and Newell. "Let's turn the basement into a clothing exchange," Baroni said. Many in the riot fires had lost all their possessions, including clothing. The city responded with emergency shelter, but few local people had more to wear than the clothing on their backs. The Sts. Paul and Augustine clothing exchange was set up. Baroni and Newell noted that many of the articles brought into the basement to be exchanged for garments of the right size seemed to be fresh off a rack, unworn and neatly creased. "We had a lot of hot merchandise on our hands," Baroni said. "We didn't ask for any proof of purchase."

The clergy of Washington's inner-city performed well under the difficult circumstances of the riot, and Newell said Baroni deserved enormous praise for the role he played during the entire period. Newell gave Baroni credit for the food distribution center and clothing exchange ideas. "Because of Baroni's insistence that we plan for something like this, we were looking pretty good and nobody raised any questions about us," Newell said. "In every community we were bathed with the acceptance of having been ready and right."

*         *         *

In the months that followed the riot, as rubble was slowly cleared away and essential services returned, Baroni began to think more about his future at Sts. Paul and Augustine. No longer did he feel as comfortable as he did before April 4 in walking the streets. No longer did he encourage white volunteers as tutors and social workers. They feared to enter the neighborhood and he was concerned about their safety. "After what happened," Geno said, "I couldn't blame them. You could just feel that everything had changed."

He also felt a certain failure. He worked for more than seven years to bring a touch of civility to the ghetto, and then overnight it exploded on him. In the months after the riot, Baroni went through several severe illnesses. He was depressed and lonely, and felt alienation surrounding him. He was forced to stay in bed for several weeks during the summer of 1968. The doctors said he suffered from nerves and exhaustion. He had controlled his fear during the riot; now it caught up with him.

To further aggravate Baroni, issues inside the Catholic Church were coming to a head. The theological dispute between the old guard and the young Turks in the priesthood largely centered around the role of individual conscience. The older men tended toward black-letter law. Their view was that through the centuries certain rules had been worked out for men and women to live by, and violations of those rules were sins.

Sins involving sex seemed to occupy a special category. In the case of birth control, for instance, it mattered not if the married couple chose to practice artificial contraception for reasons that to them were quite valid, including such specific cases as serious risk of physical harm to the woman from pregnancy, an inability to afford additional children, or the desire to space children.

The use of artificial contraception was a mortal sin, condemning the participants to hell unless they confessed their sin to the priest and had it absolved. Finally, in 1967, a major birth-control controversy erupted. Some counseled people that under some circumstances, such as a threat to the health of the mother and inability to financially support additional children, birth control was not only appropriate, it may be mandatory as a moral act.

Young priests of Washington got into the birth control issue in their monthly Sunday night meetings which they dubbed "Scotch and Scripture." In 1967 there was widespread expectation that a commission appointed by the Vatican to study birth control would conclude that the church would alter its centuries-old position in light of modern needs and theology.

Meanwhile, Baroni and many other Washington priests wanted to learn more about the birth control issue. Many signed up for a special course at Catholic University. It was held on Monday afternoons and the teacher was Father Charles Curran, a noted Catholic theologian.

But a bombshell exploded in the spring of 1968. The bishops of Washington, Delaware, Maryland and Virginia, known collectively as the Delmarva Conference, issued a statement dealing with the special method of teaching religious belief called catechesis. In effect, the bishops confirmed the law against birth control and ordered their priests not to deviate from the traditional position whether preaching, teaching, counseling or hearing confessions. The priests rebelled, drafting a statement of their own. Baroni agreed with the priests' statement, but he told Gingras that he hoped the birth control controversy would not blow up. He believed it would involve most of the young priests who preached and practiced the social gospel ministry, his friends and allies. Baroni's concerns began to unfold with the release later that year of the encyclical *Humanae Vitae*.

The news set off a firestorm. Some 44 priests, most of them in active social gospel ministry, signed a dissenting document and went public. One by one, the priests were called into the Latin School off Connecticut Avenue in northwest Washington and asked to withdraw their signature from the dissenting document. Those who refused to do so were punished. Some were ordered out of their rectories. Some were forbidden to preach, teach or hear confessions.

Baroni was on vacation in Trent, Italy, when the dissenting document was issued and the examinations in the Latin School started. Many of his friends in the priesthood implored him to join them and sign the paper. He refused, and went into seclusion. Several dissenters were sorely disappointed. They hoped Baroni would give weight to their appeal for intervention by Bishop Joseph L. Bernardin, executive secretary of the U.S. Catholic Conference. Baroni's refusal to join the dissenters was a harsh blow. Grieved, Baroni nevertheless held fast. He explained: "Birth control was not my issue. I had other issues, housing, poverty, injustice." He intended to continue to provide privately and in the confessional the same advice he had been offering, he told friends, but would not publicly dissent. "My effectiveness would have been over, even if I had been allowed to stay," Baroni pointed out.

The dispute produced tragic and bitter consequences. The archdiocese lost many of its brightest young priests. The cadre of social activists built up over five years was destroyed. O'Boyle, too, was hurt. He retired not long after the controversy, and his service to the archdiocese of Washington was often measured in light of the birth control controversy.

For Baroni it was a deep personal tragedy. When O'Boyle arranged Baroni's promotion to monsignor a few months later, there were whispers of payoff. Baroni overheard these whispers and they saddened him. He was also hurt that some friends never forgave him. One told him: "You were always talking about the justice of decent housing. Where were you when your fellow-priests were thrown out of their rectories onto the streets?"

Baroni didn't know how to answer that question. The birth control controversy and the loss of good friends, the Washington riots that started around the corner from his rectory, the assassinations of Dr. King and Robert F. Kennedy left Baroni physically and emotionally exhausted.

He was seized with frustration and anger. He thought O'Boyle had acted harshly and unjustly with the dissenting priests. A few times that fall, as he came face-to-face with the reality that there was injustice and lack of compassion within the very institution he sought to serve, he thought about leaving the priesthood.

# 7

## Out of the Ashes

Madonna House in nearby Aquia, Virginia, was the refuge Geno sought in the fall of 1968. While studying for the priesthood, Geno read about Catherine de Hueck, and the Friendship House and Madonna House Movements. A wealthy Russian emigré, Catherine and her husband arrived in Toronto, Canada, in 1921. That same year Catherine founded Friendship House, a movement to work against racial discrimination and injustice. She established the first Friendship House in the United States in 1938 in Harlem. She said she picked Harlem because it was a "very stony portion of the great vineyard of the Lord" with its "poverty, misery, race discrimination and much hardship and sorrow." In 1943, she founded Madonna House, a lay apostolate in the movement for social service and justice.

Baroni was fascinated with the movements and told his seminary friends they were examples of what the church ought to be doing. During his first visit to a Friendship House, to Combermere in Ontario, Canada, during his low point as a young priest in Altoona, Geno found it a good place to forget about fears and frustrations. The baroness gave Baroni the run of the Madonna House grounds on the banks of Madawaska River. There he walked across fields, spent quiet hours in the small chapel, ate communally with Madonna House members, candidates and visitors. He poured out his heart to the baroness. He wanted to be a good priest, to celebrate mass, to absolve sins, to comfort the afflicted, to visit the sick, to preach the gospel, he said, but he wasn't very good at it. And, besides, he wanted to do much more, things that weren't accepted in Altoona and Johnstown by his pastors.

Expressing discontent at the restrictions of a parish rectory in a stable, working and middle-class community, he said he wanted more action on social issues. Baroni talked to the baroness about his ideas that the church had to be on the frontline in the war for social change. He wanted the church, specifically the local bishops and priests, to endorse labor unions and to back their strikes against greedy managers. Instead, he found that church people tended to side with managers against workers.

Baroni told the baroness that the church offered the promise of salvation to the poor through observance of the ten commandments, prayer and sacrifice, but that didn't go far enough. The church provided money to people short on their mortgage, food for the hungry, old suits and shoes for unemployed, free schoolbooks and supplies for children of misfortune—again, all wonderful works of charity, but that still wasn't enough. The church did not deal with the underlying problems of poverty and discrimination.

Baroni told the baroness that perhaps he should join Dorothy Day's Catholic Worker Movement in New York. "I could work on the Bowery," he said. The baroness pointed out that much of the Catholic Worker Movement's efforts were feeding and sheltering the human derelicts, not in forcing changes in American government and society's policies that Baroni wanted to achieve. She reminded Baroni that her own community, then called the Pious Union, was opening houses throughout Canada and the United States to spread its way of living the gospel in the world. Through the example of a simple dedicated lifestyle and work among the poor, the baroness hoped that the world would look afresh at urban and rural poverty, injustice, and peace issues.

"Would you like to join us?" the baroness asked Baroni.

"I need to think about it," he said.

Inspired by the philosophy and people of Madonna House, he informally promised a life of prayer and work toward the alleviation of poverty and the attainment of peace. Encouraged and renewed by Catherine de Hueck Doherty's friendship and support, Geno went back to Johnstown where he followed through on his plans to get psychiatric help and then go to Washington.

By the time Baroni returned to Combermere from Washington in a second trip in 1961, his plan had been successful, and his experiences in Johnstown and Altoona already a fading memory. He was receiving professional therapy for his emotional strain. He was settled in Sts. Paul and Augustine Parish, and liked it. When he met with the baroness in 1961, Baroni said he had given considerable thought to her invitation to join the Pious Union, and he asked to be considered as a candidate for membership.

The following summer, in 1962, he went to Combermere again. Things were still going very well for him in Washington. The work at the Sts. Paul and Augustine was challenging. He was setting up the V Street Center, and building alliances with Protestant and Jewish clerics to promote inner-city social programs. The work in Washington, he said, was very similar to the task undertaken by Pious Union members: prayer and work. On August 2, 1962, he took the promise to live a life of poverty required for a priest entering the Pious Union, and renewed the promises of chastity and obedience he made at his ordination. Baroni received the symbol of membership in the Pious Union—the cross bearing the Latin words, *Pax* and *Caritas*, Peace and Love. But he declined the baroness' offer to join the Pious Union as its chaplain. He said he felt he should be "more active in the world." He talked about his deepening involvement in social issues in Washington.

*     *     *

That involvement was evident when in 1966, Cardinal O'Boyle appointed Geno executive director of the archdiocese's Commission on Urban Affairs. A big part of the commission's job was to improve the quality of urban life. One way to go about that, Baroni said, was to provide decent housing for the poor. His childhood in Pennsylvania—during which he watched his parents struggle to acquire a home of their own—motivated Baroni to favor home ownership by the poor. His experience as an inner-city priest heightened his awareness of the rotten housing that started at the boundaries of Sts. Paul and Augustine. His success in turning empty parish space into the thriving V Street Center led him to believe that he could manage even larger development projects.

By the middle of the decade Baroni took a mighty multi-million dollar gamble. It began with walking the streets of the neighborhood around Sts. Paul and Augustine Parish: Baroni was outraged by what he saw. Baroni occasionally visited parishioners in their homes in buildings owned by the city housing authority or absentee landlords. "I couldn't stand the smells," Baroni said. "Urine and pork and cabbage. There was graffiti all over the walls, garbage and trash in the corridors. The pipes leaked." For shelter like this, he said, people came to him at the rectory and begged for money. "I had about $90 bucks a month in my pocket and the parish could afford only a few hundred dollars. There wasn't much I could do as a parish priest to raise money for these people to move to someplace better," Baroni said.

Here and there in the neighborhood were vacant single houses that could be made fit for habitation, but he knew from listening to parishioners, social workers and police that these houses were targets for vandalism. He learned that single homes were mostly owner-occupied. He immediately saw a linkage between ownership and responsibility, but there was little incentive to buy a house, and little money to do it.

"The neighborhood was deteriorating fast," Baroni said. "Houses that had been abandoned or caught fire were left to stand there as eyesores. Sometimes they would tear them down, but they didn't rebuild. They left a vacant lot with rocks and a place to collect more garbage." Many vacant houses became "shooting galleries" for the neighborhood's drug pushers and users.

It was easy enough to blame government and slum landlords for the terrible housing, but to his embarrassment he learned that some of those landlords "were his own people, Catholics living in the suburbs while they made their money off the slums."

What distressed him most was the smell of defeat in the neighborhood. Baroni could not help but measure living conditions in Washington's slums against the poverty of his youth and his parents' struggle to acquire and cultivate a precious piece of property. In central Pennsylvania when he was growing up, he said, people took great pride in their homes. "They would be little houses, not much more than the miner's shack where I was born and lived as a little kid. But they fixed them up. They painted them and kept them clean. They put the garbage in cans and if your neighbor didn't do the same thing, there was hell to pay." The difference was home ownership. Begging the city's housing authority and the absentee landlords to repair rundown housing and to let people slide in their rent payments was just not enough. As the executive director of Cardinal O'Boyle's Commission on Urban Affairs, Baroni made frequent trips to the office of Walter W. Washington, the city's development coordinator and later first black mayor, and began to prowl the halls of Capitol Hill. Baroni believed that while government had a duty to provide social services, it couldn't do everything that needed to be done. "When I first came to Washington I wanted to save the world. Then I wanted to save the country. Then I wanted to save the city. Then I realized that if you wanted to save the world and the country and the city, you had to start right in the neighborhood where people lived."

In 1967, despite Johnson's war against poverty, 32 percent of Washington's people still needed housing assistance. It seemed like everybody in the Sts. Paul and Augustine neighborhood did. When he couldn't tolerate sitting at his desk any longer, Baroni got into his dented blue Volkswagen and went to look at the problem first hand.

His resentment grew as he understood the financial reality. The archdiocese was hard-strapped to find money to maintain the black inner-city parishes. They were essentially mission churches, supported by affluent white suburban parishes. Still, other denominations were making the effort.

By the spring of 1967, it seemed to Baroni that a partnership among church groups, backed by government, could help relieve the housing problem. Clergy friends, including Bill Wendt at St. Stephen and the Incarnation Episcopal Church and Phil Newell on the Presbyterian Church staff, liked the idea. Their institutions were already in the field.

Baroni decided that the Catholic archdiocese should join the effort. He contacted Newton Frohlich, a young Washington attorney, and got him to research federal housing law and to help him form on paper a corporation that would buy 3,000 slum houses, rehabilitate them, and sell them back to individual family purchasers. Baroni's idea was to make enough profit on each house so that the corporation could be self-sustaining and growing.

Geno went to O'Boyle and asked for money to buy some houses to get started. O'Boyle was very sensitive about housing and willing to help, but he said he didn't have much money. He asked how much it would cost. Baroni hedged a bit. He talked about perhaps $50,000 to get started, but it would all come back as the houses were repaired and sold. The cardinal was skeptical, and said he would think about it. He conferred with his advisers and they recommended against it. To friends, Geno confided, "Some of them think I'm trying to make the church into a slum landlord."

The cardinal overrode his advisers and decided to back Baroni for a modest effort—reconstruction of a few houses. Baroni's design, of course, was much larger than the cardinal's understanding of it. "I had these dreams of buying up maybe 3,000 houses all over the city and rehabilitating them," he said. "I thought we could put together the largest and best government-private housing partnership in the country right here in Washington."

One of the landlords that Baroni had worked with over the years was a Catholic layman, George Basiliko. Baroni often called him and asked him to let some family in the parish slide for a month or two on rent. "Oh, Father, I've already given them an extra month. I can't give them any more," Basiliko said. Baroni persisted: "George, I know it's tough on you, but I really need it this time." Basiliko would then agree to do it, vowing that this was absolutely the last time. Baroni was forced to acknowledge that by the next month, the beneficiaries of his intervention had skipped without paying anything.

Now Baroni went to Basiliko and said his Urban Rehabilitation Corporation would like to buy some houses. Basiliko cooperated. Baroni bought some for two and three thousand dollars. "Some we got by promising to pay the back taxes. But for others we had to pay several thousand dollars." Baroni was so anxious to launch the program that he ignored warning signs. It was not the first, nor the last, time in his public career that he let his enthusiasm for a project overcome sober judgments that it would not work. "Prophets," said the Rev. Tilden Edwards, then an assistant pastor at St. Stephen and the Incarnation Episcopal Church, "have to dream and proclaim without worrying too much about the consequences."

In January, 1969, URC purchased 108 houses from Basiliko. Baroni's lawyer, Frohlich, insisted on a contract provision that Basiliko would buy back the houses if the Federal Housing Authority refused to give them high enough appraisals to cover the costs.

Baroni put together a team of architects and contractors. He was the driving force. He selected the first houses for rehabilitation, and he took an active hand in approving the rehabilitation plan. "This was really the beginning of my education about housing," Baroni said. He acknowledged that he was personally over his head, and most of the time, knew it. But he was undeterred. He had confidence that the others shared his dream and would pull it off.

Work got started in February, 1969. Baroni reported to the cardinal that the idea was going better than expected. But it was only four months before reality set in. And Baroni was forced to admit: "Our initial naivete about our role as non-profit sponsor vanished as we encountered a multitude of problems at each step." He said the land cost too much, the federal housing law had too many requirements, and the poor could not get mortgages from banks. In addition, said Baroni, "Some contractors just plain ripped us off. They figured the money was coming from the archdiocese and the government and they might make a big profit out of it."

Cynthia Fowles, who was brought in by Baroni to bring order to the project and its books, recalled another problem: "Some of the houses were vandalized overnight. The contractor would return in the morning and find that the refrigerator or range or heater he had installed the day before was now gone. We couldn't keep up with the theft."

Baroni sought to rescue the project by convincing FHA appraisers that their figures were too low. He appealed without success to President Richard M. Nixon's Secretary of Housing and Urban Development, George W. Romney. "Romney was sympathetic," Baroni said, "but he said he couldn't reverse the appraisers." Baroni placed several calls for help with friends on Capitol Hill, but they too were stymied.

Finally, about a year after the project had been started with great high hopes, Baroni agreed reluctantly that a rescue operation was needed. He withdrew his verbal commitment to buy 3,000 houses. Frohlich and Basiliko's lawyers worked out a plan for Basiliko to buy most of the houses back.

Baroni decided to continue the rehabilitation of about a dozen houses. In time, many were sold and a few were rented. But Baroni was no more successful than other landlords in collecting the rent. Now it was Geno Baroni, slum landlord.

Cynthia Fowles advised Baroni: "Two tenants who have been moved out for non-payment of rent have been turned over to a collection agency. One has been put in the hands of a lawyer, who has not taken action to date. In spite of monthly billings to delinquents, threats of eviction, visits and such other follow-up actions as our staff has taken, accounts receivable for rents total about $6,000." Like it or not, the archdiocese had also become a slum landlord dunning people to pay their rent. Now it was Geno Baroni, bad debt collector.

Although Baroni's grand dream of rehabilitating 3,000 houses failed to materialize, the pioneering priest and his corporation did chalk up several accomplishments. URC was the first non-profit sponsor in Washington to have completed homes for ownership for low-income families under the FHA's 221(h) program. In December, 1968, several of its purchasers became the first families in the nation to qualify for a new government interest subsidy under the 1968 Housing Act.

The project cost the archdiocese between $300,000 and $400,000, the records indicate. Baroni said the loss did not cause him any problems with O'Boyle.

But Baroni was distressed. He talked about leaving Sts. Paul and Augustine and resigning as director of the cardinal's Urban Affairs Office. At one point during this crisis, Baroni disappeared from the office for about ten days while crucial decisions were pending. That was a typical response by Baroni to crisis. He laid low until others absorbed the heat or made this tough decisions. Associates said they came quickly to realize that Baroni was unable to confront difficult situations or handle demanding people.

Baroni alternated in this period between the exuberant and the despondent. He poured out ideas, many visionary, but he was frustrated by his inability to achieve them. Baroni's enthusiasm could be contagious. He infected those around him with a conviction that nothing was impossible, but his moods changed quickly. Without warning, but often after a setback, he became morose, uncommunicative, even to close friends. When pressed for an explanation, he mumbled an evasion. So close were many of his associates to him that Baroni's mood swings affected their cycles, too. Baroni's depression was reflected in a letter he wrote to O'Boyle:

> I feel constrained to write this letter and wish it were not so. I know and the Lord knows my sins and I regret I may not fully realize the grief or complaints you have received or accepted on my account. However, does one cringe when implied criticism is leveled against the church's housing effort—in the name of Urban Rehabilitation Corporation—in secular terms of "money wasted." While millions have been spent by HUD, the City, Real Estate Corporations, etc., this city is witness to the failure to house the poor and their children. In fact, it has been the scandal of the Banks and Realtors, Saving and Loan Associations, and even the Wolman's, Orsingers, Watergates, etc., that have produced a city where 285,000 people do not have decent, safe, and sanitary housing necessary for human life. The Church's role is not to solve the problem of housing or the 50,000 substandard homes in our midst, yet, it does share a moral concern and the responsibility of example.
>
> While moral and spiritual counsel abound in the Gospel and Catholic tradition that our Christian duty must be discerned or expressed in terms of Christ's and His Church's mission to the poor, must we justify in secular terms what had been done for and in the name of the poor? "Tell John the poor have the Gospel preached to them—the hungry are fed, naked clothed, the homeless . . ." If we talk of the Church's service to the community and the poor in business terms—accounting, budget, investment, or in other secular terms—or in terms of "other" priorities, are we not forgetting—"the Poor are the true treasure of the Church"?
>
> As affluence and materialism and life style of the laity and the clergy increasingly scandalize the poor, their children, and even now the children of the affluent; shall we purport to teach or preach to—in terms of our empty talk and bad example? I've seen one or two new rectories recently housing a few priests that cost more than $100,000.
>
> The poor must be the first citizen of the Church—it's the only real sign of the Church's spiritual vitality. St. Vincent well said that the poor are not the beneficiaries of our charity or justice or whatever we do or try to do for, or in the service to them—the poor are truly benefactors to us.

Truthfully, Your Eminence, it's frustrating—as you know—to work for and to serve the poor. It's much easier to do and talk about other things. Your example in this area has inspired me and there is so little example, sad to say, to be found in our modern society. I am also ashamed that my own efforts are so weak.

However, you exemplify the maxim that "the man who fights for what he thinks is right to be free." I beg you to support what has been committed so that it may be concluded. Whatever is to be done in the future, I humbly accept and acknowledge as your judgment and prerogative.

Sometimes I know what Abbe Pierre (the priest who was trying to house ragpickers in France) meant when he broke down and they hauled him away to a mental hospital— muttering "God Damn the Poor!"

Thank you for listening.

Baroni never received a written reply to his memo, nor was the subject ever raised during subsequent meetings between Baroni and the cardinal. Baroni felt he had been vindicated, and if he needed forgiveness for his excess, he had received it.

# 8

# Power to the People: The Rise of the White Ethnic

In the spring of 1969, Baroni decided it was time to leave Sts. Paul and Augustine. He did not know where he might go so he tested other ideas to create opportunities. Though the Urban Rehabilitation Corp. was a failure, he thought he might have a future in the housing field. In a few months, he had a new plan.

It was to construct housing on North Capitol Street, near Gonzaga High School. Geno named the project *Sursum Corda*, the Latin invocation in the mass which summons the people to "lift up your hearts." The Sursum Corda project turned out to be a great success.

Beyond helping to convince O'Boyle that the project deserved archdiocesan support, Baroni called on old friends on Capitol Hill for government assistance. One of these friends was Carl Coan, who had helped design the backyard beyond the V Street Center. Coan was staff director of the Senate Housing subcommittee. Baroni told him, "The black working class does not have any housing opportunities in Washington. We got these housing programs that Johnson pushed through as part of the Great Society. Can't we get some of them to work for us?"

Baroni heard of Coan through a network he was building of Catholic members of Congress and aides. They brought in Gerald R. McMurray, an aide to the House subcommittee on housing. "I've known priests all my life, having been raised in an Irish Catholic milieu of New York," said McMurray. "In general, priests are very limited in their outlook, particularly their social outlook. But here was Geno, a guy who

71

seemed to me to be a tremendous example of what I thought the church and its leadership should be engaged in."

Looking for help on Capitol Hill, Baroni wore his Roman collar and said he represented the archdiocese of Washington and a rather substantial investment in housing. His emphasis, however, was on the poor rather than the church. "The black people of this city live in some of the worst housing in the United States and you got to do something about it," Baroni said. Refreshingly to some, he did not present his request as a Catholic issue. "It was all said in terms of helping the poor," a Capitol Hill veteran recalled.

Catholic priests were rare visitors to the back corridors of power in the 1960s. They avoided politics. Politicians, except at election time, avoided them. But Baroni broke the pattern. "Geno just came in and flaunted his own very individualistic traits. It just turned people right on," McMurray said. "People up here had a perception of a Catholic priest that they never had before. He was a real human person who lived and breathed and suffered and rejoiced with the people he was with."

In the months that followed his new appointment, Baroni expanded his network beyond Catholics. He added Sens. John Sparkman, Democrat of Alabama, and William Proxmire, Democrat of Wisconsin. He convinced them that Sursum Corda was worth doing. On his behalf, they called Robert C. Weaver, the Secretary of Housing and Urban Development, to grease federal approval of loans and grants for the project. Weaver called Carl Coan, Jr., son of the Senate subcommittee staff director and also a Catholic. "Walk this thing through," Weaver told Coan. HUD quickly approved Sursum Corda.

To Baroni, this episode whetted his taste for politics, and he developed political connections for the rest of his life. Baroni, with his strange waddling walk, notoriously unpressed and frequently tomato-paste stained suit, warm smile and sensitivity to political realities, became one of the most effective lobbyists on Capitol Hill. He never registered with the Justice Department, but he was a pro when it came to pushing his causes. The lessons he learned on Capitol Hill in working on the Sursum Corda project helped him land a job downtown.

It was only a short drive across northwest Washington from Sts. Paul and Augustine to the headquarters of the U.S. Catholic Conference at 1312 Massachusetts Avenue, but it was an abrupt change in atmosphere. There was never a dull moment at Sts. Paul and Augustine. The V Street Center, Baroni's permanent legacy to the parish, was active from early morning until late at night as hundreds of people streamed in and out for appointments and meetings. Clerics of various denominations bumped into one another while rushing along the hallways. Phones rang constantly and with money to hire secretaries in short supply, callers were likely to get through directly to the person they wanted.

Baroni was the great guru at the V Street Center, the master of it all, recognized by everyone as the man who spun off ideas faster than he could articulate them.

Things were different at 1312. There was a hierarchy and Baroni was not high on it. The staff, used to cardinals, didn't look twice at an ordinary monsignor, even one as disheveled as Baroni. Besides, it was hard to figure out that Baroni was a monsignor. Although he used the title in correspondence and documents, he was never to acquire the red-buttoned and trimmed cassock that denotes the rank.

Where the V Street Center was interdenominational, frenzied, chaotic, and excited, 1312 was organization charts, switchboards, regular hours and Catholic. It didn't take Baroni long to learn that at 1312 people were expected to send neatly typed memos, speak softly and in complete sentences, and respect rank with its privileges.

Baroni adapted. He prudently hired for his staff people who could keep his schedule books and translate his random thoughts into paragraphs. Richard Krickus became his consultant, or writer. Sister Rita Mudd, a former women's college president in Montana, became his general manager.

Baroni's assignment was to help produce a plan of urban action for the U.S. Catholic bishops. In the late 1960s, the bishops watched with growing concern as the United States drifted into two societies, one rich, one poor: one black, the other white; one with opportunity, the other a boiling cauldron of despair. What Baroni and his allies experienced underscored the need for national action. The bishops saw the growing divisions within their own ranks. As they promoted the just cause of blacks, they felt counter-thrust from alienated whites. From Catholic whites across the country, the bishops got a message that, like it or not, they were part of the urban scene too.

The magnitude of the task facing the bishops was spelled out on March 3, 1968, when a commission appointed by President Johnson and chaired by former Gov. Otto Kerner of Illinois reported: "Our nation is moving toward two societies, one black, one white—separate and unequal. Reaction to last summer's disorders has quickened the movement and deepened the division. Discrimination and segregation have long permeated much of American life; they now threaten the future of every American."

Baroni's task was to develop a package of proposals on the urban crisis within the framework of modern Catholic thinking, as exemplified by the teachings of Popes John XXIII and Paul VI. It was, said Pope

Paul, "a most exalted task, for it is the task of bringing about the true peace in the order established by God. If someone who has the riches of this world sees his brother in need and closes his heart to him, how does the love of God abide in him?"

That was exactly the sort of question Baroni had asked for years. But Geno recognized the gap between recognition of the theory and development of concrete proposals to make it work.

Looking for ideas, Baroni invited to Combermere that summer priest friends he had gained through the years. They were members of an organization called the Catholic Committee for the Urban Ministry, known by the acronym CCUM. These men, who worked in some of the nation's worst slums, talked about the growing crisis. The riots of 1967 which Kerner investigated, and the riots of 1968, including Washington's, may be the beginning of an urban revolution in this country, said the CCUM men assembled. Aware of the first sproutings of urban terrorism abroad, they wondered if it could happen in the United States.

The Democratic Party was in serious disarray. Richard Nixon, the Republican, had won the presidential election over Democrat Hubert H. Humphrey. Nixon had received strong support from traditional Democratic constituencies, including urban ethnic Catholics, labor and young people. Perhaps liberalism had run its course. At the very least, Baroni observed that the social welfare programs promised by Johnson's War on Poverty had failed, and the Vietnam War had done nothing to shore them up. The priest started to rethink his own political philosophy. He had always believed government could do it all, but now he began to wonder about the possibility of a cooperative effort involving government, the private sector and the community. He had the nagging sense that change was needed, but he didn't know exactly what.

Returning to Washington, Baroni plunged into drafting a report to the bishops. Working closely with him as co-chairmen of the urban task force were three others, Father Don Clark of Detroit, president of the Black Catholic Clergy Caucus; Andrew Gallegos, representing the Spanish-speaking community, and Monsignor Aloysius Welsh, staff director of the USCC task force.

Baroni, Clark and Gallegos had a difficult assignment. Each was designated to represent a definite interest group—Baroni the whites, Clark the blacks, and Gallegos the Hispanics. The three men recognized the potential for conflicting interests. While each worked toward a course of action for the American bishops that would serve and protect all three groups, each became identified as the advocate for his particular group. It was not an easy situation, and as the deadline approached for delivering a report, it was clear to all that they could not agree on a single presentation to the bishops. They made a decision to draft an overall statement, and to submit individual statements.

The bishops gathered in the Statler Hilton Hotel at 15th and K Streets in downtown Washington on November 11, 1969, to hear the report of the task force on urban problems. Baroni, Clark and Gallegos together reminded the bishops that "the Catholic Church has traditionally been an urban church. Indeed, it was an inner-city church, with a body of knowledge and techniques useful to achieving the assimilation of poor people into the mainstream. This knowledge is relevant today, and adaptable to the new urban poor."

The task force recommended creation of another task force to give direction and drive and material support to a need, Baroni said, "that is as great as going to the moon." Baroni said each diocese must provide leadership in developing a moral response to the human needs of the poor by setting up "an urban task force to coordinate church officials, agencies and parishes to develop an agenda for the 1970s."

Baroni could speak with authority about such coordination. He had done it, and more, at Sts. Paul and Augustine parish. At 39, Baroni had more practical experience with the problems of contemporary urban America than anyone else in the room that day. In many ways—impact, timing and setting, innovation, Baroni's own career—this was the most important statement that Baroni was to make. This is what he read to the bishops:

## Agenda for the '70s

The mission of the Church, a believing institution, in today's world, must be developed in a constantly evolving metropolitan and urban society. Whether a person lives in the center of our cities, or in the suburbs, or in a farm village, his life and the life of his community are significantly shaped by the metropolitan and urban character of our modern world.

## What Are the Dynamics of Urban Growth?

Nearly one-half of all people in the United States in the year 2000 will live in dwelling units that have not yet been started and on land that has not yet been broken (and the year 2000 is not so far away—as close to our futures as the year 1940 in our past).

— —Every month in the United States we are adding roughly 300,000 people, a city the size of Toledo.

— —Every year we add a new Philadelphia.

— —In twenty years we will double the size of Los Angeles and the San Francisco Bay area.

— —We will add 6,000,000 people to the New York region in the same period.

— —Since 1940 Baltimore has added to its population a city larger than Milwaukee.

— —In the next twenty years it will add another city about the size of Miami.

— —In the same period of time, Washington, 35 miles away, will be adding a city nearly as large as Baltimore.

Such are the dynamics of our urban growth. It has been said that in the remainder of this century we will build, new, in our cities, the equivalent of all that has been built since Plymouth Rock. What a challenge and opportunity this presents for the Church in an increasingly metropolitan and urban society.

## The Urban Crisis—"Inevitable Group Conflict"

"The urban crisis"—at its core, is a human crisis. "The urban crisis" has become our major domestic issue and had focused on those minority groups which have been left at the bottom of the social scale.

Now, there is a need to pay new attention to the white urban ethnic groups as well, if we are to move toward the reduction of "inevitable group . . . conflict."

Little attention has been given to the anguish of the socially and politically alienated "middle American":

— —The second and third generation—almost poor;

— —Descendant of the largely Catholic ethnic immigrant;

— —A major source of vocations and traditional backbone and support for the Church;

The ethnic "forgotten" American:

——Heavily burdened by a lion's share of taxes;

——Dissatisfied with poor community and government services;

——Fearful of job security;

——Concerned with the prohibitive cost of college education for his children.

As probably the most ethnic and cultural pluralistic nation in the world, the United States has functioned less as a nation of individuals than of groups. This has meant inevitable group competition, friction and conflict. There is a desperate need to reduce and prevent the confrontation—the group conflict—the polarization—between the white urban ethnic groups and the minority poor.

## The New Coalition

If we are to develop a new agenda for the 1970s:

——We must go beyond the civil rights struggle of the '60s.

——We must stop exploiting the fear of the ethnic, middle Americans.

——We must bring together a new coalition to press for new goals and new priorities for all the poor and the near poor, including the blacks, the Appalachians, the Indians, the Spanish-speaking, and the white urban ethnic groups. . . . Then we can develop a true cultural pluralism in this country and reduce the "inevitable . . . group conflict."

## The Moral Response

At the heart of the urban crisis, a human crisis, is a moral crisis. While we admit that our nation has the material resources, the technology, the economic and industrial know-how and the wealth to provide a more human existence for every man, woman and child, something spiritual is lacking—the heart, the will, the desire on the part of affluent America to develop the goals and commitments necessary to end the hardships of poverty and race in our midst.

This is the greatest scandal of our affluent society: that we tolerate millions of poor people living in our midst without hope, some because of poverty, some because of race, and some because of both.

## The National Will

This lack of national will, this lack of a national purpose or desire, this lack of a moral response to develop goals and commitments to meet our substantive problems of housing, education, health, unemployment, discrimination and so on, has created a crisis of belief on the part of the poor and youth, including many younger priests and nuns, in our democratic system of government and other institutions of society, including the Church.

We may respond "that much had been done," and much has been done by government, labor, business and the religious community to meet the suffering caused by poverty. But our combined efforts, including the numerous programs sponsored by the Church and its institutions, have not sufficiently affected the causes of our problems. Much more remains to be done.

The most crucial item on the agenda of the 1970s is a moral question:

— —What can we, the nation, or how can we, the Church, develop a spiritual response to meet our urban crisis?

— —How can we help to develop a national will, a desire, that supports the conviction that "we, as a nation, must clearly and positively demonstrate our belief that justice, social progress, and equality of opportunity are rights of every citizen"?

— —Can we lead our people to respond, not out of guilt or fear, but as Christians who believe that "the American people must reorder national priorities, with a commitment of resources equal to the magnitude we face"?

— —Can we develop the moral commitment necessary to recognize that our human crisis requires a new dimension of effort in both the private and public sectors, working together to provide for the human needs of the poor, for the human needs of a growing urban society?

## The Role of an Urban Church: Assumptions

The urban Church and its institutions represent a crucial force that might well be decisive in determining the future life-style of our rapidly urbanized nation. The following assumptions might be explored in the development of urban mission policy:

— —The Catholic Church has traditionally been an urban church, indeed an inner-city church, with a body of knowledge and techniques useful in achieving the assimilation of poor people into the mainstream. Can this be a relevant model adaptable to the new urban poor?

— —Populations in closest proximity to the ghettoes of our older industrial cities are Catholic: that is, concentrations of white Catholics either adjoin the great Negro ghettoes or dominate racially changing neighborhoods.

— —These populations, largely middle American-Ethnic-Union members, view the Catholic parish as the major, if not the only, cohesive force in their neighborhoods.

— —These populations see themselves in direct competition with neighboring Negroes for jobs, education, housing, recreation, shopping, and street life.

— —Attitudes held by these populations have deflected attention from issues most germane to their own neighborhood, namely, the needs of the poor in their own groups, and planning and renewal programs that affect the future of their own community.

— —The dioceses and parishes of the Church lack the urban policies, personnel, and organization which is required to deal with this great confrontation and have been at the mercy of social, political and economic forces which they have not been able to significantly influence.

— —Do contemporary theological imperatives provide a new base for intervention by the Church in these areas of severe social conflict?

— —Does the Church have the strength to help develop and execute programs that will have a positive effect on the poverty groups in our urban areas as demonstrated by the participation of Catholic institutions in the fields of housing, education, employment opportunities, recreation and family life? Such recent participation indicates a potential constituency in support of intervention that is as yet untapped.

## Urban Mission Policy—
## The Church and the Evolving Urban Society

The Church in the United States must develop an urban mission policy to meet contemporary human needs:

— —In the past, the Church responded to the industrial-labor crisis by developing new goals and a new social policy that is to be found in the bishops' statement of 1919.

— —The Church has responded to crises in many other ways, e.g., by the development of Catholic Relief Services.

— —Recently Cardinal (Terence) Cooke (of New York), in the spirit of *Populorum Progressio*, urged the Synod of Bishops to demonstrate our collegial concern for mankind by developing a world fund for human development.

### National Fund for Human Development in the United States

We urge the National Council of Catholic Bishops to establish an annual collection for human development in the United States. A national response by the U.S. Church would be a concrete initiative in leading the nation by way of example to develop new priorities and new efforts in meeting human needs in our society. (This would be expended mainly at a diocesan and regional level for practical programs aimed toward self-determination of all our citizens.) Such a national campaign might well serve as an educational instrument in developing a domestic social consciousness.

A small part of this human development fund could be used as a national foundation administered by the NCCB to receive and evaluate proposals from national Catholic and inter-faith sources.

### Diocesan Response

Each diocese must provide leadership in developing a moral response to the human needs of the poor by setting up and staffing an urban task force to coordinate church officials, agencies and parishes to develop a new agenda for the 1970s.

— —The development of a local urban mission policy needs concrete data and analysis to be able to set priorities and to have a documented base upon which to determine parish and diocesan positions regarding planning, poverty, human relations, urban renewal, economic development, city services, and other problems in our urban society.

— —The development of an urban mission policy includes a rationale for the training of leadership both lay and clerical for an urban ministry.

— —Above all, an urban mission statement needs to develop a process whereby the blacks, the middle-American, the Spanish-speaking, the Appalachian, all our people, can participate in developing goals and priorities that go beyond the fears of racism.

— —An urban mission policy needs to develop a spiritual response that is informed, sensitive and well-directed to creating a "national will," that will meet the human needs of the poor and otherwise alienated.

## National Task Force

At the level of the National Task Force diocesan and regional goals and plans can be collected and developed into long-range planning and program development. A small staff with a two-year deadline would make available research and planning, consultant help in training for new urban-oriented pastoral work and share results of diocesan and regional planning with areas with fewer resources.

Only by developing a national and local urban mission policy based on concrete data and analysis can the Catholic Church in the United States overcome any temporary lack of direction and give moral and spiritual leadership to demonstrate in a renewed effort, the Church's concern for its mission of service to the poor. Only then can we answer the poor, the alienated, and our anguished youth who ask, "What's the proof that Christ is present among us today?"

The agenda for the 1970s is the same for every follower of Christ:

— —How do we feed the hungry?

— —How do we clothe the naked?

— —How do we house the homeless?

— —How do we multiply the loaves and fishes in a modern and evolving metropolitan society?

*      *      *

Baroni's statement to the bishops on November 11, 1969, was right from his heart, soul and experience. It was an organized and fancy way of saying what Baroni had been telling and showing the archdiocese of Washington for more than eight years. Throughout the formal statement were bits and pieces of speeches Baroni delivered to clerical groups and parishes in Washington and its suburbs. The emphasis on the country having the resources, but not the will, to fight poverty and injustice was vintage Baroni.

His call to include non-Catholic groups as beneficiaries of the campaign for human development was drawn from his experience working with Protestant and Jewish groups in Washington. His complaint that dioceses and parishes lack the policies, personnel and organization to deal with the urban crisis was right out of messages he delivered to Cardinal O'Boyle, his friends in the Tuesday Morning Breakfast Club, and CCUM.

No doubt Baroni lifted many ideas from others, but he was the first street priest of the urban crisis of the 1960s and 1970s to win a national forum and to articulate effectively—and as it turned out, somewhat successfully—the needs of a shredded society.

Clark and Gallegos joined Baroni in urging creation of the annual collection for human development. The church had a proud record of its charitable work, Baroni pointed out, but it wasn't enough—it had to move away from serving as the "ambulance service" for society, rescuing those who lose out in government programs. Geno wanted the bishops to begin investing money to build society, even if that meant taking on government, business and labor in the process.

The Baroni proposal for an annual human development collection was adopted by the bishops the next day. They voted to create a National Crusade Against Poverty and pledged $50 million. The bishops described the money they would raise and distribute as "self-help funds," and they agreed that the money would not go for traditional Catholic charitable functions or pay tuition for children of the poor to attend parochial schools. "There is an evident need for funds designated to be used for organized groups of white and minority poor to develop economic strength and political power in their own communities," the bishops said.

The poor in America need much more than alms, the bishops said. "They need self-respect. They need the door of opportunity to open equally for them. They do not need cast-off housing and inferior education but the quality housing and education that is available for all Americans."

But it was to take months of struggling before the actual criteria for the beneficiaries could be written. Baroni played a major role in what was an intense battle within the church bureaucracy. The Catholic Charities office wanted to administer the program. Baroni wanted a separate office. He wanted to head it.

But the bishops appointed Bishop Michael R. Dempsey of Chicago to head the Crusade. Baroni was disappointed, but not for long. The bishops also decided that the issue of urban problems needed further study. Would Geno be interested in heading up such a task force for studying the issue and making further recommendations?

He was elated. The bishops' decisions were real victories, he told friends—not for himself, but for the "little people" who were finally getting a chance to be heard, the so-called "white ethnic." Some people had a problem with this term, he knew, but he accepted and used it freely. For others, though, the word stirred deep feelings bordering on racism. He learned that as he traveled over the next six months to New York, Boston, Detroit, Cleveland, Baltimore, Pittsburgh, Youngstown, Toledo, Providence, and Chicago, and saw firsthand how the Catholic community was handling—or not handling—the urban crisis.

# 9

# Who Are We?
# The White Ethnic Question

To Geno Baroni, "white ethnics" included doctors, lawyers, educators, private business owners, and corporate executives. They were the grandchildren of European immigrants who could be found in various socioeconomic strata. Some were blue-collar workers, the backbone of the labor force in most northern industrial cities, mining towns, and manufacturing centers.

But now these white ethnics were fleeing the cities. Their neighborhoods had become battlegrounds between blacks and whites. Cities themselves were in flames as blacks rioted in Newark and Detroit, Los Angeles, Philadelphia and Washington.

From riot-scarred Detroit, Baroni reported to the bishops on the formation of a Black-Polish Conference under the leadership of Father Dan Bogus and Jerome Ernst of the Archdiocesan Human Relations Commission. In one of the nation's most racially tense communities, the Black-Polish Conference said it would "promote increased knowledge of the history and culture of each community by the other through public meetings and cultural and educational programs, develop and expand the channels of communication between the two groups, particularly on matters of current community concern, not only between the leadership, but between the individuals in each community, and sponsor specific programs of mutual benefit to black and Polish communities."

From Cleveland, Baroni reported back the establishment of the Little Italy Development Corp. in the Mayfield-Murray Hill section, and the creation by the Catholic archdiocese of an urban task force. One of

Baroni's constant points was that big city dioceses should maintain an urban task force separate from the local Catholic Charities office and that the director should have great flexibility in shaping programs. He emphasized the importance of independence in this office, and by doing so, he recalled his own not-always friendly entanglements with the Chancery in Washington. Baroni said he was saved from the Chancery by Cardinal O'Boyle.

In Boston, Baroni found that his CCUM associate Father Michael Groden had helped the residents of racially-troubled South Boston prepare a community development plan. In Gary, Baroni met with Mayor Richard Hatcher and his staff and with Bishop Andrew G. Grutka.

As he traveled, Baroni carried a copy of a National Urban League poll by Louis Harris and Associates. It found that white Anglo-Saxon Protestants were more likely than Polish, Irish and Italian blue-collar Roman Catholics to think blacks were pushing too fast for equality, to disapprove of the 1954 Supreme Court school desegregation decision, and to favor separate schools for blacks and whites.

Even Whitney M. Young, executive director of the National Urban League, said the study contradicted the popular conception that there was a "white backlash" among white ethnics. Baroni told audiences that conventional liberals were unfair and incorrect in blaming white ethnics for the urban tension. To ethnics Baroni said: "They say you're part of the problem. What I say is that you're part of the solution." But it was a hard sell.

Baroni decided to illustrate what he was talking about by organizing a conference in Washington that would set an ambitious agenda. The conference was held in the Nursing School Auditorium on the eastern edge of the campus of Catholic University in northeast Washington. Baroni, Sister Rita Mudd, and Paul Peachey, associate professor of sociology at Catholic University, were the conference directors. Its purpose was to analyze ethnic factors in urban conflict, explore the use of federal and private programs and resources in economic, cultural and social development, share the practical experiences of community workers and professionals, confer with government agencies to discuss the development of cultural, economic and social programs in urban areas, and encourage clergy and lay participants to become involved in their parishes and communities. The conference drew several hundred participants.

Representative Roman Pucinski, Chicago Democrat, discussed a bill he co-sponsored in Congress to create "Ethnic Heritage" Study Centers to provide for the comparative study of white ethnics, blacks and browns. Richard Krickus, one of Baroni's closest aides, said that the white ethnic communities in northern industrial cities had stable social systems that should be preserved.

Senator Edmund Muskie, Maine Democrat, said all Americans were plagued by insecurity because of the neglect of domestic problems caused by the Vietnam War. Brendan Sexton of the United Auto Workers Union said that inflation and rising taxes made it tough on the white blue-collar worker. Dr. Otto von Mering, professor of anthropology at the University of Pittsburgh, said that the second wave of immigrants from Europe into the United States had not shed their ethnic identities in the "melting pot," but had preserved something that could be a positive force in pluralistic America. Bishop Grutka of Gary defended Catholic parishes that served members of single ethnic identity groups.

Few of the participants said or heard anything new. "Very Anglo-Saxon," Baroni said. There was little spark. Reporters ignored the platform speakers. Television stations packed up their equipment to head back to the studio. Baroni, who wanted big coverage to impress Capitol Hill and Washington's political community, was afraid the conference would fail on that account.

Some participants felt the press distorted their positions as anti-black. To most reporters, the preservation of white ethnic neighborhoods meant a refusal to allow blacks to live there. They just couldn't see Baroni's point of view, no matter how hard he tried. White ethnics, meanwhile, had their own fears about being identified with right-wing reactionaries like George Wallace.

Baroni told Jack Rosenthal of *The New York Times* that Wallace "only voices their basic insecurity by being anti. What this conference is saying is that there are positive elements in that insecurity which can be marshaled against polarization of our society."

Then Baroni's conference came to life. A nervous young social worker from Baltimore named Barbara Mikulski stepped onstage and effectively voiced the anger of white ethnics. Mikulski had come to Baroni's attention when she was a social welfare administrator in southeast Baltimore, and had aggressively opposed City Hall's plans to run an expressway through the neighborhood, which was home primarily to first- and second-generation immigrants from eastern Europe. The expressway was going to cut through a black neighborhood on the west side of Baltimore. The residents there were the descendants of slaves. They, too, owned their homes, and valued their own neighborhood with its churches, schools and shops. The blacks were organizing their neighborhood as Mikulski moved in hers. She created a group called SCAR, Southeast Council Against the Road. For the sole purpose of opposing the expressway, everyone—the European ethnics, the blacks, and some others—got together and formed a coalition called MAD, Movement Against Destruction.

A priest in the audience, an ally of Mikulski's in southeast Baltimore, said he would like to hear Mikulski's ideas on Muskie's speech. She stood up with her prepared statement. It was a vibrant, ringing declaration on behalf of the white working class. Widely reprinted later, the message became one of the major documents of the white ethnic movement.

"America is not a melting pot," Mikulski said. "It is a sizzling cauldron for the ethnic American who feels that he has been politically courted and legally extorted by both government and private enterprise. The ethnic American is sick of being stereotyped as a racist and dullard by phony white liberals, pseudo black militants and patronizing bureaucrats. He pays the bill for every major government program and gets nothing or little in the way of return. Tricked by the political rhetoric of the illusionary funding for black-oriented social programs, he turns his anger to race—when he himself is the victim of class prejudice."

Mikulski said the white ethnic "has worked hard all his life to become a 'good American;' he and his sons have fought on every battlefield—then he is made fun of because he likes the flag. The ethnic American is overtaxed and underserved at every level of government. He does not have fancy lawyers or expensive lobbyists getting him tax breaks on his income. Being a home owner, he shoulders the rising property taxes—the major revenue source for the municipalities in which he lives. Yet he enjoys very little from these unfair and burdensome levies."

She said that "the ethnic American also feels unappreciated for the contribution he makes to society. He resents the way the working class is looked down upon. In many instances he is treated like the machine he operates or the pencil he pushes. He is tired of being treated like an object of production. The public and private institutions have made him frustrated by their lack of response to his needs. At present he feels powerless in his daily dealings with and efforts to change them. Unfortunately, because of old prejudices and new fears, anger is generated against other minority groups rather than those who have power. What is needed is an alliance of white and black, white collar, blue collar and no collar based on mutual need, interdependence and respect, an alliance to develop the strategy for new kinds of community organization and political participation."

Baroni's conference at Catholic University became an historic milepost in the urban white ethnic movement. Mikulski's speech became the reference point for important ethnic movement leaders. Baroni reworked and adapted Mikulski's rhetoric to his own style and seasoned it with his own stories.

Mikulski's speech was well-covered in the press and got Baroni attention, including an invitation to the White House. Baroni told President Nixon of the recommendations of the workshop, including a proposal for a federal inter-agency task force to review possibilities for assistance to ethnic communities under existing federal programs. Nixon said he would create such a task force.

The conference and the White House invitation contributed to Baroni's growing reputation as a priest who understood tensions within big cities. Monsignor George Higgins at the U.S. Catholic Conference invited him to join in writing a Labor Day statement for the bishops. True to Baroni's convictions, it rejected "the widespread accusation" that urban ethnics "are the primary exponents of racism in our society, although we do not deny that racism exists in their ranks." The statement called on government, business, labor, the academic community, citizens' organizations, and churches to look for opportunities for social, cultural and economic community development that served to unite whites, blacks and Hispanics in big cities.

As 1970 ended, the question for Geno was what role he would play in converting the rhetoric into action.

The local and national press seized on Geno as the most effective national spokesman for the white urban ethnic movement. *Newsweek* magazine in 1970 dubbed Baroni "chief strategist for the nascent ethnic movement."

Priests and community organizers across the nation invited Baroni to their neighborhoods to help solve their pressing problems before the neighborhoods collapsed. His reputation as a civil rights activist was secure. Yet he also believed that as a white ethnic himself—he called himself one of the PIGS—he could speak the language of inner-city whites.

In the fall of 1970 Baroni proposed to Archbishop Joseph Bernardin the creation of an office for urban ethnic whites at the USCC. This immediately drew opposition from church bureaucrats and many bishops. Blacks and Hispanics, relatively small groups in the church, might need special attention, but not urban ethnic whites. They were the majority within the American church. The creation of a special office would dramatize differences instead of lessening tensions, and would highlight disputes and drive people into contending camps. Baroni did not agree. People had to be accepted as they were and feel proud about their uniqueness before they could flourish in a more unified experience, he countered.

The dispute was resolved in November, 1970, when Bernardin decided that the task force on urban affairs, of which Baroni was program director, would be phased out by June 10, 1971. Baroni publicly defended the decision.

He had been reading the newspapers and learned that the Ford Foundation planned to make a sizable grant to the American Jewish Committee and the University of Michigan for a two-year program of conferences, workshops, and financial assistance to projects aimed at fostering a better understanding of white working-class Americans.

Baroni learned that the Foundation was studying grant applications from the Research Foundation of the City University of New York for a conference on problems of white ethnic workers under the direction of Professor Irving Howe, and from the Center of Policy Research at the University of Michigan for research on white ethnic workers through interviews and surveys in metropolitan areas.

But when Baroni saw that the American Jewish Committee and the University of Michigan were planning to study white ethnics, he seethed. Most white ethnics were Roman Catholics and lived in neighborhoods where the Catholic Church was the linchpin. They would be more receptive to Catholic researchers than researchers and social workers from the American Jewish Committee and the University of Michigan. Baroni got in touch with Congressional contacts—Reps. Peter W. Rodino of Newark, New Jersey, Joseph P. Addabbo of Queens in New York City, William A. Barrett of Philadelphia, and Henry S. Reuss of Milwaukee, and Sen. William Proxmire of Wisconsin. All were Democrats.

A young street-smart politician from the predominantly Italian North Ward of Newark named Stephen Adubato telephoned Baroni that Italian-Americans should picket the Ford Foundation headquarters in New York demanding money for a study of American Jews. If the American Jewish Committee got Ford money to study Catholics, why shouldn't a Catholic group get money to study Jews?

While Baroni and Adubato devised their strategy, Baroni's friends in Congress exerted their own pressure on Ford and other foundations. For about a decade, from across the country, black, liberal and civil rights groups tapped the giant foundation treasuries for money. Some beneficiaries and critics considered the foundation money as reparations for more than a century of injustice to blacks. Others saw the money as fines paid in the form of punishment on behalf of corporations that had been discriminating against blacks in hiring.

Whatever the motives of Ford and other foundations, the money was good, and the forces of integration drank it up. Some money found its way into the hands of community organizers whose goals included the ouster of members of Congress. From the survivalist perspective of Congress, the foundations financed the opposition at the expense of incumbents. People in Congress didn't like that, and they challenged the foundations. Ford, the giant, was the best target.

Ford and other foundations are what is known as 501(c)(3) charitable organizations. They enjoy tax advantages which allow contributions to those funds to be deductions from income for federal income tax purposes. Foundations, with millions of dollars a year in income from investments, had special tax code advantages because of Congress. What Congress gave, Congress could take away. It could also apply subtle pressure on foundations to channel money to supportive constituents.

To the Democrats who controlled the Senate and House in the 1960s and early 1970s, urban ethnic whites were traditional political allies. The candidacy of Democratic Gov. Alfred E. Smith started the movement of urban ethnics into Democratic ranks in 1928. The movement was solidified by Franklin Delano Roosevelt, whose New Deal social welfare programs, especially Social Security, attracted urban ethnic whites. John F. Kennedy won that vote in 1960 and Lyndon Johnson had it in 1964.

In the 1968 presidential campaign, Catholic urban ethnic votes shifted away from the Democrats after the assassination of Senator Robert F. Kennedy. Many voters who cast their ballots in the spring for the liberal Kennedy were Wallace supporters in the fall. The trend toward the right of the white urban liberals continued in the 1970 election and looked to go on further in the 1972 election. Democrats were in danger of losing one of the sturdiest elements in their coalition. Wanting it back, they looked for ways to escape their tag as the party of the blacks and once again become the party of the white ethnics.

The Ford Foundation had political savvy. Outwardly, in the fall of 1970, it expressed satisfaction with its history of grants and its relationship with Congress, but there were concerns about all this inside the Foundation's New York headquarters. All these pressures converged when Baroni went to Higgins with a proposal: ask Ford for a grant to fund a study by the U.S. Catholic Conference of urban white ethnics. Baroni was still maneuvering to establish an office for ethnic whites at the USCC. He was making an end run around those who said that creation of an office for urban ethnics would reduce the amount of the pie available to blacks and Hispanics. Baroni did not know if Bernardin and other bishops would like the idea of foundation money supporting a USCC study, but it wouldn't hurt to try.

Higgins, working his Foundation contacts, got in touch with Robert Schrank, a senior grant officer at Ford. Baroni went to New York with his proposal. Schrank was impressed by Baroni's sincerity and knowledge, though not by his art of grantsmanship. To Baroni, the process was simple: have a good idea, sell it to somebody in authority, get the money. But the Ford Foundation doesn't work that way. So Baroni called on his friends, led by Krickus, to draft the formal proposal to Ford.

It didn't take Ford long to make up its mind. Within a few weeks, it informed Baroni that it liked the idea of a study by Catholics of white urban ethnics, but it had a problem. Ford would not give a grant to the U.S. Catholic Conference whose primary purpose was religious. Schrank suggested to Baroni that he look for another vehicle to accept and spend the Ford money.

Baroni huddled with Bishop John Higgins, Krickus and McCarthy. They came up with the idea that Baroni create a separate organization that would be sponsored by the U.S. Catholic Conference, but be independent of it. In that way, Baroni would keep intact his linkage with the Conference, but would be free to take the funds. Ford agreed. So did Bernardin.

On January 16, 1971, the Ford Foundation announced a one-year $163,831 grant to the newly-created Center for Urban Ethnic Affairs. The Center existed only on paper and in Baroni's fertile mind.

Baroni said the Center would lean heavily on urban planners and consultants and on the National Urban Coalition for assistance and technical support, as well as help in dealing with organizational problems. The Urban Coalition had given Baroni's task force $18,000 for its urban white ethnic research. Two of Baroni's allies there were Carl Holman and James Gibson, with whom he had worked in inner-city Washington. As the first full-time Center staff member Baroni chose Sister Rita Mudd as his assistant.

Mudd said that Geno "was a master at being able to get people to work together and communicate. He could spin off ideas, but details were not his bag. He'd get 50 calls a day, sometimes four at once. I wanted him to answer his mail, but it was difficult to tie him down." She said that Geno "felt he was inferior to people with degrees. I used to tell him he was better than they were. Like many ethnics, he discovered his Italian side late in life." He was a difficult boss, she said. "He had a habit of taking things and keeping them a long time. He worked long hours. He'd usually be in the office by 8 o'clock. He would already have three or four pages of phone calls he had gotten at home. He lived by the telephone. He was not much on writing letters."

But his style was effective, Mudd said. "His timidity was part of his charisma."

Support by the Catholic Conference for the Baroni task force and the Ford grant angered blacks who said that the church and Ford were caving in to the white racists. Throughout the eight years at the USCC and at the Center that he dealt with urban ethnic whites, Baroni often heard that he gave legitimacy to racists and made a mockery of his record as a civil rights champion.

The issue troubled Ford, and Higgins came to Baroni's aid through a column he wrote in 1971 for Catholic newspapers around the country:

> I recently felt obliged to defend the good name of Msgr. Geno Baroni of the USCC Task Force (and of others who share his concern about the problems facing ethnic working-class Americans) against the charge of copping out on the issue of white racism in this country. I said, among other things, that Msgr. Baroni need not apologize to anyone, white or black, for his record in the area of race relations and pointed out that he is working night and day to put together viable coalitions between black and ethnic blue-collar workers.
>
> Msgr. Baroni knows better than most of us how difficult it will be to achieve this objective. He knows that there is little hope of solving the so-called race problem in this country unless and until blacks and urban whites learn to pool their resources in a joint effort to solve their common problems. But experience also has convinced him that this will never happen until the ethnics themselves become more conscious of their own identity and more convinced of their own ability to reform the system and get off the treadmill on which they are now marking time.

Higgins pointed out that Baroni's recent involvement as the USCC's program director in the creation of the Calumet Community Congress in Gary, Ind., a coalition of white ethnic groups, was distinctly anti-racist and a triumph of moderation. Baroni had worked a near-miracle in the city, which was split into two camps, 50% black and 50% white. Once Gary, Indiana, south of Lake Michigan around the bend from Chicago, was a booming steel town, its mills first drawing thousands of white workers from Appalachia. When the American steel industry failed to modernize after World War II and increasingly lost business to foreign producers, Gary declined. White steel workers and

many blacks from the Deep South who worked in Gary were fur-
loughed. Many were thrown onto the dole. Tensions came to a head in
1967, when Richard Hatcher, a black, was elected mayor.

At a cabinet meeting, Hatcher asked his department officers, ten
blacks and two whites, what should be done about Glen Park, a section
of Gary containing 57 ethnic groups, which was demanding deannex-
ation from Gary. Several black cabinet officers said, "Let them go." The
whites said, "What do they want?"

"Why don't we give them swimming pools?" a black cabinet officer
told Hatcher. The mayor liked the idea. Then Arthur Naparstek, in
charge of federal programs in Gary, interrupted. "Mr. Mayor, you
sound just like [Mayor Richard J.] Dick Daley in Chicago. The truth is
that we're spending $120 million of federal money in this city and not
a dime is going to Glen Park. The Glen Park people think of us as the
enemy. I think we better start talking to them before we start putting
swimming pools in their neighborhoods."

Hatcher told Naparstek to go to Glen Park and talk to the whites
there. He was at the mill gates the next morning and he got an earful.
"I'd come here to work and it used to be I'd see a Pole on my left and
an Italian on my right. Now I look on my left and there's a spic and on
the right there's a nigger. That's what's wrong," one white man told
Naparstek. "I sent my kid to Indiana University and he comes back with
long hair and a beard. He's against the war in Vietnam. He's wearing
the American flag on his ass and he's smoking dope," said another. "We
don't have any hospitals left in Gary. All the doctors are getting out.
And all your health service does is run a clinic and build free neighborhood health facilities for the blacks," a third told Naparstek.

Naparstek reported to the mayor and cabinet the following week.
Hatcher said he was beginning to get the point, but Naparstek hadn't
yet made his case that the city should do more for the whites in Glen
Park. Naparstek, not knowing what more he could do, called James
Gibson, with the National Urban Coalition in Washington.

"Call this guy named Geno Baroni. He's talking the same stuff you
are," Gibson told Naparstek. Naparstek telephoned Baroni and ran
through his problem. Baroni had one suggestion: "Go out and find out
how they voted."

When Naparstek checked, he discovered that the people of Glen
Park and other white communities of Gary had voted during the 1968
Indiana Democratic primary election nine to one for Robert F.
Kennedy. Then in the fall election, they voted heavily for Wallace. It
was a complete turnaround from the liberal pro-civil rights Kennedy to
the anti-black Wallace.

These figures impressed Hatcher and his staff. They reached out to the white leaders and in time created the Gary Plan, which pledged that city services would flow to whites as well as blacks on a need basis. Naparstek credited Baroni with coming up with the idea that swung Hatcher around. Naparstek and Baroni began to talk frequently, on the phone and in person in Washington and Gary. They eventually formed a network of white ethnic activists across the country who went after Congress to change federal rules on urban spending. As then written, the rules prohibited federal assistance for housing, job training, legal-aid, and medical-care programs for most white urban ethnics.

The law was clear. Federal money should go to the poor—the blacks—and not to the "nearly poor"—the whites. A Labor Department study in 1970 concluded that whites, as taxpayers, "support these programs with no visible relief—no visible share." White ethnics of Gary and other cities told the Democratic Congress and the Nixon administration that they were "caught in the middle" between rich and poor, threatened by crime, ridiculed as hard-hat racists, outshouted by 22 million blacks.

In forcing Hatcher to pay more attention to their demands, whites felt they had won a major victory—through sheer strength of numbers. Community organizers moved to consolidate their power in an umbrella organization. Baroni was called in to help put it together. He provided money from the USCC urban task force. "After all, most ethnics are Catholics," Baroni said. Additional funds came from the American Jewish Committee and Protestant denominations.

Baroni worked closely with Gary's white community leaders. He met with Hatcher to assure him the Catholic Church was not helping to create a white racist organization that would seek to defeat him in the next election. Not only Hatcher felt threatened. John Krupa, Lake County Democratic leader, called the Calumet Community Congress "a power grab . . . motivated by the godless, atheistic forces of Communism." Republican Rep. Earl Landgrebe said, "One of the favorite tactics of Communists and other radical elements is to find a legitimate concern and take it over. There are strong indications that this is taking place in Lake County."

Baroni's superiors at the Catholic Conference and monitors of his new source of money at the Ford Foundation were disturbed at this talk of racism and Communism. They feared their man Baroni was getting them deeply into dangerous waters. One man who did understand Baroni was the Catholic bishop of Gary, Andrew G. Grutka, a 62-year-old Slovak. He attended Baroni's conference in June and now he fought to protect Baroni's reputation. Grutka said he supported both the Calumet

Community Congress and the new Black Alliance, a comparable group across town. Baroni's critics backed off. But the battle was to be re-fought many times during the years ahead.

Meanwhile in Washington, with the Ford grant, Baroni put together his urban center. He named himself director and appointed Mudd assistant director. He hired Joseph Sedlak as staff director, James Wright as community organizations specialist, Jerome Ernst as ethnic programs specialist, Ann Pisula Brown as special projects specialist, and Floyd Agostinelli to work on credit unions. Tony Tighe was named office manager and Richard Krickus, who wrote much of the USCC urban task force statement, was named research director.

As Baroni saw it in those heady early days, his first job was to raise ethnic consciousness, especially in Washington where policy decisions are made, and at the pressure points in big cities. He targeted fifty-eight northeast and midwestern cities, homes to about 40 million ethnic Americans.

Baroni drew many big-name speakers to his first workshop, among them author Michael Novak; consumer protection activist Ralph Nader; John Perkins, the assistant director of the AFL-CIO's political arm, COPE; Sens. Richard S. Schweiker, Pennsylvania Republican; Philip Hart, Michigan Democrat; Charles Mathias, Maryland Republican, and Harrison W. Williams, Jr., New Jersey Democrat. There were also Edward D'Alessio from the U.S. Catholic Conference, Margaret E. Galey from the University of Pittsburgh, Schrank from the Ford Foundation, and three reporters, Bill Kovach, of *The New York Times*, Haynes Johnson, of the *Washington Post*, and Hal Walker, of CBS Television.

Baroni believed that Novak, a young Catholic liberal who worked for Shriver at the federal anti-poverty program and supported sizable federal spending on domestic programs, was able to put into words what Baroni felt, but could not himself express on the printed page. Baroni liked Novak's argument that a coalition of blacks and ethnics was inherently more stable than a coalition of blacks and liberals.

At his first Center meeting, Baroni had a panel report on urban communities. Its members were Mary Sansone, president of the Congress of Italian-American Organizations of New York; Gary Deacon of the Southeast Community Organization of Baltimore, Ralph Perrotta of the New York project, Father Philip Murnion, director of the research office of the Diocesan Personnel Board of the Archdiocese of New York, and Steve Adubato of the Newark Cultural and Educational Center.

Steve Adubato didn't have to picket Ford asking money for white urban ethnics to study Jews, as he had threatened to do during his conversation the previous fall with Baroni. But he had enough fighting on his hands with a less gentle opponent than Ford. Jousting for political power in Newark's predominantly North Ward were Adubato and ex-Councilman Anthony "Tony" Imperiale. Insisting he was not a white racist who hated blacks, but rather a believer in ethnic neighborhoods, Adubato created an organization in Newark called Displaced Ethnic Whites (DEW). "All that's left in Newark is the blacks, Puerto Ricans and Italians," Adubato said. "If you drive us out, then you're going to have an all-black city." Adubato, in 1970 a 38-year-old former civics teacher, had an influential political backer, Congressman Peter Rodino of Newark. Each in his own way had contributed to Ford's first grant to Baroni. Adubato talked about street action. Rodino suggested he might make it hot on Capitol Hill if Ford did not make money available to Baroni-like projects.

In June of 1970, Adubato broke with the Democratic machine led by former Mayor Hugh J. Addonizzio. In the election for mayor, and in a runoff, Adubato supported the black candidate, Kenneth Gibson. "I was the only white leader with any political power in this city who was supporting Gibson," Adubato said. "I was against Addonizzio. I was not committing a political act. I was committing treason."

Adubato said that other Italian leaders in Newark were "more than angry. It was dangerous. They felt, understandably so, that I had betrayed them. It was a changing of the political guard. Not from Irish to Italian. Not from Jewish to German. But from white to black. The connotations are much different. They're sexual, social, religious, spiritual, besides racial."

Adubato said that while supporting Gibson, he was not "pro-black. I was a politician looking to be with the winner. Frankly, Gibson was also a better man." Adubato liked to play hardball. At Baroni's conference in June, he rose to ask a question of Sen. Edward M. Kennedy. Since this was an ethnic conference, Adubato said, and since Kennedy was saying such nice things about ethnic politicians, why was Kennedy supporting William J. Green for mayor of Philadelphia rather than former Police Commissioner Frank L. Rizzo. Kennedy said it was a matter of conviction and political loyalty—that Green's father had played a key role in the 1960 election of President John F. Kennedy. Adubato didn't think much of Kennedy's answer. "What is this?" he said. "The Irish are close to one another. That's the old politics, Senator."

Kennedy replied, "I guess it's inconsistent." Adubato felt he had scored a point against Kennedy. The papers played it that way. Baroni was angry at Adubato and later apologized to Kennedy.

But despite that disagreement, Baroni put Adubato at the top of the list of local community organizers applying for Center money. With the Ford dollars that had passed through Baroni's Center, Adubato expanded his organizing among North Ward Italians.

Linked to Adubato, Baroni was drawn into Newark politics. Adubato became one of Baroni's disciples. Adubato said Baroni "was teaching us that we could continue to live here in a black city, and we didn't have to be victims. We wanted to walk alongside the new black leadership, not behind it, and not in front of it. He was teaching us to avoid an 'us against them' battle, to find ways that we can fight together."

But the search for cooperation was derailed when Gibson announced plans to build a high-rise housing project in the North Ward. It would be a project for poor blacks set in the heart of the predominantly Italian neighborhood. No amount of goodwill was going to settle that. Baroni found himself in the middle of the battle. Adubato said that "people should have a right to live in the area they want, I suppose, but I'm not going to protect them, I'm not going to help them in their folly." He said his motivation was to keep this area a "decent place where I can raise my family."

Adubato said that Baroni was "not sympathetic" to his efforts to keep out the project. "Geno never put any pressure on me, but I knew that the people around him were asking him what was he doing with this racist."

Baroni said he tried to play an intermediary role, meeting both Gibson and Adubato. The important thing, Baroni told Gibson, was that Adubato was a coalition-builder, not a racist. Press on with this project, Baroni told Gibson, and Imperiale and other more militant street leaders will cause trouble.

Construction of the housing project in the North Ward was also a show of muscle for Newark's black militants, who wanted to make it clear that they were in charge of the city now and could do what they wanted with its money, just as the white politicians had done before. Gibson eventually abandoned the project.

Allegations that Baroni and his Center nourished white racists with money and moral support constantly surfaced. Baroni was scrupulous in words, deeds and grants. He constantly preached the message that blacks had legitimate grievances against American society. At the same time, he said that the terrible wound that blacks suffered in no way denied white urban ethnics the right to feel their own pain and seek treatment for their own ills.

Liberals, some blacks, and some reporters were skeptical that even as honorable a man as Baroni could pull off the fine balancing act between acknowledging the rights of blacks while serving the cause of white ethnics. But there is absolutely no evidence that Baroni ever supported, approved or pardoned white racism. This was one of the major concerns of the Ford Foundation when it first gave money to Baroni, and it remained a worry throughout. But the worry was unjustified. Robert Goldmann, an investigator for Ford, said in a December, 1975, report to the Foundation that "the Center and the local groups it has supported are approaching racial issues very gingerly. They have never said anything explicitly that they would or might build a black-white coalition on an issue, although for key Center staff, and above all for Baroni, this is indeed a major commitment. But it is far from such among residents of ethnic neighborhoods. In fact, in many of them, there is a strong undercurrent of racial feelings that could easily be tapped by Center staff as an organizing tool. The Center and its local organizers have taken great care to avoid any issue of activity that might play to these racial fears.

"In fact, the Center has been successful in a number of sites in building black and white support for a specific objective. The approach has been to start organizing among white residents. Once whites had focused on the problem and identified obstacles and solutions, coalitions with black and brown groups sometimes followed logically as the best way to go about the task at hand."

In Newark, Goldmann said, Adubato's North Ward Cultural and Education Center had only a few black participants. But Adubato himself, said the report, "has taken on several issues, such as low-income housing, civil service staffing, and the need for more school remedial programs, that align him with Newark's black leadership."

How much of a role Baroni played in calming the fears of inner-city whites in the early 1970s is impossible to assess. Any measurement would have to be against the conjecture of what the situation would have been without the intervention of Baroni and people like him. There were others in the field, but unquestionably the major voice, the principal strategist, the most effective advocate for a recognition of the legitimate grievances of the white urban ethnics in that period, nationwide, was Baroni. No one else had his sensitivity, charisma and understanding. No one else had his ability to communicate to frightened white people in the nation's big cities that their fears were legitimate, their hopes appropriate, and their ambitions attainable.

Whether Baroni changed the course of American race relations in big cities or was merely around when they changed is a question that can never be answered. But it was during his supremacy as the spokesman for the white urban ethnics that overt white racism went into decline, that racial violence subsided, and black-white coalitions began to build. For that, Baroni could take pride and claim credit.

At his Center's first workshop, Baroni told the audience that their first task was to answer the same questions that more than 40 million ethnic Americans were asking themselves: "Who am I?" and "Who are we?" They were questions that Baroni tackled with enthusiasm. More than any expert, he identified his own search for self-identity and understanding with the identity struggle faced by urban ethnics. He had lived its struggle firsthand as the child of immigrants.

# 10

# George Bush Attacks

George Bush helped to authenticate Geno Baroni's understanding of urban ethnic America, and got a bloody political nose in the process. As the nation's celebration of its 200th birthday in 1976 approached, Baroni was angry that urban ethnic Americans were being ignored. He set out to force the U.S. government to revise its bicentennial plans to pay the proper notice to the cultural and ethnic pluralism vital to American society.

Before he was through, Baroni got President Gerald R. Ford's administration to declare the death of the melting pot theory. He forced leaders of both the Democratic and Republican Parties to pay attention to ethnic issues. Baroni won a nasty personal battle with George Bush. And, as a cap to his entire theory, Baroni formed the first national organization that genuinely included white ethnics and blacks working toward a common philosophy.

Congress in 1966 authorized creation of the American Revolution Bicentennial Commission. In 1972, the commission adopted a resolution recognizing "the ethnic and cultural diversity of our citizenry and the contribution of this pluralism to America." It pledged to "actively and consistently seek the participation of all constituencies" in planning and conducting the 1976 bicentennial events. Congress in 1973 established a new federal agency, the American Revolution Bicentennial Administration, to organize the 1976 celebration.

At the same time, Baroni, as president of the National Center for Urban Ethnic Affairs, and James Gibson, president of the District of Columbia Bicentennial Commission, old friends from their days as inner-city activists in Washington, agreed that the bicentennial celebration, the way it was heading, would ignore white ethnics and blacks. The planners were aiming for a series of patriotic events like parades, speeches, fireworks demonstrations and exhibitions that minimized the contributions of white ethnics and blacks to the nation's development.

This was the high tide of white ethnic consciousness-raising. Baroni felt that the bicentennial should recognize the country's cultural pluralism, and in the process, distribute federal money to ethnic groups to record their own histories for retelling during 1976. Baroni and Gibson in June, 1974, co-sponsored the first Bicentennial Ethnic Racial Coalition (BERC) Conference. The federal bicentennial agency cooperated as representatives of more than twenty different ethnic and racial groups assembled in Washington.

The federal cooperation was significant. It was the first time that any federal agency allowed such a diverse ethnic and racial group to make policy recommendations on an official basis. "The tremendous fact that must never be overlooked," said BERC chairman John A. Kromkowski, "is that the first step toward legitimizing and institutionalizing cultural diversity as a primary criterion of participation in public-policy spheres had been taken." Kromkowski later became president of Baroni's Center.

Baroni's consultation with the White House continued into the Ford administration after Watergate and Nixon's resignation. Ford's establishment of a White House office on ethnic affairs under Baroni-disciple Myron Kuropas in the post, represented a receptivity to urban ethnic concerns. Previously the Republican Party, as well as the Democratic, dealt with ethnics through nationality divisions. Those offices were considered junior players in political strategy. The offices were intended to mollify and absorb the outrage of many Americans of eastern and northern European descent whose native lands were subjugated by the Soviet Union after World War II. The national offices ran conferences where people considered super-U.S. patriots and fervent anti-Communists could harmlessly air their anti-Soviet rhetoric without leaving much of a trace on real party politics or national policy.

At times, mainstream party leaders seemed embarrassed by the strong rhetoric of the urban ethnic leaders, but as long as they railed against the Soviet Union, they were considered harmless. Though Kuropas was firmly in the anti-Soviet tradition and a critic of the detente policies of Secretary of State Henry A. Kissinger and European specialist official Helmut Sonnenfeldt, Kuropas was also an advocate for urban ethnic neighborhoods and receptive to Baroni's ideas on how to stabilize and improve them. Baroni wanted to bring ethnic groups from the fringes of U.S. politics into the very center of political and government life.

That was impossible as long as white ethnics were considered racists set on a white backlash against legitimate black claims for civil and human rights. In his first two to three years at the Center, Baroni managed to shift the spotlight from hostility between ethnics and blacks toward legitimate grievances of the white ethnics themselves. By 1974, ethnics were feeling better about themselves, the country was listening to their complaints, and there had been small steps toward Baroni's desired coalition of the aggrieved. Baroni, William Baroody, a Nixon aide, and Kuropas arranged for a series of White House meetings on domestic policy and ethnicity. The convening of an ethnic-racial coalition for participation in the bicentennial celebration was a master stroke. BERC, under Baroni and Gibson, was the most visible evidence of the political use of an ethnic-racial alliance in public policy. For the first time, ethnic and black leaders served on committees together, not to work out differences between their groups, but to find common complaints that they could present to the national government.

Politicians tend to fear grassroots organizations that they do not control. So it was with BERC and other black/white groups. Baroni, working through Baroody, convinced Ford to convene a White House Conference on Ethnicity and Neighborhood Development in 1976. This eventually led to Ford's creation of the National Commission on Neighborhoods. Secretary of Commerce Elliot L. Richardson made an important statement for the Ford administration:

> It is time now for us to forge a strategy for the future of America which is based upon a coalition between diverse groups which recognize each other's right in a pluralistic society to build a secure sense of community and ethnic pride. This pride in the diversity of America is in no sense exclusionary. It springs from the self-confidence of a people who have achieved mastery over their destinies.

The thoughts and politics of Baroni, Kuropas and Baroody echoed in Richardson's words.

While Baroni was raising the cultural awareness of urban ethnic whites, events shaped the nation's understanding of its pluralistic background. The Black Power movement adopted the "Black is Beautiful" slogan. Studies showed the low regard in which blacks held themselves as a group. Blacks identified themselves with low self-respect, drug and alcohol abuse, illegitimacy, crime, a dependency on welfare. Studies showed that black children had negative attitudes about their culture and skin color. Given a choice of a white doll and a black doll, black girls often chose the white doll for affection and care, the black doll for service and punishment.

In the mid-1970s, the television production of Alex Haley's "Roots" captured national attention. "Roots" validated everything Baroni had been saying. Whites as well as blacks had much to learn from a study of their heritage. Haley, "Roots" writer, and David Wolper, its producer, met while serving on the bicentennial commission board.

The National Archives in Washington reported record numbers of Americans asking how their relatives entered the United States. Genealogy became the rage. Travel agents reported vast increases in the number of Americans heading to Europe to find long-lost cousins.

John L. Warner, former Undersecretary of the Navy, was appointed by Nixon early in 1974 to head the American Revolution Bicentennial Administration. "One of the most serious deficiencies I found upon my arrival," said Warner, "was the lack of significant channels of communications and support for ethnic minority organizations." He set out to change the policy and to find money for ethnic organizations to participate. Warner told two ARBA program officers, Martin Goldman and Verna E. Clayborne, to work with Baroni and Gibson. They planned a June, 1974, meeting.

It was a tough time to focus the country's attention on ethnicity. Nixon was fighting for his political life. In May, he had been to the Soviet Union to sign a strategic arms limitation treaty with Leonid Brezhnev, and in June he visited the Middle East. The House Judiciary Committee held hearings on a motion to initiate impeachment proceedings against Nixon, who revealed that he used the Central Intelligence Agency as part of the Watergate cover-up. The "smoking gun" of evidence was in the hands of the investigators. Even stalwart Nixon aide, Patrick J. Buchanan, conceded that the end was in sight.

Ethnic white and black representatives who gathered in Washington under the leadership of Baroni and Gibson and at Warner's invitation agreed they wanted to advise ARBA and to separate from the federal bicentennial operation. They said they wanted their own "community." They wanted the national community to recognize the importance and legitimacy of local communities.

"Community means belonging," the meeting planners told participants. "It is made up of people of common beliefs and purposes, common needs and interest. One is bound to a community by ethnic and cultural ties which often extend beyond simple geographic boundaries. Yet, community can simply mean the neighborhoods—a series of close economic, social and political relationships. In each instance, ethnicity has a more prominent role in our consciousness."

The desire of this group of ethnic and black leaders, working under Baroni and Gibson, to mobilize into a community did not sit well with George Bush, then chairman of the Republican National Committee. On July 18, 1974, he fired off a letter to Warner, and said he was disturbed by "critical comments made known to me" about what he called "the ethnic/minority meeting." Bush said that "the comments were disturbing enough that I wanted to advise you of them in the hope you will look into the allegations and, if the concern proves to be founded, that you will help to correct the situation." Bush continued:

> Let me say that I not only understand, but I agree with your desire to have the Bicentennial be non-partisan. I do hope some credit will be given for the magnificent way the two-party system has served our country. One main criticism of the June meeting was that the ethnic divisions of both major parties were essentially bypassed in planning the meeting and in making suggestions for the meeting. The Democrats have already written a letter of protest. Both parties were notified a day or so before the meeting, and were rather gratuitously invited to have observer slots."

Now Bush went after Baroni.

> Our main objection, however, is that in selecting Gino [sic] Baroni to chair the meeting, the Commission seems to have cast its lot with the more radical ethnic people—and people with very liberal views who would not represent the matrix of our great ethnic communities. Indeed, under Father Baroni's direction and insistent leadership, the following themes emerged:
>     . . . This group would have an ongoing purpose which would not end with the Bicentennial.
>     . . . A lasting racial/ethnic coalition—militant in nature and "Activist" in orientation would emerge. The creation of a new urban "power bloc" was envisaged.
>     . . . The Bicentennial Commission funds should be used to start up this coalition.
>     . . . Little mention was made of the traditional values which unite the ethnic groups in this country. Rather a special film was shown that left the impression that the Commission's

goal should be putting together racial coalitions for social action.

. . . Ethnics of European heritage were to be amalgamated into some kind of "minority bloc."

Needless to say, if these allegations are founded, many ethnic Americans would be offended to see the ethnic participation in the Bicentennial become an instrument for radical action.

Bush concluded his letter to Warner:

Throughout my political and public service life I have been tremendously impressed with the pride in this country shown by our great ethnic groups. They are not radical; they are not militant; and they are most appreciative of the unique opportunities that America has given them. We must not write them off by lumping them into some kind of ongoing quasi-militant coalition.

Bush's letter was leaked to Baroni, who could not have been happier since it established him as an advocate of ethnics against the political power structure.

Bush was the archetype Wasp—cool, unemotional, predictable, a prep-school graduate, Baroni's model for white elitism. As Baroni saw it, Bush didn't understand blacks or cities any more than he understood the ethnic movement.

Warner came to Baroni's defense in an August 8, 1974, letter to Bush. In a "Dear George" letter, Warner said that the "best response I can make to your allegations, is to provide you with some facts about the genesis and conduct of the meeting and the results emanating therefrom." Warner recalled that when he arrived at the ARBA he found a "lack of significant channels of communication with ethnic and minority organizations."

Warner continued:

Because of ARBA's desire to serve as convenor and not to run or dominate the meeting, we asked two gentlemen to assume the responsibility of co-chairing the meeting. One, as you pointed out in your letter, was Father Geno Baroni, of the National Center for Urban Ethnic Affairs; the second was Mr. James Gibson, chairman of the District of Columbia Bicentennial Commission. I emphasize the point that there were two persons who co-chaired the meeting; that they generally shared the duties of the chair equally; that they both discharged the duties of the chair ably and responsibly; that from my personal observation—I was present intermittently throughout—no single voice was dominant in any facet of the proceedings; that each participant was given every opportunity to express his views, and that each participant listened carefully to the statements of his colleagues.

One of the most gratifying aspects of the meeting was the discovery by the participants that they did in fact share common goals and aspirations. Following this realization they determined to constitute themselves as an independent coalition which would advise the ARBA and requested the Co-Chairmen to designate a Steering Committee. One function of this Committee will be the task of enlarging the number of coalition members to insure broader representation of the ethnic and minority communities at large. As of today, the Bicentennial Ethnic/Racial Coalition is an independent body whose advice and counsel we welcome but which is also responsible for itself, its own membership, its own processes, its own goals, and its own future. This is consistent with my basic philosophy in Bicentennial planning, namely, the U.S. Government should provide positive, not dominant, leadership.

Warner turned to Bush's allegations about Baroni:

I have taken some care to outline these facts because of the shadow your allegations cast on the good will and integrity of ARBA, the participants themselves and the Co-Chairmen, Father Baroni and Jim Gibson. Having been in attendance, I must say I was impressed by the dedication, the genuine concern and spirit of harmony and cooperation which dominated the meeting. I saw nothing that relegated any group into a "minority bloc" nor do I believe that the theme of the meeting was "militant" or "radical" in nature. As the representative of the Archbishop of the Greek Orthodox Church of North and South America stated: "These last two days, attending the conference I felt that America has come a long way. We are what we are was more or less the motif for our discussions the last two days. Who are we? I raised that question and we saw ourselves in a beautiful way. The people who were there representing the various ethnic groups and cultural groups and racial groups were quality people. They expressed themselves sophisticatedly, clearly, and had very good ideas. . . . I think all in all we had a very successful, very meaningful and very effective meeting the last two days.

Warner said he hoped Bush would be able to attend the next meeting and see for himself. Baroni said he never saw Bush at any of the meetings. Meanwhile, the Ford White House quietly passed the word to Bush to keep his criticism off Baroni.

Baroni had no quarrel with Bush's recitation of the themes which Bush said emerged under Baroni's "direction and insistent leadership." It was, in fact, true that Baroni sought an ongoing racial/ethnic coalition that would be both "militant" and "activist" toward the creation of a new urban "power bloc." That pretty much summarized everything Baroni had worked for through the creation of the Campaign for Human Development, the bishops' urban task force, and the National Center for Urban Ethnic Affairs. Creation of an ongoing coalition of blacks and whites in cities that would exercise political power to improve the quality of their lives was precisely Baroni's target.

Bush's attack drew attention to the coming together of blacks and ethnics for a common purpose. What Bush saw as a threat to the political parties, Baroni saw as a victory for blacks and whites in big cities.

\*　　\*　　\*

Although Warner's putdown of Bush and his promise of support for urban ethnic/racial participation in the bicentennial heartened Baroni, nothing much came of this immediately.

Baroni and Gibson called a second BERC meeting in January, 1975, and this time 400 representatives of urban ethnic and racial organizations attended. The District of Columbia Bicentennial Commission's newspaper, *The Century Post*, said of the meeting: "Not since the emergence of the populist movement at the end of the nineteenth century has such a diverse assembly of Americans met, agreed on commonly shared goals, and more importantly, determined to work together with the Bicentennial as their unifying framework."

Baroni set the theme for the joint black/urban ethnic effort during an attack on one of his favorite targets, the melting pot theory:

Most of us came out of the slavery experience, out of the immigrant experience. America is a nation of many, many different kinds of people. Our melting pot image of assimilation, as our young people are now reminding us, has somehow got to be challenged. And perhaps the Bicentennial, if it can do one thing, can help us redefine America in terms that it is legitimate to be a Native American, it is legitimate to come from different ethnic and racial groups and to be American, and it is legitimate to certify the cultural heritage of different racial and ethnic groups.

In fact, the different ethnic and racial groups, the mosaic of America not the melting pot, may well be the soul, the energy that can help us out of more complicated social and other issues. I think that we all must begin to realize that the polarization between different people in our society is partly a result of that melting pot theory.

Keynote speaker John D. Rockefeller, III, said he had grown from a melting-pot point of view to an understanding and active support of ethnic and racial pluralism.

But despite the upbeat talk, a year later, on August 11, 1975, Warner was forced to acknowledge that "the combined community of Native Americans, Racial and Ethnics in the United States is not fully represented in the bicentennial." Although Warner and the Ford administration talked a good game about supporting racial/ethnic bicentennial projects, they did very little about it. The ARBA said that 718 of the 5,009 projects undertaken by states dealt with ethnic/racial subjects.

Baroni was disappointed in the final outcome of the urban ethnic/ racial coalition's efforts. But he saw these as setting in motion a course by which the country would inevitably recognize that ethnic and racial groups in cities had to work together, rather than fight with one another, if they were to be saved. That was the essence of the Baroni message.

As the president of the National Center for Urban Ethnic Affairs, Baroni was the foremost proponent of a new rhetoric of cultural pluralism. Despite what he viewed as a lackluster performance by the Bicentennial Commission, the celebration nationally saw a blossoming of the urban ethnic movement in the country.

Baroni's effort stimulated urban ethnic and racial festivals throughout the nation during 1976. Although police chiefs and city officials widely predicted that those festivals would bring violence, they brought together urban ethnics and blacks in celebrations of heritage. Those festivals were the first widespread gathering of urban ethnics and blacks in many big cities since the street riots of the 1960s. In the 1968 campaign, Richard Nixon stressed the slogan, "Bring us together." Baroni did it.

*    *    *

Baroni's many activities left him little time to manage the Center. He spent much of his time away from the office. He loved to travel and accepted many invitations. Ironically for a man who spent so much time helping others find their roots, Baroni himself seemed rootless.

Even when he was in Washington, he was elusive. He was on Capitol Hill for a meeting, having lunch at the Federal City Club, hustling money from foundations, attending a session of one of the many boards of directors on which he served. Baroni thrived under pressure—the more the demand for his time and energy, the happier he was. He was easily bored. He became distracted when forced to participate in long meetings. He overscheduled, partly as an excuse to avoid having to spend too much time on any one event.

His major weakness as a fundraiser and organizer was that he talked too much. He was unable to say something once and then move along to a new point. Baroni said he was a bit like Hubert H. Humphrey, who would talk until he convinced himself that he had won everybody there to his own viewpoint.

Baroni compartmentalized his life, so that people came to know and understand him well only in one significant function. Some shared his developing thoughts on ethnicity; others heard his views on the Catholic Church; others on politics, others on fund-raising. Some went to the movies with him or to Arena Stage or the National Theater. Some he took to the A. V. Restaurant, his favorite inexpensive hangout, in northwest Washington. But no one saw all of Baroni.

He linked people together, merging individual interests into committees and coalitions. He himself wanted to be part of many projects. No committee was too small for his interest or membership. He spun off ideas about urban development, then left it to others to carry out projects. He agreed to serve on innumerable boards of directors of projects, some of which never got anywhere beyond a file jacket. As Father Raymond Kemp, who became pastor at Sts. Paul and Augustine Church, said, Baroni's method of operation was to reject no idea, encourage every idea. "Try it," was the Baroni philosophy.

But while linking people, working 18 and 20 hour days, talking to all, if even for a few minutes, Baroni kept a large amount of himself private. While uniting others, he had a private life closed to outsiders.

He raised the shades on many windows into his mind and soul, but most people could see only a small part. No one could see into everything that was Geno Baroni.

Baroni's key staff aides did not always know how to deal with him, because he was unpredictable, sometimes casually approving a costly project, and at other times quibbling over minor details. One thing was certain: Baroni wanted nothing to happen that he didn't know about. Just as he wanted to know the internal politics in some distant city, he wanted to know the events in the personal lives of his staff. If an aide had a birth or death in the family, had difficulties with a spouse, Baroni wanted to be kept informed.

He was moody. "When we became friends I saw everything," said Gerson Green. "He could not hide his feelings. If he was down, he was down, and if he was up, he was up. He was very often depressed, but when other people were around, he was in control."

*      *      *

Gerson's story demonstrates the Baroni technique. Green came to Washington in 1967 from a Polish neighborhood of Pittsburgh called Lawrenceville. Green came close to getting run out of town on a rail when, in a power struggle, he managed to defeat a local Democratic politician.

Green was hired by Shriver as director of research and development at the Office of Economic Opportunity. In these glory days of the Great Society, before the Vietnam War destroyed the federal antipoverty program, large amounts of money were available for experimental programs. Shriver and Green agreed that white ethnics in big cities had to be dealt with as a political force as part of the program to lift the burden of poverty from blacks. Shriver said he wondered if white ethnics could be reached through their parish priests; after all, most were Catholics. A Catholic himself, Shriver was sensitive to complaints that he funneled government money to the Catholic Church. So he asked Green, the son of immigrant Jewish parents from Lithuania, to deal with Catholic groups. Green invited urban affairs priests from thirteen dioceses across the country to the OEO office on 19th Street for a private meeting. OEO picked up the tab. Green did not invite anybody from the Archdiocese of Washington.

Colman McCarthy, Shriver's aide, heard about this. "You have to understand Church protocol," McCarthy said. "When you do anything with the Catholics, you have to contact Cardinal O'Boyle." At the last minute Green wrote to O'Boyle and the cardinal assigned Baroni to attend as the archdiocese's representative.

Green talked about his experience in Lawrenceville, suggesting that inner-city ethnics, who happened to be Roman Catholics, could be led into racism. Some Catholics were racist, very much a part of the white backlash against black progress. Green said that Shriver was afraid that Catholics, in their anger toward blacks claiming civil rights, would undermine the federal antipoverty program. Green asked the priests how to get Catholics and the Catholic Church involved in the antipoverty effort.

The out-of-town priests replied that, by and large, Catholics had incomes above the poverty level, but that they were willing to set up service programs that served the poor, who would be primarily black. Green told the priests they didn't get his point. He wanted Catholics themselves involved in the antipoverty program so that they would feel they were a part of it, not its enemy.

"They didn't buy it," Green said. "The only one who did was the one priest who came from a city in which the entire poverty problem was black, in which there were no ethnic white neighborhoods." That was Baroni.

"Geno agreed immediately that it was impossible to build an urban consensus without the white ethnics," Green said. There was no talk then of coalition building. Even the blacks on Shriver's staff saw any reaching out to whites as a reduction in the amount of money and effort that could be spent on blacks.

Not much came of the meeting. The priests went back to their dioceses unwilling to pledge the involvement of Roman Catholics in the antipoverty program except as managers of programs for blacks. Catholics were too proud to be seen, like blacks, as beneficiaries of federal money.

But something did come of the meeting although it was four years later. Baroni telephoned Green, who was then working in mental-hospital management. Baroni said he had just gotten a large grant from the Ford Foundation to set up a center on urban ethnic issues, and wondered if Green would join his staff. Green was amazed that Baroni still remembered him after four years, but Green hardly hesitated. He joined Baroni's staff as a proposal writer. This was the pattern for many Baroni hiring decisions. He carried resumes "in his head." Baroni was a poor salary bargainer, generous to a fault, spending money as if there were an endless supply of it. Fortunately for him, grants and contracts kept flowing the Center's way during the early 1970s. But when the spigot was turned off in 1975, serious problems developed.

"Geno was an idea man," Green said. "He wasn't a process-oriented man. He didn't have an orderly work schedule. You have to understand that this guy was spontaneous." Green said Baroni's strength was in "creating the climate" in which others could work to their potential. "In a way he had a preacher's role. Geno was a preacher. He was more of a Protestant preacher than he was a Catholic priest in that sense."

Geno also suffered because of his secrecy. "Geno was as Machiavellian as you could get. He would get himself into trouble because of that. He'd get murky and get down into himself, which was unnecessary. He didn't let people do what they have to do. We were pros. We wanted clarity. We wanted action. We wanted movement. Geno would be afraid to make a decision lest he make a wrong decision because he wasn't sure."

                              *       *       *

By 1975, the Center staff was going in as many directions as there were people, and Baroni was not happy about it. He called them "my bunch of characters," but inwardly he chafed at the loss of control. His troubles mounted. A Ford Foundation report said the Center needed stronger central management. Baroni brought in Robert Corletta to achieve it. Corletta sought to impose order on the place, but it was probably too late.

Compounding the disorder was a falling out Baroni had with one of his closest friends, Jerome B. Ernst. Both men were deeply hurt and affected by their quarrel. There were bitter exchanges. It was a sad and tragic event. Ernst had been a seminarian, a monk and a journalist before he went to Detroit as a layman in 1965 to work on Project Commitment as assistant director of human relations. Cardinal John Dearden of Detroit created the program to encourage Roman Catholics to become informed and involved about racial and urban problems. Ernst held about 150 meetings with small groups of Catholics around the city, but came to realize that he had yet to hold one in a Polish parish. Detroit had a very large Polish population, but neither the pastors nor people seemed anxious to join in Project Commitment.

When Ernst went to Detroit, three stately Catholic churches—Sweetest Heart of Mary, St. Albertus, and St. Josephat—stood on Canfield Avenue on the city's east side in the black ghetto. The Polish immigrants built those churches, at terrible hardship to themselves. In 1965, they remembered as if it were yesterday, that during the depression of the 1890s, the parishioners of Sweetest Heart of Mary mortgaged their own homes to buy their church at an auction. The church and its properties were auctioned to pay off creditors.

In 1965, as Dearden sought to deal with the urban ethnic and racial divisions in Detroit, the Canfield Avenue Polish churches still functioned, but they were in financial trouble, targets for closure. They were supported by Polish families who lived in distant suburbs who drove for Sunday morning mass to the churches and in some instances sent their children to the schools by bus during the week. These Poles saw Dearden getting ready to close the parishes. Many felt that his zeal was for blacks who were not members of the Catholic Church, and that this was carried out at the expense of loyal Poles. Many Poles were hostile to Dearden. Writing in 1965 on the 75th anniversary of Sweetest Heart of Mary, Dearden spoke about "those whom the parish will serve in the future." The Poles got the message. Their church was going to be turned over to blacks. Blacks were the future. The Poles were history, and they resented it.

The mood was captured by a Father Slawinski, who wrote pessimistically: "To be pastor in these hard times is truly to bear the Cross of Christ. . . . The Parish is shrinking and troubles are growing. Worried, the priest and people ask themselves. Can we survive? . . . It is not in our power to swim against the flood. But we must try to keep intact the Church and school . . . and leave it thus to our beloved children."

But in 1965, few of the Poles at Sweetest Heart of Mary had confidence that their children would attend the church or school on Canfield Avenue.

\*       \*       \*

As Dearden's representative, Ernst in 1965 attended an all-day meeting of the Conference of Polish Priests on race. At the end of the meeting, the chairman proposed that they issue a statement that they were open to any person joining one of their parishes. That was a thinly-veiled attempt to deflect the racism charge before it was raised. One of the priests rose to modify the proposal. "Let's just say that we are open to any responsible person." The priest seemed then to remember that Ernst was in the room. He switched from English to Polish. But Ernst got the drift. Blacks were not thought responsible.

Nonetheless the statement welcoming anyone to join the parish was enough to attract the attention of Democratic Congressman John Conyers, a black who was born on Polish Hill. Those were tense days in

Detroit. The white backlash was developing and Detroit was well on its way to becoming a predominantly black city. Conyers proposed that the black and Polish communities try to work out their differences before it was too late for both of them.

Conyers and Father Daniel Bogus became co-chairmen of the new Black/Polish Alliance, and Ernst became the staff director. "I was a simple liberal in the sense that I felt blacks could do no wrong," he said. "I saw them impoverished, powerless and persecuted and the Poles as part of that persecution. Eventually I saw that the Poles were the whites left living in the city. They weren't running out and leaving the blacks behind."

Ernest was soon critical of Conyers. He said the congressman's attitude toward the Poles was, "You all admit you are racists and then we can get down to business." Challenged that this was itself a racist statement, Conyers said that blacks had been victims of persecution and could not be racists.

Ernst was a member of CCUM and he attended the retreats for inner-city activists arranged at Notre Dame by Monsignor John Egan. Through CCUM and the urban activist grapevine, Baroni learned of Ernst's work with the Poles. So when Baroni received his Ford grant in 1971, one of his first calls at 6:30 one Saturday morning went to Ernst in Detroit.

"I remember because it seemed so strange getting a call that hour in the morning," Ernst said. "We talked for a long time. I remember getting off the phone and saying, 'I think I was just offered a job.' "

Ernst joined the Center staff at 702 Lawrence Street in the early spring of 1971. "Geno was a very dynamic person," Ernst said. "He stimulated everyone else as well. I used to hear him give the same talk, the one he used for years, three or four times a day, and it never failed to bring tears to my eyes. He knew the right cords to pull."

From the beginning, Ernst saw the absolutely essential role Baroni could fill as a bridge between blacks and urban ethnic whites. He rejected the charge—made by some blacks when Baroni created the Center—that Baroni was turning his back on blacks and changing into a minister for racists. "Geno's real agenda was with the blacks," Ernst said. "He was in no way a racist. Geno was a very sensitive person and he had black experience. His cause was the cause of the black community which did not negate the cause of the white ethnic community."

Was Baroni, with his incomplete sentences and rambling thoughts, able to communicate this approach to the staff? "Geno never gave full sentences, but there were important underlying values that Geno communicated," Ernst said. "He respected all sides of complicated issues, but there was no trouble getting the general tone of his position. He had a sense of values."

Ernst was on Baroni's Center payroll for five years. At the Center, staff roles were undefined. It was a free-wheeling operation, with everything revolving around Baroni. There were no job descriptions. Baroni recruited strong self-starting people.

Baroni had confidence in Ernst. He designated him as the executive director of the Catholic Conference on Ethnic and Neighborhood Affairs, the Center's Cleveland offshoot.

In the internal Center debate over whether emphasis should be placed on organizing communities or developing job and income-producing projects, Baroni and Ernst disagreed. Baroni liked the development approach; Ernst argued for organization first. But it was a professional disagreement.

The real Baroni-Ernst fight developed out of a Center project in Prince George's County, Maryland, a Washington suburb. The money was provided by the Ford Foundation, the Meyer Foundation and the Campaign for Human Development.

Baroni believed that Ernst misused Center money and attempted to build an independent organization in Prince George's County. In cooperation with the Baroni Center, Baroni disappeared from the office for two weeks. When he returned, he and Ernst had a meeting which deteriorated into a shouting match. They had been friends. Baroni had baptized Ernst's children and had dined at Ernst's table. "During those years I was as close to Geno as anyone else," Ernst said. "We trusted each other and worked things out with one another." But now that was over. Baroni accused Ernst of stealing. Ernst denied it. He pointed out he had even put his own money into the project.

Baroni went to the Prince George's people with his complaint about Ernst. They fired Ernst, but also wrote a letter denying Baroni's charge. In the next few months, as Ernst looked for a job, he learned that his reputation was tarnished. He blamed Baroni and in January, 1976, he retained lawyers to sue Baroni.

Through his lawyers, Ernst challenged Baroni to go public with his accusations. On January 22, 1976, attorney Arthur H. Blitz wrote Baroni: "Mr. Ernst believes that if there is to be any accusations of criminal conduct, they should be brought to the attention of the appropriate prosecuting authorities so that the matter can be brought to trial or otherwise disposed of through judicial process rather than by indictment through rumor. Mr. Ernst has asked me to consider the possibilities of civil litigation against those persons responsible for the false accusations."

The bad blood between Baroni and Ernst grieved both men, but they were trapped in their own personalities and history.

The Ernst affair worried the Ford Foundation, which came at a time when the Foundation was forcing Baroni to reorganize the Center. Eventually Baroni was obligated to establish a board of directors with independent authority to make policy. Limits were set on Baroni's freewheeling operation, and in addition, money became harder to get. Ford reduced its support. Other foundations and the Campaign for Human Development couldn't take up the slack. Baroni's strength had been consciousness-raising, not the management of development programs. Everybody knew, including Baroni, that he was an atrocious manager. Ford came to that conclusion. The Ernst affair seemed to confirm it.

In 1978, the Center had its peak payroll of 65 people. The Ford and other foundation money was no longer enough for that large a payroll. The Center staff grew in Baroni's final years there beyond his expectations or his managerial style. Baroni wanted everything to revolve around him and everyone to reflect his philosophy. But the money problem stopped that. Baroni finally consented to staff members applying to the government for grants. One result of those grants was the creation within the Center of power centers. Each Center employee with a grant felt he was entitled to control his own fiefdom within the larger Baroni kingdom. As the lord of the fief, the staff member sought to keep a distance from Baroni and to exercise authority over the staff working on the grant. In 1975 and 1976, as the Ford Foundation money dried up, leaving all employees vulnerable except those working on government grants, Baroni faced new and difficult problems. It wasn't easy for the good-hearted, optimistic Baroni to tell friends that he could no longer pay them and they would have to get work elsewhere. The Center community described as a "family" by Barbara Mikulski was disintegrating because of dependence on federal grants and a strange pattern of growth.

Intellectually, Baroni knew that movements and centers had brief lifespans. He wasn't ready to give up yet, but he began to ask around about other opportunities. While the Center's reputation and future were bleak, that was not the case for Baroni. He was recognized and honored as the father and the leader of the urban ethnic movement. He was the Moses who led ethnic Americans out of the captivity of slavery to their own fears.

Granted all his weaknesses—he was incompetent as a manager; he was inarticulate as a writer and thinker; he stole others' ideas shamelessly; he was bound by personal insecurities—he was also a brilliant strategist and political analyst; a genius at connecting people and ideas; a deeply religious man who suffered on a lonely but ever-onward pilgrimage for justice.

# 11

# From Ford to Carter

In the spring of 1976, Geno Baroni got itchy again. Jimmy Carter needed advice on how to win the votes of white urban ethnics in the presidential election. Baroni was there to provide it. The linkage was the politically sensitive abortion issue.

But first Baroni had to resolve problems at his Center. The Carter opening was an opportunity to escape a deteriorating situation at the Center. Ford Foundation pressure on him to reorganize management at the Center became uncomfortable. Especially irritating was Ford's demand for a board of directors that would oversee the entire operation, including Baroni. He liked too much being his own boss to submit to Ford easily, but he complied with the demand. He had little choice if he wanted Ford's money to keep the Center operating, but he would not give up control. He became chairman of the board of directors, as well as president and chief operating officer. Ford saw through the new arrangement, but he accepted it. There was at least the promise of some new people looking over Baroni's shoulders. The Ford people told Baroni that they would reduce their grants to the five-year-old Center. Ford program officer Schrank told Baroni that the Center should begin to "stand on its own feet."

Baroni's greatest gift to the urban ethnic movement had been himself. In the previous four years he traveled thousands of miles and visited hundreds of neighborhoods to give his standard speech extolling neighborhood values. Under his charismatic leadership, hundreds of neighborhood people stepped onto the rungs of power. But now there was less need of exhortation and inspiration. The need increasingly was for technical expertise—something Baroni himself was unable to provide. He moved the Center toward that capability. His central role diminished, and the movement took the direction that Baroni hoped—toward neighborhood leadership and control. That meant less of a place for Baroni. From friends in the ethnic movement, he heard talk that he had accomplished his mission. Because he was still delivering the same basic message and speech he started with four years before, some called him "Geno One Note." He heard it and didn't like it.

Internal conflicts at the Center between those who wanted to put the most emphasis on neighborhood organizing efforts and those who wanted to move toward community development rubbed nerves raw. Those who wanted continued emphasis on organizing said that the local groups created and shepherded by Baroni were not yet ready to move into development. They needed broader bases to raise money and show political muscle. But others at the Center disagreed with this go-slow approach. They pressed Baroni for permission to offer more counseling and support for development projects.

"Be careful. That's the right direction, but they may not be ready for it yet," Baroni said. Ford wanted the Center to move toward development and away from advocacy. Ford said it was not enough to talk about ethnicity. If leaders of the freshly-conscious urban ethnic communities wanted enduring accomplishments, they had to move from organizing toward development, particularly that of job-creating businesses. Otherwise, Ford and the development advocates said, young people would move out, leaving houses empty and the neighborhood open to the radical racial change that Baroni and the Center worked so hard to resist.

Baroni liked the development approach, but he didn't want to abandon community organizing. To do development work clearly required new technical advisers on the staff, but there were few around who had the right combination—a neighborhood background, ethnic identity and technical skills.

\*     \*     \*

Baroni found such a person in Marcy Kaptur. Baroni met Kaptur when he worked with Father Martin Hernady to revitalize the Birmingham neighborhood in Toledo. Kaptur was a 29-year-old planning professional with six years' experience on the Toledo-Lucas County Planning Commission. Baroni, Hernady and their colleague, Peter Ujvagi, knew that Kaptur had technical competence. She knew the vocabulary, rules and history of planning. She understood ingredients of plans. She was bright, aggressive and cooperative. Of Polish background, Kaptur was sensitive to urban ethnic values and goals. Very few urban ethnic people in neighborhoods had Kaptur's technical knowledge.

Baroni was always on the lookout for apostles who could carry out his gospel of ethnicity. When an opening came in a Chicago project supported by the Center and the Campaign for Human Development, Baroni helped Kaptur get the job. She brought to it technical planning tools that the neighborhood organization needed.

The neighborhood was East Humboldt Park on the northwest side of Chicago, two miles west of Lake Michigan. It was predominantly Polish. Ed Marciniak, president of the Institute of Urban Life of Chicago, wrote that the citizens of East Humboldt Park strongly believed that "the neighborhood is indispensable for the good life and that urban planners who are indifferent to the care of cultivation of neighborhoods should be resisted." Marciniak said that when Kaptur arrived, the neighborhood had been "woefully neglected and heavily depreciated." The question was whether the decline could be reversed. The neighborhood, which was predominantly Catholic, contained three Catholic churches, each large enough to be a cathedral.

After World War II, newcomers moved gradually into the neighborhood. There were Puerto Ricans, Mexicans and blacks. Stores displayed "Se Habla Espanol" signs. In the 1950s, the city cut a new expressway that forced condemnation of homes and eviction of people along East Humboldt Park's eastern border. In the 1960s, many younger people moved to the suburbs.

The Catholic parishes called on Cardinal Albert Gregory Meyer, archbishop of Chicago, for assistance to stem the outmigration. He gave the assignment to Monsignor John Egan, director of the archdiocesan Office of Urban Affairs. Egan called upon Saul Alinsky, executive director of the Industrial Areas Foundation, to organize the community. It wasn't long before the Egan/Alinsky team and the area's politicians were in conflict. Egan's activities brought him national attention. He was the unchallenged leading Catholic priest in the urban ministry when he formed the Catholic Committee for the Urban Ministry.

Meanwhile, Mayor Richard J. Daley's staff produced the Chicago 21 plan. In 1974, residents of East Humboldt Park asked what the plan meant for them. In 1975, residents created a committee to hire a planning consultant to draft a realistic, workable program to improve the area. There was public bidding and twelve established firms submitted applications. At a four-hour meeting in the summer of 1975, attended by several hundred residents, a vote was taken and a decision made to award a seven-month contract to Baroni's Center.

Marciniak said that one city planner reported that "some planners immediately began to bad-mouth the NCUEA. In the first place, they didn't know who or what the National Center was. NCUEA didn't belong to the planners' club, locally or nationally. If NCUEA was not part of the planning establishment, what could it possibly offer by way of planning expertise? A disgruntled few even hinted that the bidding and final vote must have been rigged."

Baroni was not a stranger to the neighborhood. He had been the keynote speaker at a local conference in 1971, and NCUEA officials had done previous work with the Chicago Polish community. Baroni promised East Humboldt Park citizens that he would not parachute an expert into their neighborhood and then flee as soon as the money ran out. He said the Center would work with all groups in the area. Then he made his major move. He asked Kaptur to leave the planning board in Toledo and go to East Humboldt Park as his representative. She agreed.

Kaptur's job included guiding the local planning committee and brokering disputes among contending organizations. Working over several months, the committee produced a report, with Kaptur the major author. In 1976, Kaptur, who was consulting frequently with Baroni and his colleagues back at the Center, wrote a plan that echoed Baroni's philosophy and meshed with local needs. It had these major elements:

— — The basic objective . . . is to insure the residents of the community their right to stay in the neighborhood.

— — The primary concern is upgrading of the community through repair of older buildings and construction of new homes and apartments on vacant lots without pricing current residents out of the neighborhood.

— — The neighborhood is the building block of city planning. . . . East Humboldt Park is a community of neighborhoods. . . . If there is one underlying theme throughout, it is that the neighborhood unit is recognized as the primary form of human settlement and placed in the special context it deserves. . . . Residential neighborhoods must be protected over time.

— — The concerns that have surfaced in this community through the planning process revolve mainly around how to keep this a working class area in the face of major rehabilitation and development efforts. This is a particularly important issue here because so many of this community's residents work in the industrial park south of Grand Avenue and are convenient to their place of employment.

— —In order to keep money that is already here in this area and attract a limited amount of additional wealth, there is a commitment in this plan to provide housing, either new or rehabbed, for the middle income market.

The idea of self-help to preserve and revitalize a neighborhood was right out of Baroni's textbook. His voice could be heard in the East Humboldt Park plan: "People don't live in cities. They live in neighborhoods. Neighborhoods. Neighborhoods are the building blocks of cities. If neighborhoods die, cities die."

When the plan was finished, Baroni had other work for Kaptur. He played a key role in securing for her a job the next year on Carter's White House staff. Later he assisted her successful campaign for the U.S. House of Representatives from Toledo.

\*　　\*　　\*

During the spring and summer of 1976, Baroni found it increasingly difficult to manage the Center. Though it was not in imminent danger of collapse, he worried over how he could find the money to continue present operations. He saw the possibility of a smaller staff and lower expectations. It was not Baroni's style to go backward.

He continued that summer to hire consultants, some of whom did little visible work at the Center. Baroni was building his political team. Sometimes he forgot to tell his program or budget officers that he had hired a consultant and needed some of their money to pay that consultant. Baroni was notoriously disorganized when it came to keeping payroll records. On the other hand, program officers were doing more and more business with the federal government which demanded mountains of records to substantiate claims. There were inevitable clashes between the free-wheeling and free-spending Baroni and the more structured program officers.

These clashes helped to push Baroni back toward one of his favorite techniques when under stress: disappearance. That spring and summer, he visited Combermere for a few days, and Seven Springs on several occasions. He carried within himself the full knowledge of the Center's developing problems. He did not let aides know the full story. In addition to the turmoil back at the office, Baroni was pulled in different political directions.

He enjoyed the courting from President Gerald R. Ford and his aides Bill Baroody and Myron Kuropas, and also liked his meetings over meals with Joseph Duffy and other Carter aides. For Baroni, the sad memory of 1972, when George McGovern ignored his advice, faded in the excitement of a new presidential campaign. With both Ford and Carter chasing him, Baroni felt that the urban ethnic movement was firmly entrenched in the political game.

Politicians realized that the Catholic urban ethnic vote could turn the election. Ford's staff asked Baroni what the president should do to seek out votes of Catholic urban ethnics. So did the Democrats. The Democrats had a special problem. Invariably, they asked Baroni, "How do we handle abortion?"

\*    \*    \*

The abortion issue had hovered over national, state and local politics ever since the January, 1973, decision by the U.S. Supreme Court in the Roe v. Wade case. The decision set off a political firestorm. It was condemned by the hierarchy of the Roman Catholic Church, as well as leaders of some other faiths. Even many Catholics who disagreed, as did Baroni, with the church's position on birth control were strongly against abortion. While polls showed a fairly sizable Catholic acceptance of the Supreme Court decision, the politicians believed that voters in the urban ethnic communities, socially and religiously conservative, would support the hierarchy in an abortion fight.

Baroni accepted the church's teaching on abortion. This was different from the 1968 *Humanae Vitae* fight.

Now, eight years later, Baroni had no disagreement with church teaching on abortion. He expressed uncertainty over whether a Constitutional amendment or a national statute was the appropriate way to end abortion and reverse the effect of the Supreme Court decision. When pressed in the summer of 1976 by Democratic candidates, Baroni said that he didn't like abortions, personally wanted them ended, but was skeptical about accomplishing that through the legal and law enforcement systems. Besides, said Baroni, he was so busy with neighborhood work that he had not kept up with the theological or legal debates. So, said Baroni, "Abortion is one subject I can't help you with very much politically."

But the Democrats pointed out to Baroni that unless they handled the abortion issue, they could not get elected, and that would doom many of the other programs in which Baroni had an interest. Baroni worked out an answer. The Catholic Church leadership in the United States, he said, was unanimous in its opposition to the Supreme Court decision and in support of a law change, whether through a Constitutional amendment or statute, to ban abortions. "Do not try to exploit any differences of emphasis you think you see among the bishops," Baroni said. "This is a touchy issue, but I can tell you it would be a mistake to think there are differences among the bishops or a gap between the bishops and the people on abortion."

While believing in his church's position on abortion and endorsing efforts to restrict abortion, Baroni deplored the single-issue politics practiced by many anti-abortion foes. For them, it was either you're with us absolutely on abortion or we'll work to defeat you, no matter where you are on other issues. As early as 1976, Baroni said what the U.S. bishops would declare in 1980 and 1984—that candidates should be examined on a full range of issues.

To Democrats Baroni talked with during the primary campaign and pre-convention period—Morris Udall, Birch Bayh, Henry Jackson and Jimmy Carter—Baroni's advice was to avoid the abortion controversy as much as they could and to seek Catholic urban ethnic votes on other issues, such as jobs, health care and neighborhoods, especially local control of neighborhoods.

Carter got caught up in the abortion issue just before the Democratic caucuses in Iowa in January. He was interviewed on the telephone by a Catholic priest for an article to be published in Catholic newspapers. Carter told the priest that he personally opposed abortion, but also opposed the proposed anti-abortion amendment to the Constitution. When pressed, Carter said he might support some sort of "national statute" that might restrict abortion.

Other Democratic candidates shared Carter's opposition to a Constitutional amendment. Now they saw him trying to stake out a position closer to the right-to-life movement, which had strength in Iowa. Later Carter was reported by columnists Rowland Evans and Robert Novak to have told a woman that "under circumstances I would" support a federal Constitutional amendment. Finally, to clarify his position, Carter put out a statement:

> The confusion in Iowa did not originate because of any change of position of my own. I've had a very consistent position on abortion for several years. I think that abortion is wrong. I don't think the government should do anything to encourage abortion. I believe that positive action should be taken in better education, better family-planning programs, the availability of contraceptive devices for those who believe in their use, better adoption procedures to minimize abortions. I do not favor the Constitutional amendment that would prohibit all abortions. I

do not favor the Constitutional amendment that would give states local option.

The abortion issue, Carter believed, was important to his campaign.

\* \* \*

Carter also created a controversy during the primary campaign season, and Baroni was involved in it. This developed after Baroni sent material on ethnicity and voting to the Carter issues team in Georgia. Stuart Eizenstat, a Carter aide, read the Baroni material and sent along some of the ideas to Carter. In late winter in Washington, Baroni had had a breakfast meeting with Carter. They talked about the importance of ethnicity and neighborhoods and about shared values. Carter told Baroni he understood and agreed with his ideas. "But I wasn't certain," Baroni said. "I still had doubts that this southern governor and the people around him understood very much about the urban ethnics in the industrial big city neighborhoods."

Carter was interviewed on April 2 by Sam Roberts, chief political correspondent of the New York *Daily News*. A story ran two days later. The sixteenth paragraph said: "And, asked about low-income scatter-site housing in the suburbs, he replied: 'I see nothing wrong with ethnic purity being maintained. I would not force a racial integration of a neighborhood by government action. But I would not permit discrimination against a family moving into a neighborhood.' "

The words "ethnic purity" shot across the country. Baroni said that he understood what Carter tried to say, but that the words "ethnic purity" were open to misinterpretation as code words for keeping blacks out of urban ethnic neighborhoods.

"I never used the words 'ethnic purity' and I certainly didn't give them to Carter," Baroni said. But he guessed that Carter was trying to assure urban ethnic whites that he would not push blacks into their neighborhoods.

CBS correspondent Ed Rabel asked Carter at a press conference in Indianapolis about what he meant by ethnic purity. "I have nothing against a community that's made up of people who are Polish, Czechoslovakians, French-Canadians, or blacks who are trying to maintain the ethnic purity of their neighborhood," Carter said. "This is a natural inclination on the part of people."

Carter said he never "condoned any sort of discrimination against, say, a black family or other family from moving into that neighborhood . . . but I don't think government ought to deliberately break down an ethnically oriented community by injecting into it a member of another race. To me, this is contrary to the best interests of the community."

In press conferences later at South Bend and Pittsburgh, Carter continued to defend the concept and words of ethnic purity. A staff member, Greg Schneiders, wrote Carter a note warning him that the words were controversial. Alarm bells had rung back at campaign headquarters in Atlanta. Hamilton Jordan and other top aides heard from black leaders. Among these was Andrew Young, a congressman from Atlanta and a former aide to Martin Luther King. Young issued a public statement: "This doesn't mean to me he's a racist. It means he made a terrible blunder that he's got to recover from. I just think it's an awful phrase. I don't think he understood how loaded it is with Hitlerian connotations."

By now Carter began to understand his poor choice of words. Arriving two days later in Philadelphia, he said, "I think most of the problem has been caused by my ill-chosen agreement to use the words ethnic purity. I think it should have been the word 'ethnic character' or 'ethnic heritage.'" Carter said he wanted to apologize "to all those who have been concerned about the unfortunate use of the ethnic purity. I don't think there are any ethnically pure neighborhoods."

In Washington, Baroni was disturbed at Carter's use of the words ethnic purity. He called Duffy and said Carter could even jeopardize his standing within the white urban ethnic community by suggesting a stereotype response. "Ethnicity is not racism," Baroni said. "Urban ethnics hate that idea that they are red-necked racists. That's the image I've been working to change for six years and now your candidate shows he fails to understand what we've been saying." Baroni said Carter better learn more about ethnicity and neighborhoods before he talked about them.

A few days later, a call came to Baroni from campaign headquarters. Would he fly to Chicago and meet with Carter to talk about urban ethnics and neighborhoods? Baroni went. He and Carter had breakfast and talked for more than an hour in a downtown Chicago hotel. Baroni went through his standard line. Carter was impressed. "Please keep in touch with my staff. I'll make sure they continue to deal with you on these issues," Carter told him.

Through the rest of the spring and into the summer, Baroni steadily fed information to the Carter campaign. In Washington, Duffy was his main contact. In Atlanta, Baroni dealt with Eizenstat and Landon Butler, an Atlanta businessman and Carter's political coordinator. Within two weeks after Carter won the Democratic nomination in New York,

Baroni got another call from Butler. Would you come to Atlanta and help us set up the desk which will deal with the Catholic and urban ethnic vote during the campaign? Baroni flew down with John Kromkowski.

They met first with Eizenstat, then with Butler. The Carter aides asked Baroni to pick the staff for the desk, and told him that he could join the campaign team if he wanted to.

"It would be better for both of us if I stayed outside," Baroni said. "I can do you more good by staying at my Center. But I'll be glad to give you some people for the Catholic desk." Baroni said the team of himself in Washington and a few aides in Atlanta would give Carter needed background and excellent contacts with the Catholic and urban ethnic communities.

Butler checked it out with Jordan, who approved. Within a few days, Vicki Mongiardo, a former nun on Baroni's Center payroll, was sent to Atlanta to set up the desk. In September, Baroni added another member to the desk, Terry Sunday, who left a job at the United States Catholic Conference. "I wrote briefing papers and Vicki and I arranged some campaign appearances by the Carter people before urban ethnic groups," said Sunday. They kept in frequent touch with Baroni, whose introduction on the telephone was invariably, "Did you read this morning's *New York Times?*"

Baroni also prevailed on Herman Gallegos, an Hispanic, to join the campaign staff in Atlanta. Baroni and Gallegos had worked together since the early 1970s when they met at the U.S. Catholic Conference. Gallegos helped prepare the briefing books which Carter studied before his debates with Ford. "Geno was on the phone constantly. He was hearing where Carter was having real problems and suggesting a visit there by Carter or someone else in the campaign," Gallegos said.

Mongiardo and Sunday were later appointed to the White House staff. Gallegos returned to San Francisco by choice after the election and was later appointed by Carter to the Student Loan Marketing Association.

\*　　\*　　\*

In August, Baroni told Jordan and Eizenstat that Carter should set up a meeting with Roman Catholic bishops in Washington, and helped to arrange this through his friends at the conference, Father J. Bryan Hehir and Monsignor George Higgins. Meanwhile, Bishop James S. Rausch of St. Cloud, a longtime friend to Democratic vice-presidential nominee, Walter F. Mondale, also suggested a meeting. Rausch was general secretary of the bishops' conference. Mondale passed the word to Carter. Carter heard contradictory advice. One aide wrote that nothing he could say to the bishops would lessen their concern or criticism over his abortion position. Stay away, the aide said.

But Carter was confident that the meeting would be productive and useful to his campaign. He said he could build an "intimate personal relationship" with the bishops. After all, hadn't he charmed and won over thousands of Americans in their living rooms on the way to the nomination? Furthermore, Carter accurately pointed out that the Democratic Party platform contained many provisions in line with Catholic social teaching. Carter was sure the bishops would understand and accept his position that he found abortion personally to be morally wrong, but opposed the Constitutional amendment.

In August, Carter and the bishops agreed to a meeting. The next question was where it should be held. Baroni recommended that Carter go to the bishops' headquarters at 1312 Massachusetts Avenue in northwest Washington. Carter agreed, but the bishops demurred. They envisioned the Catholic headquarters building as a backdrop for television reports and Carter campaign advertisements. Finally, it was agreed that the meeting would take place in the Mayflower Hotel on Connecticut Avenue in downtown Washington.

Carter felt well-prepared for the meeting. He studied an opening statement that Baroni had helped to shape. Baroni said the bishops were concerned about living conditions for the millions of American Catholics in urban areas. In effect, Carter was ready to lay a Baroni agenda on the bishops.

Carter opened the meeting. He said that he and the bishops agreed on a wide range of social issues. They shared a concern, Carter said, for the middle class and the working class as well as for the poor. Carter, casting his own and the Baroni agenda in his own words, said he believed in strong moral values, and those values were respected by a nation that used its resources for shelter, medical care, education and jobs. The bishops listened in silence. When Carter finished, he looked around the room apparently satisfied with his approach.

He was startled when Archbishop (later Cardinal) Joseph L. Bernardin of Cincinnati, the bishops' conference president, opened a folder and began to read a prepared statement. Carter's face remained impassive, but he was stunned as Bernardin said that until the bishops and the candidate resolved the abortion issue, there was no point in going forward on other topics. Abortion overrode all other issues, Bernardin said. To the bishops, abortion is murder, the taking of the lives of millions of unborn babies every year. Just as government must step in and deal with other social issues, so it must address abortion. And the way to do that, Bernardin told Carter, is through either a Constitutional amendment or legislation.

Another bishop took up the issue. He asked Carter if he would work to find language for a Constitutional amendment that he could endorse. Carter sought to duck the question, saying he could not comment on any language until he saw it. "I would welcome language your excellencies might prepare," Carter said. Bernardin replied immediately. The church is not in the business of drafting a Constitutional amendment. That's government's job. "I won't automatically oppose any amendment. If the lawyers can come up with the right language, I would look at it carefully," Carter said. The bishops listened.

The meeting ended with handshakes. Carter was pleased, but only for a few minutes. Bernardin went to a press conference and told reporters he was "disappointed" in Carter's position on abortion. He continued: "Governor Carter did tell us that if acceptable language could be found, he would support a Constitutional amendment." The reporters immediately ran to Carter. Had he changed his abortion position? Carter said no. He said he opposed anti-abortion amendment proposals he had seen and could not imagine one that would be acceptable to him. He said he only told the bishops that he would not totally rule out a proposal he had not seen.

The meeting was a total loss politically for Carter. News accounts focused on Bernardin's "disappointment" and Carter's vagueness. There was no mention of wide areas of agreement between Carter and the bishops on other issues.

Carter's aides got on the phone with Baroni. What do we do now?

It got worse. Ford invited the bishops to the White House. They met and Bernardin went to the White House briefing room. There he told reporters that the bishops found the president's position on abortion "acceptable." Does that constitute an endorsement by the bishops of the president over Carter? No, Bernardin responded. The Catholic bishops, he insisted, do not endorse presidential candidates. They look at the candidates' positions. The questions from reporters all concerned abortion. There was no acknowledgement that a vast gap existed between Ford and the bishops on social issues. Measured against the church's teaching, the Republican platform on which Ford was running was a disaster. But the news stories dwelt only on abortion. It was a moment of triumph for single-issue politics.

Baroni was irritated and saddened. He believed the bishops blundered in stressing abortion and ignoring other issues. He called Hehir and Higgins and activated the CCUM network. Baroni talked to Egan and Father Edward Flahavan, to Mongiardo in Atlanta and to John Carr. Mongiardo said that Carter staffers were quite bitter about the meeting with the bishops. They felt that Carter had been misguided and betrayed. They were looking for scapegoats. Who were the idiots who suggested the Carter-bishops' meeting? Fingers pointed at Baroni.

Bernardin apparently didn't feel very good about the outcome of the meeting himself. He insisted that the bishops did not endorse Ford. He accused the press of twisting the stories, but the politically-wise men around Bernardin knew better. They understood that the bishops made a serious mistake in their comments on the two meetings, and they looked for a way out before the bishops were drawn up to their necks in the presidential election campaign. Baroni joined others in pressing for a new statement clarifying the bishops' position. Finally it came. It restated what Bernardin had been unsuccessful in getting across in the White House press room. The bishops would not endorse any candidate, and conscientious voters had to look at all issues before casting their ballots in November, the bishops said. But Carter was damaged.

Baroni had an idea. Carter could not win on the abortion issue. He was wasting opportunities to go after the Catholic vote on other more appealing issues. Mongiardo passed the advice along to Jordan, Eizenstat and Butler in Atlanta.

On the Saturday morning before Labor Day, Baroni was in the kitchen of the Chevy Chase, Md., home of Mark Talisman, Washington representative for the Federation of Jewish Agencies. A former aide to Democratic Congressman Charles A. Vanik of Ohio, Talisman was known as a savvy political analyst. He and Baroni like to swap theories and gossip. Duffy, Carter's Washington representative, was also in the Talisman kitchen. The men were eating Talisman's homemade bagels and drinking coffee when the telephone rang. It was for Baroni from the Carter brain trust in Plains, Georgia.

Carter gathered his top staff that weekend in the home of his mother, Lillian, in Plains. It was called Miss Lillian's Pond House. Mondale was there, along with Jordan, Jody Powell, Schneiders, Pat Caddell, Charles Kirbo, Jerry Rafshoon, Robert Lipshutz, Rich Hutcheson, Tim Kraft and Eizenstat.

It had not been a good month since they won the nomination. Sitting next to the fireplace, Carter asked, "What are our themes going to be for this campaign?" Nobody had any good answers. They all had been so busy winning the nomination and setting up a campaign team that they had neglected the message. Carter reminded them that the campaign would begin officially in a few hours. The aides headed for telephones. One call was placed to Mark Talisman's kitchen.

Could you rush us a memo for Jordan and Eizenstat telling us precisely how we might go after the Catholic and urban ethnic vote?, Baroni was asked. We're not talking abstractions now, the caller said. We're talking election politics. "Jimmy would be very grateful." The caller said the campaign aides wanted to get the debate away from abortion as soon as they could. Could Baroni help?

Baroni went immediately to work. Within hours, he submitted to Duffy for wiring to Atlanta a packet of suggestions. Baroni said that Carter should campaign aggressively in urban ethnic neighborhoods, and that he should dwell on the bread and butter economic issues that for years attracted the Catholic middle-and working-class voters to the Democratic Party. Baroni told Carter what he had been saying publicly for years.

Eizenstat liked Baroni's ideas. The next question was how to sell them. The brain trust decided that the Catholic urban ethnic vote was so important that they would devote to it several days early in the campaign. Baroni gave them a list of possible campaign stops. Among his proposals were Steve Adubato's North Ward Center in Newark, Father Martin Hernady's Birmingham neighborhood in Toledo, sites in Providence and Cleveland, and Polish Hill in Pittsburgh.

Carter's campaign staff decided to try out Baroni's idea on the Tuesday night after Labor Day in Philadelphia, an idea which Baroni had *not* suggested. They told this to Baroni, and he warned them. The Catholic Church in Philadelphia is among the most conservative in the country, Baroni said. Cardinal John Krol is a leader in the anti-abortion movement. Test out the ideas elsewhere before you try Philadelphia, Baroni warned.

But Carter's staff had an invitation from a group called Coalition of Organizations for Action, a progressive group which had been influenced by the Baroni ethnic affairs philosophy. Baroni told Eizenstat that the people were fine. The Coalition arranged to meet Carter in the rectory of Our Lady of Pompeii Roman Catholic Church. But a few hours before Carter was due, Krol laid down his own condition. His office announced: "The archdiocese of Philadelphia has informed the pastor of Our Lady of Pompeii that if a community meeting is held with Gov. Carter on Catholic property, then the abortion issue must be on the agenda." The Coalition switched the meeting site to the Lutheran Church of St. Simeon, but it was too late to spare Carter another embarrassing spanking by the Catholic Church.

There was one more incident. Carter headed that night to Scranton in upstate Pennsylvania. Again Baroni warned the Carter people that Scranton was a hotbed of the right-to-life movement and that its bishop was a conservative who probably would vote for Ford. When Carter got to his overnight stop at the Hilton Hotel, there was a large hostile crowd outside. They carried posters with photographs of garbage cans with babies and a cartoon of Carter with a big grin holding an aborted fetus in his teeth. "This is a disaster," Eizenstat told Baroni. Carter read Caddell's polls showing him slipping badly among Catholic Democrats.

Baroni proposed that Carter visit Polish Hill in Pittsburgh, and reassured the Carter staff that Polish Hill could turn Carter's problems around. Baroni's reputation as a political savant was on the line at Polish Hill. When Baroni suggested the site, Joseph Timilty, Carter's campaign director in Pennsylvania, said no. He wanted a downtown rally in Pittsburgh. Organized labor and Mayor Peter Flaherty promised a big friendly crowd. "Yeah, of city employees, and the press will know that," Baroni said. Timilty said Carter could credit Pittsburgh's Golden Triangle—its renewed downtown district—to Democratic administrations in the city and in Washington. Pittsburgh was a model of a reborn city, Timilty said. "That's what's wrong with your campaign," Baroni said. "You should be going after ethnic voters who live in neighborhoods, not people who work downtown. Most people who work downtown are going to vote for Ford," Baroni said. "Go to a neighborhood where your voters are."

The argument between Baroni and Timilty went back and forth, until Jordan and field-director Tim Kraft decided to take Baroni's advice. Kraft asked Baroni, "Would you be willing to advance that trip?" Baroni accepted the challenge. He had never been an advance man, but he admired the work of those who went to a site ahead of the candidate, fixed the schedule, picked the spots for maximum television advantage, and worked out logistics. Baroni had read a book by Jerry Bruno, an advance man for Robert F. Kennedy, and thought that advancing would be fun. At the Center, Baroni aides told him, "Geno, you're getting in over your head." Baroni flew to Pittsburgh. With Timilty, other Carter staff aides, and Secret Service agents, Baroni cased the neighborhood.

There were 500 people on Burton Avenue in Polish Hill when Carter arrived. He worked his way down the street, shaking hands, posing for photographs, until he came to Chester Galda's butcher shop. Baroni had been there the day before.

"This is Chester, our butcher," Baroni told Carter.

"You're screwing up my business," Galda said with a laugh to Carter.

Carter wanted to know the names of the different meat products Galda was selling. At a counter in the rear of the store, butcher Jerry Helwick was selling a kielbasa, a Polish sausage, to Jenna Kulanovich. Helwick kidded her: "Don't buy it and take it outside. The Secret Service will think it's a gun."

Father John Jendzura, pastor of Immaculate Heart of Mary Roman Catholic Church, arrived. He and Baroni had talked the day before. Jendzura had lined up the nuns and schoolchildren on the front steps of his church. Jendzura took the kielbasa from Helwick and showed it to Carter.

Outside the butcher shop, Carter met Joe S. Zaporowski, born on Polish Hill in 1913. He retired in 1978 as a maintenance man for Trans World Airlines at the Pittsburgh airport. Zaporowski told Carter how the poor and retired people were having a tough time financially because of the national economy. Carter said he would change that. "But I need you to get out and vote," he said. Jendzura was waiting at the church. The school children, in their uniforms, surrounded Carter as he spoke. He talked about the beauty of neighborhoods and the importance of the values found there. It was the speech that Baroni recommended. At last, Carter appeared at a rally for Catholics that was not overwhelmed by the abortion issue.

Father John Webber, curate at the church, whispered to one of the churchwomen, "Give him the T-shirt." Carter put on a red and white T-shirt. "Polish Power," it said. Jendzura kissed Carter on both cheeks. Jimmy beamed. The photographers got it all. Baroni the advance man had done all right.

\*       \*       \*

Carter never did go to Adubato's North Ward, but Mondale did. Baroni suggested several other stops for Carter, and they were successful as Carter moved through the campaign. Geno's political reputation was enhanced. Within the Carter camp, he was known as "the priest who turned us around with the Catholic voters." Abortion receded as a Carter campaign issue.

A few days before the election, Mongiardo called Baroni. "Where are you going to be on election night, Geno?" she asked. He had no plans. "Then why not come down to Atlanta? I'll get you in the Omni ballroom where they'll be posting the figures all night. A lot of newspaper guys will be here and the Carter people will be wandering back and forth." Baroni accepted.

Baroni was not stuck in the ballroom, however. With the returns showing Carter leading Ford narrowly, Baroni was invited to the candidate's headquarters on the 15th floor of the Omni Hotel. Baroni was escorted to the Capitol Suite, Room 1522, where Carter, his family, a few close friends and some top aides watched the results on three color television sets.

"Congratulations, Mr. President," Baroni said.

"Not yet," Carter replied.

Pennsylvania looks good, Baroni said. Yes, Carter agreed, but Ohio may be lost and New York is too close to call. In the final two weeks of the campaign, Ford made an amazing comeback. Carter's thirty-point lead in the polls in the summer fell down to one or two points nationally. Ford campaigned hard in six industrial states, Pennsylvania, New York, Illinois, Michigan, New Jersey and Ohio. They were the states of greatest urban ethnic concentration, the states of Baroni's neighborhoods and people. Baroni reminded friends that he had advised both Ford and Carter how to carry them. Now it was time for the final count.

The night before, flying into Michigan for his final campaign stop in Grand Rapids, Ford got the grim figures from his pollster, Robert Teeter. The final blitz hadn't been enough, Teeter said. Carter was going to win. Ford cried, but he braced himself for his final speech, as snowflakes fell. Then he collapsed.

But the Carter people were not as sure of their polling data as Teeter was of his. Baroni wished Carter good luck and left the suite. He put his head into the Carter Situation Room around the corner. Caddell and his staff were on telephones getting local results and matching them against the projection books. It was very business-like. There was no elation.

Baroni headed for the adjacent World Congress Center, where thousands gathered to await the results. He walked around with Mongiardo, stopping to talk to newspaper reporters and Carter aides. When Jody Powell came down to brief the reporters on the candidate's activities, Baroni listened.

The networks awarded New York, Hawaii, Mississippi to Carter. Just after 3:30 in the morning, they flashed across their screens that Carter had been elected. Baroni joined others in the room in cheers and applause.

*      *      *

Baroni was on Eizenstat's list of those who helped Jimmy Carter win. Mongiardo stayed in Atlanta to help process the thousands of resumes that poured in from job seekers. She urged Baroni to submit a resume, but he was reluctant. She and Baroni talked about their own futures. Baroni urged her to go after an Administration job. She might be able to return to the Center, he said, but cutbacks by the Ford Foundation and other revenue sources were forcing payroll reductions. As for him, Baroni said, he could stay on at the Center. There was enough money from the Ford, Raskob, and Meyer Foundations, and from the Campaign for Human Development to keep him in business. He would like to have an influence on Carter's urban policy, Baroni said. He already had changed Carter's rhetoric, but didn't know how far the former southern governor and his aides would go toward addressing the concerns of the urban white ethnics.

Baroni still believed what he had said in the summer to the National Catholic Education Association: "We have to discover ourselves. We ought to discover each other. Who am I? Who are You? Who are we as Americans? Who am I, who are you, who are we as American Catholics? I don't think we have done such a good job at that. That's why Jimmy Carter and other politicians are very uncomfortable when talking about our ethnic, social and cultural pluralism."

When the Carter transition team set to work in Washington after Thanksgiving, Baroni occasionally visited. He told Eizenstat that he would do whatever he could during the transition to get the new Carter Administration off to a successful start. "I think this new Commission on Neighborhoods could be very important," Baroni said. "I have a lot of experience in that field, you know. Maybe I could help there."

Eizenstat asked Baroni to suggest the names of people who might serve on the commission, the Department of Housing and Urban Development, and the White House domestic policy staff. Although it was not announced yet, Eizenstat was to direct the domestic policy staff. Baroni promised to submit names, noting that the domestic policy staff might be another place he could help out.

Baroni submitted his names—including several from the Center staff. On his list were Mongiardo, Marcy Kaptur, Peter Ujvagi, Tommy Massero, Fred Rotondaro, Theodore Mastroianni, John Carr, Arthur Naparstek and others. About himself, Baroni heard nothing through the transition period and after the Inauguration. He was back at the Center, making speeches about the opportunities before the new administration to serve neighborhoods and urban ethnic concerns.

One night Mongiardo brought to Baroni from the transition offices the secret list of names being compiled for top jobs. Baroni read through it and became livid. He scribbled a note to her: "The book is weak, very weak on ethnic (Catholic) Americans. The book is overloaded by academics and lawyers. Very few neighborhood-oriented people. There are 27 Italian-American congressmen. Not one is mentioned in the book. Our fears are realized. The transition team ignored and neglected the ethnic factor in American society. Nearly 60 million people."

\*       \*       \*

In February, a White House aide called Baroni and asked if he would accept appointment from Carter to serve on the Commission on Neighborhoods as a member and possibly as chairman. Baroni was delighted and accepted without hesitation. He had thought through possible job offers, and this was one he felt he could handle without any conflict of interest. He might even be able to remain as president of the Center. As he saw it, the job involved travel around the country to hold hearings and meet with neighborhood leaders, academics, and politicians.

Its task would be to recommend a neighborhood policy that Carter could declare as a guiding principle for federal domestic policy. Baroni remembered that Father Theodore Hesburgh of Notre Dame University chaired the Civil Rights Commission. Baroni knew that church authorities permitted that kind of government service, and he saw no objections to his accepting a similar job.

Baroni told only a few very close friends of the possibility of his chairing the neighborhood commission. To them, it seemed ideal. He would be doing something he knew and cared deeply about, and it would give him a White House identification, strengthening his reputation as an advocate for the interests of urban ethnics. Many advised him against going into the Administration. They said his independence would be curtailed by the required loyalty. Better to be a critic outside than an apologist inside, they said.

With Baroni's permission, Federal Bureau of Investigation agents arrived at the Center to go through the files. Agents were assigned to look at the financial and operational records. They were surprised to find what others knew—that the Center had few files. The Center was Baroni. Baroni was the Center. There was no point looking at paper. The movement was the man.

Then came a problem. Carter had offered Baroni a job that wasn't empty. Ironically, Jordan had promised the chairmanship to Joseph

Timilty, the Boston politician who ran the Pennsylvania campaign and opposed Carter's tour of Polish Hill.

Baroni won the campaign battle. Now he feared he was about to lose his Carter administration job. Word of Baroni's impending appointment to the commission leaked. Now Baroni told friends he wasn't going to get it. Baroni's political backers on Capitol Hill, in the ethnic movement and in the Italian-American community got to work. Not nominating Baroni to a major spot within this administration would be a disgrace and an insult, they said. The White House staff looked around for another assignment for Baroni.

Jordan called Housing and Urban Development Department Secretary Patricia Roberts Harris. "I'd like you to find something for Geno Baroni," Jordan said. Harris bristled at what she knew to be an order. She wanted to fill her department with people of her choosing. But in reality the White House, primarily Jordan, was calling the shots.

In March, an aide to Harris called Baroni and said there was the possibility of an opening as assistant secretary for consumer and regulatory affairs. Was Geno interested? Baroni studied the office, and said it wasn't what he had in mind. Now Baroni had the administration on the spot. The rejection for the commission chairmanship strengthened Baroni's hand in dealing with the next offer. He told the Harris aide that he wanted a position that involved neighborhood policy.

A few days later, Harris called Baroni. She planned a department reorganization. She would be shifting responsibility for neighborhood policy to the assistant secretary for consumer and regulatory affairs. Then Harris tossed in the pot sweetener. That assistant secretary would be the administration official charged with overseeing the work of the Commission on Neighborhoods. Baroni would not be commission chairman, but he would, in some respects, be the commission chairman's boss.

Baroni accepted the offer from Harris, but he had one important hurdle to overcome before his nomination could be announced. He was uncertain how his ecclesiastical superior, Cardinal William Baum, would take the appointment. Baroni and Baum were not close the way Baroni had been with O'Boyle. Baroni and O'Boyle had a common background. Neither presumed to be an intellectual. They came from the social action wing of the church. Both were artful politicians who used one another, and understood that.

Baum was an intellectual and a skilled theologian, not a church politician. On his arrival in Washington Baum had blundered, buying an expensive house in one of the city's spiffier white neighborhoods.

Baroni thought that was a dreadful mistake and said so; now he had to deal with Baum over his nomination to HUD.

Baroni told Baum that he had been offered the position and had accepted it, but that he would withdraw if the archbishop felt that the position would embarrass the church. Baroni said he was not asking for permission to take the job. He did not want to put Baum on the spot for a yes or no answer. He was asking him only to say no, if that's what he wanted. The archbishop said he had no objection.

Jimmy Carter announced the appointment of Geno C. Baroni of Pennsylvania to be assistant secretary of the United States Department of Housing and Urban Development for Neighborhood, Consumer and Regulatory Affairs. The White House sent over a briefing book.

Baroni liked what he read. The transition team's recommendations to Harris included material that Baroni had pushed. He especially liked the recommendation that the Community Block Grant program—HUD's major contribution to community development strategy—be changed to allow stronger citizen participation.

Baroni marked the relevant passage:

> Present administrative regulations are very loose and permit communities to meet their requirements virtually through public hearings alone. Citizen groups would like to see this strengthened to focus resources more on poor areas and to give greater citizen input into program decisions. While this is generally supported by communities, it must be handled with great sensitivity. Otherwise, it will become bogged down in lengthy standoffs over "who controls the program—the city or citizens groups." Ultimate control and responsibility must remain with the local government.

Baroni saw this immediately as a potential source of conflict. He was correct.

*     *     *

At 9:35 on Thursday morning, in Room 5302 in the Dirksen Senate Office, the Senate Committee on Banking, Housing and Urban Affairs met to consider the nominations of Geno Baroni, Donna E. Shalala and Harry K. Schwartz. Shalala was nominated as assistant secretary for Policy Development and Research. Schwartz was nominated as assistant secretary for Legislation.

Baroni was introduced by Walter E. Fauntroy, delegate in Congress from the District of Columbia, a Washington minister. Baroni, Fauntroy said, "has shown tremendous leadership in bringing together the various financial institutions of the citizens who live in the neighborhoods, and has prevented, in many instances, the kind of misunderstanding that has been the death knell of many efforts to improve the quality of life in our urban centers." Baroni and Fauntroy were old Washington friends. Baroni wanted it to be noted as significant that it was Fauntroy, a civil rights activist from a predominantly black city, who recommended the confirmation of a man who had spent the previous six years of his life attempting to preserve white ethnic neighborhoods.

In response to a question from committee chairman Proxmire, Baroni said that Harris asked him "to broaden my concerns and my interests to reaching out from HUD to those other kinds of groups in the voluntary sector, like neighborhood groups, nongovernmental groups, who must be involved if we are going to revitalize our older cities."

There was one amusing, though revealing, episode at the hearing. Proxmire asked Baroni if his office had money from Congress to operate.

Baroni: "There are no line item funds, Senator, at this time. Hopefully internally we are going to try to see what kind of program we can put together in cooperation with Policy Development and Research, with Housing, with Community Development, and eventually develop a budget and come back to the committee." Baroni told Proxmire he had no idea what his plans would cost.

Senator Sparkman said he didn't understand Baroni's statement that there were no funds available. "Now, this is a government operation, isn't it?"

Baroni: "Yes."

Sparkman: "This is a government office you have been nominated for?"

Baroni: "Yes."

Sparkman: "You mean to tell us you don't have any funds to operate it?"

Baroni: "In the particular area that the Secretary has asked me to bring to the attention of HUD there are no line item funds. I mean there are the Community Development Block Grant grants, there are many many housing programs and so on. But there are no additional funds for specific programs that I hope to develop, Senator. Not yet."

Sparkman: "That is for the development. You do draw a salary, don't you?"

Baroni: "Oh, yes. I hope so."

Sparkman: "Well, I wanted to be sure when you talked about no funds that they were not leaving you out."
Baroni: "I appreciate that."

Not until the final months of the Carter administration was Baroni to get his hands on money that he could use to promote the cause of neighborhoods the way he desired and the way he understood Carter to favor. It was one of several sources of friction between Baroni and his colleagues at HUD.

*       *       *

The Senate quickly confirmed Baroni and two weeks later it was time to swear him in. He was about to become the highest ranked Roman Catholic priest ever to serve in the United States government. For such an historic event, Carter offered the White House Roosevelt Room, and Vice President Walter F. Mondale agreed to preside. The oath was to be administered by Chief Judge H. Carl Moultrie of the District of Columbia Superior Court.

It was to be a glorious day for Baroni. But there was one sticky problem. His father, Guido, refused to attend. For Geno, even in this moment of crowning achievement, the refusal of his father brought back the terrible memory of his boyhood difficulties with his father. Guido Baroni did not attend his son's high school graduation. Neither did Mrs. Baroni. "I wish we had," she said many years later.

Guido Baroni was not the kind of man who believed in making a fuss over his children. As a child and indeed all his life, Geno craved affection from his father. That emerged in his therapy sessions. It emerged in conversations with close friends.

Geno's brothers and sisters knew how much their father's presence at the White House ceremony meant to Geno. The brothers devised a strategy.

"We have bad news, pop," they said. "Geno's going to lose that big job in Washington because of you."

"Why me?" Guido Baroni said.

"Because you won't go to the ceremony. They think Geno is illegitimate."

What Angelo and John Baroni intended to suggest to their father was that Guido was not legitimately in the United States. In fact, Guido was a naturalized U.S. citizen.

Guido Baroni asked how he could prove Geno's legitimacy. The only way, the brothers said, is for you to go to the ceremony and sign a paper. Reluctantly, Guido Baroni changed his mind and decided to attend the ceremony.

And so on April 11, 1977, Geno Carlo Baroni swore an oath to "preserve, protect and defend the Constitution of the United States." When the ceremony ended, Guido Baroni approached the vice president.

"Where's the paper?" he said.

"What paper?" asked Mondale.

Before it could go further, the Baroni brothers intervened.

Geno Baroni had come a long way from his birthplace in the strike barracks in Griffee, Pennsylvania. Now he was on board the Carter administration, a subcabinet official, bound by the traditional rules of political loyalty to support the president and his policies. It remained to be seen how much impact Baroni would have on the nation during the next four years.

# 12

# Loose Cannon on the Deck

Geno Baroni quickly became odd man out in the bureaucracy of the U.S. Department of Housing and Urban Development. Secretary Patricia Roberts Harris' aides said two things about this portly rambling priest. When Baroni heard them, he felt both rewarded and injured. "Here comes the neighborhood," they said of Baroni, partly in derision of the singlemindedness of his approach. Baroni knew they wondered if he was a team player, ready to compromise his beliefs. He also took his identification as the neighborhoods' advocate as a badge of honor. It marked his determination to keep the preservation and improvement of America's neighborhoods high on the Carter administration's agenda.

The second thing Harris' aides said about Baroni was that he was a "loose cannon on the deck." He was not controllable. He fired at any foes, including some high up in the Carter administration, who failed to grasp and share his vision of what America's neighborhoods should be. One of Baroni's biggest opponents at HUD was Robert C. Embry, Jr., assistant secretary for community planning and development.

With dogged determination, Baroni turned around the federal government's policy toward neighborhoods. He deserves much credit for convincing first Harris, then the White House domestic staff, then President Carter, that federal policies should be reshaped to preserve and improve neighborhoods where people live, shop, belong to community organizations, and attend religious institutions.

In the secretary's private office and in senior staff meetings, Baroni constantly argued for changes in federal government policy toward cities. Baroni wanted to give an important voice to the people who live in the settled urban neighborhoods, white ethnic, black and Hispanic. "For too long, things had been done to these people in the name of good government. They were well-intentioned, but they missed," Baroni said. "Instead of saving neighborhoods, government destroyed neighborhoods." Baroni was not unlike Ronald Reagan and other conservatives in criticizing a decade of federal housing and neighborhood policy. They differed, however, on solutions.

Baroni viewed his HUD job as an extension of his work of six years on behalf of white urban ethnics and their neighborhoods. Instead of leading a pressure movement from the outside, Baroni was now inside, principally as the advocate for the white urban ethnic neighborhoods. In HUD policy discussions, Baroni argued that government had to cancel its smug notion that it could do it all for people, if only it had the financial resources. No amount of resources could revive cities, Baroni said, unless the white ethnics who live there choose to stay. And that choice depends not on standard government aid—which seemed to benefit poor blacks more than ethnic whites—but on targeted government aid which restored and strengthened white working-class neighborhoods.

Baroni described himself as a liberal Democrat, but he believed that in some respects, the Democratic Party had given the federal government more power and responsibility than it could handle. Baroni selectively saw the growth of federal power as dangerous and destructive. This, in his view, was especially the case with urban renewal, a forerunner to the urban development for which HUD was responsible. Baroni didn't want bulldozers in his urban ethnic neighborhoods.

In most matters, Baroni agreed with President Franklin D. Roosevelt's New Deal, and had few quarrels with Lyndon B. Johnson's Great Society. In fact, in the 1960s, he took advantage of those ideas. He had no philosophical reluctance to have Sts. Paul and Augustine and the Archdiocese of Washington serve as a testing ground for Great Society programs. Baroni took the money and used it to run a pre-school, a summer camp, a health clinic and tutoring.

Carter, in the 1976 election campaign, regrouped the Roosevelt New Deal Coalition. Baroni helped round up the white urban ethnics and their millions of vital votes. What tore the coalition apart in the late 1960s was a conflict within that coalition between two critical groups, blacks and urban ethnics. To many ethnics, blacks were people who wanted government to do everything for them. To the urban ethnics who supported their first Republican (Richard Nixon) in 1968, the party had sold out to the blacks, giving them everything while leaving nothing for the whites. Baroni spent the seven years before he joined Carter trying to defuse this white ethnic hostility. He developed his own rhetoric and definitions, which he was now using with Harris, Embry, and the HUD leadership.

To Harris, Baroni's words had a sound of racism. She did not classify him as such, but to her, a sophisticated lawyer, civil rights activist, Democratic politician and diplomat, Baroni, when talking about neighborhoods, was primarily talking about white neighborhoods. To Harris, the greatest need for federally-assisted housing was in the black neighborhoods. There was only so much money to go around. Move it from black neighborhoods to white neighborhoods and blacks suffer.

Baroni's drumbeat of support for involvement of neighborhood people in government decisions, at HUD and elsewhere, which affected their neighborhoods, was grating to Embry, whose job was to direct the rebuilding of broken-down neighborhoods. As Baroni saw it from the beginning, he and Embry were on a collision course.

Embry was wealthy, an Ivy Leaguer, a lawyer and a member of the Baltimore Establishment, a government official whose style Baroni regarded as too arrogant, too centralized, too bureaucratic and too old-fashioned New Dealish. "Embry says he's in charge of the neighborhoods, but he doesn't know a damned thing about them," Baroni complained to his staff. "I don't think he's ever been in a real neighborhood." Baroni said Embry's people were mayors and downtowners, not white urban ethnics.

Baroni calculated that Embry would inevitably target government money for neighborhoods that were beyond the hope of salvation. To Baroni, Embry came from the school that believed that when the neighborhood was so far gone, the only thing left was to move in with a bulldozer, knock the whole place down, and start all over. That was the Democratic Party's approach for decades. It failed to halt the erosion of urban America, and may have hastened that erosion. Baroni wanted the government to concentrate simultaneously on fresh starts for neighborhoods and on rehabilitation within neighborhoods to preserve them from deterioration.

To Baroni's demands for federal financial aid for rehabilitation of aging, though comparatively undeteriorated, white ethnic neighborhoods in big cities, Harris told Baroni, "Monsignor. There's no money for that."

"But this department is spending plenty of money and wasting it," Baroni shot back.

When Embry wanted HUD to approve federal funds for loans to assist the construction of a Hyatt Hotel in downtown Flint, Michigan, Baroni argued against it. He said HUD should spend the money in the neighborhoods of Flint where working-class people lived.

When Harris studied loan applications for construction of high-rise interracial housing for the elderly in Boston, Baroni again argued to the contrary, claiming that the buildings were being forced on established white ethnic communities where they were not wanted.

Baroni was an unconventional government official. In the social science hothouse of HUD, officials and politicians loved to throw around the expression "data-based." That means a pile of studies to support a point. The ideal is to make only "data-based judgments," that is, decisions that can be defended by research papers put together by the consulting firms which proliferate around Washington. Baroni didn't have much use for people who made decisions solely on data. He was a "seat of the pants guy," one who made observations based on experience as a street priest in Washington for eight years and as the country's leading spokesman for white urban ethnics for six years.

Baroni complained that the top staff of HUD was filled with lawyers and planners who spent all their lives in city downtowns during the day and in suburban bedroom communities at night. Their only contact with real neighborhoods, he said, was driving between home and office in an air-conditioned car with the radio on and at a high rate of speed. Some HUD officials accused Baroni of bitterness toward suburbanites.

These lawyers and planners were often the beneficiaries of Baroni's impromptu speech, filled with anecdotes about his life and experiences. It was a wonderful speech to people of Polish, Italian, Greek and Slavic heritages—the PIGS—in Toledo, Milwaukee, Baltimore and Chicago. They loved it. But what Baroni called the "pin-stripe button-down crowd" didn't understand it or tolerate it very well.

Several months after he started at HUD, he lectured Harris and her assistant secretaries for several minutes on neighborhood values. An aide slipped Harris a memo, on which was written, "Baroni is a loose cannon on the deck." Ironically, Harris carefully nourished her own reputation with the public as a strident advocate within the Administration of her department's interests. To some within the Carter White House, Harris was a loose cannon on the administration's deck. To them, she was not a team player, but a self-server. Like Baroni, Harris used the force of her own personality to persuade the White House and Congress.

From a friend in Harris's office, Baroni got a photocopy of that note which he kept and showed to friends. But Baroni did not want trouble with Harris. True to his nonconfrontational character, he wanted to get along with her and HUD's top officials. He knew how important it was to be a team player if he wanted to get anything done. However, he was also true to his convictions that the federal government was destroying neighborhoods. To Baroni, his obligation was to crusade. To the Harris staff,

Baroni had a fixation, an obsession, which they trivialized. Unable to address the substance of his argument, they resorted to an ad hominem attack. That was easy. Baroni was not a good debater. His anecdotal approach was ineffective. Moreover, it was counterproductive in a HUD board room where many of the decision-makers were lawyers.

To HUD's staff, money talked. The assistant secretary in charge of the Federal Housing Administration got more attention than an assistant secretary with no budget of his own. Baroni had to go practically hat in hand to Harris to get money to meet his obligation as the department's consumer affairs and neighborhoods advocate.

Just as Harris' people pressured Baroni to toe the line on departmental policy, so Baroni's people outside government pressured him right back to change departmental and government policy. "The people at the Center and those I had worked with in cities wanted me to be the bull in the china shop," Baroni said. It was not Baroni's style to break things, nor was it his way, either, to become an organization man.

So Baroni in HUD repeated the operating style of nonconfrontation and circumvention that he first learned while dealing with his father, and improved while in the seminary, as a young priest, and while serving in Washington as a parish priest and Center president. While in HUD, Baroni went around Harris and Embry. He continued to cultivate his friends on Capitol Hill and in the White House.

The classic example of Baroni going around the staff and breaking Administration policy came in connection with the move to create a consumers' cooperative bank. Baroni saw it as a national credit union, and he was all for it. Then he heard that a Treasury Department official was going to testify against the bank. This took place early in the Carter administration when Bert Lance, the banker from Georgia, directed Carter's Office of Management and Budget. OMB, opposed creation of the bank.

Baroni telephoned committee staff members on Capitol Hill with the thought that the Lance position—to be supported by the Treasury official—was not Carter's or the Democratic Party's. Baroni arranged to be called as a witness on another matter on the same day the Treasury official was to appear.

On the morning of the hearing, Baroni sat as inconspicuously as he could in a back row while the Treasury official argued against the consumer bank legislation. When the official was finished, one of the committee members happened to notice Baroni, and called him forward.

"Now, Monsignor, you have the job as the consumers' advocate at HUD and you're known as a friend to working-class people," the committee member said to Baroni. "What do you think about this consumer bank idea?" "Well," said Baroni, "it's a pretty good idea." He talked a bit about his long enthusiasm for credit unions and the wonderful things they had accomplished in Pennsylvania, Sts. Paul and Augustine, and dozens of cities where they had been sponsored by the National Center for Urban Ethnic Affairs.

The Treasury Department official, contradicted by another administration spokesman, was embarrassed and furious. He squawked to Lance, who got on the phone with Harris and asked her what right did a member of her department have testifying contrary to the administration's position. Harris said she didn't know anything about it. She called Baroni into her office. "Why, yes," he said, "I said I supported the idea. I was on the Hill and they asked me. I wasn't testifying for the administration. They know that. They just asked me because they knew I have a lot more experience with cooperative banks and credit unions than the people at Treasury or OMB." Harris told Baroni that as an administration official he was not permitted to speak publicly against the administration's position. He should not do it again, and from now on, Harris said, "When you go to Capitol Hill, take a member of the legislative staff with you to all meetings."

Baroni didn't like the dressing-down he received from Harris. However, he did not want to confront the secretary by carrying his battle with her to the White House. Baroni figured out a way to stop the nonsense of a muzzle. He arranged an invitation to meet with Rep. Frank Annunzio, the Chicago Democrat. Baroni notified Harry Schwartz's legislative office and at the appointed hour Baroni and a young woman from Schwartz's office arrived at Annunzio's office. Baroni properly introduced the legislative assistant and explained that she would have to sit in on the session.

"The secretary wants someone from the legislative office here so there's no misunderstanding between the Administration and Congress," Baroni explained to an alert Annunzio.

"It's certainly good to meet you," said Annunzio to the HUD legislative aide, "but in my office, you can't sit in on any meetings. You see, Monsignor Baroni is here to hear my confession. Make yourself comfortable out in the front office." Baroni and Annunzio then had their conversation about politics, Carter Administration shortcomings, and how good it was to be fellow members of the National Italian-American Foundation. Baroni soon forgot all about the requirement that he tell Schwartz's office every time he had a meeting on Capitol Hill.

Harris did not raise the requirement again. Once again, Baroni, not disputing the point in a direct confrontation, but artfully going around it, got his way.

Baroni said that he recognized he had to be a Harris team player in order to get anything done in the administration. As it turned out, he got relatively little done until after Carter moved Harris out of HUD and made her Secretary of Health, Education and Welfare in 1979. That was part of a cabinet shakeup and one of Carter's stranger performances.

It came after Carter sojourned at Camp David and made an awkward speech to the country saying that a "malaise" had settled over America, and his administration. Then he began an administration housecleaning. One of the administration's more efficient and aggressive officials, Secretary of Health, Education and Welfare Joseph A. Califano, Jr., was a victim to the Carter "malaise" crusade. Califano was booted out of HEW and Harris was switched over as Califano's replacement. Succeeding Harris at HUD was Mayor Moon Landrieu of New Orleans. From then on, Baroni's position at HUD improved.

In the beginning, Baroni wanted to be what Harris asked of him—a team player. But it was not in Baroni's nature to abandon his deeply-held beliefs about neighborhoods and white ethnics. Working under these labels—defender of neighborhoods and loose cannon—Baroni's effectiveness within HUD was minimal. Baroni realized this after only a few months in the job, and he began to wonder if he made a mistake accepting it.

Adding to Baroni's problems was his habit of leaving sentences incomplete and his appearance of coming down on many sides of a discussion. Harris and Embry, both lawyers, did not want from Baroni a restatement of the problem. They wanted his opinion, fast and clear. Instead, Baroni gave them what he gave the white ethnics—himself in all its glorious contradiction and indecision.

Baroni knew that in government, tough decisions by nature require confrontation. Top government policy-makers have to choose between people as well as ideas. Simple problems are handled at the lower level of the bureaucracy. Only the knotty problems filter up to the assistant secretary, and only the very tough problems reach the secretary's desk. Baroni did not function well either at his own level of decision-making or the secretary's. He did not like to be pinned down.

A lone wolf most of his life, Baroni had difficulty picking a staff. He assumed that his aides would mold themselves to his peculiar work habits and philosophical predispositions. So he was stunned to discover that the assistants he picked and others imposed on him by Harris were themselves interested in pushing their own, frequently independent, policies. In the language of HUD, there was a lot of empire-building and self-promotion going on by Baroni's aides, and he did not know how to control it.

Thus he was undercut from within. His staff generally did not give him the total loyalty he needed and felt he deserved. Baroni was unable to confront his internal opponents and force them out. Some of his aides were absolutely loyal, and he counted himself fortunate to have Alice Shabecoff and Joseph McNeely in key spots. But his deputies fought each other, looking more for approval from Harris than Baroni. Again, Baroni could have called them in and laid down his rules for acceptable behavior. But he did not.

Sparkman's funny questions at Baroni's confirmation hearings about money soon proved to be no laughing matter. Baroni had the longest title of any presidential appointee, but the smallest budget. He failed to cut a deal with Harris on money before he entered government. He relied on her vague promises that she would find him money to accomplish what he wanted to do—give financial support for struggling groups trying to organize neighborhoods and develop job-creating enterprises. In government terms, the $1 million that Harris transferred to Baroni his first year at HUD was a pittance. He got the money to set up counseling centers for people interested in buying their own homes. This was a logical continuation of the counseling he started with his first credit union in Altoona, Pennsylvania, in 1956.

A rule of thumb in government is that those with the biggest budgets are the heaviest hitters. In Harris's cabinet, Baroni had to deal with assistant secretaries who administered budgets of hundreds of millions of dollars a year. Many deputy assistant secretaries handled multi-million dollar budgets. Along came Baroni with his puny $1 million, and that a gift with strings attached. It was no contest in favor of the big boys.

In addition, Baroni's responsibility was largely undefined. As part of the bargain to get him, Harris gave Baroni responsibility for working with neighborhoods. But no one, including Harris, seemed to know precisely what that entailed. As it turned out, Baroni in time came to appreciate the vagueness. He broadened his own responsibility and involved himself throughout government on matters affecting neighborhoods and urban white ethnics. In the annual budget-making process, priorities were largely set by Harris with the advice of her top staff, including those who felt they had a reading on what Congress wanted. In reality, Carter and his budget bureau did not concern themselves very much with allocations within the HUD budget. The bulk of the spending was mandated by law. Harris had little discretionary control. Congressional committees, the House and Senate banking and currency committees, took a great deal of interest in the HUD budget. Congress decided how much should be spent on public housing, on rent support, on downtown renewal, on projects for the elderly. These committee members also engaged in a great deal of logrolling. They had considerable influence—more than Harris and HUD officials would admit—on where the money was spent. A member of the House Banking and Currency Committee had first grabs at money to finance a project in his or her district, or in the district of a friend. Members of the committee wanted regular HUD spending within their states.

Thus the hands of officials and bureaucrats inside HUD were guided by pressure from Congress. A congressman might not be able to force HUD to allocate money to a bad project, but members could influence the choice when there were a variety of equal projects competing for money.

The $1 million Baroni got from Harris did not go far, but it did enable him to spread some money around in neighborhoods where he previously worked through his Center.

To some of those neighborhood groups, Geno was a disappointment. They expected him, once in government, to start sending them large amounts of federal dollars. They overestimated Baroni's role as an assistant secretary and underestimated the power of career civil servants. Baroni had a lot of respect for career people, and he often used their roles as excuses to explain why one of his old friends could not get HUD money. Baroni said he had some of his worst problems with Catholic priests who came in with inadequate proposals for money and expected him to straighten them out. Often, he said, these priests competed with Jewish groups which had experience and sophistication in seeking government funds. "I had priests come in and tell me they heard there were millions of dollars available to build subsidized housing for the elderly, and would I give them some. They didn't have organizations, no plans, no architects, no counts of how many people they'd serve. Then the B'nai B'rith would arrive with everything that was needed. Who do you think we gave the money to? B'nai B'rith. I kept telling the Catholic groups to get themselves some good lawyers and development people, but they refused to do it."

One Baroni goal was to use HUD money to train neighborhood groups to be effective at getting money out of HUD, other government agencies, the Campaign for Human Development, and foundations. Baroni said that responsibility for writing proposals explaining how neighborhood organizations would use government dollars should rest on the organization leaders. It was not government's job to draft proposals for people to get government money. Such an approach, in his view, was a conflict of interest. But government should help ordinary people in neighborhoods develop techniques of proposal-writing so that their bids for government money were not simply dismissed on technical grounds.

"I argued that people in neighborhoods should have the same kind of experts available to them that Hyatt and Aetna had, or that McDonnell Douglas or Fairchild had with the Pentagon."

Six months after taking the HUD job, Baroni said his "major disappointment" was failing to change the rules to allow greater citizen participation in neighborhood revitalization decisions. In a private meeting with his CCUM colleagues, called by Monsignor Egan at Notre Dame in October of 1977, Baroni said, "We don't have adequate structured citizen participation in our guidelines or regulations. If we had a real constituency of community organizations, community groups, poor people, working-class people, whatever, black, white or brown, for cities, we could have insured that HUD provided for citizen participation." Baroni said that "one of the ten largest cities in America had eight people sit down to see how they were going to spend their $29 million, and they called that citizen participation. That's not right. That's one of the problems of our cities. That's one of the problems of our program."

Baroni was not totally pessimistic. He said that the HUD bill signed a few weeks earlier by Carter providing for $12 billion in community development block grant money over three years was an important breakthrough. He said he had been successful in getting Carter and Congress to target 75 percent of the money to low- and moderate-income neighborhoods. But unless the regulation was enforced, Baroni said, mayors would spend the money as they saw fit. "Poor people don't vote as much," Baroni said.

Baroni lumped the skills that poor people need under the phrase "neighborhood capacity-building." In an interview published in the official government magazine *HUD Challenge* in March, 1978, Baroni argued that neighborhoods with skills to negotiate for their demands would be more at peace with their local governments than communities lacking such skills.

Baroni, asked for his HUD goals for neighborhoods, said: "We are committed to neighborhood capacity-building, particularly for those groups representing poor and/or minority communities. Given adequate skills and resources, neighborhood groups are in a better position to negotiate with public officials and lending representatives. Without this capacity, organizations are limited in their attempts to get programs for their neighborhoods. It may also force local groups to remain in a confrontation situation with city hall as opposed to developing a positive relationship with it."

Through this article, Baroni hoped to send a signal to Embry and big-city mayors. McNeely, a Baroni sounding board and director of the

Office of Neighborhood Development under Baroni, saw his boss and Embry clash over substance and style.

Embry was a "real elitist," said McNeely, reflecting Baroni's view. "Embry believed in well-administered public authority, a real *noblesse oblige* kind of good government." Baroni believed that public authorities had a record of destroying neighborhoods. The argument that the federal government should go around city hall and deal directly with local non-governmental groups surfaced in the federal war on poverty. Much of the money distributed by R. Sargent Shriver's U.S. Office of Economic Opportunity went to groups that were fighting mayors. Unlike traditional government programs which mayors take political credit for, antipoverty programs followed their own channel outside the local political system. Not only did mayors not get credit, but they also found themselves in battle with organizations with an independent support base.

Embry and Baroni understood that their battle over federal support for neighborhood groups in 1977 and 1978 was a revisit to the OEO battles of the mid-1960s. This time the mayors were not caught napping. Their two lobbying organizations in Washington, the U.S. Conference of Mayors and the National League of Cities, tried to undermine Baroni's approach.

Baroni touched on this in a March, 1978, interview. Asked how his programs differed from past federal efforts addressing community concerns, such as the war on poverty and the fatally-flawed Model Cities program of the 1960s, Baroni said, "This is an important question, and one I get a lot. Some federal officials (and here Baroni primarily meant Embry) are skeptical of our neighborhood development focus because they remember that the 'anti-poverty' programs were not successful. I feel we are talking about a new program focus, with different conditions. The past federal experience with neighborhoods, despite its weaknesses, was significant, and helped us develop what we currently need to do. Weaknesses of past efforts included the 'top-down' nature of designing and administering the programs; creating a climate whereby organizations came into being just to receive federal funds."

Baroni said his plan would give assistance only to programs with a "track record in program management and/or service delivery." And rather than create organizations who use their federal dollars to fight city hall, Baroni said, "Critical to our neighborhood development activity is the establishment or strengthening of the neighborhood/city relationships. Rather than working in isolation from each other, our programs will encourage ways in which they should work with each other." Baroni and Embry were never to reconcile their contrasting views of city halls and neighborhood groups, and this kept Baroni from achieving as much as he hoped as a public servant.

McNeely said another cause of friction was created by Baroni's "vision" of a program rubbing against Embry's demand for specifics which Baroni was unable to provide. "Embry was a deliberate technician," McNeely said. "Geno would get down certain fundamental elements of a program. He would say about commercial revitalization that you had to organize the merchants and it wasn't just a fix-up program. But he didn't know the level of detail that a good manager needs to preserve his vision. Embry and others would take him apart with their questions over details."

There were times when Baroni's staff maneuvered to prevent meetings between their boss and Embry, especially when the staff thought a deal could be cut if only the two men did not get into an argument. McNeely held private meetings with Nancy Jo Steetle, a special assistant to Embry, to iron out difficulties between their bosses.

McNeely said Baroni genuinely believed that government and private institutions had damaged ordinary Americans. "There was a lack of precision and definition in fleshing out those ideas," McNeely said. "It was a reflection of his cognitive process. Geno, while talking, was revising. That's one of the reasons he repeated. He worked out his ideas by interacting with someone else, not by thinking them through by himself. Geno couldn't get to D without first explaining to you A, B, and C, and then about E and F."

Baroni learned what he thought by thinking aloud before an audience. That was his method of reaching decisions. It was a method that galled Embry and Harris. Harris stopped individual meetings with Baroni. He attended the weekly senior staff conferences, but his requests to see Harris in private were rejected. Though dispirited, Baroni plugged on. He looked for ways to get around Harris and Embry, and win concessions to neighborhoods.

\* \* \*

While fighting within HUD for neighborhoods, Baroni contended with unresolved issues of goals, objectives and personalities he left at the National Center for Urban Ethnic Affairs. Geno's creation was getting ripped apart. His creation under Ford Foundation pressure of a board of directors did not bring order to the troubled Center, and tension at the Center grew worse as Ford cut down its support.

When Baroni resigned as Center president, executive director and
chairman of the board of directors in March, 1977, to take the HUD
appointment, he did not designate his successor. The board named Robert Corletta, who had a reputation as a neighborhood planner and development specialist. In Baroni's view, Corletta could also be counted on
to manage NCUEA efficiently, something Ford and other foundations
were insisting upon. For a variety of reasons, personality among them,
Corletta soon encountered a rebellious staff. Almost by definition, community organizers are ambitious and combative. Those characteristics
are necessary while facing the hardships of organizing a community by
creating confrontational situations with local power centers. Community
organizers have to be good actors—playing out tough-guy roles. While
Baroni was at the Center, staff members tended to try to work out their
differences. Often Baroni gave them no choice. He simply disappeared
until they worked it out. But with Baroni gone, suppressed hostility
bubbled over. From his HUD office, Baroni watched this, decided he
would not get involved, and kept to his plan.

Baroni knew it was not easy to tame a staff of such prima donnas.
That was one reason why he had held authority so tightly, so that no
one of his program directors would whip his Center colleagues. It
worked under Baroni, whose position as leader was absolutely undis-
puted. The staff knew that. Corletta lacked Baroni's credentials and
authority. That was intentional.

At Baroni's departure, the board decided not to try to replace him
with another charismatic figure, but to put in his place a manager,
somebody who could satisfy foundations and other money sources that
their contributions were being properly spent. Never popular with a
majority of the staff, Corletta's problems worsened when he fired one of
Gerson Green's organizers. Not only did Green like the organizer, but
he resented Corletta's exercise of authority. Money for the grant under
question had been raised by Green, not Corletta, so Green considered
himself responsible for it.

Staff members got to the point where they couldn't talk to one
another and came close to fistfights. To Baroni at HUD went pleading
telephone calls: You started the Center. You ran it for six years. It is
your legacy. Who do you want to lead it? How do you want it led?
Who shall we fire? Who do we promote? Baroni refused to answer. This
time he did not need to run off to a retreat house until the matter
smoothed over. He said simply that as a federal official who resigned
from the Center he could not offer an opinion. Baroni's position could
have been anticipated by all participants in the NCUEA internecine
feud as well as by NCUEA's fledgling board. Six years after the event,

Baroni insisted he did not give a single hint as to what way he wanted the board to act. After a cooling-off period, Corletta and Green moved on to other organizations. The Ford Foundation approved the appointment of John A. Kromkowski as Center president. Kromkowski was a government professor at Notre Dame and a collaborator with Baroni at CCUM, the American Revolution Bicentennial Commission and as national allocations chairman of the Campaign for Human Development.

Kromkowski was a non-Washington-based Center research associate with organizing and development experiences as well as cordial relationships with all Center divisions and personnel. His local and national work as a mediator, public official and researcher was encouraged by Baroni's persistent invitations to work on a Center analysis of activities. Kromkowski accepted the challenge—to salvage or to close the Center.

Kromkowski, a former Director of Economic Development for South Bend, Indiana, dissolved the tension between organizing and economic development by decentralizing the Center's neighborhood assistance projects. He localized issues so that the debate could be resolved at the local level, not among national staff interested in parachuting their recipes into neighborhoods.

Gloria Aull, a Center board member from Baltimore and an associate of Barbara Mikulski in one of the Center's first urban ethnic projects, the Southeast Community Organization, reflected the mood of many neighborhoods when she said, "The Center in the old days tried to make us grant-junkies." Kromkowski wanted to change that.

Without Baroni, the Center focused on the completion and documentation of efforts he initiated, catalyzed and was trying to support with federal resources from HUD and other agencies. The Center worked outside government while Baroni worked inside to improve neighborhood groups. The Center's activities included training hundreds of federally-supported Volunteers in Service to America (VISTA). Baroni's creation continued to give the required attentive nurturing to the skills of neighborhood and ethnic leaders. It helped scores of new neighborhood organizations with support from the Charles Stewart Mott Foundation for fledgling groups, and developed proposals and strategies for another generation of urban revitalization. The Center explicitly resisted dropping organizers onto neighborhoods. Indigenous leaders were sought and assisted.

*     *     *

Disappointing to those who were overly-optimistic in applauding Baroni's entry into the Carter administration, his arrival did not mean a sudden government sympathy toward urban ethnic neighborhoods. It was more evident to urban ethnic activists than before that the work of neighborhood organizations would have to get stronger, and that the battles would be fought—and won or lost—at the local level. Washington, even with a Baroni in power, could not save America's neighborhoods.

It was clear that new national allies were needed to assist neighborhoods, since a much longer and harder struggle was apparent. Baroni started by trying to save the world. He came to understand that the effort began on the streets of the neighborhood. So by 1979, it was clear that each neighborhood with its own needs was functioning in a unique contest. In the sense of reviving the neighborhoods, Carter was right about a national malaise. The federal government, as Baroni soon discovered and served to illustrate, was largely ineffective in rehabilitating and preserving neighborhoods. Such ineffectiveness had been foreseen by Baroni's friends who advised him not to enter the administration. They said he would be a strong voice for white urban ethnics outside the government as a critic rather than as an inside player and required defender. These people cited the advice of Saul Alinsky, who said that organizers should shake government, not join it. But Baroni listened to his own inner voices. He later argued that he could be more effective in getting things done from within government. There may have been some self-justification in this, given Baroni's other complaints that he wasn't getting nearly as much done in government as he had hoped.

The departure of Baroni from the national scene as Center president stifled the most effective and respected voice for neighborhoods. But his departure allowed other ethnic leaders to seek places in the national spotlight. Mikulski and Kaptur got elected to the U.S. Congress. Art Naparstek left Baroni's staff to head up the University of Southern California public affairs graduate school in Washington, then went to Case Western Reserve University in Cleveland. Green went to Hartford as a community organization, then transferred to Philadelphia. Jerry Ernst directed the Catholic Inter-Racial Council in Washington. Gail Cincotta built on a successful campaign against redlining in the Austin section of Chicago to found and lead a national organization for citizens.

The concept of ethnicity worked its way into the fabric of American social thinking. Baroni sounded the death knell for America's melting pot theory and replaced it with a theory of pluralism in which ethnic group members were encouraged to connect themselves to their rich heritages, to others with similar backgrounds, and then into a wider

*Above left:* Geno Baroni at the age of 7, on the day of his first communion in Acosta, Pennsylvania. *Above right:* With his mother Giuseppina after Geno's graduation from Mount St. Mary's College in Emmitsburg, Maryland, in 1953. *Bottom:* Following his move to Washington, D.C., Geno became deeply involved in neighborhood activities. Here (front, center) he helps a group of black teenagers cleaning up a yard.

*Top:* On a muddy field in Selma, Alabama, Geno Baroni (left) chats with other participants in the historic 1965 march. The breviary he wore under his hat in case of violence is gripped in his left hand. *Bottom:* Archbishop Patrick O'Boyle with Father Baroni in Rome at the time of O'Boyle's elevation to the College of Cardinals. O'Boyle was generally supportive of his maverick priest.

*Top:* In the Roosevelt Room of the White House, Geno was sworn in as HUD assistant secretary on April 11, 1977. His parents and Vice President Walter F. Mondale were present. *Bottom:* With New York Senator Jacob Javits in a Senate hearing room. Baroni was a champion of urban neighborhood programs at HUD and on Capitol Hill.

*Top:* Geno speaks to a group from Network, a social action lobby, at a meeting in the midwest. His blackboard technique was chaotic, but his talks were effective. *Bottom:* Father Henri Nouwen visited Baroni during the latter's final illness.

community of people concerned about the old-fashioned values of family and community found in the old neighborhoods.

\*        \*        \*

Baroni made it clear during his first few months at HUD that he was going to be Jimmy Carter's emissary to the neighborhoods of America. He continued his contacts by telephone with ethnic organization leaders around the country. His first speech as HUD assistant secretary was on June 11 in Cleveland, where he was the homilist at the first mass for Father Rick Orley. Six years previous to that very weekend, Orley attended the Catholic University meeting of ethnic leaders which propelled Baroni toward creating the Center and which shot Mikulski to the forefront as a major ethnic leader.

Baroni prepared for this first address as a federal official by writing it out on page after page of yellow legal paper with a felt-tipped pen in his sprawling handwriting style. The pages, with underlining, crossouts and emphasized remarks offer a window into the difficulty he admitted he had in preparing material for an article or speech. But the finished product is graceful and classic Baroni.

In the homily, Baroni told Orley: "You have learned a lesson few if hardly any priests have learned. You have learned how to be ethnic and American." With ancestors from Poland and Hungary, Baroni said, Orley "challenged the melting pot theory of American society and the American Church in your own life, and in your work. You have understood that an individual's search for identity is one of the most basic life tasks."

When American Catholics come to understand each other's ethnicity, Baroni said, they "then will not be oppressed by fear of our neighbor who may share another culture, ethnicity, race or tradition."

A few days later, Baroni went deeper into his own roots when he returned to Boswell, a little town near his home town of Acosta in central Pennsylvania. He joked about his own academic record at Somerset High School, repeating an observation of his mother: "It's a miracle. You had a hard time graduating 30 years ago, and now you're giving the commencement address."

He reminded the audience that Carter visited HUD earlier in his Administration and "told the 2,500 people who work there to stop living in sin, get married or go back to their families.

"Right after that, I arrived in my Roman collar," Baroni continued. "People still bump into me in elevators and whip out their marriage license. I've already been asked to marry some of the HUD people."

He told the graduates of the class of 1977 that "too many people in our neighborhoods are up-tight and polarized by fear. Our political, economic and social systems have created this situation." The urban renewal program of the 1950s and 1960s, he said, was proof that "government cannot rebuild America's cities alone."

In October, at Cabrini College in Radnor, Pennsylvania, Baroni spoke about ethnicity and his own struggle to find an identity growing up in America. "The Church taught me to forget about my heritage and background," Baroni said. "A summer school missionary nun with Irish heritage tried to impress me with the notion I should consider changing my name from Geno to Kevin." In high school, he said, "I learned that Sacco and Vanzetti were anarchists and the owners of the mines had God-given rights to manage without the 'terrible union.' It wasn't good to be immigrants."

In November, Baroni spoke to the American Lebanese League in Cleveland. He offered his vision of the American city:

> I want cities with flowers in the spring and tomatoes in the summer in the yards of the working and lower-class homes. . . . where the schools open the minds of all children to the extraordinary power of a sentence and the precise glories of mathematics. . . . that dwell not just on the dollar and the need for economic growth, but that also celebrate the quality and texture of life. . . . where equality of opportunity is the fundamental fact from which all others are derived and the central point at which all observations are terminated.
>
> . . . where every young girl and boy can dream of becoming president, or, as Mr. Carter has said, the even more difficult job of mayor.
>
> I want cities full of variety and movement, peace and serenity, cities of proud and gentle women and men, of six-year-olds who are joyful, eighty-three-year-olds who are wise, and handicapped citizens who live with dignity.

Baroni scratched out a paragraph from the remarks prepared for him by his HUD speechwriter: "I want cities where salsa blends with gemütlichkeit, where Italian children learn about Jewish poverty, and where Polish children read Alex Haley."

At some stops, reporters focused on the curiosity of a Roman Catholic priest serving in federal government. In Dallas, Baroni told reporters that religious leaders must get involved in government at all levels to improve the country's morality. "Every economic and social issue is a moral issue," he said. Baroni also said that most of his $50,000 annual salary went to his parents because his father suffered from black lung disease, and to a widowed sister who had a physically impaired child.

It is impossible to analyze how Baroni's priesthood affected the way he performed at HUD, or the way he was treated by his superiors or employees. Some aides said they thought the priesthood had no effect at all, either positive or negative. A few said they overheard snide remarks about Baroni thinking he was superior in enunciating the moral issues of urban policy. Certainly Baroni was not alone in the Carter administration in discussing morality. Carter did it frequently.

Baroni was very careful to avoid a know-it-all attitude in policy debates. One of his aides was the victim of self-inflicted wounds brought on by an effort to use a moral argument against Harris. The aide, a Bostonian, substituted for Baroni at a meeting. When it came his time to speak, the customary statement would have been on the order of, "I'll check with assistant secretary Baroni and I'm sure he'll get back to you soon." Instead, this aide said that a decision by Harris affecting policy was "immoral." When Baroni returned to the office, there was a message from Harris on his desk: get rid of the Bostonian. Baroni complied. There was room in government for morality, but not for arrogance.

Baroni was quick to grasp potential danger in situations. He demonstrated that his ability to stick to his own rhetoric could cover a multitude of problems. In October, 1978, he appeared at a town meeting sponsored by National Public Radio at the John F. Kennedy Center for the Performing Arts. William Moore, a private developer, asked Baroni and fellow guest, *Washington Post* architecture critic, Wolf Von Eckardt, if it was a sin to raise a child in a city like Washington. Moore said the capital city was filled with pollution, immorality, drugs, crime and pornography, "which I think is due basically to the fact that too many people are trying to live in too small a space."

Von Eckardt replied that "life is always a hazard to your health" and that a child raised in rural Arkansas could also get hurt. Baroni, more roundaboutly, said he became reminiscent in the fall about maple trees and streams, but that people wanted to live in cities. "The challenge is to create viable, livable cities."

*　　*　　*

Baroni's persistent advocacy of neighborhoods paid off in 1978 when Carter proposed and Congress passed legislation to create a neigh-

borhood self-help development program. By government standards, the
$15 million program was trivial. It was enough money to build one of
the new supersonic fighter-bombers in the Pentagon inventory. But to
Baroni it was a major symbolic breakthrough for big-city neighborhoods.

Baroni convinced Harris to start the program. It was opposed by
Embry, the Office of Management and Budget, the president's domestic
policy council, and Congress. He built support in an unconventional
manner—he contacted priest friends in the social justice ministry in the
districts of members of the Senate and House committees handling the
bill. At Baroni's urging, several priests got their more prominent parishioners to use political influence on politicians. In one case in Ohio,
Baroni learned that a wavering congressman's wife was a Roman Catholic. Baroni got to her pastor, who talked to the woman. She in turn
talked to her husband, and on voting day, the wavering congressman
favored the bill.

Baroni had a few allies in HUD. He had steady support from
William Medina, assistant secretary for administration and the highest-
ranked Hispanic in the Carter Administration, and Donna Shalala, assistant secretary for research.

One HUD assistant secretary had an aging mother. He wanted to
place her in a nursing home, and he asked Baroni for recommendations,
who suggested a Catholic nursing home near the mother's New York
home. The next time he visited his mother, the assistant secretary
stopped by the nursing home. He liked what he saw and applied for his
mother's admission. Too bad, said the administrator, we're all booked
and there's a waiting list. The assistant secretary back in Washington
contacted Baroni, suddenly his good friend Geno. Baroni said he'd do
what he could, but when he called the administrator, he got the same
report about the full house and the waiting list. But the administrator
said that places on waiting lists could always be changed. How much
did Baroni want the next opening? Baroni said he would call back.

A week or two later, one of Baroni's proposals for housing for the
elderly was on the table, and it was getting beaten up by the senior staff.
The decision ultimately came down to the assistant secretary. At a
break, Baroni told the assistant secretary that the lack of affordable
rental housing for low-income elderly created situations like overcrowded Catholic nursing homes. When the meeting resumed, the assistant secretary came out in favor of Baroni's program. Within the
month, the assistant secretary was informed that the New York nursing
home had a vacancy for his mother.

\*     \*     \*

Baroni had less support than he expected from Eizenstat, head of Carter's domestic policy staff who played a major role in getting the HUD appointment for Baroni. He was certainly questioned more directly by Eizenstat than he anticipated in one celebrated confrontation at the White House. When Eizenstat invited Baroni to the White House to discuss the self-help bill, Baroni told aides, "Stuart is a good friend. We worked together closely in the campaign. We agree on the importance of a new policy toward urban ethnic neighborhoods. He won't be any trouble."

When Baroni's aides advised him to prepare himself thoroughly for his meeting with Eizenstat, Baroni shrugged them off. That wouldn't be necessary, he said. It will be mostly a meeting about the strategy in getting Carter to sign off on the bill and then to get it to Capitol Hill. But after Baroni settled into a chair in Eizenstat's West Wing Office, he quickly found himself on the ropes. Eizenstat peppered Baroni with a series of questions about details of the bill. Relying on his own shaky memory and aides, Baroni sought to answer. Eizenstat didn't accept Baroni's generalities, and attacked the bill from every angle, exploiting its weaknesses, exposing its political vulnerabilities. Sitting there, Baroni began to sense that now that he was in power, Eizenstat wasn't going to be much of an ally after all. The tension in the room increased. Finally Baroni interrupted:

> Stu, this is the sort of legislation that you can ask questions about all week, and you won't be sure it works until you try it. The mayors don't like it. Some people in HUD don't like it. But you have to decide if you and the president like it. It does everything that the president said he would do—return power from the federal government to the people. And you've got to decide if you have guts enough to go ahead despite what the mayors and some people in HUD say. So asking me any more questions won't make sense.

HUD aides later credited Baroni's directness with Eizenstat in forcing the presidential assistant to make a positive decision on the self-help legislation and to recommend that Carter endorse it. Eizenstat said that it was his responsibility as Carter's domestic adviser to tear apart the bill, look at every detail, probe for faults, before making up his mind on whether he would recommend it to the president. Eizenstat said later that there had been a "major uproar during the Great Society when the government tried urban programs that bypassed mayors." Such a program was the national war on poverty. In many places, it relied on neighborhood commissions, shunting city halls to the sidelines. "I wanted to make sure that if we were going to try that approach again, we would do it with a program that would be administered," Eizenstat said. "That's what I wanted to get out of Geno when I gave him far more of a grilling than I'm sure he expected."

From Embry, and from mayors directly and through their national lobbying organizations, Eizenstat heard that Baroni was reviving an approach that had been divisive and destructive, not only to elected urban leadership, but to the Democratic Party. Eizenstat told Baroni he would not recommend to Carter a program that would turn out to be a disaster. "Things like this must be done in a very careful way so we don't get the mayors up in arms, Geno," Eizenstat said.

Later, working with Kaptur, an Eizenstat assistant, Baroni supplied answers to Eizenstat's string of tough questions. Satisfied, Eizenstat recommended the program to Carter, who incorporated it into his urban policy—an achievement for Baroni, but a hard, painful experience.

Eizenstat later looked back on his days of working with Baroni with a good deal of fondness. "Geno was a very special person in that he had enormous sensitivity to the problems of people, and he combined that with an enormous capacity to do something about those problems," Eizenstat said. "He had almost a saintly quality. His love of life, his love of people really showed through."

\*       \*       \*

Baroni discovered that an advantage of being the U.S. consumer affairs advocate was that he more than any other assistant secretary could speak out forcefully in public about legislation and regulations. More than once Baroni was reminded by Harris that he had gone beyond or contradicted administration policy. This did not especially worry Baroni. He knew his own constituency and his value to the Carter Administration in serving that constituency.

When Harris chided him for what she considered a lapse, Baroni took it gracefully, reminding his close circle of friends of a lesson he long ago learned as a son of the church: "It is easier to beg for forgiveness than to ask for permission."

Harris' staff decided that an effective way to control Baroni was to require him to submit his speeches in advance. Baroni complied, and every time he planned a major address he dutifully submitted a copy of his prepared remarks. Then almost without fail he totally ignored the prepared material and delivered his standard ethnics-cities speech.

He devised a wonderful technique which let him say that he used his HUD speech. He flipped over the text prepared for him by the speechwriting staff and while in the airplane or his hotel room he scrawled on the reverse side an outline of what he wanted and intended to say. When he got up to speak, he started with his side of the paper. If he had time or felt so inclined, he turned the text over at some point and read passages from the official side. But he was not, as the bureaucrats said, a stickler for following the text. Nonetheless, he could truthfully say on his return from speaking engagements, that, yes, he had used the text they gave him.

\* \* \*

Baroni's survival of the Eizenstat inquisition did not, of course, mean automatic passage of legislation. Even presidents and Baronis are subject to the scrutiny of their own internal machinery, both at department levels and at that frequent graveyard of good ideas, the Office of Management and Budget. Neither HUD nor OMB was enthusiastic about Baroni's neighborhood self-help bill. Neither pushed very hard for passage. Baroni decided to carry the ball himself. He ran splendidly on the open field of Capitol Hill. The legislation could have been called the Baroni Act.

In a statement to members of Congress, Baroni said the small federal contribution he proposed would encourage other government agencies, private developers and nongovernmental voluntary groups to put up additional money. The federal dollars would be "leveraged"—a favorite Baroni word and concept—to produce much larger actual spending.

In selling the bill to the Carter White House, Baroni primarily used a less formal, more political, approach. He reminded the Democrats of the importance of the white urban ethnic voters in the 1978 midterm Congressional elections and the 1980 presidential election. "A few bucks can win a lot of friends," Baroni said. "It gives you the right to say to white ethnics that here's a program that was especially created for you."

Whether it was the formal or the political argument that worked doesn't matter as much as the fact that Congress passed Baroni's bill. The Office of Neighborhood Self-Help Development was assigned to Baroni's department. He began handing out the money in 1979. The bill was quite popular. By March of 1980, some 1,285 groups applied for assistance, and 125 of them got grants totaling $14.16 million.

Baroni said the 125 organizations leveraged the federal dollars with more than $198 million in private and other government funds. He said the $15 million program created over 4,500 jobs. More than 60 percent of the groups receiving self-help grants were involved in housing rehabilitation. Their efforts with self-help grants produced 5,290 rehabilitated units and 872 new units.

Some economic development projects that Baroni approved included:

— —Rehabilitation of several fishing piers, formation of a fishing cooperative and development of facilities for the processing, storage and sale of fish. This particularly struck Baroni's fancy. He recalled from his seminary reading that the Antigonish Movement in Nova Scotia created a fishing cooperative.

— —Renovation of a vacant historic brewery as a neighborhood-owned and managed office, commercial and light industrial complex.

— —Construction of a building for a farmers' cooperative to pack and store produce.

— —Construction of a factory to manufacture kits for constructing low-cost houses using a passive solar design.

In approving these projects, Baroni set in motion the creation and expansion of the sort of job-creating small businesses that he saw as inevitable steps for the urban ethnic community groups he had helped to organize. Many of the 125 projects approved by Baroni were for the creation of places where people could come together. Baroni viewed the rabbit-warren housing patterns of many neighborhoods as spoilers of common values. His approved projects included a vacant school building converted into a community center and housing for the elderly, a group of historic brownstone houses for use as a community center for the elderly, and a large Victorian house converted into a community center.

Baroni scattered the grants among 37 states, the District of Columbia, and Puerto Rico, making sure that members of Congress who were key to enactment of the legislation got projects in their districts. Several people, and projects, that Baroni worked with through the years were also on the approval list, including Ted Watkins in Los Angeles, Leon D. Finney, Jr., in Chicago, Jeff Stern in Baltimore, Stephen Adubato in

Newark, Donald Monroe, Jr., in Toledo, and Getz Obstfeld in Providence, Rhode Island.

One of Baroni's proudest legacies is the self-help project based on the $150,000 grant he made to Rabbi Samuel Lefkowitz in Brooklyn's Boro Park neighborhood. The rabbi teamed with leaders of the adjacent Hispanic community to renovate and manage 177 units of housing in a ten-block area. They leveraged the $150,000 from Baroni's fund into $6 million.

Boro Park is an area of racial and ethnic tension. Baroni was present for the ground-breaking and he later returned to review the completed project. "Maybe most of the Jews and the Hispanics don't like each other any more than they did a few years ago," Baroni said. "But at least they're talking and working together." That was his ultimate hope for all the nation's big cities. (One of the first acts of the new Reagan administration in 1981 was to kill the neighborhood self-help program. The major Baroni contribution to federal programs missed Reagan's safety net.)

\*　　\*　　\*

Baroni helped shape the administration's response to the March 19, 1979 report by the National Commission on Neighborhoods. This was the group that Baroni originally wanted to chair. Instead that job went to Jordan's political ally, Timilty, a Democratic state senator from Massachusetts. Still, Baroni was able to have a great deal of influence over the Commission. Among the 19 members named by Carter were these people suggested first by Baroni: Nicholas R. Carbone of Hartford's City Council, Gale Cincotta; Victoria Mongiardo of NCUEA; Arthur J. Naparstek, formerly of Baroni's Center and then with the University of Southern California, and Peter S. Ujvagi, formerly of the Center and then with the East Toledo Community Organizations' Sponsoring Committee.

Eizenstat was responsible for drafting Carter's statement on the Commission report, and so he called upon Baroni for help. Baroni gave it a mixed review. He liked the emphasis on neighborhood initiatives and the admission that past public policies damaged neighborhoods. But scrawling the words "inconsistent" and "contradiction" across one page of his copy of the report, Baroni called for the rejection of recommendations by the Commission on issue-oriented advocacy organizations, a type of group that Baroni himself worked with closely before his entry into government at the National Center.

Baroni agreed with the Commission's finding that "in many neighborhoods advocacy organizing continues to be the only means through which disenfranchised neighborhood residents can develop the leadership and power necessary to control their future." However, the Commission said that "because independence is vital to this process," it is important that four conditions be preserved:

——Advocacy organizations should receive their primary funding from community or other private sources.

——Federal funding for the core organizing budget of issue oriented advocacy organizations should not be so great as to threaten their independence.

——Because leadership development by skilled organizers is central to the issue advocacy process, continued independent training of organizers and leadership should be supported in order to harness the grass roots networks, voluntary associations and other human resources in neighborhoods.

——Where federal money is used to fund training of staff and leadership, legal, regional and national training organizations should be contracted to provide such training.

Baroni's quarrel was with the first two points. He did not see how effective advocacy groups in very poor neighborhoods could survive only with locally-raised funds. Such groups did not have a history of raising much money. Baroni felt that ultimately the federal government had an obligation to support these neighborhood groups, even if that meant that federal dollars were used to finance movements against the government.

Nor did Baroni like what he saw as the implicit threat in point number two that government might turn the money spigot on and off as a way to control the independence of local groups. For the moment, Baroni set aside his own knowledge of the history of the war on poverty and his understanding of the nature of politicians not to finance their opposition. His idealism on behalf of neighborhoods overran reality. Baroni was also disappointed in the Commission's failure to acknowledge the importance of such private revenue sources as the Campaign for Human Development, foundations and corporations in giving money to neighborhood organizing groups. From his own experience, Baroni knew it could happen, and should.

As the report made the rounds inside government, Baroni said that if he had been chairman, the report would have much more aggressively demanded federal support for neighborhood organizations.

*     *     *

In 1978, Baroni received $5 million for the work of the Office of Neighborhood Development, part of his responsibility under his HUD portfolio. He used it to award contracts to 212 neighborhood development organizations and to hold a series of training sessions for community development officials, which were also attended by ten mayors. On the list of organizations receiving contracts was Baroni's creation, the National Center for Urban Ethnic Affairs. It received $40,000, less than any of five civil rights groups. The largest grant—$262,000—went to the National Hispanic Coalition for Better Housing.

Eizenstat at the White House directed Kaptur, a member of his staff, and Teddy Mastroianni, on the staff of the White House assistant for intergovernmental affairs Gene Eidenberg, to work with Baroni in developing an urban policy statement for Carter. Over many months, the proposals passed back and forth between Baroni's office and the White House. Baroni wanted the president to instruct cabinet secretaries that if any of the programs they considered could have a potential impact on neighborhoods, they would have to check with the neighborhoods before they acted. "I wanted to institutionalize a sensitivity to neighborhoods throughout government," Baroni said. The draft memorandum went through about thirty rewrites, with Baroni often saying, "No, no. That's not the right way. I don't know how to say it exactly in words, but keep working on it."

Finally Baroni was satisfied, and submitted the draft to Eizenstat. When Carter announced the memo, Baroni stood by him in the White House Rose Garden. At a reception which followed, Carter told Baroni, "Monsignor, I know the major contribution you made to this Administration in putting together this statement." Baroni glowed.

As the presidential election campaign of 1980 approached, Baroni became disheartened. Early in the year he told friends that Carter would lose to almost any Republican. When the Republicans picked Ronald Reagan as their nominee, Baroni was positive that Carter was finished. Baroni recognized Reagan's political skills, and said prophetically that Reagan would take a large slice of the urban ethnic vote from Carter. "The southerners around Carter never did understand the white votes in the cities," Baroni said. "They assumed that urban whites would be scared to death of Reagan. They failed to see the differences between urban blacks and urban whites."

Baroni proposed to Eizenstat early in the year that he be allowed to spend several million dollars on neighborhood self-help programs, to set up counseling programs, and to run conferences for urban whites. Baroni said he could reach millions of white ethnics through those conferences and make the point that Carter was sympathetic to them.

The White House rejected the plan. In the campaign year, it sent Baroni around the country, often to talk to liberal groups that were certainly going to vote for Carter over Reagan. "One time I spoke to some Catholic social workers in the Midwest and there wasn't one person there probably who was going to vote for Reagan. I called up the White House and said what the hell do you have me out here for when I could do you more good back dealing with the people in the cities," Baroni said. Baroni, who had scored big with the Carter team by arranging the 1976 visit for the candidate to Pittsburgh's Polish Hill, was unable in 1980 to convince them to get Carter into big-city ethnic neighborhoods.

Mastroianni, who helped coordinate the campaign for ethnic votes from the White House, was asked about Baroni's role. Mastroianni said that "He advised and he did a lot of work. He flew all over the place. They really ran him ragged. The poor guy was in three or four cities a day. They used him to put out fires with Catholics and ethnic groups."

One night Baroni called Mastroianni: "I just came back from Cleveland and they're having some problems with health care. Can you get somebody in HHS to solve the problems?" Mastroianni tried. Baroni's political instincts were sharp, but no one in power listened to him.

In his appearances before the white ethnic groups, Baroni said, "Even though you have not gotten to the point you wanted, there has been progress these past four years under President Carter. Even if you yourself have not seen progress, your brothers and sisters have. Your ethnic group has. So don't just think of yourself, but think of the community. And when you do that, you will vote for Jimmy Carter and the Democratic Party. If you vote for the Republicans they will take everything you have worked for."

Even as Baroni actively and aggressively campaigned for Carter, he privately voiced his frustration to his White House friends. But Carter's fate was pretty much locked up in 1980. On the eve of the election, Baroni predicted a landslide victory for Reagan, and he was right.

"It is true that our interests were not well served by the way Geno was used in the campaign," Eizenstat said. "Our problems with ethnic

voters ran deep. We should have given Geno more leeway and earlier."
Eizenstat said the Democrats started losing the ethnic voters with the
1972 nomination of Sen. George C. McGovern, a critic of the U.S.
involvement in the Vietnam War and U.S. military/nuclear power
buildups. "Urban ethnic voters are very patriotic. They are flag wavers,
and the Democratic Party had lost their confidence by 1980," said Eizenstat.

Jordan said that in 1980 Carter lost the ethnic voters he won in 1976
because the seizure of U.S. embassy personnel in Teheran by militant
Iranians loyal to Ayatollah Ruhollah Khomeini dramatized the decline in
U.S. prestige abroad. In addition, said Jordan, inflation rates soared and
many jobs in smokestack industries were lost to foreign competition.
Hamilton said that Baroni could not have helped the Carter-Mondale
ticket significantly in 1980 unless he was able to free the American
hostages or revive the U.S. auto industry.

Eizenstat said that many urban ethnics saw the Democratic Party
on the wrong side of social issues—school busing, affirmative action,
school prayer, aid to nonpublic schools, and abortion. Baroni told the
Carter strategists that it would do them no good to reverse position on
those issues. To do so would not bring the ethnic voters back to Carter
and Mondale, but would appear to be pandering to special interests.

On December 22, 1980, seven weeks after the election, Baroni
wrote his resignation letter to Carter. Baroni previously said he had no
intention of remaining in the administration another four years, even if
Carter had won, but there were some who doubted that. They said
Baroni was only positioning a cushion for a soft landing. Now the letter
had to be written. A memo from the White House to senior political
appointees suggested the timing and style. This is what Baroni wrote to
Carter:

Since the American electorate expressed its wishes in the November election, I hereby offer my resignation, effective January 20, 1981.

I am pleased and honored to have served your Administration as the first Assistant Secretary for Neighborhoods, Voluntary Associations and Consumer Protection. It was a further
personal honor to be appointed as the first Catholic priest to
serve in American history in a Sub-Cabinet post, and for that
privilege I am deeply grateful.

The Urban Policy developed by your Administration
which included the Neighborhood Self-Help Act which recognizes the role of the mediating institutions in our society, has

given me great pleasure. It was an honor to have served on the Task Force which developed the National Consumer Cooperative Bank and to have been appointed by you as a Member of its Board of Directors.

It has been my pleasure and honor to serve you and to share your interest and concerns to improve the quality of life of people in our cities and neighborhoods.

With sincere affection and personal best wishes, I remain, Sincerely yours, Geno C. Baroni.

# 13

## Linkages

Though usually a lone operator, Geno Baroni believed in massed power. In the 1970s, Baroni set out to create two pressure groups. His targets were two collections of people with little history of pressure politics. They were American nuns and Italian-Americans.

*     *     *

In the fall of 1971, with Ford Foundation money supporting the Center, Baroni contacted several nuns, among whom were Marjorie Tuite in Chicago, Audrey Miller in Philadelphia, and Josephine Dunne in Washington. Jo Dunne was director of education at the Campaign for Human Development. Baroni talked about the organizations which represented the nuns. They were the aggressive National Coalition of American Nuns, the mainstream National Association of Women Religious, and the powerful Leadership Conference of Women Religious. The three pursued different agendas, but together they pointed to a potentially significant untapped constituency within the Catholic sisterhood.

The three groups were still somewhat competitive, though they worked together in 1971 at a meeting in Atlanta. At that time, the leaders talked about the possibility of a common effort to lobby for social change. Baroni encouraged this, but nothing came of it.

In December, 1971, Baroni decided to take the lead in bringing the nuns together. "I was frustrated that I hadn't been able to start a priests' group to lobby in Washington," Baroni said. "I kept telling them that it's those damned public policy issues in the public arena that hurt you back

171

home when you're talking about day care or housing or jobs or food stamps.

"And the priests said, 'Nah, we don't want to get into that.' For ten years I said to Jack Egan and Pat Flood and Phil Murnion and Ed Flahavan that we shouldn't be coming out to Notre Dame to have our meetings. It's nice at Notre Dame. It's like a country club. It's like a social thing. I said every other meeting should be in Washington and we should sit down with a senator like Kennedy or somebody on the White House like Pat Moynihan to tell us what the public policy issues are so that we could work on our constituencies. Whether it's voting rights or minimum wage or any of the things we ought to be for."

Baroni said he understood Egan's refusal to change CCUM from a support group to a lobbying unit. "We socially activist priests were getting clobbered," Baroni said. "I got it in Altoona. I got it in Washington. Egan got it in Chicago, Flood in Milwaukee. We needed to get together. That's what Egan gave us in CCUM, and it was a good thing. But the system needed more than that."

With CCUM, the best-organized Catholic social justice group, unable or unwilling to act, Baroni turned toward the nuns. Ernst, Baroni's field operations director, sent a letter to social activist nuns on December 7, 1971. He invited them in Baroni's name to attend a three-day conference in Washington starting Friday, December 17. The purpose, said Ernst, was "to plan a network of sisters to deal with social policy questions." Baroni hoped that 25 nuns would attend. He rented an art classroom at Trinity College on Michigan Avenue near Catholic University in northeast Washington.

Exceeding Baroni's expectations, 47 nuns registered. Arriving in Washington, they had a sense that the meeting would produce something to enable them to get more involved with national social issues. But they did not know what that something would be. Neither did Baroni. He and Ernst chose a strategy based on a teaching by Chicago organizer Saul Alinsky, which was to assemble tough-minded, committed people in one room for three days and to see what developed. "I was confident something would," Baroni said.

He did his usual bit the first night. He gave his standard emotional speech about his family and experiences at Sts. Paul and Augustine, the obstacles tossed by the political system as barriers against social progress, and the nuns' duty to participate in the political system. In his customary fashion, Baroni filled the blackboard with circles, squares, and lines depicting the interrelationship of government, the private sector and voluntary sector. The nuns, he said, were key members of the voluntary sector.

Baroni said that American society could be transformed only through the political process. He urged them to address several questions: How do we develop a national public will and a national political consensus for reordering national priorities? How do we render our resources for human development? How do we promote the church's social teaching as a basis for national political decisions?

The evening ended with an informal session over wine and beer, and high hopes that tomorrow would bring enlightenment on the next step.

On Saturday they went by bus to Capitol Hill where Robert Bates of Senator Edward M. Kennedy's office told them how the political process works. James Gibson, then of the Potomac Institute and a close Baroni ally, told the nuns about the black agenda for the 1970s. The questions that followed each session did not deal with substantive issues, since it was assumed that everyone there wanted progress on housing, poverty, welfare, medical care and peace in Southeast Asia. The questions focused on political procedure, and specifically on how a group of nuns could make their presence felt in the halls of Congress.

It was back to Trinity College for lunch, then sessions with David Cohen of Common Cause, Anona Teska of the League of Women Voters, Ralph Nader, and John Espositio, a Washington author. Ernst and Baroni ran the meetings. The nuns sat in a semi-circle and took notes.

By Saturday evening, after several small-group workshops, it was clear that the nuns were thinking about the question: How do we establish a national network while at the same time organizing politically on the local level? There was still sentiment in the room for the nuns remaining with their current national organizations, prodding them to do more politically. Several members suggested that a few in their ranks wondered whether it was appropriate for women religious to enter the political process, or whether the chore should be left to CCUM or another male-dominated group.

By Sunday morning, it was clear that the something they had waited for had better happen quickly or they would return home with little to show for the weekend in Washington. Marjorie Tuite was confident that a consensus existed for the creation of an organization that could promote social change. Josephine Dunne believed that the Capitol Hill visit had convinced the nuns that the effort required lobbying of Congress and the executive branch and involvement in the political process. But they struggled to make it happen.

The schedule put together by Baroni and Ernst made Sunday morning the time for decision. The general notion of a national sisters' network had appeal, but a lot of details lay in the way—How to pay for it? How to pick issues? How to build a staff? How to train people for local lobbying? How to communicate among themselves? How to work with other social action lobbyists?

Until then, Ernst and Baroni had pretty much run the meeting. Audrey Miller, a member of the Congregation of the Divine Providence of Pittsburgh, thought it was time for a change.

Miller had a proposal that would shape the organization of nuns and have an enduring impact on the role that American nuns take in the country and within the church. Her proposal amounted to a liberating act for the American Catholic sisterhood.

Miller's sensitivity to social justice issues was forged in the racial antagonisms of the 1960s. In 1967, she participated in the Archdiocese of Detroit's program for racial equality called "Project Understanding." The next year, as a teacher in Pittsburgh, she organized tenants in the city's Hill district for the Catholic Interracial Council. To broaden her experience beyond Catholic action, she joined the national staff of the United Church of Christ to work on women's issues in the division on Christian education.

Miller was sensitive during the weekend to the leadership roles taken by Baroni and Ernst and the fact that most of the speakers who appeared before the nuns were males. Over meals and at breaks, Miller suggested to the nuns that they were following the traditional pattern of subservience to male leadership, and how ironic that was for a group of women who came together to create their own political organization. On Sunday morning—at the session earmarked by Baroni and Ernst for action—Miller raised her hand. "I wonder what others feel, talking about organizing women religious, when the only leadership thus far has come from the white males," she said.

"Come on up and take over," Ernst said. He left the rostrum and joined Baroni at the back of the room. To Baroni and Ernst, nothing better could have happened. "That move is exactly what we hoped for," Ernst said.

There was an immediate surge of confidence in the room. "Once the women took over the meeting," said Carol Coston, "we said what is it that we really want to do? It seemed clear to me that a consensus was building that we should go ahead and take the step toward a national network." Coston offered a motion that the sisters "form a political action network of information and communication." Miller counted the votes. The sisters' network was approved by a 43 to 3 vote, with 1 abstention. The motion was framed in vague words because nobody in the room seemed clear on what the network would do.

The nuns created a steering committee to meet the following month at Dunne's home on Tunlaw road in northwest Washington. Miller named to the steering committee nine nuns who said they expected to be able to attend the meeting. Money was a problem for most of these women. They had to receive permission from their religious superiors to spend it.

The steering committee was given five tasks: to set up the network, to identify and screen people for the permanent staff, to establish contacts with existing organizations, to explore the possibilities for types of political action, and to plan weekend and summer workshops to involve other sisters in political activity.

The nuns voted to assess themselves $50 apiece to get the network started. They promised to look for more money from their communities and their contacts across the country. They were aware that operating a national office in Washington would cost a lot more than the $2,350 they were able to pledge.

When the steering committee members gathered in January, Baroni was there too, insisting that he be an observer rather than a participant. For Baroni, who loved to plunge into meetings and often took them over, that must have been a hard decision. But there he sat in an overstuffed chair while the nuns spent hours thrashing out the details of the network's organization. As yet it had no name, but more and more, they capitalized the word from Ernst's December letter. It became Network.

The nuns agreed that they needed one of their own to work in Washington. Looking around at one another, they settled on Coston. She asked to be excused to make a phone call. Going upstairs in Dunne's house, Coston telephoned her religious superior, and immediately received permission to work in Washington.

But how was Carol Coston to do it financially? Baroni finally spoke up. He said he had money from the Ford Foundation and other sources to create the National Center for Urban Ethnic Affairs. He said he could offer Coston a little money from that grant, and would allow her to set up a small office and make phone calls from the Center on Lawrence Street. "I came the first of April and worked for Geno April, May and June," Coston said. "It provided me a base to get Network started and Geno knew that. He was very supportive. We used to run the newsletter and use the postage machine at the office."

One of Coston's first tasks was to organize a seminar to get Network noticed and to bank more money for operations. "I don't know how we would have done the seminar if Geno hadn't been generous," Coston said. Baroni was helpful to Network's finances later that year, prevailing on Edward Kennedy and other political heavyweights to attend a Network dinner in Washington which drew more than 1,000 nuns and raised enough money to expand Network.

The existing religious women's organizations were skeptical about Network. Baroni attempted to establish Network's credentials in an April, 1972, letter to the Leadership Conference of Women Religious:

> My own concern, as you know, has been to sensitize sisters to the undercurrents of fear and frustration that lie below the surface of consciousness in America. The Archie Bunkers are unhappy. They feel neglected, put upon, left out of consideration by both government and church. If they are to resist the pull of demagogues who massage their own fears and appeal to the type of base motivations latent in all of us, they will have to have courageous leadership at all levels. We will have to develop alert, informed, dedicated persons in Middle American neighborhoods who will speak up, take the initiative and generate the enthusiasm required to convince their friends, neighbors and associates that the prophets of doom have no place in our land.
>
> Most sisters are working with this large group and have the potential for influence among them that cannot be underestimated or ignored. It would be tragic if sisters were not alerted to this and challenged to respond.

It seemed that Baroni had in mind making Network part of his mission to white urban ethnics.

Not all the nuns who created Network agreed with Baroni's assessment of the priority of the need to organize white urban ethnics. Many of the nuns were activists in the movement for justice toward blacks. They tended, like other liberals, to see ethnics in big cities as a bunch of racists seeking to destroy the civil rights movement in a white backlash. Baroni had to educate those nuns as well as many priests and lay people in his philosophy that the problems of urban America transcended race and that solutions required a political response by blacks and whites working together, not against each other.

From its humble beginnings in the art classroom at Trinity College, Network went on to become an important lobby on peace and justice issues on Capitol Hill. It helped to win Congressional approval of the cooperative bank and the extension of time for states to consider the Equal Rights Amendment to the Constitution. Network lent its reputation to the ERA extension at a time when many members of Congress were saying that Roman Catholics opposed the amendment. Thus Network served as a liberal counterforce within Roman Catholic ranks. By 1984, Network had grown from the 43 women who voted for its establishment in 1971 to more than 7,000 members.

In the late 1980s, Network turned more toward war and peace issues, lobbying against the MX missile, the B-1 bomber, and expansion of the American role in Central America. On most issues, Network's position was consistent with positions of the U.S. Catholic Conference, the bishops' organization. But Network operated independently of the USCC. Moreover, several Congressional staff aides said they found that by the early 1980s, Network's lobbyists had become far more adept at informing members of Congress about crucial issues than were the bishops' lobbyists. There is some evidence that Network was instrumental in persuading the bishops to prepare pastoral letters on nuclear arms and the U.S. economy.

Coston said that Baroni's talent was "getting people together, having a vision, and creating a climate where other people can begin to share in it. He knew an enormous number of people in all walks of life, political life and Church life, and he was generous with connecting them." Audiences, including the Network nuns, responded to Baroni, she said, because "he wasn't threatening when he was talking. Sometimes he was hard to follow and to keep the whole idea in context. I think if he were working directly with you and you were kind of a linear mind, it would be hard."

When she first worked for Baroni on Lawrence Street, Coston found him spinning off so many ideas so fast that she often felt "stupid" around him. But she later came to realize that it was Baroni's skill to develop ideas in his head and then to toss them out in the hope that others would pick them up and carry them forward.

Baroni worked closely with Network through the years, helping it to identify issues, assess the Capitol Hill mood, make appointments, and reinvigorate its own members. He led the celebration of mass at Network meetings. That was rare for Baroni, who showed a strange awkwardness about leading liturgies in public. He enjoyed sitting down and letting the nuns produce their own homily.

It may be that Network would have gotten started and prospered even if Baroni had not called the founding meeting, given it his leadership, paid its first organizer, and helped it over the years. But the fact that he did all those things strengthened his reputation as one of the Catholic Church's most important innovators of his time.

The nuns of Network looked for a word to describe Baroni. They tried creator, founder, enabler, facilitator. All were either imprecise or inadequate. So they finally came up with a title Baroni enjoyed: God-father.

\*     \*     \*

To one group of Americans, the word Godfather carries an unpleasant connotation. To Italian-Americans, Godfather conjures up Mafia, La Cosa Nostra, swarthy Sicilians wielding knives and running the rackets.

The labels were no joke to Baroni, son of immigrants from northern Italy, fighter for the integrity of ethnic heritage. He believed that the smear of Italians warped American society and the Catholic Church. Baroni believed that Italian-Americans had stood by helplessly too long while their culture was distorted, their reputations damaged, their names belittled and their aspirations thwarted by a society dominated by white Anglo-Saxon Protestants and a church run by the Irish.

Baroni identified himself as a victim of this bias against Italians. One way he did this was through the stories he told of his growing up years in central Pennsylvania. He said that the mine owners and managers held that "Wops are cheaper than props" and therefore disregarded health and safety standards for their Italian coal diggers. Baroni talked about the Irish nuns who taught him the Baltimore Catechism and wanted to change his name from Geno to Kevin, and of the Waspish school-teachers who ridiculed his imported Italian salami sandwiches and the Italian tradition of winemaking.

He talked about how few Italians there were in Mount St. Mary's Seminary and how the hierarchy was filled by men with Irish surnames who promoted their own. All of young Father Baroni's first three pastors were of Irish descent, and he had problems with all of them. One of the pastors was a great expert on Irish tradition and mythology, and could spin out glorious stories, but he didn't know quite what to make of an Italian curate. In Altoona, where Baroni landed fresh out of the seminary, there was a predominantly Italian parish. The Franciscans had it, and Baroni got what was known as an Irish parish.

Geno's parents, Guido Baroni of Tenno di Riva del Garda and Giuseppina Tranquillini Baroni of San Martino di Arco, spoke Italian in their home in Acosta throughout most of Geno's growing up years. The father and his friends from the mines spent many weekends tasting one another's homemade wines and swapping stories—in Italian—about the old country and their work. This, as Baroni saw it, identified his culture as different, as purposefully set apart from the mainstream of American society.

As an adult, Baroni said he came to understand the differences and rejoice in American pluralism. He advocated the rediscovery of ethnic roots. He glorified foreign traditions practiced in the streets and homes of ethnic neighborhoods in America. Yet simultaneously he deplored the separateness which is another aspect of pluralism. He wanted Italians, Poles, Slovaks, Hungarians, and even Irish and white Anglo-Saxon Protestants to respect and revel in their heritage, but then he expected the differences to be extinguished when it came to job opportunities and the other benefits of American society.

Of course, it was always the Baroni thesis that people of ethnic background had to come to grips with their ethnicity before they could deal with other problems, particularly those linked to the movement of blacks into their neighborhoods and schools and as challengers to their jobs.

Among the ethnic groups Baroni served, Italians were the most important. Americans of Italian descent represent seven percent of the U.S. population, about 16 million people. The majority live in big cities. In many northeastern U.S. cities, theirs were among the first neighborhoods to be eyed by blacks after World War II. Those included Philadelphia, New York, Newark, Providence, Camden and Boston. Italians in the 1980s had the third largest median family income of all ethnic groups in the United States, ranking behind only Scots and Germans, whose ancestors came to America before the first major waves of Italians.

One of the most celebrated confrontations in the 1970s came in Newark where Anthony Imperiale, an Italian-American, and LeRoi Jones and other black leaders of Newark, engaged in a violence-tinged struggle for domination of that city. Baroni helped to defuse that explosive situation by creating a third power force in Steve Adubato, the Italian-American boss of Newark's North Ward, one of the first people to receive Ford Foundation money through Baroni's National Center for Urban Ethnic Affairs.

*        *        *

Baroni had a good point that Italians were historical victims of ethnic discrimination in the United States. Conditions, however, have improved, Baroni acknowledged. No American Italian had been given the red hat of cardinal of the Catholic Church before it went in 1983 to Joseph Bernardin, the archbishop of Chicago. This shutout came despite the fact that Italians represent about 20 percent of the nation's Catholics, according to Lydio F. Tomasi, director of the Center for Migration Studies of New York.

No one identified as an American Italian was nominated by a major party for national office before the Democrats in 1984 picked Congresswoman Geraldine A. Ferraro of New York. Nor was anyone identified as an American Italian ever thought of seriously as a presidential nominee until the arrival on the political scene of New York Governor Mario Cuomo.

In New York, Cuomo turned his Italian background with its strong tradition of a sharing family into a political asset. His parents came to the United States from mountain villages south of Naples in the Campania region. Speaking no English, with little education in reading and writing Italian or basic skills, the elder Cuomos arrived at Ellis Island at the lowest social and economic strata.

They were among the about four million Italians who came to the United States between 1880 and 1920, approximately 75 percent of them from the Mezzogiorno, the underdeveloped regions east and south of Rome that remain poverty-ridden.

Mario Cuomo has outdistanced most second-generation Italian-Americans in reaching power and national prominence, but his story reveals the pattern—in America, many sons and daughters of Italian immigrants have made it big.

New York City chose Fiorello LaGuardia as its mayor four decades ago, although Philadelphia had only one Italian mayor, Frank L. Rizzo, before city government passed from a line of Irish-Americans to black W. Wilson Goode. And there never was an Italian mayor of Chicago.

But Baroni could proudly recite a litany of contemporary Italian-American successes, such as business executives: Chrysler chairman Lee Iacocca; Minnesota food processor Jeno F. Paulucci; shopping-center developer and sports entrepreneur Edward J. DeBartolo, Jr.; Avis president Joseph M. Vittoria; and Detroit businessman Frank D. Stella. In politics there are hundreds of prominent Italian-Americans, including Senators Pete V. Domenici of New Mexico and Alfonse M. D'Amato of New York; Congressmen Peter W. Rodino, Jr., of New Jersey; Joseph P. Addabbo of New York; Robert M. Giaimo of Connecticut; and Dante Fascell of Florida, and Governor Richard Celeste of Ohio.

Prominent Italian-American jurists and lawyers include Judge John J. Sirica, who presided over the Watergate cases, Carter's attorney general, Benjamin R. Civiletti; Reagan's associate attorney general, Rudolph W. Giuliani. Italian-Americans who rose to prominence in education included A. Bartlett Giamatti as president of Yale and later of the National Baseball League; John Lo Schiavo as president of the University of San Francisco; Edmund D. Pellegrino, president of Catholic University and professor of medicine at Georgetown University, and Rudolph J. Vecoli, professor of history at the University of Minnesota.

No baseball fan can ever forget Italian-Americans Joe DiMaggio and Tony Lazzeri, or such contemporary figures as California Angels executive vice president Buzzie Bavasi, Los Angeles Dodgers manager Tommy LaSorda, New York Yankees manager Billy Martin, Villanova national championship basketball coach Rollie Massimino, North Carolina basketball coach Jim Valvano, Penn State football coach Joe Paterno. Probably the greatest professional football coach of all time was Vince Lombardi.

\*      \*      \*

When Guido Baroni, Geno's father, came to the United States the first time, he thought about staying a few years and then returning to his native village, marrying his girl there, and settling down at home. He returned for the girl, but came back to America. But it was many years, Giuseppina Baroni said, before her husband became reconciled to the fact that he was destined to spend the rest of his days and die in America.

Sociologist William V. D'Antonio said that half of the Italians who came to the United States eventually returned to Italy. They were able to do what Guido Baroni could not do—make enough money in the United States to buy land in Italy.

Geno Baroni wanted to visit Italy, and he did about a dozen times in his life. But he was an American, and he intended to improve the relationship between Italian-Americans and their country of birth and choice, the United States. "Here we are, nearly five hundred years after Columbus discovered America and two hundred years after the founding of the Republic, and we don't know each other as Americans," Baroni said. "We need to discover ourselves as Americans and share that discovery." He said that Italians cut themselves off from their roots too fast. He said that other European ethnic groups such as the Poles, Germans, Slovaks and Greeks were better than Italians in asking themselves "Who are we, and where are we going?"

By 1975, Baroni had six years of experience in dealing directly with ethnic Americans through his positions as urban task force co-chairman and program director for the Catholic bishops and as president of the National Center for Urban Ethnic Affairs. He came to believe that many Italians did not enjoy being lumped into the category of ethnics. They wanted to assimilate into American culture, just as the Irish had done. Standing by and allowing that to happen unchallenged would have mocked Baroni's conviction that understanding one's ethnicity was a prerequisite to solving the nation's urban crisis. So in 1975 Baroni set out, through his Center, to develop an association of Italian-Americans that would explore what it means in today's America to be an Italian-American.

When he served in Washington in the early 1960s at Sts. Paul and Augustine Parish, Baroni said, "There were no Italians who gave me the time of day. I was working in the ghetto with blacks. I was known as the 'nigger priest.' I was not invited to the Heritage Club or the Italian Club or the Social Club. There was just one guy who was different, Joe Vaghi. He said, 'Look, I am an architect. I understand you are going to build houses for poor people. If I can be of any help, I would like to be.' "

On April 15, 1975, Baroni sent a memo to prominent Italian-Americans in Washington, and invited them to his Center on April 26. "We will discuss the Bicentennial, community projects, federal programs, media and other subjects," Baroni said. "A number of groups have asked me what has been happening in these areas and want to explore ideas on what they might want to do locally."

Among those who accepted invitations were Vaghi, psychiatrist-Jesuit Father Angelo D'Agostino, *Washington Post* reporter Chuck Concini, builder John Orfino, Dr. Robert J. DiPietro, Elio E. Grandi, and Frank Calcara. There was anger in the room. It was expressed by Vaghi, president of the Lido Civic Club of Washington in a speech he was preparing for Lido's annual Congressional reception on May 6. "American-Italians are becoming more active in civic and political affairs. They are finally beginning to realize that in numbers there is power," Vaghi said. "They are asking the question 'What does it mean to be an American-Italian and how can we as a group affect the political realities?' They are telling us unequivocally: It is not acceptable that we have not yet had an American-Italian president. It is not acceptable that we have not yet had an American-Italian as vice president. It is not acceptable that we have not yet had an American-Italian on the Supreme Court. It is not acceptable that we have not yet had an American-Italian in the cabinet of the present (Ford) Administration. It is not acceptable that we have so few American-Italians on the federal judiciary."

Vaghi told the congressional guests: "We simply encourage you to sensitize yourselves to the issues that face the American-Italian on a national level and ally yourselves to a corporate unit when possible so you can speak more effectively on these issues."

At the meeting at 11 A.M. April 26 in Baroni's office, the twenty participants contributed more than $2,000 "as seed money to employ a research man" to identify the "troublesome issues" before the Washington Italian-American community. Baroni told the group to think about the Bicentennial and how it should recognize the Italian-American contributions to the nation's first 200 years.

On May 19, Baroni called the group back together, and presented the ideas he developed over the month. He said he wanted to create a National Office of American/Italian Affairs or Concerns. The formal proposal that summer reflected Baroni's belief that people of common interest and background should band together as a pressure group for political action. Essentially, Baroni developed what was to become The Italian-American Foundation along the same lines as the sisters' group, Network.

The organizational structure of the foundation was a victory for Baroni. He had to overcome members of Congress led by Rep. Frank Annunzio of Chicago who wanted to create an Italian caucus on Capitol Hill and leave it at that. As Baroni saw that move, it was an effort by the politicians to keep the Italian-American voters divided and under their control. "Annunzio said we'll give you three typewriters and some office space, a parking space and perks like that on the Hill," Baroni said.

"That would kill it," Baroni replied. "I want it to be separate from the Hill so that it is non-partisan. They wanted to see it as a congressional caucus. I wanted to see it as an office where Italians could get and spread information and cooperation." That's what they got.

The announcement Baroni prepared that summer said that, "because most of the major decisions that affect all Italian-Americans are made in Washington, the consensus of the meeting (in his office) was that a genuine need exists for an issues-oriented office for Italian-Americans located in Washington. Congress, the administration, the federal agencies, headquarters of most national organizations and the representatives of most of the media also center in the nation's capital."

Just as the nuns did, the Italian-Americans working with Baroni called for a national forum to discuss their problems. The first forum was held that fall, and the foundation was incorporated on December 22, 1975. Joining Baroni as incorporators were Floyd Agostinelli, Geno's friend since their service together for Cardinal Patrick O'Boyle, and Paul J. Asciolla, a priest and writer. Baroni secured the appointment of Asciolla as the Foundation's executive director. Jeno Paulucci was the national chairman.

The organization was to adopt another Baroni tactic—a national dinner. That was held on September 16, 1976. Baroni was the president of the Italian-American Foundation Board of Directors, and among those he brought to the dinner were the two major party candidates for the White House, incumbent President Gerald R. Ford and challenger Jimmy Carter.

The annual dinner of the Italian-American Foundation was to become, as Baroni foresaw and desired, a highly political event. On September 15, 1984, among those attending the annual dinner in the Washington Hilton Hotel were President Ronald Reagan, Democratic presidential nominee Walter F. Mondale, Vice President George Bush, and Democratic vice presidential nominee Geraldine Ferraro. It was the only time during the campaign that all four major candidates appeared together at the same event.

Reagan and Mondale paid tribute to Baroni, who three weeks before had died in Washington's Providence Hospital. And Reagan delivered a speech on ethnic Americans, Italians, family and work.

> . . . The Jews of the roiling ghettoes, the Irish living ten to a room in Boston, and the Italians looking for work in Philadelphia, all shared some rough beginnings. But what distinguished all of these groups of immigrants is that they yielded more than their share of genius. In fact, you might say that Ellis Island was one big incubator for American greatness. All of the immigrants, and certainly the Italians, changed our country by adding to the sum total of what we are. They did not take from, they added to.

Reagan said that "these immigrants were guided by habits, principles and traditions that they took from the old country and transplanted here. They believed in the central importance of the family, the dignity of hard work, and faith in a just God who would reward effort and encourage virtue." Reagan reminded the audience of one of Baroni's classic lines: "There are only two lasting things we can leave our children. One is roots, the other is wings." Geno's mother, Giuseppina, attended the dinner that evening in Washington, and heard her son eulogized by the two candidates for president and the two candidates for vice president.

\* \* \*

Two organizations—Network and the National Italian-American Foundation. Both acknowledge their debt and attribute their philosophy to Baroni. Neither would likely have come to exist without the energy, commitment and style of Baroni. He gave them their roots and then their wings.

# 14

## St. Stephen's Crown

In 1977 President Carter wanted to improve U.S. relations with Hungary. He decided to return to Hungary its most cherished symbol—the 1,000-year-old crown of St. Stephen. Carter asked for help from Baroni to make this happen.

Baroni was an official at the Department of Housing and Urban Development, but in response to Carter's request, he became involved in highly emotionally-charged U.S. politics and international negotiations that involved the State Department, the Hungarian government, and the Vatican. Baroni, calling in chits from his years of work in the U.S. urban ethnic communities, helped Carter weather the wild political storm that his announcement caused in the American Hungarian community in the United States.

Baroni tapped his old-boy network of priests and ethnics. He later concluded that Carter's return of the crown hurt the president badly in the Hungarian-American community in his 1980 bid for reelection against Ronald Reagan. Baroni, however, defended the crown's return. He said it was the right thing to do as a contribution to improved U.S.-Hungarian relations. Besides, he said, the crown meant almost nothing to the vast majority of Americans, but meant freedom, religion and culture to the Hungarian people.

Baroni participated in negotiations which led to secret concessions by the Hungarian government, including the reunification of families, increased freedom for practicing Hungarian Christians and Jews, and improved political and trade relations between Washington and Budapest.

By helping Carter, said Baroni, he strengthened his position within the administration. Recognized as a team player, Baroni won more access to the White House staff. Baroni credited his role in returning the crown for laying the groundwork for Carter's increased awareness of the special interests and concerns of the U.S. urban ethnic community. The return of the crown, however, damaged Baroni's access to the Hungarian-American community in the United States, especially in Cleveland, where he had previously worked effectively.

Part fact, part legend, the story of the crown begins nearly 1,000 years ago. Pope Sylvester II is said to have given the crown to Hungary's first king, Stephen, when he converted the Magyar people to Christianity in 1001. The crown took on enormous symbolic importance through the centuries. No ruler of Hungary was considered legitimately on the throne unless the crown was present for the coronation ceremony. Among those crowned with Stephen's crown were Empress Maria-Theresa and Emperor Franz-Joseph of Austria-Hungary.

The crown had a turbulent history of its own. Throughout the ten centuries it was stolen by ransomers, confiscated by foreign governments, seized by the Turks and Austrians, buried for hiding at the approach of such invading forces as the Tatars, Poles and French, safeguarded in a steel-walled vault in the Royal Palace of Budapest and in iron chests. The crown came to its present-day situation because of Adolf Hitler.

The story can be more or less put together from U.S. and Hungarian historians and archivists and leaders of the Hungarian-American community. The crown was protected for much of the millennium by an elite group of soldiers, with 28 in their ranks, especially chosen and trained for devotion to protecting the crown. All promised to die for it. According to the tradition, no guard could take his eyes from the crown for a second. The guard relaxed his watch only when his relief arrived and said, "I see it."

The elite guard was commanded during World War II by Colonel Ernest Pajitas. The crown and its regalia were kept in Budapest until late in 1944 as the Soviet Army approached. The elite guard moved the relics to a series of places, including a bank vault, an air raid shelter, and then to a monastery at Koszeg in western Hungary. As the Soviet troops pressed on, Colonel Pajitas and his men moved the crown and regalia once more. It is believed they were heading for neutral Switzerland, when they were overtaken by advancing American forces. Pajitas ordered the crown and regalia buried.

They were stored in an old gasoline drum and buried at Zellhof, about twenty miles from Salzburg, Austria, and near the town of Mattsee. Pajitas and his troops were captured. At the interrogation center in Mattsee, Pajitas was questioned in July, 1945, by Major Paul Kubala, a

U.S. Army intelligence officer. Apparently anxious that the crown get into American hands, Pajitas revealed the story and the hiding place. With Pajitas pointing out the burial site, U.S. soldiers dug up the oil drum. It was mud covered and mud had oozed inside to cake two leather wrappings and their contents.

According to Kubala, the contents "were carried to my bathroom where all mud and dirt was washed off." There was the crown and regalia, consisting of a ceremonial sword, orb and scepter, more noted for their symbolism than jewelry, decorations or other measures of material wealth. Nor was the crown particularly impressive at first sight. Experts said it was actually two bands of gold bisecting above a gold diadem. It was richly ornamented with roughly-cut jewels and enamel miniatures. In another container was a robe embroidered with gold thread.

The United States took the relics to the federal repository in Fort Knox, Kentucky, where they lay until 1978 when Carter decided on a new foreign policy initiative. The United States always took the position that the crown and regalia were the property of the Hungarian government and would be returned at some appropriate time. But until Carter, no president had found any time appropriate. No U.S. president wanted to be seen making a concession to a Communist government.

Carter's new policy toward eastern Europe was called "political polycentrism" by Zbigniew Brzezinski, Carter's national security adviser. The Carter plan was to drive deeper the wedge in the growing split he saw between Moscow and the eastern European nations under its domination. Carter was out to show he could make what U.S. officials called a "magnanimous gesture" toward Hungary and the Hungarian people, while still retaining vigilance against Soviet aggression. This was still before the Soviet invasion of Afghanistan. However, it was after the Soviet rejection of Carter's nuclear arms limitation proposal and at a time when the atmosphere between the White House and the Kremlin was heating up again.

Brzezinski saw the return of the crown as a symbolic rejection by the United States of the Brezhnev Doctrine, under which the Soviet Union claimed the right to intervene in Warsaw pact states. Carter scheduled a visit to Poland. He was saying to the world that while the Soviet leaders in the Kremlin would not deal with him, he was ready to improve relations with Poland, Hungary and other Soviet bloc nations.

The Americans thought they saw significant changes in the Hungarian system which they might be able to reward and encourage through the return of the crown. The Hungarians had just honored Sandor Jaraszti, 80, a minister of the non-Communist government of

Ferenc Nagy after World War II. The hardline Communists in command of Hungary in 1958 sent Jaraszti to jail for eight years as "a leading force of the counterrevolution." Now he was being honored "for deserving acts in favor of Socialist Hungary."

In 1977, Carter administration officials were convinced that Nagy, then living in Virginia, would endorse the return of the crown. They were right. Also within the previous few months before Carter's decision, the Hungarian government relaxed its policy of censorship and punishment of dissidents. It was already the most permissive of any state under Kremlin domination. The Kadar government permitted thirty-five intellectuals to declare public support for Prague's Charter 77 human rights declaration. Not long before, such acts would have been viewed by the government as treasonable and intellectuals would likely have been arrested and severely punished. Carter administration officials conceded that Hungary still denied free speech, free press and an organized political opposition. "But you take what you can get," a State Department official said later. Ridiculed by political opponents at home as naive when it came to understanding Soviet power politics, Carter was nonetheless determined to find examples of how his human rights policy was working.

These arguments for returning the crown did not have much influence, however, with Baroni's friends who were leaders of the Hungarian-American community. Many had been driven out of Hungary after World War II by the Communists. They were implacable foes of the Communist government, unwilling to concede any differences among Communists, and determined to use every bit of power they had to retain the crown.

Previous presidents wilted under that kind of pressure, but Carter was determined to go ahead. In the fall of 1977, Secretary of State Cyrus R. Vance sent a signal to Hungary that the United States was prepared to return the crown. The administration notified the Senate Foreign Relations Committee and the House Foreign Affairs Committees. There was immediate hostile reaction from segments of the Hungarian-American community. An administration official said the "professional ethnics got to work with their newspapers and mailing lists to attack our decision." Typical was the reaction of Louis Halmagyi, editor of the *American Hungarian Life* newspaper in Chicago. "I hate Carter," said Halmagyi. "To return the crown to the Communists was a slap in the face at the freedom-loving people of Hungary and all Hungarian-Americans."

Under fire from her constituents, Rep. Mary Rose Oakar (D-Ohio) opened a fight against Carter on Capitol Hill. Generally a Democratic

Party loyalist, Oakar felt she had no choice but to resist Carter loudly and aggressively. Lawsuits were filed to halt the transfer of the crown. Undaunted, and, it turned out, foolishly, Vice President Walter F. Mondale agreed to host a meeting in the White House with Hungarian-American community activists. "It was a disaster," a Mondale aide said. "They shouted at him. I thought at one point some of them were going to get up and start waving their fists. The Secret Service was very edgy for Mondale."

Baroni was at the meeting. He sat in a chair along the wall and made no comments except for a few asides to administration colleagues about the bad politics of the whole affair. They agreed with him.

Carter made a prearranged but unannounced visit to the meeting. He explained that the crown was being returned to the Hungarian people, not to the Communist government. The president insisted that it was a decent people-to-people gesture that would have the long-term effect of improving human rights conditions for the people of Hungary and provide Hungarian leaders with more reason to soften their close links to Moscow. "It was pretty much a wasted effort," a Carter aide said. "There was no convincing them that our position had a grain of sense."

There were veiled hints to Carter and more direct warnings to congressional Democrats and White House aides that the Hungarian leaders would make the return of the crown a political issue against the party in 1978 and against Carter in a 1980 reelection campaign. As insensitive as they were on political relationships with the ethnic community, Carter people could count. They won the critical state of Ohio in 1976 by a margin of only 11,176 votes. Ohio's economy was growing worse, partly due to imported steel that undercut Ohio's mills. The auto industry was in a slump. With the blue collar vote already in jeopardy for the Democrats, the loss of Hungarian-American voters in Cleveland would make victory impossible.

The U.S. Census Bureau said that in 1978 there were 1.4 million registered Hungarian-American voters. Eighty percent were registered as Democratic. Carter and his aides huddled over what to do. Vance insisted that the United States could not bow to political pressure. He said it would be a slap in the face to the Hungarian government. If you cancel the deal, Vance told Carter, the Soviet Union will gloat.

Baroni was invited to the White House for a strategy meeting by Stuart Eizenstat, assistant to the president for domestic affairs. The invitation was arranged by Marcy Kaptur and Vicki Mongiardo, former Baroni employees at the National Center for Urban Ethnic Affairs. They pointed out that Baroni had worked with the Hungarian-

American community in Cleveland. "I was in Cleveland and I ran into the Hungarian community because it was right up against the blacks. This was before I was in government, when I was at the Center," Baroni said. "One of the worst places for me was Cleveland, where whites had guns in their basements in the so-called Hungarian neighborhood, Buckeye. I heard some of the toughest stuff there, not just about blacks, but about Communists. They said the civil rights movement was Communist inspired and look what happened to our country. They said blacks are being used and our neighborhood is going to hell and our church is falling apart because everyone is running away. It was tough and it really shook me."

Baroni said one of his lowest moments in the ethnic movement came one night in Cleveland when "a speaker at a church meeting said, 'Hitler didn't finish the job in Europe.' I met somebody out there who told me about this Hungarian working in Washington at the State Department. When I came back I looked him up. His name was Csnand Toth. His father had been the editor of a paper. Csnand was an intellectual liberal who was very good on civil rights and understood foreign policy. He had worked on a development project in Latin America. He gave me another view on the return of the crown." Baroni said Toth "thought that the crown should go back."

Baroni raised the issue of the crown with friends at the U.S. Catholic Conference. The inquiry prompted an approach to the Vatican by Archbishop Joseph L. Bernardin. Bernardin was told that the Vatican had no objection to sending the crown back if certain conditions could be met. Those conditions included liberalization of rules governing activities of Hungarian Catholic bishops and priests.

Hungary was a violent battleground for the Catholic Church after World War II. Cardinal Joseph Mindzendty resisted the government, was arrested, and imprisoned. He was released in 1965 and took refuge in the U.S. embassy in Budapest, where he stayed until his death in 1975.

Through intermediaries, the Vatican informed Baroni that since the death of Mindzendty, relations between the government and church had improved. The Vatican said it was all right for Carter to return the crown.

Baroni carried this message through Eizenstat to Carter at the White House. He also passed the word to his priest-friend in Toledo, Father Martin Hernady, a Hungarian-American. Hernady said he was at first inclined to oppose the transfer of the crown, but when he got assurances from Baroni that the Vatican approved the idea, and that conditions favorable to the Hungarian people would be attached to the deal, he endorsed it. That was very important for Carter politically. The sizable Hungarian-American community of Toledo raised no objections. Hernady's leadership was credited.

Baroni asked Hernady and another Hungarian-American formerly on the Center staff, Peter Ujvagi, to phone Hungarian-American newspaper editors and other opinion leaders. Hernady was reluctant, but Ujvagi cooperated. "I can't say the tide began to turn because of what we did, but we at least slowed it down," Baroni said.

Baroni told Eizenstat that he was able to gain backing for the Carter decision by promising Hungarian-Americans that the crown's return would be matched by concessions from the Hungarian government. Negotiations were opened between U.S. Ambassador Philip M. Kaiser and the government of Janos Kadar in Budapest. Kadar sent out his own signals. His wife had just recently visited Rome and attended the 80th birthday mass for Pope Paul VI. The government permitted American evangelist Billy Graham to preach without restriction in Hungary.

The Hungarians and Americans negotiated terms for the crown's arrival ceremony and public display. The cardinal, the chief rabbi, Protestant bishops, and leaders of the intellectual, cultural, academic and scientific communities were to be invited to join representatives of the government in accepting the crown. The ceremony was to be televised live throughout Hungary. "For six hours the heads of government and the heads of the religious bodies will be together as equals. That is a very important symbolic gesture," a State Department official told Baroni.

In late December of 1977, Baroni was invited by Carter to travel to Budapest with the crown and to attend the ceremony as a member of the official party. Matthew Nimetz, the State Department Counselor, said that Carter picked Baroni because of his contacts with the ethnic community. "It seemed a logical choice," Nimetz said. Baroni saw it as a reward for the support he lined up for the crown's return from the ethnic community.

Baroni was given the right to nominate a representative of the U.S. Catholic Church. The State Department decided it would be correct to have U.S. Catholic priests join Hungarian Catholic priests at the events. Baroni chose his old friend from the U.S. Catholic Conference, Monsignor George Higgins. Well-known to State Department officials, Higgins had been an adviser to the U.S. delegation to the Belgrade Conference reviewing implementation of the 1975 Helsinki agreement on European security and cooperation and human rights.

Higgins had just been through a contest to try and force him into retirement from the U.S. Catholic Conference after 34 years as the articulate and visible spokesman for the Catholic Church in the United States on labor and public policy issues. Baroni felt Higgins needed a boost to his morale. Baroni wanted to show the bishops that Higgins was still a major figure in the Church.

On a cold January night, Higgins and Baroni checked into the May-flower Hotel on Connecticut Avenue in downtown Washington. They were instructed to let only a few trusted people know of their travel plans. Bags in the lobby, they were told, by five the next morning. U.S. security officials were afraid that last-minute efforts might be made to prevent the crown's departure. The political office at the White House had its own apprehension. It did not want another storm of protest.

With daylight still two hours away, Baroni, Higgins and other official U.S. representatives were taken to Andrews Air Force Base in suburban Maryland. One of the sleek blue and white Boeing 707 jetliners from the presidential fleet was warmed up for their arrival. Inside the cabin, in a steel case, were the crown of St. Stephen and the regalia. As the members of the official party walked past the case, they patted it gently.

After a stopover in England for refueling, the airliner with its package and the U.S. delegation landed in Budapest. The official ceremony took place the next day. Vance and Senator Adlai E. Stevenson (D-Ill.) were in the center of the first row. Baroni was right behind them.

Even at that ceremony, Baroni built his network. Learning that the State Department was looking for a translator, Baroni recommended his contact, Toth. The recommendation was accepted.

While in Budapest, Baroni visited the Catholic cathedral and the central synagogue. "I still have the yarmulke from the rabbi," he said in 1984.

Baroni said he had no regrets over easing the way for Carter to return the crown, even though it probably hurt the president politically in 1980, and certainly affected Baroni's relations with some of his Hungarian-American co-workers in the ethnic and neighborhood revitalization struggle. But Baroni was philosophical: "The crown is now displayed in a museum and people can go see it. The elderly can take their grandchildren and talk about their tradition, their heritage."

Nimetz recalled that Baroni was "definitely the most effervescent guy on the trip. All the way across the Atlantic he kept talking to everybody about the ethnics in the United States. He had a great political sense."

One of Baroni's concerns when he entered the Carter administration was that he would be used as a "token" for ethnics and Catholics. In this case, Baroni insisted, he was not used. "I played a constructive role in bringing off an important foreign policy initiative," he said. "Carter's decision was good for the country and for the people of Hungary."

*     *     *

Some Baroni critics said he was "used" as a priest by Carter during the crown affair. But Baroni saw his work as politician, Carter administration official, and organizer and spokesman of urban ethnic Americans in big cities as his mission as a Roman Catholic priest. He rejected, and all his life fought against, the traditional role of the parish priest as the only model for the American Catholic Church.

Yet he accepted with only slight resistance an order from the Vatican in 1980 which forced him to declare that he would leave the Carter Administration at the end of its first term in January, 1981, even if Carter were reelected to a second four years in the White House.

Baroni disagreed with the Vatican directive that priests should not serve in public office. He noted that Pope John Paul II, the Polish-born bishop of Rome, deeply engaged in politics, even involving himself in negotiations between Polish Prime Minister Wojciech Jaruzelski and leaders of the Solidarity workers' movement.

Baroni had trouble understanding the distinction between the role he was forced to abandon—as an advocate for public policies that benefited poor people in urban neighborhoods—and the active legislative lobbying by U.S. bishops on abortion and federal aid to nonpublic schools. As the bishops adopted a statement on nuclear arms and moved toward a document on the U.S. economy, Baroni wondered what differences there were between his political activities and theirs.

Baroni saw these political activities by the pope and the bishops as appropriate and needed. He could not help wonder, though, if there was any distinction other than rank between what they did and what he did in the Carter Administration.

"I saw that my responsibilities and my position as a priest did not stop at the altar rail," Baroni said. "I couldn't talk about Heaven inside the church while all around on the outside, where people lived, it was Hell. We couldn't isolate ourselves as priests from the problems of justice and dignity just outside the church door."

To Baroni, his responsibility as a priest required him to address the systemic causes of the problems which the people of God, in and out of his church, faced. If that put him confrontationally face-to-face against City Hall, so be it. If that forced him to seek friendly politicians in corridors of Congress, so be it. If that required him to campaign for candidates for public office whose views matched his own, so be it. If that meant entering the federal government, so be it.

And if Archbishop James A. Hickey, as spokesman for the U.S. Catholic Conference on Central America, was required to testify on Capitol Hill against Reagan Administration policies in El Salvador, that was fine with Baroni too. Using a lifetime of political experience, Baroni helped the archbishop prepare his testimony. Hickey was grateful.

To Baroni, marching in civil rights demonstrations, lobbying for higher minimum wages, protesting by laying a coffin on the Capitol steps, creating the Campaign for Human Development, and working to reinvigorate cultural identity and to build urban coalitions were legitimate priestly roles.

"I have never said that every priest should do what I did," Baroni said. "All I've argued is that I, because of my background, was ready and willing to do these things, and that they were part of my priesthood."

Eight months after joining the Carter administration, Baroni spelled out his position in a November 8, 1977, letter to Father William Downing. "There is a pressing need for all clergy to take an active role in our governmental systems," he told Downing, a Jesuit working for the U.S. Department of Housing and Urban Development's Chicago office. "Because all of the economic, social or political issues raised in the community are ultimately ethical or moral issues of justice, equality and charity, there is an implicit necessity that clergy people become involved." It was Baroni's most succinct statement of his views on priests in public office.

When Baroni took the Carter job, he was sensitive to statements by many in the Catholic Church, lay people, priests and clerics, that a priest had no business in public office. But as he saw it, when he accepted Carter's nomination, there was enough ambiguity in the Vatican's position to let him go ahead. To those who asked about his relationship with the Archdiocese of Washington and the priesthood, Baroni said he served in public office only after he cleared the matter with Cardinal William Baum of Washington.

Baroni was generous to himself in his interpretation of Baum's position. At the very least, Baum's position was unclear and indecisive. When he got the bid to enter federal service from Harris in 1977, Baroni wrote a letter to the cardinal, his religious and ecclesiastical superior. Baroni said in the letter that he wanted to take the Carter job and would unless the cardinal objected. When he did not hear from Baum, he interpreted this as tacit approval by the cardinal. Baum was not asked for, and did not give, overt approval to Baroni to take the job.

If the cardinal and Baroni had gone to church law, they would not have found a clear and unequivocal total prohibition against the acceptance by a priest of appointment to an office in the federal executive branch. But when Baroni took the job there was a strong indication of the church's overall view toward a priest in public office. That view was: Don't do it.

Canon 139 of the Code of Canon Law of 1917 said: "1. Clerics shall also avoid those occupations which, although not unbecoming, are alien to the clerical state. 2. Without an apostolic indult (special permission), clerics shall not practice medicine or surgery, or act as public notaries, except in the ecclesiastical Curia, and they shall not accept public office which involves the exercise of lay jurisdiction or administrative duties. 3. Without permission of their ordinary, clerics shall not undertake the administration or the management of the goods or the property of lay persons, or secular offices which involve the obligation of rendering an account; nor shall they act as procurator or advocate, except in ecclesiastical court, or when their own interests or the interests of the Church are involved, in the secular court. Clerics shall not take any part, even as witnesses, without necessity, in the secular criminal cases involving the possible infliction of grave personal punishment. 4. Clerics shall not solicit or accept the office of senator or deputy, without the permission of the Holy See in those countries where it is required, or, in other places, the permission of their own ordinary as well as of the ordinary of the place where the election is to be held."

Provisions 2 and 3 of the Code of Canon Law of 1917 would seem in a narrow reading to apply directly to Baroni at the time he accepted Carter's nomination. Clearly the public office entered by Baroni involved the exercise of lay jurisdiction and administrative duties. He was responsible for a staff and several million dollars of taxpayers' money. He had to report to the Secretary of Housing and Urban Development, the Office of Management and Budget, and the President of the United States. He had to guarantee that the employees under his charge were obeying the rules and the money was being appropriately spent. Baroni swore an oath he would do that.

On point 2, it was entirely a matter of judgment if Baroni's role was "alien to the clerical state." He saw his HUD work as a continuation of his work as an inner-city priest, task force director at the United States Catholic Conference, and as a consultant to parishes while at the National Center for Urban Ethnic Affairs.

Baroni identified with other priests and nuns in public office. Most prominent in 1977 was Father Robert Drinan, a Jesuit, first elected on November 3, 1970, to the U.S. House from Massachusetts. Before running the first time, Drinan sought and received from his Jesuit superiors and the Boston Chancery assurance that any service in the House would be compatible with his status as a priest and a Jesuit. In the key primary campaign, Drinan dismissed the matter of the propriety of a priest running for public office as a non-issue. Drinan quickly acquired a reputation as one of the ultra-liberal members of Congress, as a persistent critic of U.S. involvement in Vietnam, and as an advocate for increased federal assistance to help the needy. A lawyer, Drinan served on the House Judiciary Committee during the impeachment proceedings against President Nixon in 1974 and voted in favor of the articles of impeachment.

In 1977, when Baroni took his Carter administration office, Drinan was in his fourth term in the U.S. House. To those who questioned Baroni about his role as priest and politician, Baroni cited Drinan as an example of how the church felt about a priest in politics. Drinan, unlike Baroni, had to face the voters, and in the process of getting reelected, had to consider political ramifications for his district of the hundreds of votes he cast each year in Congress. Drinan, further out on a political limb than Baroni, was Baroni's protective flank.

Baroni cited the church's casual attitude in the early 1970s toward the presence of John McLaughlin, then a Jesuit priest, on Nixon's White House staff. McLaughlin was there as Watergate came crashing down on Nixon, and was one of the most aggressive White House aides in insisting that Nixon had done no wrong. McLaughlin's toughest test came after the release of transcripts of conversations among Nixon and his men in which the participants used some salty language. McLaughlin rushed to defend the language as entirely appropriate for men in high office in the privacy of their work space. Whatever the merits, McLaughlin looked and sounded ridiculous.

There were other examples that Baroni cited of people subject to canon law who served in public office. Father Theodore Hesburgh, president of Notre Dame University, held one of the country's more sensitive positions for fifteen years, as a member and then chairman of the U.S. Civil Rights Commission. He was appointed chairman in 1969 by the newly-elected Nixon. During the first four years of the Nixon Administration, Hesburgh strongly disagreed with the administration over substance and tactics relating to the achievement of equal opportunity for all Americans. When Nixon was reelected in 1972, one of his earliest acts was to dismiss Hesburgh as chairman. Hesburgh then resigned as a commission member. Hesburgh said of his Civil Rights Commission experience that it was a "lonely spot" for a priest, but "Even so, looking back over my 40 years as a priest, those fifteen years of service on the Commission were among my most priestly and apostolic—I do not regret one single day of this service."

Hesburgh held many other appointed positions in public life, including membership during the Ford Administration on the Amnesty Board which dealt with civilian and military personnel who violated the law during the Vietnam War and on the Select Committee on Immigration and Refugees.

Hesburgh, Drinan, and McLaughlin, as well as Baroni, began public service prior to the issuance in the spring of 1980 of a new Vatican statement on priests in public office. That was a much clearer ban on priests serving in public office than the 1917 Code of Canon Law.

In 1980, Pope John Paul II told priests and nuns in politics to get out. He told them to refrain from political statements and from taking sides on sensitive political issues. Many in the U.S. Catholic Church saw the papal decree directed primarily against Drinan. U.S. Church officials said the pope and the Vatican curia sent several signals to Drinan, which he chose to ignore. As a consequence, the pope issued his blanket statement.

The pope said there are different roles for priests and lay people in the political arena. He said priests should preach the gospel message, which includes a call for justice and peace, but that the priest's role as a symbol of justice and as an agent for reconciliation does not permit involvement in a partisan office where disputes over objectives and tactics are inevitable.

In John Paul II's view, the task of the priest was to inspire and motivate; the task of lay people was to run the secular in accord with moral principles. Addressing Brazilian priests in Rio de Janeiro on July 2, 1980, the pope said, "The priest's service is not that of a doctor, of a social worker, of a politician or of a trade unionist. . . . The priest has his essential function to perform in the field of souls, of their relations with God and their interior relations to their fellows."

The situation was muddied rather than clarified by a document on Religious Life and Human Promotion published in 1980 by the Vatican Congregation for Religious and for Secular Institutes. The document acknowledged that the issue of priests in politics is "a matter of heated debate and is sometimes misleading." Then the document went on to say that politics in its broadest sense requires responsible and active involvement by "all citizens."

But if politics, the document continued, "means direct involvement with a political party, then certain reservations must be made in view of the vocation and mission of religious in the church and in society, so as to arrive at correct criteria governing a possible involvement."

In the Vatican statement, there was enough flexibility for Baroni to say, as he did, that the church's view toward priests in public office did not apply to him.

In 1980, Drinan submitted to the decree, announcing that he would complete his current term because he was under obligation to the people of his district, but would not run again. In Wisconsin, Father Robert F. Cornell, a Norbertine priest and a Democrat who had served two terms in the U.S. House before being defeated in 1978, announced that, bowing to the pope's order, he would drop his plans to run again in 1980.

Baroni told the *Wall Street Journal* on May 8, 1980, that he was studying the pope's decree. Baroni said he heard nothing about it from his own authorities, and that he assumed the order did not apply to appointed officials such as himself.

In Washington, a spokesman for Archbishop Jean Jadot, the apostolic delegate and the pope's representative, said that the Vatican was applying general church law to the U.S. situation and was not singling out Drinan for removal. Jadot's spokesman said the pope was concerned about priests engaging in partisan politics and about priests, nuns and brothers involved in political causes. The spokesman said it made no difference to the pope if the causes were liberal or conservative.

The spokesman added that, strictly speaking, application of the general church law did not apply to priests holding nonelective, policy-making positions. "The Vatican decree speaks to elected public officials," the official said. That seemed to cover Baroni, as far as the Vatican office on Massachusetts Avenue was concerned. The apostolic delegate's spokesman and Baroni seemed in accord.

But within a few weeks, Baroni let it be known that he intended to leave the Carter administration, even if Carter were reelected, at the end of the first term. He denied that he was pressured by church authorities. Baroni insisted that he had decided on his own to withdraw from public office before the Vatican announcement, and his decision was not influenced by it. However, Baroni did not announce his intention until after the Vatican announcement and his letter to Carter followed the Vatican announcement. In addition, the impending statement by the Vatican was on the church grapevine and Baroni heard it.

Baroni said he agreed with the Vatican statement, and promptly added his own refinements to it. What the pope intended to say, Baroni explained, was that priests should not engage in partisan politics as candidates for public office. While saying this, Baroni was helping his friends get elected to Congress by raising money for them and assisting in their campaigns. He pushed pieces of legislation and lobbied for his interests on Capitol Hill and in the federal bureaucracy, usually in the name of Archbishop Hickey and the Archdiocese of Washington.

Baroni, of course, did not advertise his special interpretations of church rules and his differences with the Vatican. Witness this typical exchange at a meeting in February, 1983, of local directors of projects supported by the Campaign for Human Development. At the time, Baroni was a special assistant on urban affairs to Hickey.

> Baroni: "It's in the political arena where decisions are made that affect people's lives. . . . Christians cannot be absent from the political arena. Now they say priests shouldn't get in politics. I agree with that. I don't think priests should get into politics."
> Question: "What do you mean? The pope gets into politics?"
> Baroni: "I think if we get into it, we shouldn't talk about it."

While serving as special assistant to Hickey, Baroni worked with friends at the U.S. Catholic Conference on a policy statement dealing with the church's role in the U.S. political system. While the statement, which was finally approved by the bishops in March, 1984, did not specifically address the question of priests in public office, it did spell out an ambitious political agenda for the church.

> The Church, the People of God, is . . . required by the Gospel and its long tradition to promote and defend human rights and human dignity. This view of the Church's ministry and mission requires it to relate positively to the political order, since social justice and the denial of human rights can often be remedied only through governmental action.

The statement said the church's role in the political process includes these measures: education regarding the teachings of the church and the responsibilities of the faithful; analysis of issues for their social and moral dimensions; measuring public policy against gospel values; participating with other concerned parties in debate over public policy, and speaking out with courage, skill and concern on public issues involving human rights, social justice and the life of the Church in society.

The bishops added:

> We specifically do not seek the formation of a religious voting bloc; nor do we wish to instruct persons on how they should vote by endorsing candidates. We urge citizens to avoid choosing candidates simply on the basis of personal self-interest.

Rather, we hope that voters will examine the positions of candidates of the full range of issues as well as their integrity, philosophy and performance.

This veiled admonition to look at a candidate's entire record rather than on a single issue such as abortion was dear to Baroni, and he pushed for the inclusion of the statement during his meetings with bishops. Baroni found an analogy in the loss to the diocese of many of its young aggressive social ministry priests in 1968 when they rejected the birth control encyclical *Humanae Vitae* and were punished by Cardinal O'Boyle. Baroni said both the priests and O'Boyle focused erroneously, and to their mutual loss, on the single issue of birth control. As a result, many lives were hurt and the church lost some of its best up-and-coming priests, Baroni said.

He said that unless the church emphasized the importance of looking at a candidate's entire record, many Catholics would focus on the single issue of abortion. That would mean defeat of many progressive members of Congress, people who on other issues reflect progressive Catholic thinking.

\*     \*     \*

In speeches even before he joined the Carter administration, Baroni argued that the Catholic Church had been involved in politics for a very long time, and it was not necessary to go back to the de' Medicis to find examples.

In the United States, for at least a half century, Baroni said, the Roman Catholic hierarchy expressed positions on justice and peace issues, both of which, he noted, were primarily issues of morality. More recently and in his field, Baroni said, Pope Paul VI spoke of cities and neighborhoods in a May 14, 1971, apostolic letter:

There is an urgent need to remake, at the level of the street, of the neighborhood or of the great agglomerative dwellings, the social fabric whereby man may be able to develop the needs of his personality. Centers of special interest and of culture must be created or developed at the community and parish centers, and spiritual and community gatherings where the individual can escape from isolation and form a new fraternal relationship. To build up the city, the place where men and their expanded communities exist, to create new ideas of neighborliness and relationships, to perceive an original application of

social justice and to understand responsibility for this collective
future, which is foreseen as difficult, is a task in which Christians must share.

Baroni said that as priest and politician he did precisely what his
pope asked of him. Paul VI's letter of 1971 came when Baroni charted
a direction for his life and it strengthened his resolve to continue his
priestly ministry to urban ethnic whites as president of the National
Center for Urban Ethnic Affairs.

Baroni's career choices were criticized in his home diocese of Altoona and his adopted Archdiocese of Washington. "A number of priests
in Washington let me know they thought I was sticking my nose into
politics when I should have been, like them, working in a parish," Baroni said. That statement rang true for the 1960s, when Baroni supported
home rule in the District of Columbia, marched in civil rights demonstrations in the South and in Washington, and exhorted priests to join
him in political action on Capitol Hill. It was true in the early 1970s
when Baroni proposed precise and sweeping changes in government
policy toward neighborhoods. The criticism gathered strength when
Baroni entered the Carter administration. As the Catholic priest who
held the highest ranking office in Federal government, Baroni was a
target for political and theological conservatives who saw him breaking
an unwritten American ban on priests in politics.

Baroni said public service was his priestly obligation and ministry,
but others sniped at him. One shot came from Altoona, the city where
in 1956 Baroni served for the first time as a priest. It was there that he
started a credit union and supported a union organizing attempt, both of
which he regarded as part of his priestly obligation.

In Altoona, Monsignor Thomas Madden, writing in 1980 in the
*Altoona Catholic Register*, vented his hostility toward Baroni and Drinan:

> Last week we offered a prayer of thanks to God for the min-
> istry of Pope John Paul, upon the completion of his exhausting
> visit to Mexico. A closer reading of the major addresses that
> the Pope gave shows that he offers no support to the social
> technicians, whether priests or nuns, who are wasting their
> lives in the political arena. In effect, he is telling people like
> Monsignor Geno Baroni to get out of his HUD job and Father
> Robert Drinan to get out of Congress. They are not engaged
> in priestly work. Whether the political activists heed his call
> remains to be seen. The liberal press has given his proclama-
> tion of traditional theology a cool reception. But this very fact

is a warm accolade. Fractious bishops, priests, nuns and laity
can readily win headline space with rebellious laments. This is
all the more reason for us to close ranks in support of the Holy
Father.

Baroni kept the clipping from the *Altoona Catholic Register* in his desk
and showed it to visitors as an example of what he had to contend with,
especially, he noted, "from the Irish clergy." He hastened to add he was
overstating his complaint against the Irish, not only because his best
friends in the priesthood were Irish, but because many of the very top
social activists in the Catholic Church were Irish. People like Bishop
John McCarthy of Houston, George Higgins, John Egan, Timothy
Meehan, director of urban affairs in New Haven, and Michael Groden,
urban planning director in Boston.

In typical Baroni fashion, he complained that U.S. cardinals and
bishops systematically kept social activist priests from promotions and
power in the institutional church. "Higgins should have been a bishop.
Instead, they threw him out," Baroni said. Higgins denied he ever
wanted to be a bishop, and said Baroni and other social activists liked to
imagine themselves "on the fringe" of the church when they were "in
fact at the center of its teaching and practice." Besides, said Higgins,
McCarthy was a bishop, and he, Egan and Baroni were monsignors.

Baroni traced his style of priesthood back to his childhood and his
view of his father:

My father was an organizer for the mine workers' union. He
supported John L. Lewis and Franklin D. Roosevelt. I remember on Sundays we would come home from mass and my father would ask us what the priest had talked about. We would
tell him, and it usually was sex or drinking or money. My
father said he didn't have problems with any of those things,
so why should he bother. My father wanted priests and a
Church who would talk about injustice and poverty, conditions
in the mines and bad housing, low pay and medical care for
sick miners.

In the seminary, Baroni said, he studied the writings and life of
Monsignor John A. Ryan, the social philosopher and reformer. Ryan
supported Roosevelt in all four of his campaigns, and gave the benediction at two inaugurations. Ryan accepted Roosevelt's appointment to
the Industrial Appeals Board of the National Recovery Administration.
Baroni said that in the Mount St. Mary's seminary library he read the

Bishops' Program of Social Reconstruction, written by Ryan in 1919. The document called for minimum wage legislation, health, unemployment and old-age insurance and other pieces of legislation then considered Socialistic or radical. Later they became law. In 1920 Ryan became director of the Social Action Department of the National Catholic Welfare Council. Baroni said Ryan's writings and life had perhaps the most influence on his own life.

However, Ryan was an exception, tolerated by church leaders, Baroni said. He was "not part of the mainstream, any more than were the social activists of the '60s and '70s." Baroni was aware that throughout U.S. history there had been Catholic bishops and priests who advocated political positions that he would have opposed. He noted that in 1894, Archbishop John Ireland of St. Paul, Minnesota, campaigned actively for Republicans in New York State, provoking a strong condemnation of his activities from the state's Catholic bishops.

When Baroni grew up in the 1930s in Pennsylvania, many Catholics listened on their radios to the ultra-conservative Father Charles Coughlin of Royal Oak, Michigan. In 1930, Coughlin formed the Radio League of the Little Flower and spoke out on political and religious topics. He opposed the policies of President Herbert Hoover and supported the election of Franklin D. Roosevelt as one who represented true social justice. But later Coughlin turned against Roosevelt and vented virulent anti-Jewish beliefs. In 1936, Coughlin formed his own political party known as the National Union for Social Justice.

Coughlin targeted Monsignor Ryan, calling him "the Right Reverend New Dealer." As Adolf Hitler moved to conquer Europe, Coughlin supported him with pro-Nazi and anti-Jewish talks. After the start of World War II, Roosevelt wanted to stop Coughlin as a danger to the war effort. The church helped Roosevelt when Archbishop (later Cardinal) Edward Mooney of Detroit ordered Coughlin to stop his radio show. Coughlin complied. His newspaper, *Social Justice*, was banned from the U.S. mails under a provision of the 1917 Espionage Act. Coughlin returned to being a parish priest and was rarely heard from again. He died in 1974.

*       *       *

Baroni recalled for audiences that his first sermon as a young priest in Somerset was political. He told the congregation at his first public mass: "Not by Bread Alone Does Man Live, But by Credit." Baroni's story may well be apocryphal, typical of his pattern of reconstructing events to support his point. However, there is no question that very quickly after his ordination he was in hot water with his pastor, leading members of the parish, and the bishop for his involvement in issues that went beyond the narrow confines of the usual interests of a young parish priest. In championing the interests of striking railroad workers and supporting the right of police and firefighters to organize, Baroni found himself during his first few months in Altoona branded as a trouble-making renegade priest.

In a 1983 interview with Michael Creedon for the journal *Social Thought*, Baroni said his career of working for neighborhoods and community "all started as a parish priest":

What is the role of the parish priest in the neighborhood? When I was ordained, I watched poor working people borrowing money from finance companies and paying 30 percent interest and I thought that was sinful. I started a credit union and counseled people on how to manage money and loaned them money. It was a self-help group and it was done with dignity. But I had to keep talking about the philosophy of self-help. They kept saying, "Father, you do it. We think it's a good idea, you be president." I refused. I said, "you elect a president." We lose if we begin to do things for them. True, there are cases where it is necessary to do for them; perhaps they have a disability and don't know where to go and couldn't go anyway. That's charity and it is absolutely necessary. You have to make government meet its entitlement programs, but there is also an arena where you must tap into the human agent.

Baroni was asked why he left Altoona, and he replied:

Altoona was a railroad town, and there was a strike of railroad workers. They were looking for a priest to offer a prayer and bless the strike, and I went. I had just been ordained and I'm on TV. The Pennsylvania Railroad called the Chancery office and I was a marked man right away—a troublemaker. My pastor said, "You'll never be a bishop by getting into social problems. It's too controversial. You'll ruin your career." So I was worried about a career in the Church? That's not why I got ordained.

When he came to Washington in 1960, Baroni met Father John Cronin, a progressive on the staff of the bishops' association. In the

Ryan tradition, Cronin wanted the bishops to lobby for national legislation that promoted social justice, including increased protection for workers, a higher minimum wage, and aid to the poor for medical care, shelter and education.

At a seminar at Catholic University, Baroni met priests involved in politics across the country. "There was none of this putdown that priests don't do that sort of thing," he said. "I met priests there who were doing it every day." He continued:

> The traditional way priests dealt with politics was to call up an alderman and say, make sure the parking lot is clean on Sunday morning if it snows and I'll tell the people nice things about you. The truck came in time for the six o'clock mass on Sunday morning. The potholes outside the rectory got fixed and the street lights around the convent always worked. The priest would call up and get somebody a job with the fire department or the Post Office or the cops. In return, the priest might say a few things privately to some parishioners and soon it was out all over the parish that Father liked candidate so and so. But that whole thing has changed, and it had to. We got to move from that toward the public policy issues. It's those damned public policy issues in the public arena, like daycare and housing and jobs and food stamps, that really count. I can walk a guy through a welfare line and get him a few bucks to pay his rent or feed his kids. Raise the minimum wage or create jobs or job training programs in a piece of legislation and you do for thousands what I could do for one. It just makes sense that in this society, answers to critical human problems are usually found in politics.

Baroni said that as he moved toward the systemic approach to inner-city problem-solving, priests in Washington said to him, "Nah, we don't want to get into that."

The Washington priests, said Baroni, "were good when it came to collecting old underwear or food or money from their suburban parishes to take care of the poor in the city. But that was their approach: to 'take' care of the poor, not to join them in demanding better social services and jobs. The priests in the suburbs wouldn't attack government because their parishioners were the government."

During the 1960s in Washington, while a priest at Sts. Paul and Augustine Church and as director of Cardinal O'Boyle's Commission on

Urban Affairs, Baroni tried to be both parish priest and social activist. He believed he was not very effective as a parish priest in the traditional sense. His unease at hearing confessions, his low self-esteem as a homilist, and his awkwardness at public liturgies led him to believe he was not emotionally or temperamentally suited to be a parish priest.

Paramount in Baroni's complete conversion to social activist, however, was a conviction that the traditional role played by the priest and the church would not provide answers for the urban crisis he saw building all about him.

\*     \*     \*

Chicago, December 28, 1983—Monsignor John Egan is reminiscing about his friend and fellow-worker for social justice: "Geno's agenda was the church. He was a churchman first, last and always."

Egan listened to a question. Wasn't Baroni a very unconventional churchman? He never did become pastor of the parish in that mythical town he used to call East Snowshoe. He didn't often say a public mass. He hadn't formally heard confessions for many years. He didn't function in the traditional sense of being a parish priest.

Egan: "Neither do most college presidents. Neither do professors in our universities across the country. But I would put Geno's spiritual direction and the amount of it against anyone's. I think we will never know the number of public figures who maybe came in the cool of the evening or the early morning hours to seek out Geno's wisdom. I think he heard more confessions than he thought he did. The interesting thing about Geno was that he never stopped preaching."

Visitor: "But not from the altar."

Egan: "Who says you have to preach from the altar? I don't remember Jesus doing it. No, Geno wasn't that parish priest in East Snowshoe. Thank God he wasn't. That would have put a bridle on Geno, and the church and the world and this country would be poorer because of it."

\*     \*     \*

Washington, July 5, 1983—Father J. Bryan Hehir, director of the office of justice and peace at the U.S. Catholic Conference, talks about Baroni:

One thing his ministry has done is bring under the umbrella of the bishops and the rest of the church things people used to have to do outside the umbrella. That's the catalytic kind of force, the kind of work he's done. You have to look at his ministry for the past 20 years, right up until today, in light of and along with the theological development that's gone on in the church, precisely on this question of the church in the world.

Hehir strongly supported the notion that the Roman Catholic Church has an important role to play in making the world a more just and safer place. He was a driving force inside the institutional church in shaping the bishops' statement on nuclear war. This former student of Henry A. Kissinger at Harvard had many enemies. Among them were people who fear the church will be too dovish, too willing in a blind rush toward a weak nuclear policy to risk enslavement to a nation less scrupulous. Hehir's enemies argued that the role of the church is to offer moral guidance, and the role of priests is to remain on their side of the altar rail with the sacraments.

The church, said Hehir, has always been "worldly" in the sense that it maintained a diplomatic service and had a strong social teaching. But the issue was always the implementation of the teaching. For centuries, church leaders had spoken of justice and peace, sought to persuade their own people and others on moral issues, but rarely involved themselves or their own institutions in direct action to attain justice and peace.

What Baroni did, said Hehir, was to "get that social ministry legitimated as a central aspect of the church's life, moving it away from the periphery. The kind of work that Geno did on civil rights is probably the best example of that. He was working in the black communities and working on the civil rights question before somebody like Cardinal O'Boyle felt the pressure to have the church visibly present. O'Boyle had done certain things on his own in terms of desegregation and that kind of thing. Then all of a sudden the civil rights thing exploded as a national issue with a moral dimension and somebody said, Where is the church?

"At that point Geno is already the church on that issue. He can be called upon to bring the church visible at a national level into the debate, into the process, so that he legitimates the process that has now become legitimate and regarded as central to the church. Geno was doing it before it was regarded as legitimate and central."

Baroni moved the church away from providing the breadbasket to the poor to using its voice to ask why the poor had no bread in the first place, Hehir said. "When you start testifying, when you start asking about why they need the food baskets or why haven't they got the money for the rent or why do they pay rent and live in bad housing and start raising zoning questions, that becomes a different kind of ministry. It's still the church in the world. But it's the church in the world trying to reshape the structures of the world that influence and impact people's personal lives, their dignity and human rights."

Baroni helped the church come to see that its job, said Hehir, "is not simply to pick up the pieces of defective social arrangements, but to reshape and restructure and redesign those social arrangements. That's a religiously significant task. That's part of the ministry of the church. That's what we mean by social justice. And as part of the ministry of the church, priests must have a role to play in that ministry."

It was not an easy task for Baroni and other priests in the social ministry in the 1960s and 1970s to win approval for their activities from their bishops, Hehir said. "You always had to spend half your life justifying your existence." The accomplishments of Baroni and other social ministry activists, said Hehir, extended beyond the United States. Their actions encouraged the U.S. bishops to be more insistent that the Vatican II Council enunciate the church's commitment to work constructively in the world.

Baroni's participation in political causes and his service in public office were proper for their time, Hehir said, but they are not likely to be duplicated by a priest in good standing for a long time to come, if ever again. "Anybody today trying to do what Geno did is going to get nailed. Basically the Catholic Church is very conscious of being an institutional presence in society. That presence is embodied in certain people. It's connected to things like the habit, the collar. When you put someone in a national administration at a given point at a given time, you identify the institution of the church with that administration, with that program of action." The church hierarchy, said Hehir, does not want a "bracketed priesthood."

Sitting off to the side, Baroni listened to Hehir. Baroni could be silent no longer. "I think that it's interesting that not one single priest asked me how I got the job in Carter's administration or wanted a job like that. It was a rarity."

Hehir said that priests and nuns who seek to follow Baroni into a high-level government job or who run for public office, "will not enhance the social ministry of the church. They will endanger it."

\*    \*    \*

Archbishop Hickey of Washington had been talking to a visitor about Baroni. Was Baroni's an appropriate ministry for the modern Roman Catholic Church? he was asked.

"Sure it was," said Hickey, without hesitation. "He was simply putting into practice his Christian principles, the Christian teaching of the church, social justice. It was a unique ability he had, certainly not one that everybody had, or every priest is called to. Of course it was."

\*    \*    \*

Baroni was in Providence Hospital fighting his final battle against cancer. He was alert and attentive. Do you have any regrets that you spent so much of your life in politics, that you helped Carter get elected, that you served in his administration?

"No to all of them," Baroni said.

# 15

---

# Geno's Parables

Geno Baroni's basic speech was marvelous to hear and watch. It required eyes and ears open, a willingness to believe in him and to sus-
pend skepticism about what he told you, and an openness to enthusiasm.
Baroni was a superb performer. He was warm, witty, earthy on occasion, now and then confusingly professorial, emotional, and always sincere. Baroni's great contribution to the white ethnic movement in the
1970s was himself, given and dramatized through his speech.

His Center sponsored conferences, supported field workers, offered
guidance to community organizers, produced a flood of publications and
theories. It laid an intellectual foundation for a theory of ethnicity which
analyzed and justified the hopes and fears of white urban ethnic Americans.

Without Baroni's persona, the Center would have been nothing.
Without Baroni's personality and style, the white ethnic movement may
have succumbed to white racism. Through his speech, Baroni lifted
much of the taint of racism from the white ethnic movement. Baroni
was not a racist; he represented American ethnics. Therefore, American
ethnics were not racist. That was the syllogism, and Baroni made it
hold.

Baroni's speech personalized the white ethnic movement around
Baroni—The message and the messenger became one and the same.
The speech could not be read by anyone else. Several who tried to
deliver Baroni's speech, when he was forced to cancel an appearance,
failed. The importance of the speech was not in the individual combinations of words, but in the total package. Only Baroni could deliver
that package.

Baroni's platform style was folksy, chatty. He distrusted himself with formal addresses. That's one reason why he disliked giving homilies in church.

As a printed document, the Baroni speech bordered on the incomprehensible. He ignored ordinary rules of syntax and grammar, and he left sentences dangling and paragraphs incomplete. He went from point to point as a bee moves among flowers, stopping just long enough to collect nectar for honey and to leave behind pollen for propagation.

He said his speeches didn't work as written documents because he was a poor writer. That's not true. When he worked slowly and patiently, Baroni was not a poor writer. It's just that he didn't want to slow down or be patient long enough to write. Speeches were the perfect vehicle for him. Readers tend to focus on the written word. Speech audiences get the whole package—the words, the delivery, the hidden coded meanings. Baroni gave them the works.

Written documents have other characteristics that ill-fitted Baroni. They invite a second reading. Readers tend to demand a structure that permits and encourages a logical thought progression. Readers slow down, speed up, read again. Readers, at the moment they are reading, are more in control than the author.

Speeches are different, and Baroni made the most of his speech. He controlled the event, imposed his own logical progression, created and recreated events and presented them as facts when close examination would have revealed them to be impossible and fictional.

This is not to say that Baroni lied—he didn't. He believed the stories he was telling had a basis in fact. Perhaps they did not happen just as he said; perhaps the characters he named did not, in fact, exist. For Baroni, the stories he told and the characters he invented or altered to suit his purposes, were true to life. That was the important thing. Truth in detail wasn't as important as truth in the message.

Baroni offered several explanations and justifications for his stories. He said they were intended to do what a good anecdotal lead does in a newspaper story—draw the reader into the story by humanizing the issues. Sometimes Baroni said he told his stories to make people laugh, "like a comedian," he said.

Sometimes he said he told stories as parables, short fictitious stories that illustrated a moral attitude or a religious principle. Jesus Christ built a religious faith with considerable help from parables. They were precedents for Baroni.

\*        \*        \*

Geno had one basic speech. It wore well, but those who heard it often tended on repeat hearings to be more amused than moved.

Several nuns in the early 1970s heard Baroni deliver his speech and were so impressed they made him an offer. They were planning a gathering of superiors of the major women's religious communities in Atlanta, and they asked him if he would come down and give a five-day seminar on ethnicity. They told him their conference would be held in the Hyatt Hotel in Atlanta, that he would be expected to conduct his seminar two hours each morning, then would have the rest of the day off for visiting, sightseeing and relaxation. "It would be good for you, Geno," the meeting organizer told Baroni.

He accepted. When aides at the Center heard that Baroni was holding a seminar for five straight days, they warned him against it and advised careful preparation. He said he would be ready.

The first morning in Atlanta, he was a tremendous hit. The nuns applauded as if it were the greatest speech they ever heard, which, in fact, it may well have been. They talked about it the rest of the day, and when they passed Baroni in the hallways, they told him how pleased they were and how they were looking forward to the second day of the seminar.

The second day came. Baroni had notes of fresh points he wanted to make that day, but soon he slid right back to the basic speech. The same stories, the same rhetoric. That day the speech got less applause, but the organizers at the back of the hall had an explanation. Maybe he thought he would have a different audience the second day. They conferred with Baroni, reminded him that he would have the same crowd the next morning at ten o'clock, and suggested the need for fresh material. "I have it," he said. "I'm well prepared for tomorrow."

Tomorrow came, and once again, Baroni presented his few new points, then launched into the basic speech. This time the reaction was less polite. The nuns mumbled among themselves. Some left. There was a lot of loud talking at the back of the room.

Once again the organizers had a meeting with Baroni. They said the speech was wonderful, but don't forget that on Thursday, you will have the same audience you had on Monday, Tuesday and Wednesday. You need to enlarge your material, come up with some additional points, the nuns said. Baroni promised he would. But he didn't have enough material, and he knew his own habits.

So that afternoon he telephoned back to aides at the Center. He did not know it, but one of the organizing nuns had already called a contact at the Center and advised him of what was going on. Baroni told his aide in Washington, "It's beautiful down here in Atlanta. You would love it."

The aide replied, "I'm glad you're having a good time, Geno. I'm sure you're making very impressive speeches. We miss you back here, but we're very busy."

Baroni: "Maybe you'd like to come down and participate."

The aide: "I would, but I have heavy schedules the next couple of days. You'll have to do it by yourself."

Baroni: "I think it's important that you be here and meet these nuns. They're fantastic. They could learn a lot about the Center from you."

The aide: "I would like to meet them too, Geno. Maybe the next time."

Baroni paused, and the aide decided to stop the teasing.

"You want me to come down, Geno, and speak at the seminar?"

"If you want to," said Baroni. "You might want to come tonight."

The next morning, the fourth day of the seminar, the organizing nuns paced nervously in the back of the conference room as Baroni again made his new points, then drifted into his basic speech. The nuns looked around frantically. Attendance was down; it was going to get worse. Then the aide from Washington walked in. The nuns escorted him to the front row. Baroni saw him, and with relief, told the audience that he had finished laying out the big picture, now his aide was here with details. Baroni turned the microphone over and sat down.

*      *      *

Baroni did not have a written copy of his basic speech. His technique was to write key words on yellow legal paper or a large index card and glance at them periodically to remind him of the order of stories or points he wanted to utter. In later years, he joked that he spoke just like President Ronald Reagan—from two-by-five-inch index cards.

The key word system freed Baroni's eyes to stray from the paper on the rostrum and pass over the audience. He maintained eye contact, part of his magic in linking himself with his listeners. He added regularly to his key word repertoire, gleaning ideas from newspapers, books and spoken words of others. He massaged an idea in a series of speeches, tested the audience for reaction, adjusted with new formulations, until finally he felt he had it right. That idea was then ready for the index card on a regular basis.

Baroni's files contained scores of tapes of his speech delivered at different sites. No biography of Baroni would be complete without the text of his basic speech. The text here was taken from a tape of an appearance he made at the Potter's House on Columbia Road in Washington. He addressed a racially-mixed, liberal, urban audience. By the definition of the 1980s, many would be classified as Yuppies. Baroni got a good reaction, and he said he enjoyed the experience. There has been some slight editing for clarification. The speech goes somewhat beyond the string of stories he usually employed at meetings with urban ethnics. Its value lies in the analysis Baroni offered about his work. Baroni, knowing that many of his colleagues from inner-city Washington days and reporters would attend, gave this speech more care than his standard speech. But it was typical of the speeches that he had delivered in the first half of the 1970s to groups all over the United States:

"I guess like most of you who have been through the last ten years or at least many of us who have been here in Washington, D.C., I kind of came to Washington during the campaign of 1960, at the time of John Kennedy's election, and was very excited about the possibilities or promise of the American dream. I ended up the 1960s and began the 1970s wondering if the American dream was not becoming the American nightmare for everyone. I think we are in that kind of a crisis.

"Here are some significant events for me and they're important to what I'm working in and trying to talk about. In the '60s, we saw the tragic death of President Kennedy, Martin Luther King, Jr., and the civil rights workers—and their dreams. We saw the death of Robert Kennedy, civil disorders, the rebellion of the cities. We heard and read the Kerner Report—'a divided society.' We saw the growing moral conflict about Vietnam sap our energies and resources as a people, as a nation. We saw and felt all these things.

"We began to look at our ecology and we began to look at our nation. We began to see there was a great scandal of the so-called affluent American society. The scandal that we had tolerated: millions of people living in our midst without hope, some because of poverty, some because of race, some because of both.

"We've lost our sense of national purpose. As Americans, we're asking, 'Who are we? Who am I?' We've become, many of us perhaps, quite cynical. We saw in the 1960s two fantastic revolutions happening in our American society. On the one hand, we saw the youth revolt of, not all by any means, but a significant number of youths who began to rebel and develop the Woodstock, the counter-culture, the youth revolution against the war and many more than that very concerned about the quality of life.

"On the other side of the spectrum, in our cities, we saw the rebellion, the economic rebellion, the riots; but also a cultural explosion on the part of the black community, the brown community, the Chicano community, the Indian community. And so as these things began to happen and as we turn into the 1970s and we began to go to meetings and meetings began to break up into different kinds of groups.

"Blacks began to say they had to assert some kind of new awareness, self-respect, pride. Groups, conventions, conferences in Washington usually broke down into a Black Caucus or a Chicano Caucus and so on. This began to happen with quite a bit of regularity and I began to wonder about the cities, wonder about the war, wonder about whether or not we could create an urban society where we could live, wonder about what kind of mission it would be in an urban complicated technological society, what men might even hope and work for.

"I began to think about a lot of things. I began to think especially that perhaps the whole idea of American society, the whole concept of America as a nation, had been wrongly taught and perhaps even more significantly, maybe very much wrongly lived.

"And the one very important point as I began to look at northern cities and then to look at Newark. After Mayor Hatcher got elected in Gary, Indiana, I was asked to go out there with some friends from Washington and see a divided city. Literally not only to read what the Kerner Report says, but also see and feel a polarized, frozen society, black/white. I began also to wonder whether or not in the 1960s we looked at America as a society that was rich and poor and black and white. America perhaps is more than that.

"The National Commission on Violence talked about inevitable group conflict in our urban cities. I began to ask myself what's an option to this inevitable group conflict. I've been in Newark a number of times and literally found Newark is a complicated, racial, social and political cauldron. It could blow, not in the riots of 1967, 1968, but more devastatingly in a human kind of explosion.

"Can our cities be any kind of a place to live? Is there an inevitable group conflict? And in looking at that and in getting some kind of anxiety, I began to say who's left in Gary? Who's left in Pittsburgh? Who's left in Detroit? Who's left in Newark? Newark is the city of growing brown and black population. Who are the whites left in Newark? The white people left in Newark happen to be, not bankers, not professionals, not lawyers, not doctors. They don't happen to be industrialists. They're not even the heads of Prudential Life in Newark.

"The white groups living in Newark happen to be a very much first-, second-, or third-generation eastern/southern European; happen to be very much blue-collar; happen to be very much that group so-called 'the middle American' that is an exploited and courted group by politicians. It's been abused by the press and the media. The so-called middle-American, sign of majority, that large group between $5,000 and $10,000. That group caught between poverty and affluence. And so we had as a result of the 1960s a division of our society not just in terms of black and white, not just in terms of rich and poor.

"We had a big polarization in the United States. On the one hand, we had the upper-middle-class, whether it be Birchite or liberal or in-between. Then we had the youth culture, the children of affluence. Then we had the poor, particularly the black urban poor, the Chicano, Indian poor. And then, in our last group, we had all the others who weren't upper-middle-class, or youth culture, or poor.

"That large part is between $5,000 and $11,000, which makes up nearly a hundred million people. And within this group of a hundred million, forty million of them are what we might call ethnic American in my own definition, even though I think we're all ethnic Americans.

"At the White House Conference on Youth in Estes Park, I was a delegate to the race task force. It was interesting how the kids broke up. They broke up immediately as blacks, as Chicanos, as Indians, as Puerto Ricans, as Cubans, and then the European-American ethnics. The only ones left were whites; upper-middle-class who are traditionally known as white Anglo-Saxon Protestants who absolutely refused to be identified as white Anglo-Saxon Protestants and spent two hours trying to figure out what name they'd call themselves. And they ended up calling themselves the Nonethnic Caucus, thereby identifying themselves as an ethnic group.

"And those groups went away by themselves because the Indians, particularly, told the blacks and Chicanos to stop talking so the Indians could talk and so they could hear the Indian point of view. And it was very interesting that they went away. Everybody went away and could do their own thing. And only by looking at things from their own perspective, in their own dimensions, and their insight, could they come back and try to translate to one another.

"But what we're saying is this: in Newark, in Detroit, two out of three people in Detroit are either Polish or black. You talk about Gary, you talk about Pittsburgh, you talk about northern urban industrial and manufacturing cities of the north that are critical to the urban crisis. You're talking about blacks. You're talking about browns. In particular, you're talking about whites who are left in the city who are very heavily first-, second-, third-generation ethnic Americans.

"When the kids came back from Chicago in 1968, they began to talk about the police. They viewed police as pigs and in the George Washington University seminar I was writing on the blackboard and I said,

'Let's look and see who those pigs are—PIGS.' The police in Chicago are literally PIGS in the sense they are Polish, Italian, Greeks and Slovaks. And the children of affluence stopped very quickly, in the sense of not wanting to become intellectual or cultural or elitist bigots. So literally 65 percent of the Chicago police department are PIGS. In Pittsburgh, in Philadelphia, in New York, in Newark, and we must include the Irish. So when you look at the northern cities, you see rich and poor and you see black and white and brown and you see more than that.

"And I want to talk about four dimensions of the urban crisis and what may be some possibilities of avoiding inevitable group conflict if we can. And these four dimensions, one I have begun to talk about already, and that is economic. I used to go home in 1965 and talk to my brother-in-law, who is the youngest of sixteen brothers and sisters. They're from the western Pennsylvania mines too. Five of the brothers are policemen, and my brother-in-law works on trucks.

"So I come in from Washington and he says, 'Oh, here comes Father Geno Baroni from Washington. How are the blacks? We're making it. Why can't they?' That was 1965 conceit. And we got into a little dialogue, you know, a discussion about we and they. Everybody knows who we is and everybody knows who they is. And my mother, who's four foot, nine-and-a-half inches, said: 'Shut up, everybody. This is Thanksgiving. Sit down and eat the spaghetti. This is supposed to be a happy family. What is this dialogue? Stop shouting. This is America.'

"So that conceit of 1965 very fast disappeared with the white working-class worker who began to feel the price of inflation. He began to feel the squeeze and there are three dimensions of that squeeze. I've been in housing. There's no money in housing for anybody right now, the way we're going. Two out of five Americans can no longer afford to buy a house, including the mailman, black or white. And that's supposed to be a part of the American dream.

"Health care. 43 percent increase. Cost of education. My brother-in-law who makes $8,500 with five kids says, 'Hey, how much does it cost to send a kid to Georgetown?' He ain't sending those kids to Georgetown. His kids are going to go to Johnstown-Junior-Pitt and work, you know. At the same time, one operation in one family wipes out a family. I know families of eight thousand dollar bills, and so forth. So that anxiety about health care, cost of education, housing and all of that—that old rat-race for the American consumer goods and so forth, plus the fear, the fear of inflation, the fear of the high cost of living. That's a bit of an economic squeeze. I disagree. I think he's wrong.

"The second factor is the so-called working-class. I think we've got a great middle-class myth mentality about America. The second factor is the working-class groups. Not all ethnics are working-class and not all working-class people are ethnics. But I'm talking about that large group who live in northern urban cities who happen to be very heavily working-class and very heavily ethnic in my sense. And what's happened socially? Jackie Spence knows about Steubenville, East Liverpool, Camden, Massillon, Youngstown, Cleveland and all those places. Now in Youngstown, you don't read *The Washington Post* and *The New York Times*. In Youngstown, you read *The Youngstown Vindicator* and they hardly carry David Lawrence once a week.

"So the average working guy watching the television is seeing how the social revolution is going. He's seeing documentaries about Woodstock and about Kent State and about the war and demonstrations and the long hair and the kids and peace. And he's seen the black revolution on the three-minute newscast. He's seen that for ten years and he's beginning to wonder what is all that about. 'Those kids at Kent State. They got what they deserve.' They began to see anxiety. 'I want to send my kid to college but I don't want them to come back looking like that.' Like what? Well, like Abby Hoffman or Jerry Rubin. Not really that. The workingman is very much the really low man who wants his kid to go to college but he's afraid his kid will come back hating the family and giving up the value system.

"In Waterbury, Connecticut, the man said, 'I took my kid to J.C. Penney's and dressed him up, bought him all these clothes and sent him to the University of Connecticut. Now he comes back in dungarees with no shoes and no clothes. What're they teaching him there?' So there's an anxiety about that in the working-class who wants his kid to go.

"There's that anxiety wondering what the black revolution is all about. There's that anxiety about dress. There's that anxiety about a lot of things. But beyond the economic and beyond the social, the biggest anxiety of all, I believe, in the working-class white community of our nation is the cultural anxiety and that's an anxiety that's shared by everyone. I think the children of affluence have begun to ask, 'What's in America? What's the price of being Americanized?'

"My parents came to this country with a lot of hopes and a lot of belief in 'the American dream' to escape the oppression or poverty or whatever. They settled in a little town in western Pennsylvania that's near a place called New Hope. But I wonder what the price has been of being Americanized.

"When I was in the first grade, I used to take my genuine Italian salami sandwich and if I put it on the window sill of the three-room school and the sun got a little hot and it started to smell and the teacher says, 'Get that damn stinking garlic salami outta here and eat that good

All-American homogenized, tasteless, odorless Safeway baloney, you know. And I used to think she was talking about my name.

"But in the third grade. You know how those teachers used to ask, 'What did you do for the weekend?' I said I made wine. 'Well, how'd you make wine?' 'With my little feet.' She was an ecologist even then. She said, 'With your feet. That's not sanitary. That's not healthy.' So I went home very much ashamed and protested to my father that I wasn't going to make wine anymore with my feet.

"He asked why and I said 'cause the teacher said so. So OK, he went to the company store and bought a little pair of white boots so we could make our wine. This is the price of being Americanized.

"You see, I read all those Andrew Carnegie books and I had all the great American teachers and I read everything in that school and everything taught me one thing: Church, public society, that everybody's supposed to be an American. Everybody's supposed to throw off the slings and arrows of misfortune and be somebody and make it economically.

"That was the most important thing and everybody was gonna be the same and everybody was gonna fight the enemy—Communism, whatever that is. So my parents didn't want to teach me any language. They wanted to skip a whole generation so I'd be an American. There was nobody prouder than my father when my brother Angelo went to Korea. Johnny went to Vietnam. The same Johnny recently came back from Vietnam and burned his uniform. (Author's note: John Baroni is a career Air Force enlisted man who never burned his uniform.)

"Who are his cultural heroes? Who are the cultural heroes of the working-class? Do they relate to Woodstock, Abby Hoffman or Jerry Rubin? No. Do they relate to the black cultural heroes: Malcolm X, Martin Luther King, Angela Davis, Bobby Seale, Huey Newton? No. They're cultureless.

"My name is Geno. My brother's name is Angelo. Guess what my nephew and nieces' names are? Craig; Scott. And I've one named Rocky Ruggerio. Pretty soon they'll be Portnoy.

"But I have a nephew in northeast Philadelphia and my mother still kisses the statues and the nephews and nieces laugh at her. They've been burmacized. So while Americanizing process, the price of the blue star. In the First World War, 12 percent of the casualties were Polish-American, although they only made up 3 and 1/2 percent of the population.

"That's something the blacks and the poor whites have in common today. There's a price you have to pay to become accepted, for becoming Americanized.

"But more important than culturally is the whole question of what do you have to give up. I'm talking about value systems. I'm talking about life–style. I'm talking about a rat-race in order to make it economically. So the working-class, raised and trained and geared to by every institution to make it economically, to make it, make it, make it economically. The biggest graduates of Georgetown are those who make the most money. Or anywhere else. And that's something we have in common with the working-class with the children of affluence and the black community. They begin talking about a life-style. They begin talking about a soul. They begin talking about value systems.

"But how else could you relate to my mother about the flower children except through her own culture which is an old proverb she talks about? When you have two loaves of bread, what do you do? You keep one loaf for the body and sell one loaf of bread and buy flowers for the soul. I wonder how through that culture could you relate what flower children were all about. But how can you relate in the face of growing economic anxiety, growing social anxiety and growing cultural anxiety about 'Who am I?'

"What is sane? What is beautiful? What do we celebrate? What do you emulate in American society? What is our national purpose? What is our national identity? And just who am I as an American? What does that mean?

"One lady in northeast Philadelphia I know said, 'I got eleven kids. My old man came from Ireland, you know, and my great-grandfather came from so-and-so. Four of my kids say they're Irish. Five say Portuguese. The other two say they're Portuguese-Irish and the one kid who says he's an American is all screwed up.'

"So what is this country coming to? And who is an American? And I think the whole question of identity, as an individual, as a group, as a people, is a very important question. And I think you can't measure it. Many of us thought that the intellectual climate was the way to go, that Americans would go past religion, past everything else. So the way of life was intellectual. But you should look at the *New York Review*. The *New York Review* guys can talk to guys from *Commentator* [sic] and vice versa. But the guys at the *New York Review* and their publishers in New York can't talk to their truck drivers, you know. Most of the intellectuals of our colleges can't sit down and talk to the husbands of their good motherly secretaries. That probably is the new ecumenical movement. But what I'm saying is that we've seen the revolt in our youth group, as we've seen the revolt in the black, brown and Chicano communities. Are we going to see some kind of radicalization in the white working-class? Will that radicalization be positive or negative? Will someone capture the resentment of the white working-class when they begin to question the price of being Americanized?

"My brothers and my sisters can't cook at all like my mother and father. I'm used to snails, lizards, dandelions and squirrel. Rabbit was my favorite food. And I ate all those things because I was poor. Now you've got to have a fancy restaurant to find good snails, mushrooms and so on.

"What are my sisters and nephews into? Hot dogs, hamburgers and potato chips. These are simple things. But the biggest thing of all is what is the way of life. What is enjoyment of family, of trees, of children, of poetry and music? Many people in the working-class don't have time. They're in the rat-race, in the rat-race to make it to all-suburbia. And the children of all-suburbia are walking the streets of Georgetown, up and down, looking for what? Looking for the old community. Looking for the old neighborhood or looking to create a new community, hopefully.

"And we've got to create a sense of community. I married Merita Calaherd to Eddie Sabaleski outside of Washington. When she had her first baby she had a nervous breakdown. There was no grandmother in the neighborhood who would say in her third month to eat more honey or more salt. Or some other grandmother who would say, 'No. You eat more grapefruit.' Or an aunt who would say, 'When I had my first one, I did this. . . .

"Instead, her husband came home three nights out of the week and said, 'I've got to go back to work' or 'I've got to fly to someplace else' or 'I've got to be away this weekend.' Or he looked at her crooked and she started crying. And she lost the whole fantastic cultural base of an older community which she still needed.

"The economic system, the culture system, the dollar sign of the American culture for these people has not been enough. And what happens now when you go back to Newark, you go back to Gary and Mayor Hatcher? Jim Gibson and Harvey who's somebody you know went out to help Mayor Hatcher. They came back and said, 'Baroni. They're all your people out there. They want to secede. They're talking about drawing a line through Gary.' Black Gary will be a new city. White Gary, whatever is left, and so on.

"And people have now turned from hope to fear. What do you do in the midst of black rage and white fear? Then we have an inevitable group conflict that's going to fight for jobs and housing and schools and street lights. And then, more importantly, what is needed is economic, social and foreign policy after Vietnam.

"The working-class, ethnic and otherwise, is between $5,000 and $11,000. That nears 70 to a 100 million Americans or more. That working-class will help to determine American policy. We begin to ask ourselves are we going to build 28 million units of housing in the next ten years? Are we going to meet the human needs of hunger, housing, education, health needs of the poor in all our American cities? Are we going to do that? Where are we going to get the national will? Where are we going to get that public moral will that says take the money out of ABM (anti-ballistic missile systems) and the defense?

"If we've got the technology and we've got the resources, the gross national product and the economic know-how, what's missing? Something that's missing is the soul, the guts. How do we create that? When you go in Newark and you see a city that's dying, see people there who don't believe that it can live even if a doctor told them so, even if we had all the money.

"Where are we going to get the human resources to rebuild, to re-create an urban society that can create some kind of decent life-style? And I think that the whole concept is why we look at the whole thing economically, culturally, socially and politically. What's happened politically in the last ten years? There's been only one place in the northern United States where the working-class and the very heavily ethnic group has a choice, only one place and that's in Gary. In Gary in 1964, 1968, a man named Wallace went to Gary to the white working-class and he catered to every single fear, economic, social and cultural. And he went to other cities.

"In 1968 Bobby Kennedy decided to go to Gary against the advice of a lot of his friends. He said, 'You've got to go there or you can't go anywhere.' And so the difference was very significant. Bobby Kennedy catered to the workingman's hopes. He said, 'We've got to build an America for everybody or we're not going to have one for anybody.' And he catered to that hope, that promise, that might still be. He catered to all of us, to our hopes. Many politicians, too many politicians in Washington, national and otherwise, have catered, exploited and courted the economic, social, and cultural fear of white working-class ethnic and otherwise. And that's a great disaster and a great danger.

"Many of my liberal friends say they no longer can tell black jokes, only Polish jokes. The media has made fun of—the movie *Joe* is a devastating example—the need of stereotyping the workingman and also stereotyping the hippies in the worst possible light. A disastrous portrait of a young person trying to develop a life-style and a disastrous portrait of a workingman. Every single vicious stereotype is all condensed in one word and one voice and one bar. And the media has done that continually. So you have a whole large group of people who feel that they've been ignored, who feel that they've been neglected and who feel that they've been put down and made ashamed of. And they've begun to wonder themselves about their own identity, especially when you wash it out, especially when you're ashamed.

"The Jews can talk about their self-hate. The Irish can talk about their guilt and so do other groups. All groups have their own kinds of problems and particularly problems about their own identity. We either are healthy about our past or we ignore it or we respect it. What has happened in cities like Newark and Gary, many people have become ashamed of, many people have become negative, many people have become fearful. Many people have lost their sense of awareness. They've lost their sense of identity. They've lost their sense of pride. They've lost their sense of self-respect and find it increasingly difficult to deal with someone who looks different, who's in a different life-style.

"What is a different life-style? What is a different culture? What we have to say is this: It is not a melting pot, that America is the most ethnically and culturally pluralistic country in the world. Let's respect our own culture, our own heritage, and let's try to develop some respect for someone else's heritage and culture. Let's try to develop a multiracial cooperative rather than a competitive kind of society.

"Who's going to stop my brothers and sisters from this rat-race which is consumerism, of making it? Who's going to wage the war of repression in the main law of the working-class? We have a political problem. We have a cultural one. We have a social one. We have a racial one. We have an economic one. And I say there's only one option to the inevitable group conflict and that is to reorder our national priorities.

"But if the war ended yesterday, would the American public take that $30 billion Southeast Asia war economy and use it for health care, the housing, and educational facilities, and transportation, ecology and things that we desperately need?

"So who's going to dream the new dream? Who's going to develop a new kind of hope? What other option is there in our cities? We don't have anybody who can talk to LeRoi Jones in Newark except one guy— Tony Imperiale, who responds by getting a gun. It's very hard to find a Steven Adubato who can stand up to LeRoi Jones and say, 'Look, don't call me a no good racist. I was born here. I learned it here. But I don't own any mortgage companies. Now, I live in this city. Your kids are on drugs and my kids are on drugs. Are we going to live together? How are we going to do it?'

"In Detroit it took three years, from 1968–1971, working separately with a black and a Polish group until they agreed. The first thing they agreed on was to respect one another's culture and heritage. And then they agreed on the issues. The question is: Can we develop social and economic policies that will develop converging common issues? Can we develop a sense of identity, a sense of respect for somebody else's way of life, a sense for our own value system, and so on?

"How can you teach my nephew, Rodney Ruggerio, about black history when he has an historical amnesia about himself? You can't talk to kids in Steubenville College about why the Black Panthers, why Angela Davis, why Huey Newton, why black rebellion. You can't talk to those kids at all about that. They're very uptight about that. It takes a very smart teacher to understand and recognize that somebody in Steubenville has to go back and look up the Republic Steel strike, the coal strike, the coal mine struggle, the Molly Maguires in Pennsylvania, the riots, the violence of this nation and the real history of this country.

"It has to relate to that experience and that background, parents and grandparents. And only by relating to that grandparent can some kid come along and say, 'Man, my great-grandfather was in the Molly Maguires. The Black Panthers have nothing on us.' Why can't the Irish-American understand where Bernadette Devlin comes from? It's for the same reason that the Italian-American, the Irish-American, can't understand where Angela Davis comes from or why there is an Angela Davis. Why can't we understand?

"So there has to be a lot of work done in developing that kind of material. There's a lot of new black material with white working-class kids who're still in the second and third generation who're having a hard time because the white kids in a sense are also culturally deprived from their history, their background, their experience. It's always been put down. Your grandmother spoke Slovak. How many funerals have I attended in towns like Johnstown and Altoona and the high-school sophomore was ashamed of her mother and going through all kinds of Polish and Slovak customs at a funeral say, 'Mother, we don't do that any more. Don't embarrass me'? And so we're still on that treadmill in American society and we still have that dimension.

"The whole question is this. The question is a religious one. Who are we? Who am I? What's our American identity? What's our national purpose? When are we going to re-order our national priorities?

"I've seen people who have found their sense of identity and it's released a whole new sense of human resource, a whole new freedom. The people have been hung up with their identity.

"People who don't know who they are are not free and can't deal with themselves or someone else. This is particularly true of many whites from ethnic communities who tried to find their identity in a black community, tried to find their identity somewhere else. Dr. Robert Coles of Harvard and I spent a whole day discussing it, of the experience of going south and working with the children who were spit upon. We also had to go see the parents of the kids who spat on the black kids. He looked at both sides of that black/white thing in the south. He came into Harvard and he went to the Roxbury ghetto and he went there as a research person. The black community could tell him when to come and when to leave. And it was comfortable for him. He had a hard time passing Somerville, Massachusetts, which is white working-class and it bothers him very much. Why? Somerville, Massachusetts, is one of those places which has the highest Marine recruitment in the country. Those kids coming back from the Marines are second, third, fourth generation mixed ethnic Americans who don't have an historical base.

"They don't belong to a union movement. They don't have an historical perspective. They don't have a healthy feeling about themselves and who they are. There's a vacuum there. There's a connected cultural chaos there.

"So we have these kinds of dimensions. What are the alternatives? I say the alternative is to find that human strength, that human hope, that human vision, that human resource, positive and not negative. Find peoples' hope and cater to that hope and massage it and bring it alive and not to cater to peoples' fears and we must do that culturally and we must not ignore peoples' social and economic needs.

"My brothers and sisters are for everybody being on health care, but if one of their grandmothers needs a little bit of health care, don't exclude them. Working people who make $1.50 or $2.00 or $3.00 an hour can't see how somebody can do it on $1.50. If somebody had a broken foot, it's hard for them to deal with someone else's problem who's worse, who has a broken back. Both problems have to be dealt with. They're not the same.

"So I think we learned from the black community, the Indians, the Chicanos. The Chicanos keep telling me, 'We want into the American mainstream, but we find it's polluted. We have to give up our whole way of life, our whole life system.'

"Why can't we have a multi-diverse, a pluralistic, value system way of life and respect these life systems and stop being so competitive and develop a mutual interdependence? Can we do it? Is that the only option to conflict and chaos? Can we find a new identity? Can we find a new national purpose? Can we create a society that meets the human needs of the poor, which is always a test of standards?

"This is a good question to ask ourselves. There have been millions and millions of Americans who have been frauded into the price of being Americanized and now that energy is frozen and untapped.

"Very often in many cities like Newark they're very uptight and negative and very easily exploited and courted by politicians. How do you unleash that energy away from fear, toward hope and new dreams that maybe the American promise can work and that's a great contribution that the ethnic American could make in helping to resolve the urban crisis."

\*   \*   \*

## Cancer's Options

"One of the great things about human beings is you create and exercise your own options. And that applies to cancer as well.

"I'm in the middle of radiation, sick as a dog, lost 40 pounds, and they said, 'There's nothing this radiation can do for you.' And I said, 'Well, then, what the Hell am I taking it for?' And the doctor said, 'When you get done with this, we're going to give you something that's even worse, chemotherapy. That's going to make you sicker.'

"I said, 'What the Hell. I'm going to exercise another option. So I went to a doctor who said nothing worked. So when it was time for the chemotherapy, I said, 'No.'

"Let me tell you about doctors. You have all these old ladies whose doctors are dead. My mother had a doctor for 25 years and she had diabetes. She did what she pleased. Now her doctor's dead, and she's alive. She eats a lot of cornbread."

# 16

## Cancer

In July, 1981, at Georgetown University Hospital in Washington, Geno Baroni awakened after surgery. His sister, Rose, and two doctors, James Cantrell and Peter E. Petrucci, were by his bedside. "I had the tubes in my nose and in my veins," he said. "I looked up at them and started to say something when Jim Cantrell said, 'Not now. We'll talk later.'" Baroni missed the customary post-operative good cheer. "I remember thinking just before I fell back to sleep, 'Oh, oh, this one is bad.'" He was right.

He had awakened after 1973 and 1980 operations for cancer to find surgeons ready to advise, "We got it all." But in 1981, only a year after his second bout with cancer, he was ill with the disease again. There was no "We got it all" this July day in Georgetown.

"That's what they're taught to say, we got it all, whether they believe it or not, and they expect the patient to grab at it and believe it," Baroni said. "Too often the doctors feed the instinct for denial which keeps people with cancer from getting a realistic view of their situation." Baroni hated the cancer which killed him. But he never denied it. He confronted it courageously.

Baroni's third episode of cancer, unlike the 1973 and 1980 cancers, was inoperable. It had metastasized throughout the outer abdominal wall. Baroni was about to begin a period of intense pain and suffering. He was to undergo radiation therapy and chemotherapy that sapped his body, tormented his mind, and altered his personality. But finally he was brought to deal with what he called "the ultimate healing"—death.

While undergoing treatment for his third cancer, Baroni struggled for meaning in his life and his work. This book is in large measure the result of that struggle. He regarded the hundreds of hours of interviews he sat for as "a life review." On several occasions, he told his interviewer, "You are asking me questions about things I have not thought about for years. I'm glad I'm forced to think them through now."

Baroni's third and final cancer was peritoneal mesothelioma. It is commonly called asbestos cancer of the stomach. Baroni's doctors found in him an abnormal, seemingly unrestricted, growth of cancer cells in clusters on the outside wall of the stomach. The cancer had started to spread throughout his body. At best, he was told, radiation and chemotherapy can buy you time through a remission. Baroni was to have several remissions, but the cancer grew inexorably. Remissions cheered Baroni, though he knew they were temporary. There were times when his vibrant and optimistic spirit flagged, when he came close to despair, when he asked, "Why, God, me?"

He was 50 years old when his third cancer was diagnosed. In his position as an adviser to James A. Hickey, the archbishop of Washington, Baroni's calendar was filled with speeches, consultancies, Capitol Hill hearings, reunions with old friends in the church, the urban ethnic, neighborhood and civil rights movements, the press, and politics. Baroni saw the 1980 election of Ronald Reagan as a disaster for the country, but he saw it for himself as a mixed blessing.

He was out of government, where he had not been comfortable, and was back in his own natural element—as an adviser, an analyst, a gifted wheeler and dealer unencumbered by responsibility for a bureaucracy and policies he disagreed with. His job once again was to think, goad and connect people.

Before the diagnosis, Baroni talked with friends about the 1984 election and some way he could get back into his old niche. "No more jobs in government for me," he said. But he admitted a deep desire to make contacts with former Vice President Walter F. Mondale's inner circle, and to get there if he could. Baroni had worked for Carter's reelection, all the while predicting that Carter would lose. He did not agree with liberal friends that Reagan would fail as president and be out after the 1984 election. He recognized in Reagan a masterful politician who struck the right chords.

Baroni admired Reagan's political skills, his ability to read the mood of the voters and to address it in ways that Carter and his people had not comprehended. The political bug in Baroni was very much alive.

But his energy dropped. He felt that his abdomen was bloated. He experienced sensitivity and occasional sharp pain in the spring of 1981. "I felt tired and when I fell asleep in my chair reading the newspaper, I suspected something was wrong." He still called friends in the first hours after midnight and exchanged political gossip. He put his government retirement money into a house in Vienna, Virginia, and lived there with his sister, Rose, her husband, Joseph, and their two sons, Stephen and Joseph.

Baroni resumed checking into his office at the archdiocesan headquarters in northeast Washington every day. His government papers were filed by his secretary, Kay Shaunesy, and an associate, Mary Anne McNerney. Baroni spent most of his time downtown, on Capitol Hill or in any of the various offices where he was welcomed.

His doctors ordered Baroni into Georgetown for a sonogram, the test which uses sound waves to locate tumors. It was negative as to lumps, but it showed fluid gathering around the liver. "The doctors laughed and said I had a drinking problem," Baroni said. "They said I had something wrong with my liver and they wanted to do a biopsy and check it out. I laughed at that bit about the drinking problem. I told them that when I was growing up, we made our own wine and I had a few drops in water from about the time I was two weeks old. I could always take the booze or leave it. Not like some of my Irish friends. They couldn't handle it at all.

"All my church friends were Irish," said Baroni. "They took pitchers of whiskey straight with a little water. If I drank one glass, I couldn't see straight. They'd be at it all night, never faze them. Next day they'd be the first ones up."

Baroni reminded his doctors of a study by Andrew Greeley, the priest and sociologist in Chicago. Greeley found that Americans of Scandinavian descent had the worst drinking problem. The Irish, Poles, French, Germans and English were next. "But when you got to Mediterraneans, the Italians, Jews and Spanish, we went right off the chart because the incidence of alcoholism was too low," Baroni said.

Baroni's doctors ordered a laparoscopy procedure. He received a local anesthesia. An incision was made in his abdomen and a laparoscope was inserted. It confirmed the presence of fluid and the absence of a tumor. "I didn't think I had cancer because I didn't have a lump," Baroni said. Cantrell recommended exploratory surgery. It was performed by Dr. Peter E. Petrucci.

Baroni suspected the worst the day after surgery when Cantrell and Petrucci arrived at his bedside. "I read it on their faces and on my sister's face. You can't hide that kind of news. The doctors told Baroni he had a rare cancer and that they could not cut it out. They wanted to begin treatment with radiation and anticancer drugs.

"I was stunned," Baroni said. "Here I thought I had a liver problem, no cancer because they couldn't find a tumor, and they're telling me I have a very rare cancer that they don't know much about and probably can't do anything about. I asked how long I had. Cantrell said it could be six months. He just passed that by quickly. He said it could be years, whatever."

Baroni said later that as a general rule people with cancer should be told they have the disease. The doctors should tell the patient, he said, about treatment and outlook, including life expectancy. "There are exceptions for certain people, but I think you got to know," Baroni said. "Especially with cancer, people used to know anyhow when they weren't even told, because they suspected it. I used to see people as a priest. They knew. I knew. The family knew. But technically they didn't know, so you didn't talk about it. Nobody said anything. But you can tell from all the extraordinary stuff that's going on. It is far better to deal with it upfront than to deny it. The biggest thing we do, particularly with cancer, is to wish it would go away. You want to say, 'It isn't true. It can't happen to me.' "

"You got to deal with it," Baroni said. "You got to accept it. Then you got to learn to live with it. You got to learn to live with it like it's a chronic disease, like people got to live with a wheelchair or multiple sclerosis or blindness. The people who accept it, I don't mean resigned to it passively, go on living."

The next eight weeks were a challenge to Baroni's determination to deal, accept and live with his cancer. He didn't know during those weeks if he would be able to survive the treatment his doctors now prescribed for him. Baroni moved back to Virginia. Daily he traveled to Georgetown University Hospital for radiation. He looked back on the eight weeks of treatment as the worst period of his life. "I had pain I could not imagine before. I screamed and moaned. I wasn't able to sleep. I couldn't eat, but I wanted to vomit."

The doctors drew lines across Baroni's chest and abdomen when they took him to the nuclear medicine unit. The daily treatments were brief. He was positioned on a table, told to lie still. The staff left the room. He heard a few clicking noises. Then the staff turned him over and repeated the process. For the first few days, when the radiation was aimed at the chest, there was discomfort, but Baroni drove himself back and forth to the hospital. He slept more than usual, but he got back to reading the newspapers avidly. He was on the phone with friends and managing to keep up with church and political news.

The pain worsened after the second week. He became so weak and shaky he could not drive between Vienna and Georgetown. "I never thought of Geno as one of those men whose masculinity suffers when they can't drive," a friend said. "With Geno, his inability to drive was one of the worst blows." Baroni credited his sister, Rose, a nurse, with getting him through the period. There were nights when she had to administer heavy doses of narcotics to knock him out. On occasion he pleaded for more.

Several of Baroni's friends thought he would die during the radiation treatment. The friends established a support network, but he was mostly unable to respond. He was nasty to some, but Baroni's friends did not bruise easily. They persisted in telephone calls and letters, insisting that he keep up the fight.

It was during this period that a package of information about mesothelioma arrived in Cantrell's hospital office. The package was prepared by Marcy Kaptur, studying for her doctoral degree in urban planning at Harvard and the Massachusetts Institute of Technology. Cantrell said Kaptur's research was "as fine a product as a brilliant medical student could produce." Kaptur had combed the medical libraries in Boston for information about mesothelioma.

After eight weeks, the doctors said they could do no more, that any additional radiation would destroy the healthy part of his body beyond endurance. The treatments ended and the waiting began. Baroni, meanwhile, read Kaptur's research and grew curious about his disease. He speculated on what caused it. His first theory went back to his days as a young priest hearing confessions in Altoona. He was a very nervous young man sitting in the darkened confessional box listening to people confide their sins. The box was lined with asbestos boards to cut down the sounds. "I remember breaking off pieces of the board and putting them in my mouth," said Baroni. "It was a nervous gesture."

His second theory was that he was exposed to cancer while a child in Acosta. He remembered hanging around the Pennsylvania Railroad repair shops where asbestos was used as brakelining for railroad cars. When he worked at the plywood factory in Jamestown, N.Y., in the summer between graduation from high school and entrance into Mount St. Mary's College, "I wore asbestos gloves to handle the hot boards in the presses."

He recalled the summer of his 11th year working with his father to build their home in Acosta. He helped his father lay asbestos shingles on the roof. "I have no idea what caused it, and neither do the doctors," said Baroni. "But I can't help wondering."

The doctors suspected a link between the mesothelioma and the two previous cancers. The first was in 1973. A malignant lump was removed from his mouth. The second was in July, 1980. He felt a lump on his neck. Baroni checked into the University of Virginia Hospital at

Charlottesville. Two days later doctors removed the lump and adjoining lymph nodes. The surgeons told him after both operations they were confident they had removed the entire cancer.

After the operation that discovered the mesothelioma, Baroni had no illusions. He knew that barring some incredible breakthrough of science he had only a few years at most to live. He was determined to make the most of them.

"My first decision was to figure out how I could deal and live with my cancer," Baroni said. He read about thirty books on cancer and found them inadequate. He wished he could write one himself. He said he got little comfort from his friends, who seemed to be more ill at ease talking about his cancer than he was. "For some, it was obviously too painful." Vicki Mongiardo, his friend and longtime colleague at the ethnic center and in the Carter administration, broke into tears whenever Baroni or someone else mentioned his cancer. Friends tried to cheer him by telling him he looked great, when he knew he looked awful. He went to work at the Pastoral Center of the Washington archdiocese, but fellow priests and lay co-workers were not much help. They often seemed determined to preempt discussion about his health by bringing up business subjects.

Baroni tried to shock acquaintances into discussing his disease. People hailing him on the street with the question, "How are you?" were likely to get back the response: "Not so good. I have cancer." Baroni found their reaction unsatisfactory. "They would sympathize briefly, then get on to some other subject, and end the conversation with the standard Washington line: 'Let's have lunch sometime.' "

Others who knew about his cancer would say such things as "You look well. You're not supposed to look this well. Are you really sick?" Baroni said statements like that discouraged conversation. Baroni delivered mixed signals too. The mesothelioma, with its dire prognosis, altered his thinking. "I realized that I need someone that I could talk to, and who would really listen, about my fears, and my worries, and my hopes. I figured that was somebody who had been through the same experience." Baroni heard about a group of cancer patients at the Washington School of Psychiatry.

It was organized in 1980 by Dr. Robert Kvarnes, a psychoanalyst who directed the school for 26 years. Kvarnes developed prostate cancer in 1979 and underwent radiation. The next year, the cancer had spread to his bones. Kvarnes spent his professional career helping others learn how to come to grips with their own deep-seated problems. As he faced his own grave illness, he realized that it was time he apply his own therapy to himself.

The group had three other regular members: Dr. Morris Chalick, a psychiatrist with skin cancer; Dorothy Joyce, administrator of the treatment clinic at the Washington School of Psychiatry with ovarian cancer, and Gail Polsby, a clinical social worker with bladder cancer.

The five met Thursday mornings from nine until noon every week. They allowed only the complications of their illness to keep them away. Baroni found in the group something he felt he could not get elsewhere, a free and honest sharing of the fear and agony of cancer. He saw it as an extension of his ministry as a priest and human being.

Baroni's priesthood put him on the defensive, forced to explain how a merciful and all-loving God could allow cancer to afflict the human race. Baroni offered no theological explanation or justification. He merely shrugged his shoulders at the question, and said, "It's just human nature." He would have liked a better explanation. But theology was not his strong point. Nonetheless, he struggled to make sense of the situation. "In the old days," he said, "people didn't raise questions about why God did something or other to them. They accepted it and they had their family and friends and community to help them get through it." To Baroni, the old days were the days, real and fantasized, of a simpler life in pre-immigrant Europe or his Pennsylvania boyhood.

His shrug of the shoulders and explanation that cancer could not be explained except as "human nature" failed to satisfy, Baroni conceded, many of the cancer patients who called upon him for comfort. He had a lengthy conversation over lunch at a shopping mall in Tyson's Corner, Virginia, with a woman who pressed him to explain how a God who permitted human beings in the prime of life to be struck down with cancer could be called good and loving. Baroni said God does not intervene in natural events. She asked him, "But why does a God who loves people cause them to suffer this much?"

"I don't have any problems with that."

"But do you believe God loves us?" the woman persisted.

"I don't have any problems with that," Baroni said again.

Baroni acknowledged later that he was as hard-pressed as the woman to understand why God allowed people to be stricken by cancer, especially during their productive years. He said he believed in a natural flow of events, that he rejected the notion that God chose certain people in advance to die of cancer. Nor does God intervene in the human flow, Baroni said. But he hoped and prayed for such intervention. That was dramatized by his 1982 trip with his mother to Lourdes and occasional visits to faith healers. Baroni found prayer awkward and discussion of it and other theological issues painful and embarrassing. Part of this stemmed from his lack of self-confidence about his formal education, including his seminary training.

Baroni had no doubt about his ability to read the mood of Congress, to assess people as friends or foes, to forge networks, and to play the political game. He was confident in his ability to survive in the institutional church. From his crises with Hannan over civil rights, O'Boyle over Pope Paul VI's birth control encyclical, and Baum over a priest in politics, Baroni learned the fine art of clerical maneuvering.

But on personal issues like prayer and the justice of a God who created cancer, Baroni was ill at ease. He saw no conflict between his religious beliefs as a Catholic and injustice and lack of mercy in the world. One of the group members pressed Baroni on whether he thought there was a hell. When he answered, "I have no problems with that," she accused him of evading her and giving a glib reply to a seriously-intended question. Baroni was hurt. He felt he should have been able to convince her on the basis of his own belief.

Baroni was jealous of fundamentalist Christians. He recalled peering as a child through the windows of a Pentecostal church in Acosta. "We called them the 'holy rollers.' We saw them with people on the floor, and the singing, and snakes and the whole bit. We may not like it or we thought it was silly or dangerous or failed to do anything for people. But we had to admire and envy the faith those people had."

The Kvarnes group functioned on the theory that cancer was more than a crazy growth of unwanted cells that could only be brought under control with surgery, radiation and chemotherapy. The Kvarnes group members, including Baroni, believed that cancer could be controlled by the mind. Baroni likened the Kvarnes theory to faith-healing. Baroni was of two minds about faith healing. He wanted to believe it. There was skepticism, but also hope, in his mind and heart during the journey to Lourdes. On some occasions, Baroni explained this trip as an effort to appease his mother, who believed in the possibility of a miracle for her son. Baroni insisted on these occasions, "I didn't go there expecting to be cured of cancer."

With others, Baroni pointed out the evidence at Lourdes of miracle cures. Asked whether he thought divine intervention was plausible, he said, "Anything is possible, but I'm not counting on it." Belief in a miracle cure through an act of God or injections of laetrile was dangerous, Baroni said, if it was used as a device for failing to come to grips with the reality and urgency of the cancer. To Baroni, a life review and reconciliation with the living were vital steps in dealing with the cancer.

Kvarnes told members of his Thursday morning group and fellow psychiatrists that he was impressed by the evidence that cancer could be prevented, controlled and even reversed if the individual's will is strong enough. "We're going on the hunch that what we're doing makes a lot of sense," Kvarnes told Colman McCarthy, a columnist for *The Washington Post*. Kvarnes continued:

> It will be a while before we compile a record that would sway any skeptical physician. There's an absence of a caseload. Say you have 100 cases that you worked on. You can report that 78 percent of the time you get this, in 21 percent you get this, and in one percent that. We don't have those kind of data at all. The hunch that we're going on is that the person's attitude affects the way that the body works against the cancer cells. The mediating agent seems to be the immune system. We're going on the pretty strong hunch that we can, by our efforts, influence the way the immune system works. I say hunch because it's not something that's verified by our or anyone else's statistics.

"I don't go as far as Bob Kvarnes intellectually," Baroni said. "If you got bit by a poisonous snake and sat there and said, 'I'm the greatest and God is going to heal me,' you'll die. The facts of life are fate and faith. You could walk across the street in Israel and get hit by a stray bullet and be as innocent as could be. If that bullet hits, it hits."

Baroni liked to tell a story about Monsignor Egan of Chicago. "Jack Egan had his heart attack in Ireland right across the street from the finest cardiac hospital in the country. If he had been somewhere else, say all the way across Ireland, he would have died before they got him to the hospital. So it's fate. Fate and faith are like the salt and pepper you put into a stew," Baroni said. "You mix them in. If you put too much of one or the other in, you'll choke or it will taste bad or you'll get sick. Fate and faith are strong stuff and you have to be careful about them."

Gail Polsby, mother of two adopted children, saw in the Kvarnes program an opportunity to talk on a regular basis with people who understood the "hard and lonely time" that cancer patients go through. That was also one of Baroni's motivations, irritated as he was with the inability of his family, co-workers and friends to deal with talk about his cancer.

Baroni felt qualms as a Roman Catholic about his refusal to suffer in silence. "We were always taught to keep our mouths shut about our sickness," said Baroni. "We were told to pick up our cross and carry it without complaining. That's the old Catholic way. There was something to it. You couldn't live and expect other people to live as if you were going to die the next day. You had to do some pretending for the mental health of others."

Times changed, Baroni said, but not necessarily for the better. In the old days, he said, people had a support system. "If somebody got sick or lost a job, my mother was over there with a few potatoes and a piece of meat. Or some neighbor would take them a bucket of coal, and somebody, the priest or the neighbors, paid the rent, or the landlord let it slide. People had support systems. When a neighbor died, my mother went over to wash the house because you didn't want people coming into a dirty house. Then she'd bake a ham. It was always when somebody dies, bake them a ham."

The collapse of the support system in America was a recurring Baroni theme. He pinpointed the historic strength in ethnic urban neighborhoods of such institutional support systems as churches, unions and fraternal organizations. They helped create interpersonal support systems through which people came to one another's aid. "My mother who took a pan of soup to a neighbor back in Acosta was a support system," Baroni said.

Baroni saw a destructive cycle. When support systems deteriorated, the neighborhood declined. Likewise, when external forces damaged or destroyed the neighborhood, the internal systems collapsed. Thus Baroni saw a connection between deterioration of a neighborhood and decline of the family, the alienation of the individual from society, and subsequent loss of moral standards. Baroni theorized about a linkage between his cancer and the collapse of the support system. That system, he said, meant that sick people found consolation in the traditions of the community. Sick people knew they were understood and loved. They did not have to reach out to strangers for support. In these days, said Baroni, therapy groups replaced neighborhoods as a source of support.

As on so many other occasions during his life, Baroni took a personal tragedy and saw in it a systemic problem that required solutions larger than the individual involved. The intertwining among personal elements and community responses was at the heart of the Baroni philosophy. "Self-help is self-determination and self-reliance," he said in the introduction to *Neighborhoods: A Self-Help Sampler.* "Self-help brings people together to focus on the needs of their neighborhoods and their community. Through self-help people are able to generate support for their work from local and federal resources."

Baroni knew that dying was an individual act and no person could know in advance how he would face his own death. Through the Kvarnes group and in other ways he reached for help. "Even the bravest need a support system," Baroni said. "The brave may have faith in themselves and confidence in an afterlife. But with cancer you're so alone."

While struggling to sustain life, Baroni tried to accept death. He complained that the church had not learned how to deal with death. The church revised its liturgies for the sick and the dead during Baroni's lifetime. He liked that, but thought it did not go far enough. The church offered a new version of the old sacrament, extreme unction. It had been reserved for those in extremis. It amounted to a virtual concession that the anointed person was in the terminal stage of life.

The new sacrament called the anointing of the sick remained within the context of an eternal future of heaven or hell. Death is still its premise and serious illness its occasion. But there was more emphasis on getting well to continue life and a slight deemphasis on accepting death gladly as the entrance step toward eternal happiness. Baroni said he liked the new rite because of its focus on "healing" rather than death.

To deal with death, Baroni went outside the Catholic Church to the St. Francis Center, a counselling service for death and dying founded by his Episcopalian priest friend, William Wendt. Baroni was intrigued by the deaths of two politicians. He admired the way that Philip H. Hart, Democratic senator from Michigan, died in his Virginia home in the company of his wife and children. Hart arranged his own funeral service, including selection of a plain pine box as his coffin. But Baroni was distressed by the death of Hubert H. Humphrey. Sometime after the former vice president died, Baroni was at the racecourse at Laurel, Maryland, where he met Dr. Edgar Berman, one of Humphrey's political advisers and personal friends. Berman described for Baroni Humphrey's final months of suffering, including his search for a miracle cure.

"Phil Hart came to accept that the final healing was death," Baroni said. "Hubert saw death as a defeat and he could never accept any defeat," Baroni said. "I wish I could go Phil Hart's way. I know I don't want to go Humphrey's way."

Hart was counselled by Wendt and others at the St. Francis Center. Wendt and his colleagues were good listeners and questioners. They gave to the dying the impression they have all the time in the world to hear them talk. For his counsellor, Baroni picked Julie Severance, a former Catholic in her 40s.

He turned to Severance in September, 1983, when he began to experience bloating and new pains in the stomach. The doctors told Baroni they thought the cancer had spread to the intestinal tract. A tumor blocked the tract and surgery was needed. Severance met with

Baroni in the parlor at St. Matthew's Cathedral Rectory on the day he got the bad news. Under the circumstances, he seemed remarkably content. "There are still things I would like to accomplish. There are still dreams which I would like to make real," Baroni said that day. "But I think I better look at it like I'm in a World Series. I'm ahead three games to two, but I'm losing the sixth game."

"Are you sure it's not the fifth game instead of the sixth?" Severance asked.

"No, it's the sixth. I'm just glad it's not the seventh."

"Geno accepted the inevitability of death," Severance said, "but he was not ready to do the dying right then."

Baroni's tranquility after receiving the bad news did not surprise Severance. "I have been talking with him for 18 months and have never heard any rage," she said. "Of course, he may rage in private." Baroni picked up this point with a story. "A woman I know, a terrific athlete, got cancer and got awfully angry when she couldn't run her three miles a day or play good tennis any more. She said to me, 'I'm so mad I want to kill or hit somebody.' I told her to get a rubber hose and to beat the hell out of the furniture and to let her anger escape that way."

Baroni did not use a rubber hose against furniture to exhaust his emotional stress. He found comfort in work, insisting that he wanted to remain active on Hickey's staff until he died. Baroni wanted a quick and painless death. He spoke enviously of people with heart disease. "They can die in bed at night never knowing what hit them or they can be walking along the street or driving a car and it's all over, just like that," said Baroni, snapping his fingers. "They don't have to worry about lying in bed with a tube coming out of here and another one out of here with all those people standing over you and waiting for you to die."

"People with bad hearts," he said, "don't have to worry about pain and drugs that you can't get enough of. They don't have to worry about being there hour after hour knowing that you're never going to get up and work or read the newspaper or have another dish of pasta. That's what's kept me going through my treatment, the knowledge that it will probably work and I'll be able to read *The New York Times* and have a big dish of fettuccine Alfredo. But when that hope is gone, what do you have left? You have the fear of the unknown. I don't know how much pain I can take. I know that I don't do well with pain, that I can't fight it by myself. I can feel it coming and I'm afraid of it. That's why when they talk to me about more radiation or chemotherapy, I ask them, 'But will it do any good?' Because if there's no hope that it will do any good, I don't want it. That's the point when I got to face the reality that the only healing is the final healing—death."

An insomniac throughout his life, Baroni became even more unable to sleep at night as his illness progressed. This mystified him and his doctors. He thought that the cancer would weaken him and demand that he slow down in body and mind. Instead, Baroni accelerated. He over-scheduled events that forced him to perform before people, in one-on-one lunches, at conferences, at political meetings. He sought events where he would be known, asked about his cancer, but challenged to get on with the larger purpose of the assembly. As long as he could, Baroni was determined to keep busy and useful.

"I'm not going to sit in my room and wait until I get sicker," he said. "I have to keep believing I have a future. I can't make wild promises to people that I'll do things a year from now," Baroni said in the autumn of 1983 to Rabbi Eugene Lipman of Washington's Congregation Temple Sinai. Lipman said that when Baroni left his home that day, he cried.

Baroni resolved to resist the tears and the inevitable as long as he could, in his own way.

Baroni told Severance that his most important priority was the completion of this biography. Severance asked Baroni in 1983 to list the unfinished work of his life in the order of importance. Baroni did not hesitate. "The book is number one on the list," he said.

During his final three years Baroni spent more than 200 hours in interviews with the author of this biography. He was a difficult person to interview. He did not like to say, "I don't remember" or "I don't know," though he was urged to do that when it was the case. His tendency, when asked questions that he didn't want to answer or didn't know the answer to, was to slip into an anecdote. He was hard-pressed to answer "why" questions. Unwilling or unable to explore his own motives, he recited facts or changed the subject.

Several methods were used to jog his memory. Other people were interviewed and Baroni was questioned about their recollections. Did he remember the same way? Was his recall different? His frequent response was to tell complimentary stories about the person who had been interviewed, not to deal with the question before him. Another method to elicit information from him was to prepare a transcript of a prior interview, then ask him to expand on it. After a while, it became clear that he did not intend to read the transcripts. He said, "I've been busy. I haven't been able to get to it."

But that wasn't always the case. He was very precise on his un-happy experiences as a young priest in Altoona and Johnstown, and offered an amazingly detailed account of the pastors under whom he served. One day he volunteered the names of several psychiatrists and therapists who worked with him during the bad months in Johnstown, in Baltimore at the Seton Institute, and during his dark days in Washington. "Some of them are still around. Call them up," Baroni invited.

During early interviews, Baroni said there were things in his life that he thought were not appropriate for the book. He said one of those things was how he got to Washington. "I don't know if I really want to talk about that in the book," he said. There were many stories in circulation about that. The one that some of his friends liked was that he had blessed a strike in Altoona and had been thrown out by the bishop who was under the influence of the mine owners. The story fit nicely into Baroni's life as a social activist struggling and risking for the working-class and the poor.

The story got into print during the middle 1960s, five years after Baroni arrived in Washington and his assignment to Sts. Paul and Augustine Parish. The writers of those accounts did not include in their stories the sources for the report on the exit from Altoona. It is probable, but admittedly conjecture, that Baroni was the source. But an examination of available transcripts and tape recordings of his speeches from that era does not turn up any instance in which Baroni publicly said he was thrown out of Altoona because he blessed a strike. Baroni made no effort to stop the spread of the story, and it was often used in introductions of him. The story was told at his funeral.

When asked for this biography for his recall of his departure from Johnstown and Altoona, Baroni said, "It didn't exactly happen that way"—that he was thrown out by a pro-coal company bishop. Baroni volunteered considerable detail on his difficulties as a young priest with his pastors. He used names freely, but in writing this book, some names were deleted to shield identities and preserve reputations.

In 1983, Baroni arrived for an interview over lunch at a restaurant in downtown Washington and said he had been thinking about the psychiatric care he had received through his adult life and how that should be treated in the book. "I don't want a psycho history," he said. "But I think the business about my problems and my therapy belongs in the book. It might be useful to some people. If I could make it, then others can make it."

\*         \*         \*

To many of Baroni's friends in trouble over the years, the words—"If I could make it, you can make it" and his admission of undergoing psychiatric care were consolation for their own distress. Baroni had one special case—a woman he first met in the early 1960s in Sts. Paul and Augustine. She appeared to be on the thin edge of sanity. Finally she was admitted to St. Elizabeth's Hospital in Washington. From there, several times a week, sometimes every day, for more than ten years, the woman telephoned Baroni. She took no guff from rectory housekeepers and secretaries. When she wanted to talk to Baroni, she got through.

"On some days, she was fine," he said. "She could carry on a conversation. We'd talk for a few minutes about the church or the neighborhood or old days, and I think it did her some good. But on other days, she would ramble and I'd just listen and keep saying yes and her name."

Baroni returned from out-of-town trips and found a stack of messages that the woman had called. She had priority among his return calls. He gave her his home number and now and then the phone rang in the early hours of the morning. As his cancer worsened, he asked, "I wonder who'll talk to her after I can't."

*        *        *

It is absolutely clear from interviews with Baroni and others that while he may have been on the verge of a nervous breakdown in 1960 in Johnstown which merited psychiatric treatment, he never suffered from a psychosis or neurosis. At one time Baroni went into deep psychoanalysis. That and milder therapies were part of a search for self-discovery which Baroni constantly pursued. In later years, he was rarely in the sort of crisis that required serious therapy. He looked on the almost constant therapy he received over two decades as a preventive measure against the kind of crisis he experienced in Johnstown. "He was as stable as you or me," said someone in a position to evaluate Baroni. That is not to say that he successfully avoided personal crisis. He had his share of human failings, as he often readily conceded.

"Who am I?" he asked himself, friends and audiences throughout the country. He identified his search for self-identity and understanding with the identity struggle faced by urban ethnics, caught in conflict between old-world values and new-world customs and expectations. To Baroni, young urban ethnics faced the "Who am I?" question every time they wondered if they should buy a house in the old neighborhood with their parents and church and other familiar marks or in a suburb. For Baroni, the choice was simple: Stay in the neighborhood.

In an article called "Ethnicity and Public Policy," Baroni wrote that except for the book *Beyond the Melting Pot* by sociologist and later U.S.

Senator Daniel Patrick Moynihan and sociologist Nathan Glazer, and writings by Father Andrew Greeley, few experts accepted the importance of the ethnic factor in American life.

"I believe," Baroni wrote, "that all segments of American society are in the process of redefining themselves by asking, 'Who am I?' and 'Who are we?' as Americans. As our society continues to struggle with its national sense of identity, commitment and purpose, understanding the ethnic factor may well be the key to understanding our northern urban cities. Man needs to know his own story," Geno said, "to develop his own perspective if he is to be free to relate to others." This was Baroni talking about himself and the urban ethnics whose mission he undertook.

Baroni said that urban ethnics in the late 1960s suffered from four categories of anxiety:

——Economic anxiety: illustrated by rising inflation, fear of unemployment, job security, etc. The lower middle income urban ethnic knows he can no longer afford the house he wanted. He is also worried about inflation, job competition, the cost of health care for his family and education for his children.

——Social anxiety: reflected in the attitudes toward new life-styles of youth on the one hand and ghetto rebellion on the other. The country is in the midst of vast and rapid social change. Few, if any, institutions helped him understand social change or how to deal with it. Many others catered to his fears rather than attempt a ministry to his alienation, legitimate needs or hopes. He found that he could not relate to media oriented radicals or Woodstock or college kids in revolt, and now he finds himself trying to understand dimensions of the increasing number of blacks and browns with whom he shares the city.

——Cultural anxiety: produced by the melting pot myth and the Americanization process that dictates everyone is to be "the same." But in reality he lives in the most ethnically and culturally pluralistic country in the world where he never has been taught to respect a variety of life-styles, including his own background and heritage. Man needs to know his own story, to develop his own perspective if he is to be free to relate to others.

——Political anxiety: reflected by mass media politicians who ignore the legitimate needs of the worker—or massage his economic, cultural and social fears instead of challenging his hopes. His suspicions of the politicians begin to grow with each broken political promise and with each political lie that brands him as the scapegoat for all the social and racial problems of society.

Baroni's enthusiasm for therapy was essential to his belief that human beings should live an "examined life." He believed it was the essence of human existence to probe the depths of one's soul, life and imagination.

The ethnicity which Baroni probed had its own identity problems. Clearly ethnicity is not quite political or religious, but it is very political and religious. Nor is it correct to analyze ethnicity from one ethnic perspective. The Poles have their view; Italians another; Germans another; Irish another. Baroni, who felt rather than intellectualized, was bound up in the political and religious aspects of ethnicity. It was only fitting that he should have had as much trouble answering the question "Who am I?" as did urban ethnics in their troubled neighborhoods and alien suburbs all over America.

In a chapter for the book *Pieces of a Dream*, Baroni explored the question of ethnic groups' self-image. "We Indians, Blacks, Hispanics and the children of immigrants are in the midst of redefining ourselves," he said. "Who am I and who are we as Americans? We need a new self-image. We need a new way to think about ourselves. Will our nephews and nieces want to remember what their parents wanted to forget? Will we continue producing plastic plants or real flowers? What happens when we are culturally bankrupt? Will we become like white bread, no crust and little substance?"

Baroni was determined not to become like white bread. He succeeded.

Much of the material from the interviews is incorporated in other sections of this biography, but some passages didn't quite fit or reveal enough in themselves to justify a distinct treatment. Here from the transcripts, are some of Baroni's thoughts:

Baroni was talking about Mary Houston, the social worker he hired to run the V Street Center: "She wasn't naive or romantic as a lot of the volunteers may have been."

O'Rourke: Were you naive and romantic?

Baroni: I think you have to have some of that. If you aren't a little bit naive or a little bit romantic, you don't do anything because you see all the obstacles and the roadblocks.

O'Rourke: Did you have people telling you that things couldn't be done?

Baroni: Yes. They would say "That is crazy" or "What are you trying to do? They will tear the place apart" or "You can't do that. It won't work" or "It is too much work." You have to remember that in the 60s, we really did think we could do anything, or we thought we should. (July 1982)

*

O'Rourke: What is the role of the church in politics?

Baroni: The church creates the climate through which people act politically. It is not enough for pastors to call mayors and ask for jobs for people. The role of the church is to help convene people. Whatever you do around the altar should contribute to that. That is why the Pentecostals are growing. People need loyalty. We need a new version of being Christian, something that can turn on the young Catholic kids. (September, 1982)

*

O'Rourke: Should cancer patients get better information from their doctors?

Baroni: I think you gotta know. People know anyhow, but don't talk about it. It's better to deal with it directly. The biggest thing with cancer is that people deny it. Cancer has its own shroud of dread. It's unlike a heart attack. You got to learn to live with cancer like it's a chronic disease. It's better for people to accept it. It's like a cloud. It closes down a lot of things. (January, 1983)

*

O'Rourke: Were you religious when you were at Sts. Paul and Augustine?

Baroni: I didn't have enough time to be religious. I used to think that I'd read the morning paper and it was a meditation. (January, 1983)

*

Baroni: Alice Shabecoff has this friend Myra who knows the cancer statistics. So I talk to her.

She says to me, "You know you're three months past the maximum for this cancer already. By the statistics you should be dead by now."

I said, "Oh, yeah." I didn't know if I was going to laugh or cry. I did both. Intermittently. (February, 1983)

*

O'Rourke: Do you think there is an afterlife, a heaven and a hell?

Baroni: Don't get me into describing it. I'm convinced that we're not a tree or a plant and that this life is all of it. We're a higher being. We have a spirit. There's something forever and ever about it. There's something that's got to be immortal and it's not a physical thing or physical kind of place. (February, 1983)

*

Baroni: In the last couple of years, I've gotten interested in the horses. I'm very good with the odds. My Irish friend Tim Meehan said to me, "I'm going to take you to the track, Baroni. You haven't lived until you've done that." Here I am 48 years old before I make my first bet. I didn't know one horse from nothing. But when I first started figuring out odds, I won $1,900 in one day. I won $950 on an Exacta. (February, 1983)

*

Baroni: I wake up every day and say I'm glad to see the sun shine. (February, 1983)

*

Baroni: I went to a dinner in Washington for 2,500 people and we all had filet mignon. They had an open bar. Probably cost them 50 or 60 grand. Everybody was white, all were middle-class or rich. What for? To hear Arthur Burns say the minimum wage was a disaster. (February, 1983)

*

O'Rourke: You still have hope of beating the cancer?

Baroni: Yeah. There are two words I've been picking up and I've been using now. There's a deathogenic mentality and a lifeogenic mentality. That's why Cranston made such a smart move yesterday taking that one issue. He took that nuclear issue. He's going to be identified running for president just on that. It's a big issue. But it's deathogenic. It's hard to focus on the nuclear issue all of the time. Because there's so much denial. And that's what happens to this disease. (Senator Alan Cranston, California Democrat, announced his candidacy for the party's 1984 nomination for president and said he would campaign primarily on the issue of the control of nuclear weapons. He was not successful in winning the nomination.) (February, 1983)

\*

Baroni: I would have loved to be an Old Testament prophet, to get up there and raise holy hell. When I was at my best in terms of talking, I would sometimes get into that. I would be screaming and yelling about the system, the injustice, the walls ought to come down, and we ought to march. (February, 1983)

\*

Baroni: I have a lot of rage. Very few people have seen me that way. Mostly I do it in my head. I say to myself, "Damn it. I really should write a letter and tell them off." Or I say, "I can't tolerate this and let me tell you why." Sometimes I say, "In all charity, let me tell you why." But I do it in my head. It's very hard for me to do personal anger, very hard. But I also think it's healthy to let it out. Otherwise you pay a shrink.

O'Rourke: But you Italians are supposed to be able to let your anger out.

Baroni: That's a stereotype. That's like all the Irish turn to booze or politics. That's a stereotype about the Italians letting out anger. In my family, I didn't. I'm a passive aggressive. (February, 1983)

\*

Baroni: Look at the opportunities I've had. Look at the things I've gotten into. I know who a Brzezinski is. I've been sworn in by a vice president. A snotty-nosed kid. It's kind of only in America. In the church and in the secular community, I've gone up and down a ladder. A friend of mine said, "Baroni, you're a guy who can handle a lot of levels." Last night I sat on a floor with a guy who's almost foaming at the mouth, who should be back in St. Elizabeth's. And with a guy who's trying to come off drugs and kept smoking cigarettes during the mass. Yesterday I had lunch in the Jockey Club with some people who had dinner the night before with the Reagans. Sometimes with this cancer, I say to myself, "Good God, am I getting punished for my life?" I say, "Come on. That's silly. You know better than that. It's what you do with it that counts." (February, 1983)

\*

Baroni: When people would come to me to get married, I wouldn't give them a laundry list of stuff. I'd tell them: "You two love each other. I'm just a witness. You're going to share that love and your friends are going to share it. And whatever your life is, for better or worse, is going to be a vocation of love. You're going to have to do something with it. Don't be selfish. Get involved. Share what you have with each other, with your children, your family, the community." (February, 1983)

\*

Baroni: I sent these two staff guys out to an Indian reservation in Montana to set up a credit union. And it snowed. They got drunk for two days. The guy who was with them to talk about the credit union was a Mormon. So we blew that credit union. (February, 1983)

\*

Baroni: I've been thinking about starting a healing group, healing for people who are walking around after they just hurt somebody or somebody hurt them, and they're just carrying it around. It sits there and it's unresolved and it shatters or busts marriages and friendships.

O'Rourke: What does religion have to do with that? Isn't that work for a psychiatrist?

Baroni: Religion can help. A psychiatrist may have to deal with some of it. Religion can tell people not to blame somebody else, or to forgive. It's pretty tough to forgive somebody who's shafted you. (March, 1983)

\*

Baroni: There was this priest friend of mine visiting his old man and the old man kept looking at his watch. Then he said, "Excuse me," and he went out. When he comes back, the son says, "What was all that about?" And the old man says, "I had to talk to the mailman. I talk to him every day. If I don't talk to him, sometimes I don't talk to anybody. His name is Harry." There's a tremendous loneliness, a terrible lack of connection, in this kind of society. (March, 1983)

\*

Baroni: The immigrants who came here from Europe were poor people. They didn't come over here for a thrill. They came out of desperation. They were starving. They were out of work, whether it was Italy or Poland or Ireland. The people who came were peasants. The well-off didn't come over here. The poor came looking for opportunities. Same as the boat people from Southeast Asia or the Haitians or the Salvadorans. Same kind of motivation, looking for opportunity. (March, 1983)

\*

⚞ Baroni: I have these great friends. They're liberals and they want their kid to go to a school where he can meet blacks. They're integrators. So the kid goes to school and what does he find? In the cafeteria, in the classrooms, the black kids sit on this side of the room and the white kids sit on the other side. They don't talk. Occasionally they bump into one another at their lockers. The teachers don't do the stuff. It won't work by accident. Somebody's got to create the situation in which they meet one another. But our society is not doing that. (July, 1983)

\*

Baroni: *The New York Times'* editorial pages can't stand ethnic diversity. So the paper runs five pages of recipes on ethnic food. (July, 1983)

\*

Baroni: This lawyer comes to me and says he wants to help out with the inner-city problem. Can I find for him some kids he can take to the zoo? Take to the zoo. I said to him, "I'll bet you don't take your own kids to the zoo. I need a lawyer to put some papers together so some blacks can start a business." He just looks at me. He doesn't want to do that. (July, 1983)

*

Baroni: I'm watching this television documentary by Hal Walker about the riots on 14th Street. He's trying to figure out why the blacks rioted and burned up their own neighborhoods. There's a commercial. Fly Eastern to Bermuda. So then we're back on 14th Street and Walker's showing these pictures of the slums. Then there's this next commercial. It's a guy driving his new station wagon into a house on a cul de sac and there's his wife and kids grilling in the back yard. You want to know why people riot? (July, 1983)

*

O'Rourke: Is America any better on race today than it was in the 1960s?

Baroni: We're very racist. What bothers me today is that we're more and more separate. It's going to build up to another 1960s. Reagan is adding to it. He's building a society in which privilege is blessed. Sure a black guy can get a room in the DuPont Plaza Hotel now. But most black Americans have very little opportunity. (July, 1983)

*

Baroni: They're doing a lousy job rebuilding Pennsylvania Avenue. I would make every other block residential. Apartment houses, places for the elderly, families. I'd tell these developers no more contracts for office buildings and hotels unless you put apartment buildings here and townhouses here.

O'Rourke: What will the cities of this country look like in the year 2000?

Baroni: They could be like the Renaissance Center in Detroit, with enclaves with walls around them. There may be some blacks who make it. But the poor people will live outside the cities and those poor people will be predominantly black. (July, 1983)

*

O'Rourke: How do you see the Catholic priesthood changing over the next 15 or 20 years?

Baroni: We will get to married priests, then women priests, then maybe a "special priesthood." There will be a variety of priests. We will have to redefine roles. There is no theological reason why a married person can't be ordained. Or a woman. I don't see any reason for objecting to that, except for institutional reasons, tradition. (July, 1983)

\*

Baroni: I was never much of an athlete, but my life as a priest was like something out of sports. I never saw myself as a first-string player. I was never the quarterback or the star. I was the water boy and the manager. I picked up the socks and I handed out the Band Aids and I taped peoples' ankles. That was my involvement. (September, 1983)

\*

O'Rourke: How did you decide to become a social activist rather than remain a parish priest?

Baroni: I've been doing a lot of thinking about that. The sermon on the mount was for me one of the most radical ideas ever. The sermon on the mount is one of the most powerful socioeconomic guidelines you can have. When I talked at seminaries, I would say to the seminarians, "You ought to read the Bible in one hand and the newspaper in the other." Newspapers drive you crazy with this problem and that problem. You apply the gospels to what you read in the paper. (October, 1983)

\*

Baroni: I went to a meeting of charismatic Catholics in Potomac. Very affluent people. The testimonies at the prayer meeting were all personal. They spoke about private acts, rights and wrongs. But they didn't talk about people who are hurting in the sense of being victims of an unjust society, and anything that they might do about that. The gap is horrendous. (October, 1983)

\*

Baroni: There is a large measure of hypocrisy in this move to get a school prayer amendment into the Constitution. I think it is dangerous. When I went to school, we were all expected to say a few psalms and sing a few hymns every day. They were all out of the Protestant Bible. Then the priest in church would raise hell about it and say we shouldn't be reading the Protestant Bible. So what were we supposed to do? I have great sympathy for people being intimidated by this issue. (March, 1984)

*

Baroni: After I started working with urban ethnic whites, Dr. Harold Isaacs of Massachusetts Institute of Technology came to me and said, "You may become a demagogue" by rousing the inner-city whites.

O'Rourke: Did you have any thoughts about being a demagogue?

Baroni: I was afraid of the demagogues who already existed. (May, 1984)

*

Baroni: Whether it will come this year or next year, I don't know. But we'll talk some more and do more work.

O'Rourke: I'm grateful to you for the cooperation you've given me in writing this book.

Baroni: It's been good for me too. You forced me to face some things that I had buried. (August 26, 1985, 8:30 the evening before Geno Baroni's death)

# 17

## The Final Battles

Geno Baroni first met Archbishop James A. Hickey of Washington on September 15, 1980. Carter was running for reelection but Baroni intended to leave the federal government on January 20, 1981. He wanted to return to the active priesthood. He said he did not know if the Archdiocese of Washington, to which he was officially attached, had a place for him.

While Baroni was in the government, Hickey had arrived in Washington from Cleveland and replaced William Baum as archbishop. However, Hickey and Baroni had not met. Baroni was pleased that Hickey moved the central office of the archdiocese from downtown to a former seminary in northeast Washington. Hickey wanted to live there himself. While waiting for his apartment to be finished, he lived in Baum's house on Rockwood Parkway in northwest Washington.

Baroni believed that Hickey, coming from Cleveland, had a sensitivity to concerns of inner-city ethnic Americans whom Baroni championed. Baroni checked Hickey out with old friends in the ethnic movement and got back positive reports. In Cleveland, Hickey had spoken out on behalf of neighborhoods and the poor.

Above all, Baroni wanted to be active again as a priest. "My roots were there," he said. "I began to think that it might not be so bad to be a pastor of a parish after all," he said. Gone for the moment were his claims that he was not well-enough educated, sufficiently up on dogma and liturgy, and temperamentally suited to be "a pastor in East Snowshoe or someplace." He talked to friends about becoming pastor of a parish on Capitol Hill. Perhaps he could be co-pastor with Bryan Hehir, Baroni said.

253

"We could make it the parish for Congress," Baroni said. "I could talk about neighborhood and domestic issues. Bryan could talk about war and peace and nuclear arms and other international issues." Who would raise money and administer the parish? Baroni was asked. "We'd have to have somebody else to do that," Baroni said.

Baroni doubted his ability to function without his base as a priest. He knew his access to powerholders in the executive branch and Congress depended to a large extent on his institutional identification with the Catholic Church. Monsignor Baroni could get past more secretaries than Mr. and former Father Baroni.

Once he decided he wanted to get back to a diocese, he passed the word to Hehir, Higgins, and John Carr and Father Raymond Kemp on Hickey's staff. An appointment with Hickey was arranged.

"We visited from 11:30 until 2:30," the archbishop recalled. They had lunch. "I was seeing all my priests, but Geno, as I recall, asked to see me," Hickey said. "When I came here from Cleveland I wanted to meet and spend an hour with each one of the priests serving in the archdiocese. Baroni told the archbishop of his experiences in the early 1960s at Sts. Paul and Augustine Church. "He told me something of the story of his being there during the riots," Hickey said.

"He indicated to me," said the archbishop, "that he wanted to get back to his work directly as a priest. He said, 'I'm not just sure I'll be able to be in a parish again. I've been out of the daily chores, the daily rounds of duties.'"

Baroni told the archbishop that he wanted to create some kind of an institute, preferably at Catholic University, to train community organizers and developers within the moral traditions of the Catholic faith. He said he saw the institute as a place where people with a well-developed social justice conscience could learn the mechanics of neighborhood work. Likewise, those already on the firing line who knew about the daily mechanics could be grounded in a philosophical and ethical approach. Beyond those assignments the institute could serve as a clearinghouse for the urban ethnic neighborhood movement, Baroni said.

The archbishop listened as Baroni laid out his aspirations, then leaned across the table and looked intently at Geno.

"Geno, you know, that's good work, and if that's ultimately what you decide you'd like to do, I'll certainly allow you to do it," said Hickey.

"But, Geno, I really need you myself."

There was silence in the room and then, as the archbishop described it, "there was the most beautiful smile on Geno's face."

"I wanted him," said the archbishop. "He really felt wanted that day. It really was the beginning of an extremely warm friendship. I knew I could count on him. I knew that if something was going wrong, he'd tell me. I knew if I got into a fight, he'd stick with me. I knew he'd give me good advice. He knew the city and he knew the country."

\*       \*       \*

The announcement came December 18. Baroni was to become special assistant to the archbishop for community affairs on February 15. Hickey said in a statement, "I welcome Monsignor Baroni's return to our archdiocese, to the service of the local church. I look forward to sharing his talents and expertise in a community with many diverse needs."

The decision had been made, the title arranged, but the scope of Baroni's work remained unclear when he reported to the pastoral center in February. Hickey and Baroni got along very well. Baroni was careful to wear his black suit and collar on the job, to keep silent at meetings until called upon to speak, and to tread softly in the corridors of the pastoral center.

"Geno obviously had to feel his way around this place very carefully. He was unsure how some of the priests in the archdiocese would accept him," a priest friend said. Baroni was not universally admired by the archdiocesan priests. Several remembered him from the 1960s when he had the reputation as a maverick who got away with far more than they expected they could. He seemed immune to the standard discipline of the church. Never a pastor, a self-professed failure at ordinary parish work in Pennsylvania two decades before, a player to the grandstands in the eyes of some, Baroni was nonetheless welcomed back and given an office in the pastoral center, apparently with access to the archbishop. There was grumbling in the ranks, and Baroni heard it. He could not shrug it off, but there wasn't much he could do about it.

Hickey actually called upon Geno for help before he left the Carter administration. That was in December when four churchwomen were killed in El Salvador. "That affected me very deeply because two of those women were women I had down there from Cleveland," Hickey said. "I had asked the sister to stay on. Had I not asked, they would have been home the previous June. So I was very much moved by that."

Amid the uncertainty of what happened to the women, Hickey called Baroni for assistance. "He was a great help because he was still with the administration. He knew all the right buttons to push to get information, often at the level of assistants to people rather than the top office itself."

Shortly after Baroni joined the staff in February, he was asked by the archbishop to help prepare him for Capitol Hill testimony against the Reagan administration's position in Central America. Specifically, Hickey opposed U.S. military intervention and U.S. financial aid for military purposes. Hickey was criticized for sticking his and the other bishops' noses into a political and international issue. Baroni gave Hickey a statement from the 1971 world synod of Catholic bishops: "Action on behalf of justice and participation in the transformation of the world fully appear to us as a constitutive dimension of the preaching of the Gospel, or, in other words, of the Church's mission for the redemption of the human race and its liberation from every oppressive situation."

\*     \*     \*

Baroni was only a few weeks on the job at the Pastoral Center when he felt the stomach pains that turned out to be cancer. The archdiocese provided Baroni a comfortable two-bedroom apartment in the rectory of St. Matthew's Cathedral on Rhode Island Avenue in downtown Washington. But Baroni rarely stayed there. He joked that the bed was too hard. Usually he went to the Virginia home he shared with his sister and her family.

With Hickey's approval, Geno accepted appointment to the Meyer Foundation of Washington, an organization supported by the bequest of Eugene Meyer, former publisher of *The Washington Post*, and his family enterprises. For Baroni, it was a homecoming to the political power structure of the capital city he had challenged and served in the 1960s. Board members approved the distribution of Meyer Foundation money to grant applicants they considered worthy. Baroni resumed his affiliation with the National Italian-American Foundation and became a consultant at $2,000 a month to the University of Southern California graduate program in Washington. The USC program was headed by Arthur Naparstek, who had worked for Baroni at the Center for Urban Ethnic Affairs. Baroni's task was to consult and lecture on urban development strategy. In 1982, he rejoined the Urban Ethnic Center he founded as a board member.

Baroni headed back to Capitol Hill, this time not as a pleader for his own causes or for the Carter administration, but as a representative of the Catholic archdiocese. He was a frequent and welcome visitor to the offices of such old acquaintances as Senator William Proxmire and Representatives Peter W. Rodino, Joseph P. Addabbo and Barbara Mikulski, all Democrats. "He always called first and asked if I had a couple of minutes," said Gerald L. McMurray, staff director of the House subcommittee on housing. "He was very well-informed. He picked up a lot of information while protecting his sources. He was serious about his work, but he was just a great guy to talk with for a while."

Baroni wanted to take advantage of his political contacts and experience at HUD to help the archdiocese get federal support for housing programs. For years he had been distressed at failures by his fellow church people to secure government money. He said other religious denominations were much better organized than his in applying for project support.

Monsignor Ralph Kuehner, a pastor in a northwest Washington suburb, developed a plan to build a 100-unit project to house the elderly. It was to be on land adjacent to a Silver Spring parish, Christ the King. Keuhner and Baroni asked Hickey to have the archdiocese sponsor the project. Hickey delayed a decision. Another group then received approval of a grant to build housing for the elderly in the same area. Baroni and Kuehner withdrew their request.

The slowness and failure of the institutional church sometimes resulted from an ignorance of procedures. "The Protestant churches and the Jews have lawyers and lobbyists looking around and putting in bids left and right," Baroni said with more than a twinge of jealousy. "They get people on the Hill to put pressure on the administration and the bureaucrats to get approval. If something's wrong with the proposal, the Protestant groups and the Jews send their people to fix it up. They know how things are done."

But the Catholic hierarchy, said Baroni, won't work in the right way to win approval of Catholic projects. Part of the reason, he said, was a deeply-ingrained view that something was wrong with dirtying one's hands in the political marketplace. He said that with 50 million Catholics, a large number of Catholics serving in Congress, and the Reagan administration sympathetic to Catholic concerns, the time was right to move for whatever federal assistance was available.

He said one big problem with the church in the United States was its dedication to works of charity, yet wariness of working with government on development programs. He often told a story about chastising suburbanites in Catholic parishes for "sending the poor your old used underwear when what they really need is the advice and skill you use every day in your jobs downtown."

Ever since taking a leadership role in creating the Campaign for Human Development, Baroni was both an admirer and critic of the notion that the church should focus its efforts on charitable work through the national and locally affiliated Catholic Charities offices. As an admirer, Baroni paid tribute to the men and women who collected and distributed money, clothing and furniture for the poor, paid their emergency bills, and steered them through the bureaucratic maze of the welfare system. But as a critic of Catholic Charities, Baroni said that providing immediate relief to pressing individual needs was laudable, but insufficient, and he thought that Catholic Charities should acknowledge that and join in an effort to change the American system. At times he thought that even the Campaign for Human Development was too wedded to the charities approach, that it failed to take risks on community organizers and developers who would challenge the political system.

In July, 1983, Baroni spoke of his concerns at the College of Notre Dame in Baltimore at a meeting of people joined under the name Voices for Justice. The organizers described the participants as Catholic leaders at the parish, diocesan and national levels who wanted to explore the issues, skills, strategies and relationships needed for applying Catholic social teaching in the United States in the 1980s.

On a hot Saturday morning, Baroni talked to several hundred participants about his cancer. He said they all lived in a "deathogenic society." But the fear of dying must not stop them from talking about death and facing its inevitability. He spoke of his treatment, radiation, surgery, pain, chemotherapy and drugs. He said that for him, "regardless of the outcome, sooner or later, there is the experience of civilized terror" that hits everyone facing death.

In the church and in neighborhoods around the nation, Baroni said, he heard voices for justice. Then turning to what he hoped would be understood as the main point of his address, he said, "If I have time or health for the 80s, I would like to hear a stronger voice of justice from Catholic Charities and the Campaign for Human Development." He later explained he hoped his statement would be interpreted as an appeal for Catholic Charities and the Campaign for Human Development to work more closely together.

"If I had time in life to share the inheritance that has been given to me—not in words, but by example," he said, "then I would join those of you who inspire new hope to create an institute of public policy and development. Our weakness is not being prophetic. Our weakness is our naive knowledge of the forces of evil and their strength and sophistication," he said. "Catholic groups in particular are politically naive in the national public policy arena."

Baroni said that not since 1919, when one of his heroes, Monsignor John Ryan, issued on behalf of the bishops a strong statement supporting labor unions and social welfare programs, had the Catholic Church in America sounded a strong voice for justice.

"We have no agenda in national policy and no strategies for development of community in our parishes and neighborhoods," Baroni said in one of his more pessimistic analyses of contemporary U.S. Catholicism. This was no casual shoot-from-the-hip speech by Baroni. He labored for many days over what he would tell the group, writing it out on yellow legal paper, crossing out thoughts, inserting words and ideas. He sensed that it might be the last time that he spoke to a large audience of Catholic social activists. Most were friends with years of experience. They understood one another and Baroni knew that whatever he said would get a wide circulation in the Catholic action group. At the time, he was putting pressure on his friend, Father Marvin Mottet, head of the Campaign for Human Development, to be more aggressive, to take higher risks in giving financial support to neighborhood groups. "CHD is becoming too much like Catholic Charities." Baroni said.

The significance of the dispute extends beyond the purely theoretical argument over how the contributions of American Catholics to their church should be raised and distributed. As Baroni said in his address, Catholics were increasingly both more affluent and more politically powerful. He argued that the money and the power should be used to change society, not just pick up the broken pieces of humanity.

\*       \*       \*

Baroni considered himself a political liberal, but he was not locked in a static political position. Constantly open to new ideas, ever willing to explore new approaches, he was not bounded by the political borders of Roosevelt's New Deal, Truman's Fair Deal, or Johnson's Great Society. Baroni's political philosophy moved from traditional New Deal liberalism toward a new point on the spectrum at which three sectors, government, private and non-profit, played equal roles. In his attacks on Big Government, Baroni could sound as critical as Ronald Reagan.

"What does Big Government do?" he said. "Big Government tries to limit people's options and control people's options." He called government programs that handed out money directly for urban renewal programs "Disasterville in Washington." He said planners with no understanding of communities tore them apart with superhighways, unwanted housing and development projects. He attacked policies that failed to respond to needs as seen by the people who lived in the community. This was an old theme for Baroni: that neighborhoods were wiped out because of government policy. But in his post-government days, Baroni went even further than before in condemning what he called Big Government.

Not that he expressed admiration for Reagan. In June, 1982, addressing a training program for economic development workers at Mount St. Mary's College in Emmittsburg, Md., Baroni said, "If you lived in Washington in the last couple of years, you wonder what's going on in this country. We really have a Robin Hood in reverse. Robin Hood used to steal from the rich to give to the poor. But now we have a Robin Hood who steals from the poor to give to the rich. And it's actually quite tragic how the country's being divided."

At the same time, Baroni knocked the Democratic Party's traditional emphasis on federal programs. "All the old programs are worn out and run out of gas," he said.

Baroni was early to spot Reagan's planned destruction of federal social programs. He looked at the 1981 tax cut and the budget proposals in 1982 and 1983 and predicted that the federal budget deficit would soon grow so large that pressure would build in Congress and the public to cut back on domestic programs. In his final years, Baroni spoke often of what he viewed as the insane, indecent and immoral buildup of military forces at the expense of the poor and the neighborhood people he loved.

At the Voices for Justice meeting in Baltimore, Harry Fagan, a friend to Baroni from the urban ministry, then working in New York, said of him: "He's an instinctive genius. He does not do a lot of heavy-duty reflection. He has the courage to go with a lot of his instincts."

Baroni and Fagan, informally chatting, turned to Baroni's experience in the Carter administration at the Department of Housing and Urban Development. "HUD's a failure because it just does the bricks and mortar and runs," Baroni said. "It doesn't have what these people (in the Voices for Justice) have. We have the amenities. We have soul."

\*       \*       \*

Aware that time was running out, Baroni wanted to institutionalize his own philosophy. Geno latched onto what he thought might be a sure vehicle. He described it in a May 6, 1982, memorandum to Archbishop Hickey:

From our earliest discussions, housing has been one of our common concerns. For several years the Mercy Sisters have been considering the housing problem and have reviewed many proposals. Prior to my illness I was involved in the Mercy Sisters' study and recently I was invited to submit my own proposal.

I am happy to report to you that after a three-day meeting this week, the Mercy Administrative Team and the nine provincials of the General Administrative Conference have unanimously accepted my proposal for the establishment of the McAuley Institute. To establish the McAuley Institute the Mercy Sisters have committed $1.8 million dollars. I hope to serve the Institute as Chairman of the Board or in some leadership title role. Hopefully the Institute can help us locally as we struggle with our own local efforts in the midst of a critical housing crisis.

In a poignant note, Baroni told the archbishop: "Your encouragement and personal support prompted me to this effort. I deeply appreciate your continued concern and prayers during these special days as I face death and learn to live."

Baroni's effort started when he learned that a community of religious women, the Sisters of Mercy of the Union, sold its motherhouse in Potomac, Md., for $1.8 million, and considered using the proceeds to build housing for the poor. Baroni, anxious for a new project, offered to help. It turned out to be a disappointment for both Baroni and the community's leaders. It ended in bitterness.

The nuns started their project with the best of intentions. "After Vatican II, the community decided it was not right to keep a big piece of property and a lot of money tied up in it while people were going homeless," said Carol Younoszai, a spokeswoman for the project. "We sold the property to the U.S. Post Office. The question then was what to do with the money." The community was started in Dublin in 1832 by Catherine McAuley, who was active in sheltering the homeless in that Irish city. In that spirit, the nuns initiated a study. "Not all" members of the community favored the idea, a later report said. The project leaders stipulated that the project lawyer be a woman and another board member from Catholic Charities be a man. "There was a feeling right from the beginning that the women should determine and run their own project," one participant said.

Sister Theresa Blaquiere came from Benton Harbor, Mich., to Washington to direct the study. Baroni approached her and said he had experience and ideas that the sisters might use. They agreed to work together.

Word that the community had $1.8 million to distribute ran like a prairie fire through the ranks of those involved in sheltering the homeless. "We could have given away all the money in two weeks to worthy groups," a participant said. But Baroni had other plans, and the nuns listened. He talked about "leveraging" the money to turn the $1.8 million into a much larger package. "He was vague on how this would be done," said a participant, "but he made it sound plausible."

What Baroni said was that the nuns should take their money to a major insurance company—he recommended Aetna—and ask it to add to the project an amount several times the $1.8 million. With this larger amount in pocket, Baroni said, the nuns could go to another big lender and get even more money. "It all sounded like a pyramid scheme, but Baroni kept pushing it and soon he had a lot of people convinced it would work," a participant said. The nuns decided to call their project The McAuley Institute, after their order's founder. So enthusiastic were the Institute's directors that on July 23, Sister Rosemary Ronk, according to the minutes, "asked Geno to be the first chairperson of the Board of Trustees. Geno accepted." He was given large powers, the minutes of that meeting noted. "With this position as Chair goes that authority designated by the by-laws of the McAuley Institute, Inc., to act for and in the name of the McAuley Institute, Inc., and to bring to the attention of the Board those proposals, recommendations, policies, and decisions which foster the goals and purposes of the McAuley Institute, Inc."

Baroni was to be paid a $6,000-a-year personal stipend and given an additional $6,000 for expenses. He was offered an office and the use of the Institute staff for his business. Baroni, in the days following, rode on Cloud Nine. He had a new title, a new challenge, and a new place to operate from. A friend who ate lunch with Baroni during that period said he looked better than he had in months. "He talked about leveraging the $1.8 million into tens of millions of dollars and starting a string of shelters for the homeless all over the country," the friend said.

With his new authority, Baroni contacted leaders of other religious communities and directors of archdiocesan investment funds around the country. He said he got Bishop Rembert Weakland of Milwaukee "very interested" in the project. The bishop had a reputation in Baroni's circle as someone who would use the diocesan accounts in a leveraging arrangement. Weakland later was chairman of the committee of Catholic bishops which issued a pastoral letter on the U.S. economy.

Baroni told colleagues in the urban ministry that the institute would offer 18-month full-time internships "to train new practitioners for jobs in packaging development ventures and in managing community economic development organizations."

Baroni assembled a panel of advisers. His list included McNeely, his former assistant at HUD, now an economic development consultant in Baltimore; Gerald McMurray, the House banking subcommittee director; Kathleen Rotondaro, an associate through their links to the National Italian-American Foundation; Father Michael Groden, a friend and longtime social activist in Boston, and Robert Corletta, his choice in 1976 to be president of the Center for Urban Ethnic Affairs. "What happened," said an institute source, "was that Geno took over." Four members of the Sisters of Mercy of the Union were on Baroni's advisory panel. It was clearly dominated, however, by his choices.

Several nuns resented Baroni's aggressive moves. They emphasized that his job was to raise money for the institute from other sources, and to "search out possible alternatives for leveraging institute funds." Baroni wanted to move quickly. The nuns hesitated. "It may have been a case," a person involved in the process said, "of Geno recognizing that he had only a short while left to live. He was anxious and willing to take risks that the nuns were not."

Clashes broke out between Baroni and the nuns over policies, responsibility and planning. The nuns said they wanted the right to manage their own money. Baroni said they told him they wanted a woman in the job. A few months after he accepted the chairperson's job with grand dreams of raising tens of millions in leveraged funds, Baroni's role ended.

In a letter to him on Oct. 31, 1983, Sister Theresa Blaquiere and four other women wrote Baroni: "We know that the parting of the ways was painful for all concerned. We recognize that there were differences over how the plan for the Institute should be implemented, and over questions of leadership and authority. However, our common dream of an Institute which would encourage and assist Catholic support of low-income housing has been realized."

The women said they had followed Baroni's plan, gotten commitments from Aetna and other leading financial institutions, and were "moving toward a product which has the potential of leveraging many millions of dollars for low-income housing." They told Baroni: "We realize that our past relations have been marked by errors of judgment and hurt feelings on everyone's part. It is our sincere wish that time and grace will heal and perhaps restore a measure of good faith between us. In the meantime, please know that you are in our prayers and that your efforts are remembered gratefully."

Baroni said later he was pleased that the institute adopted his suggestion on leveraging. He regretted that he had not been able to seize the opportunity to develop a national plan. He said that small groups working individually, no matter how sincerely, could not accomplish as much as groups setting aside rivalry and pride to form a single large powerful force.

His initial selection as the institute's chairperson was just one of several events which gave Baroni a sense of mission and achievement in the fall of 1982. He resumed making speeches. He survived the chemotherapy and radiation treatment and surprised his doctors with his survival. He enjoyed his therapy group and increased contacts with cancer patients.

Baroni maintained his friendship with Father J. Bryan Hehir, an intellectual giant at the U.S. Catholic Conference. Hehir was then doing the groundwork for presentation in 1983 of a pastoral letter by the U.S. Catholic bishops on nuclear arms. Though Baroni initially knew nothing about the subject, he and Hehir had many provocative discussions about nuclear arms. Baroni's contribution was the political analysis of how the letter should be presented and how it would be received by the Reagan administration and the press and public.

Baroni's tendency was not to hide his contacts or activities. In an artful way, he let others know in time that he was working with Hehir on the bishops' nuclear statement. The friendship between the two priests kept alive Baroni's talk of them running a parish on Capitol Hill as joint pastors. As time went on, Baroni discussed this proposal in the sort of half-jesting, half-serious manner that he used for trial balloons. The idea was never acted on by Baroni, Hehir or the Chancery.

\*　　\*　　\*

Baroni loved to travel and as his intimations that this would be his final illness mounted he kept looking for "one more trip." He especially wanted to visit Italy once more to see relatives. He explored the possibility of going to Spain to study cooperatives. He said he always wanted to visit Asia.

In late summer of 1982, the U.S. Catholic Conference was invited to send representatives to South Africa to meet with Catholic bishops and others. South African Catholic bishops wanted moral and political support from their American colleagues for their campaign to end apartheid, South Africa's system of legalized racial segregation.

The Catholic Conference assigned Hehir to the trip. Hehir asked Baroni if he would like to go along, and would his health allow it. Baroni said yes to both. They spent two weeks in South Africa and met numerous white and black opponents of apartheid, including Anglican Bishop Desmond Tutu, winner in 1984 of the Nobel Peace Prize for his anti-apartheid activity. "Bishop Tutu asked that there be solidarity and support from church people for their voices crying out against injustice," Baroni said in a report to Hickey after his return. Baroni said Tutu saw a "collision course. He used the word Armageddon in describing the struggle."

Baroni collaborated with the author of this biography on a report on his visit. It said, "It does not take a first-time visitor to South Africa long to see the evil and tragic effects of apartheid. For nearly two decades, I have seen incredible poverty and human suffering in the worst slums of this nation, from Washington to Watts. As a priest, as a community worker, as a Carter administration official, I have been to communities and in homes where physical filth and decay overcame my senses. One could find in some of those homes a sense of despair, an anger with the American system that had allowed such conditions to develop. But I never saw slums in this country equal to those I found in Crossroads, a shantytown for blacks."

Baroni went to Crossroads on a cold rainy night. "I went into a large tent filled with smoke from cooking fires tended by women wrapped in blankets." He joined a priest from Ireland who told him that the blacks of South Africa would someday rule the nation. Baroni recalled the priest saying that the blacks "resent" U.S. support for the racist white South African government.

On Sunday in South Africa, Baroni was asked to deliver the homily in St. Charles Luana parish, about thirty miles from Pretoria. "I told them I was an immigrant coal miner's son," said Baroni, "and I told them about the struggles in the United States to bring equal rights to our black minority." He told the black congregation that apartheid is "a sin, that social and economic problems are moral problems because they are questions of justice, of right and wrong. The Catholic Church in every land must take part in the struggle for a just and free society."

Baroni and Hehir were invited to the funeral of a black labor leader in the township of Soweto. They had necessary permits to enter the community. But at the front door of the church they were grabbed on their arms by white security police and ordered to drive out of Soweto. They complied.

"South Africa is a violent nation steadily moving, many fear, toward revolutionary acts. It is the violence of the tiny shack when families with young children are forced to live in conditions that violate human dignity. It is the violence of overcrowding, of frustration, fear, humiliation. I have seen that violence explode on the streets of Washington and Detroit and Newark and Philadelphia," Baroni said.

In December, 1984, four months after Baroni's death, Hickey issued a statement during Human Rights Week. "Our defense of human rights is not an option for the church, but an integral part of our ministry. Our popes have spoken out against apartheid for decades," Hickey said. "Monsignor Geno Baroni, who served as my assistant for community affairs, went to South Africa and Namibia on his last trip before his final illness. He came back with stories of incredible injustice, discrimination and exploitation. He shared with me the struggles of the church in South Africa. He challenged us as Americans to use our freedom to help our black brothers and sisters to obtain theirs. His challenge to work for justice, for human dignity and human rights takes on special meaning since he left us."

Arrested in an anti-apartheid protest outside the South African embassy that month were Father John Mudd, pastor, and parishioners of Sts. Paul and Augustine, the inner-city parish where Baroni worked from 1960 to 1969.

\*         \*         \*

Politics at home was never far from Baroni's attention. In the fall of 1982, his former employee at the Center and Carter administration colleague, Marcy Kaptur of Toledo, ran for the U.S. House as a Democrat.

Kaptur ran for a seat that had been held for 26 years by Democratic Rep. Thomas (Lud) Ashley. Normally, the Democratic candidate would win easily in heavily blue-collar Toledo, but Kaptur had special problems. She had been away from Toledo a long time and her Republican opponent pictured her as a carpetbagger. He also associated her with failed policies of the Carter administration, asserting they led to high inflation and rising unemployment.

Kaptur had the support of City Councilman Peter Ujvagi, another former Center employee, and the quiet backing of Father Martin Hernady, pastor of St. Stephen's Church in the ethnic section of east Toledo. Optimistic after their defeating Ashley in the Reagan landslide, Republicans targeted the district for heavy spending and campaign appearances by senior party leaders.

From Washington, Baroni in September and early October called Kaptur or one of her lieutenants daily. He asked to be kept fully informed of campaign decisions. When Kaptur needed money for TV ads, Baroni raised it from his Washington friends. One ticklish moment came when the Democratic National Committee refused to give Kaptur a full $5,000 allotment because she differed somewhat from the party's leadership on abortion. Kaptur said she supported the U.S. Supreme Court decision allowing abortions up to the 26th week of pregnancy, but opposed the use of federal funds to support the procedures. The Democratic committee supported federal funds for abortion. Baroni made telephone calls to committee officials and other party leaders to persuade them to release more money to Kaptur. More money was released.

Finally, Baroni could no longer stay away from Toledo. He flew there and spent several days before the election suggesting strategy to Kaptur and Ujvagi. There was a report that the Republicans on the Sunday before the election would blitz the district, especially church parking lots, with broadsides attacking Kaptur as a carpetbagger who supported abortion. Baroni helped draw up a counter-broadside emphasizing Kaptur's membership in the Catholic Church and her attendance at Catholic schools in Toledo.

Teddy Mastroianni, one of Kaptur's campaign managers and later her administrative assistant in Washington, said he assigned Baroni the job of driving around the district to make sure the Kaptur campaign signs were in place. Baroni did it with enthusiasm. On the Saturday night before the election, Baroni accompanied Kaptur to a dinner and during the evening Baroni in his Roman collar worked the tables for Kaptur. It was pure partisan politics. Baroni loved and welcomed every minute. As the returns rolled in election night, Baroni was with Kaptur and her senior staff, enjoying the triumph.

When Kaptur came to Washington, Baroni advised her to seek a seat on the House Banking, Finance and Urban Affairs Committee. Then he contacted several senior Democrats to win their support. Kaptur got the seat she and Baroni wanted.

*     *     *

As the Democratic House and the Republican Senate in 1981 worked on Reagan's budget, Baroni prepared for Hickey a statement that precisely reflected Baroni's own views on the role of the federal government. He said that the outcome of the Congressional debate "touches on the basic issues of justice. To the extent that its outcome upholds the common good or yields to selfish interests, this debate will also test the moral strength of our nation."

Baroni called Reagan's program of budget and tax cuts "ambitious." He said that Catholics as all other citizens want to control inflation, restore economic growth and limit spending. But other questions must be asked, Baroni said: Does the program meet the requirements of fairness and equity? Does it place the burden on those most able to carry that burden? Does it support family life or make it even more difficult? Does it make easier or more difficult efforts to provide food, housing, employment and health care for all? Will all segments of the community share in its proposed austerity, or only the poor, minorities, the young and the elderly?

\*       \*       \*

Despite his awareness that death approached, Baroni in 1983 looked forward to the 1984 presidential election campaign. He calculated how he could help the Democratic candidate defeat President Reagan. Baroni by 1983 thought that the Democrats would nominate former Vice President Walter F. Mondale of Minnesota. Baroni liked Mondale, thought him likely to be a better president than Reagan, but feared that Mondale lacked the right touch and words to win critical votes from urban ethnic Catholics. In 1983, Baroni brought together Kromkowski, president of the Center, and Fred Rotondaro, president of the National Italian-American Foundation, to create the National Leadership Conference on Ethnic Affairs. Baroni hoped that Jeno Paulucci, chairman of NIAF and a Minneapolis bank executive and friend to Mondale, and Ed Marciniak, Center chairman and longtime ally to Baroni, would rally prominent and wealthy ethnic Americans around the country to revitalize the urban ethnic coalition with Mondale as the political beneficiary. Baroni's idea was a campaign fund in disguise for Mondale. Baroni told organizers to tell potential contributors that a revitalized neighborhood ethnic coalition could only have an important impact on the 1984 election if it had unity, organization and an agenda.

In a March 25, 1983, letter of invitation to a Washington meeting, Marciniak and Paulucci spoke of the need to adopt a multi-ethnic agenda for the 1980s. They noted that their boards of directors reflected a wide spectrum of economic, social and geographic, as well as political, backgrounds.

Discussion at the meeting reflected the concerns of urban ethnics as manifested in political power and influence. They complained about "unflattering and often distorted stereotypes of ethnic Americans" in the media and said that to secure rights for all Americans, it was necessary to achieve appointment to public office of those who are "representative of and sensitive to America's ethnic diversity."

The meeting turned out to be Baroni's final efforts to create a multi-ethnic coalition. His pioneering work was acknowledged by William McCready of the National Opinion Research Center; Irving Levine, director of the American Jewish Committee and Institute on Pluralism and Group Identity; and Michael Novak, author of *The Rise of the Unmeltable Ethnics.*

Kromkowski and Rotondaro convened ethnic leaders from around the country in Washington. They were surprised that the level of agreement on the ethnic issue was as strong as the level of support they found for Reagan. What they found in 1983 became fact in November, 1984, when the urban ethnic vote went heavily for the Republican ticket. To connect the agenda with electoral power would require political and policy sophistication that Baroni advocated and challenged his various constituencies to pursue. The accuracy of his early warning about the ignored and neglected at the core of the Democratic coalition underscored Baroni's keen political intuition. Catholic social activists recognized once again Baroni's genius as a political analyst.

\*　　\*　　\*

New honors came to Baroni. Common Cause, the citizens lobby in Washington, gave him its public service achievement award. Common Cause cited Baroni as "a tireless leader in the battle to improve the quality of urban life." The Italian government honored him with a medal as a distinguished son of Italy.

Talking in 1983 about his approaching death, Baroni said doctors gave him six months back in 1981, but he was still alive. "They don't really know," he said. "They could be wrong."

His death, he said, was "the final healing." He imagined his last days. He was not very good at tolerating pain, he said, and he hoped he would not have to suffer. Nor did he want to be kept alive interminably on artificial life-support systems.

He said he was not welcoming death, but neither was he railing against it. He said he had been "through anger and rage and passed to acceptance. But the anger is always there." Hehir and Egan said they found Baroni saddened that his cancer was taking him away from work he loved doing. Baroni spoke to them about his "unfinished agenda." But Hehir and Egan said they detected no anger at God or despair in Baroni.

"I'm trying to deal with the anger and acceptance," Baroni said. "The only way you'll get any peace is with some kind of acceptance."

"Have I told you the story about the day I was sitting in the old clinic?" Baroni asked over lunch Feb.3, 1983. "There must have been 15 people in the doctors' waiting room and everybody was sitting there reading. This lady was talking to another lady, and her daughter was right there. One lady was leaning over me to talk to this lady. The mother was so sick and so little she was just bent over. Her head was down to her knees. Once in a while, the daughter would look at her, and say, 'Are you all right, mom?' Some other people in the room were talking about one hospital being better than another and one doctor being better than some other doctor. I was listening to it all and watching this old lady.

"Finally, this old lady erupted. She just screamed, 'I don't want anymore. I've had it.' Everybody stopped, looked around, and the daughter said, 'Oh, mother, don't act like that. You're embarrassing me.' So I turned to her," Baroni continued, "and I said, 'Look, I feel the same way. I wish I could scream. I'm sitting here. I don't want it either. It's OK.'

"That's what I mean," said Baroni. "Where does that point come? When is the acceptance and when is there a finality, if there is a finality?"

Baroni read about death. He studied Elizabeth Kübler-Ross' *On Death and Dying* and said it gave him understanding of the need to accept whatever comes. One of his favorite books was *Living and Dying Gracefully* by Father Herbert N. Conley, an Episcopal priest, dean of St. Andrew's Cathedral in Hawaii, the president of a real-estate firm, married and the father of three children. Baroni underlined several favorite passages. One was: "Giving man a chance to prepare for death, to even see it with some honest expectancy and to find that the sick being has become an altar of Eucharist, of eternal thanksgiving, that is what it is all about."

It was ironic, said Baroni, that here he was, a Catholic priest, finding consolation in the words of an Episcopalian priest, receiving counselling from Episcopalians Father William Wendt and Julie Severance and attending a therapy session led by a Jewish psychiatrist. "Why is it that we Catholics don't have things like that?" Baroni said. Many Catholics, he said, reached out for such a ministry. Baroni said he would like to provide it.

During the next several months, he appeared several times before groups of people stricken with cancer. One appearance was the Crossroads group at Providence Hospital in Washington on May 6, 1983, where he said: "I was anointed five times and one of the things I think priests have trouble with is that they don't know what to do, so they anoint you. Some of my best friends came in, and I think I got anointed five times in a week."

Baroni told the Crossroads group that he made inquiries about his disease and learned that the last person in Georgetown Hospital who had mesothelioma in the lungs was Mrs. Margaret McNamara, wife of Robert S. McNamara, the Secretary of Defense during the Kennedy and Johnson administrations.

"I went to her funeral at the National Cathedral and then three months after Margaret died, I was elected to take her place on the Meyer Foundation Board. Then three months after I took her place on the foundation, I get the same disease that she had. I think that's an interesting coincidence of odds. I was then 50 years old. I came to my senses in terms of what the doctors say—'Maybe six months, maybe seven months.' This is the kind of situation where they couldn't operate. It would metastasize. I didn't have any problems in terms of crisis of faith. I was raised in a pre-Vatican II seminary in Emmitsburg and so when I was back in Pennsylvania in a parish, we had three hospitals to visit. So I was in and out of hospitals all the time, and I like that."

Baroni recalled that as a young assistant priest at Sts. Paul and Augustine Parish he was given the assignment of working as a chaplain at Children's Hospital of Washington. "That was awful because doctors in those days would tell you to tell the parents that the child had leukemia, had six weeks, six months, or six days, and then the doctor would disappear. It was an older way of doing things and it was a horrendous experience for me."

Baroni talked about cancer treatment. "The treatment was worse than the disease for me. I refused to take chemotherapy for awhile because they told me there was no medicine that worked, and I said, then why should I take it? I was always one of those believers that if the doctor said this, you wanted to believe him. When the doctor said there was nothing he could do for me except take this chemotherapy stuff, I really thought much more work had to be done. As an activist, we've been organizing some patients. I think one of the most dehumanizing things to a person as an individual, both spiritually and physically, is what some of these treatments do to you. Take even chemotherapy. It just dehumanizes your system. You're worse than an animal in a sense and you wonder if there's a relationship between tolerating this treatment and/or trying to say, 'Well, it's good because you have to deal with the disease.' "

Baroni said cancer patients tend to stay away from other people. "You begin to sense that cancer is a dreaded disease and there's a lot of fear, and one of the problems that patients have is tremendous denial.

A friend of mine, a woman, came up to me the other day, whispering and she said, 'You don't notice my wig?' I said that I don't pay attention to women's wigs unless they're on backward or something. I can tell with men, though. I guess I'm sensitive to that because I'm losing my hair. She said, 'I have cancer, but don't tell anybody.' I said OK."

Baroni told the Crossroads group that he and they "come out of a believing tradition, a tradition of faith." But that was not enough. "I was concerned about what my feelings were, so I called a psychiatrist friend of mine. He had cancer too. So we started a group."

His father, said Baroni, didn't need a group. "He didn't believe in hospitals or anything like that either. He died at 86. But I think in our kind of society, where we're so disconnected, a group is needed." Doctors, he said, do not understand "a lot about people's feelings, emotions and concerns. I think we as Christians don't know a lot about people's emotions and fears because we treat them in a different way." He said he had recently visited with the cancer-stricken husband of a friend. "When I went in there I reacted like the traditional priest. I wanted to get my book out and say all the prayers. Then I realized, that's our tradition, but it isn't enough.

"So I sat down and talked to this gentleman for a little while. He had surgery. He had chemotherapy. He had radiation. He had more tubes sticking out of every hole in his body. He said, 'I don't want any more of that.' He said, 'There's only one healing for me' and I said, 'What's that?' "

"And he said, 'The final healing, the healing of death.' "

"I thought that was a great insight. But how did the family and the clergy react? They said to him, 'You look pretty good today. You look better.' One of his sons came in and said, 'Pop, you're going to get better and after you come out of the hospital, we're going to dinner at McDonald's or Pier 7 or someplace.'

"I decided to talk with the family. 'You know,' I said to them, 'you really ought to talk to your father and husband about letting him go. I think you ought to give him permission to go.' They had never really thought about that. They never really talked to him about arrangements."

Baroni recounted that Severance helped him prepare an obituary and funeral arrangements. In the process of reaching the final healing called death, Baroni said, there should be a life review to identify those things "that sometimes we've done in the past that we wish we could go back and do over, especially things like rejection. That's the toughest healing. People sometimes have been rejected, or we've said something or done something to parents, to children or relatives, or friends."

Baroni talked about having a "fantastic dream" while he was on drugs. "It was beautiful. It was peaceful and I didn't know where I was. It was a glorious place and I said, 'Gee, I'm glad to be here. There's no conflict. There's no tension. There's no problems. It's a place of justice.' And I woke up and got mad. When I woke up, I felt so bad I wanted to go back to this place. And I said, 'Maybe that's heaven.' "

It is "very healthy" for those with cancer to "get angry," said Baroni. The Old Testament tells, he said, about "those characters who got angry with God." A woman in his therapy group has thrown her husband out of the house and beats her children in an expression of her anger, Baroni said.

"We have to break that anger. She's got to be angry with God, whatever she believes. She's got to be angry with herself. She's got to be angry with her family She's got to deal with that anger. After the anger will come depression, and then after that will come negotiation, and then after that will come acceptance." People from a religious background are told they have no right to be angry, Baroni said.

"We have a lot of models of people dying badly, but we don't know enough models of people dying well," he continued. He said he found release from the fear of death through guided imagery, a process by which the mind is forced into imagination, and he used this to put his life together. "One piece is over here, one piece is over there, and I've left some pieces behind, and maybe a little wreckage, little bumps here and there and a few scars.

"I can do guided imagery and I can get back to my best friends, back in Pennsylvania. I can get my father. I can get St. Francis. I can bring anybody I want. It becomes a habit and it becomes a technique that I can do these things to fill in the gaps. "

As part of his appearance before the Crossroads group and before other groups and with individuals, Baroni went into a guided imagery. He did it quite naturally and easily. Comparisons of tapings of several of the guided imagery sessions shows that Baroni went through the same lines, almost word for word.

The Phillip referred to by Baroni is Phillip Dupre, his high school and college friend who died while solo piloting his aircraft, and who often provided refuge for Geno in Seven Springs, Pennsylvania. The meadow Baroni refers to during the session is a meadow on the Seven Springs property where he often walked during his visits to the Dupres.

Closing his eyes, slumping in his chair, his eyes on his abdomen, his legs out straight and relaxed, Baroni began to say in a soft but distinct voice this accounting of his guided imagery:

I am very conscious of my relaxing. I'm very conscious of my breathing. Be aware that you are breathing, that you have life, and you can feel your breathing. I can feel my arms heavy. I can even feel the blood running down my arms into my hands. I can even get my hands to feel warm.

This is a beautiful day and you can follow me or you can do it on your own. With my eyes closed I go back to Pennsylvania to a beautiful meadow. I'm walking in this meadow with a dear friend who died about three years ago. My closest friend. We grew up as kids and went to high school together. I witnessed his wedding and the wedding of his oldest daughter, and two months later I participated in his funeral.

I go back and I'm in a meadow and I'm looking at the dogwoods, the flowers, and I watch the trees moving. Phillip and I are there. The sun is warm and because I'm so out of shape, I get tired. We find a log and we sit down on the log and I'm watching the trees and the flowers, the beauty of the world, and I'm so happy to be with him. I can remember it like it was yesterday.

And while we're in this meadow on top of the valley, across the valley is an old house. We get up and walk across the meadow and we come to this old house and it's abandoned. We go inside, and as I go inside this old house, I start looking around and I realize that I'm inside my own body. Sometimes when I think of this old house and I think of my own body, I think of going through it with Phillip, my friend. Sometimes I think I meet somebody there, a master, a teacher, with a light.

So we take this little light with the master, teacher, and go through the house. I go through my body, and, of course, right away I want to get the part of my body where the cancer is.

I come, in my imagination, to a big room. There are a lot of doctors in white coats. They've got all these x-rays on the wall and they're pointing out these little spots, the little tumors. And then I imagine these cells, the bad cells, the cancer cells. And then I imagine the white cells, or the macrophages, or the red blood. I imagine the healthy cells in my immune system. The body really heals itself as much as anything. But there's a war going on inside of me between good cells and bad cells, between the cancer cells running away, going wild, spreading around, and there's a struggle.

I can imagine part of the good cells, almost like Pac Man, chasing the dead cells. I imagine the conflict that's going on, the tension. I encourage my body. I encourage my good cells because there's something in the mind that triggers off these cells. Everybody has bad cells and our body does it every day. Millions and millions of cells and the way we get cancer is when those bad cells get ahead of us and start tumors or metastasize and the good cells can't put them out.

I'm encouraged by this struggle and I'm also encouraged that I can talk about it to my friend Phillip, about my struggles, my fears. I can talk about it to the master, it's Jesus or someone else. I sense that my body is a home for the light, divine life, the life that God has given us. But I also know that the body is physical. In a sense, we're all terminal and death is a sure thing that we have in common, black, white, rich, poor, man, woman. And so if I get afraid I can ask Jesus to remind me that I'm connected to this divine life, and this divine life is within me and I'm looking for the God within myself.

I go right into the center of my being and in the center of my being I feel that the light is in the room and the master is there and that if I want to talk with him, I can talk, I can ask any questions. I know the light is within, I can feel the warmth of it, permeating through my whole body, and a feeling of love and well-being, and a feeling of peace.

I know that I can always return to this place within myself whenever I choose to meet with the master and experience the light because I know he told me that I am created by the divine light and that I'm sustained by divine light and protected by the divine light and surrounded by the divine light and I am ever growing into the divine light.

I know that this experience is mine to return to in my mind and soul whenever I choose, whenever I am feeling troubled, and that this knowing will change me.

And so, having experienced this, I take my time to return from this room to the present, and when you're ready, gently stretch and open your eyes. Take your time and very gently, when you're ready, stretch and open your eyes.

Often Baroni sat still, his eyes closed, for several minutes until others in the room stirred and made noise. Then he opened his eyes and looked about. In his own home and sometimes with individuals, Baroni played music at low volume while he was talking. His favorite was Pachelbel's *Canon in D*, which repeats a brief melody.

Severance, who taught the method to Baroni, said guided imagery was not appropriate for everyone. She also suggested to Baroni that the power of the mind over the body was immense, but uncharted. Baroni said he did not believe that the mind could destroy the cancerous tumors and return him to good health. "But who knows? It's possible," he said. He acted like a man who wanted to believe.

In the summer of 1983, Hickey asked Baroni to join him in con-celebrating the 31st annual Labor Day mass at Sacred Heart Church in Washington. Many of the nation's top labor leaders traditionally attended the service. Hickey asked Baroni to deliver the homily. Hickey anticipated that it would be Baroni's last public mass, and he was correct.

Baroni agonized over what he should say. He asked friends for drafts and protested he was doomed to fail. He rejected advice that he simply be himself in the pulpit. In the end that's what he was. He spoke simply. Most of the people in the church that day knew Baroni was gravely ill. There was a prolonged silence after his homily, then an outbreak of applause from a standing congregation. This was Baroni's final public homily:

"I want to thank Archbishop Hickey and the members of the Committee for inviting me to share this great honor today. I have only been in the pulpit once in the last two years, so you're taking a great risk with me today, and I thank the archbishop for taking that risk.

"Mayor (Marion) Barry, my brothers and sisters in the American labor movement, dear friends in Christ. We're here on this Labor Day, this solidarity day, to honor several voices of justice. We're here, one, to honor the tradition and heritage of the free American labor movement and its leadership in the great struggle for economic justice for all Americans. We are here, second, to honor one of America's great Christian prophets and a voice of justice, Dr. Martin Luther King, Jr., who challenged America to fulfill its moral promise for racial justice and equality for all people. We are here, third, to honor the church's support for organized labor and participation in the American struggle for economic justice and human rights.

"We're here at this particular church because outside in the little park is the statue of Cardinal Gibbons who symbolized American church leadership in support of the American workers' right to organize. In fact, Cardinal Gibbons went to Rome to plead with the Holy See, in the face of great opposition in his day, to allow American Catholics—mostly immigrants—the right to join American labor unions. What kind of a time would that have been if the church would have forbidden American Catholics to join the American labor movement?

"We're also here to honor the leadership of the archdiocese under Cardinal O'Boyle, a voice of justice, who developed a labor policy that supports the rights of workers to organize into unions and advocates union labor contracts in archdiocesan building programs. Chief Justice Earl Warren of the Supreme Court told me that Cardinal O'Boyle's integration of the Catholic schools, beginning in 1948, influenced the 1954 Supreme Court school desegregation case. We also know that Cardinal O'Boyle led the American church in the civil rights struggle, in the face of great opposition, by his leadership and participation in the 1963 March on Washington.

Today we are honored that the proud tradition of the archdiocese continues in the magnificent parish participation in the 1983 March on Washington for jobs, peace and freedom, under the leadership of Archbishop Hickey, a new voice of justice in our midst. Yes, we have many grateful reasons to be proud, to be honored, as we celebrate this Labor Day. While we can be proud of the voices of justice that have influenced the church and the nation, a more important question is: Where do we as Americans and Catholics, go from here? Let us begin with today's gospel.

"When Jesus came back to his home town of Nazareth, he spoke the words of the prophet Isaiah: 'The Spirit of the Lord is upon me, therefore he has anointed me. He has sent me to bring glad tidings to the poor, the release of prisoners, to announce a year of favor from the Lord.' They marvelled at what Jesus spoke. But when he spoke to them about the specific application of the word in his own hometown, they got angry with him, and in their indignation, they literally led him out of town. It wasn't the first time Jesus' words made people angry, and it wasn't the last time that Jesus was led out of town.

"Isn't this true in our own time? What happens when a Christian challenges the economic status quo by the gospel and with the social teachings of the church? It happened to Jesus in his own hometown. When Cardinal O'Boyle said he was going to integrate the Catholic schools, we heard some people say, 'Never!' When Dr. King spoke the gospel in Montgomery and Birmingham, Alabama, he so upset the status quo that he went to jail. It was the clergy who wanted to run him out of town and he answered the clergy by quoting Jesus in today's gospel, in his famous letter from the Birmingham jail. Yes, we need new prophets. We know what happened to Jesus, and we know what happened to Dr. King.

"I am not a prophet. But what would happen if we took today's gospel and the social teachings of the church, from Pope Leo XIII in 1891 to Pope John Paul II's encyclical *On Human Work* in 1981, and applied them to the greatest social challenge facing American society and the American church today—the unjust American economic system?

"First, let us look at some facts. There are ten million seven hundred thousand people out of work today. Fifteen percent of the American people are poor. More than thirty-five million poor are captives, oppressed in mind and body and soul by poverty. It is a sinful scandal that here in the United States, the richest and most powerful nation in the world, that so many millions of our white, black and brown sisters and brothers are poor. It's even more tragic that 33 percent of the poor are black, 25 percent are Hispanic, and every one in three families headed by women lives in poverty.

"How do we begin to respond to the facts of unemployment, poverty, and economic injustice? We must listen to the guidelines given to us by Pope John Paul II in his 1981 encyclical *On Human Work* and his specific application when speaking of the rights of workers to organize in his native Poland. We hope today will not only be our Labor Day, but we pray for the solidarity of workers all over the world—in South Africa, in Poland, in the Philippines, in Central America, everywhere—who struggle to live in their God-given dignity. The central purpose of Pope John Paul II's encyclical *On Human Work* is to highlight the fact that human work is a key. Human work is the absolutely essential key to the whole social-economic question.

"In developing this overarching theme, Pope John Paul keeps returning to two essential notions: One, 'Work is for the person, not the person for work.' I repeat, 'Work is for the person, not the person for work.' Hence the evil of any system, whether capitalist or collectivist, is that which reduces work to a mere instrument. Secondly, Pope John Paul says, 'There is a priority of labor over capital. Capital is for labor, not vice versa,' he said. This is an error of 'economism' that considers labor only according to its economic purpose. The encyclical also reminds us that workers not only have a right to organize in every industry, but workers have a right to organize everywhere. Pope John Paul says that workers not only have the right to organize, he regards unions for all workers as indispensable in the struggle for social order and solidarity. Since only 20 percent of American workers are organized into unions, and since opposition to unions is still very much part of our American tradition, the pope's greatest statement on this subject is of critical importance to us as Americans and as Catholics.

"While the American bishops are beginning to discuss a document on the economic system, I would like to propose that Catholics come together from labor, from management to organize a National Catholic Conference for Economic Justice, and that at the level of the diocese, we organize Catholic economic justice councils. Both locally and nationally, we need to begin the dialogue to explore the practical application of the gospel and the social teachings of the church to critique our American economic system. John LaFarge made a similar challenge in the 1940s and 1950s when he prompted a few Catholics to discuss and act on the moral implications of racism and discrimination, and the National Catholic Conference for Interracial Justice was born, and also Catholic Interracial Councils were formed in many dioceses.

"But today the question for most average American Catholics is: How do we preach the gospel? How do we preach today's gospel and the social teachings of the church in our families, in our parishes, in our church? How do we educate and prepare to act as Christians in facing up to the toughest issues of economic justice and racial equality which face American society? Will the new voices of justice come from our families? Our parishes? Our church? Or will our silent voices continue to scandalize the poor, the oppressed and the unemployed? Because we are more affluent and more educated as Americans and as Catholics does not mean we will be more just.

"In my own experience, the two examples of family and parish are critically important. My mother and father could not read or write any language, but they were the first voices of justice in my life. I was born 52 years ago in a tarpaper strike-barracks shack in a Pennsylvania coal camp because my parents were evicted from a company house by the coal mine owners because my father supported John L. Lewis, and was an organizer of the coal miners' right to organize into a labor union.

"The second most important voice of justice in my own life was the parish experience of St. Augustine where I was honored to serve between 1960 and 1970. At St. Augustine's, black people of great faith taught me by their life and their history of racial discrimination, in and out of the church. And yet, even today, we can walk but a block from this church and see and hear and learn what I learned from 14th Street and St. Augustine's parish. Can we not see the overcrowding? Can we not see the bad housing? Can we not see unemployed men and women and youth? Can we not sense the violence of life in this marvelous achievement of mankind called the 'capital city'? Yet only 15 or 20 minutes from here are some of the most affluent neighborhoods and parishes in the country.

" 'Action follows teaching by way of experience,' Pope John XXIII said. We must encourage parents to be the first voice of justice for their children by way of example and experience. We must encourage our parishes to organize to bridge the gap and begin the dialogue between the rich and the poor that separates our human family. We must encourage our parishes to organize and to begin the dialogue between black and white, brown and yellow, and the new immigrants—lonely, afraid, and too often unwelcomed in our midst.

"Finally, as some of you may know, I have been doing much life review in the last two years, and I'd like to take this opportunity to ask you for prayer for a personal issue of justice. Like so many other cancer patients, I have wondered about how much surgery, radiation and chemotherapy a person can take. I have also learned by faith that in the final analysis of one's life there is only one final healing—death—and we know that final healing will be just.

"From my own life review, could I share with you a prayer, my own prayer, that comes from some disappointment. I have been a priest for 27 years, with many joys, but this prayer reflects a sorrow for my own life, my own struggle.

"On this Labor Day, Lord, I pray: 'Help me to know that our limited charity is not enough. Lord, help me to know that our soup kitchens and secondhand clothes are not enough. Lord, help me to know that it is not enough for the church to be the ambulance service that goes about picking up the broken pieces of humanity for American society. Lord, help us all to know that God's judgment demands justice from us as a rich and powerful nation.

"Yes, who will hear the words of the Lord? Who will hear the words of the Lord in today's gospel? On this Labor Day, let us pray that the Holy Spirit will provide new gifts to meet new needs. Let us pray that there will be new voices of justice, new prophets who will hear the words of the Lord and stand up, as Christians, to say: 'Yes, the Spirit of the Lord is upon me. He has sent me to bring glad tidings to the poor.' "

# 18

# The Final Days

"I want to go home," Geno Baroni told his friend and death-and-dying therapist Julie Severance the week before Thanksgiving, 1983. Julie drove Baroni to Seven Springs. Baroni spent two days with the Dupres. He reminisced with Lois Dupre about his boyhood days with Phillip. He talked with Lois and the rest of the Dupre family about football, trees and politics. He gave Lois a book, Alice Walker's *The Color Purple*. There was a remarkable thing about Alice Walker, growing up as a black child in the poverty and injustice of the Deep South, Baroni told Lois. Alice Walker, he said, never knew she was supposed to be anything other than what she was. And sensing that, she was not unhappy. Baroni still struggled with the central question of whether he was what he was intended to be. There was a gnawing sense that he had not become all that he could. His doubts lingered.

He was quite ill by now. The pain returned. He had little appetite. He was always tired. He was reluctant to drive his car. But he hated the idea of giving it up. That would have been surrender. He fretted that he could not read as much as he used to. He was interested in politics and government, but he couldn't devour the newspapers or work the phones.

At Seven Springs, the Alice Walker book got Baroni talking about his parents. They, too, were poor and the victims of discrimination and unjust treatment. But they were happy because they had a sense of themselves. A sense, he said, that he was seeking to find for himself.

Baroni didn't want much to eat. He wasn't really up to taking a walk around the resort complex. But he visited the jacuzzi whirlpool. For a half hour he luxuriated in the swirling warm water. Then Chrissie

Dupre, one of Lois and Phillip's daughters, came in. She was back from California where she studied foot reflexology, a system that sees a linkage between the feet and other body organs. Chrissie asked Baroni if he would submit to one of her foot massages. He agreed and had the first and last foot massage of his life. "I wish I had discovered this earlier," he said.

On Saturday morning, Baroni took a long look around Seven Springs. "He didn't admit he was saying goodbye," Severance said. "But that's what he was doing. He was admitting to himself that this was his last trip to Pennsylvania, that he would never return."

Baroni, in farewell, wrapped his arms around Lois and the Dupre children. There were tears in his eyes.

Severance drove him slowly through Somerset, by the grave of his father, and to the house in Acosta. Mrs. Baroni had not seen her son in several weeks. Now she looked at him and saw deterioration. She knew, too, that Geno would never be back to the family home. Geno and his mother talked about his work in Washington, about his brothers and sisters, about her life with her neighbors in Acosta. He told her about new treatments for cancer that were being developed all the time, and the always present possibility of remission.

They went upstairs to the room he had shared with Angelo, and had slept in so many times during his escapes from the difficult days as a young priest in Altoona and Johnstown, during his triumphal return as a rising young star in the archdiocese of Washington, as a national figure in the urban ethnic movement, and as the highest ranked priest ever to serve in federal government.

On the second floor of the Baroni home he looked at the framed notices of blessings bestowed on his parents by several popes. Baroni had arranged that. He looked at a photograph of himself and of John F. Kennedy. He sat at the kitchen table as his mother prepared him a cup of herbal tea. He pointed out to Severance that there, on the wall, was a photograph of Arco, his father's home town. And Geno said to his mother that he wanted to make another trip with her back to the family in Italy.

"Maybe next year," Giuseppina Baroni said.

"Yes, next year," said Geno.

*     *     *

They had gone to Italy in 1981. That was a trip, Baroni said, that his mother insisted upon him making. He really didn't feel up to going, he maintained. Besides, he said, he was busy with his new responsibilities for Archbishop Hickey at the archdiocesan pastoral center in Washington. But his mother was adamant, Geno said, that they travel to the shrine in Lourdes, France, where miracle cures had been reported.

At her kitchen table in Acosta in 1985, a year after her son's death, Giuseppina Baroni remembered the journey to Lourdes. Geno, she said, wanted to go back to Italy with her. He arranged the tickets and notified the relatives they were coming. It was a good visit, she said. She had a joyful reunion with her sister, Gena, after whom her son was named. Geno, his mother and aunt talked about the death of the girls' mother, Giuseppina's assignment to an aunt's home, baby sister Gena's separation to an orphanage.

One morning of the visit, Mrs. Baroni recalled, Geno said he wanted to do some business at a travel agency. When Geno returned, he had tickets for himself and his mother to travel by train to Lourdes. "It was the first thing I ever heard about it," Mrs. Baroni said. "Geno said he wanted to go to the miracle place." She agreed to go. The two of them went to the shrine at Lourdes and prayed.

*     *     *

Immediately after his Thanksgiving trip home, Baroni went to Boston where doctors at Sydney Farber Hospital put him through a battery of tests. He was jubilant when he got the news that there was no evidence that the cancer had spread to the liver. Baroni had talked to enough doctors to know that infection of the liver meant that the disease had spread throughout the body and there was nothing that could be done. He returned home to Springfield.

Weakened, he stopped going to his office at the Pastoral Center. Kay Shaunesy, his secretary, kept him abreast of office developments. He missed the regular Thursday meetings of Hickey's cabinet. He stopped visiting Capitol Hill. He turned down invitations to dinner. He put off those asking him to make a speech a few weeks or months down the road.

"I got a call from Farber in Boston," Baroni said in December, 1983. "They're recommending surgery. I went for a week without an attack. They say I'm so strong I can stand it."

"Do you want it?" he was asked.

"Well, I don't know," he said. "What are my options?"

He read about the invasion by U.S. Marines of the Caribbean island of Grenada. "I went there once with Madonna House," he said.

"It's a poor little island, hardly developed." He predicted that the invasion would help President Reagan politically. "The conservatives love it," he said.

By Christmas the sickness returned in force. His mother and old friend Jo Dunne accepted Rose Baroni Hebda's invitation to Christmas dinner with Geno and Rose's family. Geno never came out of his room during the meal. Those who loved Baroni knew that he wanted to join them at the table. Whenever they looked in on him, he was in bed, staring at the ceiling or dozing. Late in the afternoon, he appeared, fully dressed.

"I think we ought to have a picture," he said.

They smiled as they posed. Then Geno went back to his room.

A week later he returned to Boston for the surgery. Afterwards the doctors told him the results were inconclusive, but on a positive note, they said that examination of the liver during surgery showed no evidence of cancer. This was enough to raise his spirits. He consented to a procedure by which radioactive materials would be dripped onto the cancerous intestinal wall through a tube inserted through the abdominal wall.

After two weeks of such treatment, Baroni was transferred to the Boston archdiocesan seminary to await results of the treatment. Weak, unable to get about without great pain and exhaustion, Baroni was unable to cope with the demands of the seminary. The Assumptionist brothers there set up a nursing service. But it was not enough. In February, Baroni was transferred to St. John of God Hospital in Brookline.

On Ash Wednesday, he received a letter, "Dear Monsignor, I understand you are in my home town where I hope you will keep an eye on those presidential races. We Democrats need all the help possible to change the Neanderthal philosophy of the present White House tenants. I certainly hope you are comfortable and are obeying your medical advisors. I'm aware that this has been a difficult time for you. The thoughts and prayers of all the Kennedy family are with you. And I hope that if there is something I can do you will let me know. Locally you may get in touch with your friend, Edie Martin, at 223-4655. My very best wishes to you. Sincerely, Ted." Senator Edward M. Kennedy added in his own hand: "Always the best to you."

Baroni for the first time in his adult life was not keeping a close watch on the presidential campaign. He had been so tired that he could not stay awake to see the results from the New Hampshire primary. Although *The New York Times* and *Boston Globe* were delivered to him daily, he rarely read beyond the lead headline.

One regular visitor in Boston was theologian and writer Henri J. M. Nouwen, professor of divinity at Harvard Divinity School. "Henri Nouwen has been teaching me that being patient is being in the place where you are at, wherever that is," Baroni told the author of this biography on Ash Wednesday. "This is the place where I am at. That has been quite a transition. Changing from an active person to a passive one."

"And have you made that transition?" he was asked.

"I am trying to do that in my head in a lot of ways. I am letting things go. I have dropped a lot of projects. I don't really have that much interest in the phone. My whole framework for my life before this came from the part of the gospel of the Good Samaritan. You know the guy who stopped and picked that guy up and took him to the inn. I've always judged things in that light. If I gave a drunk a hard time, I would later think the Good Samaritan wouldn't have done that.

"You go from being superactive and your whole mindset is to get involved and do this and do that. When I was in the parish, I think what made me healthy in Washington is that I identified with the victims in terms of seeing and believing that there is Christ, even if he was smelly or in a urine-filled hallway and rotten housing, or with the abused hard-luck persons. I saw them in a Christian way as 'victims.' " Baroni said he saw Christ in the faces of the suffering. "Now I have moved into a different milieu in my life," he said. "I have to figure out about my own pain, affliction and suffering. And that is a whole mystery."

"But do you still hope to get out of this hospital and resume your work for the suffering?" he was asked.

"Oh, yes," he said. "It is an interesting dilemma, I think, for the Christian. You say, 'Okay, I want to do God's will.' So does that mean you ask for a healing or is that being presumptuous with God? Do you say to God, 'Do whatever you want'? Or do you say, 'God, I need your help'? You can get yourself into a trap," said Baroni, propped up in his St. John of God Hospital bed. "I don't think God wills people to hurt or to suffer. I think what God wills is love and healing. There is a mystery here." Jesus Christ was a miracle worker, Baroni said. He cured the sick; he raised the dead to life. But he also suffered and died. "The passion and suffering and that whole mystery, he allowed to happen to him."

The visitor asked Baroni if he did not do his work against suffering and injustice in God's name.

"Yes. That was my rationale for being a priest and doing a lot of the things I was doing," he said. "People would say, 'What the hell are you doing?' I remember the story of some woman with a couple of kids who was evicted and I put her up in a cheap hotel and she got raped. I went bananas. And that's how that housing thing got into my gut. When I saw five or six people trying to share two beds in a room where there was no heat and the ceiling was coming down and the landlord was evicting them. They were paying too much rent anyhow. That would stick in my gut. I would say, 'That's not right.'

"I always thought housing was the toughest thing to do. You give people a food order and tell them to go buy some groceries or you could get them on welfare or send them to the hospital if they are sick, but the damned place to live, the shelter, the living in an inhuman situation, bugged me all the time."

Baroni and Nouwen spent most of their meeting time at St. John of God Hospital praying together. Baroni said he found consolation through prayer, the celebration of liturgy and meditation on the passion of Christ. "What do I do now going from being an active person to being here day after day after day being passive and things happening to me?" Baroni said. "Now my life is treatments, affliction, medicine, pills, shots, and the high tech, the antiseptic care of hospitals. When you are nauseated around the clock and you bring up everything until there is nothing, you feel like a non-human being. It is horrendous."

To Baroni, the pressing question was whether there was eventual victory over the disease. "To try to understand the mystery of suffering and to try to tie that up as a Christian is difficult. The one thing I do know is that when I have gotten fearful, that fear can be overcome by love, by people and by knowing of God's love and Jesus' love." This was the first time in more than 200 hours of interviewing that Baroni spoke directly of God's love and Jesus' love. Repeatedly he had said that his work for justice and peace had been in the service of God because it was God's work on earth. Now on this Ash Wednesday in the hospital on the edge of Boston, he spoke emotionally of his love for God. For the first time also, he spoke with passion about his own fear.

"I find myself terrified at times," he said. "I wake up in the middle of the night heaving away and in great pain and I say, 'What the heck is going on?' " Then, saying he had abandoned himself to the will of God, he said, "I found a kind of peace. The fear left. My theory is that my life right now is part of the passion. Jesus allowed things to happen to him. And that is a part of life."

Baroni was asked if he had ever felt despair.

"I wouldn't say despair," he said. "You get terrifying fears. Despair is a tough word. But maybe you could say, what the heck, you get very discouraged. I can get myself into a frame of mind that is pretty good about where I am at this moment in my life. Christ gave an example of suffering and it is the only one I know of where there was a hope of victory over suffering and over death and affliction."

Do you believe there will be a victory over your suffering?

"Of course," he said. "But I get to a point where I am terribly miserable and the medicine is not working and I am in tremendous pain. Then I have fear. It isn't a fear of death. I don't think it is a fear of death. I think it is a fear of this going on, of more pain. I ask, how much longer is it going to go on?"

Are you seeking to be resigned to the situation?

"I don't think 'resigned' is a good word. Too many people say, 'It is God's will for you to suffer.' I think that is wrong. You may be in a situation where you say, 'I'm never going to get well.' But I don't know that I would use the word 'resigned.' I might accept the fact in the way Jesus accepted what happened to him. But there is a negative connotation to the word 'resigned.' "

Does it mean giving up?

"Yes," said Baroni. "I think there can be a giving up. I think there is a 'letting go' that is legitimate. I think that is acceptance rather than resignation. To me, acceptance still involves a hope for victory, not a giving up."

On this Ash Wednesday morning, Baroni attended mass in the hospital chapel and complained about the homily. By Baroni's analysis, the homilist failed to understand the real meaning of Christ's resurrection. "I think I could have preached a good sermon this morning," Baroni said. "These forty days of Lent represent the forty years of Moses and God's trying to pull God's chosen people together. These forty days represent in capsule Christ's life, which was spent trying to pull humankind together. If you want to understand life, you have to understand that mystery."

On this Ash Wednesday, Baroni was asked, are you resigned to death or are you still fighting to recover from the cancer?

"Of course I'm fighting," he said. "I want to go eat fettuccine Alfredo. I want to go back and visit my relatives in Italy. I want to get involved in things. I wonder what I would do differently. You celebrate life even though death is inevitable. You celebrate life even if you are hooked up to a tube and you have to take this liquid stuff.

"You have to have hope. Hope is the only thing that keeps you going. Hope is eternal. You know that although you lost 60 pounds, that you aren't just flesh and blood. There is something else besides flesh and blood. There is a me. There is a spirit and God is there within me. I can identify with the people I see on television news getting shot at in Beirut, and their homes being bombed and people beating the hell out of each other."

Baroni said he was making a transition from an active to a passive life, but reserving the right to plunge again into the everyday world of the poor and downtrodden. "I have to have contact with human beings. I have to be in touch with people and I have to do things," he said.

His hospitalization and conversations with Nouwen showed him, he said, that he was "more contemplative than I would have thought." He said he wasn't the sort to go away and live in a Trappist monastery. "Even if I were to be completely well again and get out of here, that would not be one of my options."

There was little time for contemplation in Baroni's life as he fought for the poor and disenfranchised. "I've never had regrets about my work. I've had regrets of failures. I should have done better in this or that situation. Or I messed up somewhere. Or I should have done more. Or I shouldn't have been so shy. I should have been more aggressive. I wish I had had a better education. I wish I had a better start in life. I had to overcome a lot of crap. But I never regretted getting into housing or unemployment bills."

*    *    *

Baroni's suffering was made worse by the awful suffering he saw around him in the hospital. He feared that for him, too, the suffering could get worse.

One roommate at St. John of God was an elderly retired plumber who said whatever came into his mind. "Hey, Geno," he shouted. "I'm bleeding." Or "I've got to shit." Or "God damned son of a bitch. There is blood coming out of my tube." Baroni rang the nurse and asked help for his roommate.

One day the roommate asked Baroni, "What do you do?" "I'm a Catholic priest," Baroni replied. "How long you been a Catholic priest?" "About 28 years." "Jesus Christ," said the plumber, "and this is what you get after 28 years as a Catholic priest."

*    *    *

Baroni gave an interview in the hospital to Betty and Art Winter. It appeared in *Praying*, a supplement to the *National Catholic Reporter*, in the spring of 1985.

Baroni talked about his involvement—both as patient and as minister—in healing liturgies, and about his use of imagery to "meet Jesus, the divine light. That would become part of my meditation, part of my prayer. The divine light is within us, within me. I'm part of the divine light. I'm related to the divine light. I'm a child of God."

"What would you say to Jesus?" the Winters asked.

"Come with me. This is a temple of the Spirit, and it's hurting. I'm hurting. I'm hurting. I'm in pain. Jesus, help me to know your victory, your promise, your hope. Jesus, I love you. Jesus, love me. Jesus, forgive me. Jesus, help me. Jesus, I hope in you. I want to share the divine light. I want to be with you. I want to know you. Don't forget me."

Baroni told the Winters that in his imagery he introduced Jesus and his friend, Phillip Dupre. Baroni continued, "Give me patience. Take me day by day. Am I supposed to stay at Georgetown Hospital? Am I supposed to go to Sloan-Kettering? Am I supposed to go to Boston? Am I supposed to fight back? Help me with the fear. Help me with the doubts. Your love overcomes the fear and the doubts. Your will is your love. Are you taking me to another place? If so, help me to cross over to find peace. Help me to know your love, your will."

The Winters asked Baroni what Jesus said to him in reply.

"I am the way. I am the truth. I am the light. Have hope. He smiles. I say, 'Can we hold hands? Can I be with you?' He smiles. I say, 'Will you give me patience?' 'Yes.' 'Will you give me hope?' 'Yes.' "

\*       \*       \*

In March, Archbishop Hickey in Washington heard that Baroni's condition was deteriorating steadily. The end was coming soon. Within a matter of weeks, the doctors said, Baroni could be totally dependent on life-support systems.

Hickey and the Baroni family did not want Geno to die in Brookline. The archbishop flew to Boston and went to St. John of God Hospital. "Geno, come home," Hickey said. "Your friends miss you. Come down to Washington where we can stop in and see you."

Baroni agreed immediately. He was flown to Washington and taken to Providence Hospital. He rallied. The medical staff trained him to use the electronic device which provided him intravenously with nourishment and medication. He practiced walking around the hospital room with the tube from the device attached to his arm.

Baroni's friends from the social action movement around the country were alerted that he might be able to see them. Hickey suggested that Baroni be transferred to the nearby O'Boyle Residence for retired priests. "I don't want to be thought of as retired," Baroni said. But finally he consented to look at it.

He went there with John Carr, director of the archdiocesan social affairs office. Baroni said it might not be too bad after all. He could keep his own hours. He would have access to the dining room. He would have a phone. And he could have visitors there.

Baroni headed back to Providence for a few more days' training with the equipment. Confident that the move was certain, Carr bought Baroni a television set. The social action friends made airplane reservations and planned a weekend party at the O'Boyle Residence.

Baroni never turned on the television set. The friends never came.

On Memorial Day Geno Baroni was hit by an attack of hiccups that lasted 48 straight hours. The doctors could do nothing. Tears rolled down the faces of family and friends who stood by the bedside and watched him suffer.

Baroni's condition deteriorated rapidly. He lost weight. His hair fell out. He struggled to stay awake for visitors. From Congress Mikulski and Kaptur came by regularly to apprise him of Democratic Party events on the eve of the nomination. Dunne and McNerney shared around-the-clock bedside duty with Geno's sisters, Rose and Mary.

Baroni told his political visitors that he approved the nomination of Rep. Geraldine A. Ferraro of New York as Mondale's vice presidential running mate. But Baroni predicted that the Mondale-Ferraro ticket would lose to Republican candidates President Ronald Reagan and Vice President George Bush. Mikulski gave Baroni a Mondale-Ferraro button, which he pinned to his hospital gown. For several days, he pointed the button out to visitors. "It's a good ticket," he said, "but I don't think they can beat Reagan."

Baroni said he wasn't as convinced as many politicians and reporters were that the presence of a woman on the ticket would help the Democrats. He expected that a lot of ethnic Americans, including fellow Italian-Americans, would vote against the ticket because they did not like the idea of a woman in the White House. Baroni said a successful woman in public life threatened men who saw their sense of authority challenged by Ferraro's candidacy. "If the Democrats lose, and I expect they will, Ferraro will get the blame," Baroni said.

He warned that Ferraro, as an Italian-American, would be smeared by her political opponents for possible ties to the criminal underworld. In that, as was often the case, Baroni was proven prophetic.

Hickey visited Baroni two and three times a week. He often came with Carr. On one visit the two men thought Baroni was in a coma. Suddenly, he came to consciousness and started assigning responsibilities to those around his bed. He told Carr to check on a lottery ticket he had bought. He told Hickey to get to work establishing a credit union.

\* \* \*

Angelo Baroni frequently drove down to Providence Hospital from his Downingtown, Pennsylvania, home to sit by his brother's bedside. Rose Baroni Hebda instructed Angelo: "Try to get Geno to eat." Until one day that is forever etched in Angelo's mind, he had not been successful.

On that day, Geno, who appeared to be sleeping, opened his eyes and looked at Angelo.

"Oh, hi," said Geno in his gentle voice.

"You got to eat something," Angelo said. "You need some strength."

"What do you have to eat?" asked Geno.

Angelo looked about. "I have a plum. You want it?"

"Sure," said Geno, surprising Angelo. Angelo cut the plum, removed the stone, and handed it to his brother. Geno ate the whole plum.

"How about something to drink?" said Angelo.

"I want a Pepsi," Geno replied.

Angelo rushed to a vending machine, got a Pepsi, and Geno drank it.

Then with a satisfied look on his face, Geno Baroni laid back and returned to sleep. He was never to take food by mouth again.

\* \* \*

Baroni's condition worsened. His sisters and brothers knew that soon they would arrange and attend his funeral. Rose Hebda asked Carr to talk over funeral arrangements with her brother. Severance, as part of counseling, had discussed funeral arrangements with Baroni many times.

In early June, Carr visited Baroni in Providence Hospital and raised the subject. "Yeah, we got to talk about that," Baroni said. Off and on over the next few weeks, the two men planned the funeral services. Baroni said he wanted to be buried with his parents in Acosta. The archbishop said he would be glad to arrange a burial place for Baroni in the archdiocese of Washington, but would go along with Baroni's desires.

Baroni said he wanted the wake and funeral mass celebrated at Sts. Paul and Augustine Church, not at the cathedral. He asked that the Sts.

Paul and Augustine choir sing, and decided what it should sing. He picked the memorializers for the wake and the homilist for the funeral.

Although Baroni was writing his own funeral arrangements, he did it with detachment, as if he were working on another in a long list of conferences. Baroni cautioned that he did not want anyone to know at that time that he was in the process of drafting his funeral arrangements. He felt it would disturb his mother especially. Besides, said Baroni, he wasn't giving up the fight. There could always be remission.

Baroni told Carr to hide their working papers so that none of the family members could find them. Carr put the papers into a brown paper bag which he stuck into a rear corner of a closet in the hospital room. Baroni called his funeral arrangement papers "the brown bag papers."

*      *      *

Baroni died in Providence Hospital on Monday afternoon, August 27, 1984. He was 53.

At the bedside were his sisters, Rose and Mary, his brother, Angelo, and Archbishop Hickey. Geno's mother had returned to Acosta a few days before for treatment of a diabetes condition.

The funeral took three days. Baroni would have enjoyed it.

It began Thursday night with a wake service in Sts. Paul and Augustine Church. (The parishioners were then in the process of changing the name back to St. Augustine, the name of the black parish which was merged with St. Paul, the white parish, about the time of Baroni's arrival in Washington in 1960.)

Before the service, Mrs. Rosie Patterson, an elderly black woman, slipped into a pew near the back of the church. She remembered Baroni, the young priest walking the streets, handing out money to the poor, starting a Head Start program for young people, more than 20 years before. There was never a priest like him at Sts. Paul and Augustine, she said. "You don't forget things like that. To him, it didn't make any difference if people were black or white," she said. "I went to mass one Sunday in the 1960s when the father stood up there and said that it was disgraceful that all the black people were in the church. 'Why don't you go to your own church?' he said.

"One time I went to confession and the priest asked me, 'Are you white or colored?' 'Colored,' I said. He closed the door on me. In those days if you were colored, you went to a different church. But at the colored church, there weren't any confessionals. There wasn't any way of going to confession."

But separating the races was not Father Baroni's way, Mrs. Patterson said. "When he walked up the street, five or six people would take hold of his cassock. And they weren't kids. He'd reach out and he'd hold five or six hands. The people loved him. He never looked down on people. If he saw a child, he would say he had a penny and he'd give it away."

Baroni's body, clad in vestments, including a white chasuble, the outer vestment worn at mass, lay in a casket in the center aisle at the foot of the main altar. Hundreds walked past, some bending over to kiss Baroni on the cheek or to seize his hand.

The church was full when Hickey opened the liturgy. "Peace be with you," he said. "We gather in sadness and gratitude." It was time, he said, to pray for Baroni, to comfort his mother and other family members, to support one another at a time of personal loss, and to "remember and celebrate a life of great accomplishment, extraordinary compassion and unique leadership. We are grateful for his contribution to the church, for his prodding and pushing, his excellence in his priestly ministry. We pray we may be fulfilled in the excellence he gave us," Hickey said.

Baroni predicted that no urban activist priest would ever be named a bishop, but the next speaker proved him wrong. Bishop John McCarthy told the congregation, "You're a strange looking group." He looked out on a church filled with Baroni's people, whites and blacks and browns and yellows, young and old, Catholic and Protestant and Jewish and non-believer, men and women, affluent and poor. "Geno Baroni was not a revolutionary," McCarthy said. "He took the system and tried to make it work. He wanted a society based on justice and love."

But there was another side to Baroni, said his longtime friend McCarthy. "What a character. Think of his room. Like a flood had just been there. He filled it with copies of *The New York Times* and the *Washington Post*. When he walked into a room I wanted to laugh. He looked like he was made up for a Charlie Chaplin movie."

McCarthy remembered Baroni's lectures, his circles and triangles and connecting lines and isolated words scrawled on it. "He never wrote on it anything that had anything relevant to do with his talk," McCarthy said. "He was constantly concerned about injustice and he lived with pain, but he was marvelously funny."

McCarthy looked down at the vestment-clad body in the casket. "I'll bet 60 percent of the people in the church never saw Geno vested as a priest." Some people, he said, think of priesthood as something happening to Geno, "like having the mumps." But he was a priest, said

McCarthy, "in the best sense of the word. He looked at the total of civilization and said our structures ought to reflect what God has called us to—love and laughter, joy and sorrow, an end to injustice."

Baroni, said his friend, the Irish bishop, was a "sign of reconciliation and love, and it is the role of the priest to be essentially that, to stand there as a reminder of who we are. He was willing to live his life as a sign."

James Gibson, Washington activist for a generation, was the next speaker. Gibson directed a neighborhood development program when he and Baroni met. They worked together in 1976 to form the urban ethnic-black coalition to celebrate the nation's bicentennial. Later they served on the board of the Meyer Foundation. In 1983, Gibson and Baroni went on foundation business to Cleveland and Toledo. "At the end Geno told me he loved me because I was a good man," Gibson said. "Now that he is in the community organization in the sky, I can tell him I love him."

Wendt said one day Baroni told Protestant clergymen they had better watch out, "Italian Catholics were even worse than Irish Catholics." He remembered how Baroni secured Cardinal O'Boyle's permission to march in Selma with Dr. Martin Luther King. "Geno sprang the Roman Catholics free and led them to victory."

The Rev. Walter E. Fauntroy, minister as well as the District of Columbia elected non-voting delegate to the U.S. House of Representatives, called Baroni "a jewel of a man. We gather to celebrate his homecoming, this gentle giant of a man. We need not worry. We shall see him again."

Kaptur called Baroni "a master politician." She said his "unfilled desire was to travel around the world to undeveloped nations." After the death of President John F. Kennedy, Kaptur said, Baroni "raised and inspired another generation of torch bearers. Most of us are what we are today because of what he released in us."

Carr said of his friend, "Geno was frequently exciting, occasionally frustrating, never boring."

The *Washington Post* in its lead editorial of August 30 reviewed Baroni's distinguished record in Washington and described him as a "priest of the streets" and a "short, round figure of a white man of the cloth, touching bases as well as hearts. . . ." The *Post* said Baroni's "canny sensitivity to the concerns of people of all colors and ethnic groups made him a builder of effective coalitions working to improve housing, health care, education and police relations." All those who knew Baroni, the paper editorialized, "will miss his special insight, his concern for the neglected and the powerless and his unswerving faith in the ability of people to get along with each other. Thanks to his presence on the streets and in the centers of authority, Washington is clearly a better place."

\*        \*        \*

The funeral mass was celebrated the following night in Sts. Paul and Augustine Church. Cardinal O'Boyle, in his 80s and in failing health, attended.

Baroni made his last trip out of the country, to South Africa, with Bryan Hehir. The two friends spent hours over bottles of wine and Italian food, solving the problems of the church and the world. Hehir was a principal architect of the Catholic bishops' statement on nuclear weapons, and he sought advice from Baroni on how to handle the pressures under which he was forced to work.

Tonight it was Hehir's responsibility to deliver the homily. "The fact of death always clarifies the meaning of life," he said. The Catholic Church teaches, he said, that those who expect life in the next world should renew their commitment to this world. "Geno staked his life on the expectation of a new earth. Geno did not wait passively for a new earth. He believed it was up to us to develop the kingdom, built in truth, justice, love and peace."

Hehir said Baroni "stood at the edge of the church because it is there that the church meets the world, many worlds. There are different ministries. He straddled the jagged edge of life where the church meets the human person. He knew that's where he was supposed to be." Baroni's task was "not to distance himself from that edge, but to draw us all to that edge."

Hehir said that Baroni—"a great priest, an enormously gifted politician, an artist"—was a man who "acted by instinct, something you don't teach." Baroni could enter a human situation and feel the flow, Hehir said. "It must have been an awful burden, but it was a touch of genius."

Baroni believed that people on this earth must build the kingdom of God. "You can't wait for it to come," Hehir said. "His challenge was not to break walls, but to build bridges and bonds, to empower those who have no power.

"Many people saw what Geno did as secular," Hehir said. "They do not understand the meaning of priesthood, to stand on the jagged edge of life." Baroni knew and demonstrated, he said, "that the meaning of life is to give it away. We can't grieve the brevity of Geno's life. We just celebrate its achievements. It was quality over quantity. Many live much longer and do not leave this world richer."

The assembly and choir sang in Latin, the language that 40 years earlier in Somerset High School Baroni failed to conquer.

Hickey spoke again of Baroni's assistance to him. "He persuaded even archbishops to take steps they were sometimes afraid to take, to make investments they were reluctant to consider. He challenged us to become involved, to find common cause with the poor and the powerless." Baroni is "listening to us tonight and hoping we won't get it wrong again."

District of Columbia Mayor Marion Barry, a street fighter for racial integration in the 1960s, said he was introduced to Baroni by someone who said, "You must meet this radical priest. He's almost as radical as you are." Barry called Baroni "one of the most gentle, humane, compassionate radical priests I ever met."

Rose Baroni Hebda, Geno's sister, spoke for the family. She thanked O'Boyle for letting him come to Washington, and she thanked Sts. Paul and Augustine Parish, where Baroni found himself as a human being and as a priest.

*        *        *

In his final months in Providence Hospital, Baroni talked about his unfinished agenda. While never acknowledging that he was not going to complete his agenda, he talked wistfully about all the things he would like to tackle and accomplish if his health permitted. The principal items on his agenda dealt with community and economic development. While condemning the Reagan administration for turning its political skills and power against the interests of the poor and urban neighborhoods, Baroni conceded that government alone could not be expected to relieve the nation's poor and bring new hope, jobs and justice to cities.

He spoke pessimistically of the return to power of those, who like himself, wanted federal government to lead the way on issues affecting the poor and cities. Much more than many liberal friends, Baroni believed that the private sector could be counted on in this regard. He continued to promote the idea that neither the private sector nor the government, nor both acting together, could do the job. A third force was required—the community sector made up of organizations, including church groups. The notion that churches, including his own, could, must and should do more in community and economic development was one of his major contributions to the public policy discussion.

Baroni wanted to continue this discussion and the search for cooperative approaches involving government, the private sector and the community sector through an institute. He did not object when visitors suggested it would appropriately be called The Baroni Institute.

As he envisioned the institute, it would be affiliated with Catholic University in Washington. Community activists and those who want to make their careers in community organization would be brought to it to study, to learn from practitioners, and from one another. His idea went beyond the strictly academic or intellectual. He saw the institute as a forum in which people who knew what they talking about because they had done it themselves came together to search for new and better ways, and to win recruits.

Baroni did not see his institute serving only Catholic interests. He regretted that the church had been so inadequately prepared for the great migration of blacks into white neighborhoods in the 1960s and 1970s. The flight of the white Catholics to suburban parishes, leaving the cities behind in a swamp of racial hostility and poverty, was a scandal to Baroni. His life, moreover, was devoted to building coalitions that transcended racial, ethnic and confessional differences. The institute in his imagination would renew that approach.

Father Raymond Kemp, one of Baroni's acolytes in Washington, said that one of Baroni's legacies was the inspiration to "Try it." Not all ideas that look good in theory work in practice, Baroni said. An institute, he said, would be a place where strategies were developed and tested, and those in the struggle in the field could have their wounds balmed and their successes honored and shared.

\*   \*   \*

In the spring after Geno's death, Archbishop Hickey and the Baroni family represented by Rose Hebda and Angelo Baroni called Geno's friends together to talk more about the institute. The list included Mikulski and Kaptur from Congress, Bryan Hehir, Catholic University President William J. Byron, S.J., Sargent Shriver, McNeely, Carr, Nancy Sylvester of Network, Kromkowski from the Center, Gibson from the Meyer Foundation, and two Center colleagues, Naparstek now at Case Western Reserve in Cleveland, and Rotondaro of the National Italian-American Foundation.

They met at the Pastoral Center. Byron said he welcomed Baroni's desire that the institute be at his campus. Baroni wanted it there as a place where the theoretical and the practical, the morally optimal and the pragmatic could be discussed and reconciled. He left pieces of what he expected the institute to do and be scattered among his colleagues. He wanted either a place or process—a variety of practical and research activities under the umbrella called The Baroni Institute.

Kromkowski prepared a memo for the meeting that formalized Baroni's objectives for the institute:

——Create and orchestrate an interdisciplinary as well as practitioner attentive effort devoted to understanding and improving urban America. Particular focus would be given to humanistic, religious and cultural opportunities for wholesome self-understanding and productive work, vibrant community-based development and secular and religious celebration of urban life and various cultures in America.

——Strengthen competency and achievement of teachers, researchers and community-based practitioners through seminars, workshops, sponsored research and publication as well as continuing education, leadership training, support-group learning, and consultations.

——Convene timely conferences and workshops on topics related to American life and culture which would rivet problems to policy and then activate coalitions for appropriate actions and remedies.

——Initiate, direct, sponsor and broker applied research and problem solving through an authoritative network of researchers that is porous enough to attract new talent.

——Disseminate information through reports, monographs and books.

——Provide and/or direct referrals for on-site assistance and advisement services to organizations and institutions engaged in urban ministry and community-based initiatives.

——Assist organizations and institutions founded by Baroni to interact with each other.

*     *     *

Baroni's genius was his sense of how to use the instincts and gifts of human beings. He did this viscerally, not intellectually. He was not skilled at linear articulation of his ideas. He could not explain how he linked people together for a common purpose. He was no theologian or moralist. But he lived God's mission on earth and awakened countless numbers of people to the imperative of working for social justice.

Baroni moved in patterns rather than straight lines. He knew the general direction he wanted to go. But he was proceeding through uncharted territory. He was the pioneer of many things, particularly effective advocacy of the legitimate grievances of urban ethnics and the revitalization of their neighborhoods.

He had a vision of what he wanted society, particularly the neighborhoods of America, to look like. While he could not write down or speak bureaucratically of that vision, he could spread the good news in other ways. The tragedies of his life enhanced his basic love of humanity. His inability to make decisions was an invitation to others to struggle honestly toward their solutions. His ambiguity and embroidery of stories were elements of a conscious strategy to broaden rather than limit the political coalition that he saw as essential in contemporary America. He spoke in ideograms which simplified the complexity he recognized. He was a genius at communications.

His non-confrontational style, originally acquired in dealing with his father, was a strength; he frightened no one (except for Vice President George Bush, perhaps) and held out his arms for a loving embrace to all. That style frustrated many, but it served Baroni well. It sheltered him from intolerable pressure. It preserved the central core of his message by protecting it from peripheral disputes.

Baroni was a loyal son of his church. Standing on the jagged edge where the church meets with world, he connected the ideal with the real, the promise with the current. He made service to the world a sacrament of the church.

\*  \*  \*

The funeral procession on September 1, 1984, took a side trip past the U.S. Capitol and the White House, then carried the body of Geno Baroni back to Acosta for a final mass in the church attended by his mother, Giuseppina.

Just before the casket was closed, one of Geno's nephews slipped into it that morning's edition of the *Washington Post*.

Baroni was buried in Husband Cemetery, next to the grave of his father, Guido. They lie under a spreading Norway maple, whose roots break through the earth. The Baroni cemetery plot overlooks the Somerset interchange of the Pennsylvania Turnpike.

A black marble stone marks Baroni's grave. It bears an etching of Geno, smiling in a Roman collar. On the stone on one side are the words: "Msgr. Geno C. Baroni, October 24, 1930, August 27, 1984, Ordained a priest May 26, 1956."

On the back is a selection from Geno Baroni's final public homily on Labor Day, 1983, at Sacred Heart Church in Washington:

Let us pray that the Holy Spirit will provide new gifts to meet new needs. Let us pray that there will be new voices of justice, new prophets who will hear the words of the Lord and stand up as Christians to say: " 'Yes, the Spirit of the Lord is upon me. He has sent me to bring glad tidings to the poor.' "

# Index

301

# INDEX

313

Religious Life and Human
Promotion, 198–199
Religious men. *See* Priests
Religious women. *See* Nuns
Reuss, Henry S., 89
Richardson, Elliot L., 102
Riots in Washington, D.C., 54–
58
Rizzo, Frank L., 96, 180
Roberts, Sam, 125
Rockefeller, John D., III, 108
Rodino, Peter W., Jr., 89, 96,
180, 257
*Roe v. Wade*, 123
Romney, George, 67
Ronk, Rosemary, 262
Roosevelt, Theodore, 204
*Roots* (Haley), 103
Rotondaro, Fred, 135, 268
Rotondaro, Kathleen, 263
Ryan, John A., 203–204, 259

Sansone, Mary, 95
Sacred Heart (Altoona)
Baroni at, 10–16
credit union of, 12–13
ethnic polarization at, 10–11
O'Leary as head of, 11
Schiavo, John Lo, 181
Schneiders, Greg, 126
School prayer, 251–252
Schwartz, Harry K., 138
Schweiker, Richard S., 95
Scranton (Pennsylvania), 132
Sedlak, Joseph, 95
Selma (Alabama), 43–44, 50–53
Seton Institute, 8
Seven Springs (Pennsylvania), 17
Severance, Julie, 238–239, 240,
270, 272, 281
Sexton, Brenda, 86
Shabecoff, Alice, 149, 245

Shalala, Donna E., 138, 160
Shaunesy, Kay, 230, 283
Sheen, Fulton J., 17
Shrank, Robert, 91, 95, 118
Shriver, R. Sargent, 30, 110
Sirica, John J., 180
Sisters of Mercy of the Union,
261–264
Slawinski, Father, 113
Smith, Alfred E., 90
Social activism. *See* Social justice;
Civil rights movement
Social justice
Baroni's career in, 251
and Catholicism, 34
and Miller, 174
and news media, 40–41
South Africa, 264–265
Sparkman, John, 72, 139–140
Spence, John S., 36, 41, 47, 48
St. Augustine's (Washington,
D.C.)
acceptance of Baroni at, 8–9
blacks in, 8, 22, 25–27
and civil rights movement, 44–
47
departure of Baroni from, 71
first selling of, 22–23
merging of, with St. Paul's, 25
new church of, 23
parishioners of, 8, 22
poverty surrounding, 25–27
second selling of, 23–24
struggle of, 22
and V Street Center, 28–29,
31–33
St. Columba's Parish
(Johnstown), 18–20
St. Francis Center, 238
St. Leo's Parish (Altoona), 16–18
St. Paul's (Washington, D.C.),
23, 25

5259 3592